MW00532518

THE JAZZMEN

THE
JAZZMEN

HOW DUKE ELLINGTON,
LOUIS ARMSTRONG,
AND COUNT BASIE
TRANSFORMED AMERICA

LARRY TYE

MARINER BOOKS

New York   Boston

HarperCollins books may be purchased for educational, business, or sales promotional use. For information, please email the Special Markets Department at SPsales@harpercollins.com.

FIRST EDITION

Designed by Chloe Foster

Library of Congress Cataloging-in-Publication Data has been applied for.

ISBN 978-0-358-38043-6

24 25 26 27 28 LBC 5 4 3 2 1

To my inspirational trio:
Dottie Tye, Jill Kneerim, and Bill Frusztajer.
I miss each of you.

CONTENTS

PART IV: OFFSTAGE

PART V: RACE MATTERS

PART VI: LAST ACTS

PREFACE: A ROAD MAP

THIS IS THE story of three revolutionary American maestros, the jazzmen whose music throbs at the soul of twentieth-century America.

You know their names: Duke Ellington, Louis "Satchmo" Armstrong, and Count Basie. And you probably think you know their stories. Duke was the man who seduced the country with "Mood Indigo" and six thousand other tunes composed on his Steinway Grand, and who wound up on a U.S. coin and a U.S. postage stamp. Satchmo was a multitalented rhythm maker—trumpeter, vocalist, and leading man on the silver screen—who charmed us when he crooned "Mack the Knife," and whose "Heebie Jeebies" we instantly grasped despite its indecipherable English. Then there was the Count, the most inscrutable of the threesome, who proved—with his trademark flicker of the brow and tinkle on the treble—that the best place from which to conduct a band is a piano stool.

Yet much as we may think we do, we don't know any of the three. Not really. The story of Duke Ellington, the grandson of slaves who was christened Edward Kennedy Ellington, was layered, nuanced, and embellished not just by his managers but by his own behind-the-scenes image polishing. Louis Armstrong's father took off when he was an infant, his teenage mother temporarily took to hustling, and he was raised by his grandmother, great-grandmother, and a family of Lithuanian Jews named Karnofsky. William James Basie, the son of a coachman and laundress, also grew up in a world unfamiliar to white fans, one he dreamed of escaping every time the traveling carnival swept into town and from which he finally engineered a getaway with help from renowned jazz pianist and humorist Fats Waller.

What is far less known about these groundbreakers is that they were bound not merely by their music or even the discrimination that they, like all Blacks of their day, routinely encountered. Each defied and ultimately overcame racial boundaries not by waging war over every slight, which would have accomplished little in that Jim Crow era, but by opening America's ears and souls to the magnificence of their melodies. White men who wouldn't let a Black through their front door wooed their sweethearts with tunes from the Count, the Duke, and gravel-throated Satchmo. White women who dodged Blacks on the sidewalk gleefully tapped their high heels in the isolation of their living rooms. Even the most unyielding of rednecks flipped on their radios to hear "One O'Clock Jump" as they sped their trucks through the rolling hills of the hinterlands. Race, for once, fell away as America listened rapt.

In the process Messrs. Basie, Ellington, and Armstrong crashed through racist ceilings, making both musical and social history. All would be toasted by presidents from the race-baiting Richard Nixon to the biracial Barack Obama. As their irresistible tunes still keep our feet tapping to this day, the lives of these jazzmen resonate in the way they quietly upended the way musical dynasties are constructed and how human rights are secured. The sound of their evolving jazz dialect formed a cultural fulcrum that no outraged protester or government-issued desegregation order could begin to achieve.

Each of these unique and improvisational men did that in his own way. Armstrong was over-the-top and genuine, and he appealed to our nostalgia. Ellington was moody, aristocratic, and futuristic. Basie, with a temperament both reticent and heartfelt, was smack-dab in the moment. Those dispositional differences help explain why, even as they professed reverence for one another, they seldom connected on the bandstand or off.

Yet what the trio had in common stands out even more, and added to their collective impact. They were born on society's underside within five years of one another, at the advent of the twentieth century. All stayed front and center on the musical stage for more than half of that century, forging melodic models that hadn't existed and elevating jazz into a pulsating force for spontaneity and freedom. And each faced a color bar that extended beyond the legally segregated South. "I don't eat with niggers," a tall Yalie announced emphatically as Duke sat down with young fans in the dining room of the Ivy League college. "I didn't dare look at Duke," his flustered host recalled later, and "nobody said anything until Duke said, 'Well, let's enjoy our dinner.'" Satchmo, for his part, recalled that where he grew up, after "white Trash" guzzled too much bad whiskey all of a sudden "it's Nigger Hunting time. *Any* Nigger."

The conductors fought back unselfconsciously, interested primarily in making a living and staying alive. They took their rip-roaring harmonies and unthreatening personalities to white audiences that had never seen Black men up close in that way and certainly had never loved them like they did Duke, Satchmo, and the Count. Their anthems made visible the invisible stories of Black America, from slavery through segregation and de-segregation, infusing them into the American songbook and psyche. In the process they created a genre that Armstrong called Black American Music and Ellington dubbed Negro Folk Music. "The Negro," Duke explained, "is not merely a singing and dancing wizard but a loyal American in spite of his social position. I want to tell America how the Negro feels about it." And he did, as did his friends Armstrong and Basie.

This book lies at the intersection of two American stories—one about this country at its most hidebound and straightlaced, the other about jazz, the all-American music form, at its most locomotive and sensuous. We'll follow those contortions in the enclosed and electrifying settings of honky-tonks and concert halls. How better to bring alive the history of African America in the early- to mid-1900s than through the singular lens of America's most gifted, engaging, and enduring African American musicians? And although this is a book about struggle, it has a triumphal windup. Count Basie, Satchmo Armstrong, and Duke Ellington were as much archetypes for Black music as Joe Louis was for Black boxing and Paul Robeson was for the Black stage—and much as Louis and Robeson became symbols of their art rather than just their race, so our musicians were known not as great Black jazzmen but as great jazzmen. Barrier breakers, indeed.

I have been aching to tell this story for a quarter century, since my year as a Nieman Fellow at Harvard. First semester, I took a survey course on jazz, which reinforced my love for that music with knowledge of its greats, in-cluding the three this book focuses on. Later that year, I talked my way into a seminar on Duke Ellington taught by Mark Tucker, a visiting professor from Columbia and an Ellington biographer and devotee who helped me and my classmates see his brilliance as a composer and bandleader as well as his passion for civility and justice.

Four questions might rightfully be asked about the pages that follow: Why are all my title characters jazzmen, with no women, and why these three men? Why revisit this fifty-year-old story now? And why trust an au-thor who barely knew the difference between harmony and melody?

Jazz women are a quiet but essential part of this narrative, same as they were in early jazz history and in the orchestras of Basie, Ellington, and Arm-strong. I recount the spellbinding stories of Billie Holiday, Mary Lou Wil-liams, Lillian Hardin Armstrong, and others in a chapter on side women and throughout the book. I make clear that my choice of title characters is subjective, and that a parade of other musicians—from Holiday and Williams to Dizzy Gillespie and Miles Davis—also were compelling changemakers. As for timing, there is no moment more fitting than this era of racial reckoning to look back at three figures who stood for the very racial justice that is in the spotlight today.

I've tried to make a strength out of being a newcomer to music history, filling in my gaps by tracking down and talking to 250 of my subjects' aging bandmates and friends, relatives and biographers. I dug deep into musty files at jazz archives, public registries, and newspaper libraries around the world and especially where they lived and worked, from New Orleans and Kansas City to Chicago, New York, Red Bank, and Washington, D.C. There are hundreds of volumes on my shelves of musical biographies of Armstrong, Basie, Ellington, and their bands. My book zeroes in on their lives off, not on, the bandstand, and what America was like in a period I have written about repeatedly, from the Roaring Twenties through the Swinging Sixties. I explore how this threesome framed their times even as they were framed by them. And it wasn't just America: across the planet, Duke, the Count, and most of all Louis became symbols of American culture on par with Coca-Cola and Mickey Mouse.

Armstrong, Basie, and Ellington all wrote memoirs telling their stories, but the latter two especially gave us mainly travelogues and were deliberately opaque about their private lives and feelings. Even the prolific Satchmo offered in his published works mere hints of his wit, temper, and lifelong conviction that Black is beautiful, which belied his stereotype as an Uncle Tom.

In the pages to come I tell the stories of the venues where these music men played and how they got to their gigs, lived their nearly nonstop lives on the road, managed their finances, and quietly rejoiced with friends, family, and God. In the end, the Count, the Duke, and Satchmo all emerge as worthy of their spots on the Mount Rushmore of jazz, at least as much for the change they made as the music.

None, however, was a saint. Not even close. In the parlance of their time and in line with many in the entertainment professions, they were philanderers and adulterers—Armstrong full-throatedly, Ellington as a quiet libertine, and Basie in a way that was apparent mainly to the wife who repeatedly threatened to leave and did at least once. They drank, got high, played the ponies more than was healthy, and cavorted with gunslingers. Too little time was spent with their children or wards, and too much on the move even when that wasn't necessary. Often they enabled and elevated their sidemen and women, but other times band members were exploited or plagiarized. Their secreted sins, which I discuss at length, made my trio more fully dimensional if less virtuous, and more able to understand their imperfect listeners even as they were less suited to preach to them.

That leaves us to wrestle with some contradictions. Too often written off as minstrels, these sweet-sounding icons were instead exemplars of Black exceptionalism. They gave us songs that were the ideal remedies for the blues of everyday life, inspiring us not just to swing but to rise up. Negro folk music emboldened and galvanized young Negroes from the Deep South to the Great Plains and, as Martin Luther King Jr. attested, served as the soundtrack for the civil rights movement. This troika of Pied Pipers made jazz the New World's rollicking rejoinder to priggish European classics, and helped transform the twentieth century into the American century in music. Ellington's soulful arrangements were Shakespearian. Armstrong, with a heart as big as Earth, a heavenly smile, and a suitcase full of nicknames including his favorite, Satchmo, became the Mark Twain of song. The Buddha-like Basie was our musical everyman.

For all three, careers that began as escapes ended as devotions—to their swooning fans, to lives spent crossing continents and conventions, and, most of all, to music that moved the world. Their message was uplifting as well as prophetic. "Love, baby, love. That's the secret, yeah," said Satchmo, who was embraced by queens and crown princes along with vipers and vamps. "If lots more of us loved each other, we'd solve lots more problems. And then this world would be a gasser."

JAZZMEN CHRONOLOGY

APRIL 29, 1899: **Edward Kennedy Ellington** is born in Washington, D.C., to James Edward Ellington and Daisy Kennedy Ellington, sturdy members of that city's Black bourgeoisie.

AUGUST 4, 1901: **Louis Armstrong** is born to Mayann Albert and Willie Armstrong in a rickety cottage in a New Orleans slum called the Battlefield, although the exact date of his birth remains one of the most-argued happenings in jazz.

AUGUST 21, 1904: **William James Basie** is born in scenic Red Bank, New Jersey, to parents Harvey and Lillian Basie, both upstanding domestic workers.

DECEMBER 31, 1912: **Louis** is arrested for firing his stepdad's six-shooter to scare a youthful rival, then sentenced indefinitely to the Colored Waif's Home for Boys, where he'd live for eighteen months that he'd later say saved his life and launched his career.

SUMMER 1914: **Edward**, known from a young age as Duke, writes his first song, "Soda Fountain Rag," while in high school.

JULY 2, 1918: At age nineteen, **Duke** marries his childhood sweetheart Edna Thompson.

MARCH 11, 1919: Edna gives birth to their son, Mercer Kennedy Ellington.

MARCH 19, 1919: **Louis** marries Daisy Parker, a match that seemed doomed from the start but didn't legally end for another four years.

SUMMER 1919: Bandleader Fate Marable hires **Louis** to play on his summertime Mississippi River cruises, giving the young trumpeter a taste of life beyond New Orleans.

AUGUST 1922: Mentor and bandleader Joe "King" Oliver summons **Louis** to join his orchestra in Chicago, where he becomes the talk of Chi-town.

FEBRUARY 5, 1924: **Louis** marries Lillian Hardin, a piano-playing bandmate who'd go on to become a composer, an arranger, a singer, a conductor, and, for her husband, a publicist.

FALL 1924: **Basie** abandons the boredom of New Jersey for the bright lights of Harlem, where he played the piano when and wherever he could, including with a traveling burlesque show called Katie Crippen and Her Kids.

NOVEMBER 12, 1925: **Louis** records the first three of a genre-bending series of songs with the first band of his own, the Hot Fives.

1926: **Basie** is back on the road, this time with a vaudeville troupe.

OCTOBER 1926: **Duke** signs up with agent Irving Mills, who catapults him and the band to new fame and a substantial fortune.

DECEMBER 4, 1927: The **Ellington** Orchestra begins a career-changing four-year run at Harlem's Cotton Club.

DECEMBER 4, 1927: Mildred Dixon's dancing duo debuts at the Cotton Club the same night as **Duke**'s band, and she soon becomes his live-in mistress. She is the first in a line of paramours who include Fernanda de Castro Monte, Betty McGettigan, and Beatrice "Evie" Ellis, the longest-lasting who acted like and often was mistaken for his wife.

SUMMER 1928: **Basie** joins the Blue Devils, a terrific territory band run by double bassist Walter Page and based in Oklahoma City.

OCTOBER 23, 1929: **Basie** makes his first recording with the Bennie Moten Orchestra, the best of the blues-based bands in the Midwest.

JULY 21, 1930: **Basie**, whom friends called Billy, Willie, Bill, and finally Count, marries Vivian Winn, who is part of the Negro social and literary circles in Kansas City and clashes nearly from the start with her then hard-drinking husband.

JULY 9, 1932: **Louis** sets sail on his first European tour, a kickoff to endless trips across that continent, Africa, Latin America, Asia, and other far-flung spots that would earn him the moniker Ambassador Satch.

JUNE 1933: **Duke** begins his first British tour, performing at the London Palladium and meeting the Prince of Wales and Duke of Kent.

MAY 1935: **Louis** hires as his manager Joe Glaser, the tough-guy booker who'd become his lifelong manager and friend.

1935–6: **The Count** is invited to lead a house band at Kansas City's Reno Club, rightfully described as "one of the town's most unsavory holes," and he forms his nine-piece Barons of Rhythm. By early 1936 there is a radio hookup that lets fans listen from as far away as Chicago and New York, including John Hammond, who becomes Basie's enabler much the way Glaser was for Armstrong and Mills for Ellington.

OCTOBER 11, 1938: **Louis** marries his third wife, Alpha Smith, with whom he'd had a long affair while married to Lil.

1941: Early in the year, **Duke** records "Take the 'A' Train"—written by Billy Strayhorn in 1939—and it becomes the **Ellington** band's signature tune.

OCTOBER 12, 1942: **Louis**'s fourth and final marriage, to Lucille Wilson, is the one that lasts.

FEBRUARY 6, 1944: Diane Basie is born to parents **Count** and Catherine. But the sweet girl with curls isn't the healthy child every parent prays for. Cerebral palsy leaves her muscles too weak to walk, while an intellectual disability limits her speaking. Most children like Diane were institutionalized then, but the Basies say never.

MARCH 1, 1949: **Louis** is delighted when his native New Orleans crowns him King of the Zulus for its annual Mardi Gras parade, an honor that helped convince *Time* magazine to make him its lead story. He is the first jazz musician to grace that coveted cover, which is especially gratifying since seventeen years before, *Time* called him "a black rascal raised in a waifs' home" whose "eyes roll around in his head like white, three-penny marbles."

JULY 13, 1950: **The Count** marries Catherine Morgan, a vaudeville dancer whom he'd first laid eyes on ten years earlier, whom he said he'd married eight years before he did, and with whom he'd had Diane six years before the wedding.

That same year of 1950, facing economic pressures, **The Count** downsizes his band of fourteen, known as the Old Testament, to just seven players. Two years later it was up to seventeen, ushering in his New Testament era.

JULY 7, 1956: The **Ellington** band stages a revival at the Newport Jazz Festival with its rip-roaring performance of "Diminuendo and Crescendo in Blue."

SEPTEMBER 17, 1957: **Louis** rails against President Eisenhower and Arkansas governor Orval Faubus for their failure to protect Black students who were integrating an all-white high school in Little Rock.

MAY 4, 1959: **The Count** and Ella Fitzgerald are the first African Americans to collect Grammy awards, at the Grammys' inaugural ceremony. One of Ella's two wins that year was for her performance of the Ellington songbook, while Basie topped the dance band and jazz categories.

SEPTEMBER 1959: The NAACP awards **Duke** its cherished Spingarn Medal for "the highest or noblest achievement by an American Negro during the previous year or years."

1964: Martin Luther King Jr. salutes the transformative power of music and music makers like **Duke, the Count,** and **Louis**. "Jazz speaks for life," the civil rights leader writes. "It has strengthened us with its sweet rhythms when courage began to fail. It has calmed us with its rich harmonies when spirits were down."

SEPTEMBER 16, 1965: Calling them "the most important thing I have ever done," **Duke** performs the first of his Sacred Concerts at Grace Cathedral in San Francisco.

APRIL 29, 1969: President Nixon hosts a seventieth-birthday bash for **Duke** at the White House and awards him the Medal of Freedom.

JULY 6, 1971: Months after his final performance at New York's Waldorf-Astoria Hotel, **Louis Armstrong** dies in his sleep.

MAY 24, 1974: Weeks after his seventy-fifth birthday, **Duke Ellington** dies in New York, succumbing to lung cancer and pneumonia.

APRIL 12, 1983: Catherine Basie dies suddenly. **The Count** spends the next year mainly on the road, mourning her and maintaining a rigorous performance schedule.

APRIL 26, 1984: **Count Basie** dies in Florida, at age seventy-nine, of pancreatic cancer.

AUTHOR'S NOTE

I USE THE PRESENT tense in quoting people I interviewed, the past tense in quoting those whose words came from earlier writings and recordings. I employ terms like *Negro* and *Indian* when writing about the eras when that was how African Americans, Native Americans, and others referred to themselves. I kept Louis Armstrong's idiosyncratic and expressive spelling and punctuation. And my footnotes and endnotes generally are abridged listings of sources, with the full references in the Bibliography.

PART I

SETTING THE STAGE

SATCHMO'S BATTLEFIELD

THE BOOKEND MOMENTS of Louis Armstrong's early life are easy to identify. The first came when his seventeen-year-old mother delivered him in a rickety cottage on a dusty alleyway in a New Orleans slum called the Battlefield, named for its chaotic collection of church folks, thieves, hustlers, and shoeless children. The next occurred thirteen adrenaline-fueled years later when, on a chilly New Year's Eve, he was arrested for firing his stepdad's six-shooter to scare a youthful rival, then sentenced indefinitely to the Colored Waif's Home for Boys. Both events were marked by fireworks, as if onlookers somehow knew this was a child who'd someday light up the world. Even more remarkable is his living to tell about that adolescence, given how many of his pals from that Back o' Town neighborhood did not.

Yet those formative years also are shrouded in riddles, starting with the foundational question of the year of his birth. The answer depended on who was asking and when. In 1910, census takers were told he was eight, which meant he was born in 1901 or 1902, but when polltakers came knocking again a decade later they learned he'd astonishingly aged by eleven years. The Social Security Administration shows two different birth years—1900 and 1901—with his local newspaper agreeing with the former while the Waif's Home preferred 1901. All the dates shared two things: they were supplied by Louis or his mother, and they concurred that he had come to life on July 4, as a flag-waving America was celebrating its birthday.

In 1988, seventeen years after Armstrong's death, an intrepid researcher unearthed the musician's baptismal certificate from the dusty files of New Orleans's Sacred Heart of Jesus Church. It attested that this "niger illegitimus," or Black child of unwed parents, was born to Gulielmo (William)

Armstrong and Maria (Mary) Albert on August 4, 1901.* Case closed, or so everyone presumed. But questions persist: What if the old women who reported his baptism got the dates wrong, or the priest was tipsy or simply misheard? Were the fireworks Louis's mother supposedly heard instead gunshots? Was this all a ruse by Armstrong and his agent to spread the irresistible tale that he had burst from the womb on Independence Day at the dawn of a fresh century?

It was not a random image this verbal contortionist crafted for himself but one he knew played perfectly into the perceptions whites had of Blacks. It was a persona of agelessness and fecklessness, one where a family's entire history could be made up as it went along and where poor families often turned to honorary dates when they couldn't afford to celebrate or didn't remember actual ones. Pinning down the year, month, and day of Satchmo's birthing should have been a straightforward matter of checking public records in his native New Orleans, but in the post-Reconstruction Confederacy it was easier to track the bloodline of a packhorse than of a Negro citizen. The Black man in the era of Jim Crow was a phantom, without the dignity of a real name (hence the nickname Satchelmouth, among others), a steadfast mother (Louis's doctored her birth date in successive censuses), or an age certain ("I didn't ask Mama about all that," he explained to an interviewer. "I was just glad to be here!").

Playing to social conventions the way he did with his age and so much else is just half the story of Louis "Satchmo" Armstrong, although it is the half most told. Growing up in the Deep South, he knew better than to flout the rules directly, so he did it circuitously, feeding Uncle Sam and anyone who asked shadowy information about his provenance. In the process he masterfully exploited his uncertain birthday to ensure the world would remember his breathtaking being. Whatever the month or year, he told us, "jazz and I got born together and grew up side by side when we were poor."†

Poor he was. New Orleans had informally been carved into quadrants— Front o' Town, Uptown, Downtown, and the Battleground's Back o' Town, which was the Blackest, swampiest, and most impoverished. That was where Armstrong's grandparents put down roots, where his parents were living with Josephine, his father's mother, and where he was born in a one-story,

---

* Louis would later write that he and his sister, Beatrice, were "bastards from the Start." Armstrong, *In His Own Words,* 20.

† Satchmo fan Tony Bennett rightfully said whatever his actual birthday, "the day Louis Armstrong was born ought to be a national holiday." Bennett and Simon, *Just Getting Started,* 24.

four-room frame house on an unpaved lane called Jane Alley. One bedroom doubled as a living room, and the toilet was outdoors. The neighborhood was densely packed but relatively quiet, although it got grittier and more treacherous in every telling by biographers and by Louis himself. "The toughest characters in town used to live there, and would shoot and fight so much," he wrote in his first memoir. "There were bars, honky-tonks and saloons, and lots of women walking the streets for tricks to take to their 'pads,' as they called their rooms."

His second home, a brick tenement in the Black red-light district, was a better fit with the blighted area that Louis remembered. "We were *All* poor. The privies (the toilets) were put into a big yard, one side for the men and one side for the women," he said. Then he told a favorite joke that captured his reality: "I remember one moonlit night a woman hollared out into the yard to her daughter—she said (real loud), 'You, Marandy, you'd better come into this house, laying out there with nothing on top of you but that thin nigger.' Marandy said, 'Yassum.'"

Money wasn't the only yardstick of deprivation. Before the Civil War, New Orleans was America's busiest market for buying and selling slaves, but it also was home to more than ten thousand Blacks who were born into, bought, or were granted their freedom. Already a gumbo of French, Spanish, Canadian, Caribbean, African, and British influences, the city continued to welcome outsiders—Irish fleeing the famine, Jewish merchants, more Italians than anywhere outside of New York, along with Creoles, the free offspring of French or Spanish fathers and chattel mothers—and they in turn challenged inbred thinking on everything from politics to race. The result, during Reconstruction, was a blurring of color lines in ways unthinkable in most of the rest of Louisiana. Jim Crow—the system of segregation named after a cowering slave in an 1820s minstrel show—certainly thrived in New Orleans, where even freed slaves had owned slaves, but so did Booker T. Washington's gospel of Black self-help. Everywhere from businesses to brothels was racially segregated, but that separation was as much by tradition as law, and there was a surprising commingling of colors where Louis lived. As of 1896, an unheard-of 72 percent of the city's eligible Blacks had registered to vote, and two of them—Oscar Dunn and Pinckney Benton Stewart Pinchback—were the first African Americans to serve as governor in any state.

Unfortunately for Louis, that laissez-faire mindset had begun fraying by the turn of the century, and it unraveled entirely just as he was coming into the world. Post–Civil War reforms were collapsing, as whites who wielded power in the fallen Confederacy began to tear down Negroes' new freedoms. The brief postwar honeymoon of racial coexistence lasted longer in New Orleans than in most of the South, but the backlash finally came there, too. Most restaurants and amusement parks barred Blacks, as did schools, cemeteries, and hotels. Literacy and property-ownership requirements along with a poll tax so severely curtailed suffrage that by 1902, fewer than 3 percent of Blacks were able to register in a city where they constituted a quarter of the population. That same year riots engulfed New Orleans, set off when a Negro day laborer named Robert Charles killed several police officers who had confronted him, and ended with thousands of white vigilantes indiscriminately beating, burning, and murdering Blacks in a presaging of the Tulsa race massacre a generation later. The message was clear: New Orleans was a white man's city.

Young Louis got his first taste of the new Jim Crow order at the tender age of five, when he took his first ride on a streetcar with an elderly friend of his mother's. "I walked right up to the front of the car without noticing the signs on the backs of the seats on both sides, which read: FOR COLORED PASSENGERS ONLY," he remembered half a century after. "Thinking the woman [I was with] was following me, I sat down in one of the front seats . . . Quick as a flash she dragged me to the back of the car and pushed me into one of the rear seats."

Even within his Colored world, there was a hierarchy. Castes were set partly by skin tone in what one historian called a pigmentocracy. Jet-black shades like Louis's were a marker of poverty, inferiority, criminality, and illiteracy. So was Armstrong's ancestry: the boy whose earliest nickname was Little Louis wasn't from the ennobled classes of Creoles or free people of color, but a grandson of lowly plantation slaves. Likewise the Sanctified or Holiness churches where he spent the most time, and that nurtured his love of music and his African roots, constituted the bottom rung of the social pyramid, below Methodists, Baptists, and AME Zion. And diseases of the day—from yellow fever and smallpox to eventually the Spanish flu—hit hardest then, as now, in precincts whose residents were destitute and dark-skinned.

Such hard knocks played out in his family and life from the first. His father, William or Willie, left home for another woman less than two years after Louis's birth. The turpentine factory worker was, in his son's recollection, strapping, handsome, and useless. "My father did not have time to teach me anything," Louis would recall. "He was too busy chasing chippies." His mother, Mary Ann—whom he called May Ann, Mary-Ann, and Mayann—

tried harder as a parent but with only marginally better early results. She left not long after Willie, moving to the Black tenderloin district. "Whether my mother did any hustling, I cannot say." But he did say so, repeatedly, calling it "selling fish" and appreciating that "she certainly kept it out of my sight."*

That left grandmother Josephine Armstrong to raise him for his first five years. She did it lovingly, threatening but seldom delivering whippings, ensuring he went as often as was practical to school, church, and Sunday school, "teaching [him] right from wrong," and making sure he knew about "the lynchings and all that crap." She exposed the boy to the magic and mystery of voodoo and brought him along when she did housework for wealthy whites, letting him frolic with their kids. "Hide-and-go-seek," he said, "was one of the games we used to play, and every time we played I was It." It wasn't his mother on whom Louis first imprinted, it was "Granny," who schooled him in resilience with the help of a virtual village of aged Negresses including Mrs. Laura, Mrs. Martin, and "Old Lady" Magg.

At age five, he reunited with his birth mother in the hovel she shared with cousins in Black Storyville, a smaller, grittier counterpart to the famed whites-only vice district that aimed to contain prostitution by legalizing it in a thirty-eight-block zone. Willie had returned long enough to father with Mayann a child called Beatrice, whom Louis called Mama Lucy and didn't meet until she was three. The family summoned him back then from Josephine's because Willie was gone and Mayann was deathly ill. She'd stopped turning tricks, instead earning her living working for rich whites the way her mother-in-law did, but she still hit the bottle.† "When Mayann got the urge to go out on the town," Satchmo recalled, "we might not see her for days and days."

Preteen years are supposed to be a time when play matters more than work, and adults shelter you physically and emotionally. Little Louis never had those luxuries, but he seldom felt sorry for himself. He was too busy and didn't know any different.

Mayann didn't have the money to buy Louis shoes, and in their neighborhood, where children would play in between the gutted houses, his feet were defenseless against nails and tin cans, boards, broken bottles, and windowpanes. "We were young, healthy and tough as old hell," he said, "so

---

* Whatever his mother's occupation at a given moment, Louis was proud that "everybody from the churchfolks to the lowest roughneck treated her with the greatest respect." Armstrong, *Satchmo: My Life*, 8.

† She also hit Louis and Beatrice when they'd earned it, as he recalled, "She had to whip the hell out of us both. And, man, she hit like a man." Jenkins, *Louis Armstrong's Black & Blues*.

a little thing like lockjaw did not stay with us a long time." He was less san-guine when, several years later, the milk truck he was working on ran over his foot, grinding it into the broken oyster shells lining the road. "My big toe was torn wide open and tiny, sharp pieces of shell were driven into the wound." Friends encouraged him to sue the milk company but he didn't, and "the toe got well and the boss gave me a present."

Mayann expected him to help supply groceries, and he eventually com-piled an employment résumé that would have been impressive if he were an adult. Yet he mined joy from the drudgery. He washed dishes at Thompson's Restaurant (eating enough ice cream, pastry puffs, and doughnuts so that "the very sight of them nauseated me"). He unloaded banana boats until a huge rat jumped out of one bunch. ("Since then bananas have terrified me.") He sold newspapers up and down city streets, yelling, "Paper! Paper! Read the New Orleans *Item*!" (Debate still rages whether the papers were stolen or he was a legitimate helper to white newsboys.) The list went on: cleaning gravestones on Decoration Day, handing out ads for dances, and collect-ing spoiled potatoes, onions, and poultry from garbage bins, cleaning them, then reselling them to restaurants. When a job went bad he could always find work as a hauler at Andrews Coal Yard, courtesy of one of Mayann's many boyfriends, whom Louis longingly referred to as stepdads. ("All I had to do was turn my back and a new 'pappy' would appear.") His earnings could then be multiplied, or lost, in blackjack, African dominoes, or a card game called coon can.

He would even emulate the flesh peddlers who were celebrities in his community. He'd gotten to know several of the neighborhood ladies when, as a small boy, he sold them red dust scraped from bricks that they mixed with pee and used to scrub their steps. The one for whom he procured, Nootsy, was "short and nappy haired and she had buck teeth." She offered him a sample and, when he said no thanks, she pulled out her pocketknife and "stabbed me in the left shoulder and the blood ran down over the back of my shirt."

His first and best bosses were Lithuanian Jews named Karnofsky who, like other Jewish refugees, supported their dozen-strong family by picking up work more established immigrants didn't want. That meant peddling rags, bottles, and bones, hawking stone coal, and selling secondhand cloth-ing and hardware. In a late-life memoir, he proudly listed opportunities the Karnofskys gave his seven-year-old self—to venture into otherwise verboten white Storyville to try out his first musical instrument, a ten-cent tin horn that, along with his singing, attracted rags buyers; to break with them Tillie's challah or matzah, then listen to her soothing Russian lullabies; to hear the prayerful davening that would help inspire his nonsense scat singing; and to be embraced by the first white family he knew close-up, who "kept reminding me that I had Talent." He acknowledged them in his writing—"I will love the *Jewish* people, *all* of my life"—and by wearing around his neck forever a Star of David.

He didn't stay in school beyond fifth grade, and his long work hours never allowed much time even for music classes. He was, after all, the secondary and sometimes the primary breadwinner for Mayann and Mama Lucy. His greatest joy was the music he'd hear through the window of Funky Butt Hall and on the streets of Black and white Storyville. New Orleans was the epicenter of what was then called ragtime or jass, and Louis was quietly absorbing all that he could. Nearly everything good or bad in his world eventually turned up in a tune, from "Farewell to Storyville" and "Back O' Town Blues" to "Coal Cart Blues," where he sang,

> *Of course the cart was hot and*
> *It almost kill me . . .*
> *I've got those coal cart blues.*

He also had his own hustle, a vocal quartet with lead singer Little Mack, bass Big Nose Sidney, baritone Redhead Happy Bolton, and Little Louis as tenor and master showman.* Placing his hand behind his ear, he moved his mouth side to side to generate what he termed "beautiful tones." "We four were 'singin' fools,'" said Louis. "Then [we'd] pass the hat . . . The pennies and nickels and dimes just rolled into our little caps and then we would count them and divvy up and have some real nice change to take to our mothers."

Roam the rough streets as often and as young as he did, however, and trouble would surely follow. In the fall of 1910, he and several buddies were arrested for being "dangerous and suspicious" characters.† They were allegedly trying to steal scrap metal from the ruins of a burned building, presumably to sell at a neighborhood junk shop. Nine-year-old Louis was an accomplice, recruited by a more seasoned scavenger. Still, he was banished to the Colored Waif's Home for two and a half weeks before being released

---

* That light and lilting voice stood in sharp contrast to the raspy growl that became his trademark. He said the change came after he caught a bad cold but, given his sister's soundalike growl, it likely was genetic.

† The label "dangerous and suspicious" was a favorite of New Orleans police at that time. Email to author from Ricky Riccardi.

to an unnamed aunt. And that might not have been his first time in custody: a Louis Armstrong was arrested for allegedly stealing a pair of shoes in the French Quarter in July 1906, when he would have been just shy of five. While it's impossible to know whether that was Little Louis—there were two other Louis Armstrongs in New Orleans—he would later say he couldn't recall how many times he'd been in jail and insist that "I didn't steal—much." Arresting the youngest of Black schoolchildren wasn't uncommon then, and it might explain why Louis was branded dangerous and suspicious when he was apprehended in 1910.

The path ahead would be treacherous, given what was happening to fellow brick throwers, knife wielders, and stealers of pipes and shoes. Willie Telfry, arrested with Louis in 1910, led a crime-filled life. Another acquaintance, Arthur "Red" Brooks, died in a shootout with a railroad guard. Two more, identified only as Jack and Peter, perished prematurely and violently, one at the end of a prison noose, the other "killed dead." One after another, the prostitutes and hustlers who befriended him came to tragic ends.

What saved Louis was an event that he grieved in the moment. On a clear New Year's Eve in 1912, he and his balladeer buddies took to the streets to serenade celebrants. New Orleans's noisemaking tradition involved not just fireworks but firing guns into the air, and as midnight approached, Storyville was filled with mainly white, well-lubricated revelers. Louis came ready, having retrieved a .38-caliber pistol from the bottom of Mayann's cedar chest. The four entertainers were "just singing and minding our own business, when all of a sudden a guy on the opposite side of the street pulled out a little old six-shooter pistol and fired it off. Dy-Dy-Dy-Dy-Dy-Dy. 'Go get him, Dipper,' my gang said. Without hesitating I pulled out my stepfather's revolver from my bosom and raised my arm into the air and let her go." They were, he would later claim, the shots that "started my career." It worked so well in scaring away the rival shooter that Louis reloaded and fired six more bullets skyward, at which point "a couple of strong arms came from behind me."

The arms belonged to Detectives Edward Holyland and his partner George Dellman. Ignoring Louis's pleadings—"don't arrest me . . . Let me go back to mama . . . I won't do it no more"—they loaded him into a paddy wagon brimming with drunks, thieves, and harlots. At the juvenile court building Louis was booked, processed, and taken to a Negroes-only detention cell. New Year's morning, Judge Andrew Wilson took less than twenty minutes to review Louis's history of delinquency and hand him a stiff penalty: an open-ended stay at the segregated reform school. The *Times-Democrat* picked him out of the series of juveniles arrested as New Orleans ushered in 1913, reporting, "The most serious case was that of Louis Armstrong, a twelve-year-old negro, who discharged a revolver at Rampart and Perdido streets. Being an old offender he was sent to the negro Waif's Home."

He'd later say his arrest saved him: "I *had* to quit running around and began to learn something." At the time, however, it seemed to spell the end not just of his freedom but any hopes for a future.

———

Reform schools generally produce one of two outcomes: turning soft offenders into hardened ones, or offering a way out of delinquency. An inspiring case of the latter was George Herman "Babe" Ruth Jr., whose twelve years at St. Mary's Industrial School for Boys in Baltimore made clear that he could pitch a baseball almost as hard as he could hit it. Sixteen years later, something similar happened to Satchel Paige at the Alabama Reform School for Juvenile Negro Law-Breakers. "If I'd been left on the streets of Mobile to wander with those kids I'd been running around with, I'd of ended up as a big bum, a crook," the legendary fireballer said decades later. "You might say I traded five years of freedom to learn how to pitch."

Little Louis experienced an equally breathtaking transformation at the Colored Waif's Home in a backwater district of New Orleans, thanks mainly to the efforts of three Black males: Joseph Jones, Peter Davis, and Louis himself.

In 1905, the Louisiana Child Saving and Reform Society joined forces with the Colored Branch of the Society for the Prevention of Cruelty to Children to help right the wrong that saw youthful Blacks sent to adult prisons while young whites had a reform school suited to their ages and needs. A year later Captain Jones, a veteran of the Spanish-American War, drew on his Victorian temperament and military bearing to bring that vision to life. In early years a police whistle, and later a bugle, woke the two hundred or so boys under his command as the American flag was raised and the "Our Father" prayer was recited in unison. The bugle sounded again for supper, chores, and bedtime, and the boys drilled regularly with wooden guns. They planted gardens of tomatoes, potatoes, turnips, and other produce, supplementing their diets and raising money for the Home. Staff checked new arrivals for lice, which they removed by shaving heads and burning clothes. Many of the boys also had enlarged and possibly infected glands, bad teeth, and mental deficiencies, and a third of them couldn't write or read. Classrooms housed as many as eighty-four students. While lessons focused on elemental literacy and math, that was more than street kids like Louis had gotten in their years of sketchy attendance at grammar schools.

The mission was reform, but the setting made clear it was a prison. Barbed wire ringed the complex, which was surrounded by six cemeteries and a malaria-breeding swamp. Escapes generally didn't succeed, and boys knew that the punishment could include a blistering whipping delivered to naked bodies with the whole school watching.

Louis rebelled from the moment he was issued his uniform of overalls and a jacket with "Boys Home" stenciled across the chest. He didn't answer when old-timers gave him the rookie greeting, "Welcome, newcomer." He sat at the long dinner table with fellow inmates but refused to eat the habitual white beans, dark bread, and molasses. He grit and bore his fifteen hard lashes on the hand for breaking what he said was a minor rule. "It went mighty hard with me for a while," he'd recall, "after being a kid that had had my way and come and gone as I wanted."

Just how much coming or going he did at the Waif's Home—and who came to him—were matters of shifting opinion. Mama Lucy and Mayann were there three times a week whereas "my father had never paid me a single visit," he wrote. But his half brother Henry remembered that he and Willie were regular visitors, and Louis would always ask, "Daddy, when you gettin' me out?" In Louis's telling, his behavior was exemplary, earning him visits to his mother on his own, but Waif's Home music director Peter Davis said Louis went AWOL at least once, although it only lasted a day.

At first, Davis seemed to have it out for Armstrong: "He would whip me every time he had a chance and every time he'd whip me he'd make these remarks, 'You're one of those bad boys from Liberty and Perdido Streets and I don't like you.' So I figured there wasn't any use saying anything to him. I just stood there and took my beatings like a little man." Over time, Louis made clear he was better than his surroundings and Davis showed he was more forgiving than Louis assumed. The thirty-two-year-old musician never pinpointed precisely what he saw in his eleven-year-old ward that marked him as a musical talent, but he offered clues. It started with his singing in the Sunday school quartet, where Louis was, in Davis's words, "the boss and director." He also could "buck dance" while other boys clapped.

"[Mr. Davis] watched me all that time," Louis remembered, "and he come up to me and said, 'Would you like to play in the band?' I said, 'I don't know how to play nothing.' I'd been around to the parades and things, but singing was my life. Finally he give me a tambourine. So I fool with that for a while. Then he give me a snare drum . . . Then they give me an alto horn. You know, it goes *umpah, umpah* all night. Then I got the bugle and just picked it up and started playing—blew reveille, mess call, taps every day. Finally the little cornet player went home and Mr. Davis taught me how to play 'Home Sweet Home' on that."

The cornet—a more rounded cousin to the trumpet—cemented the bond between instructor and apprentice. It was the best-loved of the many instruments Davis played and reminded Louis of the tin horn he'd tooted on the Karnofsky wagon. Louis was soon visiting the Davis home, getting his first taste of European music and of note reading, performing duets with Peter's daughter Ida, and occasionally sleeping there, with teacher and student walking back the next morning to the Waif's Home.

Davis now had the protégé every preceptor longs for. It's even easier to measure what Louis got out of the arrangement. Playing in the band conferred status on the boys, along with a pass to visit the world on the other side of the barbed wire. The troupe performed at picnics and parades, Uptown, Downtown, and Back o' Town. Ordinary band members wore white pants, blue gabardine coats, and black easy-walkers, but Louis, who'd been elevated to leader, had a sharper uniform: cream-colored trousers with cap to match, brown stockings, and brown easy-walkers. In fewer than five months he'd transformed himself from one of the bad boys to, as he put it, "the most popular boy in the Home. Seeing how much Mr. Davis liked me and the amount of time he gave me, the boys began to warm up to me and take me into their confidence." The ultimate seal of approval was the handles they gave him that reflected his prodigious chops and would last a lifetime: Gatemouth and Satchelmouth.

Louis's musical achievement and Davis's endorsement made it easier for the Home to let him out in June 1914, eighteen months after he'd arrived. His release was engineered by the white family his mother worked for, Louis said in his first memoir. In his second, it was his father and Willie's boss at the turpentine factory who were the keys. Whatever made it happen, a decidedly different person walked out of the Home than had walked in that portentous New Year's Day. He could read, write, and think in ways he hadn't before. He knew now how to scrub floors, iron and cook, and make a military-tight bed. After spending his first eleven-plus years with women as his caregivers and companions, he now had male role models in Joseph Jones and Peter Davis. They instilled in Louis the importance of discipline and determination in a Jim Crow era that tried to deny Blacks their self-respect. With talent and charm like his, he was told, this urchin from the Battlefield could make not just good but great. Best of all, for the first time in his life Little Louis got to be a boy even as he was becoming a man.

"I came to think as much of that school as other men think of the college they went to," he said. "Pops, it sure was the greatest thing that ever happened to me," he added later. "Me and music got married at the home."

———

After the Waif's Home, Louis lived with his father, which might have been a condition of his release, and it didn't work out any better than the first brief time the two lived together. Willie seemed interested mainly in landing a cook and babysitter for Henry and William, the boys he'd had with Gertrude, for whom he'd twice abandoned Mayann. With the arrival of a third child, all parties agreed it was time for Louis to be back with his mother.

Louis also returned to a patchwork of menial jobs. His passion, more than ever, was music, but it would take another four years and the end of a world war before he could do that full-time. Meanwhile he played and sang any place and time he could, from honky-tonks to second lines, a New Orleans tradition at big days like funerals where the deceased was escorted to the cemetery by loved ones, a ragtag jazz band, and, increasingly, by Little Louis Armstrong. He quietly absorbed the rich and varied strands of musical America, tooting his horn of the moment alongside friends Black Benny, Nicodemus, Hobo Crookit, Cocaine Buddy, Ikey Smooth, Lips the Camel, and Nasty Slim.

During those years, a series of older mentors each added something unique to Louis's musical education. In Charles Joseph "Buddy" Bolden, Louis discovered not just jazz royalty but the quintessential improvisational cornetist doubling as bandleader. Willie Gary "Bunk" Johnson taught him how to diminish chords and embellish stories. Nobody gave more than Joseph Nathan "King" Oliver—showing his protégé how to insert a plumber's plunger to modify a horn's timbre, don a handkerchief under his hat to beat the summer heat, revel in heaping servings of red beans, rice, and hock bones, and carry himself with unmatched dignity. "The king of all the musicians was Joe Oliver, the finest trumpeter who ever played in New Orleans," Louis said. "I was just a little punk kid when I first saw him, but his first words to me were nicer than everything that I've heard from any of the bigwigs of music."

Other words he'd remember came from Black Benny Williams, the bass drummer, ladies' man, and fairy godfather disguised as street tough who in their early days handcuffed himself to Louis to ensure his young friend didn't get lost in crowds. Later, Armstrong's muscled muse offered two bits of guidance that Satchmo passed on to everyone who'd listen. "As long as you live, no matter where you may be—always have a *White Man* . . . can + will put his Hand on your shoulder and say—*'This is "My" Nigger'* and, Can't

Nobody Harm' Ya." And: "Always remember, no matter how many times you get Married.—Always have another woman for a Sweetheart on the outside."

Louis didn't need prodding on the multiple-lovers front. His first, at age fifteen, was Irene, a twenty-one-year-old prostitute he described as "raggedy as a bowl of slaw." "We fell deeply in love," he said, and "lived together as man and wife" until he discovered she already had a common-law husband with a temper and a razor. Which brought this advice from his mother: "You'll know better next time—Never to go into a man's house and go to bed with his woman." Louis promised, "*Mother* I will never do that again"—although of course he did.

His affair with Daisy Parker lasted longer and evolved into an official marriage. Like Irene, she was twenty-one, a strumpet, and had a boyfriend Louis found out about too late. Also like Irene, Daisy was skin and bones, which she disguised by donning artificial hips that Louis called "waterwings." Their relationship was passionate and at times riotous. "All she knew how to do was fuss and fight," Louis recalled. "But it's a funny thing about two people being in love—whatever little traits there are, no matter how unpleasant they may be, love will drown them out." So fresh from a bedroom romp at Kid Green's Hotel, "we went straight down to City Hall and got hitched." The nuptials seemed doomed from the start, but they wouldn't legally end for another four years.

Outside of his mother and sister, the attachment from those years that lasted longest was with a boy named Clarence, the son of his cousin Flora Myles. Flora, her father, Isaac, and her six brothers and sisters grew up next door to Louis, Mama Lucy, and Mayann. Everything about the Myleses was tinged in mystery, including the spelling of their name (sometimes Miles, Myler, or Myers) and their relationship to the Alberts (Flora's deceased mother, Frances, might have been Mayann's sister). What was clear was that at thirteen, Flora became pregnant, which Louis said was "through an old white fellow who used to have those colored girls up to an old ramshackle house of his." Clarence temporarily took his pedophile father's last name, Hatfield, and Louis became bonded to the boy from the first, even if he never could keep Clarence's story straight. Louis implied that Flora died just after childbirth, although she lived another nine years. He'd call Clarence his adopted son, and Clarence called himself Clarence Louis Armstrong, although there is no evidence of a formal adoption. And there's no clear record in New Orleans of the elder Hatfield.

Clarence was the closest thing Louis ever had to a child of his own, even if he was just fourteen years older than the boy. And while family ties and unstinting affection are mainly what drew him to his cousin's son, guilt might have played a role. That's because when Clarence was just three, he lived in Louis and Daisy's tumultuous two-room flat over an upholsterer's shop. During a downpour the child was playing on their back porch, which Louis knew was prone to flooding. While he and Daisy listened to "Tiger Rag" and other recordings, Clarence wandered onto the deck, fell a full story onto his head, and for the rest of his life was what Louis and the doctors called "feeble-minded."

Louis's first real escape from New Orleans, and from his adult-like burdens, came in the fall of 1918, as the Great War was ending. He accepted work in an all-Black orchestra on a steamship that ran up and down the Mississippi, playing soft waltzes. Cruising the mighty river, he would imagine the lives of Tom Sawyer and others he read about in books by Mark Twain. While the boats were strictly segregated—no mingling between musicians and guests, and Black patrons welcome only on Monday nights—the job gave Louis a glimpse he'd never had of the wider world. He was mesmerized by the tall buildings in St. Louis. ("I could not imagine what they were all for . . . colleges?") He left home weighing just 140 pounds, but for the first time he had money to eat 'til he was sated. ("I had to buy a pair of fat man's trousers.") His bandmates taught him to read music, which validated the riverboats' reputation as floating conservatories and let him stop bluffing with unfamiliar scores.

Satchmo and his fellow balladeers also managed to chip away at Jim Crow everywhere they docked. "We were the first colored band to play most of the towns," he recalled with pride. "At first we ran into some ugly experiences while we were on the bandstand, and we had to listen to plenty of nasty remarks . . . Before the evening was over they *loved* us."

Three years on the river convinced Louis he could make it outside New Orleans and made him want to try. Mama Lucy had abandoned New Orleans for Florida by then, and his marriage to Daisy was all but over. He'd remain ambivalent about his native city for the rest of his days, unable to get it out of it his bloodstream even later, when he was boycotting its racism and pettiness—but for now he'd had enough. The next chance to flee his hometown came in the summer of 1922, when his mentor Joe Oliver sent a telegram that set off fireworks in his soul if not on his street: "COME IMMEDIATELY LINCOLN GARDEN CHICAGO JOB FOR YOU THIRTY DOLLARS A WEEK. KING OLIVER."

THE COUNT'S SHROUDED
ROOTS IN RED BANK

AT FIRST GLANCE, Bill Basie's family tree seems pretty straightforward.

There are his parents, Harvey and Lillian, upstanding domestic
workers living in scenic Red Bank, New Jersey. In 1898 comes their first
child, Leroy, who died of tubercular meningitis at the too-young age of
twelve, followed in 1904 by little brother Bill, who would go on to become
the Count of Swing. But dig a little further, and the storyline becomes deeply
tragic.

Leroy in fact was born two years before Lillian and Harvey were married. In what seems to have been an effort to avoid embarrassment, he was
dispatched as an infant to the nearby boardinghouse of a Colored fortune
teller, where census takers listed him as Leroy Bason. Newly unearthed genealogical documents reveal that a year and a half later he was joined by
Samuel Bason, who succumbed to a lingering case of severe malnutrition
seven months after he was born and two weeks after Lillian and Harvey were
married.

Records from that era are sketchy, especially for Negroes, but these files—
from the New Jersey and U.S. censuses, newspaper accounts, and death
certificates—point convincingly to the Basies having had three children,
not two. Samuel's last name on his death record is Bacy, and his parents are
Henry Bacy and Lillie, likely aliases used by Harvey Basie and his new wife
Lillian. By the time Leroy died, he and his parents were living together and
all were using the name Basie. Having children out of wedlock wasn't uncommon, but it could be shameful for children of upright families like Lillian's and Harvey's. Stashing them away with another family—one named in
newspapers for crimes including stealing, public drunkenness, and assault—

would have been painful, with that hurt bleeding into unimaginable guilt when Samuel essentially starved to death and Leroy died of an illness often linked to improper diet.

All of which raises questions about the soon-to-be maestro: What did he know about his family's tortured story? When and how did his parents tell him? Can being raised in a family shrouded in secrets help explain the Count's enduring reticence to divulge details of his own private life, which he long insisted was no-drama, no-mystery, and nobody's business but his?

Asked in his later years whether he had siblings, Bill said, "I did have one brother, but I knew very little about him." In that same interview he also said, "You ain't supposed to ask those questions."

———

The version of his early years that Bill Basie preferred was the one that he told in his memoir and in the few long interviews he granted journalists over the years. It was bare-bones, sanitized, and recurrently unreliable in particulars both small and big, starting with the backgrounds of his parents.

Lillian Childs was born in Virginia twelve years after the Civil War ended, in a Reconstruction era of hopes raised, then dashed. Her parents—Samuel Childs and Annie Williams—had likely grown up as slaves or freed slaves, but the records aren't clear on the lives they lived. What is known is that Lillie and her older sister Victoria made their way to the manufacturing town of Red Bank. At age twenty-three, dressed in white satin, Lillie wed Harvey Basie at that town's Pilgrim Baptist Church. (Bill says his information on Lillian as well as Harvey came from the family Bible and family lore, which made him mistakenly believe that the wedding was four hundred miles away in Virginia, that his mother was two years older than she was, and that her name was Lilly Ann as opposed to Lillian.)

Harvey's lineage is clearer. His father, Edmund Basie, and mother, Ellen Williams, like Lillian, were born in Virginia albeit during the antebellum era, then moved to New Jersey. Harvey, born in 1874, was smack in the middle of a brood of seven, all of whom attended school to ensure they could read, write, and have other opportunities denied their parents. Harvey had a passion for bicycling and an entrepreneurial spirit that led him to jobs ranging from coachman to groundsman, handyman, and property manager for two of Red Bank's preeminent families. He tried running a barbershop and advertised services outside of his day jobs, including small repairs and gardening. He helped bring to Red Bank a Colored YMCA, was a leader in his Baptist church, served as second lieutenant of the Black lodge of the Knights of Pythias fraternal organization, and, at a time when most Negroes were devoted to the party of Lincoln, he was president of the Negro Eastside Republican Club of Red Bank. He did well enough to buy a home in Red Bank's Black enclave, but he never climbed higher than the lower-middle class—and to reach even that rung, Lillian had to work as well.

Bill's relationship with Harvey was close but never warm. The son had three lasting memories of their time together: being caught drinking gin, dashing his dad's hopes of a father-son business mowing lawns and cleaning houses, and siding with his mother when his parents separated later in life. (Bill was blind to that growing estrangement, as he was to many things in his youth.) Harvey's response then, as Bill recollected: "If that's the way you're going about it, that's the way it'll have to be. Because, after all, she's your mother, and I know you love her, but she was my sweetheart and my wife." Harvey came closest to revealing his flatlined feelings about the Count in a toast he delivered years later: "He is my son, with whom I am well pleased." Bill was equivalently muted when an interviewer asked how his father had reacted when Bill left behind sleepy Red Bank for the lights of Broadway: "I guess he seen that there was no use, you know, [making] me turn another way . . . [He] didn't discourage me."

The bonds between Lillie and Billy ran far deeper. "My mother, God rest her lovely soul, used to take in washing," Bill wrote. "Her having to do that rubbing and scrubbing over those hot suds and all of the squeezing and starching and shaking out and hanging out and taking in and ironing and pressing to help my father make ends meet . . . Sometimes just the thought of all those baskets of laundry was almost more than I could bear, and I would just go over to her and hug her and say, 'One of these days. You just wait and see. I promise. You just wait till I grow up.'"

Lillie's burdens went well beyond the body-bending work she did for those white households, as Billy must have recognized. There were the irreparable losses—of Leroy, the son she openly mourned, and of Samuel, about whom she furtively anguished—and the oversized hopes she unmistakably vested in her surviving child. It was something she could only have talked about with Harvey, and neither left written records of their states of mind. But the adult Count Basie would never forget how Lillie responded to his boyhood promises to make good and do right by her: "[I] remember myself hearing what she always used to say back to me. I never will forget that. 'I'm already proud of you, Billy,' she used to say, sometimes stroking me on the cheek, and patting me on the head, and sometimes holding me by both shoulders. 'You're a very big help to me already. You're a good boy, Billy. You're such a good boy, and you will go far in the world, and my prayers will go with you and be with you.'"

His best memories from Red Bank, as with most youngsters, were holiday sounds, tastes, and smells. "My mother loved to make cakes and pies," Bill said, "so there was all that nutmeg and vanilla and cinnamon and chocolate in the air. My mouth still waters when I remember those cakes and with all that coconut icing and those jelly layer cakes and those potato pies and custard pies. And all mixed in with all of that, you could also smell the celery and the sage and black pepper in the chicken or turkey stuffing."

His worst days were in the classroom. "School, I'm sorry to say, was not my thing," he wrote. "I didn't go any higher than junior high school . . . I used to stay in one grade so long it was shameful. Kids would come into kindergarten and grow on up and catch up with me and then leave me sitting there in the same class . . . I didn't pass in my homework or anything. I didn't take any tests. I didn't even have any report card anymore. It was ridiculous. I guess my parents must have said to hell with it."

It wasn't that Billy—or Willie, as he sometimes preferred then—lacked passions. His first was show biz, specifically the carnival. He liked the dazzle of the big-tops and their clowns, acrobats, parade bands, and once-wild animals. He liked merry-go-rounds and Ferris wheels. Most of all, he dreamed about leaving town with the carnies, no matter where they were headed. It was the characteristic wanderlust of youth, along with the bane of being an only child in an often frosty household. Regardless of the reason, as he wrote afterward, "I just wanted to be on the road with a show so much so that I would have gone along just to be a water boy for the elephants."

The love of spotlights and footlights also took him as often as he could to Red Bank's Palace moving-picture theater, which featured not just silent-picture idols like Rudolph Valentino, Buster Keaton, and Mary Pickford, but live comedy, songs, and dance. He swept the auditorium and lobby, polished the rails and fixtures, put up extra seats and scrubbed the below-stage dressing rooms used by vaudeville acts, and greeted entertainers at the train station, showing them to their hotel. Eventually he graduated to projection room helper. One day, the house piano player who accompanied that era's silents didn't show, and Willie volunteered to sit in.

This was his big moment. He didn't have the regular player's experience, but he had been taking lessons forced on him by his mother, who scraped together the twenty-five-cent fees. While his interest waxed and waned, his ears heard not just the beat written on the sheet but ones in his head and toes. His hands tinkled the keyboards with ease and poise. He was a natural.

Exercises demanded of him were straightforward, but he delivered more. "All I had to do was have somebody else playing something and I could start right in and repeat it," he remembered. "That wasn't anything for me. And of course, in those days you also picked up things from piano-player rolls."

It was more opportunism than epiphany, the way things generally are for the young. Willie Basie was no more drawn to the piano, or to the joys of ragtime and jazz, than Little Louis Armstrong was seduced by horns. Those attractions came later, no matter what romantics and screenwriters claim. Willie was as desperate to experience the world beyond Red Bank as Louis was to escape the Waif's Home and the bad-boy track that landed him there. For Willie, a band was an even better way out than the carnival, and he was showman enough to pull it off.

And much as Armstrong would experiment with a series of instruments before finding the trumpet for which he is famous, so Basie's first love was trap drums. His dad bought him a set with a small snare and bass, along with a hanging foot pedal. It was William Alexander "Sonny" Greer, a native of nearby Long Branch and later Duke Ellington's percussionist, who unknowingly moved Basie off the drums. "I had sense enough," Willie said, "to know that I'd never be able to do what he did up there."

Shy as he was, Willie also was ambitious, and he managed to talk his way into gigs in town with groups like the Colored Young Men's Association, where he soloed on the piano in his childlike knee britches. Red Bank, which took its name from the red soil of the Navesink River, was known then for its textiles and tanning, not for the quaintness that today makes it the Garden State's answer to Greenwich Village. The 1910 Census showed it had 7,398 people, and 844 Negroes, which to Bill Basie wasn't enough of either. While his first move was only ten miles down the road, to the modest seaside community of Asbury Park, it seemed to him like a metropolis with its population of 10,150—1,934 of whom were Black.

Like any artist trying to prove his worth, he was game to do whatever it took. That meant parking cars at a roadhouse called the Hongkong Inn when a more seasoned player unseated him at the piano. Customers sometimes were drunk enough that they passed out in their vehicles, and Willie would get them comfortable, then help himself to whatever tip he felt he deserved. He also pilfered armfuls of just-baked rolls from the wicker baskets delivered in the early morning to restaurants, and he slept on a bench at Joe Brown's Pool Room, a magnet for musicians on Asbury Park's Black West Side. As his longtime guitarist Freddie Green would later say of the two of them: "We could have been a jazz musician or a criminal."

Eventually Willie found more part-time piano gigs. He and his Red Bank pal Elmer Williams, who'd go on to become a big-time tenor saxophonist, enjoyed free lodgings at a thriving bordello run by Elmer's uncle Ralph. Basie never specified what they did when they weren't sleeping, but he hinted: "We made a lot of good friends out there and got a lot of experience that was very useful to a couple of youngsters starting out in the world of show business."

Things occasionally got tough enough that he and Elmer had to return home. By then it was clear that "I didn't want to go to school anymore, and I knew good and well you couldn't lie around home living off your parents. I had to get out of there and also out of Red Bank, and music was my ticket."

The first place he punched that ticket was fifty miles and a world away, in New York City, a magnet for entertainers of every sort and for Bill Basie as he was turning twenty in 1924. He'd already bought a secondhand jazz-back suit whose high waist and slanted pockets were just the thing for a young man aiming for sharpness. He had expected Harlem to be wide-open and was surprised when the only way he could get into the famed Alhambra Theater was through a Colored entrance on the side and the only section from which he could watch the show band was the balcony. "I hadn't expected to find anything like that in Harlem," he said, "but that is the way it was, and the Alhambra Theater was not the only segregated place along that part of Seventh Avenue." The Theresa Hotel was verboten for Blacks. Frank's Chophouse was "strictly lily-white," as was the Braddock Hotel where the New York Giants stayed.

Basie played whenever and wherever he could, including with a burlesque show called Katie Crippen and Her Kids. His act included dramatically running his hands up and down the keyboard, throwing his arms into the air while flashing his fingers, and standing up without skipping a beat as his right hand played the melody and his left alternated between a single note and a chord played an octave higher. It was a mixed-race touring group, and before Basie and his mates headed out for their first road trip, the manager sat them down to explain the ground rules: "There will be absolutely no [miscegenation]. He said if this sort of thing is caught, there will be an immediate dismissal of all parties concerned. Then he said something like 'But other than that, this is going to be one great big happy family.'"

Willie had grown up knowing that Jim Crow wasn't just a Southern affliction. New Jersey might not have had Black codes or other legally mandated racial segregation, but separation was built into the culture and enforced without hesitation. He'd seen the way his parents had to dissemble to get along with their white bosses. He lived on Mechanic Street, on the Black side of Red Bank's tracks, and while his school was integrated, "you couldn't miss the fact that ofays and souls went to different churches and some other things."* Still, he said looking back at the admonishment of the Crippen manager, "it really sort of surprised you that they were hung up on something like that."

Everything about that first trip was an education for the young Basie: the elegant Pullman sleeping cars the troupe had chartered ("that was my piece of cake"); the hectic but electrifying life bouncing from Philly's Casino and Pittsburgh's Gayety to the Lyric in Dayton, Star and Garter in Chicago, and more Gayetys in St. Louis, Kansas City, Detroit, Buffalo, and Rochester ("the good times were rolling"); and the "nice-looking girls" he met in after-hours joints ("of course, there was a little tasting going on").

Back in New York, he got to hear and sometimes know music makers who would become legends, from Duke Ellington and Bill "Bojangles" Robinson to Ada "Bricktop" Smith. His break came when he befriended the Harlem stride pianist and organist Thomas Wright Waller, whom everyone called Fats. "One day he told me to come on and sit over there with him. So I got under the rail, and he started showing and telling me about the stops and things like that and the important things that made the organ different from the piano," Basie remembered. "That's how it was with me and Fats. That's the way he taught me, and those were the only organ lessons I ever had."

After more than two years in New York, and just four years after Louis Armstrong left New Orleans, Bill Basie was ready to head out to new adventures and find himself as a musician, a bandleader, and eventually the Baron of Boogie Woogie. He'd come most of the way out of his shell and now knew for sure what he wanted to be—a showman, but the no-drama kind, unlike his high-energy counterpart from the Great Southern Babylon. "I'll never be able to do justice to what it all meant to me," he wrote in his autobiography. "I had been around long enough and gotten into enough to call myself a New York musician. Maybe I wasn't raising any hell, but I was there, and in my mind I was one of them. So when I would get a chance to go on those little out-of-town dates that came up every now and then, I was not from Red Bank anymore. I was from New York."

---

* *Ofay* was Black slang for a white person, *souls* was a later era's shorthand for Blacks.

3

DUKE'S CAPITAL EXPERIENCE

I T WAS A performance young Edward enacted whenever relatives were visiting. In a calculated pause at the top of the steps the lanky teenager ran his hands through his textured black hair, adjusting the carefully creased trousers that brushed the tops of his spit-shined shoes. Then he would glide slowly down the stairway, step by choreographed step, as the onlookers below looked on in bemusement. Never mind that he had overslept, missed the start of school, and his mother and aunt were fidgeting frantically in the corner. The show must go on. The maestro must receive his due. As the olive-skinned ninth grader reached the bottom landing he issued his instructions. "Stand over there," bellowed the boy with the bearing of a nobleman, pointing to a wall or doorway. "One of these days, everybody in the world is going to call me Duke Ellington, ze grand, ze great, and ze glorious Duke Ellington." He wrapped it up with final directives: the boys should bow, the girls curtsy, and everyone "applaud, applaud." At which point it was time to go to school.

Years later his family would describe the performance in detail. Cheeky, they agreed. Maybe even swollen headed.

But everything the boy had prophesied came to be. Crowds would race to see the grand and glorious Duke. Bells rang. Kings and queens, along with presidents and prime ministers, begged to play alongside him and toasted him as America's unrivaled musical genius. And while others might have been astonished by the laurels bestowed on a butler's son who dropped out of high school and learned his art in pool halls, not conservatories, Duke took it as his entitlement. "He foresaw his destiny," his cousin Bernice Wiggins recalled. "He made it."

Few in the Battlefield who grew up alongside Little Louis Armstrong imagined that one day he would be the high priest of jazz. Nobody in his Red Bank parish dreamed that soft-spoken Willie Basie would make girls feel giddy, not to mention grow worthy of a regal title like Count. But Edward Kennedy Ellington of Washington, D.C., was something else. Not only did he display in his earliest days precisely the blend of dignity and conceit that would become hallmarks of his career, but he was dubbed Duke as early as middle school.

Just who gave him the noble honorific, along with when and why, depended on which of his renditions you chose to believe. Like Louis Armstrong, he masterfully spun yarns. And like Bill Basie, there was more to his childhood narrative than the world has been led to believe, possibly much more. Duke's sister, Ruth, who was closer to him than anyone, said, "I have often described him as having veils behind veils, behind veils, behind veils. I think that he developed that kind of facade because he was so hypersensitive, that he knew he was so vulnerable to injury. And therefore he did not expose large areas of himself at the same time. Just opened up some small little facets here and there."

But a closer look at his earliest years suggests he was less of an enigma than Ruth and others made him out to be. A swashbuckler from the start, he believed in himself and in having fun with his audiences. He did revel in laying out who he was in bits and pieces, but that was because he was experimenting with new ways to assemble what he felt was an entirely original totality. To him, it wasn't a contradiction to be an artist as well as a showman, and he confided that to more people than even Ruth knew.

"I don't believe in categories of any kind," he said, referring not just to his music but his life. And he lived up to being what he pridefully called "beyond category."

————

His self-possession, along with most everything else about Edward Kennedy "Duke" Ellington, traces back to the singular force in shaping him—his mother, Daisy.

Her parents, James and Alice Kennedy, came from Virginia. According to family lore, he was the son of a slave woman and a senator who owned the plantation where James and his mother were caged, while on the same estate Alice was the indentured daughter of a Cherokee Indian and a Black man. James was freed before the signing of the Emancipation Proclamation, Alice afterward, and they moved to Washington and had a family consisting of Daisy and what Duke said was either fourteen or nine siblings.* From there

* Ruth said it was twelve, her cousin said eight, the 1900 Census said ten, and Ancestry .com says nine.

the story gets more cinematic and perhaps fanciful. James made a fortune as a builder even as he found the time to rise to captain in the District's mainly white police ranks. The family had blood ties to abolitionist Frederick Douglass and to blood bank pioneer Charles Drew, along with closer ones to doctors, lawyers, and school principals.

It was hard to fathom that Daisy was barely a generation removed from bondage. Her sensibilities were puritanical and her interests eclectic. She played piano—hymns, ragtime, and up-tempo waltzes, but no blues. She shunned lipstick and birth control, and favored old-fashioned pince-nez eyeglasses. Unlike Lillie Basie, the cultivated and attractive Daisy only worked intermittently, helping her husband. A "real Victorian lady" was how her daughter described her. Her fawning son said, "No one else but my sister Ruth had a mother as great and as beautiful as mine."

Few of those adjectives applied to James Edward Ellington, whom Daisy wed when she was eighteen and he was seventeen. Her family worried that she was marrying down. His parents were from South Carolina, where they likely were enslaved. They moved to North Carolina, where James was born in 1879, then to Washington, with the family eventually growing to what Duke said was eighteen children.* While Daisy graduated from high school, Duke said his father—friends called him J.E.—didn't finish eighth grade, and Ruth said he never went beyond third. J.E. was as joyful as Daisy was reticent. A "Chesterfieldian gentleman, you know, who wore gloves and spats. And very intellectual . . . Self-educated" was Ruth's recollection. Duke: "He was a party man, a great dancer (ballroom, that is), a connoisseur of vintages, and unsurpassed in creating an aura of conviviality."

For twenty years, he served as a coachman, butler, and sometimes confidant to Middleton F. Cuthbert, a wealthy white doctor whom J.E.'s mother had worked for and whose patients included Du Ponts and Morgenthaus. He catered or staffed receptions at embassies across the capital and—as journalists would recount in every profile on Duke—at the White House. He'd bring home not just prime steaks and terrapin, but china and silver the Cuthberts gave him and that he used to teach his children proper table-setting etiquette. And his work wasn't limited to service. During World War I he rented rooms to women who had come to Washington to help in

---

* Duke's first biographer put the number at fourteen, while Ruth counted ten. Some of the confusion is likely due to how many of the children died early in life.

  With more than two dozen first cousins traipsing through the Ellington household, Ruth and Edward got used to calling their own parents Uncle Ed and Aunt Daisy.

the war effort, and afterward he was a blueprint maker in the Navy Yard on the Potomac. As a sign of both his upward mobility and his occasional financial setbacks, the Ellingtons didn't stay in any one place very long, residing at sixteen different addresses over twenty-four years. They fit squarely into the Black bourgeoisie, never reaching the upper rungs of doctors, lawyers, or Pullman porters, but never sinking to the slum-like conditions endured by Washington's so-called alley dwellers.

Two turning points shaped the first two years of Daisy and J.E.'s marriage. In 1898, their first child—a boy conceived before they were married and delivered four months after—was stillborn, so rattling Daisy that she had difficulty leaving the house. The next year, on an unseasonably warm spring day and with help from a midwife, Edward Kennedy Ellington pushed his way into her world and became her life's devotion.

She "never took her eyes off precious little me, her jewel," Duke recalled, with Daisy pampering him, dressing him in a royal-blue, double-breasted uniform, and staying glued to his bedside through minor cuts and a bout of pneumonia. "When I was five years old, my mother put my age up to six so that I could get into first grade," he added. "She dressed me, and sent me off to school just a few blocks away. She didn't think I saw her, but I did, and every day she followed me, all the way to that school. After school, she was waiting for me at the front door of our home, if she wasn't waiting in front of the school door."

It's not by chance, perhaps, that like Louis and Bill, Edward had a mother who doted on and believed in him. This was essential for these three, since their fathers played a secondary parenting role or none at all. From Daisy, Duke learned willpower and rectitude. J.E. taught him polish and flair.

Not surprisingly, the parents attended different churches, with Edward recalling, "Every Sunday we first went to my father's church, Methodist. Then my mother took us to her church, Baptist." Rather than becoming a flash point, the messages of faith reinforced each other. "Their respect for each other was a lesson itself. You don't forget that kind of teaching. They left me such a heritage of belief that after they were gone it was natural I should turn to the Bible for help, again. I read it through four times," said the dutiful son. "I pray regularly, when I arise, when I retire. I pray my thanks for whatever He gives me: a thought, a bar of music, food . . . I figure that when we are born we are only given a lease, that's all. We're all accountable to Him at the end of the lease time. We're not supposed to arrive at the end all scarred up by anger and hurt and self-pity."

The city of Duke's birth influenced his attitudes on everything from religion to race at least as much as the Count's and Satchmo's had influenced theirs. The District of Columbia represented a border area separating the old Confederacy from the Mid-Atlantic North. It was not just the capital of America, but of Black America, with its eighty-seven thousand Negroes ranking tops in the nation in sheer numbers and constituting a third of the city's population in 1900. Blacks could aspire to being not just teachers at a school in their neighborhood, or clergy at one of the Black churches dotting the district, but to working across the federal government, which paid better, offered more security, and eventually saw 10 percent of its workforce filled with African Americans. The city was home to arguably the best Negro college in the nation, Howard University, and its Black cultural and arts activities anticipated the Harlem Renaissance by a generation. Congress had freed slaves there nine months before President Lincoln issued the Emancipation Proclamation. There were Jim Crow laws, but they were more relaxed than in most of the South. Schools and recreation facilities were racially separated, and covenants limited where Blacks could buy homes, but streetcars and public libraries were racially mixed in a way that would have drawn white outcry in New Orleans. The Ellingtons' Shaw neighborhood was the center of the Black business district, where they could see a movie, eat in a restaurant, rent a hotel room, or shop in a department store.

Washington's largesse had limits, however, as became clear during the administration of the first Southern-bred president since the Civil War, Woodrow Wilson. He authorized cabinet secretaries to segregate their departments, predicting that would reduce "friction" among workers. By the end of 1913, Black employees in several agencies had been relegated to cloistered workspaces and Coloreds-only bathrooms and lunchrooms.* Fewer good jobs were open to them, and some were reassigned to divisions slated for elimination. To ease such screening, Uncle Sam for the first time required photographs on civil service applications. And on July 19, 1919, tensions that Wilson helped stoke spilled onto the streets in four days of riots during which white veterans and mobs attacked Black businesses and residents.

The violence reached within steps of Ellington's neighborhood, but Ruth and Duke weren't hurt physically and their parents had erected an emotional buffer: an Ellingtonian exceptionalism that gave them faith they could do anything, no matter that they weren't rich or that their Black skin made them a target for white rioters. "We were always taught that we were the best,

---

* Duke's father likely witnessed the effects of that segregation when he went to work at the Navy Yard in 1920.

and so we couldn't do anything but the best," said Ruth. "I heard it from someone on the street that whites and Blacks didn't like each other, I had never heard it at home . . . I think some of the kids said to me be careful of the white kids, if you see them then walk on the other side of the street, and I really had not heard that . . . That is why Edward and I both don't have this feeling . . . I find that I forget who's what color."

Today, that sounds myopic and perhaps naive, but at the time it was the credo espoused by America's best-known Negro educator, Booker T. Washington. He argued that rather than trying to topple a fiercely entrenched system of Jim Crow, Blacks could battle back more effectively through economic improvement, self-help, and focused teaching. That was precisely what the D.C. schools were doing in the early 1900s, offering a larger dose than any in the nation of Black history and prideful learning to students like Duke. He remembered his eighth-grade English instructor's simple dictum: "Everywhere you go, you're representing the race. And you command respect. You don't ask for it . . . You never beg for it. But you command respect with your behavior." Duke never forgot that message, which "was more important than the English" classes. And he took it to heart, the more so since it was reinforced at home. He believed that Black was beautiful, and a principle to live by, long before that became the mantra of Black militants.

Two high schools were open to Edward then: Dunbar, an academically elite institution and America's first all-Black public secondary school; and its archrival, Armstrong Manual Training School, which concentrated on industrial, trade, and domestic skills. Duke enrolled at the latter, which seemed a better fit with his interest in drawing and his middling scholastic skills. His grades there were average in math, history, and English, poor in the sciences, and he somehow pulled a D in the only music course showing up in his records. He favored pulp magazines over textbooks in those years, especially Westerns and the plots and counterplots of Sherlock Holmes. Still, he managed to win an NAACP-sponsored poster contest along with a scholarship to the prestigious Pratt Institute in Brooklyn, which he turned down. A degree like that would have been Daisy's dream come true, but Duke had his own dreams and was having too much fun to defer them.

While he would insist in a late-life interview that he graduated from high school, Duke didn't, although he waited until his senior year to drop out. Half a century later he was granted an honorary diploma. Mark Tucker, who published the most complete chronicle of Ellington's early years, says he might have inflated his credentials on his own, or more likely, his publicity man did so.

Duke would always say he'd experienced "three educations"—the Bible, school, and the street corner, implying that the most influential was the last and that his favorite classroom was Frank Holliday's Poolroom. It offered the perfect counterpoint to his mother's parlor and ideal preparation for a career that would expose him to the full range of social strata. The legal age for admittance to Holliday's was sixteen, but Duke snuck in at fourteen. "Guys from all walks of life seemed to converge there: school kids over and under sixteen; college students and graduates, some starting out in law and medicine and science; and lots of Pullman porters and dining-car waiters," he remembered. "These last had much to say about the places they'd been. The names of the cities would be very impressive. You would hear them say, 'I just left Chicago,' or 'Last night I was in Cleveland' . . .

"The main thing about the poolroom, too, besides all the extraordinary talent, was the *talk*. Frank Holliday's poolroom sounded as though the prime authorities on *every* subject had been assembled there. Baseball, football, basketball, boxing, wrestling, racing, medicine, law, politics—everything was discussed with authority."

———

By that time, a chum named Edgar McEntree had dubbed him Duke, deciding, in Edward's retelling, that anyone eligible to constant companionship with the social-climbing Edgar deserved a highfalutin title. But Duke didn't need friends or even his parents to remind him of his grandeur. Everything he did underscored his innate and unshakable self-confidence.

His passion for sports matched his love of drawing in those teenage years. He was a good enough baseball player to handle second or roam center field, and he wielded a slugger's bat. He loved football, too, and ran track. He also found time for a series of jobs, from summertime dishwasher and egg-slinger in Asbury Park, New Jersey, to painting scenery at the Howard Theatre, to jerking sodas at the Poodle Dog Cafe. During World War I, he was a messenger at the Navy Department, then the State Department. And at the ballpark that hosted the Washington Senators he peddled popcorn, peanuts, chewing gum, candy, cigars, cigarettes, and scorecards. By the end of the season he'd been promoted to barking, "Cold drinks, gents! Get em ice cold!"

Music started as a sidelight and ended as the main show. Both of his parents, his grandparents, and other relatives played or sang. The piano often was the most essential piece of furniture in middle-class Black homes, and the Ellingtons had two. Their neighborhood enjoyed a reputation as the Black Broadway, with theaters, dance halls, and movie houses. Duke took his first lessons as early as age seven, for thirty-five cents, with the fittingly named Marietta Clinkscales, but he couldn't wait until he finished the barely absorbed exercises in European lullabies so he could race to the ball field. He couldn't read the sheets to start, but took the time to learn when memorizing became onerous and when he realized music's fringe benefits: money and girls.

A natural-born entrepreneur, he crafted a marketable blend of painting and piano playing. Ads in the phone book reeled in customers who came looking for a band and who left with promotional posters, too. He booked four to five musical groups, sometimes playing with them at society balls, embassy parties, or, more often, bare-bones dances in parks or fraternal halls. Around the time he was turning twenty he had enough money to buy not just a car but a house on Sherman Avenue. And wherever he went, his suits weren't the secondhand sort Little Louis and Willie Basie favored. Duke's were herringbones with pleats in the back and a matching tie perfectly knotted and neck tight.

From descending the household steps with aristocratic flair, to parading through the halls of Armstrong High, Ellington had always loved a grand entrance. Now a friend named Black Bowie preceded him to whatever club or dance hall Duke was booked into and trumpeted, "Duke Ellington is going to be here this evening." When Duke actually arrived, another companion would fling the door open and command, "Get out of the way, 'cause here comes Duke!"

"Those were the days when I was a champion drinker. I was eighteen, nineteen, or twenty, and it was customary then to put a gallon of corn whiskey on the piano when the musicians began to play. There were four of us in the group, and one hour later the jug was empty. At the end of every hour the butler would replace the jug with another full gallon of twenty-one-year-old corn," Duke remembered. "I was beginning to catch on around Washington, and I finally built up so much of a reputation that I had to study music seriously to protect it . . . I went on studying, of course, but I could also hear people whistling, and I got all the Negro music that way. You can't learn that in any school."

It's no accident that Duke remembered as much about his sign painting and band booking as his early piano playing, and nothing at all about the composing that would become legendary. It'd be nice to imagine Edward Ellington showing youthful signs of musical genius, like the child prodigies Wolfgang Mozart, Felix Mendelssohn, and Stevie Wonder. But in that respect Duke, for all his boyish bravado, was like Louis Armstrong and Count

Basie, for whom music was more of a salvation than a calling. Duke could have made a living drawing signs or portraits, managing bands or other businesses, or perhaps acting on the stage.

His teenage piano gigs seemed less like a career path than a lark, or a spirited lesson in street smarts. "There was a dance somewhere every night," recollected cornetist Rex Stewart, who was coming of age in Washington at the same time and would play for more than a decade with Duke. Their youthful stomping grounds were "the closest thing to New Orleans's Storyville," said Stewart. "You had to know what the social climate might be before venturing into a hall where you were not known, as the natives were mighty clannish in those days. Sometimes you might have to leave a dance without your overcoat, your hat or even your head! Ambulances were rarely seen in a colored neighborhood . . . and the victim generally bled to death."

With Duke, playing proved a magnet for girls. J.E. had paved his son's sweet-talking way ("he knew exactly what to say to a lady—high-toned or honey-homey"), and piano playing opened opportunities. "I learned that when you were playing piano there was always a pretty girl standing down at the bass clef end of the piano," Duke said at his elegant best. More crassly, he confided to an interviewer that "I started out playing for pussy, not money."

Edna Thompson was one of the earliest and prettiest girls. She'd grown up across the street, and was his playmate, then a classmate, sometimes sitting right behind him or next to him at school picnics. Edna developed into a more disciplined piano player and helped Duke learn to score and read. She hoped to become a music teacher, but her attachment to him derailed that dream. Edna said they fell in love in high school, where Duke "had just learned the difference between girls and boys." In his version, he lost his virginity at the callow age of twelve. Both were nineteen when they married, and a little over eight months later they had a baby boy, Mercer Kennedy Ellington.

The teenage parents didn't have it easy, but they made do until, as Edna recalled, the "second baby came. It was too close to the first and died. We were very young then. Kids, really. I think we both thought Mercer was a toy." A mournful history was repeating, of babies born out of wedlock and dying at birth.

Four years before Duke got a son, Daisy finally gave him a sibling. Or did she? Biographer A. H. Lawrence, who said he was close to Ellington and his family, speculated a quarter century ago that Ruth was Duke's daughter, not Daisy's. Jazz historian and Ruth friend Dan Morgenstern agrees. So did Ellington's young friend and confidant Robert Udkoff, who disclosed that suspicion to his daughter. Their reasoning is this: A sixteen-year gap between Duke and Ruth was inexplicably long, and over that span Daisy's feelings cooled toward her husband. That thirty-six, Daisy's age when Ruth was born, was old to be having a child in 1915 and would have been especially challenging for someone who, seventeen years earlier, went into a tailspin after delivering a stillborn baby. That Daisy was so devoted to Duke that she would have covered for him if he'd fathered a child out of wedlock, at just sixteen, with an unidentified mother. That Duke boasted about being sexually active as a preteen and being promiscuous forever. And that Duke's solicitousness of Ruth over the years was more like how a man would behave toward his daughter than his sister.

Lawrence's publisher dropped that hypothesis from the book after complaints from Ellington family members, although not before it made its way into a British newspaper—and a chronology at the back of the book refers to Ruth with quotation marks around the word *sister*. Mercedes Ellington, Duke's granddaughter, says she's heard the rumor but that keeping such a secret would have been exceedingly difficult, and neither her father Mercer nor her aunt Ruth gave her any indication it was true. If it was, she and others acknowledge, the only ones who would have known for sure were Daisy, J.E., Duke, and the child's birth mother.

What is certain is that Duke grew up with conflicting attitudes about women that would last a lifetime. There's no evidence that he physically mistreated any of the multitude he wooed, but neither could he fully commit to any, even his first and only wife, Edna. "I would say that, apart from his mother and sister, he had a basic contempt for women," wrote Mercer, who himself had trouble committing to women and alternated between adoring and abhorring his father. "Once he uncovered a weakness, or brought them to heel, so to speak, he passed on to someone else."

PART II

MUSICAL LIVES

4

NIGHTSPOTS

S TEP INTO DUKE Ellington's Cotton Club any night of the week in
the jazz-mad 1920s and you'd behold not just feathers, flappers, and
high-flying legs, but America at both its rip-roaring finest and its most
narrow minded.

The electrified "COTTON CLUB" sign made it easy to spot, especially
for tourists from River City and Rocky Mount who had the nightspot at the
top of their must-see lists. Just the idea of being in Harlem's Jungle Alley—
speakeasy capital of the planet and Valhalla for white downtowners eager for
a saucy evening in Negro uptown—was titillating. Wasn't that Mayor Jimmy
"Beau James" Walker stepping out of the silver-trimmed Duesenberg, with
his showgirl mistress Betty Compton on his arm? Could that be the Last of
the Red Hot Mamas, Sophie Tucker, at the table near the stage with Jimmy
"the Schnoz" Durante and Countess Mountbatten of Burma?

When the show started, it set listeners' feet tapping just like it had back
home, when CBS Radio brought Duke Ellington and His Cotton Club Orchestra into their kitchens. *Theater Arts Monthly* had rightly promised in
1934 that those who made it to the real thing would find a horseshoe-shaped
champagne-popping tableau seating seven hundred: "The big bass drum
boom, boom. Enthusiastic wails writhe from the cornet—another flash from
two dozen tawny, brown legs, whip-snapping . . . One by one, our cherished
biases [about Blacks and big cities] are taken off like arctic overcoats. It becomes natural to laugh and shout in the consciousness of an emotional holiday." Like the magazine writer said, there'd be time enough when the show
was over and the bus was boarding to slip back into "one's hat, coat, and
niceties" and become anew "staid, proper, and a community pillar."

No wonder audiences swooned.

But to the keen eye, the setting conveyed something much more layered.
Sixty years after the Civil War, the stage design at these United States' most

glamorous cabaret could be called faux plantation. The bandstand had been built to look like a white-columned mansion, with scenery depicting cotton bushes, weeping willows, and slave quarters. The menu, which paired Harlem-inspired fried chicken and barbecued spareribs with time-honored filet mignon and lobster, was served with a flourish by waiters whose tuxedos were red and whose skin was, to a man, black. Dark tones were okay for servers meant to look like butlers, and for exotic male dancers, but not for the scantily clad can-can-kicking chorus girls, who had to be at least five foot six, twenty-one or younger, and "high-yaller." (Although the unofficial guideline was nothing darker than a brown paper bag, the dancers described themselves as "tall, tan and terrific.")*

The antebellum fantasy didn't end there. While all the performers and stewards were Black, no patron was. Thickset bouncers enforced that rule with help from Manhattan's finest, who, like law enforcers elsewhere, were alarmed by miscegenation or even mixed-race fellowship. Warnings weren't needed for Ellington, whose band kept the beat for the shows at midnight and 2 A.M., enticed patrons to the dance floor in between, learned how to play "under-conversation" numbers for those who preferred conversing to cutting a rug, and trailblazed the growling "jungle music" that his bosses wanted from him and his nine Negro sidemen. (The Jungle Band was a pseudonym the orchestra used then on its phonograph records.)

Those codes were mandated by custom, not by law, as they would have been down South. What statutes there were meant little to the Cotton Club's racketeer bosses. Owney Madden, the British-born owner with a girlish voice and the rap sheet of a cold-blooded butcher, liked Ellington's jazz almost as much as he liked charging a usurious $30 for a bottle of bootlegged bubbly (more than $500 in today's currency). No matter that the Eighteenth Amendment to the Constitution banned the manufacture, transportation, or sale of alcohol during that Prohibition Era. In the Roaring Twenties, after all, nothing truly was prohibited. It was a moment when F. Scott Fitzgerald and Gertrude Stein's Lost Generation committed themselves to forgetting the horrors of World War I, celebrating a soaring stock market, and—donning raccoon coats and hip flasks—dancing cheek-to-cheek to the syncopated rhythms of hot jazz that was conquering America.

---

* That tawny color line was cracked in 1932 by Lucille Wilson, a dark-skinned chorus dancer who later became Mrs. Louis Armstrong. Satchmo himself is said to have been kept from performing there in the club's early days because his skin, too, was considered "a little too Negro." Haskins, *The Cotton Club*, 151.

Anyone who balked, or couldn't hold their booze, was quickly set straight by Madden and his wise guys. "When the show was on—and they did have a wonderful show—no one was allowed to talk [loudly]," Ellington recalled. "I'll never forget. Some guy would be juiced and start talking, Yap-yap-yap-yap. And the waiter would come: 'Sir, would you please'—and the next thing the captain would come over, and the next thing you know, the head waiter would come, and then the next thing the guy would just disappear. A great place."

But did Ellington really believe the Cotton Club was a great place, with his band perched on what looked like the veranda of a fossilized Southern plantation, picking up half dollars tossed at their feet as tips and playing music that seemed to emanate from the heart of primeval Africa? Surely not. Yet just as surely he had few options in those early career years, when white folks loved being transported back to their vision of the good old slave days and Black folks had to endure it. Duke, as usual, made the best of his sullied circumstances. "Even before the band sounded a note," the *New Yorker* noted, "it delivered a statement: impeccably dressed in matching tuxedos and boutonnières, its members were of a class with the biggest swells in the room. And Ellington was the swellest of all: unfailingly soigné, magisterially presiding over the urban jungle, he stood untouched and never lost his smile."

He hadn't looked quite so swell when, in his midtwenties, he first arrived in New York from Washington early in 1923. He did travel in style—riding the plush parlor car, consuming a first-class dinner on board and tipping the waiter excessively, then taking an expensive taxi uptown to meet his friends—but that took his last penny. Now he and his D.C. buddies had to hustle to survive, shooting pool for money during the day, flitting between watering holes at night. "The minute we got two dollars, we'd quit, go home, dress up, order two steak dinners, give the girl a quarter, and have a quarter left for tomorrow," Duke recalled, making it sound more romantic than it must have been to not know where they'd sleep or whether they'd eat. "We would never send home for any money, because we knew that would scare our people to death, and stories about our splitting a hot dog five ways were more of a gag than anything else."

He persevered. For every low-budget rent party he played—covers and drinks were each twenty-five cents, with profits saving the host from eviction—there was a real gig in Atlantic City or a dance, a concert, or both in outlying burgs like Salem and Haverhill, in Massachusetts. His best and steadiest runs were at Manhattan's Hollywood Cabaret and Club Kentucky, the name the Hollywood reopened under in 1925 after the second of two fires. Slumber in those days came when you could find a couch, and drinking was done from what he called "the gladiator perspective." Looking back in his 1973 memoir, he wrote, "I don't drink booze anymore. I retired undefeated champ about thirty years ago, and now I call myself a 'retired juicehead.' I drank more booze than anybody ever."

As his outlook sobered, he took what he called his "next big step" at the Cotton Club, which in 1927 was looking for an orchestra that could doll up the nightspot's image and make owner Owney Madden even richer. Madden's first choice was King Oliver, the New Orleans–to–Chicago cornetist-composer and Louis Armstrong's mentor, but he was having problems with his Dixie Syncopators (disbanded after being stranded in Baltimore), his teeth (a gum infection cost him all his choppers), and his outsized ego (he said the good offer wasn't good enough). That gave Duke his break. While five other bands auditioned, Owney failed to show up on time and only managed to hear Ellington. One hurdle remained: Ellington was under contract to perform in Philadelphia. Madden's men called City of Brotherly Love bootlegger Max "Boo Boo" Hoff, who called enforcer Julius "Yankee" Schwartz, who relayed a simple message to the Philly theater manager: "Be big about this, or you'll be dead." The theater man opted for life and let Ellington go.

"A classic example of being at the right place at the right time with the right thing before the right people," Duke said of his hiring. His band arrived in dramatic fashion, on the midnight train the very day he was due to start at the Cotton Club, December 4, 1927. They put on a ragged show that first night, but soon learned their cues, ironed out the wrinkles, added new members, and garnered headlines. Just how far they had come was memorialized by British composer, bassist, and scribe Patrick Cairns "Spike" Hughes. "Duke and his band are the only two things, apart from Toscanini, which have exceeded my wildest hopes of New York," he said. "I must confess that I could go on writing from now until the Judgment Day on the topic of Duke as a person and an artist, of the way he starts his numbers by rippling away at the piano until the band is set to go, of how he accompanies tap-dancers, of how his personality, as he sits in front of the band, expresses every mood of his own glorious music, and of the thousand and one other things that go to make him one of the most delightful and vivid characters of our time."

In the middle of his Cotton Club stay in 1930 and in one of his first interviews, the thirty-one-year-old Ellington talked about the music he was composing and playing. He knew the mutes and other inflections that gave his band a growling jungle sound were controversial with Black columnists and intellectuals, but he believed to his core that it was uplifting rather than demeaning his race. No pallid symphonies or operas here, but rather hair-raising arabesques, breakneck dance tunes, and mournful melodies that struck an African chord. "I really couldn't play very well the things white people played. So I decided that, since I must play, I should have to write something I could play myself," he told the *Christian Science Monitor*. "I am just getting a chance to work out some of my own ideas of Negro music. I stick to that. We as a race have a good deal to pay our way with in a white world . . . It pleases me to have a chance to work at it."

He also pushed back, in his soft manner, at restrictions like the ones that kept Blacks on the Cotton Club stage but out of its booths. That had always been a more nuanced policy than advertised, offering Negro celebrities like Paul Robeson and Ethel Waters tables near the kitchen, and admitting Black interns from Harlem Hospital who were on call in case entertainers drank too much, overdosed, or needed Dexedrine to stay awake. None of that helped Daisy Ellington, who could watch her son when his band played Broadway, but not at the speakeasy where he earned his living. With Edward's nudging, his mother, father, sister, young son, and closest friends were at last added to the exemption list.*

Much as he loved the twenty-dollar tips, rave reviews, and the racial entrée afforded by his closeness to the Madden mob, it was the wireless that catapulted Duke from a Harlem-centered luminary to a national one. Initially limited to local broadcasts, Bill Paley's fledgling CBS network soon picked him up, and by 1930 he had moved to the biggest and best, NBC's Peacock Network. From its inception, radio had linked urban America with the heartland, and North with South, but the medium had never been this bold in its programming. For many white Americans, hearing Ellington at the Cotton Club was their introduction to Harlem, to jazz, and to a Black artist. That weekly exposure ensured the devotion of not just the rubbernecks from the boondocks, but of music fans around the nation and eventually the globe.

---

* Ebony-toned composer W. C. Handy was among those who were turned away, even on a night when he could hear his own music blaring inside, while Duke's future doctor, Arthur Logan, was admitted as a bow to his light complexion and his posting at Harlem Hospital. The Cotton Club's exclusionary policies, along with his love of Ellington's music, motivated jazz fan Barney Josephson in 1938 to open New York's first integrated nightclub, Café Society, which earned the moniker "the wrong place for the right people." Lewis, *When Harlem Was in Vogue,* 209; and email to author from Adele Logan Alexander.

Word got out even earlier along the Great White Way and among the intelligentsia. Ellington's Cotton Club shows attracted luminaries ranging from George Gershwin to H. L. Mencken and William Faulkner. Sunday night was Celebrity Night, when Broadway went dark and stars like Al Jolson and Sophie Tucker came to watch Duke. When acclaimed Russian-born composer Igor Stravinsky stepped off the boat in New York Harbor, his welcoming committee asked what he'd like to do: "I want to go and hear Duke Ellington play at the Cotton Club."

The club was known then as the Aristocrat of Harlem, and Edward Ellington was, too.

All of this happened at a special moment in Harlem's history. By the early 1920s, the neighborhood in Upper Manhattan was displacing Washington as the Negro capital of America, fueled by the migration of more than one hundred thousand Blacks from the South and animated by a renewal of Black literature, theater, scholarship, fashion, and political awareness. Called then the New Negro Movement, and later the Harlem Renaissance, the zeitgeist embraced most of African American culture but wasn't sure how it felt about jazz and definitely didn't like the Cotton Club or its slumming patrons pretending to be two things they weren't: Black and hep. Preachers and columnists worried that their neighborhood was becoming a spectacle if not a ghetto. Social workers blamed the hot tunes for the surge in juvenile delinquency. Even the mainstream *Ladies' Home Journal* was asking, "Does Jazz Put the Sin in Syncopation?" College professors, meanwhile, accused musicians like Ellington of lacking the relevance or reach of African American literary icons like Zora Neale Hurston and Langston Hughes.[*] Apparently none of the experts had consulted with Hurston, who married a jazz musician, or Hughes, whose art was called jazz poetry. The facts also argued otherwise. More people tuned in to Ellington's broadcasts than turned out for the sum total of all of Harlem's lettered and visual artists. As important, Duke was doing just what the Renaissance aspired to: turning Negro folk art into all-American art.

The evolving names of his band mirrored the way he bounced be-

---

[*] The critics were right that Harlem was becoming infused with music and booze: by 1929, according to the *New York Amsterdam News,* the neighborhood was home to eleven "class white-trade night clubs," including the Cotton Club, and more than five hundred "colored cabarets of lower rank." And their warnings were on the mark about Harlem degenerating into a slum, although that was driven by poor migrants and lack of housing and opportunity, not by jazzmen or their fans. Hasse, *Beyond Category: The Life and Genius of Duke Ellington,* 114.

tween venues, record labels, and front men. He came to the profession as Duke's Serenaders and left Washington as Duke Ellington and His Washingtonians. From then on it was difficult to keep track: Kentucky Club Orchestra, Harlem Footwarmers, Lonnie Johnson's Harlem Footwarmers, Chicago Footwarmers, Earl Jackson and His Musical Champions, Jungle Band, the Ellingtonians, Six Jolly Jesters, Sonny Greer and His Memphis Men, Joe Turner and His Memphis Men, Whoopee Makers, Ten Black Berries, Duke Ellington and His Orchestra, Duke Ellington and His Rhythm, Duke Ellington and His Famous Orchestra, and Duke Ellington and His Cotton Club Orchestra.

Whatever the name or place, Duke was settling into backstage routines that his fans would never see but might have relished. After his second Cotton Club show finished in the nearly dawned morning, Duke would play cards with bandmates, chorus girls, and club bosses. They began with whist, a trick-taking precursor to contract bridge. Pinochle, a blend of tricks and melds using a forty-eight-card deck, was a carryover from trains and hotels. Rummy was the least taxing, a perfect match as everyone tired or got distracted by eating, talking, and drinking bootlegged beer or bourbon. Then it was to bed, or perhaps a quick stop at Connie's Inn or another nearby speakeasy.

Wife Edna and son Mercer were seldom in the city in those early years, and never in Duke's dressing room—which was a good thing, since Mildred Dixon was usually there. Mildred's dancing duo had made its Cotton Club debut the same night as Duke had, and the two would work and sleep together for years. Like his future paramours, Mildred was stunning—short and slim, with dark eyes and light skin. She seemed fascinated by everything Duke said—"Yes, yes, go on"—and was his truest love until the next one blossomed. In between long-term mistresses there was Polly Adler, the West Side madam whose clients included a mayor and mobsters, movie stars, and, when he wasn't playing the piano as her entertainment, a young bandleader with a regal name and an insatiable libido.

By the time he left the Cotton Club in February 1931, Duke was transformed. He'd arrived in Manhattan nearly a decade before as an underappreciated son of the District of Columbia, and even there few fathomed him or his music. By the end of his three-plus-year Cotton Club run he reigned as America's most acclaimed Black bandleader and a knight of Harlem, although he'd spend less and less time there in the years that followed. His memoir included this salute to his adopted city: "Amid all her tickertape and traffic, New York is the dream of a song. New York is a place where the rich walk, the poor drive Cadillacs, and beggars die of malnutrition with thousands of dollars hidden in their mattresses.''*

He had developed some healthy and productive habits during his Cotton Club years that would last a lifetime—composing and arranging hundreds of recordings, along with fine-tuning his skills as an accompanist on the piano and orchestrating a band that had swelled from ten to twelve. He toppled some racial barriers, resigned himself to others, and showcased his artistry at America's most celebrated cabaret and, courtesy of the wireless, throughout the country's hinterlands. Duke had nurtured his vices as well. He'd largely abandoned his family, the same way he would his mistresses, and had married the mob, telling himself both were necessary sacrifices for a swinging musician and a racial pioneer. He'd also taken to using the royal we, a measure of the vanity and fantasy of nobility he had evidenced from boyhood.

———

The Reno Club was as downscale as the Cotton Club was up. Instead of silk-stocking swells, the Kansas City speakeasy catered to cattle ranchers, wheat farmers, and shipping clerks. No filet mignon here, just chili, franks, or the pig snouts and hog maws available just outside at John Agnos's lunch wagon. The frills were gone, too—no scenery, staging, or costumes, and just a handful of chorus girls and an occasional tap dancer, not that anyone much noticed, with the L-shaped saloon darkened by smoke, and little room to dance or even stretch. If the Cotton Club was modeled after the master's Big House, the Reno was the chattel's cabin.

The hot-as-hell hole-in-the-wall did, however, share several things with its rich cousin back east, starting with the vice. Drinks flowed during Prohibition much as they had before and would after, with beer sold for a nickel, domestic Scotch (or a hot dog) a dime, and an imported single malt (or a hamburger) fifteen cents. Reefers cost a half dollar while prostitutes charged three times that, although it was less for just a dance. "If you want to see some sin, forget Paris and go to Kansas City," journalist Edward R. Murrow wrote in those Roaring Twenties. The godfather of that iniquity was Thomas Joseph Pendergast, an Irish American bootlegger whose family owned the

---

* Ellington loved to pen poetry about neighborhoods he relished, including Chicago's South Side: "It was a community with twelve Negro millionaires, no hungry Negroes, no complaining Negroes, no crying Negroes, and no Uncle Tom Negroes. It was a community of men and women who were respected, people of great dignity—doctors, lawyers, policy operators, bootblacks, barbers, beauticians, bartenders, saloonkeepers, night clerks, cab owners and cab drivers, stockyard workers, owners of after-hours joints, bootleggers—everything and everybody, but *no* junkies." Edward Kennedy Ellington, *Music Is My Mistress*, 131.

Reno and who oversaw a Democratic machine that dominated the politics in and around Kansas City—known then as Tom's Town—as well as its cultural and business life. T.J. rolled out red carpets for jazz and booze, in contrast to the teetotalers who ran most of Missouri and all of neighboring Kansas. And he welcomed Blacks into his organization and his club, but only on the crowded balcony, in a jam-packed area behind the kiosk, or playing in the band. Musicians were grateful for the steady work, no matter that their weekly pay was only $15 and that they worked from eight at night 'til four in the morning except Saturdays, when quitting time was eight the following morning.

While different in so many ways, the NYC and KC cabarets each played a seminal role in the history of jazz and therefore of America. Much as the Cotton Club helped turn an unfledged Edward Ellington into a true Duke, the Reno was where Willie Basie was crowned Count and where his sputtering career got a jump-start. Each club also suited the bandleader it hosted: the elegant Cotton featured the polished and patrician Duke, while the bare-bones Reno presented the no-frills Count. Basie, like Ellington, would move on from his baptismal venue after just three years, but he'd never forget Kansas City or Club Reno.

"It was a good place to work," Basie recalled. "I liked the atmosphere down there. There was always a lot of action because there were at least four other cabarets right there on that same block, and they all had live music and stayed open late." As for Kansas City, Basie called it "a cracker town, but a happy town."

That happiness was partly a function of how the Kid from Red Bank landed in the Paris of the Plains, the result of a peripatetic life playing in aptly named territory bands. Starting in the 1920s, these dance ensembles crisscrossed established circuits, bringing the novel sounds of jazz and swing to any hotel ballroom, gin mill, or Elks club that would book them for a night or, rarer and better, a week. The troupes found their most receptive audiences while barnstorming across the wide-open Southwest. Newly paved roads carried them in raggedy buses and jam-packed jalopies from Austin and Amarillo to Tulsa and Norman, dusty burgs and jerkwater towns too remote for big-name bands to venture, with as much as a thousand miles between bookings. They rarely saw any money up front, relying on a cut of the gate, bootlegged whiskey, and a warm meal. But to young musicians like Bill Basie, it was heavenly. He got to follow the sun and money wherever it took him. No need to be pinned down by parents or lovers. Wayfaring let him live each day as it came, seeing the panoramic deserts, mountains, and plains of his country while he honed his chops in what amounted to a no-madic conservatory.

Basie had gotten his first taste of national touring between 1925 and 1927, when he played with Katie Crippen's vaudeville show. In 1928 he took another step away from the region of his birth when he signed up with Walter Page's Blue Devils, which proved a stepping-stone to the best of the blues-based orchestras in the Southwest, led by Bennie Moten. Most territory musicians never made it out of the music world's version of the minor leagues, but at age twenty-five, Basie was in the bigs and eager to get bigger.

The end of 1933 brought the end of Prohibition, which should have meant good times for nightlife, nightclubs, and traveling bands like Moten's. But the Great Depression continued to strangle the economy, especially in the drought-stricken Dust Bowl. As territory bands broke up, their members sought better prospects, often in Tom's remarkably resilient town of Kansas City. While Pendergast deftly maintained his political grip and managed to replace the profits he'd earned from bootlegging and the protection racket, Bennie Moten proved less successful as a wheeler-dealer.* He had hoped to merge his band with another leading one, but his men weren't having it. They voted out the beloved Moten and replaced him with the mild-mannered pi-ano player, Bill Basie.

Was Basie the reluctant beneficiary of an unplanned mutiny? That was how he told the story: "I can truthfully say that when I went in there to that meeting, I didn't have any idea at all that Bennie Moten himself was going to be the one getting fired . . . Then before I could get over that, they had picked me to take his place." In truth, Basie was a conniver from the start—strutting his stuff for the manager when a contracted player was on break, showing up uninvited to rehearsals, or palling around with anyone he thought could advance his ambitions—and he used his mild-mannered disposition to make it look more like pull than push as he rose from piano man to band-leader. "I'll just say I didn't intend to let anything stop me, and that should tell you something about Bill Basie," Bill confessed about his early efforts to join Bennie. A day after the coup, Basie changed the band's name to Count Basie and His Cherry Blossom Victor Recording Orchestra. But less than a

---

* Pendergast's new hustles were building big public-works projects (mythmakers dubbed it Pendergast Prosperity) that meant big contracts for his cement company, and having his wholesale company supply over the counter the table liquor he'd provided under it during Prohibition. He also continued to collect protection money from gamblers specializing in everything from numbers running to horse betting and table games.

year later band members abandoned Basie and returned to Moten, and the Count followed, drawing on his charm to rebuild Moten's trust. He stayed on until Bennie's untimely death in 1935, during a routine tonsillectomy.*

Basie had made Kansas City his home by then. He fit in comfortably since he'd started coming in the mid-1920s. The city was hopping, a Wild West town that burned its candles at both ends. Pendergast made sure that the liquor always flowed and that nothing impeded the merrymaking. The sprawling Ford plant hummed late into the evening. Ships steamed in and out of its port at the junction of the Missouri and Kansas Rivers, and its teeming stockyards and a train station serving twelve lines were second only to Chicago's. St. Louis might call itself the Gateway to the West, but KC really was by the time Bill Basie arrived. It also had been where Dixie met Yankee since before the Civil War, when the Union Army held the city and much of the countryside preferred the Confederacy. Yet it still had its Arcadian flavor, with glass-and-tile drugstores and big backyards, orange juice stands, and a skyline that seemed to sprout out of the wheat fields. Even the barbecue—pig, possum, and raccoon slow-cooked over a hickory pit, slathered with a peppery molasses sauce, then wrapped in newspaper like British fish and chips—had a kick that became legendary.

Kansas City's forty thousand Negro residents—10 percent of its total population—orchestrated the jazz, belted out the blues, seared the barbecue, and supplied much of the sweat that fed the local economy. Jim Crow did limit where they lived, worked, and played, but not as rigidly as in New Orleans, not much more than in Red Bank, and not with lynchings. Many Black musicians ended up there the same way Basie did, via territory bands, while others were migrants from the South known as Exodusters. Once there, a surprising number decided to stay. They were won over by active chapters of the NAACP and the Young Negro GOP Club, a full-throated Negro newspaper called the *Call,* lots of proud Black Baptist and African Methodist churches, a concentration of courtly Pullman train porters, and an all–African American baseball team called the Monarchs. It was the best in the Negro Leagues and maybe anywhere, featuring Leroy "Satchel" Paige, a pitcher so hard-throwing that catchers softened his sting by cushioning their gloves with beefsteaks, and James "Cool Papa" Bell, a center fielder fast enough to steal two bases on a single pitch.

---

* One reason Moten took Basie back is that the Count composed for the band a song called "I Lost," apparently a whimsical admission to his bad behavior. Driggs and Haddix, *Kansas City Jazz,* 129–30.

A lover of ribs, riffs, and rundowns, Basie found Kansas City irresistible.

His fresh identity as a Kansas Citian was accompanied by a new and for-ever moniker. The storied version is that a radio announcer bestowed it in 1936, believing that Bill Basie deserved as noble a nickname as Duke Elling-ton and King Oliver. Or was it four years earlier when the band was billed as Count Basie and His Cherry Blossom Orchestra? Or when, bedecked in his first tuxedo, he joked that he looked like Count Dracula? Or perhaps when Bennie Moten would tease, "Aw, that guy ain't no 'count." Basie, who helped fuel all four narratives, offered a fifth and most revealing one in his memoir: he coined the title himself, after jealously watching fellow musicians pick up theirs. "I decided to name myself the Count," he wrote. "I actually had some little fancy business cards printed up to announce it. COUNT BASIE. Beware the Count is Here."

Wherever it came from, the highborn title didn't match his lowdown be-havior. He drank too much, partied too hard, and was too unreliable, as he admitted and witnesses confirmed. "That [Basie] band didn't believe in going out with steady black people. They'd head straight for the pimps and prostitutes and hang out with them," said Gene Ramey, a double bassist who was in Kansas City at the time and later played with the Count. "Basie was down there, lying in the gutter, getting drunk with them. He'd have patches in his pants . . . and holes in his shoes, and you see him walking down the street, trying to be a dignified beggar."

Vivian Winn was more surprised than anyone by the Count's lapses. Thin, pretty, and light-skinned, she worked as a clerk at an all-Black el-ementary school that summer of 1930, when she became Mrs. William Basie.* She'd been part of the Negro social and literary circles in Kansas City, and presumed her soft-spoken and dapper new husband was made for that world. So did the aspiring Bill, momentarily and mistakenly. Growing up in a family built around secrets, he had learned to keep his outlaw side under wraps. And he had no social or literary side. A year into their marriage, the pair set off in their new Pontiac to tour the East with the band. Halfway through, Vivian returned in tears to Kansas City. In Jan-uary 1934, just three and a half years after they were wed, a story on page one of the *Call* announced that she was seeking a divorce.

Her petition painted a distressing picture. The very day they were married,

* Her light complexion might have given the marriage registrar concerns about whether it was a mixed-race marriage, which would explain why she had to attest on the form, "I am a full Blooded Negro."

the Count abandoned her "without provocation, cause or justification . . . leaving her without income or means of support and has since refused to live with her as husband and wife." The bandleader often left home for "unreasonable" periods of time and refused to say where he was going. He displayed a "harsh and ungovernable" temper and used "quarrelsome, vile and abusive language, which caused her great embarrassment and mental anguish." For a year before their separation, he was "addicted to habitual drinking," she added, asking the court to restore her maiden name.

There is no record of an official response by the Count, but in his memoir he wrote: "As for what was happening with me and the ladies during those early days in Kansas City, I figure that ain't nobody's business . . . I was just out there hitting on whatever I could get next to, with no strings attached. Of course, if any of them had strings attached to somebody else, I'm damn sure not going to mention that." It was classic Basie-speak, making clear that his skeletons would stay closeted. No remorse for any pain he'd caused, or reflection on what he'd do differently if there were a next time. He simply called his marriage to Vivian "a mistake. In fact, that was the biggest mistake I had ever made." As if to underline the point of how little she'd meant to him, he said he couldn't remember the date they were married (July 21, 1930), and he misspelled her last name (Wynn in his autobiography, Winn on their marriage license and everywhere else).

A year after their divorce, Basie started at the Reno Club, which a prominent reviewer described as "one of the town's most unsavory holes." It was in the shadow of police headquarters and the new county courthouse, but there was no worry about interference from either so long as club owners paid the Pendergast mob on time and in full. The Count accepted his club's racial separation because he had to, but he balked at plans to rope off white entertainers from Colored ones at jam sessions: "Oh, no, we don't go for that!"* As for the immorality and graft, Basie was a realist, knowing those made the Reno and fifty other nightclubs on Twelfth Street enticing to whites from places like Independence, Missouri, the same as Harlem's Cotton Club was for whites from New York City's East Side.

But what really reeled in the Reno's patrons was the music—and oh, was there music. The sound that would be christened Kansas City style throbbed

---

* Basie called those jams, which ran from about 3 A.M. to 7 A.M. Monday mornings, Spook Breakfasts. The name "didn't really have anything to do with color," he explained. "We kept late hours, spooky hours." It also didn't have much in common with the Cotton Club's Sunday Celebrity Nights. Basie, *Good Morning Blues*, 162.

with a propulsive rhythm, repeating riffs, along with reach-back-to-cotton-field blues, honky-tonk ragtime, and the call-and-response phrasing brought to these shores by enslaved Africans. Big bands pumped out the noisy tunes like "Moten's Swing" and "Messa Stomp" that would bring all but the most necrotic listeners to their feet whirling and swaying. Open any door or window in the Jazz Capital of the World and you'd hear melodies that floated in time. The best came in the mid-1930s from Basie's nine-piece Barons of Rhythm, which included such superstars as the Blue Devils' leader and double bassist Walter "Big 'Un" Page, tenor saxophonist and hipster Lester "Prez" Young, and the portly vocalist Jimmy "Mr. Five by Five" Rushing. Some called it stomp, others jump. By any definition, it was Basie who spotted the talent and assembled this all-star band, who pounded the piano with a loose-limbed abandon too seldom seen later, and whose name would be attached to the earthy Kansas City jazz that drew on the lived experiences of ghetto Blacks as well as working-world whites.

Basie's sound and his name quickly spread beyond Kansas City. As it had for Duke Ellington, radio brought the Count's music first across Kansas and Missouri, then to taxi drivers in Central Park, jitney cabs on Chicago's South Side, and others tuned in to the Reno's high-frequency-channel broadcasts. One special listener was John Hammond, a music critic and producer in New York who'd later help launch Bob Dylan and Aretha Franklin. "I went to my car every night to listen to Basie," Hammond recalled, pronouncing the band "the best I had ever heard . . . This sort of unbuttoned, never-too-disciplined band is the foundation from which inspired jazz solos spring." Basie remembered that the young white talent scout came across the country unannounced to the Reno in 1936, ordered the bandleader a gin over ice, and stayed for two days. By then, Basie said, "I already knew that he was all for us. So he made his report back to New York, and that sort of started a lot of things for us."

Hammond's visit signaled the end of what Basie called "nine fantastic years" in and out of Kansas City, a place where he'd faltered as well as flourished. It also dawned on the maestro: "I really wasn't William Basie or Bill Basie the piano player from Red Bank anymore. From now on and for better or worse I was Count Basie, the bandleader out of Kansas City."

_____

If the suitably swank Cotton Club launched the sophisticated Duke, and the harum-scarum Reno kick-started the happy-footed Count, it's fitting that Louis Armstrong, the aspiring musician from a New Orleans shantytown known more for his horn playing than his band leading, should be rocketed skyward from a sunless, unventilated studio. OKeh Records' portable workspace was in Chicago's Loop, on the fourth floor of a brick warehouse in a shabby neighborhood of wall-to-wall storehouses, wholesalers, and newspapers, where the constant din of trucks, wagons, and full-throated newsboys filled the air. The musicians had two choices to get their equipment upstairs: lug it up themselves, or borrow the freight elevator. At most sessions there was an audience of two: one engineer and an equally lonely producer. There, Armstrong and his mates cut thirty-eight discs aimed not at all of music-loving America, but at the narrow all-Negro market derisively known as race records and especially at Blacks in the not-so-old Confederacy.

The recording process was as slapdash as its setting was rudimentary. Performers came straight from their late-night gigs, sometimes back-to-back-to-back shows that ended at three in the morning and left them adrenaline charged but sleep deprived. Records were made of shellac and, on average, captured just three minutes of sound. Fees were flat and low. OKeh's acoustic technique, called Truetone, was better than the vestigial one that industry founder Thomas Alva Edison used half a century earlier, but not by much. Musicians gathered at large horns set up around the room. The recorders acted like funnels, dispersing sounds to a stylus that cut them directly onto a rotating disc.* Any mistake meant starting over. OKeh reasoned that it was bad to "expert" the music makers and inhibit their freedom. It also was expensive. And while OKeh was the industry leader in race records, its standards were low, sloppiness was tolerated, and part of the attraction was that Black artists could be underpaid and overworked.

But Little Louis transcended those bleak circumstances, the same way he had in the Battlefield and at the Colored Waif's Home. The music that his Hot Five and Hot Seven bands set to wax in that cramped studio would become a yardstick against which all other jazz would be measured, then and still. It crafted a new language for the callow genre and transformed an all-ensemble approach into the art of the soloist—the highest art when that solitary performer was Louis Armstrong.

At twenty-four, Armstrong was the youngest of the combo that inaugural night of record making on November 12, 1925. He'd lured in his pals for these sessions pitched to Southern tastes: trombonist Edward "Kid" Ory, whose band he'd joined after King Oliver left Louisiana; two talented

---

* A trumpet, especially one played with Louis's volume and clarity, was one of the few instruments able to be captured well by these primitive recording horns and discs.

Johnnys, Dodds on clarinet and St. Cyr on banjo and guitar; and pianist Lil Hardin Armstrong, Louis's wife of twenty-one months. It was his first time recording with a band of his own, and listening to him egg on his bandmates makes clear how he relished the role: "Oh, play that thing, Mr. St. Cyr, lord. You know you can do it." It wasn't just fellow musicians that he was inviting in to the merrymaking, but his prospective audience. The band laid down just three songs that night—"My Heart," "Yes! I'm in the Barrel," and the most memorable and first to be released, "Gut Bucket Blues." If those had been the only tracks they ever committed to wax, it would have made a compelling footnote to the Armstrong catalog, but the quintet returned to the studio twice in February and, on the twenty-sixth, it etched itself into history.

"Heebie Jeebies," a lilting ditty, opened with Louis warbling "I've got the heebies, I mean the jeebies." Then he inserted "eef," "gaff," "mmff," "dee-bo," "rip-bip-ee-doo-dee-doot," and other nonsense syllables that sounded more like a musical instrument than spoken English, and that he sang while making funny faces. Was it, as Louis insisted, that he dropped the sheet with the lyrics and, not remembering them, made up plosive vocables? He told the story so joyfully that people assumed it couldn't be so, but it might well have been. It wasn't the beginning of scatting; Louis had done that himself with his kids quartet, and the technique traced back to Irish lilters and German yodelers. But this Hot Five version spread faster than the Great Chicago Fire. Forty thousand records sold within weeks, along with Heebie Jeebies shoes, hats, sandwiches, and a dance choreographed to accompany the song. Drummer and later vibraphonist Lionel Hampton was one of many boyish musicians walking Chicago's wintry streets in hopes of catching cold and echoing the gravelly Louis, while Bing Crosby, Ella Fitzgerald, and Sarah Vaughan were but a few of the adult crooners copying his hi-de-ho-style chatter and irrepressible cool. "You would hear cats greeting each other with Louis' riffs when they met around town—*I got the heebies,* one would yell out, and the other would answer *I got the jeebies,* and the next minute they were scatting in each other's face," recalled Armstrong friend Mezz Mezzrow. "Louis' recording almost drove the English language out of the Windy City for good."[*]

---

[*] Louis's real revolution wasn't in inventing scat but in teaching fellow crooners to forget all the rules they'd learned. "Before Armstrong, popular singers inhaled deeply, puffed out their chests and projected," Daniel Okrent wrote in *Time* magazine. "After him, most have tried to do what he did so magnificently: find elation or sadness or humor in the song and let it issue forth as a purely human statement." Okrent, "Pops Is Still Tops."

His Hot Five and Hot Seven bands would go on to become the most influential in jazz even though they played in public just twice. Those four
years of work in the closed confines of a recording booth served as an ideal
laboratory to watch a young Louis Armstrong expand and deepen his skills
as an instrumentalist, a singer, and, most of all, a soloist and star.* Those
thirty-one scattered days, more than his thousands of live performances in
smoky nightclubs, are what the world remembers best from his inventive
Chicago years. Looking back, it's clear he saw the sessions as jamming more
than innovating, and that the comedy and even mugging still were there.
St. Cyr, who observed it up close, remembered the technical challenges and
the schoolboy-like glee: "We could not play at ease as the musicians do now
as we had no microphones then, and we had to play into a horn which was
attached to the recording machine. There were several of them, one to the
piano, one to the reeds, and one to the brass, and one to the banjo. I would
be sitting on a small ladder, or on several packing cases stacked on top of one
another. Boy! We did it the hard way but it was fun."

Kid Ory, another firsthand witness, said that "one reason those records
came out so well was that the *Okeh* people left us alone . . . And then of
course, there was Louis himself. You couldn't go wrong with Louis."

It wasn't like Armstrong had retreated to the sound booth because he
was short on venues eager to spotlight him. Just the opposite. His studio
sessions would help transform recordings from being ads for live shows
to having value of their own along with an eventual worldwide reach.
Meanwhile his stream of in-person performances since he hopped off the
train from New Orleans that steamy summer afternoon in 1922 convinced
bandleaders and nightclub owners that Chicagoans would love to hear
him, given the chance.

He'd stepped into the city at a magical moment. Chicago was bounding
back, recovering from a Spanish flu that killed 8,500 of its residents, from a
world war that took another 4,000, and from a race riot that was the deadliest in the country during that Red Summer of 1919, claiming twenty-three
Black lives along with fifteen whites. By 1922, it had become America's railroad hub. Its stockyards processed more meat than anywhere on the planet,
while its electronics industry made it the Silicon Valley of that time. Steel
mills churned, construction boomed, and although its Second City moniker

---

* It's also likely where Louis developed his passion for sound technology, one that turned his
home into a recording studio for not just his music but his musings and that saw him taking
on the road the best and most expensive tape recorders.

originally derived from its being built afresh after the Fire of 1871, it now challenged New York for the title of America's most vibrant metropolis.

Black Chicago flourished, too. Its numbers swelled from 44,000 in 1910 to an astonishing 234,000 in 1930. Historians would label this Great Migration northward of Southern Blacks the Flight from Egypt, and Chicago was their Promised Land. That wasn't accidental. The African American porters on George Pullman's sleeping cars knew firsthand the opportunities in Chicago, where many had moved, and on work trips back South they hailed the Windy City's enticing food choices, its sky-high wages, and the homes they'd bought in swank neighborhoods like Morgan Park. Their very vestments, diction, and polish suggested possibilities unimaginable to a Negro sharecropper near Montgomery, a mill worker in Atlanta, or even to a Duke in Manhattan. "The way dining-car waiters and Pullman porters spoke of the city as 'Chi-kor-ga' fascinated me," Ellington wrote, "and they told very romantic tales about the night-life on the South Side."

The porters' proselytizing was reinforced by the *Chicago Defender,* which by World War I had become America's largest-selling Black newspaper and Chicago's most persuasive champion. It remade Negroes into "race men." The paper splayed lynchings across page one with all the bloody particulars, portrayed Confederate whites as princes of darkness, and pled with Southern readers to escape to the (relatively) civilized North. Porters gathered bundles of *Defender*s before going southward, then left them with contacts along the route. From there, they circulated to barbershops, churches, and individual subscribers in cities and hamlets across Dixie. When white businessmen and farmers tried to disrupt this network, Negroes folded newspapers into groceries and other wares as copies stealthily passed from reader to reader. By 1920 the *Defender* had a paid circulation of about 230,000, two-thirds of it outside Chicago.

One more thing made it easy to sell the city: music that kept Chicagoans Lindy Hopping and foxtrotting from sunset to sunup. The trainmen brought with them records that never made it to Southern music shops—of the self-proclaimed inventor of jazz Jelly Roll Morton, bluesy Sippie Wallace, and, in time, the wax discs that Little Louis Armstrong cut in OKeh's studio on West Washington Street. Even more riveting than the recordings were the stories, especially about the Stroll. That was how everyone referred to the brightly lit blocks on State Street between Twenty-Sixth and Thirty-Ninth, in the heart of the Black South Side, where, in the 1920s, there were more jazz clubs, cafés, cabarets, and vaudeville houses than in Harlem or Back o' Town. At the mixed-race black-and-tans, Coloreds and whites crowded together around the bandstand in unheard-of intimacy, dressed to the nines.* In an era before TVs, cars, air-conditioning, and suburbs had taken full hold, this was where adventuresome teenagers and their parents flocked to taste the good times. "Unless it happened in New Orleans, I don't think so much good jazz was ever concentrated in so small an area," said Eddie Condon, a white jazzman coming up then in Chicago. "Around midnight you could hold an instrument in the middle of the street and the air would play it."

Condon was right. Bronzeville, Chicago's Black metropolis, didn't disappoint most Southerners who planted roots there in the first decades of the twentieth century. But while Condon came and went as he pleased in that Black Belt, Blacks weren't welcome in much of white Chicago. It was no accident that 80 percent of Blacks lived on their own side of the tracks, with the poorest relegated to overcrowded cottages nearest the trains' sickly fumes. Other new arrivals—professionals, entrepreneurs, and musicians like Joe Oliver—moved into the sturdier, better-situated houses and apartments that white residents had fled. The city founded by a Black man, Jean Baptiste Point du Sable, offered a mixed blessing in that post-Migration, pre-Depression era. On the one hand, Bronzeville was a self-sufficient city-within-a-city, with thriving businesses and entertainment. On the other, Chicago's turn-of-the-century stewards had crafted covenants that made Negro migrants from the South feel at home in a way they'd hoped not to. They were largely banished from white skating rinks and nightclubs, YMCAs, churches, PTAs, Kiwanis clubs, chambers of commerce, department stores, and unions including the influential Chicago Federation of Musicians. While Chi-town boasted the nation's most powerful African American political machine and impressive numbers of Black policemen, firemen, doctors, and lawyers, nearly all worked and lived on the South Side. To some it seemed a booming parallel universe, which it was; others lamented that their new home was becoming America's most racially divided megalopolis.

Whites and Blacks mixed most regularly in the underworld. If the 1919 National Prohibition Act seemed to signal the triumph of religious fundamentalists, the way it was flouted in cities like Chicago suggested that permissiveness was the on-the-ground order of the day. Notorious mob kingpin

---

* In its earliest incarnation, *black-and-tans* meant just that: Blacks, along with tan or mixed-race customers. Later the term came to mean an intermingling of races, sometimes as equals and often with separate seating. Gays frequently were welcomed as well at these liberal-minded establishments, which made them even more loathsome to conservatives.

Al "Scarface" Capone kept the booze flowing and music playing in Chi-town. Bootleggers replaced legitimate distillers, and speakeasies proliferated as law-abiding bars and restaurants went dry. In the style of Kansas City boss man Tom Pendergast, Chicago Mayor William "Big Bill" Thompson formed brazen alliances with crooks like Capone. And the Vice Commission's shutting down the famed Levee red-light district only ensured that brothels and bars would disperse more widely and had to be marginally more discreet.

It's impossible to fathom how big-city Chicago must have looked to a young man like Louis, who'd boarded his train from the Big Easy in 1922 with a cardboard suitcase and a small cornet case in one hand and the other gripping a trout sandwich prepared by his heartsick mother, Mayann. It may have been July, but Louis was ready for anything, wearing a heavy coat and long johns. And while he must have felt like a rube having to ask a redcap at Twelfth Street Station to steer him to Lincoln Gardens, where King Oliver was waiting, he was raring to launch his new life.

He started as second cornetist behind Joe Oliver at the dance palace in the heart of the Bronzeville jazz district, with an all-Black audience savvy enough to see that Louis was the real star of the Creole Jazz Band. Before long he was packing in mixed-race crowds at the Sunset Cafe, where he met Joe Glaser, the tough-guy boss who'd become his manager. He was a featured soloist when Erskine Tate's orchestra gave voice to silent films at the 1,250-seat Vendome Theater, picked up the beat when the stately Vendome staged reviews and concerts, and, to oblige Tate, switched from the cornet to the mellower trumpet. At the Black-owned Dreamland Cafe, he was billed as Louis Armstrong: The Greatest Trumpet Player in the World. Other venues grabbed him when they could, from the Savoy to the Royal. To make a living, but also because it was fun, budding talents like Louis would go from gig to gig to gig, playing until 11 P.M. at the Vendome, for instance, then walking four blocks to the late show at Dreamland, then looking around for an after-hours spot or two.

Armstrong used all those bookings to test out routines that would become trademarks over a half-century-long career. His voice became as important a musical instrument as his cornet and trumpet. He'd back up bands or movies when he had to, and front them when he could. He'd demonstrated his sense of humor with "Heebie Jeebies," and in the vaudeville shows he would do anything—*anything*—to keep an audience smiling, including dressing in drag or pretending to be a preacher. Then there were the impossible high notes that made listeners jump onto tables and chairs, howling. First it was Fs, then Gs, As, and finally the extraordinary top Cs, blasted fifty times, a hundred, or his mind-boggling record of three hundred spiraling from a skyward-pointing trumpet in a style that cemented his reputation and battered his lips. "For many years I blew my brains out," he said. "Hitting notes so high they hurt a dog's ears, driving like crazy, screaming it."

Adjustments had to be made along the way, starting with his stomach. He'd grown up eating bare-bones red beans and rice when he was lucky and whatever he could scavenge when he wasn't. Now he could afford as much of anything as he wanted. How much he thought about food was suggested by his song titles like "Cornet Chop Suey," "Potato Head Blues," and "Struttin' with Some Barbecue." (The last was also about his second favorite topic, women, with ads showing a Black chef holding a knife in one hand and the waist of a white woman in the other.) Private bathrooms also were a novelty. "In the neighborhood where we lived we never heard of such a thing as a bathtub," he explained, "let alone a *private bath.*"

Helping him adjust was his bandmate turned mistress turned second wife. Lillian Hardin had more going for her than any woman Armstrong had ever known, and less than she claimed. She was a talented pianist, composer, arranger, singer, bandleader, and, for Louis, publicist. She also was a fabulist, claiming to have earned a music degree at the esteemed Fisk University and been named class valedictorian. (Fisk: "I doubt she could've been valedictorian since she never graduated.") She recognized in the tenderfoot from New Orleans someone with the manners of a country boy and talent of a prodigy. She was part of what drew him to Chicago, when the cagey King Oliver sent Louis her picture, sensing she was his kind of dark-skinned beauty. Once he got there she taught him how to dress ("I went downtown and bought him a bramble gray overcoat and a twenty-dollar velour hat"), how to style his hair ("he had *bangs* . . . they were sticking right straight out and I said, 'Whoa, Little Louis'"), how to eat (helping him shed fifty pounds), and how to assert himself with his mentor Joe Oliver ("I don't want you playing second trumpet. You've got to play first . . . You can't be married to Joe and married to me, too").

"I could hear Louis coming home whistling for, oh, much more than a block away. He had the most beautiful shrill whistle and all those riffs that he later made in his music, he used to whistle them," Lil recalled. "I said, 'Maybe some day that guy'll play like that' . . . crazy thoughts but it turned out all right. You never know when you're crazy the right way, huh?"

Louis took nearly all of Lil's advice, but it sometimes made him bitter. He loved her, but resented her dictatorial streak. So late in 1924, when he got his second offer to come to New York from white America's favorite Black bandleader, Fletcher Henderson, Louis bolted. He arrived at the height of the Harlem Renaissance, and his thirteen months there served as a finishing school for him and an education of a different sort for "Smack" Henderson. "One passage began triple fortissimo, and then it suddenly softened down on the next passage to double pianissimo," the bandleader remembered of Armstrong's first rehearsal, when Henderson called for a medley of Irish waltzes. "The score was properly marked 'pp' to indicate the pianissimo, but when everybody else softened down, there was Louis, still blowing as hard as he could. I stopped the band, and told him—pretty sharply, I guess—that in this band we read the marks as well as the notes. I asked him if he could read the marks and he said he could. But then I asked him: 'What about the "pp"?' and he answered, 'Why, it means *pound plenty!*'"

It was a great story and true from Henderson's vantage point. The veteran bandleader was everything Armstrong wasn't: light-hued, college-educated, and high-browed, and he took at face value his plump young trumpeter with the thick-soled high-top shoes, assuming he couldn't read music or perhaps anything. *Pound plenty* is in fact musician slang for "hit it hard," and that could have been how Armstrong interpreted it. But Henderson's biographer points out that by then Louis was an accomplished reader of music and men, and probably was pulling his boss's leg "as an attempt to break up the tension that Henderson created by pointing out the mistake." That missing of the minds—along with his wife missing him—helps explain why, in November 1925, Armstrong quit Henderson and the Big Apple, heading back to Lil and Chicago.*

He was the headliner this time around, and within two weeks of being back he was off to the first of his early-morning recording sessions at the cramped but now all-electric OKeh studio. The personnel would change, most notably with Earl "Fatha" Hines replacing Lil on piano, and so would the size of the band (sometimes it was four, six, or eight musicians, although the only name change was in 1928, to the Hot Seven). If "Heebie Jeebies" showed at that inaugural session how campy Armstrong could be, it was the June 28, 1928, recording of "West End Blues" that revealed his potential to transfigure his genre. Louis's minstrel-man demeanor of 1925 was a true reflection, but only by half. Three years on he also was a revolutionary, capable of lifting jazz out of the bawdy dance hall and taking listeners on a

---

* At his farewell party, Louis said he got drunk and vomited on Henderson's tuxedo shirt. "I was afraid Fletcher would get sore at me," he wrote later, "but all he said [was]—'Aw—that's allright *Dip*' (my nick name at that time)." Armstrong, *In His Own Words*, 94.

thrilling aural journey. King Oliver composed the twelve sleepy bars of New Orleans blues, but the world rightfully remembers only Louis Armstrong's three-plus-minute, 78 rpm rendition. Some phrasing suggests opera, some is melancholic twelve-bar blues. Offbeat notes linger. Phrases droop. High B flats and C's throb and chill. He offers every fan something: a golden-toned opening cadenza that has been called "the most important fifteen seconds in all of American music," a soulful and intentional scatting duet with the clarinetist, and a spine-tingling and near-perfect last chorus.

"It was the first time I ever heard anybody sing without using any words," said jazz diva Billie Holiday. "But the meaning used to change, depending on how I felt. Sometimes the record would make me so sad I'd cry up a storm. Other times the same damn record would make me so happy." Clarinetist and composer Artie Shaw credited the recording with changing his life: "I couldn't believe my ears. No one had done that on a trumpet, before him. No one knows how he *got* to that. I *didn't* understand that, and I *still* don't." With "West End Blues," Shaw added, "I began to see vistas in music, in popular or in jazz playing, that I had not even *imagined* or *conceived* of."

Armstrong was imagining new vistas, too. While he'd stay in Chicago another year, he'd already changed in ways that made the second-string cornetist who'd stepped off the train from New Orleans six years before nearly unrecognizable. His timing was pitch perfect, as always—leaving shortly before the stock market took its historic tumble and Elliot Ness and his Untouchables took down Capone's jazz-loving mob. King Oliver was already gone, and Lil would be soon. The silent movie and jazz ages were both winding down. While he had played mostly for Black listeners during his time on the South Side, the whole world would soon be his oyster. And while Harlem and Hollywood were his immediate destinations, neither would be the home that the Second City had been, or reshape him nearly as much.

––––––

Duke, the Count, and Satchmo inhabited largely separate domains in those formative years. In an era of trains, buses, and automobiles, New York, Kansas City, and Chicago seemed even farther apart than today. But when the regal jazzmen did cross paths, each avowed his devotion to the others.

Early on in Manhattan, Duke would head to a Harlem bar called Edmond's "every night and stand on the opposite side of Fifth Avenue and listen to Count Basie wail. It was wonderful except for the fact that I was too young to be allowed into a place like that. One day, I shed my adolescence by putting on long pants. They thought I was a grown man and let me in. I fooled them, and I'm glad, because I finally got to stand alongside the piano and watch the great Count Basie." Duke was kidding about his age, since he was five years older than the Count, but not about his love for his fellow pianist.

The feelings were mutual. Basie recalled playing his last date in Kansas City at Paseo Hall, a grand ballroom in the center of the Black community with polished wood floors and, that November night in 1936, a headliner named Ellington. The Count was the warm-up act, and as he was boarding his bus before Duke's set, the high-flying Ellington came outside for a quick greeting for the upstart Basie. "Go ahead," Duke said, not knowing that he was talking to the man who'd soon be his fiercest competitor. "You can make it." It was just four words, said with politesse and a dash of haughtiness, but Basie would neither forget nor distrust them: "Nothing nobody else could have said would have meant that much to me. Because he was the boss. He was in a class by himself."

Trying to compete with Duke was "like being in the ring with Joe Louis and having your fans cheering you on from the ringside while you're getting your brains beat out," Basie explained. "He never did drop it on me. He never did. I know what he could drop on you, and if he put any of his really heavy stuff on you, damn if you could play your own things as well as you usually could, because instead of hearing yourself, you'd be up there hearing *him*."

Louis, meanwhile, would sit around with his Chicago pals listening to Duke on the radio. "It was a sort of special deal," Zutty Singleton recalled, with Ellington extending everyone's conception of just what jazz could be. Later, Louis would sit in with the Count whenever he could, although they never cut a record together.

Duke and the Count showered love back on Satchmo. "Louis was the epitome of jazz and always will be . . . He had tremendous gifts and a likable personality that won him friends everywhere. His imagination was matched by his technical ability, and he played high notes on his horn such as had not been heard before. And it was not only trumpet players who tried to imitate his phrasing, but trombonists, saxophonists, and clarinetists, too," Ellington said. "I loved and respected Louis Armstrong."* Basie first heard Louis in Chicago in the mid-1920s, and "hearing him in person was something else. Those were the days when old Louis used to hit all of those high Cs like he couldn't stop. They didn't call him the king for nothing."

---

* Duke performed onstage tributes to Satchmo, with an Ellington band member actually wearing a handkerchief like Louis did. Email to author from Ellington biographer Harvey Cohen.

Such worshipful words were heartfelt, and were backed up by how transparently they shaped one another's choices of songs and sidemen. Yet from those early years to the ends of their careers, these musical icons' actions spoke louder. They played together only occasionally, and socialized rarely. That was partly a function of their jam-packed schedules. Their booking agents and venues that booked them, meanwhile, viewed them as rival headliners and saw any pairings as a waste of talent and money. That's also how the bandleaders saw themselves. It was one thing for Bill Basie to team up the way he would later with white stars who drew different audiences like Tony Bennett or Benny Goodman, for Louis Armstrong to make music and films with Bing Crosby, or for Edward Ellington to record with Frank Sinatra. But the Count, Satchmo, and Duke were quietly competitive enough that sharing a spotlight with someone from a similar background—which African American titan's name would top the marquee?—was something they did infrequently and mainly when pushed.

A last and little-discussed factor was their decidedly different personalities and incipient snobbishness. That was especially apparent in the way the swanky Ellington saw the folksy Armstrong. From the first, Cotton Club Duke said all the right things about Back o' Town Satchmo, but it would take decades for him to acknowledge that Louis did more than hit high notes. Armstrong's standing as a musician of the highest order was something the less aspirational Count recognized from the get-go.

As for all three towering jazzmen appearing on stage at once—the dashing Duke and the kingly Count simultaneously unfurling upon the keys of a magnificent black Steinway, with the mesmerizing rhythms of Louis's transcendent trumpet and sonorous singing blending in—that never happened. But imagine if it had.

LIFE ON THE ROCKY ROAD

IN THE MAESTROS' sentimentalized retelling, their nomadic existence from the 1930s onward was as amorous as it was glamorous, a veritable luxury cruise along bucolic byways jammed with adulatory fans and a femme fatale or two. In truth, it was a harsh crucible, keeping the Duke, the Count, and Little Louis away from home and family for lonely months at a time. They became professional wanderers, driving all day, performing into the early morning, and learning to eat from greasy paper sacks. On bad nights for the bandleaders and their players, they caught a little sleep on the bus or in the car, their knees crammed against their chests, their bodies scrunched between sweaty orchestra mates. On good ones, they found a lodging house where everyone raced up the stairs without even stopping to register, hoping to claim a catnap before that evening's gig. The more savvy veterans would leave the lights on to keep the cockroaches and bedbugs in their crevices. Layering newspapers atop whatever compressed material served as a mattress was another trick; the crinkling sent the vermin scampering.

Navigating the hostile terrain of Jim Crow America meant knowing which hotel or eatery would serve Coloreds and where there was a Negro family offering room and board. The lifestyle came naturally to musicians from the South like Armstrong, who had mastered the rulebook of segregation, but it took some getting used to for (relative) Northerners like Count Basie and Duke Ellington. They got considerable help from *The Negro Motorist Green Book*, yet until they learned a community's particular patchwork of racial laws and customs, walking down the street could land them in jail or worse.

Monte Irvin, a Negro League star who traveled a parallel circuit in the 1930s and '40s, recalled stopping at a café between Birmingham and Montgomery, Alabama. As he and his teammates approached, the white owner started shaking her head. "Why are you saying 'no' if you don't know what we want?" he recalled asking. "Whatever it is, we don't have any," she said.

"It's awfully hot," he persisted. "Can we just use your well in the back, [we'd] like to get some cold drink of water?" When she agreed, they drank up, then "thanked her very much and she didn't say anything." Driving away, Irvin looked back and saw the owner breaking the drinking gourd in pieces. "How could she hate us?" he wondered. "She didn't even know us." Duke's band encountered something unsettlingly similar around the same time in Lynchburg, Virginia. The white owner of a seedy hotel said they could stay, but "you'll have to pay for the sheets," recalled Bob Udkoff, who handled the arrangements. "I said, 'Well, what do you mean, pay for the sheets?' He said, 'Well, I gotta burn them afterwards.'"

Mike Zwerin, a jazzman who should have had it better because he was white and came along a generation after Duke, Satchmo, and the Count, summarized life on the road this way: "You skim more than read, pass out rather than fall asleep. You work when everybody else is off, breakfast in the evening, dinner at dawn. Disorder is the order."

It wasn't all torment, of course. These self-described gadabouts got to see their vast country in a way few Americans did then, and almost no Blacks. For each instance of anguish there was one of exhilaration. Hundreds of white fans turned out in farming villages and mining towns in what for many was their first encounter with a Negro—and boy, what an encounter it was on both ends. The farmers and miners got to hear the most intoxicating music on Earth from brassy cornet players and driving saxophonists, exotic trombone mutes, squealing trumpets, and sultry clarinets. The musicians, meanwhile, were earning a living doing what they loved, being treated like celebrities, and tuning up for the day when they could do both back home in Kansas City, Chicago, and New York.

Our trio of jazzmen preferred to remember the highs, but between the lines were hints of the horrors and how they held out. "Years ago I was playing the little town of Lubbock, Texas, when this white cat grabs me at the end of the show—he's full of whiskey and trouble," Armstrong recalled. "He pokes on my chest and says 'I don't like *niggers!*' These two cats with me was gonna practice their Thanksgiving carving on that dude. But I say, 'No, let the man talk. *Why* don't you like us, Pops?' And would you believe that cat couldn't *tell* us? So he apologizes—crying and carrying on . . . And dig this: that fella and his whole family come to be my friends! When I'd go back through Lubbock, Texas, for many many years they would make ole Satchmo welcome and treated him like a king.

"Quite naturally, it didn't always turn out that pleasurable. I knew some cats was blowing one nighters in little sawmill stops down in Mississippi, and one time these white boys—who had been dancing all night to the colored cats' sounds—chased 'em out on the highway and whipped 'em with chains and cut their poor asses with *knives*! Called it 'nigger knocking.' No reason—except they was so goddamn miserable they had to mess everybody else up, ya dig? *Peckerwoods*! Oh, this world's mothered some mean sons!"

Ellington had his own encounters with the "skin disease"—his euphemism for racism—including after a show in St. Louis with a policeman who said enthusiastically, "If you'd been a white man, Duke, you'd have been a great musician." Managing a smile, Duke replied softly, "I guess things would have been different if I'd been a white man."

Like the others, Basie knew the feeling of being the hottest show in towns where he wasn't sure he'd be able to get a meal or a bed. "The indignities we experienced on the road over so many years of touring were impossible for some of us to forgive and others to forget," he said.

"If I haven't spent a lot of time complaining about all of these things, it's not because I want anybody to get the impression that all of that was not also a part of it. It was. So what? Life is a bitch, and if it's not one damn thing, it's going to be something else," the Count added in his autobiography. "The fact is that I really didn't run into very much along that line that I didn't already know about. In other words it was not news to me, so I just went on trying to do what I was doing."

———

In that turbulent World War II era, the jazzmen gave the nation a much-needed lift. They toured practically full-time. Consider Count Basie's schedule in 1938: he began by playing for a New Year's Day dance at Boston's Roseland-State Ballroom, bounced the next day to a dance pavilion in Waterbury, Connecticut, and on January 3 recorded in New York for Decca Records. The rest of the winter was a grind, and the spring was worse. During one stretch, the band performed on forty-five of fifty consecutive dates, nearly all one-nighters that they dubbed hit-and-runs. At year's end they'd been to seventy-six cities in twenty-four states, from Maine to Texas.

Their audience was anyone who could afford them. One night they'd dazzle high-flying collegians from Cornell or Wellesley, the next it was high schoolers in Basie's hometown of Red Bank. The numbers hardly ever varied, and the show generally ran three and a half hours. Occasionally they'd chuck out the set list for a "battle of the bands," a contest that generally was staged in a large ballroom, where fans and/or expert judges declared the winner and the only assured prize was bragging rights. On January 16, 1938, the Aristocrat of Rhythm (Basie) faced off against America's Outstanding

Swing Band (Chick Webb's). "It was a fight to the finish," according to one review. "Handkerchiefs were waving, people were shouting and stomping, the excitement was intense."

In the parlance of his old territory bands, there was now no territory in America that wasn't Basieland.

Ellington's schedule rivaled Basie's that recessionary year of 1938. He bounced from Manhattan and Philly to Toronto, Fort Wayne, Buffalo, Pittsburgh, Steubenville, New Brunswick, Newark, New Rochelle, Providence, Schenectady, Shrewsbury (Mass.), Salem (N.H.), Marshfield (Mass.), Old Orchard Beach, Binghamton, Lancaster, Asbury Park, Baltimore, Johnson City, Bemus Point (N.Y.), Clayton (N.Y.), Scranton, Harrisburg, Boston, Albany, Durham, Norfolk, Newark, Cleveland, Dayton, Nashville, Jackson (Tenn.), Memphis, New Orleans, Jackson (Mich.), Bunkie (La.), Kansas City, Cincinnati, Erie, Detroit, Chicago, Evansville, and Montreal. Just keeping straight the cities and time zones was dizzying. Some venues were elegant, like New York's Persian Gardens at the Ritz-Carlton or the Viennese Roof at the St. Regis. Many were on the Chitlin' Circuit of all-Black clubs, or in church basements, amusement parks, and, on New Year's Eve in Montreal, a Lions Club "frolic and dance" to benefit its welfare fund. Duke orchestrated the band despite a fever of 101.5 on a night that, like many, started with a vaudeville show.*

As for Armstrong, he never wanted a night off and seldom got one. Three hundred days a year on the road was, he said, standard over a fifty-year career, which would have meant fifteen thousand performances. Even accounting for his customary embellishing, that probably was an undercount.

A pace like that would have been exhausting in an era of jet travel, but all they had were plodding trains, buses, riverboats, and cars. Stops could be five hundred miles apart, with almost no nights off.† It's no surprise that Black musicians translated TOBA, the Theater Operators Booking Association, as Tough on Black Asses. The standard accounting was that one year on a normal person's calendar took two and a half years off the life of a nomadic jazzman or woman. One of Ellington's longtime trumpet players was so tired, he said, that "when I left Duke, I slept almost a whole year."

The bandleaders needed the jam-packed schedules to cover the costs of

---

* The Chitlin' Circuit was for Black performers what the Borscht Belt was for Jews: a homogeneous audience that embraced them at a time when much of America wouldn't.

† The jazzmen's union finally pushed back against the bookers, imposing a limit of four hundred miles and six nights. Ward and Burns, *Jazz: A History of America's Music,* 250.

a dozen or so musicians, plus staff, but they also loved it. "As far as all the traveling and bumping around is concerned, that just means that I'm still lucky enough to be doing what I was always dreaming of doing way back when I was still in my boyhood days playing hooky from school and hanging around listening to the show people and helping to take water to the elephants when the carnival used to come to Red Bank," said Basie. "I know that some people think of all this as the same old grind. I don't, and I never have."

One night in particular captured the joy Basie felt on the road, in circumstances that would have unsettled less determined performers. His band rolled into the lakefront burg of Manitowoc, Wisconsin, the heart of Green Bay Packers country, on a night in 1972 when the Packers were facing off against the Detroit Lions in TV's game of the week. A set broadcast the gridiron action from one end of the armory while at the other end the band sat morosely, knowing it'd be at most the game's soundtrack. Basie merely leaned forward and ordered, "Play." For an hour he gave the football-mad audience his best and, little by little, fans headed across the large hall toward the music. Then they phoned friends to join them. Near the end of the evening the host borrowed the microphone to announce that the Packers had won. There was a polite cheer, then someone yelled, "How 'bout 'April in Paris' again?" The laid-back Basie smiled and whispered, "Touchdown."

The three hardworking greats learned to find their comfort when they left the stage late at night. "I'm a hotel man," Duke told an interviewer. "I like living in hotels. I'd like to live in the best fuckin' hotel I can live in, in the best suite, and just live there and order food, and never eat in the dining room." If the hotel couldn't find a king-sized bed, he'd pull together the two twins. He told another journalist: "The road is my home. I'm only comfortable when I'm on the move. I get restless standing still. New York is just where I keep my mailbox. I'm never in the city unless I'm performing there or in town to sign contracts."

More patrician than populist, Ellington lived in better hotels over the years than his sidemen did, or than Basie or Armstrong. All three eventually hired road managers as well as valets to ease their burden. Each also developed particular quirks that made their backbreaking life on the road more comfortable. For the Count, it was sleeping with the light on and knowing how to catch forty winks at the slightest opening. Before bed, Bill would dig into his paper bag brimming with fried chicken, cakes, cookies, and fruit, all of which tasted best if eaten while watching TV reruns of *Bo-*

nanza. Armstrong and Ellington treasured Westerns, too, and relaxing in front of the TV, which was still a novelty through the 1940s. Duke brought an electric piano to his red-carpet hotels, along with a small television set. He hated air-conditioning, which he worried would generate drafts that made him sick. But he loved lying in bed with his ear glued to the telephone, which he called "the greatest invention since peanut brittle," and lingering in the shower, which he said was "a blessing from heaven after a long night on the road. I would luxuriate under them, sometimes staying long enough for my fingertips to wrinkle like prunes." Louis always had two bags packed: the alligator-skin one bore his precious trumpet and the other, which looked like a diplomat's, included a writing pad, gargling lotion, lip salve, throat lozenges, and mineral water. His favorite hotel meal involved sending out for Chinese, then washing it down with a beer.

Books would have been a compact and compelling way to relax during their travels if any of the three had been real readers. Ellington claimed a collection of nearly a thousand books on topics as lofty as prehistoric African art, but those volumes seemed mainly for show and, in some cases, as grist for his compositions on Negro history. (His passion for Emily Post how-tos on etiquette was real, as was his devotion to comic strips.) Armstrong boasted an even bigger and more eclectic home library—from *War and Peace, Of Mice and Men, World's Great Men of Color, Ask Your Mama,* the Bible, and a text of organic chemistry, to two books on Adolf Hitler. ("If you want to hate someone, Pops," he would say, "you got to know why you hate him.") While Louis had clearly worked his way through many, his trunks and suitcases were filled with music, not books. The Count, meanwhile, never even pretended to be a bibliophile, although his library did include *The Complete Illustrated Guide to Gambling.*

Satchmo hadn't put down strong roots anywhere, so he naturally felt more at home on the road even after his doctors warned against an arduous touring schedule, and maybe especially then. But his last and longest-lasting wife recognized what was missing even if he didn't. One Christmas Eve, "I got a little small Christmas tree and I got all the decorations for it, and set it up in the hotel room while Louis was at work," Lucille said. "He took one look at it and he just clammed up, you know? Louis isn't very emotional; he doesn't say much when he's overwhelmed . . . We finally went to bed. And Louis was still laying up in the bed watching the tree; his eyes just like a baby's eyes would watch something . . . I said, 'Well, I'll turn the lights out now on the tree.' He said, 'No, don't turn them out. I have to just keep looking at it.' . . .

"I kept that first little tree until way after New Year's, putting it up every night and taking it down every morning, in a dozen hotels. And then when I did take it down for its last time, Louis wanted me to mail it home. It was a real tree, not an artificial one, and I had to convince him—I really had to convince him—that the tree would dry up."

Among Negroes, only the Pullman porters saw more of America, and even they just rolled through places like Fargo, North Dakota. But Duke Ellington stayed on one winter night in 1940 for a concert at the Crystal Ballroom that drew about seven hundred fans who, for the price of $1.30, got to hear the orchestra hitting on all cylinders. The entire population of North Dakota was only .03 percent Black then, and there were just thirty in Fargo. Racism certainly existed there, but wasn't as all-consuming as in other parts of the country. The locals' attention was focused more on dust storms and farm foreclosures. There was no TV to take people's minds off the raging war, little money for the motion pictures, and not much else to do in a city that celebrated its political and cultural isolation. That left jazz.

Duke Ellington's concerts that winter in Fargo, along with ones in nearby East Grand Forks and Duluth, showed heartland America that Black musicians could play before large audiences without the sky falling, fans rioting, or artistic standards being compromised. And performances like those proved to white entrepreneurs that musicians like Duke, the Count, and Louis could put money in their pockets.

Getting to know was a two-way street. Their time up-country exposed the bandleaders to a raw and uninhibited America that was unfamiliar to people who'd grown up in New Orleans, Washington, D.C., and Red Bank. They watched ranchers lubricated with beer fight to get closer to their bandstand, sometimes with guns drawn. They got to know Frank Sinatra, who brought the Basie band to mob-run Las Vegas and told his bodyguards, "If anybody even looks funny at any member of this band, break both of their fuckin' legs." Their up-close look at another icon of the era, Cary Grant, proved less flattering: Armstrong performed at the heartthrob's thirty-eighth birthday party in Hollywood, where guests, Grant included, came in blackface.

Duke, who loved to eat almost as much as Satchmo did, learned that in Taunton, Massachusetts, he could get "the best chicken stew in the United States." For chow mein with pigeon's blood, "I go to Johnny Cann's Cathay House in San Francisco. I get my crab cakes at Bolton—that's in San Francisco, too." Chicago had a restaurant with ribs he deemed better than anywhere west of Cleveland and the best shrimp creole outside New Orleans. And in Louisville, "I get myself a half-dozen chickens and a gallon jar of potato salad so I can feed the sea gulls. You know, the guys who reach over your shoulder."

If there was time on the road, and their schedules synced, the Black musicians would challenge Negro League baseballers to a pickup game. When no pros were around, they'd organize their own games of softball, baseball, tennis, or basketball with waiters and bartenders, policemen, firemen, or competing bands. A seemingly bottomless tub of beer kept things friendly. "Duke could really hit that ball, but he almost had to take a *bus* to get to first base," said Clark Terry. As for the Count, "Basie desperately wanted to be a part of the team," his guitar-playing pal Freddie Green recalled, but knowing the way he fielded and hit, "ten players unanimously relegated him to coaching third base."

To Basie, Ellington, and Armstrong, music meant movement, and their freedom to roam was more liberating than a running back breaking into the clear.

———

Their travels also attuned these three bandleaders to the bold hues and subtle complexions of America's color lines. "No niggers" protocols were everywhere.* No dining in Chicago's Loop. No entry at night, and sometimes at all, into Goshen, Indiana; La Crosse, Wisconsin; and thousands of other "sundown towns." No jazz or other concerts that might attract undesirable racial elements to the Opera House in San Francisco or anywhere near the University of Chicago. Don't even think about interracial fraternizing at Count Basie concerts in Oakland, per order of the OPD. No references in New Orleans to Ulysses S. Grant or other Union generals in what was still called the War of Northern Aggression. No entry other than through the kitchen at casinos on the Vegas strip, and no going to the beach in Miami Beach unless you had a hard-to-acquire pass.

Those bans were far from the worst of it. A terrifying night in the 1920s for Chicago's Whispering Band of Gold still echoed decades later. "Some rich man hired them to play for a party, and some of the guys, the cops caught them and beat them up and beat the guy up that was giving the party," said Eddie Barefield, a saxophonist who played with Armstrong and Ellington. "Some of the guys were crippled for the rest of their life and some of them died from it." Then there was the night, in St. Louis, that somebody brought Duke's band strawberry pies laced with broken glass. "You learn who to drink with, who to eat with, certainly who not to lay down with," explained Ellington singer Tony Watkins.

———

* Sometimes those codes were spelled out on signs reading, "No Niggers, No Jews, No Dogs."

It never surprised the Negro musicians when, as soon as they pulled up, gas station owners locked their restrooms and insisted their gas tanks were empty.* Or when the swimming pool at their motel was drained of water just as they arrived and refilled as they were leaving. Or when, arriving in Dallas at dawn, record producer Quincy Jones noticed that the tallest church had "a rope hanging around the steeple with an effigy of a black dummy saying, 'Keep going, don't stop here.'" Or even when someone put a raccoon in Louis Armstrong's hotel bed. "There's a coon in my room," Louis told the manager, who replied, "Just one minute, Mr. Armstrong, we'll get that nigger out of there."

The South, of course, was particularly unwelcoming to vehicles packed with Black music men and bearing license plates from places like New York and Illinois. "The white Southerner always fears the 'contamination' of his 'good Negroes' by the northern Negro," said Preston Love, a sax player and Basie sideman in the mid-'40s. But when it came to racism, Armstrong observed, "up North, the accent was different, but the melody the same." Things got so heavy for Ellington cornet player Rex Stewart that he despaired: "I'd like to go to a valley hemmed in by mountains, just me myself. That would be Utopia."

Satchmo used his wit to couch his outrage. "It's all right, folks, it's just the phone," he chuckled into the microphone when dynamite tossed from a passing car rocked the auditorium where he was playing to a mixed-race but segregated crowd of three thousand in Knoxville in 1957. On another occasion he explained, "You take the majority of white people, two thirds of 'em don't like niggers. But they always got one nigger that they just crazy about . . . They just love his dirty drawers." He learned early on, he added, "Even if we colored ones were right, when the cops arrived they'd whip our heads first and ask questions later."

In later years, itinerant musicians could read up on the dos and don'ts of their Jim Crow surroundings in the *Green Book* or *Travelguide*. Before that, there was the grapevine. No need to post Vacancy signs; word spread quietly about the network of doctors, undertakers, and other Negroes who'd open their homes, much as they had for runaway slaves with the Underground Railroad, and as they would in the civil rights era. Preachers told

* When jazz vocalist Dinah Washington was turned away from a gas station once during a trip South—"We ain't got no ladies room for no niggas!"—she pulled a pistol from her glove box and said. "Oh, yeah? Well, since you don't, then you just take your gas out of my car because I'm not paying for it!" *Autobiography of Clark Terry*, 135.

funeral directors, who told barbers, beauticians, bartenders, and the best secret keepers, Freemasons. That was how bands learned about Mom Sutton in Atlanta, who'd rent a comfortable room, serve a meal complete with greens, mashed, and biscuits, and let you watch her tending a hot stove and taking regular swigs of gin, saying, "You gotta fight fire with fire!" In Philly, Mother Havelow rented out eight rooms in her large brownstone, but only to top musicians, who also got to play pinochle with her. If she liked you, "she'd even turn her head when you brought in a guest," recalled bassist Milt Hinton. Then there was the Sterling Hotel in Cincinnati, a beloved but bedraggled dive with a house rat the size of a cat whom the cartoon-loving musicians christened Jerry.

The more roadblocks they encountered, the more the gypsy bandsmen improvised. They carried with them pots and pans—along with baloney sausage, Ritz crackers, and sardines—for towns that didn't have Mother Havelows or Mom Suttons, and they learned to use aluminum foil and a hotel iron to grill cheese sandwiches. They'd get light-skinned or white mates to order food for them, hoping nobody got suspicious when they asked for fifty hamburgers to go, or to rent a hotel room, with darker-hued teammates climbing through the window. They also learned how to sleep in farmers' fields, on top of the car, or alongside caskets in funeral parlors. Whatever it took.

Humor helped deflect the tension. "One brazen 'cracker' standing by his gas pump (undoubtedly with firepower on his hip to back him up) emitted an incendiary, 'Boy, we don't serve niggers here,'" Freddie Green remembered. From the back of the bus came this muffled response: "That's good, you [mother fucker], 'cause we didn't order any." In Shreveport, two cracker sheriffs warned Armstrong that "we have a case against you and when you finish playing tonight we want that trumpet. Is that clear?" Armstrong: "Clear as a whistle." He wasn't sure what the case was but did know the value of his horn. So "I tricked them so pretty. When they asked me—'Where's your trumpet?'—I pointed to a trumpet case and said: 'There it is' . . . It wasn't. I gave them Joe Jardan's (one of my trumpet men's trumpet instead of mine) and that was that—Tee hee. Cute? You see, Joe and I made the switch during our intermission, right under their noses. So they weren't so smart after all."

Sex was another release. "To be factual," said Rex Stewart, "all of the fellows had little black books crammed with addresses and telephone numbers of fillies from coast-to-coast." Vibraphonist Terry Gibbs remembers a band whose players slept in their bus and "in the morning the ground around the bus would be covered with condoms."

Did all the antics and distractions undermine their dignity? That was a touchy subject for Ellington, Armstrong, Basie, and nearly all Negro performers in that pre–civil rights era. While their tolerances varied on many topics, there was a consensus when it came to "Tomming": it was taboo. Sure, put on a great show for white fans. Okay, too, to make them laugh between songs or acts. Even to ignore the ignominy of being addressed as "boy" or "nigger." They would do a lot to support their wives and kids, which was not easy for Negro men in that era—but never to the flash point of behaving like that storybook shuffling house slave, Uncle Tom. So they calibrated their performances to ensure that the kidding never got in the way of their playing. In fact all three maestros at first resisted touring the South.

Duke Ellington took it a step further. He had become adept at turning his cheek when provoked, saying, "You have to try not to think about it, or you'll knock yourself out." But there was only so far he'd turn, which helps explain why, in the 1940s, he packed a snub-nosed .38. His road manager, Al Celley, said he never planned to use it, but he "would know how to," and he renewed his permit annually. Looking back on those early decades of traveling the country, including deep into Dixie, Duke told a TV interviewer: "We went down in the South *without* federal troops."

GETTING THERE

THE FUSSY BRAHMINS of Boston and the fierce Goliaths of Wall Street were uniformly smitten with George Pullman's plush velvet-appointed sleeping coaches because they knew the Negro porters and dining-car men on board would unfailingly treat them like royalty. The porters routinely slipped an extra sheet over their blankets to ensure their faces didn't chafe. What's more, the Black staffers shined their shoes, nursed their hangovers, cleared their compartments of rogue insects, clipped their hair, and served Old Fashioned Kentucky Colonel Mint Juleps to wash down the Welsh rarebit or any of 132 other culinary delights on the elegant dining car's menu. Most important, these men knew well how to observe but not bear witness, and to listen but not overhear during the four lonely nights it took to cross the continent.

Duke Ellington, Satchmo Armstrong, and Count Basie chartered Pullman cars for those reasons and one more: to save their necks from the lynching noose.

The safety factor had partly to do with getting where they were going. In an era of segregated buses, trains, and ships, it was only when they had their own railroad carriages, and were served by fellow Blacks, that the bandleaders could really relax while traveling. Otherwise they were banished to what Armstrong called the "James Crow Cars" just behind the coal-stoked engine, with noxious fumes, limited seating, and no heaters, washbasins, flush toilets, water coolers, dining options, or even a cushion to rest upon. That the Pullman porters loved these jazzmen was a bonus, and the musicians grew to return that affection. They would play their pianos, clarinets, and trumpets late into the night in the club car, where elegantly outfitted train workers doffed their caps and inhaled the beats.

The true saving of lives, however, came when the maestros reached their destination, especially in unfamiliar cities below the Mason-Dixon Line.

Arriving by normal transport they faced the perilous search for a bed and a meal. Wrong choices could carry deadly consequences, with white-on-Black violence reaching new peaks in the early 1900s. Even the music makers' fame couldn't fully protect them. But arriving by Pullman—especially when the bands had prearranged to have their coaches park on a sidetrack during their full stay—meant a safe haven to return to after and even between performances. They knew there'd be a warm meal waiting, along with a freshly laundered bed, friendly Black faces eager for the lowdown on that night's activities, and, when the bandsman was accompanied by a lady, the same discretion porters showed the Brahmins and Goliaths.*

It was a luxury every orchestra relished but only a few could afford, and nobody cashed in quite like Duke Ellington: "To avoid problems, we used to charter two Pullman sleeping cars and a seventy-foot baggage car. Everywhere we went in the South, we lived in them. On arrival in a city, the cars were parked on a convenient track, and connections were made for water, steam, sanitation, and ice. This was our home away from home. Many observers would say, 'Why, that's the way the President travels!' It automatically gained us respect from the natives, and removed the threat and anticipation of trouble. When we wanted taxis, there was no problem. We simply asked the station manager to send us six, seven, or however many we wanted. And when we were rolling, of course, we had dining-car and room service."

Armstrong said the greeting he got from the trainmen when he was leaving New Orleans for Chicago made him cherish them forever: "All the pullman porters and waiters recognized me because they had seen me playing on the tail gate wagons to advertise dances, or 'balls' as we used to call them. They all hollered at me saying, 'Where are you goin', Dipper?' 'You're a lucky black sommitch,' one guy said, 'to be going up North to play with ol' Cocky.' This was a reference to the cataract on one of Joe [Oliver]'s eyes."

Basie, meanwhile, remembered his first time on a Pullman. "That was my piece of cake," he said. "Lots of times, instead of me getting into my bed, I

---

* While the musicians slept in comfort in Pullman cars, the porters who served them had to scrounge for lodging between assignments. In most big cities the Pullman Company provided beds, for free or a nominal fee, in rooming houses, old or empty sleeping cars at the rail yard, or the YMCA, which was more welcoming to Negroes than hotels were. In Omaha in the early 1900s those quarters consisted of three double-decker beds on the ground floor of the Pullman office, which the men said was damp and had no bath. Salt Lake City had two rooms at the Wellington Hotel, one with four single beds and the other with chairs. In San Francisco, the company assumed porters could go across the bay to Oakland, where it had beds, or that San Francisco hotels would put them up for free in the hope that porters would send passengers their way.

used to sit and look out the window most of the night as we rambled from one place to another. That was music to me."

———

Riding the bus instead of the train meant fewer impromptu jam sessions, less shielding from the cruelty of Jim Crow, but also less expense, so it was the way most musicians—eventually even the high-rolling Ellingtonians—got around. And unlike the train, which depended on tracks, a motorbus could take them right to the door of small-town gin joints and dance halls.

In their early years, all three bandleaders made do with second-rate buckets of bolts. Seats didn't recline, cabins lacked air-conditioning or working heaters, and innards rattled. Need a bathroom? There were none on board, and because so many filling stations refused to unlock their restrooms, the men learned to pee from the open door, holding on for dear life. Bad roads added to the challenge, especially in winter. "One fellow I recall had become so accustomed to the jolting bus," said Rex Stewart, "that it was days before he could sleep in his own bed!"

Then there were the drivers, usually whites whom small-town sheriffs were less likely to pull over or lock up. "We had this one guy who used to drive sideways. Used to sit up there at the wheel with his feet out in the aisle," remembered Ellington clarinetist Jimmy Hamilton. "I guess he was afraid he was going to miss something going on in the bus, so he sat that way. We used to call him 'Old Sidesaddle,' but he sure scared me some—driving that way." As the money got better, the buses came with more seasoned drivers and more amenities, including bathrooms, air-conditioning, and state-of-the-art heaters. The leaders also began using charters, generally from Greyhound, but the government would commandeer those transports to move troops during World War II.

Private buses, like private train carriages, shielded musicians from the country's harshly segregated public transport system, but only to a point, as the Armstrong band found out during a Southern tour in 1931. According to a Memphis paper, Satchmo and his mates refused the bus company's reasonable request to change vehicles so theirs could be repaired, and "exhibited" six pistols to send their message, at which point the police carted them to jail. Thankfully history has set straight that record. The problem was twofold—that the band's shiny new Greyhound was "too nice" for the uppity Colored boys, and that the wife of the band's white manager was riding with them, violating Southern mores. "You're in Memphis now," one arresting officer said, "and we need some cotton-pickers." A second, pointing to the Black musician sitting with the white woman, egged on his partner:

"Why don't you shoot him in the leg?" After everyone was booked, a third constable warned, "You ain't gonna come down to Memphis and try to run the city. We'll kill all of you niggers."

Louis and his men got the last words. Sprung from jail by the local theater manager, they performed a nationally broadcast concert attended by the very detectives who'd tormented them. "I'm now goin' to dedicate this tune to the Memphis Police Force: 'I'll Be Glad When You're Dead, You Rascal You,'" Armstrong announced. Band members played as they were told, but were scoping out escape routes they were sure they'd need once the police realized their faces were being slapped. They would have been even more anxious had they known that nearly three-quarters of the Memphis force then were KKK members, and the chief was the local Grand Wizard. But after the performance, as the band's trombonist recollected, several policemen—who must not have made out lyrics like "I'll be tickled to death when you leave this earth, you dog!"—rushed to tell Armstrong, "We've had a number of important jazz orchestras come through Memphis . . . but none of them ever thought enough of the Police Department to dedicate a song to us! We appreciate it, and want you to know that at your next show we will be reserving the first several rows for ourselves and our wives."

Encounters like that were common in the Jim Crow South, but something similar happened to Louis three decades later, in liberal New England, when he was heading to a concert at the Tanglewood music center in western Massachusetts. The transport that June day was a yellow school bus with rigid seats and no air-conditioning or toilet. "After we reached Connecticut, Pops had to go to the bathroom," recalled photographer Herb Snitzer, who was riding along. "We stopped, and he went into a restaurant. When he asked where the bathroom was, he was told it was off-limits to blacks. I guess they didn't recognize him. But as Pops walked back to the bus, a car screeched to a halt and a couple of college kids ran over to him to get his autograph . . .

"When he returned to the bus, he was furious. I had not yet seen a look like that on his face. To make Pops furious was something, because usually he was so mellow. I will never forget the look on his face. The most famous entertainer in America, and he couldn't use the bathroom because he was black."

So many were their challenges that, in later years, they referred to themselves as the first freedom riders, a reference to the Black and white activists who, in 1961, protested the segregation of interstate buses by riding side by side through the separate-and-unequal South, with some nearly dying for their troubles.

Each maestro adapted to bus travel in his own way. Louis had an initiation rite for fellow riders: handing them a packet of his favorite laxative, Swiss Kriss, then making the bus stop once it worked its surprisingly speedy magic. He brought a typewriter on board, and became adept at answering fan mail while others slept and the bus bounced. He also blamed the cramped transport for the varicose veins he developed in later life. The Count wasn't sure his heavy bus with the spare tire on the back—which his men called the Blue Goose—would make it across narrow bridges or ones with overhangs, so he'd jump off, walk across, and reboard on the far side. That, however, was the only time he pulled rank or abandoned his band of brothers. Not so Ellington. Musicians who played alongside the noble Duke sometimes rode in suits and ties, as befitted a band where style mattered, but their leader was no small-*d* democrat, going first-class whenever he could and without his mates.

Despite jazz's reputation as laid-back and ad-libbed, there was nothing improvisational about seating protocols, as anyone who breached them learned in an instant. On the Blue Goose, Basie got the front-row seat across from the driver. When he rode the bus, Duke also was up front, with his hat over his eyes so he could sleep or pretend to. Louis liked being the last to board. Veteran bandmates knew the smoothest ride was in the midsection, between the axles, so that was where they claimed seats. Rookies were relegated to the cheap seats old-timers didn't want, generally in back, and had to share their two-seater. "For my initiation in the Basie band, I was assigned as Jimmy Rushing's seatmate. He was a huge cat, whose nickname was 'Mr. Five by Five.' Five feet tall and five feet wide," said Basie trumpeter Clark Terry. "His butt took up all of his seat and most of mine. The cats cracked up about it. But after a while, my trial period was over and I was allowed to move to a seat all by myself where I could spread out and relax."

Everyone spent so much time riding between one-nighters that whether they liked it or not, the bus became their refuge. They ate on board, slept there, and often changed clothes in their seats. The military was the only other place where men were thrown together in such close quarters for so long. Basie trombonist Benny Powell so cherished that informal support system that he renamed the Blue Goose the Iron Lung.

Distractions helped pass the monotonous hours. Guitarist Freddie Green schooled himself on compositional techniques from his seat. Singer Joe Williams fiddled with his cameras. Eddie Jones, the scholarly bass player, studied calculus. Others played the Dozens, a game where they'd poke fun at one another or anyone else they knew. Negro and Major League baseball were favorite topics of conversation, politics less so. Once the bus rolled, many musicians would head to the back row—"the clubhouse"—set a suitcase between the seats, and deal hands of Tonk and stud poker. A dice game called Fours was another favorite. Liquor flowed. The odor of marijuana wafted down the aisles. Sometimes the gambling action took to the floor, like when Billie Holiday was with the Basie band in 1937. "I was on my knees in the bottom of that bus from West Virginia to New York, a few hundred miles in about twelve hours," she recalled. "When we pulled up in front of the Woodside Hotel everybody was broke and crying. I was filthy dirty and had holes in the knees of my stockings, but I had sixteen hundred bucks and some change."

Still, it wasn't worth it, she concluded: "Nobody bothered to tell me I'd have to travel five hundred to six hundred miles on a hot or cold raggedy-ass Blue Goose bus."

———

Passenger cars were another option for the roving music makers, although in the early days most were secondhand and, in Armstrong's description, "raggedy." His was a Hupmobile, and in 1929 he and his bandmates departed Chicago as a fleet of four bound for New York City by way of Niagara Falls, sleeping in their vehicles. Along the way they watched with dismay as a generator blew, a gas line leaked, and an accident created "an Awful Wreck." While Louis's car made it to Manhattan in one piece, "the minute we were Crossing '42nd and Broadway—My Radiator Cap Blew off—And Steam was going every place," he wrote. "The 'Cops' came over and saw we had a Chicago License on our car, and asked us, 'Hey there have you boys any 'Shot Guns in that Car?' We gladly said 'No Suh Boss.'"

The Hupmobile was actually nicer than the "Tin Lizzies" used by territory bands like the ones in which Basie played. Nobody had money, so a dozen not-small musicians would scrunch in, with anyone who couldn't fit balancing on the running board. "When the weather turned cold and the wind started coming through the cracks we used to wrap newspaper round our legs," the Count said. "It was rough out there."

As the money rolled in and their handlers could take better care of them, the cars improved and the musicians drove themselves less and less often. Armstrong had a Packard big enough for him to sleep in. Much later, his manager secured a limousine so he could rest, but he'd never gotten used to luxury and often swapped seats with his bus-riding bandmates. Duke embraced opulence, which in this case meant a big white Chrysler Imperial, an Imperial LeBaron, a stately Pierce-Arrow, and other expensive models picked out by him or his longtime sax man and chauffeur, Harry Carney. Abandoning the bus was easy for him, Duke said, because "there's so much shit going on [there] all the time. You know, I mean, 18 maniacs . . .

"When I'm in the car with Harry, I know I'm going to be free from telephones and from having to deal with business problems."

Carney said the two-man road trips began by accident. "After riding on the bus for so long, and having to stop and go when someone gave the word, I decided if I had a car I might have a little more freedom . . . At first, it was my intention to make short hops in and around New York, and in the Eastern area. Then I found I was enjoying it so much, and Duke was riding with me almost every day. That was how it started, until I found I was jumping all over the country . . .

"We leave after the job and we like to go two hundred miles at least without stopping. Duke always says, 'Let's get some miles under our belt' . . . Duke sleeps occasionally, but not as a rule. He's a very good man to have along. He sits in the front and he does a lot of thinking. He'll pull out a piece of paper and make notes. We do very little talking, but if he thinks I'm getting weary he'll make conversation so that I don't fall asleep . . .

"One thing about traveling: it always gives you something to look forward to," added Harry, "even if it's no more than going to another town to see the people there you know."

Musician and photographer Gordon Parks rode along once and was captivated by the Ellington-Carney interplay: "The three of us were approaching San Francisco early one morning after an overnight drive from Los Angeles. In the distance, the Golden Gate Bridge floated eerily in the dawn mist rising above the bay. Harry called Edward, who was asleep in the backseat. 'Hey, Big Red, wake up and look over yonder. Looks like something you might want to write about.' Duke stirred awake, wiped his eyes and looked at the bridge. 'Majestic. Majestic. Goddamn those white people are smart,' he mumbled and fell back to sleep."

———

As World War II yielded to the Cold War, big bands switched mostly to air travel for domestic flights and a combination of air and sea for overseas trips. But they held on to an emotional connection to the railroad. It evoked a warm nostalgia for their early days on the road, and always tied them to the history of Black freedom and locomotion. Trains figured in African American spirituals, fueled the Great Migration, and, in an earlier time, inspired slaves to dream of escaping North.

When emancipation finally came in the 1860s it was a fantastic moment.

Four million Negroes were suddenly released from bondage and able to taste their first liberties. They could work where they chose at whatever wage they could negotiate. That first flush of freedom must have felt like a blind person finally getting to see, or a lifer unexpectedly getting out of prison. Then reality set in. While they no longer were chattels, most of the four million never escaped the South's shackling systems of sharecropping and tenancy. Those who headed North found the long hours on the floors of iron mills and textile factories as punishing as working on the plantation.

The railroads, by contrast, had been eager for Colored labor since before the Civil War. Afterward many freedmen abandoned their feudal farms for relatively lucrative rail jobs. They worked not just as laborers but as firemen, shoveling wood and coal to feed insatiable locomotives, as well as brakemen, setting hand brakes and coupling together cars. They helped load baggage and freight and, on occasion, drove the train.

That experience caught the attention of George Pullman, a Gilded Age entrepreneur who in the late 1860s was raising the bar for ornate overnight travel by staffing his trains with men unhesitatingly devoted to service. Former slaves were just the thing, Pullman reasoned. First, they were a bargain. He paid his porter and dining-car men just enough to keep them fed, clothed, and disinclined to sample other employment options. Second, they would be pliant. Who better to cater to passengers' every caprice, from fetching a sandwich at sunup to mending torn trousers in the middle of the night, than men whose entire upbringing had been a long lesson in vassalage? He knew his low wages would compel porters to rely on tips to survive—giving them another incentive to provide the best service imaginable and raise as few protests as possible. That submissiveness also ensured, for at least the first half century of George's enterprise, that his Negro porters would follow orders the way he wanted, resist unions he detested, and be grateful for the jobs he dispensed.

Pullman's primary motivation for hiring only Negroes, however, had to do with the social distance he believed was needed between porters and passengers. To truly feel comfortable on his sleepers, passengers had to see the porter as someone safe. Ideally it would be a man you could look at but not notice. An invisible man. Which, given the social divide between Negroes and whites in those years after slavery, meant an ex-slave. To underline that otherness, Pullman managers favored swarthy-skinned applicants over creamier complexions. No danger then of a porter ever being mistaken for a passenger. In the words of one porter, the Pullman Company wanted "the blackest man with the whitest teeth."

George Pullman's hired help didn't care about his motives. What counted was that here was the first Northern industrialist to give thousands of Negro men the chance to escape Reconstructionists, Klansmen, cotton fields, laws of segregation, and their own well-meaning parents whose experience as slaves blinded them to what the brave new world might offer. They traded in overalls for midnight-blue jackets and crisp-visored caps, riding the nation's most ornate railroad carriages and seeing the full sweep of a land that had just granted them their first taste of independence. On the sleeping cars they were king, even if that regal standing ended when they pulled into the last station. So cherished were those jobs that most made it a career, and many passed it down to sons and grandsons, brothers and nephews. And on the rails they met Americans of money and influence—presidents and starlets, Wall Street wizards and university chancellors, and, best of all, the maestros whose music they delighted in.

The jazzmen loved them back. Like Negro League ballplayers, Pullman porters were part of a Black aristocracy that Duke Ellington had aspired to ever since he'd shot pool with them in the Washington of his boyhood. As for the red-carpet trains, they were an even better sanctuary than luxury automobiles, a place where "my ideas soar and I am not limited by what I can touch and reach." Duke would sit next to the window in what appeared to be a trance, staring for hours at telephone poles, listening to the metallic rhythms of the wheels, delighting as "the firemen play blues on the engine whistle—big, smeary things like a goddamn woman singing in the night." All of which, he added, made him "a train freak."

His time on the train was more than an obsession, it was an inspiration. "Choo-Choo," in 1924, was the first in his series of tunes from the tracks. Others that he composed on his own or with help included "Daybreak Express," "Happy Go Lucky Local," "The Old Circus Train Turn-Around Blues," and "Build That Railroad," whose lyrics reflected his twin passions: "Build that railroad. And sing that song."

One downside of Duke's ease in riding the rails was that he was even more likely to oversleep there than in other settings, requiring road manager Jack Boyd to be even more enterprising at waking him. That didn't always work, as Boyd recalled: "Once in San Francisco, Ellington slept that way and when he got off the train he was so sleepy he got in a line of men that were being herded into a van. They were prisoners for San Quentin. When Ellington tried to get out, the guard wouldn't let him. Damn if I should of rescued him! Should of let him go to prison. It would of taught him."

Basie and Armstrong loved trains, too, and took them any time they could during those decades of depression, war, and recovery. Their lilting and swaying songs helped America make it through, reminding the nation of its dynamism and heartiness. And its love of trains. Basie's choo-choo playlist included "9:20 Special," "Night Train," "Super Chief," and "Midnight Freight." Armstrong favorites were "Hobo You Can't Ride This Train," "The Mail Train Blues," "Alabamy Bound," and "Railroad Blues." The sound of locomotive musicians helped sleep-deprived insomniacs across the land nod off from the comfort of their bedrooms.

On board there were the familiar games of cards and dice, and, if they were lucky enough to be on one of George Pullman's sleepers, the luxury of playing in their pajamas and ordering snacks from the dining car. "My eyes bulged at the amount of money in the poker game," said Rex Stewart. "Most of the time there'd be two tables—one an unlimited stakes game and the other a 25-dollar table stakes game. They called the first one the Big Top and the small game the Side Show. Duke and [singer] Ivie Anderson were the rulers of the Big Top, they not only had the card sense and skill, they also had the money to make a faint-hearted player turn down the best hands when they decided to put the old pressure on."

There was horseplay, too, the kind that made their road weariness more tolerable. "After the job that Pullman would be absolutely bulging with food and drink and girls would be up and running up and down, falling over you, and we'd have so much fun," remembered Harry "Sweets" Edison, Basie's trumpeter. "At one place, when our next stop was Los Angeles, Basie had the valet buy him two or three orders of fried chicken, sandwiches, some bananas and so on, and lay them in his room. Naturally he had the drawing room on the Pullman. Well, about two o'clock in the morning I and somebody else—I forget who—got hungry. So we got out of our berths to see if we could find something to eat. When we opened Basie's door, he was fast asleep and we saw all this chicken and everything. So we sat and feasted on Basie's chicken . . . When he woke up around, I guess around 4 o'clock, he felt hungry . . . and found the remains. He came out of his room, woke everybody up and called them—you know what—'All you mothers are fired; I don't give a damn who did it. This is my room and you had no business coming in, eatin' the chicken and all my fruit. You could have saved me a banana.' . . . I was just lying there smiling."

Private Pullmans made musicians like Edison and Stewart feel like Diamond Jim Brady, especially ones with enough seniority to claim a cherished lower berth. But when the train bills came, the bandleaders had to somehow pay. It was less the time on the move that nearly sent them to the poorhouse than the weeks the sleepers sat motionless, serving as hotels-on-wheels and letting the music makers glide over Jim Crow. That was especially problematic for Ellington, who traveled with his band name emblazoned on the side. A private baggage car carried chests of scenery, microphones, lights, and other vital equipment; six crates filled with Sonny Greer's timpani, vibes, cymbals, and drums; Ivie Anderson's three cases, one each for stage gowns, street clothes, and coats; and everything of Duke's. His threads and music filled five trunks, with another custom-made container just for his shoes.*

The heyday of Pullman travel, for the jazzmen and others, temporarily receded with the onset of World War II. Much like he did with charter buses, Uncle Sam needed Pullmans to shuttle soldiers across the country, which meant there no longer was room for the big bands. That wasn't the only hit the war took on the fun. Musicians were being drafted. The shellac needed for records and the rubber needed for tires suddenly were in short supply. Gasoline was being rationed. And the country was distracted, with many no longer having the time or inclination to swing.

---

* The three maestros weren't the only ones to rent Pullmans, or even the first. Cab Calloway did it for months at a time, with a baggage car big enough to transport his green Lincoln Continental. Bessie Smith, the Empress of the Blues, one-upped the men by buying her own sleeping car.

SETTING THE THEMES

SELDOM IF EVER has a melody so compact (112 words and thirty-two bars) and so romantic (yearning for windswept pines and splashing steamboats) generated such rage, most of it aimed squarely at Louis Armstrong. It was Louis, after all, who made "When It's Sleepy Time Down South" both a jazz standard and his signature song, despite flagrant racial stereotypes like these:

Darkies crooning songs soft and low . . .
Folks down there live a life of ease
When old mammy falls upon her knees

The Black press saw red. Many Negro fans kissed their favorite trumpeter goodbye, while activists burned their copies of Armstrong's recording. To them, this single tune confirmed their long-held doubts about Satchmo: that he was nothing but a groveling apologist for the Dixieland of his birth, in the tradition not just of Uncle Tom but Aunt Jemima.

That backlash was understandable, but as often with the paradoxical Armstrong, it missed the points. Yes, "Sleepy Time" was a minstrel-like sugarcoating of a monstrous era, but it helped nervous whites cross the racial chasm the same way Duke Ellington's jungle music did at the Cotton Club. Moreover, "Sleepy" made way for revolutionary numbers like "West End Blues." No need to remind Little Louis—who'd survived Jim Crow New Orleans and defied racist cops in Memphis—about the inhumanity of slavery and its aftermath. And did the naysayers know that "Sleepy Time" was written by Black writers and performed by civil rights icon Paul Robeson?

Satchmo acknowledged the anger but felt it sold him short, given his aspirations not just for himself but for his racial brethren. His reaction was not to give in but to dig in, hoping he could defang the stereotypes. From the time he first sang it in 1931 through the end of his life, "Sleepy Time" remained the tune he opened or closed with and that fans requested most. He made 194 recordings of it over forty years, sang it over the airwaves, and incorporated it into countless dances and stage performances. In later years, he generally substituted "folks" or "people" for "darkies," and he sometimes opted for an instrumental version rather than one with lyrics, but occasionally he reverted to "darkies" either because he forgot or he thought his censors had.

In 1951, while he was cutting his most celebrated rendition of "Sleepy Time," he growled at Gordon Jenkins, his arranger, "What do you want me to call those black sons-of-bitches this morning?" Around the same time his manager, Joe Glaser, got Louis "to agree to discuss the matter [of lyrics] with an emissary from the NAACP. The emissary turned out to be a very slick, well-tailored young black who looked and sounded like he must be right out of Harvard Business School," recalled Ernie Anderson, a jazz writer and Satchmo friend. Armstrong's valet showed the NAACP man "up to the dressing room where Louis sat in his undershorts with a knotted white handkerchief on his head. The young black tried to explain to Louis that the record was demeaning to blacks. Louis replied quite forcefully, 'Two niggers wrote it!' When he heard this line the young Harvard cat visibly wilted."

In later interviews, Armstrong tried to clarify why "Sleepy Time" was worth fighting for: "I, being from the south, I know the life, and the words live. You know, cats in the sunshine, they lazy, layin' up against the tree and all that stuff there. That's all in that song and it's facts. And the music is pretty . . . As long as I live, 'Sleepy Time Down South' will be my lifelong number, cause it, it, it lives with me."

Louis had no real need to pick a fight over "Sleepy Time." He recorded more than one thousand songs and wrote more than fifty, including early hits like "Potato Head Blues" with lyrics that didn't offend anyone, and "Swing That Music" with feel-good verses like "I'm as happy as I can be / When they swing that music for me." He'd have become a hero to churchgoers had he picked "When the Saints Go Marching In" as his signature melody, or to journalists and activists if he'd opted for "Black and Blue." Fats Waller composed the latter, with lyrics by Harry Brooks and Andy Razaf, but nobody who heard his mournful rendition doubted that Louis was singing his own story:

*I'm white inside, but that don't help my case*** . . .*
My only sin is in my skin
What did I do to be so black and blue?

"Black and Blue" would be immortalized in Ralph Ellison's novel *Invisible Man*. But that came later, decades after he'd introduced it in a 1929 musical revue, and it never rose to the level of a trademark tune.

That "Sleepy Time" stayed front and center was Louis's decision, and it was partly a commercial one. He felt it was time to court white audiences, which he did in ways that suggested he was okay with his second-class status and accepted their ascendancy. He'd been featuring the song in live performances and on records since 1931, and in 1942 made it into a "soundie," a three-minute film that could be watched on coin-operated projectors in nightclubs and restaurants. This one showed Armstrong as one of the darkies of the song, sitting on a cotton bale, wearing a plaid shirt and farmer's hat. But it took another ten years, and the release of a celebrated Decca record, for Black leaders finally to shout ENOUGH. "The name of trumpet player Louis Armstrong joined the list of the 'We Ain't Ready' people in show business when it became known that he has made a new recording for Decca Records in which he sings the radical epithet 'd____s' in referring to colored people," pioneering correspondent James L. Hicks wrote in the *Baltimore Afro-American*. New York radio stations, along with NBC and CBS, fell in line, promising never to air a tune with such an offensive word.

The debate over "Sleepy Time" begs this obvious question: how could someone as keen as Louis Armstrong so misread the words he was singing, failing to see how old mammys and crooning darkies were racist canards? It's easy to say it was a sign of his times, and it may have been back in 1931. But this Decca release and the outcry that ensued came in the 1950s, when that explanation no longer washed. And it wasn't just Black newspapers clamoring for Armstrong's head. As early as 1935, Ed Sullivan of the *Washington Post* ended a column of short takes with this line: "Louis Armstrong and Aunt Jemima go into the Park Avenue [Hotel] . . ." Enough said.

Readers might have chuckled, not realizing how slights like that wounded the well-meaning but slightly naive songster. Louis thought mainly about the melody, and rightfully felt that it was his sweet bluesy renditions that

---

* While Louis's lyric was "I'm white inside" for the first twenty-five years he sang the song, by 1959 he'd made a telling edit, belting out, "I'm *right* inside." Riccardi, *What a Wonderful World*, 235.

mattered to most listeners. He'd made his name partly by scatting nonsense words, so he didn't pay the attention he should have to the actual lyrics which, in his crooning of "Sleepy Time," were crystal clear. The blend of joyfulness and guilelessness that had taken him to the top of the jazz world would, he believed, ensure that Black fans saw beyond the minstrelsy and understood that his embrace by a white world would lift them, too. They did, ultimately, but that took time, and in the meantime he took a lot of grief.

"Sleepy Time" was, in the end, an appropriate theme song for Louis Armstrong, albeit not in the way he'd intended. It demonstrated the pull his native New Orleans had on him, in spite of his quietly pushing back against its racism and nativism. It helped make him the most recognized Black entertainer on the planet even as he became a pariah in parts of Black America. With Satchmo, it never was just one thing and often was contradictory. "Sleepy Time" foreshadowed what would be a career-long if falsely framed debate over whether Louis Armstrong was an artist or an entertainer, a racial pioneer or an Uncle Tom. His hurt over the reaction to "Sleepy Time" triggered flashes of anger at fellow Negroes for failing to see past the figurative masks he wore onstage. "That's why they say a bunch of niggers is like a barrel of crabs," he confided to a friend. "Because as soon as one gets to the top, all those motherfuckers reach up there and grab him and pull him right back down. That's what they do."

Louis's last words on the topic, however, were audacious, which was even more his signature. Recording a medley of his hits in 1932, including "Sleepy Time," he altered the lyrics and sang, "When it's slavery time down south."

———

Count Basie's award-winning theme song fitted him as perfectly as "Sleepy Time" had suited Armstrong. "One O'Clock Jump" was an up-tempo, twelve-bar blues. It had no controversial lyrics. In fact, it had no lyrics at all until some innocuous lines were added some ten years after his original composition.

In Basie's telling, the inspired instrumental emerged fully formed one enchanted Sunday evening during his two-hour radio broadcast from Kansas City's Reno Club in the mid-'30s. "We might be on the air playing for an hour and a half and run out of tunes, and when the announcer used to say what are you going to play next, I'd just start off something and pick any kind of title," the Count explained in his memoir. "One night we were on the air and we had about ten more minutes to go, and the announcer asked what we were going to do, and I said I didn't know. We were talking off the mike because there wasn't but one microphone in there anyway in those days, and that was the one the announcer was on. I said, 'I'm just going to just start playing,' and he said, 'What is this?' and I saw how many minutes to one o'clock it was getting to be, so I said, 'Call it the "One O'Clock Jump."' And we hit it with the rhythm section and went into the riffs, and the riffs just stuck."

As always with Basie, that wasn't quite the full story. "Head" arrangements like that often spontaneously combusted among improvising musicians who'd memorize what they'd done but not write it down, either because that wasn't their style or because they didn't know how. In this case there were building blocks, starting with a key phrase the Basie crew copied from the great stride pianist Fats Waller. Arranger Don Redman expanded on it, and a recording by McKinney's Cotton Pickers struck a chord with Buster Smith, Basie's alto sax man. Smith picks up the story: "We were fooling around at the club and Basie was playing along in F. That was his favorite key. He hollered to me that he was going to switch to D flat and for me to 'set something.' I started playing that opening reed riff on alto. Lips Page jumped in with the trumpet part without any trouble and Dan Minor thought up the trombone part. That was it—a 'head' . . . That was the first writing of the tune."

Smith and other band members also diverge from their leader in other key parts of the how-it-happened. Smith had already named the tune "Blue Balls," but that was too ribald to fly on-air. The band assembled and perfected the song at the Reno, where it became an instant hit, but the broadcast that conferred its name and fame didn't happen until weeks later—and in Little Rock, not Kansas City. It was the radio announcer, not the Count, who, noticing the time, came up with the censor-satisfying title of "One O'Clock Jump." While all that took place in 1935, it wasn't until after Decca Records' 1937 recording that the arrangement was written out, with trumpeter Buck Clayton copying it from the record, and it took eight more years for Lee Gaines to supply the lyrics.

As for the credit, that went to Basie, not to co-composer Smith, who left just before the band hit it big. "When I saw Basie later, he said, 'I don't want you suing me so I'll give you $5, and we'll drink this fifth of gin,'" Smith recalled of the era when such exploitation was routine. "'Next time we record it I'll play any of your tunes you want me to.' He did, too."

However it came together, "One O'Clock Jump" lifted listeners out of their chairs and onto the dance floor right from the start. Basie's piano set the mood and pace, settling the era's swingingest rhythm section into its groove. Following at their pulsating best were dueling tenor saxophonists Herschel Evans and Lester Young, trombonist George Hunt, and trumpeter Buck Clayton. Riffs breathed new life into old-style blues. What began with intimate and engaging piano and sax solos ended with a riveting ensemble that begot Basie's first true hit.

Decca's 78 rpm version lasted just three minutes and two seconds, although live on-air they could go on longer, with band members improvising for up to thirty minutes. "Jump" sometimes opened as well as closed shows, like the best of signatures. The ostensible "King of Swing," Benny Goodman, was smitten with the tune. Record producer John Hammond, Goodman's brother-in-law, would play Basie's Decca recording on his expensive Capehart phonograph and "Benny listened. And listened. He let the record play over and over, absolutely knocked out by 'One O'Clock Jump.' He was finally persuaded that Basie was a big deal, indeed." Goodman's rendition of "Jump" was his first record to top one million in sales, and it was part of the bill at his historic concert at Carnegie Hall in 1938.

Trumpeter Harry James liked "One O'Clock Jump" enough that after his band recorded it in 1938 it inspired him, a year later, to write "Two O'Clock Jump," which would become one of his theme songs. Lionel Hampton used the original "Jump" as his signature, although not for long. Others who played and recorded it included Al Hirt, Louis Armstrong, and Duke Ellington, with the latter claiming the tune was an outgrowth of his own phrasing of an early blues number.

In 1979, "Jump" was inducted into the Grammy Hall of Fame, and later it was listed in the recording industry's "Songs of the Century" list. It was played on TV shows and in films including *Harlem Nights, The English Patient, The Gong Show, Reveille with Beverly,* and *Bon Voyage, Charlie Brown (and Don't Come Back).* "Jump" wasn't Basie's first theme song—that was "Moten Swing," followed for a short time by "Blue and Sentimental"—but it endured the longest, reaching millions.

Sure, he claimed more credit than deserved even as he asserted his modesty. Most of what he said was true, however, and in the end "Jump" was Basie at his best—swinging and inspiring others to sway and swirl into the early hours and on into the coming decades.

―――――

That Duke Ellington's theme song featured trains was a no-brainer, given how much he loved them. What's surprising is that it wasn't one of his own compositions, given how many of them were set on the tracks.

And beyond the world of railroads there were even more logical choices for his signature, all written by him, all hits with his fans, and all with lush backstories of the kind Ellington loved to tell. He wrote "In a Sentimental Mood," for instance, in 1935 in Durham, North Carolina, when "we were having a bit of sipping and this was a rather gay party with the exception of two girls and one fella, and it seems that they were all friends of mine. One girl had been engaged with this young man for a long time and suddenly her best friend was now, you know, going to take him away from her." Duke told the duo, who flanked him at the piano, "You two are too good of friends to let something like this come between you. And ['Sentimental Mood'] is what I played for them." The girls, of course, kissed and made up.

An even more likely candidate would have been "Harlem Air Shaft," from 1940. As Ellington explained, "You get the full essence of Harlem in an air shaft. You hear fights, you smell dinner, you hear people making love. You hear intimate gossip floating down. You hear the radio. An air shaft is one great big loudspeaker. You see your neighbor's laundry. You hear the janitor's dogs. The man upstairs' aerial falls down and breaks your window. You smell coffee. A wonderful thing, is that smell. An air shaft has got every contrast."

His favorite was "East St. Louis Toodle-oo," recorded in 1927 and adopted as his first standard bearer. It was inspired by a sign he'd seen in New England, for a dry cleaner called Lewandos, Duke said, and "every time we saw it we'd start singing: 'Oh, Lee-wan-do!'" Or maybe the idea came from trumpeter Bubber Miley, as Duke wrote in his memoir. Miley "always had a story for his music, such as: 'This is an old man, tired from working in the field since sunup, coming up the road in the sunset on his way home to dinner. He's tired but strong, and humming in time with his broken gait—or vice versa.' That was how he pictured 'East St. Louis Toodle-oo.'"

But it was "Take the 'A' Train" that became Duke's longest-lasting theme tune, from its recording in 1941 until Duke's death thirty-four years later. And while its backstory was only partly about Ellington, it was riveting. Duke invited Billy Strayhorn, a young musician from Pittsburgh, to visit him in New York to talk music, and Strayhorn decided to impress the maestro by turning Ellington's directions on how to get to Harlem into a song. The tune—complete with lyrics like "take your baby subway riding—that's where romance may be hiding"—was "born without any effort," recalled Strayhorn, and came to him faster than the train itself. "It was like writing a letter to a friend."

Billy got the job. Duke got his closest-ever collaborator. And the Ellington band would get its defining song. None of that happened overnight, however, and might never have happened at all without broadcasters and songwriters engaging in a battle of titans. At issue were the fees radio stations paid to the American Society of Composers, Authors and Publishers

(ASCAP), which represents music makers. In 1940, ASCAP said it was going to double its broadcast fees; stations retaliated by vowing that as of January 1, 1941, they'd stop using records or sheet music of ASCAP members, and that included Ellington.

Duke was desperate. He turned to his son Mercer and his pseudo-son Billy, neither of whom belonged to ASCAP and therefore could write tunes that the band could play and stations could air. The callow composers billeted themselves at the Sutherland Hotel on Chicago's South Side. Buffeted by a gallon of blackberry wine, they developed an entirely new playbook. "At one point, [Billy] was having some sort of trouble, and I pulled a piece of his out of the garbage," recalled Mercer. "I said, 'What's wrong with this?' And he said, 'That's an old thing I was trying to do something with, but it's too much like Fletcher Henderson's.' I looked it over—it was "'A' Train"—and I said, 'You're right.' It was written in sections, like Fletcher Henderson. But I flattened it out anyway and put it in the pile with the rest of the stuff."

It's unclear when Ellington first laid eyes on it, but he was naturally inclined to like anything about the railroads and was frantic to find music for the band. He didn't just pick up the tune, he made it his trademark, replacing "Sepia Panorama," which had recently replaced "East St. Louis Toodle-oo." While its lyrics would vary over the decades, his favorite version was a sixty-word one by Joya Sherrill, a high-schooler from Detroit who, like Strayhorn, performed "'A' Train" at her tryout, impressed Duke, and eventually landed the job as his singer. "Hurry, hurry, hurry, take the 'A' train," Sherrill implored, "to get to Sugar Hill way up in Harlem."

"'A' Train" featured an upbeat trumpet solo and infectious scatting by Ray Nance. It blended the propulsive energy of a train and the sweet sophistication of Ellington's Sugar Hill neighborhood, with its tree-lined streets and Victorian mansions. It climbed onto and up bestseller lists, was played in films including *Paris Blues* and *Reveille for Beverly* along with four musicals, and was recorded by Ella Fitzgerald, Mel Tormé, Louis Armstrong, and Count Basie.* Broadcaster Willis Conover adopted it as his theme for *Jazz Hour* on Voice of America, which reached tens of millions of listeners worldwide during the Cold War. Ellington always received credit for his presumed part in the composition, Strayhorn got too little thanks for his unambiguous

---

* While Duke preferred Sherrill's words, Fitzgerald and others used lyrics written by Strayhorn, with possible contributions from Lee Gaines. Gaines was a founder of the Delta Rhythm Boys, the band that recorded the first vocal arrangement of "'A' Train."

authorship and too much for words he didn't write, while history has pretty much forgotten Joya Sherrill's role.*

Although its choice as Ellington's signature disappointed some benighted critics, who wished he'd reached for something more sophisticated, "'A' Train" proved that Duke had mastered pop as well as high culture. It let him pay tribute to his love of trains and of Billy Strayhorn, whom he called "my right arm, my left arm, all the eyes in the back of my head, my brainwaves in his head, and his in mine." Fittingly, a down-tempo version of "Take the 'A' Train" would be performed not just at Billy Strayhorn's funeral but at Duke Ellington's.

---

* After studying handwritten manuscripts and other evidence, Strayhorn biographer Walter van de Leur makes a compelling case that Billy composed and arranged all, or nearly all, of "'A' Train." Van de Leur, *Something to Live For.*

But if Duke got too much credit for some songs, he got too little for others he likely ghost-wrote during the broadcast ban. "I have trouble with the idea that Mercer really wrote all those songs of that era," says Harvey Cohen. "But [Duke] sure needed them at the time—and liked the idea of giving his son the royalties." Cohen email.

THE LANGUAGE OF JAZZ

NICKNAMES CAN TELL stories. Typically, the focus is on who coined the tag, and why. But we learn even more about a person from the labels they choose for themselves.

While Duke Ellington attributed his moniker to a boyhood pal, young Edward never needed to be reminded of his majesty. How else to explain his boyhood edict to his family that he was "ze grand, ze great, and ze glorious Duke Ellington"? Eddie Ellington faded into memory, if he ever really existed. Going forward, his sister and parents were allowed to use the formal version of his given name, Edward; bandmates could address him as the Governor, Guv'nor, or Guvvy; and the real-life Duke of Wales christened him the Duke of Hot.* Case closed.

Same with Billy Basie. He wasn't to the manor born, but wished he had been. So, as he confessed and his business card confirmed, he crowned himself Count not long after arriving in Kansas City. He took on even more imperial nicknames over the years: Chief, Holy Man, and the Jump King of Swing.†

Louis Armstrong's nickname had a more convoluted, and less pretentious, narrative. His early handle was Little Louis, a reference to his age and, over time, a riff on his expanding girth. Other youthful epithets included Shadmouth, Dipper, Dippermouth, Gatemouth, and Satchelmouth. The last three were commentaries on his enormous chops—or were they? Satchelmouth was rumored to go back to his days dancing for pennies in the Battlefield. Scooping up the coins, he stuck them in his mouth for safekeeping. A pal who supposedly saw it all dubbed him Satchel Mouth.

---

* The title Duke of Ellington was suspiciously close to Duke of Wellington, who may have been an inspiration for Edward's appellation.
† Sometimes it was Holy Main, or just Holy, all courtesy of Lester Young.

In later years he picked up other monikers, from the less-than-flattering Boat Nose, Hammock Face, Slow Foot, Rhythm Jaws, Sackaface, Henpeck, Brass (or Iron) Lips, Laughin' Louie, and Fats Armstrong, to Ambassador Satch, which journalists liked. Louis called people whose names he didn't know or forgot Pops, a name that friends and one biographer turned back on him. His mother called him Louis, never Louie, but two of his wives, his manager, and bandmates liked the less formal form. In Louis's picturesque telling it was Percy Brooks, the tongue-tied editor of a British music magazine, who contracted an old nickname into the most celebrated sobriquet in song. "I got off the boat and he shook my hand and said to me 'HELLO SATCHMO.' I had never heard the name before . . . I love it." He did indeed, enough to emboss it on his canary-yellow stationery, to assign it to his specially blended cologne, and to tell journalists it was part of his name and didn't require quotes.

"Call me anything at all," he added. "Just don't call me too late to eat!"*

The origin stories of these nicknames have been argued over for decades, but whether they are true is ultimately beside the point. What matters is that the maestros told them like they were, and that their narratives reflected their personalities. Duke embraced his regal nickname and the formal Edward. The Count dropped Billy and Willie early in life, although he let some old friends call him Bill Basie. And Louis, who may have been the most august of all, preferred his most lyrical and scat-like pet name, Satchmo.

———

In the world of jazz in the first half of the twentieth century, everyone had a nickname, whether you were a headliner or a second banana. The more esoteric the better, to separate insiders from hangers-on. Generally the names signaled affection, but not always. A tag shaped perceptions and created expectations for the named and anyone using it. Sometimes you could hint at things in a handle that you couldn't state openly. Nothing was too preposterous.

Pet names had figured in Louis's world beginning in boyhood, with his mother calling him Fatty O'Butler, him calling her Mayann, and everyone calling his sister Mama Lucy. He marched in funeral parades alongside the likes of Rainhead, Black Sol, Black Lute, Big Sore Dick, and Foots Ariel. La-

---

* Satchmo's nickname and explanations for it are reminiscent of Leroy "Satchel" Paige's. So is Louis's saying, "I been blowing that horn for fifty years and I never looked back once." Satchel's famed version was, "Don't look back, something might be gaining on you." Gleason, *Celebrating the Duke, and Louis*, 53.

dies of the night were everywhere, with hard-boiled names like Mary Jack the Bear, Bucktown Bessie, Buck Tooth Rena, Yard Dog, Crying Emma, Cold Blooded Carrie, Lily the Crip, Boxcar Shorty, Three Finger Annie, Big Butt Annie, Bird Leg Nora, Gold Tooth Gussie, Miss Thing, and Nootsy, who worked briefly for Louis.

Some bynames would effectively replace a person's given name. Nobody would recognize Duke's drummer as William Alexander Greer; he was simply Sonny. He'd been named after his dad and, to make clear the distinction, the family called him Son, then Sonny. When his pal Ellington wanted to get his attention, however, he was Nasty. ("He called me that because I had always defended him against all comers through the years.") Another moniker captured even better Greer's towering accomplishment and self-admiration: Mr. Empire State Building. And who knew trumpeter Cootie Williams really was Charles Melvin Williams? Charles vanished and Cootie took over at a young age when, after watching a brass band play in the park, his father asked what the boy had heard: "Cootie, cootie, cootie."

On occasion it was tit for tat. As a sign of esteem, Billie Holiday dubbed Lester Young, her closest of pals, Prez, short for President of the United States, or more accurately President of Jazz. He called everyone Lady and called her Lady Day, which friends would use more than her birth name of Eleanora Fagan or her professional name of Billie Holiday.

Many monikers had self-evident roots. Slim singer Joya Sherrill became Skinny. Scorching trumpeter Oran Thaddeus Page became Hot Lips, and sweet-sounding trumpet player Harry Edison became Sweetie Pie, then Sweets. Sweet-tempered Billy Strayhorn became Swee' Pea because he reminded fellow musicians of the single-toothed baby in *Popeye* comics (Ellington flipped it to Peaswee'). Saxophonist Johnny Hodges ate, ran, and looked like a rabbit, hence his most often-used nickname (others included Jeep, Little Caesar, and Squatty Roo). Ray Nance's multiple talents—on the trumpet and violin, along with singing and dancing—made him Floorshow. Sax man Ben Webster's beefiness led to the Brute, while the bags under his eyes yielded Frog. Trombonist Joe Nanton could do with one hand what took others two, and performed illusions with his plunger mute, hence the first half of Tricky Sam; the other half is inscrutable. Milton Mesirow, who wrote and played under the name Mezz Mezzrow, had handles ranging from Poppa Mezz and Mother Mezz to Father Neptune. The most apt was Reefer King.

Having a nickname bestowed on you signaled that you had arrived—or, in the case of Nelson Harrison, had yet to. When the trombonist was a newbie with the Basie band, veterans commissioned him Shithouse Nelson.

There were tags for songs, too: when Duke wanted the band to play "So-phisticated Lady," he called for "Sophia." Likewise for roadways: Midtown's Fifty-Second was Swing Street. Some handles smacked of irony: the Gag-writers Association named 250-pound crooner Velma Middleton "Miss Pe-tite of 1946." Some groups acquired unofficial labels: the younger set in the Ellington band was known as the Mod Squad.

Names for the leaders grew more poetic and adulatory over time. Arm-strong was called the American Bach, Chocolate Gabriel, Pied Piper of Them All, Mighty Satchmo, Uncle Satchmo, and, in Africa, Satchee-mo.* Basie be-came Daddy Basie, Base Man, Bateman, Base, Tink-a-Tink Man, Mr. Hold-It-Together, Picasso of Jazz, Kansas City Killer, and, in Frank Sinatra's ode to the Count's splank-splank-splank-boom lick in "Fly Me to the Moon," Splank or Splanky. Ellington, who loved to coin handles for others, embraced two of his new ones: Maestro and the Joe Louis of Song Champions. (He liked less Fatso, Monster, Tubby, Phony, Stinkpot, Apple Dumpling, Dumpy, Dump, Puddin', Head Knocker, Sandhead, and the Artful Dodger).†

———

Jazzmen had their own lexicon, reflecting their takes on music, life, and fel-low artists. The musicians never used it with the public, and even if fans overheard they would not have understood. Which was the point. The secret language allowed performers to talk about their audience without it over-hearing, the way immigrant parents used Yiddish, Polish, or Italian to keep things from their English-speaking children. Or children use pig Latin, and jive, to keep things from parents. For bandleaders and members, the argot meshed naturally with the music they played, since jazz itself was an under-ground language. Their wordbook fostered intimacy even as it conferred secrecy. It was a shorthand for making sense of their world.

Some expressions they brought from the Negro community, and the small-town South. *Ofay* was a not-so-fond way Blacks referred to whites.‡ African Americans in the North referred to the South they'd left behind as *Galilee*. A *handkerchief head* was a close relation to an Uncle Tom. So was a

---

* The nickname Louis cherished most was Papa, which was what his nephew Clarence called him.

† Duke, in Southern tradition, added May to lots of names—Daisy May, Evie May, Willie May, and, for his old revolver, Sweetie May. Tucker, *Duke Ellington Reader*, 272.

‡ *Crow Jim* was a term coined for antiwhite bigotry, with some white jazzmen feeling side-lined by the growing recognition of the central roles Blacks played in jazz history. But the rise of Ellington, Armstrong, and Basie didn't displace their white contemporaries like Glenn Miller, Tommy and Jimmy Dorsey, Gene Krupa, Benny Goodman, and Guy Lombardo.

sandman, although it was all right, the Count advised, to "do a little sanding to get next to a chick." Uncle Tom, meanwhile, had become a verb: *tomming.* The opposite of a Tom was a *race man* (or woman), according to the *Chicago Defender.* Musicians preferred *Negro* to *Colored,* and later to *Black,* much the way they favored *lady* over *woman.* Beware of *nasty types* or anyone slick enough to have *oil on his bottom;* both were *as unwelcome as an undertaker at a marriage breakfast.*

They had special terms for music, and especially for jazz, which became a verb as well as a noun and adjective. A *cutting contest* described a battle of pianists or bands to see who shone brighter or riffed longer. Up-and-coming players disparaged the old guard as *moldy figs. Taking a Boston* was another way of saying "getting off" or, more simply, "swinging." *Jazz* could also mean fornication, and an earlier spelling was *jass.* The musicians turned *funk* on its head, from its earlier definition of dejected to earthy and in-the-groove. *Dixieland, traditional, Chicago style, hot, swing, Kansas City, bop, progressive, modern, cool, West Coast, mainstream, hard bop, funky, soul, avant-garde,* and *Third Stream* were some of the ways critics categorized jazz—and reasons why Ellington hated categories.

Drugs and drink, ubiquitous in that world, merited their own vernacular. *Vipers* like Louis Armstrong smoked *gage, tea, mota, muggles, weed, reefer,* or what Louis called simply *some of that good shit. Potville* was the name given to the deadliest of burgs where the only thing to do was get drunk or smoke gage, preferably hand-rolled into a fat *bomber.* The Basie band called wine and gin *tops and bottoms.* A *liquor head* was a drunk, a *dipsy* was a drunk looking for sex, but you could count on a *100-proof guy.*

The vocabulary used for sex and women in those male-dominated bands generally skewed toward the loutish. *Chili bandits* were the girls who chased musicians; *sporting women* were whores. When a good-looking lady passed by, bandsmen would say *want some, want some,* and for less attractive ones they'd mutter *want none, want none. Barbecue, canary,* and *pigeon* were slang for woman, *vonce* for sex. Even *squares* wanted to check out the *gams* (legs) on a *pretty brownskin with a shape on her hittin' ninety-nine.* A superabundance of good things left you with the *Too-Sies*—too much money, too much drinking, too many women, at too young an age.

Basie had his own way of saying things. *Grays* were white people. Negroes were *Oxford grays* or *oxes.* For laughs, he and the band would say or sing *Yo' mammy don't wear no drawers,* sometimes before playing the insult-trading game the Dozens. *Pass the peanuts* meant a new song wasn't going to work, so don't bother trying a second time.

Nobody played more word games than Armstrong. *Whaling* was having sex, which he talked about almost as often as he did it. He used expressions like *yassuh, no suh, boss,* and *cullid* to outfox the police or bigots. A *butter-and-egg man* was a small-time big shot, a *paperman* played written rather than *head* music, and an *alligator* was a listener (sometimes a white jazzman trying to learn—or steal—from Black ones). *Mugging light* was soft swing, *mugging heavy* was the opposite, and *gutbucket* was swinging to the blues. *Prostitutes* were high-class *whores,* and twice the price. A *physic* was a laxative that, like most everything, Louis pronounced with an accent as suggestive of Brooklyn as of New Orleans. He also was credited with coining this list of idioms: *jive, solid, scat, chops, mellow, Pops, face, cat, daddy,* and *half-fast,* which meant neither too swift nor too sluggish.

"There are more than four hundred words used among swing musicians that no one else would understand," explained Louis, who was part polyglot, part prophet. "They have a language of their own, and I don't think anything could show better how closely they have worked together and how much that they feel they are apart from 'regular' musicians and have a world of their own that they believe in and that most people have not understood."

Satchmo also had his own special way of expressing regret, vowing never to do again whatever it was he'd done "as long as I'm colored." He promised, too, never to be *dicty,* which referred to snobbery at its worst.

Ellington's glossary was long and less dicty than his general mannerisms, although his bandmates tapped it more than he did. *Juice* and *charge water* were other ways of saying "liquor." *Short* denoted a cheap car, *rubber* a good one. *Blow my top, flip my lid,* and *bust my conk* made clear you'd enjoyed yourself, and when food was the topic, it was *knock a scarf. Bug disease* was when you let the irritations of daily life bug you, which he tried hard not to. *Kittens, bantas,* and *dresses* were ways of saying "girl"; *pants* was short for "boys." He considered himself a master of *Skilapooping,* "the art of making what you're doing look better than what you're supposed to be doing." *Hip* "actually means, when someone is hip, he's wearing hip boots. This is the original of it. He's wearing hip boots, which means that he can walk through shit up to his ass, and not get full of it . . . You can't give me no shit because I've got my hip boots on."

Saxophonist Toby Hardwicke had no illusions about Duke's use of *we.* "Ten years ago, it was, 'We do it this way' and 'We wrote that,'" explained Hardwicke, who rejoined the band in 1932. "Now the we was *royal.*"

ON CENTER STAGE

WITH MOST JAZZ kingpins, it was difficult to be sure when they were swinging at full throttle. With Bill Basie, the tell was his ten toes.

Those calloused and curled digits, planted squarely under his piano seat, foretold whether a song had the vital elixir, the rhythmic perfection, the sheer *it*. His bandmates watched for a hopeful nod of his close-cropped head, a flicker of his bushy brows, or perhaps a doubling of his fists. But they knew the true proof lay in any movement of his toes. Would it be enough to lift both feet? Would they thump or just flutter? Some musicians actually suspected he had radar hidden in his shoes.

He'd learned the truism of toes watching Fats Waller work his magic on the organ at Harlem's Lincoln Theater. "You play with your feet," Fats instructed his youthful apprentice. It wasn't merely the pedals that mattered, but the patter. When Basie looked down, the stride stylist chided, "No, don't do that. You'll never play it if you look at it."

Now that he was on center stage, the Count's weren't the only toes that counted. Everyone listening—dresses and pants, moldy figs and beboppers— had to be bobbing theirs. Then moving to the dance floor. Once they got there, the rest was a gut reaction—stomping, swaying, and swiveling with the Jump King of Swing.

"If you have a Count Basie record playing and your left foot isn't tapping," said jazz radio host and scholar Dick Golden, "you better go see your doctor because something must be wrong with your circulation." Critic Gary Giddins concurred, saying, "Basie knew if he had your foot, your heart and mind would follow."

That was different from our other maestros. Duke Ellington would jump up from his piano seat, his right hand levitating before striking a chord from on high and launching one of his self-composed ballads. Louis Armstrong jump-started his audience by reaching for a powerfully high E, F, or that elusive A flat, placing jazz in the command of the soloist. The Basie Machine drew from a narrower palette of colors and moods. But in Basie's hands, less really was more. On the bandstand, he displayed a cool economy of motion. Inhibitions evaporated. Even fellow musicians weren't sure what was coming. Then, with a single pop of a key and twitch of the toes, he introduced an intoxicating riff that levitated his horn players, drummers, and string men, together with everyone on the dance floor.

All Basie wanted to know was: Does it swing? "I didn't say foot-tappin'," he clarified. "I said foot-pattin'. That's a lot more solid." And solid it was—enough to make his band of brothers the swingingest machine of the dance-band era.

Trumpeter Clark Terry marveled at how Basie's minimalism worked like a sixth sense. "With the simple drop of his finger, the band hit. 'Zow!' It felt like we had knocked down the Great Wall of China," said Terry, who played with both Basie and Ellington. The Count "had a way of getting that feeling through the whole band without having to use linebacker tactics—no showbiz antics of batons or jumping around, or dancing, or running back and forth . . . Playing with Basie, I felt and heard the music better than I ever had before. Man, his swing was powerful! Then sometimes it was elegantly dynamic. During his easygoing renditions, there was a soul-stirring feeling. His four-four rhythm swayed a head-nodding and ear-bending groove, an easy foot-tapping bounce. Then during his up-tempo renditions he created a finger-popping force that made you move.

"Unmistakable. Undeniable. And *very* signature."

That trademark simplicity served as cover for all the things the Count didn't want to or perhaps couldn't do. He was a lazy songwriter, leaning on others to work out his ideas and score his songs. He had enough ambition to run a band but lacked patience, rejecting any number that required rehearsing more than once. An inbred caution and inclination to play it safe held him back, at least at first. His two-fingered approach to piano playing aimed to conserve rather than dish out energy, in contrast to two-fisted hard drivers like Fats Waller, Willie "the Lion" Smith, or Basie himself in his younger days. No genius here, at least not one as self-evident as with the early Duke or Satchmo.

All that suggested the Count Basie Orchestra would be another flash in the pan in a business that offered few second chances, even to onetime kings like Joe Oliver or the erstwhile red-hot Blue Devils. But anyone paying attention also could see signs of evolution, even of brilliance.

His piano playing took on new purpose starting in the mid-1930s. His left hand now either held notes or kept still. His right tinkled short, staccato phrases in the upper register. The punching and striding were long gone. "Yet through some strange quirk of musical logic, the [new] version is more forceful," jazz educator Mark Tucker said. "The pruned chords and more relaxed pacing let in air so the notes can breathe. The accents are fewer but more incisive. Here are the hallmarks of the classic Basie style: wit, economy, suspense, and most of all, swing."

The fewer notes the Count played, the more heed and heft he put into each. His simple plink-clink became such trademarks that listeners could identify a Basie tune after just a pair of chords placed squarely on the beat. "Count Basie could do more with two notes than any musician I've ever known, and was the master of the in-the-pocket tempo," said Basie arranger and friend Quincy Jones. Territory musicians like the Count distilled their Wild West sound to its refined essentials when they got to KC, which fancied itself the Jazz Capital of the World. "The adage in Kansas City was—and still is—*say something* . . . not just show off," said Basie contemporary and double bassist Gene Ramey. "*Tell us a story and don't let it be a lie.* Let it *mean* something, if it's only one note."

Basie's own reasoning for his new approach to the piano was characteristically bare-bones. "I don't want to 'run it in the ground,' as they say. I love to play, but this idea of one man taking one chorus after another is not wise, in my opinion. Therefore, I fed dancers my own piano in short doses, and when I came in for a solo, I did it unexpectedly," explained the Count. "I think a band can really *swing* when it swings *easy,* when it can just play along like you are cutting butter."

That new keyboard style fit with his evolving conception of the bandleader's role. No more showboating, like he'd done with the Blue Devils and Benny Moten. Even his uniform got a makeover: gone were the patched pants, replaced onstage by a tie and suit and topped off by a yachting cap. He'd proven his chops, gotten the band he aspired to, and now that orchestra, not him, had to be front and center. His piano playing still mattered. The goal this time, however, was to give bandmates needed support, creating lead-ins to and background for their solos. The musical equivalents of shouting and banter gave way to whispering and even silence.

In a world that named everything, the Basie approach amounted to leading from behind. It happened quietly enough that few outside the band noticed. The roly-poly Count had an intuitive grasp of psychology and a precise vision for his growing troupe: "I want my 15-piece band today to work together just like those nine pieces did. I want 15 men to think and play the same way. I want those four trumpets and three trombones to bite with real guts. BUT I want that bite to be just as tasty and subtle as if it were the three brass I used to use."

Brilliant wind-section soloists like Lester Young and Walter Page helped cement the band's success. So did Freddie Green on guitar, "Papa" Jo Jones on drums, and Basie on keyboards, with the Count setting the gold standard for percussionists. As advertised, it was the All-American Rhythm Section. It "put wheels on all four bars of the beat," one critic noted, creating a flow over which the other instrumentalists rode like they were on a streamlined cushion. Basie was the navigator. He plinked the blues-rooted cadence, then leaned over and chuckled to bass player Milt Hinton, "Go ahead, hog, you're gonna take it anyway," or whispered to guitarist Green, "Kid, swing that music!" With an understated magic, the group that would grow to seventeen became an ensemble of rhythmic unity. Audiences listened attentively to Duke and Satchmo, but when the Count played, they danced.

Time magazine tried to capture that magic: "After the Count played a phrase or two on the piano, the rhythm section began to boost the beat while cymbals sizzled in the background. Five saxophones took up the melody, sweetly and a bit hoarsely, and then seven brasses began to clip into it with cross rhythms. Suddenly the snare drum cut loose with the effect of a burp gun, and the whole band leaped into ear-crushing chords and rammed home the climax."

Looking back half a century later, Gary Giddins remembers how "I finally got to see with my own eyes the fact that they'd get an arrangement, and it was just a nothing arrangement. They would rehearse it without Basie. It could have been fifty different bands . . . Then Basie walks in at the piano and transforms the whole goddamn thing. I mean, he crosses out everything that he thinks is baroque or excessive . . . And everybody just pops up, everybody in the band, they just, you know, their posture changes in the chairs. It was unbelievable."

His sidemen and women could have landed jobs with Duke Ellington or Cab Calloway, Chick Webb, Fletcher Henderson, or any of the other towering big band leaders, and many did or would. But most saw their time with Basie as their best. It was when they played mainly for other Blacks, and for the single-minded purpose of swinging. Basie believed that the band that partied hard together offstage would play well on, said "Papa" Jo Jones: "You hung out with the Basie band, you knew two things were gonna happen: you drank some booze and went to bed with some women! Hanging out with Duke Ellington was *nice*, it was *culture*, you know, I could get that at Carnegie Hall, but there's never been a band like that Basie band."

It also was democratic. Ellington the bon vivant experimented and stylized, giving audiences a taste of jazz's destiny. Armstrong explosively transported listeners to their ragtime and blues roots. Basie, by contrast, stayed on the button in the here and now. His modesty made him both exciting and relatable. Anyone could understand his kind of jazz. He encouraged sidemen to improvise, with his rare solos inviting the next soloist to join the party. The piano talked for him, and he considered himself less the leader than a part of the rhythm section. Louis wanted center stage. Duke saw himself as a grand impresario. The Count remained a bona-fide populist.

There were limits, of course. Nobody ever forgot who was boss. "The minute the brass gets out of hand and blares and screeches instead of making every note mean something, there'll be some changes made," Basie warned.

So was he aloof or involved, a democrat or an autocrat? The answer is: yes. His music, like his personality, embodied contradictions. He was intensely private but spent his life in the public arena. His swinging brand of jazz blended nuance and tsunami. He spoke volumes in low tones and abbreviated notes. He was self-effacing and ambitious, outwardly dialed back and at heart white-hot. Those new to the band saw just the smile, not the behind-the-scenes rivalries he stirred up—telling Herschel Evans, "Lester Young says you're a siss," and telling Young, "Herschel talks about your family like a dog"—believing that was the way to get the best out of both sax men. Such riddles and enigmas were the paradox of jazz itself, and the Count seemed to have solved it. A jazz-crazed public lined up now not to hear steamrolling Bill Basie the piano player, but to float in time with the electrifying Count Basie Orchestra.

"If a Martian arrived here today and asked you what jazz is," says longtime jazz radio host Tom Reney, "you're gonna play him Count Basie."

————

Edward Ellington had the passion to match Bill Basie and like him relished swinging, but their approaches were as divergent as jazz allowed. The Count was all sense and instinct, as embodied by his happy feet, whereas Duke was cerebral. He had to be, as the jazz world's singular quadruple threat.

Any one of Ellington's talents—tickling the ivories, conducting an orchestra, composing tunes, or arranging compositions and orchestrations— would have made him a man to remember. On the piano, his two-handed stride matched the percussive heights of his idols, Willie "the Lion" Smith and James P. Johnson. As a bandleader, he kept his orchestral collective at the front of the cutthroat pack for half a century, and reworked songs nearly every time a new member joined his band. But it was his composing—six thousand tunes in all, from ballads to blues, spirituals, show tunes, and brief interludes—that put him in the company of musical greats of any era or idiom.*

As with Basie, Ellington's evolution began with the piano. It was the orchestra-unto-itself instrument aspiring big band leaders assumed they had to play, especially if they were Black. That proved true for everyone from Sam Wooding to Fletcher Henderson, Jelly Roll Morton, and Bill Basie.† Duke had always thought of himself as the leader even when, in the early days of the Washingtonians, he wasn't. And according to his son Mercer, "he didn't consider himself a piano player. He only considered himself a piano player in the earlier days when he used to sit down and challenge James P. Johnson, and you know have his sessions round New York, but it happens inevitably that once a musician gets into writing he abandons the abilities that he has on an instrument."

The elder Ellington confirmed that assessment. "[Billy] Strayhorn is a good piano player, you see, I am not. No, you see, I'm a jive piano player. I am the same thing I was when I started out. In the days of the piano plunkers, when a guy was walking to a party, a house rent party or whatever the hell it was, and he's supposed to be a piano player. So they say, 'Okay, so and so, sit down, blow something.' So they'd sit down. And they had things that they would do," Duke told an interviewer, displaying his characteristic false modesty and underselling his out-of-sight stylizing. "There's no greater actors than a piano-plunking piano player, man. Because they'd sit down and . . . smoke a cigarette and they'd take their time."

As always ze grand Duke was being glib. His piano playing was better than he said and many critics thought. His style was Spartan, like the Count's, but strong, bold, and mysterious. He liked to give people a show, the way Bill Basie had in his Reno Club years. Ellington "has a way of letting his right hand hang limp at his side and then swinging it up in the air before striking the notes, seeming to 'hit' a chord from a distance," recalled fellow pianist

---

* Estimates on how many songs he composed vary widely. The clearest answer comes from the Library of Congress, which says, "Ellington, frequently working with Billy Strayhorn, created over 1,500 pieces of music—nearly 6,000, if brief musical interludes are included." Library of Congress, "Today in History—April 29."

† There were, of course, exceptions, from drummer Chick Webb to vocalist Cab Calloway and sax man Andy Kirk.

Teddy Wilson. "Actually, the motion itself means nothing: what happens when you actually contact the keys is quite different to what is happening in the air."

Almost from the start, he acted as quarterback while he played. Again like Basie, he led from behind, seeing the whole field, piloting from his piano stool, anticipating and providing the support soloists needed, loving to improvise and scramble, and making the band the real star. He relished his image as a low-key boss, one who could marshal his players without raising his voice. "You shout for different reasons. Sometimes you shout to further the enthusiasm. And then you shout probably as a result of sort of a reprimand, a protest against what you've just heard. You know, I mean, it's just utterly ridiculous," he said. "I can't use my strength, I'm too damn fragile for that." Another favorite Duke-ism: "I'm easy to please. Just give me the *best*."*

At times he used his hand to conduct rather than plunk, catapulting himself onto center stage. "Leading a band was the expression of a lifelong need to perform before an audience," said Smithsonian curator and Ellington biographer John Edward Hasse. "He loved putting on a show, being theatrical, relished the high-wire aspects of improvising and performing, the element of controlling his realm, the challenge of winning the next audience—they were truly in his blood, and he was compelled to perform. He would have been miserable if he had retired."

His best work happened out of public hearing or sight, when he was arranging the tunes and the show. In that context his band, as he told people, was his plaything, his hobby, and his toy. He'd reimagine the music to fit not just any instrument but individual band members' personality strengths as well as their musical imperfections, writing in the score their name rather than their instrument. He appreciated the drunken wah-wah growls Bubber Miley could get from his trumpet. Same for the funky jungle sounds Sonny Greer could produce with his elaborate drum kit. It didn't matter if the sideman had been with him from the start, was new, or was just passing through. That helps explain why his sound evolved in the masterful way it did, even when the playlist stayed the same.†

---

* He also was astute enough to know that yelling never would have worked with a team as talented as his, as Harvey Cohen points out. Cohen email.

† He even sang a bit. "He's got three numbers that he's recorded," recalled Mercer. "He thinks very highly of himself hahahaha for what he did. One of them is called 'Moon Maiden,' and there's another tune called ['Tell Me It's the Truth'] . . . In the old days it was a requisite as a piano player to sing, otherwise you couldn't get the job." Interview of Mercer Ellington, June 19, 1983, Yale.

As good as he was at playing, leading, and arranging, Duke's greatest creative genius lay in the music he wrote. As a teenager, he soaked up what he'd heard in the drugstore and turned out "Soda Fountain Rag." His love for jamming and for the blues yielded "C Jam Blues." His deep faith gave us sacred gifts like "Come Sunday" and "In the Beginning God." Ellington ballads celebrated African flowers and Harlem gin mills, sophisticated ladies and churning locomotives. He could instill new energy into the three-minute pop songs that were standard for 78 rpm records, and craft concertos and tone poems that lasted an unheard-of fifty minutes. He was as comfortable on Tin Pan Alley as in Carnegie Hall, enthralling foot-thumping jitterbuggers as well as intellectuals who exercised only their ears and minds. To him, composing was as compulsive and instinctive as breathing—he scratched out ideas on manuscript pads and scraps of cocktail napkins, hummed them just loud enough to intrigue his companions, and kept a portable piano at his bedside.

He also learned to use his band as a laboratory for his compositions. That let him test them hours after he wrote them. Did they sound as good with an orchestra as they did in his head? It worked well enough that he kept the band together fifty-two weeks a year for a full half century, even when he couldn't afford to.

At the root of it all for Ellington lay his love of stories. Unlike William Faulkner, Ernest Hemingway, and William Shakespeare, with whom he sometimes was compared, Duke generally told his without words. "Ellington writes naturally for instruments alone," R. D. Darrell observed in an influential and adoring review in 1932, comparing him to Mozart, Wagner, and Schubert. "Words may sometimes be added to his pieces, but always unhappily . . . The human voice is not disdained, but in his works it operates only in an instrumental technique, wordlessly, one might say inarticulately if it were not for the definite articulation of its expressiveness . . . Ellington has emancipated American popular music from text for the first time since the Colonial days of reels and breakdowns."

There, too, he defied expectations. Early on, others generally added whatever words there were, but later he did it himself, said his son: "One of the great developments of Ellington was his power to do lyrics . . . He would do his own things and then he'd discuss it, and that's about the time when he felt he was going somewhere. Rock came in and he said you spend all that time developing a sense of how to write poetically and with some artistry and suddenly here comes a way of music where the more wrong it is, the hotter the song becomes . . . His greatest achievement that most people don't think of was his three sacred concerts because practically every lyrical word in there, that's in the concerts, was written by Ellington."

Duke relied on his instincts and followed his own rules, the first of which was to make careful listeners think—about their lives, their country, and the place of the Negro in Africa and America—the way he did with numbers like "Uncle Tom's Cabin Is a Drive-In Now." Not the normal fare of pop songs, which was part of what appealed to Duke. "He was a self, what they call a self-made man," said granddaughter Mercedes Ellington, a dancer and choreographer. "He didn't, you know, say that, 'Oh, I want to be like another Frank Sinatra or I want to be like another Lawrence Welk or whatever.' He created his own persona."

His second precept was reminiscent of rival Bill Basie's first. The Count might have had America's most spine-tingling dance band, while Duke fancied himself the leader of an unrivaled orchestra, almost in the continental sense, but that didn't mean Ellington didn't want his music to swing. "If [Duke] wanted something to swing, it was going to *swing,* and he was going to swing your behind right on *out* of there," testified Basie. Ellington made that clear in a 1931 composition that became an anthem for the Swing Era: "It Don't Mean a Thing (If It Ain't Got that Swing)."* "When I'm making my arrangements or composing something new, I try to think of something that will make my hearers feel like dancing," Duke said. "It's a primitive instinct, this dancing business, perhaps; but it also signifies happiness and the desire to step around a little means that people are not bothering very much about the cares of the world, at least for the moment. And I like to see people happy. I like to think that I'm contributing something that promotes at least temporary happiness."

He got to witness that one night when a woman came to his show in a wheelchair. "At the end of the dance, she got up and ran to the bandstand and thanked us all," he remembered. "She didn't realize she was standing up. She'd left her wheelchair. No kidding . . . She said the music had gotten into her soul and her bones."

Rule three: do it like a duke. He was handsome and dapper, polished and regal. His onstage bearing, wit, and manners made clear his seriousness. He commanded respect without having to ask, the way his eighth-grade English teacher had taught. All of which helped lift jazz from the low art of gin mills

---

* Trumpeter Cootie Williams says the title was a takeoff on the advice he'd perpetually give Duke. Duke said an earlier trumpeter, Bubber Miley, coined the phrase, believing that "if it didn't swing, it wasn't worth playing." Carter Harman interviews of Duke Ellington.

and honky-tonks to an art form worthy of performances at New York's Cathedral of St. John the Divine and San Francisco's Grace Church.

The last rule was to pretend there were no rules. "I discarded most of the rules I had learned," he said, "and found greatest success in doing things that my harmony instructors had warned me against." His compositions fused jazz and classical traditions, embraced ballet along with ballads and blues, and stretched choruses beyond their normal thirty-two bars. "[This music] is 98 per cent emotional and cannot be written down on paper," he explained. "It observes no conservatory laws, but smacks a little of the barber-shop quartette [*sic*] and the mass singing of slaves."

Ellington's reach and depth—playing and composing, writing rules and chafing at them—required a one-of-a-kind intellect. Scientists have actually tried to trace a link between the great jazz artists and the structural networks of their brain. The closer they seem to get, the more we are left to ponder. What did Duke inherit from Daisy and J.E.? What was picked up in parlors and poolrooms? Duke himself said, "There is no format for the activity of the brain. If it doesn't happen in the mind first, it doesn't happen."*

In the end it's not science, but the mystery of the arts and the history of African America, that helps us understand the musical legacy of Duke Ellington. Nobody on the music scene then or ever drew from a broader palette of themes and moods to paint his songs and define the DNA of jazz. As British critic Spike Hughes wrote in 1933, his is "the music of a race that plays, sings and dances because music is its most direct medium of expression and escape. Duke Ellington alone has brought this music out of the semi-twilight of small night-clubs into the broad daylight of the outside world." The following year Constant Lambert, another Englishman as well as a composer and critic, went a note higher in trumpeting this Duke's accomplishments: "Ellington, in fact, is a real composer, the first jazz composer of distinction, and the first Negro composer of distinction . . . He has crystallized the popular music of our time and set up a standard by which we may judge not only other jazz composers but also those highbrow composers, whether American or European, who indulge in what is roughly known as 'symphonic jazz.'"

———

Simply put, Louis Armstrong was all heart, an oversized heart that revealed itself whenever he stepped onstage. Nowhere did the inner light of his soul

---

* An autopsy done on Duke showed that he "had so many extra folds in the brain that he was unique, physiologically unique," said his nephew Stephen James. Author interview of Stephen James.

shine more brightly than when he communed with a live audience. His thirty or so original songs were two hundred times fewer than Ellington produced. He arranged and wrote lyrics, too, but not often and generally just tweaking existing words. He was a bandleader on and off, but lacked Basie's or even Ellington's knack for, and interest in, conducting.

His thing was his horn. Starting with the Hot Five bands, he shifted the focus of jazz from a collective enterprise to solo performances that stole nearly every show where he was the soloist. He created a new vocabulary for his instrument, picking just the right notes (his favorite keys were D♭ and A♭) and lifting them to their uppermost range (sure to startle audiences, then dazzle them). His timing was pitch-perfect—knowing when to softly caress as if his instrument was his angelface, when to unleash a bracing intensity that inflated his throat and swelled his neck to the size of a goiter, or when to simply rest. Pretty was his goal, and he set a standard not just for trumpeters but for the clarinet, bass, trombone, and drums. Duke said he wanted Satchmo on every instrument. It was instinctual for Louis, feeling the beat then remolding it. Strong teeth helped. So did supple lips, a powerful chest, an unmatched work ethic, and a heart that seemed to bubble out of the bell of his trumpet.

"In Armstrong's work there is a new kind of confidence that had never existed in Western music, an aural proof that man can master time through improvisation, that contemplation and action needn't be at odds," said poet, columnist, and critic Stanley Crouch. "Armstrong found that he could hear a chord, digest it, decide what to play, tell his lips, lungs, and fingers what to do, and express his individuality within the mobile ensemble as rhythms, harmonies, timbres, and phrases flew forward around him . . . He became a hero of epic proportions to fellow musicians. One remembers first hearing him sound like an archangel from a riverboat, another touching him just as he was going on stage and feeling an electric shock. Yet another recalls him taking the measure of a challenge at a cornet supper in Harlem and standing the listeners on their chairs, tables, and plates as he played notes that were like they were hot, silver solder splashing across the roof that supports the heavens."

No matter the tune, "it all came out magnificent," added Louis's friend Jack Bradley. "Louis could play the New York telephone directory and it would come out magnificent."

His musical vocabulary and melodic storytelling drew from funerals and christenings in New Orleans, Chicago blues, New York's Tin Pan Alley, Tillie Karnofsky's prayerful Jewish lullabies, and his grandmother's revitalizing gospel that made his "When the Saints Go Marching In" swing like it never had. He blended all that in a way that liberated it. "The great ones, they always know much more than their generation, because they know the generations before them," said trumpeter and Armstrong acolyte Wynton Marsalis. "He understood what all those great trumpet players were trying to play. From King Oliver, he got his conception of dignity. From Vaughn Johnson, the common smoky tone. From Buddy Bolden, the sense of the trumpet player as a leader. He distilled all their styles into this one superstar."

Alone among these three giants, Satchmo's vocal styling was every bit the match of his instrumental chops. The two mirrored each other. Louis played trumpet solos with his voice. He had fun with rhythm and syncopation. He bent lyrics, shortened and lengthened phrases, and interjected improvisations. It helped that he knew how to coax the sounds he wanted from the newfangled microphones, and cared as much about recordings as live performances. The results were as accessible to Ellington's music intelligentsia as to Basie's foot thumpers. As his health limited his ability to blow, starting as early as his thirties and worsening by the decade, Armstrong sang more. Never had an artist managed both so brilliantly. "It would," as Crouch said, "be like if Beethoven stood up from the piano and started to sing!"

The miracle was he did all of that without what anyone at the time was looking for in a vocalist. His intonation was rightfully compared to a sawmill, a cement mixer, iron filings, a gearbox full of peanut butter, a slice of sandpaper summoning its mate, and a horn wailing through gravel and fog. To the young musicians who wanted to echo him, it sounded like he had a bad cold. He actually started out sweet and gentle, but over time and with practice became deeper, gruffer, and, eventually, the most recognized voice of the twentieth century. "It is almost inaccurate to use that word [singing] to describe Louis' vocal renditions," said Armstrong scholar Dan Morgenstern. It is "utterly mad, hoarse, inchoate mumble-jumble . . . They often seem to be the result of a chaotic, disorganized mind struggling to express itself, but those who know anything about modern music recognize his perfect command of time spacing, of rhythm, harmony, and pitch and his flawless understanding of the effects he is striving to achieve. He is the master of his peculiar art."

Frank Sinatra agreed. So did Tony Bennett, Mildred Bailey, Billie Holiday, and scores of singers of up-tempo, blues, ballads, and pop, all of whom were convinced, as one of their best, Billy Eckstine, said, that Louis was the body of water from which their tributaries flowed. It's hard to imagine the vocalizing of Bob Dylan, or James Brown, without Louis Armstrong having shown the world that singing didn't have to be pretty to be expressive. "I'm proud to acknowledge my debt to the Rev. Satchelmouth," said multimedia crooner Bing Crosby. "He is the beginning and end of music in America. And long may he reign."

It was a nonmusician who captured best Satchmo's musical legacy. "It seems to me that the essence of Louis is that he feels in his soul the ineffable tragedy of human existence and manages to communicate it to the aware, perceptive listener," said actress and activist Tallulah Bankhead. "I entertain the notion that Louis hasn't the foggiest idea of his own greatness. Yet he's the authentic creative man . . . His beautiful, heartbreaking horn with the pure, clear notes embroidered in the tasteful classical patterns; his comedy, his humor, everything about Satchmo gasses me! I suppose it might be interesting and possibly even expected of me to evaluate Louis Armstrong as an actor. If I were to draw an analogy, I should mention Charlie Chaplin."

PART III

IT'S AN ENSEMBLE

THE SIDEMEN

THERE'S A SECRET in the jungle that every creature knows: the lion's got no power without all the other cats. That was the case even for a Duke.

Jimmie Blanton's double bass so electrified audiences that recordings featuring him alongside the equally gifted tenor saxophonist Ben Webster would playfully retag the Ellington Orchestra as the Blanton-Webster Band. Bubber Miley's "wah-wah" trumpet convinced listeners that he'd invented the plunger mute as well as Duke's Cotton Club sound. Sonny Greer's drums, gongs, and cymbals drove the rhythm section, Cootie Williams's power-packed jump blues made listeners forget when Miley left, and nobody played a sweeter clarinet than Barney Bigard. Then came the multitalented Billy Strayhorn who was, as Duke put it, "my favorite human being."

All were good enough to have starred in or even conducted their own bands, and some eventually did. But no sideman had more influence on Duke Ellington than Harry Carney. Not that anybody realized that at the time.

The bashful Bostonian lacked Miley's flair and Blanton's flame. No one ever dreamed of renaming the band after him, or suggested that he was El-lington's alter ego or muse, the way they did with Swee' Pea Strayhorn. Few appreciated that the self-contained gourmand was jazz's outstanding bari-tone sax player, the Ellington Orchestra's top cat, and the one band member who never got on Duke's nerves.

That was because Carney understood better than anyone the dos and don'ts of the hundred-proof sideman: never ask for center stage or let your light blind the leader's. Always be there when you're needed, ideally without having to be summoned. Keep your mouth shut unless you're blowing your horn, and do that powerfully yet simply. Then there were these last cardinal rules for survival: drink as much as you want, carouse until dawn, get high as the treetops, just don't get caught. With those, too, Carney was the quiet master.

When he went on the road with Duke in 1927, Harry was just seventeen, so immature that he needed his mother's permission, and she needed to think twice about Duke's sweet-tongued assurances. Harry was in awe of Duke, which was exactly how Ellington liked things. When Duke needed a clarinetist, a bass clarinetist, a sax man, or even a singer, Harry stepped right up. Carney was already on the bandstand every evening when the rest of the band trickled in. If Ellington wanted a break, Carney conducted; during intermission, wholehearted Harry signed autographs, schmoozed with fans, and answered journalists' questions while other musicians took a nip or a toke. Ellington liked nothing better than the near silence that reigned when, beginning in 1949, the two of them crisscrossed the country in Carney's Chrysler Imperial.

"Carney doesn't talk much. We drive and drive. And I look at the countryside," said Duke. "This gives me lots of time to establish mental isolation for thinking, planning, and writing my words and music." What amazed band PR woman Patricia Willard was Carney's capacity to drive after drinking: "I used to see Harry put it away; drink out of the bottle and then get on the road and drive the car and, I don't know how he did it—because I don't think he ever had an accident." As for Harry, he said his ambition was to "stay with Duke until I get too old to play and then I'll say: 'Duke, you have my permission to fire me.'"

Carney was as unflappable as he was affable. Whereas other bandsmen had nicknames like Nasty and Little Caesar, Harry was simply Youth, a reference to his initial callowness and ongoing good behavior. Years later, when the band was in Zurich, Harry and trumpeter Ray Nance were leaving a jewelry store when the owner realized that three precious stones were missing. The police arrested the two Black musicians and held them until a salesgirl realized she'd misplaced the gems. The sidemen were released, without apologies. The next day Harry returned to the store, explaining, "I thought of the poor shopowner who had so unjustly suspected us. I could imagine how bad he must have felt about it all. Well, to show him that I wasn't angry with him I went back to that shop. I bought the most expensive watch that I could find. The man in the shop looked happy and so was I."

No wonder Duke adored him.

What made Carney's even keel especially appealing was that the rest of the Ellington men tended to rock the boat. Cootie Williams and Cat Anderson were known as the bookends of the trumpet section, which sounded neighborly but to those in the know meant they so despised each other that they played back against back, not exchanging a single word for eleven long years. Anderson and cornetist Rex Stewart broke that record, not speaking for fifteen years. Trombonist Juan Tizol and bassist Charles Mingus would have been better off if they had settled into stony silence; instead they traded fiery and racially tinged words, then, depending on whose reconstruction was right, one or the other drew a bolo knife, fire axe, lead pipe, or switch-blade that could have ended either or both illustrious careers. It did end Mingus's stint with the band.

Trumpet player Buck Clayton, a stalwart of Basie's band of brothers, was astounded at the Ellington ensemble's unbrotherly ethos. "I found out one more thing about Duke's band," he said. "If there is fifteen musicians that enter a restaurant they take up fifteen tables as everybody takes a ta-ble for himself." Mercer Ellington called his father's orchestra "a troupe of ballerinas . . . Instead of the camaraderie developing because they stayed with Ellington so long, they felt that by having been with him so long, they had passed by their own opportunities, and they blamed it on him, and detested him for keeping them there."

There also was comradeship, of course, but what discord existed resulted from a natural clash of headstrong temperaments. Duke didn't choose side-men because they were sweet-natured; his single yardstick was whether they had the right stuff. He liked to observe them playing poker, which he said offered a peek at their musical soul. "His God was talent," explained long-time drummer Greer. "He could single out a guy who you would say, 'This cat can't play nothing.' But he could see something in him. He was just a genius like that."

Ellington never pretended that his orchestra was a democracy. When band members made do with Pullman berths, Duke allowed himself a pri-vate roomette. When they rode the bus, he traveled in Carney's luxurious Chrysler. While sidemen were decked out in pearl-gray suits or, for mati-nees, brown slacks with cream jackets and white shoes, their boss sported white tails or a single-breasted white suit with an orange tie. All of which carried a message: *I'm the sovereign.* He ruled like the proverbial iron fist in a velvet glove, reining in disparate egos and alternating between caretaker and taskmaster. He used the same understatement and insinuation that he brought to conducting, which often failed to stanch the dissension in a band comprised of the high-strung, low-strung, and strung-out.

At times the orchestra's rage was aimed squarely at its leader. Tizol, Bigard, and others believed Duke didn't adequately credit or compensate them for their compositions. Johnny Hodges, whose riffs Ellington turned into leg-endary songs, made his resentment known by turning onstage to the piano and miming the counting of dollar bills. No doubt Duke's appropriation of bandmates' material sometimes amounted to outright theft, and when he did pay it could be as little as $15. But the situation generally was murkier: Duke borrowed notes, words, and ideas from his soloists, arrangers, and co-creators. Yet it was what he did with them—parsing and tweaking, orches-trating and augmenting—that elevated them to greatness. Nobody else had that knack for moving audiences and cash registers.

Bigard knew that but still resented that his boss "never gave the boys in the band the credit they deserved . . . It wouldn't cost him nothing to credit them." Strayhorn, who was victimized more than anyone by Ellington's klep-tomania and plagiarism, justified them: "So this guy says you and he wrote it, but he thinks he wrote it. He thinks you just put it down on paper. But what you did was put it down on paper, harmonized it, straightened out the bad phrases, and added things to it, so you could hear the finished product. Now, really, who wrote it? . . . The proof is that these people don't go somewhere else and write beautiful music. You don't hear anything else from them. You do from Ellington."

The nail-biting over money was about more than credit. There simply wasn't enough to go around for musicians, even in the best bands like Elling-ton's, to be paid what they were worth. Or to justify life on the rocky road. Sidemen earned more than Negro males could in nearly every other line of work open to them back then, with the possible exceptions of the Post Office and the Pullman Company, but it still was less than they wanted or deserved. A two-tiered payroll also created tension. Stars who were being courted by other bands and who were tighter with Ellington got more, and were paid whether or not the band was working, while everyone else got less and went unpaid when there were no gigs. Ironically Hodges, even as he was staging his quiet protests, earned the highest salary in the orchestra—more than $20,000 in 1961 ($200,000 in 2023 dollars), which was 50 percent more than the next-highest-paid sidemen, Harry Carney and Lawrence Brown.

Duke wanted people to believe he rose above such frays, never getting up-set enough to fire anyone, but that didn't square with the facts. Trombonist Lawrence Brown said Duke canned him over a money dispute (then rehired him, for no extra money). He fired the venerated Mingus after his run-in with Tizol, dismissed Bubber Miley when his drinking got in the way of his playing, fired pioneering saxophonist Sidney Bechet for his lack of punc-tuality and discipline, and replaced drummer Bobby Durham for reasons no one ever knew. Flautist Norris Turney wasn't axed, but after he publicly defied Duke, the bandleader "waited until the situation duplicated itself, and then he needled Norris so much between numbers that Norris became furious, packed up his instruments, and left the stage during a performance," recalled Mercer. Ben Webster, a talented tenor saxophonist, hogged Duke's spotlight, got the cold shoulder for it, and left the band in such frustration that, on the way out, he reportedly took scissors to one of Duke's suits.*

Other band members quit without Duke wanting them to. Williams left in 1940 and Stewart in 1945, both after eleven years with Ellington. Bigard and Tizol left around the same time, each after fifteen years. The departures resulted from disputes over money, the musician being drafted by the military, or run-ins with Duke over a woman or rights to a song. So great was the turnover that between 1943 and the end of 1950, the orchestra had fifteen different trumpeters. Yet none of the losses during the 1940s proved insurmountable, and most who left eventually came back.

No matter who stole from him, the gracious Ellington made out like he'd never stoop to swiping musicians from other bands. Yet he did. To nab Ben Webster, who was playing for Cab Calloway, Duke told Webster to quit Calloway, pretend he was unemployed, then Duke could and did hire him. He was even more blatant in pilfering Clark Terry from Count Basie, then covering his tracks. Yes, Ellington revered Basie, but he knew the music business was brutally cutthroat, and he saw how good Basie was at spotting and nurturing talent. "I figured that Duke didn't get to where he was by being dumb. So I thought about what he said I should use for an excuse—fake being sick and lie to Basie. I decided to do it," Terry sheepishly recalled.

Every band had comings and goings, but the magnitude of Ellington's losses in 1951 seemed to signal the end of the band along with its leader. How, critics and fans wondered, could Duke replace the simultaneous losses of Hodges, Brown, and Greer? His alto saxophonist, trombonist, and drummer were defining performers with a combined total of seventy years'

---

* Some say it was a razor and a sports jacket. Clark Terry reported that Webster also slapped Duke, and Don George said Webster left and returned to the band six times: "He just got drunk, called Duke a motherfucker and quit." *Autobiography of Clark Terry*, 149; George, *Sweet Man*, 100; and Teachout, *Duke: A Life of Duke Ellington*, 254.

One sign of Ellington's short fuse was when, at a public rehearsal in 1972 at the University of Wisconsin, he told his musicians to start in the key of E. When only half did, he shouted, "No! E! E as in Ellington! E! E as in Edward! . . . E as in excellence! E as in elegance! as in Edward and Ellington! E E! E as in all good things!" John S. Wilson, "Duke Ellington, a Master of Music, Dies at 75."

service. Hodges lured the other two to join a band he was forming, and that would include ex-Ellingtonians Joe Benjamin, Al Sears, Harold "Shorty" Baker, and Nelson "Cadillac" Williams.

Duke responded tit-for-tat, stealing replacements from the band of trumpet player Harry James. Reporters called it the Great James Robbery, and it netted Ellington his old valve trombonist Tizol, along with drummer Louie Belson and alto sax man Willie Smith. "All three of us went to Henry James and said, 'Harry, we got a chance to join Duke Ellington.' And he looked at all three of us, and said, 'Take me with you.'"

Of all the hundreds of musicians who played alongside Duke, no one had a more multilayered and nuanced relationship with him than Billy Strayhorn. He was an arranger and a lyricist, a sounding board, a source of inspiration, a reader of Duke's mind, and, in the minds of many, his adopted and best-loved son. On the outside, the two couldn't have been less alike. Ellington, who stood slightly over six feet, was, in the words of Lawrence Brown, "an exploiter of men and a seducer of women," including Brown's wife. Strayhorn, at just five foot three, was as bashful as Duke was commanding, as modest as Duke was brash, and a homosexual in an era when almost no one even discussed such things, much less accepted them, especially Billy's father.*

Photographer and musician Gordon Parks marveled at their symbiotic relationship, having witnessed when Duke and Billy co-composed a tune in a San Francisco hotel room after watching on TV a late-night horror film:

> At about one-thirty Edward switched off the television. "That flick," he said with a yawn, "was the worst. No other has aroused my imperial displeasure so thoroughly." He picked up some manuscript paper and handed it to Strayhorn. "Gather up the genius, Swee' Pea. The maestro is limp at the heels." He then flopped down on the couch. Turning to me he mumbled wearily, "You are about to witness a remote and covetous collaboration between flower and beast." Five minutes later he was snoring deeply. Strayhorn worked.
>
> It was well past three when Strayhorn shook Edward's shoulder: "Wake up, Monster. I stopped on C minor. Take it from there." Edward rose slowly, yawned and stumbled over to the manuscript. Strayhorn took the couch.
>
> "C minor. C minor. How indelicate of you, Pea. C minor." Edward

---

* Jazz, as pianist and activist Fred Hersch has pointed out, was "a club for macho guys." Fred Hersch, "Fred Hersch's Life In & Out of Jazz."
  While the jazz world knew Strayhorn was gay, fans did not.

was mumbling himself back to consciousness. "Working with you is like tearing one's heart in half. C minor. How dull. How unimaginative to awaken one and assign him to such an ordinary chord. You are a slaughterer of the innocent." Strayhorn snored peacefully now. Edward worked. In a couple of hours he roused Strayhorn and they worked together. And so it went until the piece was finished at dawn.

It was the closest musical collaboration Edward would ever experience. What Billy got from it was more complicated, according to a friend: "Billy could have pursued a career on his own. He had the talent to become rich and famous—but he'd have had to be less than honest about his sexual orientation. Or he could work behind the scenes for Duke and be open about being gay. It really was truth or consequences, and Billy went with truth."

Were they sexual partners as well as musical ones? Some thought so, but that's unlikely not just because Ellington was a ladies' man, but because of what Duke told Mercer about "his belief in a Faggot Mafia . . . How homosexuals hired their own kind whenever they could, and how, when they achieved executive status, they maneuvered to keep straight guys out of the influential positions . . . Throughout his career [Duke] had attachments and warm relationships—though never of a romantic nature—with effeminate men, homosexuals."* Was that a cover? Lena Horne, who knew well both Duke and Billy, said, "Their relationship was also very *sexual*. Don't misunderstand. It wasn't physical at all. But it was very, very sexual. Billy loved Duke and Duke loved Billy. The problem is, Duke treated Billy exactly like he treated women, with all that old-fashioned chauvinism."

Ellington was by Strayhorn's side when, in 1967, Billy was dying of cancer and poisoning himself with alcohol, even pouring booze directly into his own feeding tube after his esophagus was removed. As to the nature of their connection, Duke was characteristically opaque: "We had a relationship that nobody else in the world would understand."

In the face of knotty links like the one to Strayhorn, and contentious ones to so many of his other musicians, Ellington cherished the ease of riding in quietude with Harry Carney. Carney wasn't all innocence, as he shared many of Duke's vices. Both loved playing the numbers, and Harry phoned in his bets along with Duke's. On one government-sponsored trip overseas

---

* It wasn't just Mercer who remembered Duke talking about the "faggot mafia." Robert Udkoff said Duke told him that "homosexuals control the theater and Broadway. And they only allowed you to get in if you were one of them." Robert Udkoff interview, March 11, 1991, SI.

during the Cold War, the State Department's Tom Simons remembers, "I walked into [Harry's] room trying to get him out of bed and he was there with a gorgeous blonde woman . . . He was a wonderful man, but he kind of sheepishly came up to me to ask if I could come get her on the plane with him where we were going. And this was somewhere on the subcontinent, and I told him, 'No, the U.S. government's not gonna, not gonna pay for that.'"

Harry would remain with his mentor and traveling buddy until Duke's last breath—an inconceivable forty-seven years—which was longer than any sideman stayed with the Ellington band or any other in jazz history. Their bond worked both ways: Duke was, for Harry, some blend of father and big brother. When Duke was buried in 1974, Harry reportedly said, "Without Duke I have nothing to live for."* True to his forecast, four months later Harry died.

———

Freddie Green was the anti–Harry Carney. While Carney offered Duke Ellington an escape valve, freeing both of them from the troublesome details of overseeing a big band, Green burrowed into and took care of such minutiae for Count Basie. Need an advance or a loan? Ask Freddie. Unsure what tempo to hit, or whether to play an encore? Freddie'll know. Wondering if anyone noticed when you stepped out of line on the bandstand or off? Steel yourself for the Ray, that dagger-like dart of Freddie's steely-dark eyes.

If Carney was Ellington's therapist, enabling Edward to clear his head, Green was Basie's consigliere, doing the dirty work that Bill hated to do and couldn't. The outcome was the same. Both leaders knew it was only within their own band that they could find someone who understood their peculiar challenges, and who always was close at hand. Thus the two men, the aristocratic Count and Duke, deployed these handpicked confederates so they themselves could stay above the fray, preserving their bodies, psyches, and jovial images to preside for half a century. The burdens didn't go away, they just went to someone else. Carney chauffeured Ellington on roads that were bumpy and long, figuratively and literally, even as he was blowing a brilliant baritone sax. Green acted as the Basie band's pseudo-manager while serving as Mr. Rhythm in the All-American Rhythm Section. The Count's advice to new sidemen joining the band was succinct: "Listen to the guitar player."

"We got along as a family," explained the tenderhearted Green. "I was

———

* Even as he was saying that, Harry kept on playing for Mercer when he picked up Duke's baton.

always the peacemaker. I was always the one saying, 'Wait a minute now, don't do that, don't do this' . . . We wouldn't let things get out of hand no kind of way." Basie agreed, on one occasion calling his guitar strummer his "left testicle" and on another saying, "Freddie Green has been my right arm for thirty years. And if he leaves the band one day, I'll probably leave with him."

Just three years after saying that, Basie in 1950 responded to economic pressures by downsizing his band of fourteen to just six players, and Green didn't make the cut. The loyal guitarist was devastated, calling that interregnum the "most miserable" time of his life and saying, "At night, I dreamt about the band." To make ends meet, he worked two jobs—during the day as an elevator operator at a Columbia University dormitory, at night playing with Lester Young and his combo at Birdland. A couple months later Green surprised the band at the airport and, when Basie asked why, Freddie answered, "I give you the best years of my life and you think you are going to leave me here . . . no way!" That was all it took: a sextet suddenly became a septet.

Those two months aside, the Basie band's camaraderie was legendary, both in its fourteen-member, soloist-focused incarnation from 1935 to 1950 that became known as the Old Testament, and in the more collective-minded, polished era that commenced in 1952, numbered seventeen, and, for easy reference, was called the New Testament. Sidemen referred to one another as brothers and to Basie as a father figure. "You all could meet at one place at the same time, at a bar, and not know how you got there," said Buddy Tate, a saxophonist and vital part of the Basie band of the '40s. "We loved to be together off of the stage, off the stand, off the bus . . . If a guy wasn't cool, he stuck out like a sore thumb in that band. It wasn't long before he got in line." Trumpeter Sweets Edison was there for thirteen years, left when others did in 1950, then returned on and off for the rest of his career. Why go back on the exhausting road? "In one word, Basie. I wouldn't have gone out with anyone else."

Clark Terry remembered finishing a performance in New York in about 1950 and being told he had to fly to make the next show in Boston, a prospect that petrified him. "Basie said, 'Aw, man. You've *got* to get on this plane. That's the only way you're going to make this gig tonight,'" Terry recalled. "When Basie saw how scared I was, he said, 'Come here with me.' I followed him into the men's room, where he pulled out a half pint of gin. He handed me the bottle and said, 'Here, drink some of this.' I took a slug, then handed him the bottle, but he pushed it back to me. He said, 'Drink some more' . . . Before I knew it, we had killed the whole bottle. Then he said, 'Now come and let's get on this plane and go on up to Boston and make some music.' I said, 'Okay, let's go.'"

Al Grey had his own story of becoming a Basie believer. "One day we were in line, this is when you had to jump off the bus and run in and get in line because you know that the bath [in the hotel] is going to run out . . . Everybody was always jumping in front of me because I was the new boy," recounted Grey, who was with the band in the '50s. Basie, he added, could see how upset the young trombonist was and said, "'I'll tell you what I'm going to do. I'm going to let you come down and have a bath in my room and there's an extra room over here, the suite, and you can stay there tonight.' And this is like he became like my father. Because then I would listen to everything he had to say."

The work was exhausting for the Basie group, as it was for all big bands then. Sidemen had to pick up their own hotel and restaurant tabs, which left little to send home. Each night's set list was nearly identical, three hundred nights a week, and the bone-weary musicians could barely distinguish between dance clubs or even cities. Many sidemen had to moonlight writing arrangements for the band; when recordings were made they got paid just for that date, with any royalties going to the leader. The rare dressing room was cramped and dingy, and the only refuge between long sets was the bar next door. They generally got two weeks a year of unpaid vacation. It helped that they were doing what they loved, and that they could see that the Count, whose expenses were huge, wasn't rolling in dough. But still.

Unions were making things better for white musicians by midcentury, but less so for Blacks. It wasn't easy to come by the federation cards required in places like Chicago and Kansas City. In New York, newcomers needed a police permit to work more than three days anywhere that served liquor, which meant being fingerprinted, getting a mug shot, and paying $2 for a cabaret card that required renewal every two years. Rather than going into city coffers, that money was funneled to the police pension fund.

"I was so damn poor that I borrowed Maceo Birch's raccoon-skin coat, which didn't fit, but still it was better than anything I had, which was nothing. My heels on my shoes were so run over that sometimes I would back out of a building rather than walk out forwards and let everybody see how bad my heels were," said Buck Clayton. "So it was only natural that we were friends with every loan shark we could find, and between the loan sharks and the pawnshops we were able to make it for a while . . . Basie said to me one day, 'Don't worry, Buck. One day you'll be wearing an overcoat that will cost a hundred dollars.'"

The Count reveled in his reputation for pampering band members, and for remaining a sideman at heart, but he also could be a steely taskmaster. Like Ellington, Basie never technically fired anyone. That was a fine point lost on drummer Sol Gubin, who got a night off when he didn't feel well but never got his job back. Another drummer, Gus Johnson, developed appendicitis at Christmastime in 1954 and sub Sonny Payne became his permanent replacement. And when baritone saxophonist Charlie Fowlkes broke his leg, he got the news in the hospital that he'd been sacked.*

Basie was renowned for landing America's most accomplished musicians. Less known were his bets on lowlifes like Clinton Brewer, hired as a music arranger in 1941 after his release from a prison where he'd spent nineteen years for killing his first wife. Five months later Brewer was back in prison, having confessed to stabbing to death a new romantic interest, then stuffing her into a closet where her sons discovered her when they got home from school.

But Basie set limits, with violence as with everything, as saxophonist Don Byas learned. "Byas told me that this is how he was fired from the band," says Gary Giddins. "He was very drunk one evening—I don't know where they were, I guess they were in a hotel—and he took out a gun. I don't know why he carried a gun but he took out a loaded pistol. And he had the whole band lined up against the wall. And Basie just walked right over to him with his hand out. He said, 'Don, give me the gun.' Byas is like crying, he says, 'Base. You know, I love you. I'd like to give you the gun. But if I give you the gun, you're gonna fire me.' And Basie said, 'Don, I'm gonna fire you whether you give me the gun or not. So gimme the gun.'

"He gives him the gun, and [Byas] said, 'Basie, really, you're gonna fire me? You're gonna really fire me?' And Basie says, 'Don, there are very few rules in this band. But one of them is don't pull a gun on the boss.'"

The Count's most notable signing was the free-floating Lester Young, whose sax sounded as delicate as a flute and who Basie said "never had a bad night." Young, however, felt his playing and arranging weren't getting the recognition they warranted, he didn't get the raise he'd requested, and he wasn't growing. "Basie was like school," Young explained. "I used to fall asleep in school because I had my lesson, and there was nothing else to do. The teacher would be teaching those who hadn't studied at home, but I had, so I'd go to sleep."

---

* A young trumpeter from Chicago who lipped off to Basie wasn't technically fired because he hadn't actually played with the band—and wouldn't. Basie "gave him his ticket home and told him good-bye," said drummer Butch Miles. "He never did play a note." Rowe and Britell, *Jazz Tales from Jazz Legends*, 40.

Few agreed with Young's critique. Most of Basie's crew said that the Count set the gold standard for musical opportunity, bonding, and just plain fun. For instance, the band made a game out of surveying the audience for men with toupees. "Lester would be going, 'Row three, seat seven.' 'No, no, that's his real hair.' 'No, no, no, it's a rug.' And they had this thing going and they would be spotting. Because if you're playing the same show four or five times a day, what do you do to keep interested?" recounted English bassist and critic Alyn Shipton. "Harry Edison went to prison in Boston when the band, in a restaurant, bet him that he could knock a guy's toupee off with a bagel. So they're sitting in this restaurant and Harry, who is a dab hand, threw the bagel. The wig goes off and falls on the table. It's a white guy. So Harry ends up being arrested and sent to jail, and the band had to get him out."

Nobody knew more stories like that than Freddie Green, although he was generally as buttoned-up as the Count. But this consummate team player and most cherished sideman let his feeling show a bit at Basie's funeral in 1984, lamenting, "Now that he is gone, what am I going to do?"

Drummer Arthur James "Zutty" Singleton's ties to Louis Armstrong traced back to the days when Louis was wearing short trousers and the pair made up half of the Singing Fools quartet on New Orleans's rollicking streets. Rollicking also describes the next sixty years of ups and downs between maestro Satchmo and sideman Singleton.

The pair performed together in Chicago, including in the later incarnation of the fabulous Hot Five band. Zutty's righteous timing and uplifting beat were the ideal backdrop for Satchmo's operatic licks. They also collaborated on cabaret skits, with Singleton dressed as a washerwoman and Armstrong swaying side to side, pretending to be sloshed. They shared a Ford roadster they dubbed the Covered Wagon, a failed ballroom venture called Warwick Hall, and a steady stream of women whose names they couldn't remember and might never have known. Zutty was Satchmo's oldest and closest pal when, in 1929, they set out with the rest of the Carroll Dickerson Orchestra in four "raggedy" cars that would double as hotels on a pilgrimage from Chicago to Toledo, Cleveland, Detroit, Buffalo, (a detour to) Niagara Falls, and, finally and with just three cars barely running, their mecca of Manhattan.

That was where the bonds began to fray. The two were playing in the recently named Armstrong Band at Connie's Inn, a whites-only nightclub in Harlem. When the revue in which they were performing closed, the orchestra was fired, and Zutty accepted an offer to join the new house band. He said he had first consulted Louis, who told him, "I'm going to become commercial. I can make some money." So Singleton figured he'd do the same, telling Armstrong, "Friendship is one thing and business is another." Louis remembered it differently, calling Zutty a "low son-of-a-bitch," saying he "broke a truce that you're supposed to stick together," and insisting that it wasn't just him who was outraged, but "all the cats, shit, they were onto Zutty from then on."

But not all the cats sided with Louis. Before Singleton and Armstrong left Chicago there had been a third member of their "little corporation," the powerhouse of a pianist Earl Hines. "We agreed to stick together and not play for anyone unless the three of us were hired," Hines recalled. When Zutty and Louis joined the Dickerson band without him, "I was very disappointed that our little pact was broken." While Hines and Armstrong would play together again twenty years later, it didn't go well then, either, with Hines quitting the band over a contractual dispute. "I thought what I had contributed to the music business entitled me to more consideration than they offered," Hines said. Armstrong felt enough was enough: "Hines and his ego, ego, ego! If he wanted to go, the hell with him . . . Earl Hines and his big ideas."

Louis's fiery rages generally didn't morph into enduring grudges, with this pair the exceptions. "There are two musicians I'd never play with again—Hines or Zutty," he told one interviewer. "We can get along without Mr. Earl Hines," he added, and as for Singleton, "He didn't stick with nobody. He insulted me. And that's what puts the son of a bitch behind the eight-ball." Louis blamed the breaches on Hines and Singleton not being able to take criticism. He insisted he was the injured party.

Louis might have been right about Zutty and Earl having fragile egos, but so did he. From 1925 on, he was jazz's premiere soloist, taking audiences to dizzying heights with his rhapsodic trumpet and his guttural voice. That success should have made him supremely confident, the way theirs had for Ellington and Basie. Instead, the higher the seemingly happy-go-lucky Armstrong climbed, the more his wounding self-doubts and mushrooming jealousies became painfully visible. It no longer was enough to be the centerpiece of a band full of divas like the Hot Five. He'd played second fiddle to King Oliver out of deference to a mentor, but no more. He'd never liked managing an ensemble, or having to rally, rehearse, or rein in other celebrities. A veteran of the Battlefield, he nursed hidden bruises and was tired of battling. Now he wanted to be the unchallenged headliner, and to control the narrative like he did when competing stars left or were pushed out.

The midcentury Armstrong bands reflected Louis's need for stardom. Whereas Duke and the Count knew that surrounding themselves with the best musicians made them shine, Satchmo sometimes settled for lesser talent, believing that made his thunder louder and spotlight brighter. Singleton and Hines were simply too accomplished, too strong-willed. Most replacements over the decades were capable but not brilliant musicians, and few if any were potential competitors. The numbers filled in the story: more than eight hundred sidemen and accompanists came and went, surely a testament to Armstrong's indecision as well as his insecurity.*

"The band was there to back Louis, to set him off well; the rest was immaterial," said jazz scholar and Armstrong friend Dan Morgenstern. "By the 1950s," Satchmo biographer Ricky Riccardi added, "you were either with Armstrong or you could go to hell." As he jettisoned old mates, Louis was frank about where he was headed: "I'm the leader, I'll be the leader."

The sidemen who stuck around had to play by Satchmo's rules. Show up on time and don't stretch out intermissions. ("Don't let 'em cool off, boys," he'd say. "Keep that audience hot!") Earn the salary he paid (said to be among the most generous in the business). Stay sober. ("Don't fuck with my hustle," he warned a sideman who drank too much.) Most important, know your place. ("If you play bad you won't be in the band," said string bassist Pops Foster. "And if you play too good you won't be there.")

That was a touch of hyperbole, since Louis was a masterful spotter of talent and wasn't about to diminish himself with mediocre backups. But it's no exaggeration to say he didn't suffer insubordination or indiscipline. "You had to have a record of responsibility," recalls singer Jewel Brown. "If you showed irresponsibility three times in any way or form, you knew not to say nothing, just pack your bags and go." In Irv Manning's case all it took was one time. The short-tempered bassist got into an altercation with Pierre "Frenchy" Tallerie, the road manager Louis despised who'd borrowed a dollar from Irv and wouldn't return it. "One thing led to another, Irv got mad and he pushed Frenchy onto a stanchion or something. The floor had just been mopped and Frenchy slipped. Somebody told Louis that they had got into a fight and Frenchy was down on the floor," recalled clarinetist Joe Darensbourg. Brown picked up the story, saying Louis yelled, "'[Manning's] fired! Get rid of him!' . . . And Pops didn't want to know why or anything, that was it. That was it."

---

* The total of those who made any kind of recording with Armstrong at least once is 1,068, and that doesn't include uncredited session players for his guest appearances with other bands and studio orchestras. The comparable count for Ellington is 473 and for Basie, just 370. Lord, "Jazz Discography"; Willems, *All of Me;* and author's own count.

The charismatic tenor saxophonist Dexter Gordon joined the band in 1944 and stayed for a mere six months, but he said it shaped his life: "That was a thrill. Every night. He had such a big, beautiful, fat, blaring sound, just ran right through you. And that was really the reason I joined the band, to play with him. To play with him every night. The band was a mediocre type band . . . The arrangements were just a showcase for him. But, he liked me and he always gave me a chance to blow . . . Working with Louis was love, love, love."

Other esteemed musicians also signed up, especially when he went from a big band to a small one tellingly named the All Stars. Nobody doubted the star power of trombonists Jack Teagarden, Trummy Young, and Russell "Big Chief" Moore, drummer Sid Catlett, or clarinetists Edmond Hall, Peanuts Hucko, and Barney Bigard. Others, like bassist Arvell Shaw, didn't start out as frontline backups but grew into the role. "I'd just been discharged from the Navy when Louis came to town and when his bass player had to go home because his wife was giving birth, Louis let the word out that he needed a substitute for that gig only. He hired me but didn't recognize me, and when I told him who I was he said, 'What took you so long?'" remembered Shaw. What he'd envisioned as a temporary job with Satchmo lasted more than eleven years, and Shaw said it would have continued if family troubles hadn't forced him to leave.*

While Satchmo never patched things up with Earl Hines, he did with Zutty Singleton.† It happened in 1969, when both were old men and after Singleton had a stroke. Louis visited him and was struck by a photo from forty years earlier that he'd signed, "May we never part." Marge Singleton, Zutty's wife, recalled "the way [Louis] bathed Zutty and wheeled him out to the house like Zutty was a piece of gold." After Louis died, Zutty called him "the warmest, kindest man who ever lived," adding "it all came out in his music."

---

* Shaw tended to exaggerate, insisting he was with Armstrong for twenty-five years and that he went with him to places like Africa when he didn't, says Ricky Riccardi, adding, "We have a tape where Louis vents that he would never let Shaw back in the band because . . . in 1956, Shaw was saying that he was bigger than Louis and 'Fuck Louis Armstrong, Fuck Joe Glaser, two motherfuckers!' By 1961, Shaw was trying to get back in but Louis prevented it. They made their peace and Shaw was back 1963–1965 but then out again." Riccardi email.
† The night of Louis's funeral, in an hour-long CBS tribute, Hines had this to say about his onetime friend: "When I ran across Louis and we started working together, he'd steal something from me and say, 'Thank you,' and I'd steal from him and say, 'Thank you,' and that's how we got along." *Louis Armstrong, 1900–1971*, CBS News Special, July 9, 1971.

11

SIDE WOMEN

MERRIAM-WEBSTER'S UNABRIDGED DICTIONARY describes a *jazzman* as "a performer of jazz," with the term dating back to the Jazz Age in 1926. But while it provides definitions for *fancy woman, saleswoman,* and *madwoman,* it doesn't recognize the word *jazzwoman* (or *jazz woman*).

The same holds true for *sideman,* which we learn means "a member of a band," especially one playing jazz or swing, and more specifically "a supporting instrumentalist." But nada for *sidewoman* or *side woman* (although it does define *widow woman* and *little woman*).

What a dictionary includes and what it ignores offer insights into not just a nation's language but also its biases. Now, as then, America's most trusted glossary sees jazz as a man's universe. Which shouldn't surprise anyone since it recognizes a first baseman, but not the women who field that position. And while it knows about train porters, it has nothing to say about the porterettes or maids who, in the days of the Pullmans, set rich women's hair, boxed their hats, tucked in their berths, and performed other up-close tasks that could have gotten porters lynched.*

Merriam-Webster's doesn't just reflect norms, it legitimizes them. There weren't many porterettes or maids on sleeping cars, but there were some, just as there were women owners and players in the Negro Leagues. As for jazz bands, few knew or know about the International Sweethearts of Rhythm, sixteen blazingly gifted music makers who in the 1940s raised the roof at the Regal in Chicago, the Howard in Washington, D.C., and, repeatedly, at New York's legendary Apollo Theater. There's even less record

* *Merriam-Webster's* does recognize *portress,* which it says is a female porter, as in a doorkeeper or a charwoman.

of the all-girl, all-Black territory and college bands of the Swing Era. The early jazz women we do read about—from Billie Holiday to Ella Fitzgerald and Ivie Anderson—were singers, generally for big bands like Basie's, Ellington's, and Armstrong's. It is no accident that they were gorgeous as well as talented. Duke, Satchmo, and the Count thought they knew what audiences wanted, and so made sensuality a priority. They also knew that, in addition to the racial slurs that came with being Black, jazz women were belittled as warblers, thrushes, and canaries.

One of the few to break through those barriers was Lillian Hardin Armstrong. She demonstrated as early as the 1920s that jazz women could do more than sing, in her case by playing the piano, composing, arranging, and leading the band. Even so, if history recognizes her at all it is primarily as Satchmo's second wife, musical enabler, and all-round helpmate. Books on him depict her as puffed up and jealous, because she had more refined manners than he did, and she rightfully resented not getting the credit she warranted. She did embroider her academic and other records, but there's reason to believe the embellishing was partly Louis's doing, to make himself seem smart by having picked a valedictorian as his bride.*

Lil, who grew up in Memphis, played marches on the piano in grade school, hymns in church, and, after she and her mother moved to Chicago, she demonstrated sheet music at a store on State Street. Her style was what she called heavy, like Willie "the Lion" Smith, and she was crackerjack enough to be invited into King Oliver's band a year before Louis arrived in the city and on the scene. While she was only mildly impressed by him, he was so taken with her that Hot Miss Lil became part of his original Hot Five. She co-wrote hits with Satchmo, encouraged him to join and then leave Fletcher Henderson's band in New York, and helped launch his career and live up to her claim that he was the World's Greatest Trumpet Player. Later, she toured as "Mrs. Louis Armstrong and her Chicago Creolians," an all-girl band of fourteen, was house pianist at Decca Records, and performed as a soloist.

How good was this jazz pioneer? Her biographer in 2001 called her "the most important woman in jazz history," which was overreaching, but she

---

* Lil admitted in an unpublished interview that she never graduated from Fisk University, as she would claim. "Her fingering was wrong, her reading, and this or that," says Armstrong House research director Ricky Riccardi. "And so they put her like in beginners' classes, and that was a brutal blow to the ego. And after, I think, maybe three semesters, she quit." Author interview of Ricky Riccardi.

was one of the most important of her time.* A *Chicago Defender* writer came closer to the mark when, in 1934, he wrote, "to the surprise of this chronicler and the other patrons as well, likely Mrs. Louis Armstrong's all-girl orchestra does not suffer in comparison with that of her more famous hubby . . . Lil herself is a great pianist and arranger." The reviewer—a man, of course—didn't hide his skepticism that a gals' band could be anything but a "novelty," or could ever measure up to the likes of Armstrong and Ellington. But after hearing Lil a second time he found himself "a fine supporter of girl bands and musicians. They offer plenty [of] jazz and swing and will entertain you with the late[est] song hits, as capably as any of the masculine orchestras."†

Mary Lou Williams ran into similar skepticism while doing even more than Lil to make *jazz woman* a *Webster's*-worthy concept. Known in Pittsburgh as the Little Piano Girl, as a three-year-old she played spirituals and ragtime on a pump organ while propped on her mother's lap. At six, she got racist neighbors to stop throwing bricks into her family's house by giving them private concerts and brought home money that helped support seven siblings. By fifteen she was a full-time musician. Fats Waller was so delighted when he heard the teenaged Williams that he playfully tossed her into the air. Celebrated pianist Art Tatum took her on tours of jazz clubs. Later, her piano playing, composing, and arranging catapulted her to the vanguard of Kansas City swing, bebop, and, after she became a devoted Catholic, sacred music, including writing a jazz Mass that thousands heard at St. Patrick's Cathedral. Whatever the genre, she was a pioneer and innovator. When she died in 1981, the *New York Times* called her "the first woman to be ranked with the greatest of jazz musicians."

Williams's career intersected with those of Armstrong, Ellington, and Basie. In 1953, Louis offered her a job in his All-Star band; she declined, knowing that would mean sharing the spotlight. She joined the Count in mentoring young musicians in Kansas City and wrote music for his orches-

---

* Two others who would compete for that title were pianist and singer Julia Lee, the Queen of Kansas City Blues; and Lovie Austin, a Chicago bandleader, pianist, singer, composer, and arranger of classic blues.

† The *New York Amsterdam News,* another Black-focused newspaper, was less impressed, calling Lil's band "very weak." By 1935 Lil was leading a male orchestra, Mrs. Louis Armstrong and Her Kings of Rhythm. In both cases she was Mrs. Armstrong in name only, having separated from Louis in 1931. "Eddie South and Arcadians Will Head Apollo Program," *New York Amsterdam News.*

tra. While she already knew him and his gifts, when she heard the Basie band in Paris in 1954 "I couldn't sit down during the concert, I couldn't stop dancing."

She was closest to Duke, although she vacillated between adoring and abhorring him. She first ran into his band in the mid-1920s, when it was still called the Washingtonians. She wrote fifty or so compositions and arrangements for him from the 1940s through the '60s, and found his freewheeling rehearsals heavenly.* But she resented that when she needed money, Duke wouldn't hire her even though she'd bailed him out in the early '40s when ASCAP wouldn't let him broadcast his own compositions. As for Ellington personally, "I never had too much to say to Duke," Williams wrote. "I always liked being around sidemen or little people." Ouch. That didn't stop Duke, in his memoir, from calling her "perpetually contemporary" and saying, "She is like soul on soul."

Like Lil, Mary Lou had to contend with a double stigma. They were Black in the era of Jim Crow persecution, and female at a time of rampant sexism. Ellington, Armstrong, and Basie weren't exempt from such misogyny. While they employed more women than most bandleaders did, they shared the prejudice that it was unladylike to play a trumpet, a trombone, or any instrument other than perhaps the piano. The three maestros helped push Mary Lou, Lil, and other women to the top even as—in ways they might not have realized—they held them back precisely because they were women in Black and jazz worlds controlled by men. While African American jazzmen had a hard time on the road, be it finding accommodations or earning a living wage, African American jazz women had it tougher, with even lower wages, fewer options on restrooms or rooming houses, reluctance on the part of the State Department to send them on tours, and a tacit assumption that this ostensibly egalitarian music form was a male bastion.

Melba Doretta Liston made a name for herself a bit later, and without the pizzazz of Lil or Mary Lou. Liston stood out because her instrument wasn't a refined keyboard, but a hard-blowing trombone. She toured with the Basie band in 1948, one of just three female instrumental players to

---

* Adding to that freewheeling atmosphere, nearly every rehearsal played out before an eclectic audience—Duke's physician, his press agent, the band boy, a couple of former sidemen, band wives, and perhaps a policeman or two. Duke greeted each of them, kissing the women, signing autographs for the men, and relishing the spectacle. Tucker, *Duke Ellington Reader*, 323.

perform with him.* The rigors of the road burned Liston out, however, and in later life she was best known for arrangements she wrote with pianist Randy Weston.

If Mary Lou Williams, Lil Hardin Armstrong, and Melba Liston were the exceptions to the rule that women should sing and not play, diva Bessie Smith was its embodiment. Young Bessie perfected her singing on Tennessee street corners, where she and six siblings earned enough to keep going after their parents died. A generation later she was crowned Empress of the Blues as the most successful Black vocalist of the 1920s and '30s. Smith helped open the singing profession to African American women, drawing on slapstick and theatrics to get her audiences to listen to her lived stories of surviving poverty and racism, sexism and the trials of love. Of her nearly two hundred recordings, several of her best were crooned in 1925 alongside Satchmo, including "Cold in Hand Blues" and "Sobbin' Hearted Blues." She already was a star by then, while he still was Joe Oliver's masterly sideman. "Everything I did with her, I *like*," Louis said. "She had a quick temper, made a lot of money. A cat came up to her one day, wanted change for a thousand-dollar bill—trying to see if she had it. Bessie said, yeah. She just raised up the front of her dress and there was a carpenter's apron and she just pulled that change out of it. That was her bank."†

Billie Holiday also knew about the blues she sang—spending time in a Catholic reform school, fighting off a rapist, scrubbing white people's stoops, and running errands at a brothel in exchange for being able to sing along with recordings by Satchmo and the Empress. Like Bessie, Billie showed that women belonged on center stage rather than in supporting roles. And like Smith, Holiday's unorthodox but affecting singing brilliantly incorporated social critique, most poignantly in "Strange Fruit," the poem turned song that became an anthem of the civil rights movement. At the mixed-race Café Society nightclub in Greenwich Village, she always sang it as her closing number. The waiters stopped all service in advance, and the room went dark save for the spotlight on Holiday's face as she prayerfully chanted:

---

* The other two were alto saxophonists Vi Redd and Eve Duke, both of whom also sang. Ellington worked with at least fifty-three women over the course of his career, but just four were instrumentalists: Betty Glamann on harp, Patti Brown on piano, Mary Barrow on French horn, and timpanist Elayne Jones. Lord, "Jazz Discography"; and author's own count.

† Eighty-four of Louis Armstrong's 1,068 accompanists were women, and of them just five were instrumentalists, including Lil. The numbers for Bill Basie were 370 total, thirty-six women, and three female instrumentalists. Lord, "Jazz Discography"; Willems, *All of Me;* and author's own count.

Southern trees bear strange fruit
Blood on the leaves and blood at the root
Black bodies swinging in the southern breeze

While Billie gave Louis much of the credit for her elegantly cool phrasing and feeling, Count Basie actually did more to launch her to stardom. Basie was awestruck as soon as John Hammond introduced them in 1937 and she was soon working for him. "I joined Count Basie's band to make a little money and see the world. For almost two years I didn't see anything but the inside of a Blue Goose bus, and I never got to send home a quarter," she wrote in *Lady Sings the Blues*. "There were a lot of great things about the Basie band, and the experts are just beginning to pick it to pieces after almost twenty years to find out what made it so great . . . I still say the greatest thing about the Basie band of those days was that they never used a piece of music, still all sixteen of them could end up sounding like a great big wonderful one sound . . . For the two years I was with the band we had a book of a hundred songs, and every one of us carried every last damn note of them in our heads."

Basie and Billie split in early 1938 for reasons that, like most such partings, depended on who was telling the story and when. "I quit," Billie said. Her biographer said she "was fired—'asked to leave.'" The press and others blamed Hammond. Basie booker Willard Alexander claimed responsibility, saying he let her go because "Billie sang fine when she felt like it. We just couldn't count on her for consistent performance." For his part Basie, who generally called Billie by the endearingly formal William (she called him Daddy Basie), said, "I loved Billie an awful lot. I loved Billie as far as love could go."* As for her leaving, the Count wrote, "According to the story, I had let her go because I felt that it would be easier to work without a girl singer. But I think Billie left because she got a chance to make more money than we could afford to pay at that time. As for me not wanting a girl singer, how could that be true when we replaced Billie with Helen Humes as fast as we could?"

Billie and Louis shared a manager, Joe Glaser, who made a request of her he never made of the rotund Satchmo: skinny down. "He told me he hadn't booked me anywhere because I was too fat. I told him to tell that to Mildred Bailey the Rocking Chair Lady. I was big, sure, but she still had plenty of

---

* That sounded like they were lovers, but her actual lover was Basie's number one sideman, Freddie Green, who had a wife and kids. Clarke, *Wishing on the Moon*, 132.

pounds on me. But I started losing weight and finally he told me he had a job for me at the Grand Terrace Club in Chicago."

Weight was a lifelong issue for Velma Middleton, a former chorus girl and dancer who sang for Armstrong bands for twenty years. Critics mocked her size (she weighed nearly three hundred pounds), her vocal style (less than pitch-perfect), and her onstage antics (miraculous splits and comic duets). What mattered was that audiences adored her, and Louis did, too. Sadly, she suffered a stroke during a tour of Africa, and in February 1961, in just her mid-forties, she died alone at a hospital in Freetown.

These side women's experiences with the three bandleaders make clear that being pretty mattered almost as much as being racy (Velma, to some eyes, was the exception). "They used to call me the Pretty Department," said Maria Cole, whose stage name was Marie Ellington and who was no relation to Duke though she sang for his band as well as Basie's. "We got up to do our numbers and you sat there, regardless of whether you were performing or not. To look pretty," she said of her time with Duke. Ellington later acknowledged that Marie, who married singer Nat King Cole, "was so pretty it took a while for audiences to realize that she was presented for the purpose of singing rather than just to be looked at."

Kay Davis worked with Duke from 1944 to 1950, but at first he'd stand her onstage merely to hum and be eyeballed. "I used to call home at least once a week crying," she said, "because I wasn't doing anything significant." (Duke said it *was* significant, that "she had perfect pitch . . . so we decided to use her voice as an instrument.") Another reason for Kay's crying: the "baby doll pumps" singers had to wear, which "hurt our feet so we could hardly cripple out on stage." But she says Duke "was always very kind to me . . . He had a respect for me I wasn't due—about my talent . . . It was, I think, kind of amazing to him that I had finished college, you know, gotten a Masters in Music and [yet] I would go with the band . . . But this was just a dream come true. It was very exciting."

Davis and her sister side women also were taught that the way to get along with the sidemen was to be one of the boys. That meant shooting craps and playing cards on buses and trains, the way Billie Holiday did. It meant accepting the upper berths when the boys claimed the lower ones, because they had more seniority and bravado. It meant sometimes tolerating more teasing than they'd have liked, and taking care that kidding didn't descend into harassment. But most of the time, as Lu Elliott said, boys in the band "looked out for me."

Elliott's real name was Lucy, but she changed it to Lu at Duke's suggestion. "He said, 'I think it sounds much better to go out and say, "'Bringin' to you our vocalist, Lu Elliott' than saying 'Lucy Elliott.'" Pianist Judy Carmichael got different advice when she went backstage to say hello to the Count and, with a quick look and the merest of words, he made clear she should stop wearing the tight jeans that she called "spray-on pants." "I was horrified. I was the girl who wanted to be taken seriously, not to look like a twenty-something groupie trying to hit on one of the band members," wrote Carmichael, a white beauty queen and actress. "I'll never know if Basie meant to give me a particular message, but I heard what he was saying and changed what I wore from then on when I went to hear music."

Gender wasn't the only challenge facing Black jazz women. They lived with racism that sometimes was even more insidious than what Black jazzmen faced. Jewel Brown, who replaced Velma Middleton in the Ellington band, says her mother steeled her for that, teaching her "how to act among the Caucasian people. She said, 'You never want to look at a Caucasian man sitting with his wife. Look above the head, like you, like you looking but you not looking at them. And if anything, look at her, not him.'"[*]

Mary Lou Williams, who was old enough to be Jewel's mother, saw that bigotry for herself when, as a teenager in the late 1920s, she worked as a piano player at a roadhouse-brothel outside Memphis: "The clientele consisted of barrel-bellied, loud-mouthed, third-grade readers whose preoccupation was gambling and girls. A rich, big fat redheaded, freckle-faced plantation owner came up to Memphis from Mississippi with this little nurse. Every night he'd give me $5 each time I played his requests. Around the third night his girlfriend tried to take him away, saying, 'You like nigger girls?'" The female owner of the club sent Williams home, fearing for her safety. "When I returned to the job, she told me that this sick man had paid the cook $50 to kidnap me and bring me to his farm in Mississippi . . .

"I had heard many tales about black women being kidnapped and taken to Mississippi across state lines, out of the reach of Tennessee authorities. And when their parents had gone to get them, they were shot at the gate."[†]

Was it all worth it for these talented women? Lu Elliott believed it was,

---

[*] That is reminiscent of the advice young Jews were given by their parents during the Holocaust—never to look a Nazi in the eye.
[†] Williams's "completely self-written ahead of their time concept albums, *Zodiac Suite* (1945) and *Black Christ* (1964), are still studied, sold, played," says jazz historian Harvey Cohen, making clear that "the men in her life didn't totally define her." Cohen email.

saying, "I have benefited by just being able to wear the banner of having been a Duke Ellington vocalist . . . It can only enhance anything that I've ever done or will do in this business." Not so for the Queen of Swing Norma Miller: "It was just a living. I did one-nighters with Basie, and I've asked God, if you ever get me out of this, please never let me do this again."*

---

* While numbers are hard to come by, only about 5 percent of today's jazz instrumentalists are women, says Grammy Award–winning drummer and educator Terri Lyne Carrington, adding, "That number is crazy . . . The race struggle in the Black community definitely has overshadowed gender in the Black community . . . Our slogan for our [Berklee College] Institute [of Jazz and Gender Justice] is 'jazz without patriarchy.'" Author interview of Terri Lyne Carrington.

MANAGERS AND MOBSTERS

S ATCHMO WAS AS snakebit when it came to picking a manager as he was in choosing his sidemen and spouses.

First up was then-wife Lillian Hardin Armstrong, whom he stopped trusting to look out for his professional interests when their marital bonds unraveled in the late '20s. Next came Tommy Rockwell. The brash record producer transformed Louis from jazz artist to pop star, but when he and his star parted ways on next steps, Rockwell goaded him with a pistol-packing mobster who left the trumpeter cowering in a phone booth. (Louis: "They never wanted me dead, [they] wanted me blowing so they could rake in my bread.") Johnny Collins, a nervous and nervy booking agent, promised to clean up the mess. The mustachioed manager did catapult his industrious client to greater success on the stage, radio, and film, but he wasn't tough enough to protect Armstrong from real roughnecks like Rockwell. Collins went too far first by telling the music man not just where to play but what, then by assaulting him with the N-word. "Not that I haven't been called a 'nigger' before," an enraged Satchmo admonished the blind-drunk Collins as he was firing him. "But from you?"

All of which made the trumpet master rethink the counsel Black Benny Williams had given him years before, in Jim Crow New Orleans: always have a white man with his hand on your shoulder warning, "This is my nigger and can't nobody harm him."* Rockwell and Collins were white, but turned out to be more Satans than saviors. Could Black Benny have gotten it wrong?

Louis's third white man would prove to be his charm, unlikely as that

---

* Louis's recollection of Benny's advice changed a bit with each recollection. If it sounds harsh to contemporary ears, it did as well to Louis: "I don't like to hear people use that word, but that's the way the talk was at the time." Sometimes, the version was "get yourself a Jew and be his boy." Interview of George Avakian, September 28, 1993, SI; and interview of Gary Zucker, January 26, 1996, LAHM.

seemed at the time. Bertha and George Glaser had hoped their son Joseph would become a doctor like his dad, and a cultured patron of Chicago arts like both parents. Joe made it as far as medical school, but was stopped in his tracks at the first sight of blood. The truth was, his appetites ran in a distinctly different direction from his parents'. He knew just enough about medicine to set up his first con and draw his first arrest, for selling fake diplomas to medical students anxious about earning them the real way. "All the men accused," the *Chicago Tribune* reported in 1916, "are Italian physicians with large practices, except one, who is the son of a well known south side physician."

The next time his mother had to bail Joe out of jail was for driving his speedster on the sidewalk, which he claimed was to avoid the bumpy streets. George died a few years after that; Bertha became a real estate maven; and Joe soon was running what he boasted was "the biggest chain of whore houses on the South Side of Chicago" along with a lounge that was a favorite watering hole for Al Capone and his mob. This being the time of Prohibition, police raided the Sunset Cafe on Christmas Day in 1926. The judge fined Joe $200 and pronounced his club "a public nuisance" after reviewing evidence that "girls of 17 were brought to the cafe by escorts and carried off the dance floor drunk."

Seventeen turned out to be too old for Glaser. Two months later he was arrested for raping Dolores Wheeler, a fourteen-year-old whose mother, he said, "pointed her out to me and encouraged my interest in her." The jury believed the girl's version, which was that her cousin lured her to Glaser's apartment, where he "took all my clothes off me and he took his bathrobe off him and he had intercourse with me." After she washed the blood off herself, Glaser "gave me five dollars." It took just forty-five minutes for jurors to pronounce Joe guilty and he was sentenced to ten years in the penitentiary. What happened next was strange but not unexpected in the whatever-it-takes world of Joe Glaser. Wheeler retracted her testimony under circumstances even the judge found "suspicious." Then she agreed to marry the thirty-one-year-old nightclub manager. In the end he avoided jail on those counts, and subsequently on charges of raping two other teenagers. But the settlements he presumably paid the older girls, along with alimony he gave Wheeler after she sued for divorce, forced Glaser to close the Sunset, pushing him from the headlines and to the brink of bankruptcy.

His ticket back to solvency came courtesy of Black entertainers, and especially Louis Armstrong, who was as broke as Joe in 1935. Desperate for a manager to reset his career, Louis believed his best option was another white scoundrel. "I went to Papa Joe Glaser and told him I was tired of being cheated and set upon by scamps," recalled Louis, who'd met Glaser when he played at the Sunset nine years earlier. "I told him, 'Pops, I need you. Come be my manager. *Please!* Take care all my business and take care of me. Just lemme blow my gig!' And goddamn that sweet man did it! Sold his nightclub in Chicago where I had worked and started handling [me]." A handshake later they were partners, for life. Louis hated managing his bands or his business affairs. This new arrangement would make Satchmo rich and Glaser richer, and set a template for the wider world of Black entertainers and their white handlers.

How much Armstrong knew about Glaser's background isn't clear, but it had to have been a lot, and what he knew clearly didn't bother this musician who'd grown up cheek-by-jowl with racketeers and roughnecks. He might well have seen Glaser's unsavory past as an asset. The more syndicate-savvy Joe was, and the more willing he was to push people around on Louis's behalf, the better. As brawling Black Benny might have counseled, Rockwell and Collins weren't badass enough. Glaser was. "You get a gangster to play ball with a gangster, you're straight," Satchmo said.

Armstrong gave Glaser credibility with Negro celebrities. (His $25 million practice and thousand-long client list would eventually include such stars as comedian Moms Mabley, singers Billie Holiday and Ella Fitzgerald, boxer Sugar Ray Robinson, and, briefly, Duke Ellington.) The relationship lent him cachet with his underworld cronies (most loved jazz and Satchmo), *and* with his parents' upper-crust crowd (who preferred Louis's trumpet to Joe's strumpets). Most of all it gave Joe something of which he had too few: a truehearted friend.

The showbiz world didn't know what to make of this oddest of couples: a foul-mouthed middle-class kid looking for some street cred, and a Black child of the ghetto eager for respectability. While their relationship was multilayered and not always on level terms, Joe Glaser meant it when he said of Louis Armstrong, "To me he's like a son. A brother," and when he told his most cherished ward, "Louis, you're me and I'm you." Louis, who grew up essentially fatherless, returned the compliment: "Askin' me about Joe is like askin' a chile 'bout its daddy."

A normal band manager would negotiate bookings, secure record deals, and assist in other business decisions. In the jazz business in that roaring first half of the 1900s, steering the career of a performer like Louis Armstrong also meant navigating his ties to and onslaughts from the underworld, starting with his former managers.

Tommy Rockwell had helped make Louis a star, but by the fall of 1930 Armstrong felt he wasn't getting the attention he deserved from Rockwell and could from the cocky fifty-four-year-old son of a Chicago police sergeant, Johnny Collins. Collins, who'd by then had a nervous breakdown and been arrested for drunk driving, dazzled and conned Armstrong into signing up with him, no matter that the trumpeter still had ties to Rockwell as well as to the owners of Harlem's Connie's Inn and their silent partner, the vicious mobster Dutch Schultz. Lawsuits were filed, and countersuits. Empty threats were made. (Rockwell and his henchmen demanded $6,000; when Collins and Armstrong refused, the demand was lowered to $3,000, then $1,000, with Louis reportedly insisting, "Not a dime!") Real threats followed, with guns stuck into Louis's ribs and a carful of fearsome men following him everywhere.

Collins and Armstrong abandoned Chicago and its angry thugs and headed on their first tour of the South, with a private bodyguard and the knowledge that the risks this time included being a Black man in the Jim Crow heartland. In 1932 he fled farther, to England and a roaring reception. Those exhausting travels kept Louis away from the two most sought-after destinations in jazzland, Chicago and New York, which had become too hot for him given his dueling managers and their gangster crews. It was on his return from his second trip to England, on the S.S. *Majestic,* that Armstrong finally broke with Collins. It had been three long years, much of it on the lam. It wasn't just the manager's racism that doomed the relationship, but his failure to pay Louis's taxes, send the money promised to Lil, or give Satchmo the peace of mind he needed to focus on healing his ravaged lips.

That was when Joe Glaser turned back up on his radar and offered a way out. First, he took out $100,000 insurance policies on his life and Louis's. Then he abandoned the Sunset Cafe and became an official booking agent. He accommodated Lil, who'd sued Louis. He reached arrangements that were face-saving for Collins and Rockwell but gave Glaser full control over Armstrong. Deals done.

In many ways, Glaser was following the playbook laid out by his benefactor and role model, Al "Scarface" Capone. Both sprouted from solid immigrant roots, Al's Italian, Joe's Russian-Jewish. Each was engaged at a young age with brothels and the women who worked there. Both were popular white men on Chicago's Black South Side, Al for giving Negro racketeers free reign, Joe for fostering Negro performers. Each talked tough and backed it up. (Capone was a notorious leg-breaker and killer, Glaser fanned rumors that he was, too.) Associates knew Al and Joe could be counted on, whether that was to pay bills on time or pull strings at City Hall.* Both loved the money jazz brought in, the music itself, and Louis Armstrong.

Glaser, however, was more nuanced and layered than Capone. With his steel-blue eyes, thinning gray hair, white socks that drooped to his ankles, and pigeon toes, Joe seemed more like an undertaker than a gangster. He showered love on the champion poodles he collected from around the world, but treated shabbily the singers, dancers, and secretaries he continued to seduce even after he married the madam of a brothel.† He wanted to keep a low profile, given his gangland connections, yet drove around the city in a one-of-a-kind blue Rolls-Royce convertible with the vanity plate JOE.‡ He was a teetotaler and a bootlegger, a man whose fortune came from nightclubs but who tried to be in bed by ten o'clock every night. Even when his language was blue, he rendered it with careful diction and in perfect cursive.

Was the real Joe Glaser the agent who booked gay playwright Noël Coward to a record-breaking engagement in Las Vegas, or the guy who, when Coward wanted to join him at a boxing match, explained, "I like Noel. But if those guys at the ringside see me with him they'll think I'm a faggot!" He was, of course, both. So it was no surprise that, even as he made successes out of Black performers whom many white agents shunned, he was known to call them lazy shines, niggers, and schvartzes.§

In Glaser's spinning of the Satchmo narrative, he'd been there Zelig-like at various crossroads all the way back to·the young trumpet player's arrival in Chicago. It was him, he told biographer Ernie Anderson, who'd bought Louis's train ticket from New Orleans. He was the one who convinced King Oliver to free Armstrong to sow his oats at the Sunset Cafe and beyond.

---

* TV impresario Ed Sullivan said it best: "If I have Joe Glaser's word, I can go to sleep. And the performer he is booking can go to sleep, too. This is the old way of doing things. A word . . . It was better than 10 contracts." Breslin, "A Normal Day with Joe Glaser."
† Joe let his dogs roam free on the terrace of his blue-walled, blue-carpeted penthouse apartment in Midtown, and buried them under $175 headstones in a private pet cemetery.
‡ One of his favorite perks was being admitted behind the counter at Manhattan's iconic Carnegie Deli so he could fix his own sandwich, a rare and perhaps unique honor. Another was having the traffic cop near his Midtown office stop traffic to let his limo make a U-turn, as if he were the mayor. And he loved his box seats at Yankee Stadium because they were close enough to the dugout that he could lean over and bawl out the manager. Author interview of Dan Morgenstern; and Collier, *An American Genius*, 271.
§ He was equally boorish in referring to women as cunts and bitches, and talking about his fondness for "nigger pussy."

And it was the Pierce-Arrow he'd sent from his used-car lot, which normally supplied battling underworld gangs, that chauffeured Louis to the cramped studios where he cut the leading-edge records of the Hot Five.

However embellished those claims, there was no denying the support Glaser provided now for Armstrong. He rode along on bus tours, helping the band navigate the segregated South. "When we get hungry, my manager Joe Glaser (who's also my friend, Jewish, and white) would buy food along the way in paper bags and bring it to us boys in the bus who wouldn't be served," remembered Louis. Up North the routine was slightly different: "Glaser perfected a 'scouting' technique so as not to embarrass us. He'd go alone into a restaurant or diner, and ask the proprietor politely, 'Will you serve Negroes?' Ninety percent of the time he got the same answer: 'No.'" It wasn't just food: Glaser could challenge white owners of dance halls and theaters when they shortchanged Black artists.

Joe handled the bookings, keeping Louis on stage year-round and planetwide, for higher fees than ever. He arranged transportation and lodging. He did the hiring and firing that Louis hated doing, trying to ensure that band members were drug free and insisting they take physicals to see if they could handle the rigors of road life. "If he fired someone Louis wouldn't say anything, even if he liked the guy real well," recalled clarinetist Barney Bigard. "It wasn't on account of that he was frightened of Joe, or that Joe was a white guy handling him . . . He didn't want to tread on anyone's toes or hurt anyone's feelings." The result was predictable: most band members adored Louis and abhorred Joe.

Joe Glaser also knew what had done in Johnny Collins. He didn't try telling Louis how to blow his horn, although he wasn't shy about telling him who to blow it for. He sought out the same racially mixed audience that Tommy Rockwell had favored, one that liked their jazz cool, not red hot. "I used to say, 'Louis, forget all the goddamn critics, the musicians. Play for the public,'" Glaser recounted. Louis agreed: "Everybody got this image I was some kind of a wild man. Joe Glaser told me, 'Play and sing pretty. Give the people a show.'"

Offstage, Glaser paid the bills and kept successive wives happy. Once money was rolling in, the manager gave his prime client $1,000 in walk-around cash to spend on anything he wanted or give away as was his wont. No need for this star to fret about contracts, checkbooks, investments, or the IRS. Joe also realized that the symbols of success mattered to a kid who'd spent his adolescence wearing raggedy short pants, so "whenever I went to a tailor and bought two suits, in them days for $175, $200—I'd buy Louis two suits. When I went to the haberdashery store and bought a dozen shirts, I would buy Louis a dozen shirts."

Most important, tough-guy Joe kept Louis safe. No more worries about pistol-packing thugs cornering him in phone booths, following him as he traveled the country, or forcing him to stay away from musical meccas like Harlem or the Stroll in Chicago. It was simple: Joe packed his own pistols on his belt, and had pals who could scare any of Armstrong's tormenters.* "He saved me from the gangsters in Chicago, he saved me from the gangsters in New York," Louis told a friend.†

Was Glaser exploiting Armstrong? No doubt. He worked him like he was a money machine, which he was, although Louis helped set the frenzied pace, saying, "Them days off are bad—your lip gets soft and slack." He skimmed a fatter share of Louis's earnings than other managers did with their clients—some speculated that it was half, or even three-quarters—but Louis insisted, "That's the way I want it. Don't want to *worry* all [the] time about that crap!" He also used Louis to prop up his second-rate performers, as Decca producer Milt Gabler remembered: "You would take Grade B and C acts that you would break your hump over, just so you could keep Louie. It was an old trick."

The exact nature of the Glaser-Armstrong relationship remains a matter of fierce debate. George Wein, the colorful producer of jazz festivals, said Louis confided to him late in life that "the minute we started to make money, Joe Glaser was no longer my friend . . . I was just a passport for him." When he saw Joe in the hospital, and his manager was dying, Louis whispered to him, "I'll bury you, you motherfucker." Or so said Wein, who was no fan of Glaser's. Wein wasn't the only one who saw tension. Louis and Joe "couldn't be in the same room together for two minutes," Lucille Armstrong said, according to Armstrong biographer James Lincoln Collier. And Stan-

---

* Longtime *Tonight Show* bandleader Doc Severinsen knew firsthand just how ruthless Glaser could be: "He called me up one time, right after I had signed with him, and he said, 'Hey, kid, goddammit, this is Joe. Listen, you're going to Cleveland, you understand me? I got a friend that's got a club there. And you're gonna go play there. And don't ask me any goddamn questions about how much it pays because it doesn't matter. You understand me? You go there and do a good job, or I'll have you fucking killed.'" Author interview of Doc Severinsen.

† Armstrong saved himself one pitch-black night when he was leaving a speakeasy in lower Harlem. "As he stepped out onto the street, two young men jumped him from behind. One held a knife at his throat and the other said, 'Okay, give us your loot, Daddy,'" recounted jazz storyteller Bill Crow. When they realized who they were holding up "the two muggers jumped back and pleaded, 'Oh, Pops, we didn't know it was you. We're sorry, man.' Louis gave them a brief lecture and some money, and went on his way." Crow, *Jazz Anecdotes*, 239–40.

ley Crouch reported in the *Village Voice* that "one musician claims to have opened Armstrong's dressing room door one evening to find him holding a knife to Glaser's throat, saying, 'I can't prove it, but if I find out you've stolen one *dime* from me, I'll cut your goddam throat.'"

Those words are shocking precisely because they would have been so out of character. Armstrong historian Ricky Riccardi tracked down every reference Satchmo made to his manager the last two years of his life and found thirteen instances on TV and radio, and in scrapbooks and letters, all adulatory. Glaser "was the greatest for me + all the spades that he handled," he wrote a friend in July 1969. He told TV host Dick Cavett, "To me, [Joe] was Jesus." Four years before that, in a profile in *Harper's Magazine,* Louis gushed that "to hear us talk on the phone you'd think we was a couple of fairies: I say, 'I love you, Pops,' and he say, 'I love *you,* Pops.'"*

Nobody understood such trade-offs better than Duke Ellington, who knew Glaser and Armstrong. "Louis Armstrong and Joe Glaser; Joe Glaser and Louis Armstrong. Don't put the cart before the horse, they say, and at first glance you might think Louis was the horse doing all the pulling while Glaser was in the driver's seat of the cart," Duke wrote in his memoir. "Then you realize that in spite of how well Joe Glaser did for himself, Louis still ended up a very rich man, maybe the richest of all the 'trumpet Gabriels' . . . Joe Glaser watched over Louis like the treasure he was."

Yet even Joe Glaser couldn't take care of Louis Armstrong on his own. In the prewar, big band years, a chauffeur worried about the driving, letting Louis enjoy the view from the rumble seat of his Model A or the spacious backseat of his rust-colored Packard. A friend from New Orleans served as road chef. A straw boss kept band members in line, while a music director oversaw that end of the business. A band boy took care of the musical instruments. And Glaser's special relationship with Al Capone ensured that Armstrong no longer was bothered by hoodlums, at least in Chicago. "A nice little cute fat boy," is how Louis described the kingpin gangster, "like some professor who had just come out of college to teach or something."

Satchmo had several valets over the years, one of whom doubled as personal secretary, which helped with the trumpeter's reams of correspondence. Armstrong's most memorable attendant was Doc Pugh, who became

---

* Armstrong friend and photographer Jack Bradley remembered making a disparaging comment about Glaser in the later years, when Louis was married to his fourth and most enduring wife, Lucille. Armstrong shot back, first with curses, then an explanation: "First there's music, then there's Mr. Glaser, then Lucille." Giddins, *Satchmo,* 129.

a trusted confidant. "He took meticulous care of Louis's dressing room and he was in total charge of the ample pharmacopia and of all the other luggage that Louis carried with him everywhere," reported Ernie Anderson. "He was a specialist with the Armstrong white handkerchiefs. He carried 200 of these. Louis sometimes uses as many as 30 during a single performance. They were cotton and they had to be forever washed and ironed."

Frenchy Tallerie started as a bus driver, worked his way to road manager, and showed his real value to Glaser as his enforcer and spy. He'd phone Joe every day with a report on who'd visited Louis's dressing room—that could be anybody from a rabbi and two nuns to a detective, a street walker, and a guy just out of the penitentiary—reassuring the absent manager that nobody was trying to steal his most valued client.* Frenchy was the one sidemen were supposed to see when they wanted a better hotel room or more money. Pianist Dick Cary recalled approaching Glaser directly in search of a raise: "I'm sitting in the office there, and Frenchy comes in and he tells Joe Glaser that I'm a drug addict. And that was absolutely false, and I got mad as hell. I told him what I thought of him and I left the office."

Frenchy, who was white and may or may not have been French, did little to disguise his disdain toward Blacks generally and for Satchmo, who returned the antipathy. Once, riding through Kansas, Tallerie looked out the window at a bunch of white and black cows munching in a field. "Gee, I hate to see that," he said. "A black and white cow, just like a white man and a colored woman." Louis generally ignored such outbursts, but during a 1965 trip to Germany, he exploded at the wiggy road boss: "We're not in the States here. And even there you won't be able to boss us around much longer! Get out: slavery is over once and for all." Louis was right: after that tour, Frenchy was gone.

————

Irving Mills did as much to set the trajectory of Duke Ellington's career as Joe Glaser did for Satchmo, although Mills didn't last nearly as long and was more of a spinmeister than a gangster. Mills had it easier because his client wasn't a three-time loser when it came to picking managers, but Ellington did need handholding as he sought to break out of the big-band pack.

In Washington, when he was starting out in the early 1900s, Duke

—————————

* By 1944, Louis was no longer Glaser's top moneymaker. That title went to Les Brown, who led His Band of Renown and earned enough to let Joe buy a Hollywood mansion complete with pool and private movie theater. Joe, in turn, bought Brown an eight-room house in Beverly Hills. Riccardi, *Heart Full of Rhythm*, 282.

managed himself. He picked the tunes, booked the jobs, set and collected fees, and paid band members. He reached out with his era's best marketing devices—newspapers and phone directories—offering "irresistible jass" for "select patrons." While many of his patrons were indeed select—highbrows from the countryside with the time and cash for horse shows and fox hunts—others were urban and Black. He learned tricks like talking fast on the phone to make people think he was rushed. And he tapped his skills as a visual artist to run a sign-painting business on the side, then "when customers came for posters to advertise a dance, I would ask them what they were doing about their music. When they wanted to hire a band, I would ask them who's painting their signs."

He'd need more than his knack for hustling when he left the slow-paced and familiar capital in 1923, and headed to the fast-tracked, less-forgiving Gotham. His first three years there showed his talents as a songwriter and bandleader, but they required moving from club to club, then, when city residents cleared out for the summer, to mill towns and oceanside resorts in New England. The Washingtonians were known but not renowned. Duke seemed to have plateaued when, on a late night in 1926, he met Isadore Minsky—known then by the WASPy pseudonym Irving Mills, which he bestowed on himself. In Mills's colorful version, it was love at first sight when the dapper thirty-two-year-old with slicked-back hair heard Ellington and his orchestra at the Kentucky Club, a cramped basement nightspot in Times Square. A few days later Mills came to Ellington with a proposition: "How about doing records, Duke?"

Irving wasn't an obvious choice. Small and squat, he had the limited vocabulary one might expect of a young man who was born in Odessa and grew up with Russian-speaking parents in the Jewish enclave of New York's Lower East Side. There'd been little time for school after his father died, when Isadore was just eleven. He lacked the toughness, or tough friends, that made Joe attractive to Louis, but also came free of Glaser's penchant for underage girls and grown-up mobsters. Irving married at twenty-one and eventually had to support seven kids. He had a decent voice and an uncanny ability to reimagine songs he'd heard. He plugged tunes by crooning them behind the music counter of Snellenburg's Department Store in Philadelphia, nudging customers to buy, then for Broadway producer Lew Leslie, urging bandleaders to play Leslie's verses.

More than anything, Irving was a go-getter with what his parents, Hyman and Sophia Minsky, would have called chutzpah. In 1919, he and older brother Jack started Mills Music to publish songs, and they soon progressed to producing records and scouting talent. He paid desperate songwriters $20 to $30, which was a lifesaver for the musicians and a steal for the Millses.* With Duke, Irving said he knew from the first they could go great places.

He had a simple plan for the Washingtonians: Promote Duke not as a run-of-the-mill bandleader or piano player, but as a composer, an artist, and a genial genius. It wasn't a hard sell because it was true, or would be soon. No one had ever tried making a pitch like that on behalf of a Black jazzman. Would the rest of the band, used to working collaboratively back when Duke replaced Elmer Snowden, tolerate Mills's transparent bid to sideline their efforts as soloists, improvisers, and arrangers, and give all the credit to the bandleader-composer? And could Ellington really move from Negroes-only race records to the multiracial mainstream? Others had doubts, but not a natural-born fast talker like Irving Mills.

"When I got into the black thing, I figured I might as well corral something so that I could have control of something, and these people are appreciative," explained Mills, who fancied himself the Abe Lincoln of the music world. "A dollar don't care where it comes from, whether it's black, green . . . Everybody looked down at me. They said, 'Geez, he fools around with niggers. Nigger bands.' And just because I started this and it worked so good, all the other black people started to come around to me, all the best of them . . . We were always ahead of ourselves."

He stayed ahead, of his time and his competitors. He fed journalists catch phrases to describe Duke, including "Harlem's Aristocrat of Jazz" and "the Rudy Vallée of the colored race." He hired an artist to draw a caricature of the bandleader that he handed out to editors, knowing that for a Negro that would cause less controversy than a photo, and dispensed pictures of a "pretty girl" posed with the "gourds, mutes and other strange instruments" favored by Negro musicians. He linked his commercial success to community-minded causes, letting it be known that Duke "will appear anywhere in behalf of a milk and ice fund, shoe fund, boys' camp fund or any similar activity, or for the entertainment of war veterans, crippled children, aged persons or other hospital shut-ins." He and Duke burnished the Ellington résumé, suggesting that the bandleader had graduated from high school and attended a conservatory. This master of misdirection spelled that all out

---

* Songwriters like Ellington learned to steal back. Mills, Duke said, "bought the same Goddamn tune over and over and over . . . I just changed the name of it, switched the first line, the second line, or something like that. But this was all the same anyway." Carter Harman interviews of Duke Ellington.

in a marketing manual that came with this admonition to his staff: "Do NOT tear out the publicity stories from this book and give them direct to newspaper editors! They do not like 'canned' copy. Have these stories typewritten on separate sheets of paper, inserting the playdates, which makes them appear fresh and original. You will get twice the response from your editors!"

Mills's industriousness paid off big. Prior to 1930, Duke's name appeared a mere fifteen times in the national edition of the *Chicago Defender,* America's leading Black newspaper. From then until 1935, with Mills overseeing a stable of publicists, Ellington was mentioned there in 284 separate stories.

The final piece of his PR template was a style befitting royalty, and that fit perfectly with Duke's own obsession with image. It meant not just traveling in the Pullman sleeping cars that transported presidents, but dressing the part. Each instrumentalist had two sets of fancy threads, with a boutonniere for venue openings. "We were the most dressed up band in the world," said drummer Sonny Greer. "We did four or five shows a day, sometimes six . . . each show we changed complete, from head to toe, uniforms . . . Irving Mills was a very shrewd man. And he knew appearance was half the battle."

Under Mills, Greer added, "[We were] sharp as a Gillette razor blade."

It worked. By branding his client as a philanthropic artiste, and incessantly hyping him in the press, Mills got Ellington into Harlem's jazzy Cotton Club. He secured unmatched national radio play and singular tours here and abroad from the Roaring Twenties into the Threadbare Thirties. The band grew as did its record deals and booking fees. Irving knew what the public wanted, and he and Duke delivered. Yes, that meant jungle music, with light-skinned, barely clad chorus girls, but contradictions like those were an inescapable part of expanding his audience in a racially restrictive landscape. Yet along the way, Irving and Duke— whose own complexion the *New Yorker* described as coffee with a strong dash of cream—loosened those restrictions. Theirs was the first Black ensemble in a major Hollywood feature, the first in a Ziegfeld show on Broadway, and, in time, the first to replace jungle with genius as its marketing master plan.

Mills never denied being in it for the money, and conflicts of interest were baked into his relationship with his star client. Irving was on the payroll of record companies with whom he signed Duke, and he pushed Ellington to record his own compositions since, as his publisher, that meant more money for Mills. He took a fatter share of the profits than seemed fair or than he was getting from his white clients—a third for him, a third for

Ellington, and the last third for Mills's lawyer*—and claimed more credit than he was due for lyrics and compositions. Just how much he stole is unclear. Mills insisted he wrote at least part of about fifty Ellington songs, including favorites like "Sophisticated Lady," "Mood Indigo," and "In a Sentimental Mood." And he said "from the pen of Duke Ellington" was a retailing device they cooked up, "whether [Duke] wrote it or he didn't write it." Duke's son Mercer said fudging credits like that "was the practice of publishers in those days."

Like Armstrong, Ellington went along with the managerial arrangement so long as it relieved him of worry and earned him enough to buy his Pierce-Arrows, pay sidemen's salaries, cover expenses for everything from meals to the women who traveled with him, and live like a duke. "If, after home and the road and the family, there's anything left," Ellington said, "Mills and anybody else is welcome to it. Anything they can find, let 'em take." And while he'd never say so outright, Duke, like Louis, knew that in a Jim Crow world populated by Caucasian theater owners and record executives, it helped to have a white man running interference.

It was no surprise that Mills, Glaser, and so many other managers of Black jazzmen were not just white but also Jewish. Jews always played a big role in jazz, as performers like Benny Goodman and Artie Shaw, club owners like Frank Schiffman at the Apollo and Max Gordon at the Village Vanguard, gangster benefactors like Dutch Schultz and Meyer Lansky, along with a legion of producers, bookers, and critics. Jews, like Blacks, had limited opportunities in white-shoe fields like advertising, publishing, and broadcasting. Such barriers are what made the equally rebellious field of comic books so attractive to Superman creators Jerry Siegel and Joe Shuster and Batman originators Bob Kane and Bill Finger, all Jewish and all aware they were getting in on the ground floor of a rapidly growing and superprofitable field that most white businessmen foolishly wanted no part of. Blacks and Jews also shared long and rich histories of music as an outlet or escape in repressive circumstances.

While the Mills-Ellington bond stayed strong for thirteen long years, they split in 1939. Gossip flew as to what caused the breach. Was it that Mills had stopped giving Ellington the attention Duke felt he deserved, now that Irving's client list included Cab Calloway, Hoagy Carmichael, Benny Goodman, and other celebrities impressed by, among other things, all he'd done

---

* Some biographers claim the split was 45 percent each for Ellington and Mills, with the lawyer getting 10 percent and Ellington getting a share of other Mills properties.

for Duke? Or that Ellington had taken his artistry too far and no longer was producing music Mills could sell and fans could dance to? Was it that Benny Goodman beat Duke to a jazz premiere at Carnegie Hall, or perhaps the hits that Duke was taking in the Black press, where Adam Clayton Powell Jr. branded him a "musical sharecropper" who was "owned body and soul by Massa Irving Mills"?*

Ellington's earliest biographer traced the rupture to a surprise visit the bandleader paid to Mills's office when Irving wasn't there but his secretary was. "Duke sat down at the table and looked through all the books of Duke Ellington Incorporated," wrote Barry Ulanov, who presumably got this version from Duke himself. "He got up slowly, adjusted his jacket and tie, put on his hat and overcoat and walked out of the office. He never returned."† An Ellington friend added this twist: what most upset Duke was that Mills promised four years earlier to buy the most expensive casket for the pianist's beloved mother, Daisy, which would have cost $5,000, but the records showed he'd bought a $3,500 version.

Whatever lit that powder keg, it belied a more basic reality: Duke already had gleaned all he could from Mills about managing and promoting a band. Irving had worked hard for Duke, worked the bandleader hard, and he—along with his children and grandchildren—would continue enjoying royalties from Ellington songs he'd purportedly co-composed. It was inevitable, given Duke's personality and his self-reliance, that he would want to claw back control of his career in a way that never interested Satchmo. The relationship with Mills provided "a great place for him to get an education," said Duke's son Mercer. Once he had, he could strike out on his own, parting, as Mills said and Ellington publicly confirmed, as "the best of friends."

From then on Ellington employed a team to steer his affairs, starting with William Morris and his agency. A venerated vaudeville and radio booker,

---

* Powell, a Baptist pastor and civil rights leader in Harlem, would be elected as the first Black on the New York City Council, then the first Black congressman from New York. His article on Ellington in the *New York Amsterdam News* included this editor's note: "The publishers do not necessarily subscribe to the opinions expressed in this column." In fact, Powell didn't understand how the music business worked, but he'd find out ten years later when he married pianist and singer Hazel Scott.

† Mills said that Duke would already have known everything in those books since "52 weeks a year he got a statement . . . never was there a complaint . . . And the moneys that I spent on Duke for photographs, for clothes, for publicity, for things that I've done for him. I don't think that anybody ever spent on anything what I did for Duke." Interview of Irving Mills, April 23, 1981, Yale.

Morris was getting into the band business and took a personal interest in Duke. He collected a commission of just 10 percent and no royalties, which left Ellington with a substantially bigger share of his earnings than he'd had with Mills. At the same time, Duke signed an attractive deal with Robbins Music, the era's most successful record company, and, even more astutely, he launched his own publishing company.

He also assembled a stable of aides to rival Armstrong's. There was a wayfaring hairdresser, a sign not just of his vanity but of his being too busy to stop at his regular barbershop. A full-time electrician and part-time road manager knocked on Duke's stage room door every night, reminding the leader, "Five is in, folks" (the band was due on stage in five minutes). The choirmaster played the piano, arranged, and even composed. One singer set up the bandstand and helped dress Duke. Then came Jerry Sullivan, who in the era when hoods were kidnapping celebrities in hopes of collecting ransoms, "used to take Duke to work each night in his bullet proof car with a machine gun between his legs. He'd wait the show out and bring him back too."

Nobody had to tell Richard Bowden Jones how dangerous show business could be. The short dark-Black busboy at the Cotton Club, known to everyone as Jonesy, came on the road in the late '20s, first as Duke's valet, then majordomo and bodyguard. In 1938, when hoods were harassing Duke at a restaurant, Jonesy came to the rescue with guns for himself and his boss. The two "left the place shooting in the air, and when they got into the car waiting for them outside, Jonesy continued to threaten from the running board, at nothing in particular, just making fearsome noises in the manner of Western and gangster films," wrote Ulanov, Duke's first biographer.[*]

At the theater, Jonesy would stay behind as the band cleared out, picking up drummer Sonny Greer's six huge trunks, singer Ivie Anderson's three, and Duke's six, along with others for scenery, lights, sound systems, instruments, and music. At the hotel, he'd ensure the water in Duke's tub was at just the right temperature, with an easy-to-reach supply of manuscript paper, a Scotch and milk, and a bottomless tub of chocolate ice cream. "It was also part of his duties to get everybody aboard the train on time, a chore necessitating a lot of running from one part of town to another, checking and

---

* Duke was seldom intimidated by mobsters, partly because Chicago mobster in chief Al Capone and New York tough guy Owney Madden spread the word not to mess with him. For his part, Ellington said, "The gangster situation? I would never have amounted to anything if it hadn't been for my friends . . . It's ridiculous calling them gangsters." Interview of Duke Ellington, September 5, 1964, Yale.

double-checking the various after-hour spots, conditions of sobriety and overall awareness of train time," recalled Rex Stewart.

"After we hit a town, he'd help set up the stage and lights, then check the linen, send out the costumes to be pressed or cleaned, and inspect Ellington's wardrobe and try to anticipate what the Duke would want to wear . . . He loved the band and worked and worked until he dropped dead in LA many years later." When that happened, Ellington was so bereft that he kept Jones's wife on the payroll.

The most controversial member of the team was Al Celley, who took over as road manager in 1944 and played the tough guy with musicians who grew to hate him and mobsters who feared him. Not long after he joined the band, a gang stole many of the orchestra's horns. Celley caught three of the thieves, brought them to his hotel room, and said, "Now look, guys, either you produce those instruments or I'm gonna hang one or all of you out of this window by the thumbs." Trumpets and saxes magically materialized. For twenty years, Celley handled payroll, made hotel and train arrangements, and kept the show on the road. He also embezzled thousands of dollars from his boss, or so Ellington charged in a 1966 lawsuit, with Celley countering that it was Duke who owed Celley thousands in back pay and loans. Untangling the web of the band's finances and cash-only operations proved so onerous that Ellington ultimately agreed to pay Celley $6,000.

The Celley and Mills experiences helped convince Ellington that he could trust only family. He persuaded Mercer to give up being a disc jockey and music director and manage his band.* "Pop called [the radio station] and said he had dire need of me to join him and handle the business," Mercer recalled. "I soon began to get into a psychological battle with the seniors in the band. Here I was in a position where I had to overlord people who had led me by the hand to the movies, who had taken me out to the circus, who had bought me candy apples . . . I had to fight them and I had to fight Duke Ellington . . . So I gradually began to make more enemies and to live in a world by myself. I was neither fish nor fowl."

Mercer's awkward new role also made for touching times between father and son. "He would call me on the phone in my hotel room, ostensibly to

---

* Duke later twisted what happened in an interview with the *Chicago Defender,* saying that Mercer "somehow just drifted into the band and stayed. I was quite surprised . . . I've never tried to encourage anybody in my family to go into this business." "An Interview with Busy Duke Ellington," *Chicago Defender.*

argue about one thing or another, but really just to talk. I think he beckoned me mostly to keep him company, though he was too stubborn to admit that," said Mercer. "From time to time, he would ask me if I loved him, and I would tell him that I did."

The younger Ellington settled delinquent hotel bills, made sure musicians were paid on time, and put the books in as much order as possible given Duke's complete lack of fiscal discipline. "Ellington was a great bird in the hand guy. You know, he'd see cash, that was it. He didn't want to know about what went on the day after tomorrow," said Cress Courtney, the young booker who handled Duke at the Morris Agency. "He sold music for $100 because he got cash. You know, he'd sell a song outright. And he'd let other people put their names on his songs . . . All these kinds of things, you know, for cash. Which, you know, in the long run was a very costly affair."

Mercer wasn't the only Ellington whom Duke spun into his expanding musical web. His father, J.E., traveled with the band for a short time, doing make-work as a social secretary that Duke hoped would lift his spirits and did, temporarily. Grandchildren Edward and Mercedes Ellington and nephew Stephen James did odd jobs when they traveled with the orchestra. Sister Ruth played a more vital and long-lasting role, serving as president of Tempo Music, the publishing company Duke set up in 1940 after he split with Mills, while her first husband handled PR. Now both the publisher's and writer's shares of profits went to Ellington. Duke didn't care that Ruth wasn't interested in or skilled at business, or that she wanted to study medicine or teach biology. The lawyers handled the details and Ruth was grateful for the generous income. A decade later Duke created his own recording label, Mercer Records, run in part by his son and in fact, like Tempo, mainly by Duke himself, who was setting a model for artists on how to control their fates.

Even as he was doing that, Duke's perpetual need for cash to support his large band and his growing appetite for the red-carpet life led him to leave William Morris and other booking agents and turn, in 1951, to Joe Glaser, Armstrong's manager and benefactor. It was a frosty relationship from the first. Duke knew Louis would always remain Joe's top-drawer client, and Ellington wasn't used to playing backup. Joe was respectful of Duke in public, referring to him as "Mr. Ellington" and calling him a "fine, high-class genius." In private, he allegedly talked about "that crazy nigger Duke Ellington." Glaser gave Ellington the cash advances he perpetually asked for, knowing, the way any loan shark did, that his famous client would stay in line and under contract. Ellington made clear how he felt in a letter he penned to Glaser, in longhand, in December 1963: "Obviously I am a nuisance and an unnecessary addition to your kennel—and so to rid us both of this unhappy union I think it would be a good idea to discontinue our association immediately." But the letter never was mailed and the fraught relationship continued for the rest of Ellington's life.

The more managers that came and went, and the more time Ellington spent with Glaser, the better Irving Mills looked. Irving was worried how Duke would treat him in his memoir, to the point of repeatedly calling Duke's collaborator, Stanley Dance. He needn't have fretted. While not gushing like he did with others, the ever-diplomatic Duke wrote of Mills: "He had always preserved the dignity of my name. Duke Ellington had an unblemished image, and that is the most anybody can do for anybody."

———

Count Basie's first and most influential manager didn't fit the mold. John Henry Hammond was less of a handler than a spotter, an enabler, a producer, and a critic. He hadn't risen from his bootstraps and wasn't street-smart. A Yale dropout, he'd grown up in a Manhattan mansion with a houseful of servants, private schools including St. Bernard's and Hotchkiss, and a lineage that included great-great-grandfather Commodore Cornelius Vanderbilt and a namesake father who worked as a banker, railroad executive, and lawyer. Though from an establishment WASP family, John II always purposefully identified with underdogs, especially Jewish ones. He searched for Hebrew ancestors and told people, "I wanted to be Jewish."

What Hammond was was smart, and he knew it. He supported Negroes in his orbit yet was paternalistic in the way that well-meaning white benefactors could be. "The joke behind John's back, was . . . 'Oh, yes, I was in the studio at that time.' Or they would say, 'Yes, I discovered him' . . . because those are the two things that John used to say all the time," said longtime producer and manager George Avakian. "So John, who on the surface was very friendly, bubbly, and so forth, was really a strange person, very eager to grab credit."

None of that bothered Basie, who never forgot the night that Hammond came all the way from New York to Kansas City just to hear the band for himself. "There's only one John Hammond. Some people have their differences with him," the Count wrote in his memoir. "But as far as I'm concerned, John Hammond was the one who made the big difference in my life as a bandleader, no question about it. Without him I probably would still be in Kansas City, if I still happened to be alive. Or back in New York, and I don't know what for . . . John Hammond is, well, let's say he's responsible for me."

Hammond brought Basie from Kansas City to New York, along the way expanding the band from nine pieces to a more traditional thirteen-piece dance band and shaking out tired hands while bringing aboard fresh ones. The orchestra grew softer and subtler, with more solos and pacing that saved the hottest numbers for finales. John connected Bill to vocalists Billie Holiday then Helen Humes. He introduced him to MCA's big band booker and industry powerhouse Willard Alexander, who in turn convinced his prestigious agency to take on the unproven and at times unready orchestra, in the process beating out Joe Glaser and paving Basie's road not just to New York but to the musical Oz. Whatever his proclivity to embellish, it was Hammond who brought Bill Basie to the nation's attention and made him a true Count as well as a bona-fide star.

That ride had its bumps. Basie signed a three-year recording contract with Decca that looked good to him but nobody else, and while Hammond was outraged he couldn't crack the deal. There also were harsh reviews just before Basie arrived in New York. "That sax is so invariably out of tune. And if you think that sax section is out of tune, catch the brass! And if you think the brass by itself is out of tune, catch the intonation of the band as a whole!" influential critic George Simon wrote in *Metronome,* based on radio broadcasts he'd heard. "Here's hoping the outfit sounds better in person."

Hammond eventually yielded to more full-time and professional managers. As Basie looked for his next handler, it might have saved him angst and dough to have consulted Ellington and Armstrong, who were older and savvier. But that was not the kind of information bandleaders shared then, even if they respected one another like these three did. The world of big orchestras was too competitive. The needs and predilections of this trio were too dissimilar. And while they gushed about how much they liked one another, they were never close friends.

Basie instead turned first to MCA, then to the William Morris Agency. As with Duke and Satchmo, many of the Count's trusted managers going forward were Jewish—including Milt Ebbins, who helped lift him out of debt; Sam Weisbord, a honcho at the Morris Agency; and the fierce-tempered, big-as-a-house hustler Teddy Reig, who produced some of the Count's best records. Eddie "Lockjaw" Davis, who was Black, played and managed. "I would like to give [Davis] special credit for the job he did while he was my road manager . . . He was honest, which is more than I can say for some others we've had in that job over the years," Basie wrote in his memoir *Good Morning Blues.* "But he could get pretty rough when it came to personal relations. He wouldn't stand for any stuff from anybody.

Sometimes I've had to cool him down because he could rub some people the wrong way . . .

"By the way, as far as the other band managers I've had over the years are concerned, if I say what I really think about some of them, it would change this book into another kind of story," the always-diplomatic Count added. "I'll just say that all of them could talk a lot and also talk very loud and count that money and separate it. They could really separate that money. But the thing about it was when you checked up, every time you found a mistake it was always in their favor. I'm not going to name any names, but one cat made something like a twelve-hundred-dollar mistake on one goddamn payroll."

Like with Duke and Satchmo, the Count's choices of managers and assistants in part reflected what the maestro either didn't want to do or couldn't. Hence the need for a series of straw bosses to at least appear to hire, fire, and make other painful choices. And as with the others, the ever-busy Basie indulged himself—with a tailor, band boys, and a valet who went everywhere with him, as organizer George Wein recalled of the rain-soaked opening night of his 1956 Newport Jazz Festival: "Beside me, Senator [Theodore] Green upturned the collar on his raincoat in a futile attempt to keep from getting soaked; he looked like a basset hound. I was worried about the health of this elderly statesman, so I looked around for something with which to shield him from the elements. I soon spotted an umbrella, in the hands of Basie's valet—a young African-American kid standing at the edge of the stage. I approached him and asked if he could please hold the umbrella over the senator.

"'I'm sorry,' he said. 'This is Count Basie's umbrella.' It was only after some cajoling that the young man agreed to hold the umbrella for Senator Green until Basie came off the stage. This valet apparently knew all about pulling rank. He strongly believed that a Senator—no matter how distinguished or well advanced in years—should always defer to a Count."

CRITICAL AUDIENCES AND
PROFESSIONAL CRITICS

G ARDEN-VARIETY INSULTS COULDN'T pierce the thick skin of musicians like these three, long accustomed to bigoted slurs and crude critique. But when reviewers blithely demeaned them as un-cultured clowns, or savage beasts, something snapped.

Later in their careers, Duke, the Count, and Satchmo would become the darlings of music reviewers, with white critics worldwide tripping over one another to toast their genius and, in the process, demonstrate the writer's broad-mindedness about race. It wasn't that way at first. All three bandleaders confronted a regular racist assault dressed as commentary as pundits guard-edly danced their way around this threatening new form of Black music. The quickest way to undermine a rising African American genius was to dismiss him as a primeval animal.

"Armstrong is the ugliest man I have ever seen on the music-hall stage. He looks, and behaves, like an untrained gorilla. He might have come straight from some African jungle and then, after being taken to a slop tailor's for a ready made dress-suit, been put straight on the stage and told to 'sing,'" Han-nen Swaffer, one of Britain's best-known drama critics, wrote in the *Daily Herald* in 1932. As for the audience, "five out of six people seated in a row in front of me walked out while [Armstrong] was on; so did two people on my right—and several others at the back." That left "pale aesthetes . . . and the young Jewish element at the back was enthusiastic."

A competing London rag, the *Daily Express*, described Satchmo's singing as "savage growling [that] is as far removed from English as we speak or sing it—and as modern—as James Joyce."

Armstrong absorbed the attacks without publicly responding. He knew it was futile to take on journalists who bought their ink by the barrelful, and that even negative write-ups built his following. He'd grown up being told which urinals, schools, and friends were off-limits to Negroes like him, and he knew his bid to break through to white audiences would open him to abuse. But it stung, and years later he explained that "when I was coming along, a black man had hell." He boasted how he'd snapped back against one hateful reviewer: "I told that bastard, 'You telling me how to blow my god-damn horn and you can't even blow your goddamn nose.'"

The racial condescension was by no means limited to Satchmo. A year earlier, the *Cleveland News*'s Archie Bell said this of the Ellington Cotton Club Orchestra: "These chocolate-tinted folk have something distinctly artistic and fine to offer, when they adhere to their own idiom." Likewise, British composer and critic Constant Lambert diluted his praise with the patronizing observation that Duke "is definitely a petit maître,* but that, af-ter all, is considerably more than many people thought either jazz or the coloured race would ever produce."

Even John Hammond, Basie's enabler and a social crusader, reverted to racial stereotypes in trying to tell Black musicians like Ellington how to behave. "Ellington is fully conscious of the fact that Broadway has not treated him fairly, knowing many of the sordid details," Hammond wrote in 1935. "And yet he did not lift a finger to protect himself because he has the completely defeatist outlook which chokes so many of the artists of his race."

Hammond's takedown might have been well-meaning but it was misin-formed. Duke delivered a titanic response with each new riveting compo-sition telling the story of his race. While he preferred to speak through his piano and his orchestra, two years before Hammond's rebuke, Duke told a Scottish journalist, "You have no idea of the fury with which people have attacked me through the press and by personal letters. One man wrote say-ing that as my music is at present it is an insult to the word." Duke's counter was that much the way bagpipes captured the spirit of Scotland, so "my contention about the music we play is that it also is folk music, the result of our transplantation to American soil, and the expression of a people's soul just as much as the wild skirling of bagpipes denotes a heroic race that has never known the yoke of foreign dictatorship."†

---

* A fop, dandy, or minor talent.

† Leonard Feather, then a critic as well as press agent for Duke, took on Hammond directly in the publication *Jazz*: "I think it is a dirty rotten, lowdown no-good shame that somebody like John Hammond, who has done so much to eliminate race prejudice in music, should be so completely befuddled by personal prejudices himself. Hammond's prejudices against certain

Basie also was occasionally singed by racist reviewers, although he took less flak than the other two because he maintained a lower profile in those early years and kept his focus on Black audiences and Black reviewers. Yet even the Count couldn't escape Jim Crow's strictures. At a 1938 faceoff at Madison Square Garden with purported King of Swing Benny Goodman, Basie and his band "practiced some plain and fancy carving at the expense of Benny Goodman's reputation," wrote reviewer George Avakian.* Sadly, because he was Black and Goodman white, "Basie wasn't even mentioned on the tickets and half the posters. He got $400 for the date. BG got $2,500."

Basie's response to the slights and the barbs was, as always, boiled down and low pitched: "I learned a critic is nothing but a human being."

Regardless of what the commentators said, most fans loved all three from the get-go. "He knew how to work an audience. He knew to make an audience eat out of his hand. He was so charming," choreographer Alvin Ailey said of Duke, although that description fit the Count and Satchmo as well. "One thing I remember, he was on the bandstand, conducting and playing all the tunes and all that and suddenly he remembered that somebody was there who had just gotten married so he called their names and he called them up to the stage and he made this couple sit on the stage while they played 'Auld Lang Syne' to them and 'Satin Doll.' He did a little dance for them . . . He was a kind of king."

Ellington, Armstrong, and Basie mapped out music not just to bop and listen to, but to make out to, as couples of all ages and backgrounds well knew. Whites in America, it was said then, imitate Indians as children and Blacks as teenagers, and nowhere was that more true than in restless, rebellious music halls. Everybody tuned in: English kings, princes, and princesses; First Lady Eleanor Roosevelt and first man of American composition George Gershwin; people ranging from hip urbanities to laborers and heartland farmers who drove, hitchhiked, or walked great distances, with dimes they'd squirreled away, to experience the delight of hearing in person jazz idols they'd gotten to know through vinyls and the wireless.

The trio moved from playing to Negro audiences to black-and-tans and other mixed-race settings. In the end, their venues were packed mainly with the whites who could afford the concerts, Broadway shows,

---

musicians and bands are mostly motivated by his inability to run their bands or their careers for them." Tucker, *Duke Ellington Reader*, 174.

* Carving is the height of musical one-upmanship, with one band trying to blow the other offstage—and a reviewer's applauding the band that delivered that thrashing was the sincerest flattery imaginable.

and motion pictures. Even if the price didn't deter Black fans, Jim Crow certainly did.

Armstrong, who actively courted whites dating back to his days on the riverboats, was hurt when Black audiences who'd once celebrated him as their cultural icon began turning away in the 1940s. "One time he did a gig in Texas. He told me, 'Down the street [African American saxophonist] Louis Jordan was playing, and there was only a couple dozen people at my place, and his place was *turnin' away niggers!*' And that really hurt him," reported friend and photographer Jack Bradley.

Cross-racial appeal posed its own challenges, as critic and *Invisible Man* author Ralph Ellison saw in 1929 when Armstrong came to Oklahoma City: "The bandstand in our segregated dance hall was suddenly filled with white women. They were wild for his music and nothing like that had ever happened in our town before. His music was our music but they saw it as theirs too, and were willing to break the law to get to it."

In the early years, lucky fans sometimes got a two-fer. "Down South fraternities and sororities are really big," explains Nelson Harrison, a jazz historian who played trombone with Basie. "They would have these Mardi Gras's and these dances, and they would hire the Basie band on one end of the ballroom and the Ellington band on the other end of the ballroom. They say that when Ellington's band was playing, everybody was crowded around the bandstand listening. When the Basie band was playing, everybody was dancing." When Duke was alone, he did both, first a dance set, then a concert where tables and chairs were lined along the dance floor. Black kids who came "were dressed to the nines. I mean, it was such a major evening for them," recalls Gary Giddins. "Whereas the white kids were dressed the way we were always dressed, in jeans and T-shirts."

Photojournalist Gordon Parks never forgot his first sighting of Duke, when Parks was seventeen, and Ellington was playing at Minneapolis's Orpheum Theater: "He had arrived in a cream-colored LaSalle convertible driven by Big Nate, a racketeer off the Northside. Elegantly attired, Ellington alighted and began making his way through a bunch of admirers. I scrambled up and shoved a piece of paper into his face for an autograph. Big Nate shoved me back, saying, 'Get the hell out of here, kid!' Ellington had gently reprimanded him. 'We don't treat our public like that, Nate.' He motioned me forward, asked my name, and signed my paper. He had dubbed me 'Sir Gordon,' and I went about addressing myself with that title for weeks."

Valve trombonist Bob Brookmeyer had a similar experience with Basie: "I was about ten years old when I first heard Count Basie live at the Tower

Theatre in Kansas City. I heard six shows a day and saw a rotten movie five times [laughter]. It was the only time I ever cut school in my life: four or five times a year I spent seven days a week there . . . To hear the first note—it was the severest physical thrill I think I've ever had. Drugs and sex and all that stuff—it was just the most powerful thing."

For Timuel Black, the Chicago civil rights leader, it happened even younger, and in a way that might have embarrassed other five-year-olds. "Mama took my brother Walter and me to the Vendome Theater on Thirty-Third and State Street. And there I heard this magnificent sound. Louis Armstrong . . . It was for me as a small child a sound so profound and embracing. I was absolutely hypnotized by the music of Louis Armstrong. That was the day I fell in love with jazz. There was only one problem. In mid-concert, I needed to go to the washroom. But, gripped as I was by the spell of the music, I forgot I had to go. Nature took its course . . . I pissed my pants, but I never regretted it, because I didn't want to miss a note of this new sound."

Twenty years later, when Black was part of General George Patton's army of liberation entering Paris, French civilians waved jazz records and yelled "Louis Armstrong!" as Black's African American unit passed. "They wanted to wave them," he explained, "to show their support."

Fans expressed themselves in fanatical ways. Some tried to grab Duke's shoe as a memento, the way they would with rock stars like Elvis. In Satchmo's case there was "clipping man," a Philadelphia admirer who made it to every concert within a hundred miles, quietly hanging around backstage hoping for a private moment, which he often got, and sending Louis copies of each newspaper story. Sometimes so many jitterbuggers crowded onto the stage that it caved in, like it did at an Ellington performance in 1940 in West Virginia, or the dance floor collapsed, as happened years later in Arkansas. Other times cowboys ended the festivities by firing their sidearms at the ceiling or insisting the band play only the gunslinger's favorite numbers.

Duke adored his fans enough to tutor them, at the close of concerts, on the proper blend of simplicity and savoir-vivre: "You are all invited to join the finger snapping craze. I see I don't have to tell you. Nobody snaps their fingers on the beat, it's considered aggressive. Don't push it, just let it fall. And if you would like to be conservatively hip, then at the same time tilt the left earlobe. Establish a state of nonchalance. And if you would like to be respectably cool, then tilt your left earlobe on the beat and snap the fingers on the afterbeat, there. Then you really don't care. And so by routining one's finger snapping and choreographing one's earlobe tilting, one discovers that one can become as cool as one wishes to be."

Not everyone loved jazz or its three nattiest ambassadors. "It could be rather curious to see negroes roll their wild eyes, gyrate, and shake with the pulsations of the drum, like the ancestral beat," a reviewer of Louis's 1934 Paris concerts wrote in the Fascist *Action Française*. "But one discovered afterwards that, beneath the appearances of scary trances, it is all blatant fakery, bad acting, pretty much unchanging, which Armstrong himself did not escape."

After their initial racially tinged skepticism, the professional critics softened over the years to the point of being difficult to distinguish from adoring fans.

Reviewers clutched for metaphors to describe Basie. He was a master at meshing egos, creating a communal blueprint. When it came to building champions, critics put the Count in the pantheon that included UCLA basketball wizard John Wooden and Green Bay Packers gridiron genius Vince Lombardi. His rhythm section was "nothing less than a Cadillac with the force of a Mack truck," while the Count himself was the best accompanist—and the most laconic. "The number one jazzman in the world today," concluded one writer. Another pronounced him "too good for comparison with any other."

They showered similar accolades on Duke. "I could go on writing from now until the Judgment Day on the topic of Duke as a person and an artist, of the way he starts his numbers by rippling away at the piano until the band is set to go, of how he accompanies tap-dancers, of how his personality, as he sits in front of the band, expresses every mood of his own glorious music, and of the thousand and one other things that go to make him one of the most delightful and vivid characters of our time," English composer and journalist Spike Hughes wrote in 1933, sounding decidedly different notes than his countrymen, who a year earlier had maligned Armstrong as a "gorilla" and a "savage." Thirty-five years later another British critic who heard him confessed, "I feel a little uneasy about my criticisms, rather like an art critic who has just dissected the *Mona Lisa*." And in 1969, a U.S. reviewer gushed, "Like motherhood, practically nobody is against Duke Ellington."

As for Satchmo, in 1949 he became the first jazz musician to be splashed across the cherished cover of *Time* magazine, a publication that seventeen years before diminished him as "a black rascal raised in a waifs' home" whose "eyes roll around in his head like white, three-penny marbles." Now it saluted him, delighting that "both jazz and Louis emerged from streets of brutal poverty and professional vice—jazz to become an exciting art, Louis to be hailed almost without dissent as its greatest creator-practitioner." Pulitzer Prize–winning columnist Murray Kempton said it even better: "Armstrong is a great river so deep that it suggests no bottom and so wide that to stand on one bank is to perceive nothing about the other any plainer than a mist." The fact that he often played with unthreatening and inferior backup musicians reinforced Kempton's conviction that Louis could "drive the purest of streams through no end of sludge."

Not all reviewers were smitten. Paul Eduard Miller wrote in 1941 that "creatively and artistically, Armstrong is dead . . . Armstrong had chosen to play exclusively for the box-office." Hammond had been even tougher on Ellington, saying his "music has become vapid and without the slightest semblance of guts." And Leonard Feather would deliver this overly personal and thoroughly damning verdict on the Count: "What has happened to the Basie juggernaut illustrates a classical pattern: you start out making musical history by accident, and wind up making plenty of money by design. Somewhere along the way, sidemen get bored and quit the band, or worse, get bored and stay on."

Early in their careers the maestros were disparaged by critics, many using racial tropes, for not measuring up. Later the charge was that they might have once been good, but had gotten old and tired. Ellington spoke for all three when he answered the attacks this way in a 1965 article in *Jazz Journal*: "If you find a beautiful flower, it is probably better enjoyed than analysed, because in order to analyse it, you have to pull it apart, dissect it. And when you get through you have all the formulas, all the botanical information you need, and all the science of it, but you haven't got a beautiful flower anymore."

PART IV

OFFSTAGE

14

FAMILY UNFRIENDLY

EVER THE CONDUCTOR, Duke Ellington occupied the center of a familial cosmos in which all the planets revolved around and were bound to him. And each of his closest relatives, at times even his adoring mother, resented him for it.

Edna, his high school sweetheart, became his wife in 1918 because she was pregnant. They lived together on and off as his career blossomed, separated when he'd had enough nine years later, and stayed wed without reconciling for half a century because it saved him from having to marry any of his mistresses. Before parting they quarreled repeatedly over Duke's infidelities, with Edna one time threatening him with a pistol and the next actually slashing him with a knife, vowing to "spoil those pretty looks" and leaving a crescent-shaped scar that ran from his left ear almost to his lip.*

Mercer, their son, knew in his bones that he wasn't the child Duke longed for: "He wanted a daughter! To have him tolerate my presence, my mother kept my hair in long braids for months after most boys my age would have had their hair cut." Later in life, it was easy to trace Mercer's ever-changing mindset about his dad. When he felt warmly toward Duke, Mercer called him "Pop" or "Fadu" (for Father Duke); other times he'd use the arm's-length "Ellington." Duke returned the coolness on those occasions, often dismissing

---

* Rumors were rampant about the source of the scar. Was it the result of a taxi crash? Had he fallen on a broken bottle? Or, as he told photojournalist Gordon Parks, did it happen "at my sixth bullfight in lower Spanishotozfol? No, in all seriousness, I got it umpiring a duel between the pink baboon and a three-legged giraffe in back of a Japanese supermarket in eastern Turkey." Parks, *To Smile in Autumn,* 121.

Ellington guitarist and friend Freddie Guy said his version came directly from Duke: "I had just fell asleep and heard my doorbell ringing. When I opened the door Duke was standing there with blood on his shirt and holding a towel to his face. He was crying. The first thing out of his mouth was, 'Edna cut me.'" Lawrence, *Duke Ellington and His World,* 135.

his only child as "the Brat." "The word 'father', like 'son,'" Mercer added, "was very seldom used in our family."

Daisy always maintained her status as Duke's beloved mom, but over time she behaved more like his wife, especially after she moved to New York to be with him. Daisy slept then in a bedroom with her daughter, not with her husband, who slept in a room with Mercer. She protested the way Duke spoiled her with expensive jewelry, furs, and flowers, and a chauffeur-driven sixteen-cylinder Pierce-Arrow sedan, but readily succumbed when Duke would say, "Mother, if you don't take these things, I won't work." And whenever Duke had a personal problem, mother and son would end up in the privacy of the bathroom, where he'd talk his heart out.

J.E., Duke's dad, moved from Washington to New York a bit after Daisy did, but he wasn't thrilled about being pushed by Duke and Daisy to retire at forty-nine or being supported by his son. Knowing that J.E. was eager for something to do, Duke gave him make-work—as chairman of the Duke Ellington fan club, then as the bandleader's $100-a-week traveling secretary. He ultimately stayed home, where, when Daisy got sick, he began imbibing to a degree that would prove deadly.

As for Ruth, Duke's much younger sister, she said he treated her like his daughter, perhaps because she was. "We were not really siblings," she told an interviewer, likely not meaning it literally but adding that throughout her young life it was Edward, as much as Daisy and J.E., who "made the decisions." Mercer's daughter Mercedes, meanwhile, said that growing up, her dad and her aunt Ruth were "like brother and sister." However confused the relationships, one thing was clear to all of the family, Ruth explained. "Everything was for Edward."

That family pattern was made explicit early on to Edna, whose parents came from a family of teachers and had warned her against carrying on with a hoi-polloi musician. Not yet twenty when they wed, she and Ellington relished the challenges of his working two or more jobs, running messages for the Treasury Department even as he tried to cut it as an ivory tickler. "We lived in one room and beans were only 5 cents a can. Some days we didn't have the 5 cents," she recalled of the time when Duke was entranced by her sparkling dark eyes, sought-after light skin, and shiny hair parted down the middle.

It wasn't just that Duke's life as head of a musical family required him to be on the road and away from Edna and his actual family; wanderlust was part of his constitution, along with a relentlessly wandering eye. Edna moved with him to New York in 1923 or 1924, leaving Mercer behind with

Daisy and J.E. in Washington. She hoped that she and Duke could dive to-gether into his new life as a celebrity, so she worked as a showgirl in clubs where he performed (her main job, she acknowledged, was to "walk around and lend atmosphere"). "[But] I was young and jealous and didn't want to share him with the public. I couldn't stand around waiting until the public had their fill of him before he could give me some of his time. If there was something important I wanted to say to him, I wanted to rush up and tell him then," she told an interviewer more than thirty years later. "Then came the big breakup. Ellington thought I should have been more understand-ing of him. I guess I should have been. I guess I've regretted—I *know* I've regretted it . . .

"Why didn't we divorce after the breakup?" Edna asked out loud, echo-ing a question that puzzled many. "I love Ellington and I'm going to stick my neck out and say I don't think he hates me. I don't want a divorce and neither does he. We're proud of the way we get along . . . I was hurt, bad hurt when the breakup came, but I have never been bitter . . . Whenever anything happens he'll call me or I'll call him. He'll open up to me when he's angry. But Duke—and Mercer takes after him in this respect—is a lonely man. He masks his emotions. Never wants you to know how he actually feels . . . We'll never be together again. The public's still there and I'm still jealous."

Mercedes offered a more realistic appraisal of why her grandfather liked being divorced in practice but not in law: "I have two ideas. One, he really didn't want to hurt her and he felt that there would still be some attach-ment if he didn't make that final break and the other is that if he did, he would have no protection against other women who were after him to marry them . . . It might have been both."

It was, and the early years of their marriage were more complicated than anyone but Duke and Edna knew. She was unfaithful to him much as he re-peatedly was with her, according to Ellington sideman Barney Bigard, who said Edna used a razor to cut Duke while he was sleeping and that Duke justified having affairs with married women because another man once cut in on his marriage. Duke continued to pay Edna's bills after she moved back to Washington and until she died—of some blend of her stroke, cancer, pneumonia, chronic depression, and the overconsumption of alcohol—with Mercer at her side, at just sixty-seven. "Mother was my favorite," Mercer said, "and I was hers."

Daisy reappeared in Duke's life not long after Edna vanished. His mother came to New York to see him perform in 1930, and a year later came for good. Duke installed the family in an apartment on Edgecombe Avenue, on elegant Sugar Hill, with a view of the Harlem River and neighbors like Thurgood Marshall and Cab Calloway. Daisy was thrilled to be reunited with and able to take care of what she called her blessed boy. She dismissed the man Duke had hired to clean the house, to which Duke replied, "Yes, mother dear." The high point of her day was when he burst through the door announcing, "Mother, I'm home to dine!"

Those good times didn't last long. Two years after Daisy got to Manhattan, doctors told her she was sick, not just with her chronic asthma but with what people then called the Big C, because they dared not even whisper the word *cancer*. By 1934 it had spread and she insisted on moving back to Washington. In the spring of 1935 she checked into a state-of-the-art clinic in Detroit, with Duke arranging bookings nearby that let him rush to the hospital as soon as his performance was over. For Daisy's last three days, her son rested his head on her pillow, holding her hand and praying until the end. "His world had been built around his mother," said Mercer. "He just sat around the house and wept for days. Eventually his suffering was reduced to the time of the year when she passed away. Then you could be very sure he was drinking. He would be on a drunk for two or three weeks and then come off it."

"I about lost me," Duke confided years later. He worked through that devastating grief the way he processed other pain or heartbreak: through his music, especially the twelve-minute, four-sided "Reminiscing in Tempo." "In it was a detailed account of my aloneness after losing my mother," Duke said of his most personal composition, one of the few for which he wouldn't allow additions or improvisations. "Every page of that particular manuscript was dotted with smears and unshapely marks caused by tears that had fallen. I would sit and gaze into space, pat my foot, and say to myself, 'Now, Edward, you know she would not want you to disintegrate, to collapse into the past, into your loss, into lengthy negation or destruction. She did not spend all the first part of your life preparing you for this negative attitude.' I believed I could hear the words, her words, and slowly—but never completely—I really did straighten up."

Even as he began to recover from the loss of his mother, his father started drinking more and eating less. J.E. had never looked or acted his age, with an eye for attractive women girlish enough to have been his daughter, wooing them with come-hither lines like "I don't know what it is about the younger generation, something about these boys that always leaves the girls looking

1956 photo of Jane Alley where, half a century earlier, Louis Armstrong was born in a one-story, four-room frame house. RALSTON CRAWFORD COLLECTION/WILLIAM RANSOM HOGAN JAZZ ARCHIVE/TULANE UNIVERSITY

Louis with his mother, Mayann, and sister, Beatrice. LOUIS ARMSTRONG HOUSE MUSEUM (LAHM)

Louis—in the middle of the third row—played the tambourine, snare drum, alto horn, bugle, and finally his cherished cornet in the band of the Colored Waif's Home for Boys in New Orleans. LAHM

A publicity photo for the Hot Five, Armstrong's first and perhaps best recording band. LAHM

Louis signs a history-making contract to host the *Fleischmann's Yeast Hour* on radio, flanked by two of his most influential managers, Joe Glaser (*left*) and Tommy Rockwell. LAHM

Louis with Clarence Hatfield Armstrong, whom he called his adopted son, in Chicago in 1933. LAHM

Louis smooching with Lucille, his fourth and longest-lasting wife, backstage at Washington, D.C.'s Howard Theatre in the early 1940s. LAHM

Pope Paul VI greets Louis in Italy in 1968. LAHM

Louis is carried like
a king through
the streets of the
Congo in 1960.
LAHM

SWISS KRISSLY

SATCHMO-SLOGAN
(Leave It All Behind Ya)

The famous keyhole image of Louis promoting his favorite laxative, Swiss Kriss, with his slogan, "Leave It All Behind Ya." LAHM

Louis plays for his young neighbors on the steps of his home in the Corona section of Queens, New York. LAHM, CHRIS BARHAM PHOTOGRAPHER

One of the few surviving images
of Count Basie's mother, Lillian.
UNKNOWN PHOTOGRAPHER/
COURTESY OF THE INSTITUTE
OF JAZZ STUDIES/COUNT BASIE
FAMILY PAPERS AND ARTIFACTS/
RUTGERS UNIVERSITY

Harvey Basie,
the Count's father.
UNKNOWN PHOTOGRAPHER/
COURTESY OF THE INSTITUTE
OF JAZZ STUDIES/COUNT BASIE
FAMILY PAPERS AND ARTIFACTS/
RUTGERS UNIVERSITY

A courtly looking Count.
JOHN W. MOSLEY PHOTO
COLLECTION/TEMPLE
UNIVERSITY

Basie performs
in 1943 for
servicemen at
the South Broad
Street USO in
Philadelphia.
JOHN W.
MOSLEY PHOTO
COLLECTION/
TEMPLE
UNIVERSITY

The Count and Catherine with their thirteen-year-old daughter, Diane, listening to a Basie band recording. DAVID MCLANE/*NEW YORK DAILY NEWS* ARCHIVE/GETTY IMAGES

The Basies watch the Count's model train round the bend in the basement of their home in the St. Albans section of Queens, New York. DAVID MCLANE/*NEW YORK DAILY NEWS* ARCHIVE/GETTY IMAGES

The Count and his pal Frank Sinatra, who toured together in the early 1960s.
BETTMANN/GETTY IMAGES

Basie with Jesse Jackson and Dionne Warwick at a concert honoring the Count at Radio City Music Hall in New York in 1982. EBET ROBERTS/GETTY IMAGES

Basie taking a cigar break. COPYRIGHT CHUCK FISHMAN

With dog Graf poolside
in the Bahamas.
COPYRIGHT CHUCK FISHMAN

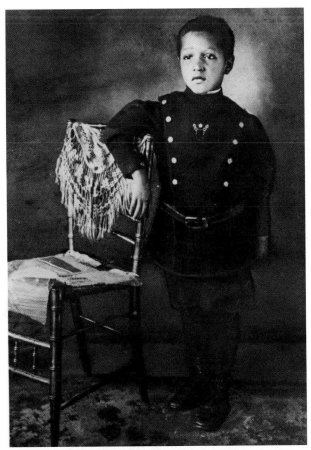

Edward Kennedy Ellington at age six, when he already was acting and dressing like a duke.

Duke running from a flock of female fans.

In Florida, Duke and the band get in some swings in front of their tour bus, with the segregated Astor Motel in the background. CHARLOTTE BROOKS/*LOOK* MAGAZINE COLLECTION/LIBRARY OF CONGRESS

Duke and the band arrive in Hollywood for the filming of Paramount's 1934 musical *Murder at the Vanities.* DRIGGS COLLECTION/NMAH

Duke was a clotheshorse. ELLINGTON COLLECTION/NMAH

Ellington with saxophonist Paul Gonsalves on a government-arranged tour
in 1963. ELLINGTON COLLECTION/NMAH

President Nixon awards Ellington the Medal of Freedom in 1969, at a White House party celebrating the bandleader's seventieth birthday.
ELLINGTON COLLECTION/NMAH

The Duke meets a queen, Elizabeth II, in 1958.
ELLINGTON COLLECTION/ NMAH

Duke dining with guests including his son, Mercer, and granddaughter, Mercedes, in 1971.
PIERRE BOULAT/ELLINGTON COLLECTION/NMAH

Duke and Louis at New York's Rainbow Grill in 1969.
LAHM, JACK BRADLEY PHOTOGRAPHER

Duke and the Count share a keyboard at Disneyland's Big Band Festival in 1964.
LOS ANGELES TIMES PHOTO ARCHIVE/CHARLES E. YOUNG RESEARCH LIBRARY/UCLA

Louis and Lucille with Count Basie and Emmett Berry at the Bop City jazz club
in San Francisco, 1950. LAHM

tired . . . My influence is more restful."* Now, however, he looked and felt haggard. A trip to a sanatorium in the Catskills didn't help, and by mid-July 1937 he was diagnosed with pleurisy, which turned into consumption, better known now as tuberculosis. Three months later, with Duke at his bedside, J.E., too, passed away.

That left twenty-two-year-old Ruth an orphan, with her big brother more than ever her guardian and surrogate parent. "Look after little Ruthie," Daisy had instructed Duke as she was dying, but he had already taken on that role. In addition to an apartment on Central Park South, he bought Ruth a four-story house on fashionable Riverside Drive that the family dubbed the Winter Palace. When he was on the road, which was most of the time, he tried to telephone her every day. "We all kind of put our arms around each other," Ruth said of that family bond.

At times, for a young Ruthie, that embrace felt more like a stranglehold. Duke decreed that she come home immediately after school, and arranged for his chauffeur to pick her up. The summer after her father died, her brother set conditions on her going to Paris to study at the Sorbonne. "There were thirty-five students and five professors to chaperone us," she recalled. "But [Duke] wasn't happy with that. He went back to Washington and got a sixty-five-year-old lady, who had grown up with my mother, and whose mother knew my grandmother, and he sent her with me." Duke called Ruth "our little doll," but couldn't see how that made her chafe. "I remember when I married my children's father he kept calling me up and saying, 'What do you need to be married for?'" said Ruth. "He had given me everything . . . I had an apartment, I had a Cadillac, I had a mink coat, I had everything . . . I, of course, was too painfully shy. This is why we never had arguments. Because I was afraid to tell him I was lonely, so I didn't say anything."

Over time Ruth became the fulcrum of the Ellington enterprise, running Duke's music company, keeping his mistresses from colliding, organizing his trophy room of medals and ribbons, and serving as his sounding board. "All my life I told him about everything, unless I felt that it were too painful for him," she said. "He did not want to hear problems. As he used to say, 'I have to think about beautiful music.' And I knew that. And my job, here in New York, was to mind the store in New York and take care of the problems. Because his job was to be creative and to be on the road."

Things were even harder on Mercer, who could barely remember the time

---

* Like Duke, J.E. seemed to have inherited his flirtatious nature. Duke's paternal grandfather still was making passes at girls from his wheelchair. Collier, *Duke Ellington*, 9.

when his parents were together. He grew up first in his grandparents' home, and later in his father's, without his father there. That lack of a solid parental model may explain why he had his first child out of wedlock and then was married three times. If Ruth related to Duke more like his daughter than his sister, Mercer was more like his brother than his son. He was just nine when his parents separated and nineteen when Ruth went to France and he was left alone in the apartment, "unsupervised, but with maid service and a Cadillac."

Over time, Duke made it clear that his career mattered more than his son's. He pushed Mercer to give up his own work whenever Duke needed his help, and he worried that having both father and son in the band business was diluting the Ellington brand. "Duke Ellington would make certain he remained on top regardless of whom he knocked down, including me . . . My father would never do anything overt or bad enough to really hurt, but if my foot slipped he would let me go all the way down," said Mercer, who found it stressful living in the shadow of Duke's talent and fame. While some might see that as "ruthless or selfish," Mercer added, "I would say it was done in the interest of the whole, of what he regarded as family. Keeping himself at the top, at all costs, put him in a position to help others."

The familial bond won out in their seesaw relationship after Mercer came aboard as road manager, and later, when he kept alive his father's band and legacy. Mercer even took on Duke's mannerisms, from rubbing his nose to pulling his ear. "As I grew to know him better, I never closed my eyes to his faults," Mercer wrote later, "but they never outweighed the good in my appreciation of him."

Duke's relationship with Mercer's daughter Mercedes and her half brother Edward offered more hints into how the bandleader saw his family and the world. "I was a kid when I first met Duke Ellington in person," Mercedes said. "In the topsy-turvy world of a touring musician's life, my family would often find themselves celebrating Christmas in July—whenever the great man (the Duke) turned up in New York, that was Christmas . . . At one point, I wanted to know what to call him . . . He said, 'Call me Uncle Edward.' He did not want to acknowledge his age. If my father wanted to get his father mad, he'd call him 'Pop.'"

Grandson Edward, meanwhile, vividly recalled half a century later the counsel Duke had given him as a boy. "'Edward, I think what you should really do is lock yourself in a room and invent something that will make a lot of money and set you up, because the only other alternative is that you become a pimp, but the hours are too long.' This is verbatim," Edward says of his grandfather's advice, which he relished but didn't follow. He also recalled a trip he took to Las Vegas with his grandfather and father: "My grandfather was going on stage. He had some money in his pocket, and he didn't want any bulges in his pants. So he said, 'Here, take this $500 and give it to me when I get off the stage.' I said, 'Sure.' It took me about three minutes to lose every cent of that $500. He came offstage and said, 'Let me have that $500.' And I said, 'I'm sorry, I just gambled it away.' And he said, 'Oh, okay.' And then he walked over to my father. And he said, 'Hey Mercer, let me have a couple bucks.' [Mercer] said, 'I just gave you $500. What'd you do with it?' [Duke] says, 'I lost it.'"

For anyone else the story might have ended there, and still have been a good one. With Duke there always was more, as Edward recalled: "A year later I went back on the road and Ellington was there. We were walking into a hotel. A couple of people took our bags and Ellington said, 'Let me have a couple of, you know, bucks, so I can tip the stewards.' I gave him, I guess it was $50 or something like that. And he gave it to them. And then he looked over at me, he says, 'That's 450.'"

With that and everything, Edward added, "He was gonna do it in his way, never a direct way."

––––––

Bill Basie knew just what kind of home life he wanted to complement his existence as a gadabout bandleader: a wife unlike his ill-chosen first, a marriage free from whatever entanglements had quietly undermined his parents', and no closeted skeletons like Leroy and Samuel, his older brothers who died too young. For a while, the Count got the whole kingdom.

He first laid eyes on Catherine Morgan in about 1932, when he was still married to Vivian Winn, the woman he later said he wanted to forget. The teenaged Catherine was one of three Snakehips Queens dancers in a vaudeville show that Basie was part of in Harlem. "I didn't actually meet her then, because she wouldn't even speak to me," he wrote in his memoir of the striking woman with long black hair, big brown eyes, and a muscular backstroke that might have taken her to the Olympics. "But I will never forget seeing Katy that first time." Their second encounter was several years later, when Catherine was a fan dancer and featured single at the Club Harlem in Atlantic City, performing as Princess Aloha from Tahiti.* "I was backstage and her dressing-room door was open, and I thought I would go in," Basie remembered. "But she saw me looking in there, and before I could say anything she started blowing the whistle on old Basie. 'Hey,

––––––

* Earlier, she performed under the name Blondy Morgan.

somebody come here. That piano player with Bennie Moten's band—I caught him trying to peep behind my fans!' I wasn't doing any such thing, and she knew damn well I wasn't. But I got the hell out of there fast.'"

The third time was nearly his charm. She'd been coming to hear him at the Famous Door nightclub on Fifty-Second Street in Manhattan, sitting quietly along the back wall. On his Sunday off, he ran into her at a bar in Atlantic City. "I walked her out to the car with my little finger hooked into hers. Then when she got in, I aimed my forefinger at her again with my thumb cocked, and that's when I said something I remember to this day. 'That's all right. One of these days I'm going to get you. One of these days I'm going to make you my wife' . . . She just looked at me and shook her head like she thought I was crazy as they drove off. But when I got back to work that next week, I looked out from the bandstand for her, and after a couple of nights she started coming back again.'"*

His persistence paid off, although not quite in the way he recounted in his memoir and other tellings over the years. In those versions, he and Catherine were married in the summer of 1942, ten years after his first sighting and on the Count's thirty-eighth birthday. "Naturally she had her own career as a dancer and singer; and that is one reason it took her so long to make up her mind to tie the knot," he wrote of his bride, who was eleven years younger than him. "I just wanted her to settle down and make a home so we could have a family . . . There was no big ceremony or anything like that. We just found a justice of the peace in Seattle . . . and we spent our honeymoon on the road with the band doing another string of those one-nighters.'"

The official records tell a different story. Catherine and Bill took out an application to get married but never followed up on it, and that happened in Baltimore, not Seattle, in 1947, not 1942.† The archives in Seattle con-

---

* During their off-again-on-again courtship, Catherine was being wooed as well by singer and sax man Dan Grissom, according to "Papa" Jo Jones, who thought Katy was too good for a "goof-off" like the Count. Jones also said that "Basie was supposed to marry Alice Dixon," a light-skinned African American from Baltimore. But "when her parents saw *black Basie,* they said, 'Nooooo!' You know how it is, the blue bloods. They said you ain't gonna marry that black son of a gun." Jo Jones, *Rifftide,* 59.

As for Catherine, she'd been wed before, for five years to guitarist Jimmy Miller, and was divorced in 1940, although, like the Count, she seldom discussed her earlier marriage. "151 Out-of-Town Pairs Get Baltimore Wedding Permits," *Baltimore Afro-American;* and *Catherine Miller v. James Miller,* Cuyahoga County (Ohio) Common Pleas Court divorce decree, April 10, 1940.

† On her application, Catherine marked "colored" in the race box, but the record keeper typed in white. That might have been by mistake. Or it could have been because Catherine's mother

firm that the couple did ultimately wed there, but not until 1950, eight years after the Count said and the world believed and six after they became parents. Why the deception? Maybe they just never had the time: the Basie band was red-hot, and taking even a modest break for a civil ceremony wasn't easy. Perhaps it was that they were living like husband and wife and, in a Jim Crow world stacked against Negroes, legal technicalities weren't worth fretting over, especially on something so personal. Or maybe it went back to Billy Basie's childhood, when his parents dissembled about their first two sons who were born out of wedlock and never made it out of childhood.

Whenever the knot was tied, Catherine indeed gave the Count everything he'd hoped for, starting with a reconnection with his father. Bill had remained closer to his mother, and after she fell down the steps and broke her neck, he rented an apartment in a stately brick-and-stone building on Harlem's Sugar Hill, moved her in, hired round-the-clock nurses, and made her comfortable until she died in 1941. His father was a different matter. Bill had always blamed Harvey for separating from Lillian, but Catherine helped him rise above that resentment. "She made a special thing of seeing to it that we acted more like father and son than we had been for all those years," Bill recalled. Harvey outlived Lillian by nineteen years, and Catherine was the one who "made sure that he didn't have to go wanting for anything that we were able to provide, and when we decided to replace the old house where I grew up on Mechanic Street with a nice little one-story pad, she was the one who stuck close to the scene, checking on things, not me. As usual, I was mostly out on the road."*

Catherine set up their home in Addisleigh Park, an enclave comprised of large lots, a sprawling park, and more than four hundred houses in the St. Albans neighborhood of Queens. Babe Ruth had lived there when it was lily-white, and residents hoping to keep it that way had inserted racial covenants into property deeds and slipped notes under doors warning, "Negroes entering St. Albans." By the time the Basies moved into their seven-room English Tudor in 1946, the district was home to famous African Americans including Fats Waller and Lena Horne and was being transformed into New York's African American Gold Coast. Jackie Robinson moved in later, as did

---

was Black, her father was white, and she was light-skinned enough that people weren't sure what race she was. Author interview of Baltimore County Marriage Division; U.S. Census records for Catherine's family; and Catherine's birth certificate, December 3, 1914.

* That one-story pad was a mail-order house of the kind available from the Sears, Montgomery Ward, and other catalogs.

Joe Louis, John Coltrane, Ella Fitzgerald, Billie Holiday, Roy Campanella, James Brown, W. E. B. DuBois, and Mercer Ellington. None of them had quite the presence that Catherine did, driving around the neighborhood in either of their pair of Cadillac Eldorado Biarritzes, one white, one black, with the convertible tops making it easy to behold her single-piece bathing suit, yachtsman's cap, and dyed-blond hair flowing with the breeze. She became a leader in Addisleigh Park and in the wider arena of New York. Her friends included Gov. Nelson Rockefeller, Martin Luther King Jr., and other political figures, and she was a driving force in community groups including the Rinkeydinks, a civic and social-action organization made up mainly of the wives of performers.

Their house, meanwhile, had all the playthings that the Count cherished. There was a Hammond organ to noodle around with, and a large Lionel model train set took up half of the hideaway he dubbed the "Basie basement." He'd stand in the center at the controls, sending his locomotive careening past Lilliputian bridges, pools, tunnels, and people. When they weren't reveling in their own childlike wonderland, he and his pal Mercer Ellington, another toy-train devotee, would entertain actual kids from the neighborhood, who called Basie "Uncle Bill." He also relished hanging out with neighbor and fellow musician Milt Hinton, turning on a silent movie and sitting at Hinton's old upright piano, accompanying the way he had decades before back in Red Bank.

What Catherine gave him that he cherished most was a child. Diane was born in Katy's home state of Ohio in the winter of 1944 and, as the Count recalled, "I never will forget what a special thrill it was for me to be bringing my family home that day. Old Base and his wife and daughter."* But the sweet girl with curls wasn't the healthy child every parent prays for. Her diagnoses were ambiguous at first, but over time doctors, nurses, and therapists laid out a tall list: cerebral palsy that left her muscles too weak to walk and made her head droop; an intellectual disability that limited her speaking and was called at the time mental retardation; seizures that made her arms and legs fling uncontrollably; a condition called geographic tongue that made hers hang from her mouth and dry out; bruxism that wore down and rotted out her teeth; along with, in later life, osteoporosis, hypothyroidism, and kidney stones.

In that era, most children like Diane were institutionalized, and that was

---

* While she and Bill weren't legally married then, Catherine listed her name as Basie on Diane's birth certificate.

recommended to the Basies. But they said never. Thankfully, the Count earned enough to pay for the extra care Diane required in every aspect of her life, while Catherine had the determination and patience to help her daughter accomplish things the caretakers dismissed as impossible, mostly without help from her peripatetic husband. Diane learned to communicate with hand motions and grunts. She could say "mama," "dada," and "bye-bye," pray before meals, and smile. Music was always playing on the Victrola, to Diane's delight. With an aide's or a parent's left arm around her waist and a right holding her arm, she took long walks around the neighborhood. The Basies bought the big lot next to their house and built a fenced-in pool, where the athletic Catherine taught the challenged Diane to swim, and where neighborhood kids came to play but stayed to keep Diane company.

Bill got home maybe once in six weeks for a weekend or a rare week off from band duties. He'd hold musical parties then for Diane and her friends, with everyone singing nursery rhymes while he played the organ. On occasion, Catherine, Diane, and a caretaker drove across the country to be with him on the road. Generally he communicated with his wife and daughter by letter, "as though [Diane] could understand my words." "Dear Katy," he said in one, "hope you Diane & the gang are O.K. I'm fine but having a hard time sleeping up here. Sure wish you were here. I'm being a very good boy for a change, and instead of the cards dice and one arm bandit, I'm putting my [autobiography] in place." He wrote from hotels across the country and around the globe, generally addressing them to Diane even though his obvious audience was Katy, and often apologizing for something he'd done wrong, although occasionally expressing frustration that she'd been too critical of him.

The Count adored his daughter but she left a hole in his life and heart, as the young singer Carmen Bradford sensed when she joined the band in the early 1980s. One day he summoned her to his hotel room and gave her a $100 bill, saying, "'Now, go shopping and come back and show me what you bought.' So I went shopping and bought a bunch of crap, you know, foam fingers and snow globes . . . I came back to his room, and he said, 'Come on in! What did ya get?' . . . I showed him everything, and then he said, 'Well, let's just do this on our days off, this is between us, okay? And we'll just send you shopping, and you just come back and show me, okay?' . . .

"That went on as long as I knew him . . . I think I kinda fulfilled just an empty spot there, as far as his daughter goes, or looking at me as a granddaughter, but I think he looked at me as a daughter, you know, that he could spoil, and that's exactly what he did."

Satchmo never had a role model for good husbands or parents. He had never gotten to know his dad, spent part of his formative years with his grandmother, and watched over his mother as much as she did him. All of which made him crave a family more even than Duke or the Count, and be willing to experiment three times before it stuck.

He tried first with Daisy, a red-hot, hot-headed prostitute who could neither read nor write but knew how to wield the razor tucked in her garter and to make Louis keep coming back each time she broke his heart.* He met the petite Creole at the Brick House, a raucous honky-tonk outside New Orleans, and bedded down with her in one of the upstairs rooms at a price that he said "wasn't much." They soon fell "deeply in love," marrying in 1919 when he was a tender seventeen. "That," he wrote looking back, "was when the lid blew off." In between lovemaking and trying to make a home for Louis's two-year-old nephew, Clarence, Daisy and Louis cursed and pitched bricks at one another. Then they'd make up. "We two kids," he concluded, "should never have been married."

Their divorce five years later was almost as contentious as their marriage. She said he "deserted and abandoned" her, "failed and refused to support her" even though he "earns large sums of money" while she was "a poor woman," and lied to the court about their marriage and estrangement. He said he had "treated her kindly and affectionately," but that she "wilfully and without any reasonable cause therefore deserted and abandoned" him "and wholly refused to live and cohabit with him any longer as husband and wife." What he didn't say there, but did in interviews with his authorized biographers, was that Daisy wasn't the only one prone to violence: "The way these tough men such as gamblers, pimps, etc., got along with their wives and whores, that was the same way that I had to get along with Daisy. That was to beat the hell out of her every night and make love in order to get some sleep."

That first marriage set a pattern for the ones to follow. A brief infatuation stage would soon lead to a schism and, much later and only when necessary so he could marry again, a formal divorce. He gradually came to understand what he wanted based on what he wasn't getting, which in Daisy's case was tranquility. To him, looks would always "make all the difference in the world, no matter whether a woman is dumb or not." How a woman treated Clarence mattered, too, and here again Daisy scored high. And Louis, who

---

*Daisy never used her blade on Louis, but she sliced to pieces his cherished Stetson hat.

had grown up on streets where blood was easily and regularly shed, believed it was okay to "hit her with a few real hard ones."

Lillian Hardin, the piano player with King Oliver's band, was next up. She wasn't as educated or refined as she pretended, nor as young, but she was dramatically more sophisticated than Daisy or Louis. She and Satchmo grew up together musically and monetarily, boosting one another's egos and careers. Lil welcomed Louis's mother into their lives and home in 1927 when Mayann was dying, at just forty-four, of hardened arteries.* In return, he used part of his growing paychecks to buy a house in Chicago, his first ever and hers forever, and a vacation hideaway in the Negro-friendly resort of Idlewild, Michigan. He gave her a cherished spot on keyboards with his Hot Five, with the two eventually reigning as jazz's power couple. They married at City Hall in the winter of 1924, a month and a half after he divorced Daisy with help from a lawyer Lil arranged.

While the marriage lasted fourteen years on paper, their divorce papers made clear that only two of those were angst free. Before the marriage, her mother warned that Lil was marrying down. Shortly after, Lil would say, he "commenced a course of cruel and inhuman treatment and conducted and demeaned himself in a rough, vulgar, profane and abusive manner . . . At divers times and occasions without any cause therefore he cruelly struck, kicked, beat and otherwise extremely and cruelly injured [me]." (Later, in a taped interview, she lowered the heat, saying he slapped her, and did that just once.) In his version, she'd "wilfully deserted" him, and he "always conducted himself toward her with kindness and as a true and indulgent husband, supplied . . . all her wants and necessities."

Differences that had once seemed a source of strength now grated. Three things in particular got Louis riled up. Hot Lil cheated on Little Louis, "running around with one of the Chicago pimps while I was at work." She corrected his grammar and his manners and lectured him on how to manage his money, "rubbin' it into my mind she was smarter" and trying to remake him in the dicty image he disdained and she embraced. Worst by far, she and her mother allegedly hollered at Clarence, which in Louis's telling amounted to "abuse" and had Clarence begging to move out. That, as generally is the case in marriages that are imploding, was at most half the story. Infidelity was a two-way street, as he knew, and he relished Lil's sophistication if not

---

* Louis says Mayann's last words to him were: "Carry on, you're a good boy—treats everybody right. And everybody— 'White and 'Colored Loves you—you have a good heart.—You can't miss." Armstrong, *In His Own Words*, 90.

her snobbishness. As for Clarence, Lil's court papers—referring to her as the oratrix, or female plaintiff—said that the "backward boy child of the age of sixteen" is "living with your oratrix, that your oratrix has the expense of the support and maintenance of said child; that the said child needs the constant attention of your oratrix . . . and that [Louis] does not contribute anything whatsoever to the support of said child."

That animosity waxed and waned. Was she the so-so piano player who "did not know jazz . . . Read music, yes. As an improviser—*Hmm*—terrible." Or the "woman [who] was in my corner at all times"? Over time he welcomed her back into his orbit. For her part, she never remarried, and never stopped calling herself Mrs. Louis Armstrong, wearing the rings he gave her and making a second career out of burnishing his legend in her writings and interviews.

Wife number three, Alpha Smith, came into the picture while Louis was married to Lil, and he wed Alpha just eleven days after he and Lil divorced in 1938. Louis didn't actually want a court-sanctioned split from Lil because he knew that'd mean he had to marry Alpha, whom he already was souring on by then. That made Lil even more eager to divorce, for spite. He'd first met Alpha a dozen years before, when she worked as a domestic for a white family in Hyde Park. She started showing up twice a week in the front row of Louis's shows at Chicago's Vendome Theatre, flirting with the trumpeter. She seemed to be everything Lil wasn't: down-to-earth, passionately infatuated with Louis, and, after they were married, willing to "permit my husband to go where he pleases, drink what he pleases and when he pleases, and I furthermore permit him to keep and enjoy the company of any lady or ladies he sees fit." Alpha also charmed Clarence, who gravitated to Louis's new woman and, even more, to her ever-present mother.

This time the luster wore off even faster than normal. It was partly that Alpha was cheating on him, with the white drummer Cliff Leeman, boasting that he was paying her gas bill. "[Can] you imagine my wife 'Bragging about this Lad paying a few lousy gas bills—when I've been giving her THOUSANDS and 'THOUSANDS of Dollars for 'Furs-Diamonds, Jewelry, etc . . . It really 'Kills, One Doesn't It?" he wrote in 1942 to the gossip columnist Walter Winchell. Louis erased any doubt about his disenchantment years later when he composed "Someday, You'll Be Sorry," a song he said came to him in a dream and with Alpha in mind. It chided,

Someday you'll be sorry
The way you treated me was wrong.
I was the one who taught you all you know.

But he didn't always treat her well, as he conceded to an interviewer in the mid-1950s: "Alpha was always getting drunk. She was swinging at my mouth too often, and it always scared me. What good is a trumpet player if his chops are no good? We were on the train one night with the band and she was trying to hit me in the mouth with the lock (illustrates with his thumb) on her purse. I hit her, and my fist kept traveling through the double plate glass window . . . There were other times when I would have thrown her out of the hotel window if nobody had been around." Such stories might have been dismissed as Black Benny–style tough talking had he not made clear, in earlier marriages, that it was too much more than talk. Tragically, beating one's wife rarely attracted attention or censure in an era when law enforcement considered domestic violence a private matter and when marital rape wasn't considered a crime anywhere in the United States.*

He filed for divorce in the fall of 1942, partly to be rid of her, but mostly so he could marry his new girlfriend. Alpha was the only ex-wife with whom he would have no contact after their marriage ended, although Joe Glaser kept mailing $75 a week to Los Angeles, where she worked as a domestic. There were, as Armstrong House historian Ricky Riccardi says, "no letters, no photographed reunions, she doesn't appear on his tapes." Worse, he told *Ebony* readers in 1954 that she'd passed away, when she lived until 1960.

Lucille Wilson was proof that persistence paid off for Satchmo, and that security and serenity were possible even for a nomadic jazzman. He'd learned, after three failed marriages, to control his temper if not his libido. He had fallen in love with an especially savvy woman, one who was well-bred, mature, and knew better than to try and compete with Louis on center stage. He became enchanted with Lucille—or Brown Sugar, as she was known onstage—shortly after he married Alpha. The Bronx native spent nine years as a dancer at the Alhambra Ballroom, the Cotton Club, and on Broadway. She started her career during the Depression when, after graduating from junior high, her father's modest taxi business was floundering and she had to help support three younger siblings (she also sold cookies, which Louis scooped up). She'd been an Armstrong fan forever, and they wed in October 1942, ten days after he was officially divorced from Alpha, a record even for him. Some wondered why the ceremony was held not at a church but at the home of the mother of Louis's new singer, Velma Middleton, and why the officiate was not the Catholic priest that Louis looked for and Lucille would have preferred,

---

* Prior to the 1970s, marital rape was legal in every state.

but a Baptist preacher. The simple truth was that few priests or churches would marry a man who'd broken his vows three times.

"You know, my brother was married four times. But he only had one wife," said Mama Lucy, Louis's sister, who was married twice herself. "I was glad he had that one wife at the end of his life when he could appreciate it. He was old enough to appreciate it." Lucille, told of those comments, said, "It was the first time in her life [Mama Lucy] ever said anything nice [about me]."

Louis said his failed marriages taught him all the things that he needed and that Lucille provided him: an understanding that "[my] trumpet must come first before anybody or anything," a refrigerator stuffed with cold cuts and beer along with red beans and rice cooked his mother's way, the deep-brown skin tone that he'd been drawn to "ever since I was old enough to feel a desire for women,"* as well as explicit permission not just to talk crudely but to talk to other women. Lucille blended Lil's sophistication with Daisy's earthiness, as Jack Bradley observed: "She spoke in a very proper English unless she'd had a few drinks. Then she'd start with the *motherfuckers*." As Louis saw it, "Lucille has done such a swell job of being my wife that I doubt I'll ever want to replace her with another. She's almost an ideal type of woman . . . She doesn't bother me until I want to be bothered. She also senses the right moment. That kind of woman is rare today."

It wasn't all about him, however. Lucille got a thirteen-room house on a quiet street in the Corona section of Queens where she'd spent part of her youth, which she didn't tell him about until eight months after she purchased it for $8,000, and which she richly redecorated every ten or so years.† She had eight fur coats or stoles, a Cadillac, a charge account at Saks Fifth Avenue, and a second floor where her mother lived the last three years of her life. He promised he'd show Lucille the world, "and he kept his promise." When she went out, he'd say, "Be careful, have a good time, and do you have enough money?" He had finally learned to manage his rage, with no indication that he hit Lucille the way he had the others. Most important, she got

---

* "That old phrase about 'the blacker the berry, the sweeter the juice' holds true in [Lucille's] case," Louis said. Armstrong, "Why I Like Dark Women."

† Once she told him about the house, Lucille said, Louis asked, "How did you pay for it?" Lucille: "I have been working for thirteen years. I have a little money saved up. And so, when I approached you about a house and you were so down on it, I didn't ask you. I just took my money, and I put the down payment on the house, and I've been keeping the payments up . . . Now that you know about the house, you can take the payments over." Jenkins, *Louis Armstrong's Black & Blues*.

The house's thirteen small rooms became eleven bigger ones after a renovation in the late '60s.

to spend her life with one of the most charismatic, talented, and idolized people on the planet.

There was one thing that she refused to do and that ate at him, although he never said so: invite Clarence, with his special needs, to live with them, the way Catherine Basie insisted happen with her much needier daughter, Diane. Instead, Louis arranged for Clarence a relationship that they called a marriage with Evelyn Hazel Allen, a heavyset woman who'd managed a dance hall and was glad to oblige since Louis gave her and her love-child son, Leon, a home and a comfortable life, first in Brooklyn, then the Bronx. Clarence and Evelyn's application for a marriage license lists Louis and Alpha as his parents (he'd have liked that), says he is a musician (he aspired to be because Louis was), and makes clear they took out an application but not whether they actually wed (their form was marked "cancelled" two months after it was issued). Evelyn and Clarence occasionally socialized with Louis and Lucille, generally at a restaurant or nightclub, and she kept working as a dancer at least through 1945.*

When it came to children, Lucille and Louis agreed that they wanted one, in his case desperately, much as he had with his first three wives. Their failure to deliver may have been one reason he ended those marriages, since he always assumed the problem was with them when the evidence suggested otherwise. Optimistically, he wrote jazz historian William Russell that "if Lucille and I have more than one Satchmo—I'll name one of them Russell."

---

* Clarence followed every detail of Satchmo's career, attended Mass regularly, and had a full-fledged sense of irony as well as humor. He also was wild about baseball, playing in their yard and chattering about it—and especially about his beloved New York Mets, whose hat he wore sideways and always—with the neighborhood kids. They initially taunted him by calling him "ooga booga," but switched to "Mr. Armstrong" or "Little Louis Armstrong" when they were told of his connection to the famous trumpeter. "He was like one of us," remembers Tom Cosentino. "He was like an eight- or nine-year-old kid at heart." Author interview of Cosentino.

MISTRESSES AND MISOGYNY

OUIS ARMSTRONG TALKED openly about his short-lived career as a pimp, marriage to a prostitute, and lifelong roving eye. Edward Ellington was a shade subtler, telling nearly every winsome woman he met, "I'm so jealous of your dress, because it's closer to you than I will ever be"—then trying to disprove that hypothesis. But Bill Basie was different, in his coyness if not his carousing.

The Count knew how to keep a secret. He'd learned that lesson growing up in a home where the very existence of his brothers was a taboo topic. He and Catherine had confidences, too, like why they told the world they were married in those early years when they weren't. Now he had an unmentionable of his own: that while he assuredly loved and depended on his wife, when he traveled with the band he was a serial adulterer.

He nearly admitted that in his memoir, not with Armstrong's bombast but in Basie-like phrasing obscure enough to be safe: "You can't be Peck's bad boy as often as I have always been without getting caught every now and then. But that's another story."

Basie's friends filled in that story. On one road trip with famed jazzman Billy Eckstine, Billy and his friend the Count both tried to talk their way into the hotel room of glamorous singer Esther Phillips. Basie won. So the mischievous Eckstine "got somebody to help him move a desk out of his room, which was across the hall from Basie's, and put it up by the door so he could stand on the desk, open the transom, and stick the lens of his camera into the room. And he did," recalls Billy's son Ed. "He took a photograph of them, you know, embroiled in their passion, and Basie looked up and said, 'You're a lying motherfucker.'"

Bassist Milt Hinton, a neighbor and sometimes band member, said the Count chauffeured him back and forth to work: "If we'd finish for the night and he was standing around talking to some ladies, I'd whisper to him, 'Basie, either we leave now or you better get two of them. With the deal we got, if I come home without you, your wife's gonna know where you've been.' My joking didn't seem to matter. There were plenty of early mornings when I'd stand around for hours waiting for my driver to finish his business and take me home."

Catherine, of course, did know, and the Count repeatedly promised he'd change. When he didn't, she would banish him from the house for a month or more. On one occasion she moved out, to Texas, taking Diane with her, not telling him where they were, and instructing friends who knew to ignore his incessant queries. He labored to keep all of that behind the scenes, but in 1954 it surfaced, with the *Chicago Defender* reporting that Catherine "accused [the Count] of having a romance with a girl vocalist in the band, and declared she will seek a divorce.* Mrs. Basie . . . indicated she will soon take up residence in Reno"—the divorce capital of the world. It came to light again in 1965, when Catherine told the *Amsterdam News* that she had kicked the Count out three months earlier and that the two of them feuded "about three or four times a year."

She wasn't exaggerating, as newly released Basie family files make clear. Over the years, the Count sent Catherine a stream of letters, cables, and cards, generally on stationery from whatever hotel he was in, reflecting their ongoing marital blues. Most were contrite, like in 1957 when he addressed her as "Dear Miss Pretty" and wrote from Sweden, "Thanks baby for starting a new life for me." Sometimes he jabbed, addressing her as "Dear Catherine" in a four-page handwritten missive in 1960 from Chicago that suggested their marriage was ending: "You are so bent on getting rid of me that you are using everything you can to do so. Well Katy if you want to leave me that Badly—don't make up a lot of bullshit to do so . . . You can get rid of me but please do it right and decent and not nasty." Back in Sweden in 1962, he dashed off this: "Doll. Today I love you. Dearly Bill." The following year he got sexy: "Hi Baby. Just got up to raid the ice box, and I thought about how I'd like to go back in the room and find you with your back ass side up which is always a pretty view for me, and right now I could jump thru you."

He promised he was earning more money and would take care of the taxes along with payments for her new Cadillac. He fretted about Diane,

---

* That vocalist was Bixie Crawford. Catherine allegedly spit on Bixie and threw a drink in her face, leading Bixie to file a $25,000 assault-and-battery suit against Catherine. *Bixie Crawford against Catherine Basie,* Summons, Supreme Court of the State of New York, May 9, 1955.

who'd apparently fallen trying to walk without assistance. He pledged to be home for more Thanksgivings, Christmases, and birthdays, and to bring Katy along more often when he traveled. The notes show he was achingly exhausted by his world travels and nightly gigs, as well as lonely. When things were especially tense, he'd address the letters to Diane, knowing that would tug at Katy's heartstrings.

The correspondence is mostly one-way, but reading between the lines of Bill's letters it's apparent that Catherine vacillated between the exasperation of knowing Bill couldn't remake himself and the hope that he might. One sign of her stoicism as well as her humor was a 1952 cover of a magazine called *Tan Confessions,* which targeted Black women. Its front teased an inside story entitled "How To Live Without a Husband," written by Mrs. Arthur Prysock—but the version in the Basie files was doctored to read, "By Mrs. Count Basie."*

Most breaches eventually and miraculously got repaired. Family friend Pamela Jackson said Catherine called her regularly to say, "Take the car and go and get [Bill]. So I would have to go to the hotel and go get him and say, 'You can come home now. She's letting you back in the house now.' And he would get the biggest grin on his face . . . you know. 'Oh, I can come back home now' . . . Whenever there was a misunderstanding between [Catherine and Bill] she would go buy [herself] a new mink coat or a mink stole or a sable shawl. She'd go and change the stone in her wedding ring just so it cost him some money. She changed that stone 'til it was almost 10 carats."†

All three jazzmen justified their infidelities as an inevitable part of life on the road, and it's true that the existence of a rover presented more temptations than one focused squarely on family and community. Other revered leaders of that era, from MLK and Satchel Paige to Bobby and Jack Kennedy, all experienced that. It also was a reality of the last century that, with a less prying press, mistresses and misogyny were easier to hide from the public.

---

* Katy lived without a husband for most of her earlier marriage, with an Ohio judge granting her divorce after ruling that her spouse, James Miller, was guilty of "willful absence for more than three years" from Catherine Miller, and "gross neglect of duty" toward her. *Catherine Miller v. James Miller,* Cuyahoga County Common Pleas Court, April 10, 1940.

It's impossible to say for sure who doctored the "Live Without a Husband" article. It could have been the Count poking fun at himself, or a friend making a joke, but the message and the odds suggest it was Katy.

† One jazz scholar called that the "Carmela Soprano approach"—getting a life of luxury in return for turning a blind eye—and it wasn't just Catherine's, but Louis's wives' and Duke's mistresses'. Riccardi interview.

But in a sign of our times, the sordid deeds of all these leading lights are surfacing, to the detriment of their legacies. How, we rightfully ask now, could men so determined to heal the world cause such hurt at home? The wives and lovers of Duke, Satchmo, and the Count grudgingly came to tolerate their bad behavior because, as Catherine asked, "Where is either Bill or myself going after twenty-four years of marriage?" But the affairs left deep marks. The men said it would be different if only they could be home more; their women knew better. As the bandleaders accumulated enough money and clout to set their own schedules, being away so much became a matter of choice more than necessity. "That was a part of their existence that wasn't the greatest," said a close friend of both Bill and Katy who asked not to be named. "And it hurt her. Hurt her. Hurt her."

In the Count's case, the flirting and philandering predated Catherine, as Vivian Winn Basie could have warned her. He'd been even more of a swinger in those wild years in Kansas City and the territories beyond. Drummer "Papa" Jo Jones remembers what Bill was like then: "We go to a party and there's Bette Davis and she's sitting on the piano bench. Basie rubbed his ass against hers and said, 'I'm not gonna wash my ass for a month!' Goddamn! Basie would rather play a cesspool than play in a king's palace."

Linda Gerber, whose father Jay McShann was another luminary of the Black jazz scene in Kansas City, says that "marrying a musician is not an easy thing." Young women hung around the jazzmen, tempting them, although not much temptation was needed. Gerber's father left her mother for a woman who was younger and was white. Everyone heard the gossip—of male owners of boardinghouses staying up all night to keep their musician-guests away from their daughters and wives, and bandsmen artfully avoiding cities where paternity suits were pending. In Basie's case there were rumors of affairs with Billie Holiday and perhaps with Holiday's would-be biographer, Linda Kuehl, who died before she could finish her book.* When *60 Minutes'* Dan Rather asked the Count about the "women who hung around the band," Basie answered snappily, "You stash them questions. You are going to get a lot of people in trouble around here."

––––

* Basie deflected nearly all of Kuehl's questions when she interviewed him, which frustrated her and raised the question why he agreed to talk to her in the first place. "The interviewer got five hundred bucks, the interview subject got $2,000," explained jazz historian Dan Morgenstern. "So that [Kuehl-Basie session] became known as the $2,000 interview." Author interview of Morgenstern.

Edward Ellington worried less than Bill Basie about getting into trouble, in part because he'd been away from Edna so long that they were essentially common-law divorcees. But while he professed his love for women in florid lyrics along with a long memoir, the only way to see how he truly felt was to watch what he did. He kept a steady diet of one-nighters with a dash of three-somes. Some of his ladyloves were gangly or corpulent; others were blonde and brunette dreamboats. There were Caucasians and Negroes, matrons and their daughters, hangers-on whose names he never asked and headliners like Lena Horne and Fredi Washington. He'd hand keys to different hotel rooms to three or four ladies, deciding later which to return to. When he was finished, he'd pass his conquests to bandmates. Irving Mills once offered to bankroll whomever he picked from the lineup at a Paris brothel; Duke: "I'll take the three on the end." After his death, at least two improbable women swore plans had been made for them to become the next Mrs. Ellington. In the end, four of his mistresses stood out and offered keys to the dukedom.

The first was Mildred Dixon. Short and polished, with her wavy black hair generally tied in a bun like a ballerina's, the dark-eyed beauty from Boston was half of the famed dancing duo of Mildred and Henri. They opened at the Cotton Club the same December night in 1927 that Ellington's band did, and Duke couldn't help but notice Mil. She had everything he was looking for then—intellect and grace, the capacity to get along with band members and their sometimes temperamental wives, and a willingness to tolerate not just Ellington's refusal to divorce his wife but his refusal to stay faithful to her. His "Sweet Bebe" accepted a living situation that would have unnerved a less stalwart companion. Duke left behind his clothes and other belongings with Edna and moved with Mildred into an elegant Harlem apartment where he also moved his mother, father, sister, and son, but where he himself spent limited time given his touring.

That arrangement lasted for a decade, looking enough like a marriage that many assumed it was. When he moved out to be with his next mistress, he again abandoned his clothes, his sister, and his son. "After he and Mil had come to the parting of the ways, we realized that if we didn't change our res-idence he would never come back to live with us, or even visit us, because he didn't want to come back to face Mil," Mercer remembered. "So we left the apartment, left all the furniture and everything with Mil, and moved further up the street." As a sign of loyalty along with guilt, Duke continued for years to pay Mildred's bills and employ her at the family music company.

The next woman to capture his heart was another fair-skinned Negress who worked at the Cotton Club, Beatrice "Evie" Ellis. She was called a chorus girl, but unlike Mildred, who was an artist, all that was asked of Evie was to decorate the stage by parading around in a gown, looking beautiful the way Edna had. Duke soon moved in with her on St. Nicholas Place, just across the park from Mildred. He stayed with Evie for the rest of his life, which was three times longer than he'd been with Edna or Mildred. Yet while newspapers referred to her first as his wife, which was how he introduced her to some friends, then as his widow, she was neither.* "Evie was very much obsessed with the idea of becoming Mrs. Ellington, but somehow he was able to persuade her that if he were to get a divorce from my mother, it would be a very expensive undertaking," said Mercer. "Wouldn't she rather see him have more money? She went along with the idea and that was where she made her mistake. Instead of saying, 'I'd rather have you and be poor,' she had said, 'I'd rather wait for the money.'"

Whatever her lawful title, Evie played the role of First Lady, accepting all the good and bad that came with it. He called her "darling doll" and telephoned at bedtime wherever he was in the world, assuring her that he loved her madly, as he famously told ladies around the globe. She kept his house and kept him safe from other women who wanted him to commit, the way Edna once had, letting him tell them, "I have to go back to Evie." Also like Edna, Evie had a gun and more than once threatened to use it on Duke. She lived in luxurious settings, with a Cadillac and a bank account big enough to buy Duke pair after pair of gold heart-shaped cufflinks, but increasingly she lived like a hermit, almost as despondent and embittered as Edna. Duke needed her, as he'd concede each time he came home to her over thirty-five years, yet sadly for both of them, she never was enough.

The other women generally disappeared almost as fast as they arrived, but one who stuck around was Fernanda de Castro Monte, Duke's paramour of choice the last decades of his life. They met in 1960 in Las Vegas, where she was singing in the Tropicana Lounge and he was playing at the Riviera. Tall and striking, and twenty years his junior, she had blond hair and not just light but white skin. Duke introduced her as a contessa, and while like him she only pretended to be royalty, she actually was schooled in five languages, nearly all the arts, and the joys of caviar, escargot, and foie gras. She was mainly with him overseas, where she remained by his side except when

---

* Duke preferred that the press not refer to his women friends at all, and he did what it took to make that happen, from paying off reporters to feeding gossip columnists juicy stories on other celebrities so there wouldn't be ones on him. Their doorbell label, meanwhile, made clear that the apartment belonged to Bea Ellis and Edward K. Ellington. Mercer Ellington, *Duke Ellington in Person*, 77–78.

the State Department or other nervous sponsors hid her away, rightfully fearing that a Black man with a white woman—especially one wearing suede suits with slits at the sides, long eyelashes above thick makeup, and revealing tops—would shock his hosts in India, Turkey, and other lands where, like in much of America, that was verboten. She held court in his hotel suite, calling him Dukie and confiding to an Ellington biographer that after she met him, she abandoned her singing and "became his slave."

Her genuine life story remains a mystery. Why, for instance, would she wait for Duke at the border in certain countries, refusing to enter? Did she hail from Algeria, Brazil, Argentina, or perhaps the Bronx, which her accent suggested to some? She had a sense of drama, getting his attention at first by sending dozens of roses to his dressing room, and later by taking an over-dose of sleeping pills. To keep him close, she'd sometimes follow him into the men's room. Her expensive tastes were legendary, including glittery rings and other pricey jewelry that Duke paid for. She packed his bags, cleaned his dressing room, served as a blend of social secretary, culinary counsel, and translator, and eased doubts that crept in as he aged.

With the countess on hand, everything was an adventure, as Mercer re-called of her seeing Duke off at the railroad station: "She was very smartly dressed in a mink coat. Just as the train was about to pull out, she opened the coat. She had nothing at all on under it, and she wrapped it around him to give him his good-bye kiss. With that, she left him to cool off. He thought it wonderful, and the whole episode stimulated his imagination [to] no end. Several of the men and I—not to mention a couple of open-mouthed ob-servers on the station platform—saw it happen and could hardly believe it."

Evie and Fernanda each knew about the other. Duke made clear to the former that he had no intention of giving up his road girlfriends, especially this one, and he made clear to his sister, his son, and others close to him that infidelity was unacceptable for anyone but him. The countess, mean-while, believed Evie was his wife, not just a stay-at-home lover, but wasn't concerned.

Even the contessa wasn't enough in his last five or so years. That was when he took up with Betty McGettigan, a white Catholic mother of four from suburban Menlo Park who showed up at the Fairmont Hotel on San Francisco's Nob Hill when Duke visited in 1969, beseeching him to perform at a benefit for her local youth symphony. The two had a Chinese dinner in his room, talking past midnight, and became not just friends but lovers. Betty, who was just over half Duke's age, eventually left her husband for him.

Betty was a late-life distraction for Duke. He'd call and tell her to meet him in a far-off city, and would mail a plane ticket. She'd show up with four dictionaries and a thesaurus, for their word games, along with travel books that she'd read to him about exotic lands he was about to visit. Both were night creatures, but while she wanted to talk, he wanted to watch *Gunsmoke*. She adjusted. Given her race, they had to dream up ruses like her checking in to a room a floor below his or her ducking into an anteroom when room service arrived. She described herself as his musical collaborator; his family and managers called her his secretary. Whatever the reality, their fitful encounters—by phone more than in person—lasted longer than most of his, extraordinary for a septuagenarian who was simultaneously involved with Evie, Fernanda, and a coterie of others.

Like many of Duke's dalliances, this relationship left collateral damage of a kind he likely didn't know or care about. Betty's marriage, which she said was weak to begin with, shattered. She moved out on Christmas Eve and took with her to a motel twelve-year-old Michael, their one child still living at home. With no financial support from Duke, she found what work she could, at a dry cleaner and a bookstore. Yet looking back, she had no regrets: "I was thrown into a whole different world and I loved it. If I ever do write about him," she added, "I'll probably start it out by saying, 'I think I reminded him of him.'"

Betty's family was less resilient and forgiving. Daughter Mary remembers that her father "was devastated . . . it scarred my younger brother for a long time . . . my sister and my mother didn't talk for twenty years because of that." Before Duke arrived, Mary adds, hers was a *Leave It to Beaver* household. Afterward "it completely blew up my family!"

Mary carries her own scar. She was seventeen then, living in France, and at her mother's suggestion she connected with the band when it was in Geneva. She hit it off romantically with Mercer, whom she calls "a gentleman's gentleman," and she accompanied the band to London. What happened next was extraordinary: Duke himself "hit on me . . . he came on to me and I said, 'No! We can't—you're involved with my mother! I can't do this. And I'm with your son, you know. This is *not* going to happen.' And it didn't happen . . .

"[Duke] didn't press, he didn't push it or anything," recalls Mary. "It was almost part of room service . . . It was like, OK, well, you're here in London and I can hit on you." Mary adds that years later, when she told her mother what Duke had done, "she didn't believe me."

Duke had come to feel entitled. There's no doubt women were drawn to this rangy golden-skinned piano player, which in turn impressed the men in his orbit. They watched as the conductor roguishly doled out his charm.

He told Evie and countless others that they'd inspired his composition "Satin Doll." "My mother always told me to gravitate toward beauty, so I had to come see you" was one of the rehearsed lines that a friend dubbed "crotch warmers." Another, which worked like catnip with older women: "Whose pretty little girl are you?" The thirty-two-year-old Queen Elizabeth II asked in 1958 how long it had been since he was in Britain. Duke answered, "1933, Your Majesty, years before you were born."

Trumpeter Clark Terry "knew a couple of ladies who told me that Duke could talk to them on the telephone and cause them to have a *climax*." Biographer Don George said another lady confided, "I love him so much, I douche with Lavoris."

The come-ons worked because women made the fateful error of believing them. Betty was convinced she was *the one*, the same way Fernanda, Evie, Mildred, and Edna had been. That was part of Duke's power to control and manipulate, the same as he did with his bandmates and family. So was this Casanova a hard-edged misogynist or a tenderhearted romantic? Both personas existed within him, as he told the world in songs and writings. He needed women in his life and celebrated them, but he hedged his bets, always keeping several close and staying dead-set against being tied down. He saw the act of sex as a God-given gift, comparing it to a sensuous aria that "moves with that certainty to a distinct tempo of feeling, sings itself happily, steadily, working, working, to a screaming, bursting climax of indescribable beauty and rapture and then throbs, spent and grateful in a re-dedication for the next movement of its perfection."* But he remained wary of his carnal partners, advising, "Love her madly, Friday through Friday if necessary, respect her. But watch her. She has more ways to destroy you than the Soviet Army."

That love-hate incongruity and ticklish juggling of lovers, Duke said, "keeps my juices flowing, and that's where I get all my ideas for the music I write." While seldom alone, he often was lonely. He attributed it to the life of the roving minstrel, but that was the only existence that suited him and enabled his promiscuity. He confessed his truest lover in his memoir, in words that could have come from Louis Armstrong or Count Basie: "Lovers have come and gone, but only my mistress stays. She is beautiful and gentle. She waits on me hand and foot. She is a swinger. She has grace. To hear her

---

* Less poetically, he confided, "We can't permit anything to interfere with man's inalienable right to have a little pussy on the side." Carter Harman interviews of Duke Ellington; and George, *Sweet Man*, 28.

speak, you can't believe your ears. She is ten thousand years old. She is as modern as tomorrow, a brand-new woman every day, and as endless as time mathematics. Living with her is a labyrinth of ramifications. I look forward to her every gesture.

"Music is my mistress, and she plays second fiddle to no one."

———

Louis Armstrong could have tutored his fellow maestros in how to juggle wives and girlfriends if they'd ever talked about such things, which these three didn't. His unfaithfulness couldn't have been a surprise to his last three brides, since each had been his mistress before she was his spouse. As for Daisy, his first, she made her living at a brothel where monogamy was unheard of and everyone soon would hear of Louis's rakishness. He boastfully rivaled even the Don Juan–like Duke, with one Armstrong scholar guesstimating that he had "hundreds" of extramarital escapades—from secretaries to chambermaids—and another saying they are "uncountable."

To take one case, just before he left New Orleans he ran into Irene, an old girlfriend. After two or three drinks, "we were Right in the mood for a very fine Session of Romance. But I was very Careful in asking Irene who was her Sweet Man." Neither of them thought to ask how Daisy would feel about her husband going to bed with another woman. Likewise with Fanny Cotton, the chorus girl he met in New York while he was married to but living apart from Lil. And nightclub entertainer Polly Jones, who filed a $35,000 breach-of-promise suit claiming that Louis had committed to wed her but instead married Alpha. And Velma Ford, his secretary and "sweetheart" when Lucille was his wife, whose services, whatever they were, he deemed worthy of gifting her a Fleetwood Cadillac.

Lucille was understanding of Louis's ways, to a point. They almost reached that Rubicon in 1945, just three years after they were married. He'd moved out of his and Lucille's apartment in Los Angeles, where he was performing, and was temporarily living nearby with Mama Lucy. "All is not well, in fact all is far, far from well in the Louis Armstrong ménage here," Lawrence Lamar, head of the Negro Press Bureau, wrote in the *Amsterdam News*. "A rift that can be well authenticated here as true, has broken out with great suddenness and threatens to see the matrimonial ship piloted by the famed King of the Trumpet and his ex-chorine glamour girl wife, Lucille Wilson, crash on the shores of marital difficulties." The trigger this time wasn't Louis's proven two-timing, but allegations that Lucille was following suit, with some of Satchmo's "own alleged male friends." Louis told Lamar that he'd become suspicious when Mama Lucy was staying at the Armstrongs' place, and a caller hung up after she picked up the phone. The story ends with Satchmo's vow that henceforth he "might love all, but [will] marry nary."*

Louis almost certainly planted this problematic explanation with a reporter he knew was sympathetic. It made him seem like the victim when no proof existed then or ever of Lucille's having an extramarital affair. He was taking a huge gamble, trusting that publicly embarrassing his wife and twisting the facts wouldn't push her to make the split permanent. It suggested what a polished spinmeister he'd become, and how he realized that his stardom mattered more than facts to the press, especially in a case of he-said, she-said in an era when the gender imbalance was so skewed. His bet paid off. They stayed married for thirty years, even if going forward Brown Sugar had to tolerate adultery by Satchmo that outpaced even the Count's and Duke's.

Such perfidy laid bare Louis's outlook on women. Growing up in an all-female environment—enveloped by his mother, grandmother, sister, and neighborhood prayer sisters—he'd come to respect womenfolk, none more than Mayann. But patriarchy ruled in the Waif's Home and on the New Orleans streets, and young Louis's attitude hardened if only to keep pace. He took to heart Black Benny Williams's advice on mating, the same as he had on managers, to wit: "Always remember, no matter how many times you get Married—Always have another woman for a Sweetheart on the outside."† That, Louis explained in a letter to Joe Glaser written thirteen years into his marriage to Lucille, is "why I have several Chicks that I enjoy *whaling with* the same as I do with Lucille. And She's, Always had the Choicest *Ass* of them All." It wasn't just him, he told a Voice of America interviewer, but all jazzmen: "We musician think about nothing but ballin' all the time."

Louis did have one other thing on his mind: procreating. He wanted it to happen so badly he believed it had when one of his mistresses assured him that her baby was his, despite a half century of evidence that he was infertile. Lucille "Sweets" Preston, a successful vaudeville dancer and longtime Armstrong paramour, gave birth in 1955 to a girl named Sharon whom Louis embraced from the start, but at a distance. He wrote Sweets

---

* Another interviewer wrote, "Nowadays when there's a slight difference of opinion in the household (at which time she calls him 'Dipper') and the madam threatens to put the master out, he just laughs and laughs and says, 'I am going nowhere! You got a lot of rooms here, just give me one of those upstairs floors.'" Lucille Armstrong and Cunnington, "Life with Louis," LAHM.
† Benny didn't just live by that counsel, he died by it when he was shot by a jealous girlfriend named May Daughter. Bergreen, *An Extravagant Life,* 140.

adoring letters signed "your future husband," regularly visited mother and baby armed with gifts, sent checks to cover the rent, bought them a three-story home with a wraparound porch in Mount Vernon, New York, and filled the growing girl's private-school tuition and college funds. It was all done on the q.t. Lucille Armstrong knew, and even wrote the checks along with Glaser, yet the world remained in the dark for half a century, until Sharon—saying she was tired of being "invisible"—co-wrote a book and starred in a film. Both were titled *Little Satchmo*.

But was she? Lucille Armstrong didn't believe it. Louis, she insisted, "couldn't make a baby with a pencil," was "stupid" for believing Sweets's claims, and, as Lucille swore in an affidavit after Louis died, "the deceased never had any children." Joe Glaser was equally skeptical, proposing that Louis and Sharon compare their blood, but the tests apparently never were done. Louis, however, told himself that after decades of trying, he finally had "*Struck Oil*—and planted that cute little Baby."

Whatever his relationship was to Sweets and Sharon, Louis made clear in his 1955 letter to Glaser that he had no plans to leave his wife and no doubts that he was asking a lot of her to put up with his faithlessness: "You know deep down in your heart, that I love my wife Lucille + She love's Me. Or else we wouldn't been together this long. Especially' doing the Crazy things that I usually do *Kicks*. That's why I love her, because she's smart. The Average woman would have "Quit' my 'ol ass—long long ago. The Woman understands me and there's no, ifs' and ans' about it."

KEEPING THE FAITH

ARSONS AND PRIESTS blamed jazz and jazzmen for everything reprehensible in midcentury America, from soaring rates of juvenile crime to the scourges of drugs and sex. Duke Ellington's music is "just considered worldly," and when people become Christians, "they stop their worldly ways," counseled the Rev. John D. Bussey, explaining why the local Baptist Ministers Conference in 1966 unanimously passed his resolution opposing an Ellington performance in Washington, D.C. And it wasn't just Duke. Years before, a religion editor at the African American–focused *Pittsburgh Courier* denounced Satchmo's "sacrilegious desecration of Spirituals." *Ladies' Home Journal,* meanwhile, wanted to know, "Does Jazz Put the Sin in Syncopation?"

Given such bad blood, one might imagine that Satchmo, Duke, and the Count steered clear of the houses of God that their parents had corralled them into as children, and even God himself. They did not.

All three maestros believed in God, prayed before every meal, and read the Bible, in Duke's case cover to cover and time after time. They also wove their religion into their music. They knew the rip-roaring roots of the melodies they loved had been planted by Black Baptists, Methodists, and especially the Pentecostals. Whatever commandments they were breaking—and there were plenty, from slighting the Sabbath to serial adultery—believers and agnostics, teenagers and grandparents, were swinging to their jazzed-up renderings of hymns like "When the Saints Go Marching In." The trio's emergence as evangelists happened quietly enough that few noticed, at least at first.

Two who did were Popes Pius XII and Paul VI, who invited Satchmo and Lucille for private audiences at the Vatican that delighted the pontiffs as much as they did the Armstrongs. Pius had been a jazz fan since he was a young priest, and told Louis how much he relished his records. Paul, who was accompanied by a pair of cardinals and two Swiss Guards, asked if the Armstrongs had children. Louis shot back: "No. But we're having a lot of fun trying," a risqué reference that, rather than embarrassing the reform-minded cleric, cracked him up. The trumpeter, who was baptized a Catholic but spent his youth attending more raucous Baptist and Sanctified churches, had insisted that "I don't fall to my knees for any man" when told it was tradition to bow in the papal presence. Then, according to a witness, he was "the first of us to hit the floor."*

Bill Basie had his own religious pedigree. Two uncles were ministers, and his father was a founder and pillar of Red Bank's Pilgrim Baptist Church. The Count's use of historic call-and-response in his performances mimicked the Black experience brought over from Africa and sustained during slavery's most ferocious days. Sideman Sweets Edison compared the Basie band to church organists and singers who inspired congregants to "get up to shout . . . that's moving you spiritually." Drummer Jo Jones agreed, saying he unexpectedly stayed with the orchestra for a decade because it "operated on a strange spiritual and mental plane."

Nobody in the world of music was more God-fearing than Duke, who devoted his last years to creating a series of sacred concerts that blended musical elements from jazz, classical, choral, spirituals, gospel, and blues. Suddenly, he was getting more invitations to play in churches than in dance halls. Synagogues, too. "These are things people don't know about him," said singer-songwriter Herb Jeffries. "He had a great ministry. It was hidden in his music . . . He was practicing his ministry moving about here and there, making people happy!" When a reporter asked how could he, "as a religious man, play in dark, dingy places where depravity and drunkenness reign," Ellington whispered, "Isn't that exactly what Christ did—went into the places where people were, bringing light into darkness?"

After holding his religious feelings close for his first sixty years, Duke opened up in the last ten. Sensing not just his vulnerability but his mortality,

---

* As always, Louis blended solemnity with irreverence. On the drive to see Pope Paul in 1968, nineteen years after his audience with Pope Pius, Satchmo took out a fat marijuana cigarette and said, "Let's light up," according to publicist and producer Ernie Anderson, who accompanied the Armstrongs. Anderson demurred, but "Louis lit up anyway and smoked the whole joint himself." And while waiting for the pontiff at his summer residence, Satchmo cried, "I've got to shit." Shown to a bathroom, he summoned Lucille, saying, "Come in here and see the Pope's toilet." Ernie Anderson, "Joe Glaser & Louis Armstrong."

But looking back afterward he got serious again, saying, "I shall never forget" that day, and calling the pope "such a fine man . . . Speaks everybody's language . . . And talk about anything you wish to talk about." Armstrong, "Europe—with Kicks."

he pushed back against preachers who'd accused him of defiling their churches with his concerts. "Some people ask me what prompted me to write the music for the sacred concerts. I have done so not as a matter of career, but in response to a growing understanding of my own vocation," he wrote in his memoir. "I think of myself as a messenger boy, one who tries to bring messages to people, not people who have never heard of God, but those who were more or less raised with the guidance of the church." The sacred concerts, this most accomplished of composers and bandleaders added, are "the most important thing I have ever done."

———

All three maestros were weaned on the church, and absorbed more than most kids sitting in those pews.

Louis learned to sing attending services and Sunday school, especially when his born-again mother started taking him to a Sanctified church when he was about ten. That holiness or Pentecostal movement occupied the lowermost rung of Protestantism socioeconomically and the top of the ladder when it came to praying, swaying, and testifying. "The 'whole 'Congregation would be 'Wailing—'Singing like 'mad and 'sound so 'beautiful,'" Satchmo remembered.* "I'd have myself a 'Ball in 'Church, *especially* when those 'Sisters 'would get 'So 'Carried away while 'Rev' (the preacher) would be 'right in the 'Middle of his 'Sermon. '*Man* those 'Church 'Sisters would '*begin* 'Shouting 'So—until their 'petticoats would '*fall* off. Of course 'one of the 'Deacons would 'rush over and 'grab her—'hold her in his 'Arms (a sorta 'free 'feel) and 'fan her until 'she'd '*Come* 'to."

"My heart went into every hymn I sang," Armstrong added, and "I am still a great believer and I go to church whenever I get the chance." With so much of his later life spent traveling, and Saturday night performances typically stretching into Sunday, that wasn't often. But he didn't have to be in a sanctuary to say grace at meals or sense a celestial power. He eventually found a way to bring that ecstatic expression to listeners, starting in his youth with funeral processions in New Orleans. Nearly half a century later, Satchmo released an album the church sisters would have loved entitled *Louis and the Good Book,* with gassed-up versions of spirituals including "Go Down Moses," "Nobody Knows the Trouble I've Seen," and "When the Saints," which he recorded 106 times and had become the anthem of the Big Easy.

It wasn't just big-city Black churchgoers who saw something in jazz that

———

* *Wailing* was a word that Louis used to describe his playing, defecating, and fornicating. Charles Hersch, *Subversive Sounds,* 190.

they recognized and related to, but rural white worshippers, too. The gospel roots of the music of Satchmo, Duke, and the Count are undoubtedly a big reason they were boundlessly adored. It helped that all three maestros adhered to a creed that was distinctly ecumenical. "As far as religion," Louis explained, "I'm a Baptist and a good friend of the Pope, and I always wear a Jewish star for luck."*

The Count's Baptist roots were a bit more buttoned down, but equally inclusive and resonant, especially when they were reinforced by his wife Catherine. In oral histories and writings, one after another of his sidemen and friends used the word *spiritual* to describe his presence and what he brought to the band. "Prior to eating, he would do this elaborate silent prayer," recalls tenor-saxophonist Eric Schneider. "If the food came and he was still praying, or silently meditating, it was understood that we should go ahead and eat." And like Louis, Bill Basie put his faith into his music, with fifteen songs with religious themes or imagery, from "Silent Night" and "Christmas Jive Routine" to "Hallelujah, I Love Her So."

Duke took that sensibility to a higher level. As a child he attended church twice on Sundays, at his father's African Methodist Episcopal Zion and his mother's Baptist. As a young man he consulted the Bible twice every day, sometimes taking it into the bathtub and reading until the water got cold. Asked what one book he'd bring to a deserted island, he didn't hesitate: "the Bible, because all the other books are in it."† He told friends, "I'd be afraid to sit in a house with people who don't believe. Afraid the house would fall down." He wouldn't eat without saying grace and while he shunned most jewelry, he wore a gold crucifix around his neck and carried a St. Christopher medal in his hip pocket. His Christmas card bore a simple message, in gold lettering: LOVE GOD.

Don George, Duke's friend and sometimes lyricist, cataloged Ellington's iniquities, but he was surprised to discover Duke's sublime side during a New Year's Eve party when he encountered the bandleader alone in a small room: "He was kneeling, his eyes closed, his head bowed, his hands folded across his chest. He was praying aloud. I didn't move, not wishing to disturb him . . . He prayed for strength to keep him humble, to appreciate what he had, and to keep fame, money and women secondary to his love for God . . .

---

* He also wore two Catholic medals and kept a supply of matzo in his kitchen "so I can *Nibble* on them any time that I want to eat late at night." Armstrong, *In His Own Words*, 11.
† He offered this whimsical twist on a biblical pronouncement: "Bread cast upon the water comes back buttered on *both* sides." Ruff, *Call to Assembly*, 5.

As I listened to my brother kneeling there, a glorious feeling overpowered me, a feeling of great ecstasy. I fell to my knees beside Duke, and for the first time in my life I prayed."

Like the Count and Satchmo, Duke embraced a nonsectarian spirituality. "I was his pastor, one of his pastors. He had rabbis and Episcopal priests," said the Rev. John Gensel, a Lutheran and New York's famous jazz minister. "In religion he was neither Jew nor Greek or Protestant or Catholic . . . He was universal." Or as Duke himself said repeatedly, "Every man prays in his own language, and there is no language that God does not understand."

After his mother's death in 1935, Duke turned to his faith, but comfort remained elusive. He read his Bible three more times that year and started wearing his cross necklace. He cried for days and remained depressed for months. Writing "Reminiscing in Tempo" helped. Ultimately, he recognized that neither his mother nor his God would have wanted him to wallow.

Thirty years later, an invitation to present a concert of sacred music at San Francisco's Grace Cathedral let him share with the public his feelings about his faith and everything else that mattered to him. "Now I can say openly," he wrote, "what I have been saying to myself on my knees." In that performance and two that followed, he dressed in blinding blues and deep purples and pinks and spoke directly to his cherished God, his beloved mother, and fears of his own demise. "He was quite taken with the [nineteenth century] story of the 'Juggler of Notre Dame,'" explained Mercer. "The man was a great juggler, who would sneak into the church and juggle before the altar. As the story goes, the priests found out about it and kicked him out. God intervened and told the priests to leave him alone. The man was celebrating his presence, by using the gifts that He gave him. That's how Pop felt about the *Sacred Concerts*."

Duke said he didn't care what the public thought of his sacred works—that they were between him and his deity—but he must have been offended when some church leaders denounced his compositions as a reflection of "this sin-sick world." A Christian radio and TV host in New Jersey blasted the New York concert's sponsor for contributing "to the apostasy that will one day become the world church under the anti-Christ." A national poll in the 1960s showed that, among Black preachers, just one in five wanted to let jazz or blues into their services.

Others, however, saw rapturous jazz as a way to win back rebellious youth and disenfranchised Blacks in that riotous and separatist decade of the 1960s. *New York Herald-Tribune* critic Alan Rich said Ellington's sacred music "is a powerful distillation of emotion and emotional gesture; it speaks, whether through a singer, a piano, a solo saxophone, or a set of drums, of tremendously personal things. As such it is never removed from the purest meaning of prayer." And writing in the Catholic publication *Ave Maria,* author and journalist Joe Brieg said Duke's religious work was part of "the great central historical truth of our time—the gradual ending of the great divorce between religion and the world" that fit just right with Pope Pius XII's plea for "the consecration of the world."

The feedback that moved Ellington the most, as he made clear in his memoir, came not from a journalist or a pastor, but from a girl who approached him after one concert and said, "You know, Duke, you made me put my cross back on!"

CRAVINGS AND DEPENDENCIES

D URING HIS HALF-CENTURY career Count Basie was consumed by twin passions—for the band the world knew well, and for the ponies known only to his tight-lipped band buddies.

As soon as the orchestra checked into a hotel, the Count invariably spun around and took off. Changing into casual clothes, he grabbed his black captain's hat, flagged a cab, and headed to the nearest track to watch the fleet-footed racehorses. At rehearsals, sidemen warmed up on their own while Basie sat in the corner, poring over the racing form, calculating the odds and considering his bets. Once, when the band was in Europe waiting for a train, "a woman was standing next to us with a greyhound dog," recalled saxophonist Frank Wess. "And Basie asked the woman, 'Can he run?'"*

"Basie was the sweetest cat in the world, but a serial, black-belt gambling junkie," said producer Quincy Jones. "He'd go to the roulette table and put $100 on every number—zero, double zero, one through eighteen, nineteen through thirty-six, black and red, odd and even . . . With one hand at the roulette wheel, Basie was simultaneously placing his bets with the other hand at the closest blackjack table; from there he'd segue to the telephone to call his bookie."

A multitasker, the Count would place wagers on the ponies from East Coast to West, and as far away as Ireland, while in the middle of a high-stakes card game. "I'd finish a show at midnight," added Jones, "gamble with him for four hours, go to bed, or whatever, and wake up to find Basie downstairs still in the casino, gambling at noon, still wearing his tux from the

---

* Composer Sammy Nestico, who watched the Count spend his royalty checks at the track, wrote for his friend a song "dedicated to all the horses he bet on." Nestico called it "Hay Burner," which is an old horse that continues to eat expensive hay but can no longer win races. Author interview of Nestico.

night before. They had slot machines in the Vegas airport, and after losing everything, Basie would still be dropping quarters into them until I dragged him aboard the plane."

On the one hand, that dependency would take less of a toll than the heroin, marijuana, and other drugs that jazzmen back then took more of than any other professionals. Yet the Count's endless betting and surefire losing carried a cost. Like most addicts, he believed the gambling only hurt himself; in fact, it affected his wife, daughter, and bandmates.

Gaming debts were the biggest reason the Count folded his big band in 1950 for two years, throwing half his sidemen out of work. Freddie Green, his guitarist and confidant, kept a ledger of personal loans Green made to band members when Basie couldn't meet his payroll or no longer had the money to help troubled employees. The red ink pushed the Count to tie his musical fortunes to mobsters and hustlers like Morris Levy and Teddy Reig. "Basie had lost his ass playing horses," remembered trumpeter Clark Terry. "He was working his behind out of debt. While doing so, the cats whom he owed said, 'You can run your band for salary, and we'll take so much every week out of your bread to get you back up to par.' He had problems like that all his life.

"Terry Reig, who worked as a liaison between Basie and the record man Morris Levy, he had practically taken everything, he almost owned Basie's band."

Basie admitted in his memoir that "Kate and I were right at home with all of those little clicking wheels and felt tables and galloping bones and slot machines." But he attributed such obsessions to his wife, saying "that, by the way, was something Katy turned me on to . . . She got me interested but didn't pass on any of her luck." In truth, he'd always been a plunger, and in fact, Katy was alarmed by his overindulgence. Once, she foiled the Count's scheme to hock her fur coats to cover his hapless bets. That, along with his infidelities, prompted her to put the family assets in her name and their daughter Diane's.

It was also why the Count never considered retiring. "We may well ask what kept [Basie] out there, rolling to the piano in a wheelchair during his last three years," said jazz historian Gary Giddins. "Some who knew him well said he had to work to pay off gambling debts. Some who knew him better said he incurred gambling debts as an excuse to keep working."

Gambling was his most obvious and longest-lasting addiction, but not his only one. He'd been enough of a boozer during his Kansas City years to fritter away his money and spawn a reputation as a hedonist, a gutter-dweller, and, in the words of his then wife Vivian, "nothing but a juice-head . . . nothing but a drunkard." While he tempered the drinking when he headed east, he still "didn't give a damn," said dancer Norma Miller. "He liked to smoke weed and everything else and you enjoyed it sitting there in the corner with him."* He sometimes joined the card and dice games band members played in the back of the bus, although he seldom won.† And while his band would earn a reputation as one of the cleanest in town when it came to drugs or alcohol, exceptions were made for such notorious abusers as Lester Young and Billie Holiday even as the band bus often reeked of hairspray, which was used to dull the whiff of marijuana.

"I used to drink a bit in those days, and we also used to do little strange things in the alley back of the hotel, little things called sevens and elevens and nines and sixes and snake eyes," the Count wrote. As for calming his nerves when he got on an airplane, "I always used to expect a little help from Mr. Scotch or Mr. Bourbon in a situation like that, but I can't really say that either one of them ever really helped me. Not much. Not enough."

Over time the Count took up healthier habits, like reading comic books (he leafed through them in bed, laughing out loud, and liked them most before reformers edited out the sex and violence in the 1950s), and watching shoot-'em-ups on TV (the more gunplay the better). But he never entirely gave up his more ruinous ones. Trumpeter Dave Stahl remembers how, in the 1970s, Basie hired a limo and took him to the racetrack. And drummer Duff Jackson says that, until the end, the Count was "a champion partier."

———

Duke Ellington had a handle on his partying and gambling, but was hamstrung by his irrational fears.

He was afraid of flying. He refused to do it at all in the early years—"If God had intended me to fly," he reasoned, "he would have leased me some wings"—and when he had no choice, he reached for his prayer beads and cross necklace. Compounding the problem, boats also frightened him. He remembered the sinking of the *Titanic*, and when his ships went on automatic pilot overnight, he'd pace the deck and soothe his nerves with cham-

---

* There were rumors, never proven, that the Count loved cocaine, which was easy to get back then in Kansas City.

† During one such rolling game, players were so intense that they wouldn't move to let drummer Sonny Payne get to the bathroom. He noticed that Basie had a brand-new briefcase and decided to use it as a toilet. Basie had a rare hand of good cards and didn't want to lose it, so he just yelled, "Don't let him get the contracts wet!" Harold Jones, *Singer's Drummer*, 77.

pagne and cognac.* In retrospect, both anxieties seem ironic for a man who preferred to let hard-driving, hard-drinking bandmate Harry Carney chauffeur him around.

Bad experiences often mushroomed into superstitions that stayed with him. He was afraid of most things green, which was the color of grass and, in his mind, associated with tombstones. He forbade yellow manuscript paper because he once was holding such when he had an accident in an elevator. He hated brown even worse since it was the color of the suit he was wearing when his beloved mother died.[†]

Drafts could cause colds, which he couldn't afford, so he kept the windows shuttered in his hotel rooms. Doing that, he said, carried a bonus: keeping out lightning. And he didn't believe in watches because he didn't want to rush through life.

Duke neither gave nor accepted gifts of slippers, shoes, or even socks, which he felt risked the recipient or presenter ending the friendship. "I made the mistake once of giving him a gift for his birthday, a pair of shoes. He says, 'No, no, no, don't do that, don't do that. That means you're going to be walking out of my life,'" remembered drummer Louie Bellson. "So I exchanged those for a blue sweater." The same thing applied to anything that cut, like a knife, which might sever a bond.

He also avoided dropped buttons or repaired trousers. "If a button is hanging by a thread or—even worse—has fallen off, that garment will never be worn by Duke again. It is up for grabs among the fellows in the band," said Rex Stewart. "Some of the men in his good graces who have coveted a beautiful top coat or sports jacket have been known to deliberately twist a button loose."

A few of his fears were common for performers, like it being bad luck to throw away opening-night telegrams from well-wishers, read reviews in the dressing room, or, when backstage, whistle or eat peanuts. The worries over buttons and knives were common folklore worthy of scientific names, *koumpounophobia* and *aichmophobia*. His greatest fear was death, to the point where he wouldn't discuss it or abide others doing that in his presence. He didn't make out a will or take out life or accident insurance. He postponed penning finales to his compositions, and procrastinated writing his

---

* The first time Duke was reported to have paced the decks like that was on his way to Europe in 1933 aboard the R.M.S. *Olympic,* and it wouldn't have eased his nerves had he known that it was a sister ship of the *Titanic.*

† Duke's favorite color was blue—Navy or French, cornflower, baby, or royal—for his walls, bedding, and clothing down to his shoes.

memoir. "If you write your autobiography, you die," Mercedes recalled her granddad saying.

Some Ellington superstitions were counterintuitive. He preferred to make decisions, sign contracts, or open gigs on Friday the thirteenth, an unlucky date to many. That traced back to his having had such a great opening on a Friday the thirteenth in 1931, at Chicago's Oriental Theater. He'd also lay bets on the number thirteen, or multiples of it.

It was surprising that he'd allow such fetishes and rituals to vie with the many he already carried around through his religion. "Most of these superstitions tended to persist," explained Mercer, "but every now and then he would pick one up, say, 'Well, there really isn't anything to this,' and discard it. He wasn't really superstitious about spilling salt, but just to be safe he'd throw some over his left shoulder."

Like Basie, Ellington had experienced other dependencies, some of which harmed his bandmates. He occasionally gambled to the point of not making payroll, admitted to being addicted to women, and hated losing so much that he would bet on every horse in a race. He also drank regularly—everything from moonshine to gin highballs—starting in his teens and continuing through his twenties and thirties, although always with the cease-before-you-embarrass-yourself pacing he had learned from his father. He stopped cold in the years after alcohol helped kill J.E. In later years his preferred drinks were, at meals, weak tea and hot water with lemon peel, and on the bandstand, Coca-Cola with precisely four teaspoons of sugar.

But Ellington sidemen never tempered their guzzling. Saxophonist Otto Hardwick would sometimes go missing for days, earning his nickname Professor Booze. Trumpeter Bubber Miley crawled under the piano to sleep off his benders, using talcum powder to cover the grime he'd get on his shirt. Trombonist Tricky Sam Nanton kept his whiskey bottle in his inside pocket, using a straw to sip while the band played. Ben Webster was a mean drunk, but sober he couldn't make his tenor sax sing the way it did when he was at least partly lubricated.* Sonny Greer was so potted one night that he fell backward off his drum stand, breaking a bone and nearly his neck. And if Billy Strayhorn's cancer hadn't killed him, his dipsomania would have.

---

* "Before a record date [Duke would] talk to Ben," said Mercer. "He'd call him up on the phone and if Ben was sober he'd take him out and go get him drunk and put him to bed about 4 o'clock and then wake him up at 8 and he knew that he would be less inhibited than if he was in there stone sober." Interview of Mercer Ellington, June 19, 1983, Yale.

Duke dealt with their drinking in subtle ways. When he'd spot a sideman who was sloshed he gave him one lengthy and bouncy solo after another, letting him know that he knew and hoping to embarrass him if not sober him up. It sometimes worked, but didn't treat the underlying addiction. Other band members caught on, though, and faked inebriation to get the solos that let them show off.

Drugs posed even more of a problem. There, too, Duke often turned a blind eye. Those who got high most frequently were dubbed the Air Force, and included singer Jimmy Grissom, trumpet player Willie Cook, multi-instrumentalist Ray Nance, and, saddest of all, saxophonist Paul Gonsalves. Gonsalves drank like a thirsty fish (other band members formed the Hide Behind Paul Club, knowing he'd be drunker than them and deflect attention), regularly fell asleep on the bandstand (sometimes he woke and played supine, others he had to be carted off like a vanquished boxer), and was addicted to heroin (his body was riddled with track marks). Nearly everyone in the band was at one time assigned by Duke to sober up Paul—by putting him in a cold shower, feeding him uppers, or, in the case of the *Chicago Tribune*'s Harriet Choice, taking him to her mother's, who made dinner, limited his wine intake, then put him to bed. "I took him to the recording studio the next day," she recalls, "and Duke sent for a bottle. He was too sober."

In 1961 the law stepped in. Gonsalves and three other sidemen were arrested in Las Vegas, during a stint at the Riviera Hotel. Officers said they'd been investigating for two weeks and had found narcotics in the men's apartment. Also arrested was arranger William Henry Black, said to be carrying a concealed straight-edged razor. Ellington posted the $2,500 bail.* Nance, a repeat offender, received a sixty-day sentence, and the band was banished from Vegas for years. That wasn't the first time drugs proved embarrassing to the orchestra leader. Nine years earlier his secretary-chauffeur was arrested in New York and charged with selling marijuana from the boss's car.

Duke occasionally lost his temper with Paul, ordering him home from an overseas trip or actually hitting him in the face. But he'd quickly forget, as their father-son–like relationship turned Shakespearian. As for Ellington's general attitude about drugs, he made that clear after still another sideman

---

* Duke's superstitions kicked in with arrests, as everywhere. When a trumpet player was hauled off by the police, the bandleader banished from his playbook the tune that was being played (ironically, "Prisoner of Love"). He also instructed sometimes-flautist Jimmy Hamilton, "Don't play that flute. Every time you play that flute, somebody gets locked up." Hentoff, "Incompleat Duke Ellington."

who'd been an addict for a decade was imprisoned at the Tombs in Lower Manhattan. "I think we'd better keep him there until we leave town," Duke told his lawyer. "Him being on the street is a worse hazard than him being where he is now. If we wait until we get out on the road again, it'll be easier to detect trouble . . . You can't talk to those people because they always know more than Einstein. Besides, he's a wonderful musician and he's got three of the prettiest children you ever saw."

That attitude prevailed among orchestra leaders at midcentury. Society was just beginning to grapple with a drug crisis that would play out especially harshly on the bandstand. Psychologist Charles Winick, who surveyed more than four hundred jazz musicians in the mid-1950s, found that 82 percent had tried marijuana at least once and 23 percent were regular users. With heroin, 53 percent tried it at least once while 16 percent used it habitually. Liquor yielded to marijuana as the music scene moved north from New Orleans, and pot gave way to heroin with the entry of bebop. "Jazz musicians have traditionally been the occupational group most closely associated with the use of narcotic drugs, both in the United States and England," Winick said. "Physicians represent the only other occupational group which has . . . consistently been identified with drug addiction, but the incidence of addiction among physicians is generally believed to be much less than among jazz musicians."*

Names, as always with jazzmen, reflected their reality. They referred to towns where they performed as Potville. *Hip* in this context came from the atrophy of that joint that opium users suffered when they lay on one side and balanced their drug device on the other. Popular tunes were laced with drug-related references, from Satchmo's "Muggles" to Duke's "Hop Head." As for jazz jargon, Winick wrote, "values are reversed," with, for instance, "terrible" describing "excellence." "It is a means of expressing fantasies and discontent with ordinary language and reality. The professional names of some famous jazz musicians have a fantasy element: Duke, Count, Lord, President, Lady, King, Bird."

––––––

* Winick's scientific and therapeutic approach to drugs contrasted sharply with Federal Bureau of Narcotics boss Harry J. Anslinger's law-and-order one. In "Marijuana: Assassin of Youth," Anslinger branded marijuana "as dangerous as a coiled rattlesnake . . . How many murders, suicides, robberies, criminal assaults, holdups, burglaries, and deeds of maniacal insanity it causes each year, especially among the young, can only be conjectured." And he said musicians, especially jazz ones, bore special blame for the deadly drug's spread. Anslinger, "Marijuana: Assassin of Youth."

Louis Armstrong didn't have to read about muggles or pot. He was, as grateful fans made clear, King of the Vipers.*

His marijuana adventure began like many of his others, in Chicago at age twenty-six, and it came courtesy of the so-called alligators, or white musicians who populated Black jazz clubs. "It was at the Savoy Ballroom that Louis was introduced to pot," according to then-pal Earl Hines. "There was no air conditioning in those days, and it was summertime and very hot inside the Savoy. So everybody was standing outside in the back, and I was right there, because I was always with Louis. 'I got a new cigarette, man,' a white arranger said to him. 'It makes you feel so good.' . . . So this guy lit it up, took a drag or two, and passed it around, and nobody would take it. 'Let me try it,' Louis finally said. So he tried it. It was pure marijuana, direct from Mexico, and it had an attractive odor, a little like the smell of those cigarettes people with asthma smoke."

Louis's memory of the moment was vivid, as always: "I'm telling you, I had myself a ball . . . That's 'why it really puzzles me to see Marijuana connected with Narcotics—Dope and all that kind of crap . . . It never did impress me as dope. Because my mother and her Church Sisters used to go out by the railroad track and pick baskets full of Pepper Grass, Dandelions, and lots of weeds similar to gage, and they would bring it to their homes, get a big fat slice of salt meat—and make one of the most 'deelicious pots of greens anyone would want to smack their lips on . . .

"My Mother always told me, to try anything at least once," he added. "You either like it or you don't."

His fondness for pot grew from a distraction to an obsession. "It makes me feel 'good as 'gracious," he said, arguing that it cleansed his mind much the way laxatives did his body. "He followed a regular routine practically every night. When he was through working and no one was left in his dressing room, he'd go back to his hotel, get undressed, and light up a joint," said bassist Milt Hinton. And it wasn't just at night. "When he got up in the morning, first thing he'd do is go to the bathroom and spend a half-hour there," said photographer-friend Jack Bradley. "He'd usually light up a bomber, which is a joint about the size of a pencil, and sit on the toilet."

Everyone who worked with or even knew him had a story about Pops

---

* In St. Louis in the early 1930s, six identically garbed men presented him with a foot-long joint shaped like a baseball bat with this inscription: "To the King of the Vipers, Louis Armstrong, from the Vipers Club of St. Louis." He and Billie Holiday were known among pot smokers as Queen Billie and King Louis. Brothers, *Master of Modernism*, 391–92; and Stanley Dance, *World of Earl Hines*, 211–12.

and pot. Of him giving band members a $5 bag of marijuana along with their $25-a-week paychecks. Of workmen hired by Lucille discovering a kilo of weed in a brown paper bag he'd stashed inside a wall. Of actress Tallulah Bankhead hiding a fat, meticulously rolled reefer in a bunch of long-stemmed roses she sent to his dressing room. And of him carrying the kind of cigarette case that was a standard accessory back then, only his smokes were filled with ganja, not tobacco.

He had enough money and the drug was cheap enough that he could easily afford a supply wherever he went, generally from the notorious dealer and clarinetist Mezz Mezzrow. Born Jewish as Milton Mesirow, he married a Black woman, moved to Harlem, declared himself a "voluntary Negro," and listed Negro on his draft card. Mezz's very name became slang for marijuana. "I'd like for you to start right in and pack me enough orchestrations to last me the whole trip," Satchmo wrote Mezz from the Queens Hotel in Birmingham, Alabama, in 1932. He wasn't, of course, talking about music scores. But he was clear where he wanted the cache sent: "to the American Express Company, Paris, France. If you mail it now, it'll about get there the same time as me. No doubt you've received the money I wired you, eh?"

Much the way young musicians were inspired by him to play the trumpet or try to sing with a froggy throat, so they followed Louis the evangelist into a world that a 1936 propaganda film labeled *Reefer Madness*.* "The first inkling of that I got was Louis Armstrong," said saxophonist Budd Johnson. "'Man, Louis gets high and blows and blows!' So we all used to get high as kids." It was the same for the trumpeter Buck Clayton, whose first taste of pot was when Satchmo handed him a joint in the bathroom. Buck's mother had warned him off drugs, "but with Louis Armstrong I would have done anything . . . That night I went home and I got down on my knees and I prayed to God. I said, 'Oh God, now that I'm a dope addict, please forgive me.'"

Armstrong's romance with gage didn't always go smoothly. He was arrested on felony drug charges in 1930 in Culver City, California, when he was playing at the West Coast Cotton Club. During an intermission, he and a friend, drummer Vic Berton, tried out Berton's can of Mexican golden leaf. "They were sitting in Louie's car, smoking a joint and rolling some more, when The Man came up behind them and flashed a light into the car, and a badge, and that was it," recalled Berton's brother Ralph, who was at the club

---

* Charlie Parker and Billie Holiday would play comparable roles as Pied Pipers for heroin.

that night. "We'll take the roach boys," said one of the two detectives, who'd been tipped off by a rival bandleader. The lawmen were such Armstrong fans that they let him finish the show. On the way to the station Louis had an unusual plea: "*Please* don't hit me in my chops." Detective: "I wouldn't think of anything like that." Louis: "Okay, ride me."

At his trial, the judge admonished Satchmo to "leave marijuana alone" and sentenced him to a month in jail, but he served just nine days thanks to the intervention of the Cotton Club's owner and other pooh-bahs. Louis's legal troubles drew intense press coverage that seemed to boost rather than dampen his popularity. And while his offense was considered serious back then, his recollections were fun-filled, as were Ralph Berton's likely embellished ones. His brother and Louis didn't do their time at an actual jail, as most accounts had it, but at a jail hospital. "In practice," Ralph wrote, "this meant driving downtown after work every night, parking in the space marked VISITORS, signing in, fooling around with the night nurses, going to bed in private rooms, not always alone, sleeping till noon, breakfasting with the day nurses, signing out, and going about their business. Justice was satisfied, and so, I presume, were quite a few of the nurses."

Things went down rather differently when federal agents arrested Lucille at her Honolulu hotel on New Year's Day in 1954; her eyeglass case concealed a joint and two roaches that she'd allegedly smuggled in on a flight from Japan. "I saw Louis the next day and he was absolutely furious, ranting and raving about being stopped and how badly he'd been treated," said Milt Hinton. "'I spread good will for my country all over the world and they want to put me in jail,' he yelled." But it wasn't him who'd been nabbed but Lucille, who ended up pleading guilty and escaped with a modest fine. Her lawyer told the press that she didn't "have conscious possession of the marijuana," which was true since it clearly belonged to Louis, not her.

The matter didn't end there, however. Two weeks later Louis penned a now-famous letter to Joe Glaser, venting his spleen against the country's drug laws: "Gage ain't nothing but medicine." He railed against his wife's arrest: "Can you imagine anyone giving Lucille all of those headaches and grief over a mere small pittance such as gage, something that grows out in the backyard among the chickens?" And he lamented the way they'd humiliated an altruist like him: "What colored or white . . . are doing as much for humanity's sake as I am?" Telling his manager he had "never been as serious with you, Mr. Glaser, as I am about to get right now," he had a very specific request: "You must see to it that I have special permission to smoke all the reefers that I want to when I want or I will just have to put this horn down, that's all. It can be done. Nothing impossible, man."

It's impossible to know whether Glaser tried to pull strings to do what Armstrong asked, although it would have faced stiff odds since America then was toughening rather than loosening its antimarijuana laws. It is, however, known that Satchmo never was busted again for a habit he continued until his last years. Glaser, meanwhile, was "scared to death Louie would get busted and he'd lose the goose that lay the golden age," said Jack Bradley. Their running argument about pot, Bradley added, went like this: "Glaser would scream and Louis would say, 'Fuck you.'"

It is no coincidence that not long after he wrote to his manager, Louis started on another memoir, one whose focal point was marijuana. He didn't finish it until 1959, and it wasn't published during his lifetime although parts found their way into print forty years later. Just why it vanished for so long is uncertain; it could have been lost, or Glaser could have squelched it, petrified that straightlaced fans would be offended by Louis's homage to the drug he lovingly referred to as gage, muta, pot, and "that *good shit*." "It's a thousand times better than whiskey," he wrote.[*] "It's an Assistant—a friend a nice cheap drunk if you want to call it that . . . Good (very good) for Asthma— Relaxes your nerves . . . Great for cleanderness . . . Much different than a dope fiend."[†]

The debate over pot raged then, and hasn't cooled down even as Armstrong's dream of legalization has been realized in state after state. We know now that it can be addictive, like it was for Louis, and can aggravate depression, like it may have for him. It is healthier than the blend of heroin and alcohol that helped kill Billie Holiday, Charlie Parker, and Paul Gonsalves, and served as a psychoactive crutch, much the way gambling did for the Count and submitting to superstition for Duke. Marijuana cigarettes irritated the lungs and aggravated the heart the same as the Camels Louis smoked and advertised ("so rich-tasting yet so mild"). There was nothing more import-

---

[*] While he said he was rip-roaring drunk only two or three times in his life, he did enjoy bourbon and slivovitz. Giddins, *Satchmo*, 42.

[†] Another story that circulated over the years had then vice president Richard Nixon encountering Satchmo at the airport in New York in 1958 and escorting him through Customs, unaware that the bandleader's suitcases contained three pounds of cannabis. Told later what he'd done, Nixon reportedly asked, "Louis smokes marijuana?" Armstrong scholar Ricky Riccardi said, "In the beginning, I wanted to believe it because it's such a good story," but after fact-checking Nixon's and Armstrong's schedules and other circumstances, "I wavered and now I think it's pure fiction." Riccardi, "Ambassador Satchmo Meets Tricky Dick?"

ant to Satchmo's playing and singing than his breathing, which occasionally presented problems including pneumonia, and his heart, which gave out in the end.

Louis apparently gave up gage the last few years of his life. "Many years ago I quit messing around with that stuff. Got tired looking over my shoulder and waiting for that long arm to reach out and somebody say, 'Come here, Boy. Twenty years in the cage!'" he informed an interviewer in 1967. And he told Jack Bradley, "Hey, man, I gotta tell you something—Mr. Glaser and the doctors finally convinced me to stop smoking shit." Then he whispered loudly, "But *don't tell anyone!*"

18

TOILET TRUTHS,
FOOD FETISHES, AND OTHER
MEDICAL MATTERS

VEN IN THE giddy world of jazz, most performers' business cards were strictly informational, bearing but a name and phone number. The ones that Louis Armstrong circulated were something quite other. Peering out from the card was a beaming Satchmo perched on a bathroom throne—pants around his knees, toilet paper presumably at the ready—ballyhooing the benefits of the herbal laxative Swiss Kriss with these inviting words: "Leave It All Behind Ya."

That love of laxatives was born in boyhood with something called Coal Rollers, the "little bitty black pills" that Mayann handed him, explaining that they "will throw off many symptoms and germs that congregate from nowheres in your stomach. We can't afford no doctor for fifty cents or a dollar . . . I want you to promise me you will take a physic at least once a week as long as you live. Will you promise?" Little Louis: "Yes, mother."

He more than kept that promise, becoming an apostle for purgatives much like he was for marijuana. Pot, he said, cleansed the mind, while laxatives sustained the body even as they drained it. First it was mineral salt–infused Pluto Water, then the antacid Bisma-Rex along with Swiss Kriss, a blend of plants like hibiscus and peach leaves and binding agents like microcrystalline cellulose.* He advertised it on his Christmas cards and stationery

---

* Herbs have been used as medicine in America since slave days, and more recently there's been a fascination with anticonstipation food, drugs, and devices. Popular laxatives in the 1920s and '30s—the Golden Age of Purgation—included Ex-Lax and Zam Zam. Louis was so enthusiastic that he signed his letters, "Pluto Waterly Yours" or "Swiss Krissly Yours." While such usage risked depleting him of essential electrolytes, that didn't happen, according to his doctor. Whorton, "Civilization and the Colon"; and Zucker interview, LAHM.

and trumpeted it on calling cards that he handed out—along with sample packets—to everyone from the pilot and passengers on airplanes to the British royal family. "You got the right diet, you're all right down here," he told scientists at Stanford Research Institute as he pointed to his abdomen. "No ulcers, no cancer." More lyrically, he testified that "the more you shit, the thinner you'll git. No shit."[†]

It's no surprise, then, that his favorite haunt at home was the bathroom, with floor-to-ceiling gold-rimmed mirrors that let him watch himself purge. "The laxative comes first in my life, then my wife," he told TV host David Frost. His most-read book was self-help guru Gayelord Hauser's *Diet Does It*. He and Lucille even co-authored their own nutrition guide, "Lose Weight the 'Satchmo' Way," that advocated lots of orange juice, sliced tomatoes (with lemon juice) or a salad, and generally eating "as much as you want to . . . from soup to nuts"—so long as, after lunch and dinner and before bed, you ingested a generous dose of a purgative "to cut gas, grease, and a lot of discomforts from a lot of foods and liquors that won't act right in your stomach."

He followed his own advice, dropping from 268 pounds to 170, which was a lot easier to carry on his five-foot-six-inch frame.

But there was more to the cards and the slogans than a love of the loo or a fascination with bodily functions. Even the most ordinary toilet seat was a perch of honor to a shoeless kid who grew up using a communal outhouse, with no money for doctors and his once-a-week laxative often coming from pepper grass Mayann picked by the railroad tracks, ground down at home, and had Louis wash down using water from the hydrant. He was well pleased with how far he'd come and remained loyal to those folklore remedies, some of which actually worked and all of which enhanced not just his Everyman image but that of jazzmen generally. And a steady diet of Swiss Kriss allowed him to keep eating on the run favorite foods like red beans and rice, deep-fried chicken, hominy grits, and Cracker Jack, all of which could weigh a person down if they weren't excreted soon and often.

Yet the home-health elixirs told only half of his later-life medical narrative, even if that was the part he preferred telling. The boy from the bayou who couldn't afford fifty cents for a medic now had both a personal doctor at

---

* President Eisenhower got Bisma-Rex, along with a note saying, "Man, you wouldn't of had that stroke you had one of these." Kennedy, "Music Don't Know No Age."
† Another famous Satchmo aphorism on diet: "It don't matter what you eat and when you eat, so long as you don't eat right before you go to bed." Halberstam, "A Day with Satchmo."

his side on his travels and a specialist waiting back home. Alexander Schiff, a pal of Joe Glaser's and physician for the New York State Athletic Commission, served as Louis's devoted general practitioner here and overseas. Gary Zucker, assistant chief of medicine at New York's Beth Israel Medical Center, kept extra-close tabs on Satchmo's faulty ticker. Even his teeth and lips—both recognized cultural treasures—got high-priced attention.

Here as everywhere, Louis preferred to blend what was time-tested with what was state-of-the-art. That was why in his later years, when he was in and out of Beth Israel's life-saving intensive care unit, as soon as he got snugly settled on a VIP floor he would immediately ask Zucker and Schiff for his Swiss Kriss. "I use the word *physic*—which I was taught to say from my childhood days," he explained. "Finally I learned to say *laxative*. *All* the same. Maybe more expensive than the word *physic*. They both make you do the same thing."

It's not surprising that Louis would become preoccupied with his health. He kept up a relentless work schedule, day after day, putting his mouth and body to the test with little rest, reaching for high Cs even into his sixties. And he had real issues to contend with, starting back in the Battlefield.

All kids get sore throats. When they do, few responded the way Mayann did by boiling cockroaches, straining the broth, and feeding Mama Lucy or Louis a teaspoon. When stepping on a rusty nail or broken glass raised the risk of lockjaw, the homespun solution was pepper grass simmered to a gummy paste, then lathered onto the wound. A glass of Pluto Water and a night of sweating could help, too. "The next morning," Louis reported, "I was on my way to school just as though nothing had happened."

As his medical challenges multiplied over the years, Louis became more resourceful. The biggest concern was his embouchure, a French term for how the lips, tongue, teeth, and facial muscles are applied in playing a brass or wind instrument. His technique was flawed—resting the mouthpiece on his soft upper lip in a way that crushed his teeth, and using a rim narrow enough to tighten the grip and cut into flesh—although damage seemed inevitable given how hard and long he blew. He also might have had leukoplakia, a condition where white patches or spots form on the inside of the mouth and sometimes become cancerous. Whatever the reason, the troubles started as early as the 1920s and his doctor confirmed that by midcentury his muscles had atrophied and "his lip actually became like a skin flap."

He described his throbbing jaw as "tender as a baby's bottom." At the flash point—when the craters dug too deep, the scar tissue got harder than wood, or the "heat-friction" in his mouth made him double up in pain—he put down the trumpet and sang. Other times, like at a theater in Baltimore, "I was playing my last number of the night when my lip started to bleed. I couldn't very well stop. I had to finish my show. But by the time I did, only a few minutes later, my boiled shirt was dripping with blood."* His lip troubles got so much press that horn players now refer to muscle ruptures like those as Satchmo's Syndrome. At their worst, Armstrong talked about walking away from his art.

Salvation came in the form of Ansatz-Crème, a salve made by a German trombone player that "draws all that tiredness out. So—quite naturally—your chops rest easy." The balm arrived in coin-sized orange tins, and Louis ordered so much, and dispensed it to so many friends, that the manufacturers renamed it Louis Armstrong Lip Salve. The cream joined Swiss Kriss and the other assorted packets, bottles, and applicators in Satchmo's dressing-room drugstore. Vaseline added extra lubrication for his chops, while a wire brush scrubbed the saliva and germs from his horn. Heet Triple Action pain formula "cools me down and dries me out and steadies the skin." Witch hazel on the eyelids yielded a "cooling up all the way back inside your *cranium*." A swig of glycerin and honey cleansed his pipes, Maalox eased stomach pains, and marijuana promised instant bliss. His leather wallet was crammed with five varieties of vitamins and, to stay awake on long trips, methedrine.

"It wasn't long ago I believed in all kinds of old-timey remedies like the voodoo people," he said. "Now I just use things do me some good, ya dig?"

He was sold, and so were many of the journalists he bewitched backstage, but some of those cure-alls didn't wear well. The strawberry-scented sweet spirits of nitre that he lathered on his face and lips twice a day—and swore "will take the soreness out of anything"—was banned as an over-the-counter medicine in 1980 because the Food and Drug Administration determined it could kill infants and lacked proof it worked with the issues for which Louis and others took it. And methedrine—known by scientists as methamphetamine and by street users as glass, meth, and crystal—today is recognized as a highly addictive stimulant that is illegal to manufacture, transport, sell, or possess without a doctor's (unrefillable) prescription.

Armstrong worried terribly about his teeth, especially after he learned what had happened to his mentor, King Oliver: Joe "played till his teeth got

---

* "He told me that he always had that problem, and once every four or five years he would have to remove [the callus tissue], and then take two or three months off, or six months off, for his mouth to heal," said trombonist Marshall Brown. "He told me how he was resolving the problem, which I thought was an extremely primitive way, he would literally himself take a razor blade, and remove it." Collier, *An American Genius*, 231.

so loose you could pull them out with your fingers." Same for Bunk Johnson and his problematic buck teeth. "I watched all that," said Louis, who would eventually get a mouthful of bridges and whose choppers would be written up admiringly in a dental journal. "So now, every time I have two weeks off . . . the dentist is doing something to my chops . . . the danger's gone . . . there's no chance of pyorrhea."*

Sleep never came easily to performers who worked nights and rehearsed, recorded, or romped during daylight hours. Louis seldom spent consecutive nights in the same bed. His routine naps couldn't compensate for his always fitful sleep. The solution: one of his two valets would load three tape recorders—the music was his or Guy Lombardo's—"and, as soon as Pops got into bed, the first one would be turned on . . . Within a couple minutes he'd usually be snoring," reported Milt Hinton. "When a tape finished, they'd quickly switch on the next recorder, then reload the empty. They knew even if the music stopped for only a couple of seconds, Louis would wake up."†

Many of his health issues, even the trouble sleeping, were born of his lifestyle. His chronic bronchitis, intermittent pneumonia, and enflamed tonsils surely were aggravated by toking on weed and tobacco and working in smoky roadhouses and nightclubs. His mild diabetes, gnawing ulcers, and searing kidney stones, meanwhile, couldn't have been helped by the high-fat, high-cholesterol, heavily salted foods he ate. He had loved Tabasco and other spicy sauces since childhood. Likewise with ice cream, biscuits, Chinese and Cajun foods, egg-and-liverwurst sandwiches, pigs knuckles, sardines, Vienna sausages, and spaghetti carbonara.‡ His weight seesawed, with him binging, then going back on "my baby diet . . . That include, milk and cream, constantly, or should I say, disgustingly."

———

Duke Ellington experienced two kinds of health issues over his working life, the real ones and those he imagined.

He did endure a list of verifiable physical ills over the years. He had hernia

———

* Leslie Gottlieb, whose father was Louis's dentist in the 1950s and '60s, remembered that "Daddy was working on the spacing of his teeth or on caps, I think it was. And he did something to the spacing, and Louis could not blow a note. And [Louis] said, 'Put it back, Doc. Put it back.' And Daddy made the readjustment." "Lost Tapes": *Voice of America Jazz Hour*, BBC Radio 4, 1956.

† He also liked listening to tapes of Glenn Miller, Bunny Berigan, Erroll Garner, and Pyotr Ilyich Tchaikovsky.

‡ Complimented on his hearty if not healthy appetite, Louis replied, "Man, that's just a synopsis." "Louis the First," *Time*.

troubles, getting one repaired at age eighteen and another, on the other side, in his late thirties. A hangnail was removed, without an anesthetic, when he first got to New York. In 1948 he felt a stinging pain in his side; doctors excised a benign cyst from the outside of his kidney. Another ache, in 1958, was traced to his gallbladder, which was taken out. With that and his kidney surgery he was an impatient healer, proudly retaking the bandstand in precisely nine days. His last in-patient experience in those hectic years followed a concert trip to Paris in 1963, when he picked up what he self-diagnosed as a cold and turned out to be pneumonia. "After four days in the hospital," he recalled, "they had kind of a party in my hotel when I came out."

Later, he developed vision problems, especially in his right eye. While vanity kept him from wearing glasses, he asked audiences not to use flash-bulbs when they photographed him. "One reporter did it to him one night, and he took the glass of pop he had sittin' on the piano and just threw it in his face," said Mercer. "That's the only time I'd ever seen him react desperately in front of the public."

As with Satchmo, Duke's health troubles offer a lens into the lifestyle of a world-traveling jazzman but never sidetracked him for long during his iron man–like half-century career. Given the way he abused his body, it's surprising he didn't face more serious medical challenges.

Duke was more gourmand than gourmet, favoring a diet that nutritionists described as a road map to clogged arteries but that Duke saw as a treat topped only by sex. He began meals with a healthy grapefruit, generally followed by a juicy steak, then another. Other fare that filled his plates: lobster lathered in butter, syrup-drenched pancakes and waffles, eggrolls and sweet-and-sour pork, sticky Danish pastries, fried chicken and ribs, double helpings of French fries, ham and eggs with biscuits, old-fashioned baked beans, and lettuce sprinkled with sugar. Sometimes all in one sitting. But there always was room for dessert, with his favorite being slices of three different cakes (one had to be chocolate), each with a scoop of ice cream (in an ideal world, strawberry from Wil Wright's in Southern California, eaten with the spiffy tablespoon-sized ice-cream utensil he carried with him) and a different topping (anything from whipped cream to applesauce or jelly). "In the 1940s," he recalled, "I would have my dessert as the first course— something delicate like pie à la mode. But now I prefer to have all my courses on the table at the same time."

Trombonist Tricky Sam Nanton said Duke once ate thirty-two sandwiches during intermission at a dance at Maine's Old Orchard Beach.

It's amazing that he wasn't obese, but at six foot one and 210 pounds, he was certainly overweight. Like Louis, Duke dieted regularly. In 1955 his doctor told him to "take off twenty-two pounds," he wrote. "I tore up his suggested menu and made one of my own. Mine was simply steak (any amount), grapefruit, and black coffee with a slice of lemon first squeezed and then dropped into it. With the exception of a binge one day a week, I ate as much of this and as often as I pleased for three months. When we returned to the New York area, my first date was with the symphony in New Haven." His physician "took one look at me, and said, 'Go get yourself a banana split quick!' I had lost thirty pounds."

Going to a gym or even on a stroll might have helped but, as one sideman observed, Duke "doesn't even go for sunshine. He figures he can take a pill that will give him the same benefit. We were playing Storyville on Cape Cod once and Duke got all the way out to the front porch. But no farther." On another occasion, when the bandleader was told by his driver that his car was in a garage around the corner, Ellington asked, "You mean you want me to *walk* a block? Well, I might as well, but it'll be the longest walk I've had in years." Interviewers described the way he moved in middle age as stiff, like an old man with tired feet.

It didn't help that Duke sometimes went days without real sleep. Or that he was a smoker (he cut down from a pack a day to four cigarettes, and by the end he took just a few puffs on each). The toll of that lifelong habit wouldn't show up until nearer his end.

His mental health also was precarious. He sank into deep depressions after the deaths of his mother and his confederate Billy Strayhorn. And starting in 1950 or so, he showed signs of what Mercer said was paranoia: "He blamed different things on different sets of people. In world events, he believed prominent men were often influenced to act wrongly or indulge in reprisals by women somewhere in the background . . . When something bad happened on the international level, he often saw the handiwork of people in powerful positions, communists, financiers, or both."

More worrisome, psychologically, Duke fretted that his health was worse than it was, a tendency that his family and doctors recognized as hypochondria. He called himself a "doctor freak," and said he never knew how he felt until he asked his physician. Everywhere he went he brought vitamins and potions stuffed into a satchel that Strayhorn gave him with the monogram "Dr. E.K.E." ("He ate vitamins like other people eat breakfast cereal," said a friend.) He'd interrupt rehearsals to take his pulse. At other moments he'd obsess about his feet, lying on his back to stretch them against the wall. All that made sense for someone as superstitious as Ellington, but it was surprising given that he studiously avoided stresses and strains that he called the "bug disease" and he took to heart his doctor's admonition "not to let anything bug you."

Thankfully that doctor, Arthur Logan, proved himself an understanding friend and confessor as well as a skilled diagnostician and prescriber. The light-skinned, silver-haired Logan was one of the first Black graduates of Columbia University's College of Physicians and Surgeons and would later become Dr. Martin Luther King Jr.'s physician and head of New York's anti-poverty programs. He met Ellington in 1937 at the Cotton Club, and the two stayed close for the rest of Logan's life. Duke regularly called in the middle of the night not because something was wrong, but to make sure his doctor would be available in case he really needed him. Arthur listened, offered reassurance, and, if necessary, jumped on a plane even when that meant flying to East Pakistan to treat an ailment that sounded like airsickness. "If he stubbed his toe," said trumpeter Clark Terry, "he'd call his doctor. Even if he had to do it from Egypt. He might even take a plane back to New York, as much as he hates planes."

Duke got full physicals four times a year, with regular visits in between. Whenever he saw Logan, be it in his dressing room or living room, the doctor administered a shot to the backside of what could have been vitamins or perhaps was water. "There's nothing wrong with Edward," confided Logan. "It's in his mind. If it makes him happy for me to stick him, I'm going to stick him." Logan's wife, Marian, a former cabaret singer and later a civil rights activist, observed that "of course, Edward needed Arthur. Arthur kept him healthy, so he could make his music. Edward also loved the *idea* of Arthur. He thought it was magnificent to have his personal physician with him all the time, like some sort of ancient potentate . . . Arthur went along for the ride. You know why? He loved it, too. He loved the idea of being Duke Ellington's doctor. It was all a big, fabulous charade, two grown men playing dress-up."

————

As a physical specimen, Count Basie was less than impressive. A healthy weight for a five-foot-six-inch man like him is between 128 and 156 pounds, which made him forty to seventy pounds heavier than ideal when he registered for the draft in 1942. He wasn't unattractive with his dark brown amiable eyes and thinning black hair, slender wrists and hands, heavy jowls, and a light mustache—but he didn't turn heads like the dashing Duke or even a young and roguish Satchmo. As for his health, Bill Basie's youthful boozing in the gutters of Kansas City and later-life puffing on cigars should have taken their toll, yet until his last years, the Count actually suffered fewer health burdens, physical or psychological, than his fellow bandleaders. And he dabbled less in exotic and dubious treatments.

He did have a scare in his early twenties, when a case of spinal meningitis landed him in General Hospital No. 2, Kansas City's Negroes-only facility. He never publicly discussed the illness, although the press labeled his condition "very grave" and he had to stay in Kansas City while his bandmates went on with their tour. The meningitis must have sent Bill Basie into a cold sweat, given that his big brother Leroy had died of it just fourteen years before, at age twelve.

For the next fifty years the Count seemed to live a charmed life, healthwise and otherwise. He didn't get much sleep on the buses he perpetually rode, and his main exercise was walking onto and off the stage and into and out of hotels. His preferred menu would have given his doctors heartburn but would have felt just right to Duke and Satchmo. For breakfast, he'd have ham and eggs, a tall stack of pancakes, and a big T-bone with fried potatoes. The rest of the day he went for Southern confections, especially chicken, red beans and rice, ham and turnip greens, and slabs of gingerbread or high-carb cornbread. Knowing he'd be hungry on the bus, and it'd be a challenge to find a restaurant that would serve a Negro troupe, he would fill a paper bag with crispy chicken sandwiches, cakes, cookies, and a banana, giving it to the band boy to help Bill resist the temptation to dig in often. That trick didn't work, according to Basie arranger Ernie Wilkins: "Every five or ten minutes he'd call the band boy from the back of the bus for his bag!"*

Some sidemen surprisingly looked to him for inspiration on matters of health as well as harmony. Singer Joe Williams, fourteen years younger than his boss, said he learned from the Count "to take care of the instrument, which is the body."

Age, however, brought real medical worries for Basie, the way it does for most people who live that long and hardily. He'd just finished a weeklong run at Disneyland in September 1976, and was staying with the band at the Players Motel in Hollywood. When the seventy-two-year-old bandleader woke the next day, "I felt a pain in my chest. I just thought it was indigestion

---

* A Basie trick that did work was spitting on his slab of barbecued ribs, a sure way to ensure nobody would ask to share them. Even more shocking to an assembled waiter and journalist, in France he lathered his haute cuisine with a thick layer of ketchup. Author interview of Chuck Haddix; and Horricks, *Count Basie and His Orchestra*, 18.

or something like that," he recalled. "I just felt like I needed to belch but couldn't, and I couldn't relieve the congestion or whatever it was, and when I began to sweat, I called Paul Probst, one of our staff men who travels with us . . . The next thing I knew, I was lying over in his arms, and he was wiping the sweat off me. I had a terrible pain in my chest."

Basie insisted on walking to the ambulance, rather than resting on a stretcher, and when he got there he passed out again. "It just didn't seem all that serious, and I never felt I was going to die," he said, although it was a serious heart attack and he could have died. He stayed in the hospital for two weeks and at home for four months. He took long walks and a long break from the piano, learned from Catherine how to swim and did it every day in his pool, lost twenty pounds while cleaning up his diet, and grew what became trademark mutton-chop sideburns. Then he hit the road again, but with newfound awareness of his mortality: "We have cut down on the number of working days per week whenever possible, and we have definitely increased the number of vacation breaks we take each year . . . We get from ten to fifteen days off just about every five or six weeks."

In 1980 the Count developed what he called "a hell of a case" of shingles, forcing the cancellation of a four-week tour of Japan and sending him home for another monthslong reprieve. (One friend linked that outbreak to the marital stress Basie was going through, and research shows that stress is a risk factor for shingles.) The following spring he was hit again, this time by "this arthritis thing . . . I felt it coming on, and then all of a sudden there it was. It hit me like a brick. It really shook me. Everything was spinning, and I couldn't stand up and walk, and I couldn't control *anything*. That really scared the hell out of me because I didn't really know whether I was going to make it from one minute to the next. And nobody knew what the trouble really was."

After three days in the hospital, doctors concluded he'd suffered a viral infection that "brought on this arthritis thing that I haven't recovered from yet." He never would. The crippling rheumatism made it difficult to stand without assistance, even with his new walking sticks. His wife, Katy, was so worried that she joined him on the road whenever possible. "My main way of getting around, and also for getting to and from the bandstand, was my new Amigo motor scooter," he said of the custom-designed wheelchair that he operated with abandon, joyfully ringing its bell and showing off the nameplate on his bumper. "I would drive the scooter out to the piano stool, and then somebody . . . would give me a hand in making the switch. Other than that, everything was back to normal, with us filling the same choice bookings as before and drawing the same sellout audiences that gave us the same great receptions as before."

As always, Basie underplayed things. He did acknowledge that "once you hit your seventies, you can't really expect to feel in tip-top condition every day," and that "these ailments began to slow the old sparrow down a bit." The truth was that at times his fingers stopped working along with his legs. Arranger Sammy Nestico remembered a recording session when, facing one rapid-tempo take after another of "Sweet Georgia Brown," the Count concluded that "enough was enough. He stopped the band, looked down at his fingers and muttered, 'These mutherf—ers just ain't doin' what they used t'do.' I chuckled inwardly, and with pure admiration and love, I suggested one piano chorus only. The recording continued smoothly from that point."

FOLLOW THE MONEY

To SEE THE degradations of Jim Crow in midcentury America, you only had to look at a lunch counter or the inside of a bus or a voting booth. But the financial impact of that brutal double standard was more subtle and more difficult to measure.

The money troubles of the Count, Duke, and Satchmo made for ideal bellwethers.

Ellington gave breakthrough performances in three Paramount films in the 1930s, but was paid just half of what white bandleader Guy Lombardo got in the same era for a single Paramount picture. It was par for the racist course, as Duke knew, and he took great pleasure in knowing that he and the band were so embedded into the plots of those movies that Southern theater owners couldn't easily cut them out, as was their wont. That same pride showed itself when, during a 1940s recording session at RCA Victor, his producer accidentally left a microphone on and the band heard him say, "Ready for a little Saturday night nigger music." Instead of making a scene, Ellington quietly instructed his mates, "Gentlemen, pack up," then asked to be released from his contract.[*]

Decca Records signed Basie to a deal that became the epitome of exploitation, paying him a fee of just $30 and no royalties for chart-topping tunes like "Jumpin' at the Woodside." His bandmates, meanwhile, were paid less than the modest union scale. "To me it was devastating—for both of us," said John Hammond, Basie's white producer and enabler. The Count "earned nothing from record sales."

The street-smart Armstrong gave up early on trying to fight back against

---

[*] Manager Irving Mills would later say that he'd been summoned to RCA Victor headquarters and "chastised" for "mixing the races" on an Ellington recording that featured Black and white sidemen. Cohen, *Duke Ellington's America*, 70.

bigoted record companies, theater managers, and movie producers. Instead, he took Black Benny's advice and gave full control over his finances to his "boss man," white hard-guy Joe Glaser, who gave him all the cash he needed but kept for himself a fatter share than seemed warranted. "What's money anyhow?" Louis asked wryly.

Even as they slowly made progress in breaking down racial barriers, these bandleaders remained, like all musicians of their race, barred from the most lucrative jobs in whites-only hotels, limited in parts they could play in Hollywood and on TV and radio, and squeezed by extortionist management fees. Worse, they had to bite their tongues on the sidelines while wealthy Caucasian imitators brazenly performed the very tunes that the Negro jazzmen had penned. Benny Goodman had the nerve to introduce Basie's "One O'Clock Jump" to a Carnegie Hall audience, while Glenn Miller's band rang up sales with its rendition of Ellington and Strayhorn's "Take the 'A' Train."

For three Negroes raised in poverty or close to it, the millions that Satchmo, Duke, and the Count eventually earned seemed like manna from heaven. But even that amount was grossly unfair given their stature and stardom, and a fraction of what they would have earned if Jim Crow hadn't shackled their bank accounts.

"Some times I sit around the house and think about all the places me and Lucille have been. You name the country and we've just about been there. We've been wined and dined by all kinds of royalty. We've had an audience with the Pope. We've even slept in Hitler's bed," said Satchmo. "But regardless of all that kind of stuff, I've got sense enough to know that I'm still Louis Armstrong—colored."

———

Few bandleaders were able to simultaneously manage their checkbooks and their music. Likewise, the business side of their careers threatened to defeat Ellington, Basie, and Armstrong in ways that were unique to each, and telling reflections of their personalities and circumstances.

Duke had always brought in decent money, going back to his steady and lucrative house-band job at the Cotton Club, together with night after night of bookings at choice venues nationwide. But the ledger was always awash in red ink. The 1929 crash of the stock market hit him hard, and he always seemed a short step ahead of the debt collector. It took years just to pay off his mother's and father's medical and burial bills. The Internal Revenue Service garnished his concert fees, convinced he was exaggerating his deductions for everything from tips to alcohol and flowers and claiming unwarranted exemptions for cousins, an aunt, and other relatives. He was supporting an estranged wife, a sister who liked mink coats, a son with children of his own, and past and present mistresses, and he helped out long-departed band members and up-and-coming protégés.* Duke that he was, he insisted on living beyond his means. Add it up, Mercer said only slightly whimsically, and it got "to a point where basically he had about three possessions. He had a white overcoat, he had an electric piano he used to sleep with and a steak sandwich in his pocket."

The biggest drain on his income, Mercer and everyone knew, was his determination to keep the core of his band intact not just when there were paying gigs, but year-round for more than fifty uninterrupted years. It was partly a matter of loyalty to his musicians, band boys, PR people, barbers, and other footmen, although he was a notorious tightwad when it came to raises. More important, he needed his orchestra at hand so he could instantaneously hear his compositions, knowing his longtime sidemen would adjust and improvise until the piece reached tonal perfection.

To pay those salaries, Duke held his nose and became a mouthpiece for Olivetti typewriters ("Duke Ellington at the keys") and Hammond organs ("It sounds like an organ's supposed to sound"). He reluctantly and unhurriedly penned a memoir when a publisher offered a $50,000 advance. He wrote more radio themes than almost anyone, appeared in eighteen full-length movies, continued doing wearying one-nighters, and churned out a stream of royalty-yielding standards.† Most of all, he repeatedly sacrificed his own earnings to cover business costs. He had to, as his ledgers from a representative year like 1944 make clear: he took in an impressive $405,000 ($7 million in today's dollars), but payroll, rent, legal and accounting fees,

---

* "He sent everybody to Juilliard," says granddaughter Mercedes. "He sent Quincy [Jones] to Juilliard. He sent Luther Henderson to Juilliard. He sent my father to Juilliard. He sent me to Juilliard. And he felt that that was something that he gave us that would serve us well and help us in our lifetime decisions or in our, our chosen field." Author interview of Mercedes Ellington.

† "I was short of cash, so I went to the William Morris office to negotiate a small loan," Duke recalled cheerfully. "While I was standing around, a boy came through with the mail, and handed me a letter from Victor records. I glanced at it. It was a check for $2,250. I slid it back into the envelope quick. Just what I needed, I thought . . . But maybe I had misread it. Probably it was $22.50. I opened it again. It was $22,500, royalties for 'Don't Get Around Much Any More.' I went out of there like a shot, and nobody saw me for two months." Harman, "Jazz Man Duke Ellington."

and other expenses left him with a meager profit of $11,000. In four of the years between 1953 and 1960, he made no gain at all. "It's a matter of whether you want to play music," he explained, "or make money."

The bottom line, said Ellington biographer and friend Derek Jewell, is that in his later decades "he needed to make at least a million dollars a year to break even." While he fared well compared with other Negro orchestrators, white big band leader Kay Kyser pulled down six times more and Glenn Miller five times.

Count Basie faced equally rough going. In the early years, he booked less fancy venues than Duke did, with smaller fees. And he had ongoing gambling debts and tax troubles. Trumpet player Buck Clayton remembered what it was like in those years: "We'd pawn everything we had if we were broke—suits, radios, anything." It got so bad in 1940 that, to give himself leverage with his booking agency, Basie planted with the press a story that he was about to break up his band and sign up as featured pianist with Benny Goodman. It was more than a bluff: he was $35,000 in debt and near bankruptcy. By the end of 1940, word circulated that the Count was played out.

The Music Corporation of America stepped in as a short-lived white knight, offering the discipline and direction he needed and boosting his 1941 gross to $300,000. Over the next few years he'd launch his own publishing company, the Basie Music Corporation, take featured roles in Hollywood movies, watch jukebox sales soar, tour Europe, and be crowned the Jump King of Swing.* But by the end of that decade hard times were back, for big bands, swing music, and Bill Basie. "Quality bookings were few," remembered sideman Freddie Green, "forcing Basie to travel the rough road of one-nighters again with a disgruntled band trying to survive on reduced salaries."

While he conceded that money "is very important," Basie, like Ellington, said it wasn't his main motivation, but rather "a part of the dues you have to pay to have the kind of band to make the kind of music you like."

Satchmo had more money rolling in and less leaking out, partly because he didn't have to bankroll a big band like Duke and the Count. His background also left him more steeled for hard times. But that didn't mean it was easy.

---

* All three bandleaders cashed in on the soaring popularity of jukeboxes, with the number nationwide rising from 25,000 in 1933 to 300,000 just six years later. Record sales boomed, too—from 6 million discs sold in 1933 to 127 million in 1941. Hasse, *Beyond Category: The Life and Genius of Duke Ellington*, 199.

He had to supplement his performance fees by plugging products ranging from Pepsi-Cola and Selmer trumpets to Schaefer Beer and Suzy Cute Dolls. He appeared in thirty-five feature films and documentaries along with several shorts, earning a colossal $50,000 for eleven days of shooting for the 1959 film *The Five Pennies*. These projects let him pay his sidemen well, at least by the standards of other jazz ensembles, and to keep them working even through the Great Depression. What hurt was having so many mistresses and ex-wives: "The divorces cost me plenty. After each one I had to start all over again. Right after Daisy—right after Alpha—right after Lil. Those marriages cost me a fortune not only to make and sustain but to break."

———

By the 1960s, all three maestros were in the money, with Louis the richest of all. In his Queens home, a $5,000 Sevres vase perched on a flawless block of pink marble that came from an Italian quarry and now sat across the room from furniture hand-hewn from Germany's Black Forest. A silver-blue Cadillac Fleetwood with polished fruitwood stretched out in the garage, while the bandleader relaxed upstairs on a red leather recliner, sipping Seagram's V.O. and munching on sardines and soda crackers. "Pops Armstrong is a millionaire several times over," *Ebony* announced in an article titled "The Reluctant Millionaire." The magazine writer got it half right: Louis hadn't "made less than a half-million bucks in any given year during the past 20 years," as Joe Glaser attested. But he was hardly reluctant.

The boy who'd grown up on unpaved Jane Alley now owned properties not just in New York, but in Accra, Ghana, and Las Vegas. There were insurance trusts and government bonds, paid for by bookings that yielded $5,000 a night domestically and $35,000 for several nights work in Europe. Royalties rolled in on 2,500 recordings. Lucille ordered her clothes from Paris, Rome, and Saks; Satchmo traveled like a fancy man, with forty-eight trunks stuffed with 139 tailored suits and countless silk handkerchiefs, shirts, and mufflers. Louis wanted it both ways when it came to his bankroll. He delighted when authors and journalists crowned him "the richest man of his race" or "the only jazzman—and certainly the only Negro jazzman—who ever made a million dollars." But he told *Ebony* that "even if I start making a million bucks a day it won't make me try to be something different . . . You might eat a little better than the next cat. You might be able to buy a little better booze than some wino on the corner. But you get sick just like the next cat, and when you die you're just as graveyard dead as he is."

The Count led a life of relative affluence, too, with five-or-more-figure record contracts instead of the measly two Decca once paid. He finally could buy the bar he'd coveted on the corner of Seventh Avenue and 132nd Street in Harlem, which he renamed Count Basie's. "I never would have thought that that place on that corner would ever be mine. Back during those early days I used to walk along that sidewalk and see people going in there, but I never could. You *could* go in if you wanted to and could afford the prices," he said. "It was a real gas to be the owner of your own club, especially when it was so popular."*

More important, he had enough to afford the caretakers his daughter Diane needed. He could cover most gambling debts now without bankrupting the band or hocking Catherine's minks. And he could pay for the hotels or apartments he rented when she kicked him out for philandering, then shower her with gifts so she'd take him back. There was even enough to buy the cigars he loved puffing and the model trains that let him relax.

Duke viewed money as a marker of status more than an end in itself. The amount he was paid mattered less than that it topped big band rivals like Benny Goodman and Count Basie. That generally was the case, with venue fees as well as record contracts. It became clear how little the cash itself had meant—his muddled financial management meant he seldom even knew how much there was—"when they were trying to clean up his apartment after he passed away," says Mercedes. "They found in the closet shopping bags full of cash. It was a mess."

One gauge of his prosperity was his sartorial splendor. Tailors in Chicago, California, and New York spun out double-breasted suits, along with tailcoats with cuffs but without pockets, in bright whites, blues, and salmons. *Time* magazine counted "100-plus suits of clothes," pronouncing him "fastidious to the point of frivolity." Although he already had a thousand neckties, he'd travel twenty miles to buy just the right one for the next performance, generally fat and knitted, in orange or perhaps apricot. His favorite starched shirt had a Barrymore collar with long points. His wide-cuffed trousers stood two inches above the shoe line to show off his red socks, while his custom-made footwear ranged from black ballet slippers to shoes in blue suede or crimson, squared-toe or rounded. A corset tight-

---

* The Count loved to hold court at the bar where, according to Columbia Records executive Nat Shapiro, "he will talk about baseball, prize fighting, food, Western movies on television, 'the good old days,' and his elaborate plans for an electric railroad [for his basement] . . . He will talk about the many things that men enjoy talking about in saloons, living rooms and on street corners everywhere. But about the 'meaning' of music? Never!" Shapiro and Hentoff, *Jazz Makers*, 233.

ened his gut. Talcum powder and toilet water sweetened his smell. "They may not like our music," he would say as the audience gasped. "But we sure look pretty."*

Let others worry whether the royalties were enough to balance the books, Duke reasoned. "The thing that sets him apart from most of the bandleaders and composers . . . [is] sooner or later, they let economics get in the way of creativity," said Mercer. "Ellington never did."

———

These Bible-reading bandleaders surely knew the Parable of the Rich Fool, and they remembered their own penniless pasts. So rather than hoarding their wealth, they gave away more than their managers wanted.

Duke covered distant family members' medical bills and loaned money to band members and mistresses, never expecting them to make good. On Wednesday mornings needy musicians and artists knew they could stop by for $10, while relatives could count on $100 anytime he saw them. He saved his pocket change for kids. And on Duke's order, said sister Ruth, "our chauffeur was going around the city delivering . . . money and this and that" to "people that we don't even know about."

As for Billy Strayhorn, "he had no bills: no hotel bills, no apartment bills, no food bills, no clothes or tax bills. He didn't have a salary, either. He just signed a tab. Duke paid for everything. If Strays decided that he wanted to go to Paris and have breakfast, he'd just get on a plane—fly to Paris and have breakfast and come back," said trumpeter Clark Terry. "Duke paid for all of it."

Not everyone received such favored treatment. Prized trumpet player Cootie Williams left to join Benny Goodman when Duke wouldn't hike his weekly pay by $25. Rex Stewart threatened to quit over a similar $25 request, only this time Duke relented at the last instant. "[Ellington] is both generous and stingy; thoughtful and inconsiderate; dependable and irresponsible . . . Duke's generosity or lack of it does not follow a pattern. He often picks up the tab for a large party, but will cadge cigarettes," Stewart observed. "On reflection, and I've given this a lot of thought, Ellington is the most complex and paradoxical individual that I've ever known. He is completely unpredictable, a combination of Sir Galahad, Scrooge, Don Quixote and God knows what other saints and sinners."

Basie was less complex but equally charitable. Trumpet player Dave Stahl remembers him occasionally covering the band's hotel bills even though that

---

* Backstage, of course, it was different, with Duke relaxing in a sweater with holes or an old bathrobe, slippers warming his feet and a stocking matting down his hair.

wasn't his responsibility, and he did it Basie-like, with "no fanfare." Quincy Jones recalled that when he was struggling, the Count cosigned a loan, and when he needed direction, Basie offered lessons to live by. "Basie was family to me, an idol, a father, a brother, a mentor, a manager, whatever he had to be," said Jones. "'Learn to deal with the valleys, the hills will take care of themselves,' he advised. 'And always be fair.'"

"Money," Basie explained in his memoir, "has never really been a very big consideration with me personally. I really would rather not get into any discussion about it."

Satchmo was the softest touch of all. He'd send TVs or radios to bare acquaintances, buy oil paints for poor kids eager to create, peel off $20 bills for needy cases who lined up outside his hotel or dressing room, and, just before Christmas at the height of the Great Depression, dispense three hundred tons of coal to needy Baltimoreans. He knew people were taking advantage but didn't care.* Civil rights groups benefited from his generosity. So did the Colored Waif's Home and the widow of an old-time musician who got $50 a week for years. "We don't tell too many people this, but it's no lie. Pops actually gives away—I mean gives away—$500 to $1,000 every damn week," Joe Glaser told *Ebony* magazine. "He honestly gets his biggest thrill just giving away dough. He just gives it away—no strings attached."

It's simple, Louis said: "I greases a few palms here and there. What good is all the dough doing me and Lucille just laying around accumulating?"

---

* Sometimes once through the line wasn't enough. "Here comes some guy that Louis knew from years back and he told Louis he was broke," remembered clarinetist Joe Darensbourg. "Louis gave him a 50-dollar bill and this guy walked out of the door, then he turned right round and came back saying, 'Hey, Pops, I don't care to break into this 50-dollar bill. Have you got an extra five-dollar bill for my fare?' Louis said, OK, and he gave him another five dollars. Can you believe that?" Darensbourg, *Jazz Odyssey*, 164–65.

PART V

RACE MATTERS

ARTISTS *AND* ENTERTAINERS

S OPHISTICATED ARTIST OR folk musician? Virtuoso or clown? That debate about Louis Armstrong raged in the salons of the Harlem Renaissance, in gossip-fueled newsrooms, and in living rooms across midcentury America. Did this jazz master's eye-rolling antics—his minstrel-like mugging, moaning into the microphone, waving sweat-soaked handkerchiefs, and shaggy-dog storytelling—make him even more lovable or undercut his seriousness? Was it Satchmo being his impish self, or had he taken on the self-loathing that marked the slave in Harriet Beecher Stowe's 1852 novel *Uncle Tom's Cabin,* who forever after symbolized subservience? And what was his end game—to entertain listeners of all races, or to win over whites by confirming their skewed perception of Negroes as happy-go-lucky dimwits?

His detractors decried his stage persona, but believed his film roles were far worse, reaching a wider audience and debasing the entire Black race. He serenades a horse in *Going Places.* He's dressed like Tarzan in *Rhapsody in Black and Blue,* and is a singing cannibal head chasing Betty Boop through the jungle in the cartoon "I'll Be Glad When You're Dead You Rascal You." And in *Pennies from Heaven* he's Henry, a mentally challenged farmer-musician who, when Bing Crosby offers him 10 percent of the gate receipts, answers, "There's seven men in the band. And none of us knows how to divide ten percent up by seven. So if you could only make it seven percent?"

His playing the fool like that nauseated bebop prodigy and equality advocate Miles Davis. "I hated the way [Louis] had to grin in order to get over with some tired white folks," said the trumpeter and composer, who was born into an affluent African American family a quarter century after Armstrong was born into poverty. "I wasn't going to do it just so that some non-playing, racist, white motherfucker could write some nice things about me."

Ossie Davis, the pioneering Black film star and director, remembered that "most of the fellows I grew up with, myself included, we used to laugh at Louis Armstrong . . . Everywhere we'd look, there'd be Louis—sweat popping, eyes bugging, mouth wide open, grinning, oh my Lord, from ear to ear. *Ooftah,* we called him—mopping his brow, ducking his head, doing his thing for the white man."*

The argument seemed settled to Satchmo's detriment in the 1960s, when young Blacks were crafting new visions of racial pride and rendering harsh verdicts on their timeworn elders. But they often did so without appreciating the gut-wrenching lived experiences of their parents, their grandparents, and breakthrough artists like Louis Armstrong. He grabbed the gigs and the roles he could get, which weren't many and which pried open whites-only portals for the two Davises and other Negro performers who followed. Just being there mattered in a Jim Crow world that said he couldn't be. As for his tomfoolery when he was onstage, as Miles eventually came to see, "Louis was doing that when he was around his friends. You know he was acting the same way. But when you do it in front of white people, and try to make them enjoy what you feel—that's all he was doing—they call him Uncle Tom."

Ossie also changed his heart about Louis, based on an unforgettable experience making a forgettable movie with him in 1966: "One day, we had broken for lunch, and I had decided to stay in. It was quiet, and I thought everybody else had gone out. I started back towards the set to lie down, and there near the doorway was Louis, sitting in a chair staring up and off into space, with the saddest, most heartbreaking expression I'd ever seen on a man's face . . . What I saw in that look shook me: it was my father, my uncle, myself, down through the generations doing exactly what Louis had had to do, and for the same reason—to survive. I never laughed at Louis after that. Beneath that gravel voice and that shuffle, under all that mouth, wide as a satchel with more grinning teeth than a piano got keys, was a horn that could kill a man. That horn was where Louis kept his manhood hid all those years . . . enough for him . . . enough for all of us.

"Louis, man, I didn't have sense enough to tell you this when I was a kid—I didn't even know it myself—but I love you. And I ain't the only one."

---

* It wasn't just Ossie and Myles who harbored doubts, at first. A character in James Baldwin's short story "Sonny's Blues" refers to Satchmo's "old-time, down-home crap." Dizzy Gillespie bemoaned his "plantation character." And Wynton Marsalis resented his "shuffling," adding, "I hated that with an unbelievable passion." Baldwin, *Sonny's Blues,* 25; Armstrong, *In His Own Words,* 150; and Jenkins, *Louis Armstrong's Black & Blues.*

Armstrong never pretended to be a Beethoven or Bach, but he had the ingenuity and personality that let him turn a killer trumpet, a soulful tune, or an X-rated one-liner into high art. To him, art wasn't medicine or homework, the way beboppers and other purists wanted it. It was supposed to be fun. He hated when critics made being crowd-pleasing and being top-drawer seem contradictory—"Why not take all of me baby?" he'd famously ask in a hit song of that name—and, worse still, when they painted his bid to draw in white fans as somehow selling out Black ones.

"All my little gestures, coming out all chesty, making faces, the jive with the audience clapping—aw, it's all in fun. People expect it of me; they know I'm there in the cause of happiness," Satchmo explained. As for whether he was a jester, he asked, "What is clowning? Anything to make the people get a little laugh, to put humor in your program and the note still comes out, that's not clowning. Clowning's when you can't play nothing."

Like he said, he had been hitting high notes and dispensing happiness as early as his boyhood hustles with a New Orleans street band, playing to prostitutes, pimps, and johns of all skin tones. That he was a cameraman's dream by his early teens is crystal clear in a recently unearthed newsreel from 1915 showing him hawking newspapers in the Big Easy, with his trademark wall-to-wall smile and unmistakable magnetism.* He reprieved that one-man jubilee of joy in Chicago, playing the Rev. Satchelmouth in vaudeville acts. Joe Glaser had instructed him early on to keep it simple—"Sing and make faces and smile. Smile, goddamn it."—but he didn't need a white manager or anyone else to tell him what came naturally. He would continue dazzling 'til his last years, when his celebratory rendering of the humdrum "Hello, Dolly!" shockingly dethroned the Beatles—at the peak of Beatlemania—from No. 1 on *Billboard*'s Hot 100.

Armstrong fine-tuned that trick artist-showman persona when, with Glaser's help, he started playing first to mixed-race audiences, then to predominantly white ones. He modeled his comic rapport with audiences on Bert Williams, a Black funnyman in vaudeville, on Broadway, and in Hollywood. For blending high-top dressing, singing, and dancing with low comedy, Louis looked to another African American headliner, Bill "Bojangles" Robinson. Like other pioneers of their generation, Williams and Robinson dazzled white audiences with their supreme talent, willfully remaining

---

* Experts say it has to be Louis since he was the rare Black youth hawking newspapers in New Orleans, his news-selling history jibes with where and when the film was shot, and scientific analysis of facial features points to it being him.

unthreatening.* Louis learned well, referencing his race onstage mainly as a punch line ("My makeup's coming off," he'd say as he brushed sweat from his brow), perfecting the art of mugging (his facial English harmonized with his music), and hamming up his old-Southland accent (learned from preachers at his mother's Pentecostal church).

Fans loved it. Critics not so much. Paul Eduard Miller wrote, "Creatively and artistically, Armstrong is dead." Why? Because, Miller explained in a 1941 column titled "Musical Blasphemies," the trumpeter "had chosen to play exclusively for the box-office." Orrin Keepnews, another trusted reviewer, wrote in 1948 that Louis's "responsibilities are to his art, and to all of Jazz. Without getting stuffy or arty about it"—which was precisely what Keepnews was doing—"I'd like to insist that these men, whose names are synonymous with 'jazz' to a multitude of people, have no moral right at all to let their names be used to drag both jazz fans and curious outsiders into a shoddy exhibition of pseudo-jazz."

Louis's response was characteristically blunt and brief: "You can't please everybody, but if you can please the majority, don't worry about that few."

Such arguments, at first confined to dance hall floors and ivory towers, entered the wider public consciousness when he took what amounted to the Louis Armstrong Show to the big screen. Hollywood catapulted him to international stardom and made him richer, but opened him to even more vicious charges of racial caricature, which became increasingly difficult to rebut.

The reality was more nuanced. While he too often played feeble-minded companions or yes-sir footmen, those were the only film roles open to Blacks then, as his pal Stepin Fetchit could attest. And when he finally got a memorable part serenading star Martha Raye in the 1937 *Artists and Models,* it was remembered mainly for the white Raye being ordered to don blackface to appease audiences scandalized by interracial mingling. Even that wasn't enough for one Atlanta newspaper critic, who raged, "Martha Raye, thinly burnt-corked, does a Harlem specialty with a fat Negro trumpeter and a hundred other Negroes. It is coarse to the point of vulgarity. I have no ob-

---

* Satchmo remembered of Bojangles, "You'd go back to his dressing room and Bill Robinson would be crouched around the table, tears running down his face, in real agony, and the man would rap on the door and say, 'One minute,' and Bill would stand and wipe his face, and put his shoulders back, and grin, and dance on that stage. THAT's show business!" Which is, nearly to the word, what friends would later say about Louis.

But Armstrong was determined not to repeat the lessons that led his two role models to tragic deaths—Williams via alcohol and depression, Robinson ending up penniless after making millions. Riccardi, "Louis Armstrong and Comedy Part 1," LAHM.

jection to Negroes on the screen . . . But I don't like mixing white folk—and especially a white girl—in their acts."

Louis barreled ahead despite the enforced limitations, shaping his surroundings more than they shaped him. Henry the farmer in *Pennies from Heaven* wasn't the role he craved, but it made him the first Black to get star billing in a Hollywood film. Other Negro jazzmen appeared on the big and small screens, but none got as many speaking parts or approached his output of thirty-five movies and eighteen made-for-TV films, variety shows, or specials. He appeared alongside celebrities ranging from Jack Benny and Danny Kaye to Ida Lupino, Ronald Reagan, and Mae West. Whatever the limits of the assignment, he often stole the show and the headlines, as in this *Variety* review of *Pennies from Heaven*: "Best individual impression is by Louis Armstrong. Negro cornetist and hi-de-ho expert. Not as an eccentric musician but as a Negro comedian he suggests possibilities." Sir Laurence Olivier, one of the most acclaimed actors of his generation, reportedly said that Satchmo and Charlie Chaplin "are two of the best actors I've ever seen." Even the melody he crooned to a horse in *Going Places* made a splash, getting nominated for the best-song Oscar.

Had he been white and willing, a motion-picture studio almost surely would have scooped him up.* Louis didn't mince words about how it felt to be cold-shouldered at Hollywood soirees and bullied on studio lots, the way he was by a rude callboy during the shooting of the 1952 film *Glory Alley*:† "I said, 'Why do you hand me that shit? Cause I'm colored?'"

Blacks generally had to suppress their instinct to respond to racial slights in the pre–civil rights era when Satchmo was expanding his audience. The Pullman porters could have told him that, and likely did in their long nights riding together through Jim Crow America. Most donned an invisible mask as soon as they boarded the train, letting white passengers see only their servants' faces. They put on permanent smiles as part of the disguise, along with skin so thick nothing could get under it. The rest—their identities as men, their humanity—was off-limits. That tradition of changing faces traced to slave ancestors, who risked beatings and even death if they bared their true feelings. Pullman customers and the Pullman Company got the ideal menials they sought, and the porters saved what they really felt and thought

---

* He listed a dual career—"actor and musician"—in his 1932 passport application.

† It was true even with Bing Crosby, with whom Louis appeared in movies, and on radio and TV. "We aren't social. Even in the early days, we didn't go cabareting together," Satchmo explained. "I've never been invited to the home of a movie star—not even Bing's." Armstrong, "Daddy, How the Country Has Changed!"

for off-hours time when they could stew among themselves. He and his rail-riding brothers became "the best trained men in the world at maneuvering, at getting over it," explained veteran porter Harold Reddick. "You survived by knowing that at the end of the road, when payday came, you could buy your steak and cut it as thick as you wanted it cut."

Satchel Paige and his Negro League teammates mastered similar skills. Spending so much time dueling with second-rate white teams and dodging the minefields of Jim Crow made the ballplayers pros at using charm and humor to deflect tension. Batters hit one-handed or on their knees. Satchel took his warm-up throws sitting down, with his catcher stationed behind the plate in a rocking chair. Barnstorming Negro Leaguers knew it was best not to win by too many runs if they wanted to be invited back the following year. They tuned out when the ballpark announcer told fans that "Nigger Satchel will be doing the pitching today," or when "Bye, Bye Blackbird" was broadcast as he exited the game. They tried not to let racial animosities eat away at their humanity. Their stage might be shabby but their performance remained regal.

So did Satchmo's. His mask was his smile, a full-faced, unquenchable beam that was analyzed more than the Mona Lisa's and hid an ever-shifting range of emotions. Sometimes it was straightforward joy; in other situations, as Ossie Davis saw, it shielded heart-wrenching sadness. He wore it as armor as he crossed into an often-hostile white world. (Ralph Ellison's invisible man said Louis "made poetry out of being invisible.") In the movies, he evinced whatever primitive sentiment his directors wanted in return for their fat paychecks, or whatever vanilla image Southern theater owners would tolerate. The more melodramatic the portrayal, the more he trusted that Pullman porters, Negro Leaguers, and other African Americans would recognize that you sometimes had to stoop to prevail.

No matter the circumstance, Louis Armstrong made himself more visible to his fans than the average porter did to his passengers. ("They wouldn't respect you as a man," Reddick said.) Or than Satchel Paige bared to the crowds in his stadiums. ("Nobody knows how complicated I am," he once said. "All they want to know is how old I am.") Even the most narrow-minded or dim-witted nightclub patron or movie watcher could sense Satchmo's warmth, humor, and genius. How else to account for his becoming, by mid-century, the most recognized and celebrated artist on the planet? He was a paradox and a contradiction. Trying to separate the artist from the prankster represented, with him, a false dichotomy. The two existed in splendid harmony. Armstrong fan and *Invisible Man* author Ellison recognized that "Armstrong's clownish license and intoxicating powers are almost Elizabethan; he takes liberties with kings, queens and presidents; he emphasizes the physicality of his music with sweat, spittle and facial contortions; [and] he performs the magical feat of making romantic melody issue from a throat of gravel.'"

Or as Louis himself said more concisely, "Showmanship does not mean you're not serious."

Nobody ever accused Edward Kennedy Ellington of being a clown, although he put on almost as much of a crowd-pleasing show as Louis Armstrong. But while Satchmo was upbraided for stooping too low with his stagecraft, Duke was assailed as being high-and-mighty, with long suites, sacred concerts, compositions for stage, ballet, and opera, and other polished pieces better suited to Carnegie Hall than the Cotton Club.

Why the difference? Both jazzmen, after all, doggedly wooed white audiences—Louis tutored by Joe Glaser, Duke under the equally masterful guidance of Irving Mills. Each took his music to creative heights seldom seen, and made money few fellow musicians and even fewer African Americans dreamed of.

For one thing, while Satchmo acted the minstrel, Duke played the patrician. It started with a silk-stocking wardrobe, and was enhanced by his cultured carriage. His very presence was entrancing to Negro youth looking for a high-style role model, including Gordon Parks, who grew up on a vegetable farm in Kansas with fourteen siblings. "Ellington never grinned. He smiled. Ellington never shuffled. He strode. It was 'Good afternoon ladies and gentlemen,' never 'How y'all doin'?'" remembered the photo essayist and filmmaker. "At his performances we sat up high in our seats. We wanted to be seen by the whites in the audience. We wanted them to know that this elegant, handsome and awe-inspiring man playing that ever-so-fine music on that golden stage dressed in those fine clothes before that big beautiful black band was black—like us."

But most nights Ellington performed more toe-tapping pop than sophisticated recitals, despite polished titles like "Sophisticated Lady" and "Mood Indigo." He spent more time over his long career in clubhouses than concert halls, and he insisted he didn't mind when, at the end of a dance in the

------

* Years later Wynton Marsalis would compare Armstrong to another all-American genius, saying he was "a bit like Mark Twain. They both found a way to combine down-home soul with an extremely high level of sophistication." Blumenfeld, "Second Line: Ten Trumpeters Talkin' about Louis."

farming borough of Carrolltown, Pennsylvania, he had to remind patrons that "the bar will close at one o'clock tonight. We regret to tell you we will be here a half hour later though. So if you're going to be with us, let's be fortified." Duke never denied his commercial bent, born of a love of even a dim spotlight like the one in Carrollton. "I am commercial because I've got to be," he explained. "The support of the ordinary masses for the music from me, which they like, alone enables me to cater for the minority of jazz cognoscenti, who certainly, on their own, couldn't enable me to keep my big and expensive organisation going."*

Wherever he was, people remembered Duke's white gloves and tux along with his understated magnetism, images that were reinforced when the late-night crosstown choice was the exuberantly mugging Satchmo. The contrast wasn't accidental. Ellington was too diplomatic to publicly criticize Armstrong, whom he respected although never befriended. But it wouldn't have entered his mind to copy Louis's smiling, handkerchief waving, and other showboating. For Duke, Satchmo stood as an unambiguous benchmark of the line never to cross between entertainer and hot dog.†

Ellington's own passion increasingly steered him to works that were more experimental and extended, and less fan-friendly. High-concept music like that, John Hammond sniped, signaled that Duke "has robbed jazz of most of its basic virtue and lost contact with his audience."‡ Prickly critics aside, Ellington managed to do two seemingly contradictory things at once in a way that Armstrong was too transparent to even try. Duke composed simple

---

* The men in that organization sometimes paid a price for Duke's obsession with appearance. Sideman Freddie Jenkins's right hand was mangled in a childhood accident. After joining Duke, he explained, "I started playing trumpet with my left hand. With Duke, you were in show business, and show business meant just that. You're there to perform, and nothing must interfere with the enjoyment of your patrons. You must try to hide any deformity you have which might divert their attention from what you are doing. You don't want them feeling sorry for you." Jenkins, "Reminiscing in Tempo."

† Even as he kept his distance stylistically, Ellington defended Armstrong's fun-loving style: "Some of the most severe critics say [Louis] injects too much comedy. I say that there has never been any jazz worth listening to that didn't have a sense of humor and that there is no defense against the Louis Armstrong brand of musical charm." Duke Ellington, "A Royal View of Jazz."

‡ Hammond had earlier lacerated Ellington for moving in the opposite direction. "His music is losing the distinctive flavor it once had, both because of the fact that he has added slick, un-negroid musicians to his band and because he himself is aping Tin Pan Alley composers for commercial reasons," the producer wrote in the jazz journal *DownBeat*. "He and his music are definitely losing favor with a once idolatrous public. And unless there are definite changes very soon he will be in a very precarious position." Tucker, *Duke Ellington Reader,* 120.

Tin Pan Alley tunes as well as pieces worthy of the opera house. Even when playing the hottest of them, he stayed ice-cool. It was part of his paradoxical pattern—an instinctive aristocrat with a common touch, a conservative innovator, a master of sardonic self-mockery and soft-spoken irony, and a man who, while deeply devout, rarely forgave or forgot. The mercurial Edward Kennedy Ellington seldom revealed his true self. He's "an iceberg," said cornetist Rex Stewart. "There's much more beneath the surface than above."

Even on film he remained opaque. No rapturous letting go or kowtowing like with Armstrong, and almost no acting. That would have required opening up and perhaps offending. He wrote the scores or appeared in eighteen feature films in theaters and on forty-one TV shows, losing his early jitters and becoming more comfortable in front of the camera. He was heard but not seen in nearly half his films; on-screen he generally conducted, tinkled the keyboard, looked debonair, or muttered the way he did in the 1959 courtroom drama *Anatomy of a Murder:* "Hey, you're not splittin' the scene, man? I mean you're not cuttin' out?" The exception was a 1929 musical short, *Black and Tan,* but even there Duke spoke mainly through his music as he appeared alongside his real-life mistress Fredi Washington.

Ellington occasionally acquiesced to Hollywood's racist strictures, like when lighter-skinned band members applied dark makeup for the 1930 Amos 'n' Andy feature *Check and Double Check.* ("It was awful," said the milky-complexioned trombonist Juan Tizol.) *Paris Blues* was written as the story of cross-racial romances until United Artists lost its nerve. (Those changes "took the spark out of it," said one of its stars, Sidney Poitier.) But Duke also toppled barriers, like in that same middling drama when his band became the first of its race to appear in a feature film. (The fainthearted RKO studio scrubbed the Ellington name from its publicity in Southern screenings.) The nine-minute-long *Symphony in Black* artfully blended music and a screenplay, with lyrics by Billie Holiday but without a word of dialogue. *Black and Tan,* meanwhile, was the first movie to avoid the "nauseating lowdown niggerisms" typical of Black film roles, according to the Negro *New York Age.*

———

Count Basie didn't face the slander of Tomming that Satchmo did because he didn't cackle, mug, wear funny hats, or make droll jokes. He barely uttered a word from the stage. Simplicity remained his hallmark, with plinks, planks, plunks, and a glint in his eye that few noticed. And he wasn't branded as la-di-da because he had no pretense of composing Ellingtonian high art, although many would characterize "Jumpin' at the Woodside" and "One O'Clock Jump" as such. The spotlight focused on the band, not on Basie.

That let him get away with being as much of a showman as his maestro brethren without critics objecting, and it let him draw white fans without upsetting Black ones.

It all was classic Count, leading from the rear, like a savvy shepherd tending his flock, and deftly walking the line between uppity and obsequious. He worshipped Duke and adored Satchmo, both from a distance, but knew he'd be happiest and most successful by being himself.

He stuck with that approach when Hollywood came calling. Basie appeared on the silver screen in twelve feature films, and even more on the small screen, with thirty-one made-for-TV movies, documentaries, and other shows. Some are long forgotten, like the 1938 *Harlemania;* more memorable is the 1964 *Sex and the Single Girl,* with superstars Henry Fonda and Lauren Bacall. Even with the camera trained on him, few paid attention to the cap-wearing Count, who lacked Satchmo's scene-stealing charisma and Duke's regal stature. Most directors didn't want the music to take center stage, preferring that it set a tone. The Basie band did that so well that he was asked back again and again.

Filmmaker Mel Brooks had something else in mind when he recruited Bill Basie for a cameo in *Blazing Saddles,* his 1974 satirical Western. Bart, a black railroad worker who'd just been tapped as sheriff, encounters the Count and his orchestra in the middle of the Wild West, playing their trademark "April in Paris." It's counterintuitive and random, evoking the kind of subtle laugh that made the film a classic and made straight-man Basie a perfect fit.

Race sometimes surfaced as an issue even with the Count. White sideman Buddy DeFranco was allowed to play in a short film in 1950 featuring "Sugar Chile" Robinson and Billie Holiday, but could not appear on camera alongside his Black bandmates. That, as the production company realized, might dampen bookings below the Mason-Dixon Line. More often and more lasting, the Count achieved quiet breakthroughs. He was the first Black to compose a theme song for a TV series, *M Squad,* and was invited to play at the inaugurations of three U.S. presidents. Unlike with Satchmo and Duke, the Hollywood press seldom commented on the Count's presence and never questioned it, which is just the kind of racial normalcy—and professional anonymity—that he cherished.

Nat Hentoff, his era's canniest jazz reviewer, wrote that Duke Ellington "wears so many masks that some of his intimates wonder if his own face has not all but disappeared. Louis Armstrong is not just the grinning clown he appears to be on television . . . No member of the jazz pantheon, however, smiles so much and says so little as Count Basie."

RESETTING THE THEMES

IF THE UP-TEMPO and airy "Take the 'A' Train" was Duke Ellington's signature tune in his early years, a very different number characterized the maestro later on. The song, "King Fit the Battle of Alabam," marked a rare occasion when Duke employed Satchmo-like verbal idiom and an even rarer one of him using his music to sound off on the racial violence engulfing America. Few remember the song because it played only during the six-week run of *My People,* a show staged in Chicago in 1963 during a centenary celebration of the Emancipation Proclamation. Almost as astonishing as its unflinchingly political message, the tune marked the first time in his life that Duke didn't just compose, orchestrate, and pen lyrics, but he sang the song himself. His libretto railed against Bull Connor, the racist police chief in Birmingham, Alabama, for violently assaulting youthful Black demonstrators with a barrage of fire hoses, club-wielding officers, and snarling German shepherds:

> *King fit the battle of Alabam'—Birmingham . . .*
> *And the bull got nasty—ghastly—nasty*
> *Bull turned the hoses on the church people . . .*
> *And the water came splashing—dashing—crashing*

As the song ended, a parade of placards on the stage celebrated the stories of Negroes who Duke felt had changed the world, from the predictable Frederick Douglass and Thurgood Marshall to actor Bill "Bojangles" Robinson, medical pioneer Charles Drew, and poet and novelist Paul Laurence Dunbar. Then a young girl recited an Ellington-written parable about green people and purple people bludgeoning each other to death in a battle neither side understood. "There was blood everywhere," the schoolgirl told listeners. "There was no purple blood, and there was no green blood. All the blood was red." In case the audience—and especially young Negroes he feared didn't know their history—hadn't gotten his point, Duke sent them home with a number titled "What Color Is Virtue?" That, Duke explained, "is a big question. If you answer the question, it says everything you want to say."

While the theater world didn't see any money-making possibilities, *My People* resonated with the cultural moment and with Duke's life journey. It was staged mere months after the violence in Birmingham, and just two weeks before the March on Washington that demanded jobs and justice for Black Americans. More significant, it prompted the first meeting between Ellington and Martin Luther King Jr., who came to Chicago to catch the show.

Duke, who had just woken up, "came down in his cashmere coat and wrap and his little pork-pie hat," recalled Marian Logan, a mutual friend. "Martin saw us and he jumped out of the limousine, and he and Ellington embraced . . . It was a very warm embrace." The three proceeded to the theater and watched from the director's booth a rehearsal of the song written in King's honor. "It was the first time Martin had ever heard that, and he was very impressed—very proud. It was quite a moment."

"King Fit the Battle" surprised audiences because it seemed so out of character for the avowedly apolitical and dispassionate Duke, but it wasn't entirely unforeseen. A generation earlier, in 1941, he had scripted *Jump for Joy,* a musical that he called "A Sun-Tanned Revu-sical." It celebrated Black culture and, he said, was meant to "take Uncle Tom out the theater." He left unsaid his intention that the show would end any discussion of his being an Uncle Tom. An all-Negro cast performed an evolving set of thirty songs and sketches. Instead of presenting the world from a white perspective— "dripping with molasses," as Duke explained from the stage pit, and viewed "through Stephen Foster's glasses"—on this rare occasion it showed how Blacks looked at whites.*

The material was thematically explosive, especially a tune titled "I've Got a Passport from Georgia (and I'm Going to the U.S.A.)." The performer

---

* Foster was a nineteenth-century composer known for such minstrel tunes as "My Old Kentucky Home."

Jump's wardrobe also made a statement, shining a spotlight on the Zoot Suit, with its "reet pleat and a stuff cuff and a drape shape, shoulders extended." In dance numbers, meanwhile, an athlete's jump replaced the Jim Crow shuffle. Duke said the show was "the hippest thing we ever did." Always one for circumlocution, he added, "We included everything we wanted to say without saying it." Cohen, *Duke Ellington's America,* 187–89; and Peiss, *Zoot Suit: The Enigmatic Career of an Extreme Style,* 86.

dreamed of a place where businesses would brandish noontime signs saying "Out to Lunch" instead of "Out to Lynch." The first-act finale was called "Uncle Tom's Cabin Is a Drive-In Now." One reviewer said the show portended "a new mood" in the theater and perhaps the country, one where "Uncle Tom is dead. God rest his bones." Mercer Ellington went a step further, saying the play's ahead-of-its-time message was "we were not turning the other cheek anymore . . . If we got slapped, the next time around the slap would be returned in good measure." Fans applauded, with many in the mixed-race audience coming back for subsequent performances. Celebrities John Garfield and Mickey Rooney were underwriters, Charlie Chaplin and Orson Welles had offered to direct, and Martha Raye and Marlene Dietrich were there on opening night. Even the moment and place seemed perfectly cast: on the eve of U.S. entry into World War II, at the ornate Mayan Theater in downtown Los Angeles, when Duke was in transition from Tin Pan Alley to the opera house, America was preparing to battle fascism with an army that was racially segregated, and cities like LA were so bigoted that the band couldn't find a hotel to stay at in all of Hollywood.

The musical's title tune offered a joyfully optimistic liftoff, bidding "fare thee well" to the "land of cotton." But while Jim Crow bent briefly he never broke, even in the closed confines of the Mayan. Thugs roughed up an actor, issued multiple bomb threats, and slipped a charred drawing of a coffin under the stage door. (In reluctant response, "Passport from Georgia" was lifted from the show.) One of the underwriters ordered light-skinned singer Herb Jeffries to darken up. (Duke hit the roof, and the makeup was removed.) Money never materialized for the intended national tour. (No surprise, given the influential weekly *Variety*'s slam that "Main trouble with 'Jump with [*sic*] Joy' is that it doesn't jump.") An industry recording ban kept the show's songs off the air, actors were drafted as America readied for war, and after a hopeful 101 performances, *Jump* was shuttered.

"Every setting, every note of music, every lyric, meant something. All the sketches had a message for the world," Duke said. "The tragedy was that the world was not ready."

The world was only marginally more ready a year and a half later when Ellington debuted *Black, Brown and Beige,* his loftiest extended composition and, at forty-four minutes, the longest. It was his first concert at New York's grand Carnegie Hall, and a fundraiser for America's beleaguered wartime allies in Russia. Never would Duke celebrate so dramatically the story of the Negro in America. He called it a tone parallel, meaning a narrative expressed almost entirely through music, and he didn't give that night's audience the verbal explanation that he'd share later and that made the story so much clearer. It was the most memorable performance of his career, with a standing-room audience that included First Lady Eleanor Roosevelt, poet Langston Hughes, and music men Benny Goodman, Glenn Miller, and Count Basie. Frank Sinatra visited backstage as thousands milled outside hoping to get in.

While *Jump for Joy* was Duke's effort to slay Jim Crow with satire and mockery, *Black, Brown and Beige* was deadly earnest. He'd planned to write an opera, but when he couldn't find backers he turned to the familiar form of symphony to tell a story unfamiliar to most Americans. It spanned the gamut of Black experiences—from slavery through emancipation, segregation, and increasing integration—incorporating music evocative of those times and places. And it drew on all the emotions—from gloom to joy, purposefulness to the patriotism that fit a country at war. "Just as always before, the Black, Brown, and Beige were soon right in there for the Red, White, and Blue," said Ellington, who meant to educate—not alienate—the white audience he'd spent decades nurturing.

His title's reference to a palette of shades, he explained in an unpublished interview, "has to do with the state of mind, not the color of the skin. Because when [Africans] arrived, everything was real black, you know. The Negro thought that when he was being brought here from Africa that he was being brought as food, because he was a very delicious thing . . . When they got here, they found all they had to do [was] the work . . . It got to be brown with the entrance of the spiritual . . . Gradually it got lighter. In *Black, Brown and Beige*, of course we went on up to the [color] cream . . . but it never got quite white."

Mercer had a different and more candid take on his father's use of that palette: "*Black, Brown and Beige* was his criticism of his own race. And their prejudices within itself. That there were these different castes: the black, the brown or tan ones, and the ones light enough to pass for white. And yet they wanted, as a whole, the race wanted recognition and equal rights, and yet within themselves they restricted each other."

The composition was drawn from Ellington's study of Black history, and from his eight-hundred-book collection of "Negro culture and its evolution." His lived experience contributed even more, with the last and most hopeful "Beige" section portraying a Harlem where, as Duke said, "there were more churches than cabarets" and where "there were forty-two Red Caps in New York's Grand Central and Penn Stations who had Ph.D.'s." Ellington later wished he'd blended words like those into his instrumentals-only narration because "the script itself is more interesting than the music." While most of that written scenario was told with third-person distance, Duke surely was talking about himself here:

> Your song has stirred the souls
> Of men in strange and distant places . . .
> How could they ever fail to hear
> The hurt and pain and anguish
> Of those who travel dark, lone ways
> The soul in them to languish?

Reviews of his opus stoked that hurt, pain, and anguish. The *New York World-Telegram* damned it as "too long" and "far from being an in toto symphonic creation." The *New York Herald-Tribune* said it was "formless and meaningless," adding that "nothing emerged but a gaudy potpourri of tutti dance passages" and "paraphrases on well-known tunes that were as trite as the tunes themselves." Bob Thiele, editor of the journal *Jazz*, added this jab: "*Black, Brown and Beige* is not true jazz. Louis Armstrong improvising the blues is real jazz."

Duke did have his defenders. "His wasn't just the music of a great composer whose notes fitted the men in his band, nor the thing which we call Modern Jazz or Negro Syncopation, but the anguished cry of a people calling to the Gods of our time for fair play," wrote Billy Rowe, a Black columnist for *Variety*. "Each note meant something. Each bit of lyric sang, not a song of happiness or despair, but the words of Lincoln, Booker T. Washington, Fred Douglass and all those other great Americans whose lives were built upon the pulpit of freedom for all people and all lands."

Ellington would continue using his music to talk about his country and its treatment of Blacks, yet never so honestly and with such vulnerability as in *Black, Brown and Beige*. He "sort of withdrew and was very quiet," his sister Ruth said. That inaugural performance at Carnegie Hall proved, as if it were necessary, that he was a virtuoso, and he cashed in financially and artistically. But he never repeated the full show, given how scalded he was by the reviews.* It would take twenty-one years, and Bull Connor's snarling police dogs, for him to again go down that risky road of racial critique.

---

* He repurposed parts of it into *My People* as well as his sacred concerts.

Louis Armstrong was heading in the opposite direction in his later years—from the concert hall back to Tin Pin Alley—and no tune better captured that shift than "Hello, Dolly!"

It started as an afterthought, a quick recording session done in 1963 as a favor to Joe Glaser, who was doing a favor for his song-plugging friend Jack Lee. The tune was the title number of a musical that hadn't opened yet, and Armstrong made it his own by giving it a jazz beat and replacing the second "Hello, Dolly" with "This is Louis, Dolly."* He paid more attention to another song he recorded the same day, "A Lot of Livin' to Do," from the Broadway show *Bye Bye Birdie,* which already had proven itself with four Tony awards. Louis later recounted the story to Jimmy Breslin. Lee walked into Joe Glaser's office one day and "said he had a song that was made to order for Armstrong," the nationally syndicated columnist wrote. "He then proceeded to spread the music out on Glaser's desk and start singing. When Jack Lee sings, he sounds like he is in jail. But Lee, fingers snapping and foot tapping in tune with his atrocious voice, went right at it. 'Hello, Dolly . . .' he started squawking.

"Within a few days, Louis Armstrong was walking around his house in Corona, Queens, listening to a demonstration record of the song," Breslin added. "He kept humming it and trying a few notes of it. He did this for two weeks, and all the things Louis Armstrong ever learned about music and all the places where he learned his music went into these two weeks."

Breslin knew what he was talking about. Louis poured into "Dolly" half a century's know-how as both a musician and performer. This wasn't the Hot Five Louis who in 1928 belted out the genre-defining "West End Blues," nor the one who three years later controversially crooned his soon-to-be-signature "Sleepy Time Down South." Thirty years on, Satchmo was a different music maker and man. He sang more and blew less, to preserve his tender lips and showcase his dual gifts. He'd perfected the art of sashaying across the stage, whether it was in a B-list film farce or doing a Hawaiian instrumental, and smiled in a way that some belittled as grinning. Now more than ever, he stole the show, wowed the audience, and transformed simple barbershop numbers into sensations, with no number better reflecting that reinvention than "Hello, Dolly!"

---

* The debate still rages over whether Armstrong preferred Louis or Louie. At times he favored both, but this time the choice was clear, with him emphasizing the *s* by stretching it to "Louissss."

Louis liked the song from the start, despite later suggestions that he was a reluctant convert, but the only label willing to take a chance was the relatively unknown Kapp Records. That proved to be a brilliant bet. *Hello, Dolly!* opened on Broadway six weeks after Armstrong made his recording. The musical was based on Thornton Wilder's book *The Matchmaker,* with Jerry Herman's words and music, and Carol Channing starred as marriage broker Dolly Gallagher Levi. The original title was *Dolly, a Damned Exasperating Woman,* but producer David Merrick was so dazzled by Louis's promotional recording of "Hello, Dolly!" that he made that the name of his play. Critics and fans loved what they saw and heard, and the production won a record-setting ten Tony awards, including Best Musical. It also set the mark as Broadway's longest-running show at the time, with 2,844 performances and a succession of high-spirited Dollys from Channing to Pearl Bailey, Ethel Merman, Phyllis Diller, Betty Grable, Martha Raye, and Ginger Rogers.

While Channing was singing "Dolly" onstage Kapp released Louis's recording, and the reaction was instantaneous and overwhelming. "We were out on the road doing one-nighters in Nebraska and Iowa—way out," recalled bass player Arvell Shaw. "And every night we'd hear from the audience, 'Hello Dolly, Hello Dolly.' So, the first couple of nights Louis ignored it, and it got louder, 'Hello Dolly.' So Louis looked at me. He said, 'What the hell is "Hello Dolly"?' I said, 'Well you remember that date we did a few months ago in New York? One of the tunes was called "Hello Dolly"; it's from a Broadway show.' We had to call and get the music and learn it and put it in the concert, and the first time we put it in the concert, pandemonium broke out."

Disc jockeys kept the tune on nearly constant rotation. Louis added to the buzz during his second mystery-challenger appearance on the TV game show *What's My Line?* After playfully toying with the blindfolded panel, he delighted them, the studio audience, and millions of Americans by singing "Dolly."*

The Armstrong record, meanwhile, was climbing the *Billboard* charts. On May 9 it broke through as the most popular song in the land, finishing just ahead of the Beatles' "Do You Want to Know a Secret." At sixty-two, he was the oldest musician ever to hit number one. His rendering of the song was

---

* Just days after being treated in the hospital for varicose veins, Louis joked with the TV panelists that "cat come in the hospital and said, man, they told me you had very-close veins." "*What's My Line?*—Louis Armstrong; Ross Hunter [panel] (Mar 22, 1964)," YouTube, video, https://www.youtube.com/watch?v=5PM5Xk9Hxxo.

being played ten thousand times a day just in North America. It eventually sold three million records, made Satchmo even more of a hero to golden-agers, and landed him a walk-on as orchestra leader in Barbra Streisand's *Hello, Dolly!* movie. In June 1964 Frank Sinatra toasted Louis when he cut his own version of the song with Count Basie's band. "This is Francis," sang Frank. "You're back on top, Louie, never stop, Louie. You're still singing, you're still swinging, you're still going strong."

"Dolly" had gone from being an ode to Dolly the matchmaker to a paean to Louis and his generation of jazzmen. Which was fine by him. "It's awful nice to be there among all them Beatles," he told *Newsweek*. And he confided to Breslin, "I like it real fine. It's just the thing for my teenage audience."

Another gift for Beatles fans and their grandparents was another heart-stirring tune that defined Satchmo's later years, "What a Wonderful World." He recorded it in 1967, with words but without his signature trumpet, and a year later it sold more than any single in England. It would turn up again everywhere from *The Muppet Show* and *The Hitchhiker's Guide to the Galaxy* to the 1988 film *Good Morning, Vietnam,* and in 1999 it was inducted into the Grammy Hall of Fame. Here again Armstrong tapped the optimism that was his trademark, this time with a tune written specially for him. "We wanted this immortal musician and performer to say, as only he could, the world really *is* great: full of the love and sharing people make possible for themselves and each other every day," said co-composer Bob Thiele. Louis at first balked, asking, "What is this shit?" Then he saw that what Thiele had written was about him and his take on the world, with lines like these:

> *I hear babies cry*
> *I watch them grow*
> *They'll learn much more*
> *Than I'll ever know*
> *And I think to myself*
> *What a wonderful world*

Some youthful listeners resisted. In that era of conflicts—in Watts and Saigon, at Kent State and My Lai—they dismissed Armstrong's optimism as misplaced and naive. Louis—who'd grown up at ground zero of the civil rights struggle, and called out do-nothing leaders in ways that should have offered a role model to the young activists—pushed back. "Some of you young folks been saying to me, 'Hey, Pops. What you mean, "What a Wonderful World"? How about all them wars, all over the place, you call them wonderful? And how about hunger and pollution?'" he said. "How about listening to Pops for a minute? Seems to me, it ain't the world that's so bad, but what we are doing to it. And all I'm saying is, see what a wonderful world it would be, if only we'd give it a chance. Love, baby, love, that's the secret. Yeaah."

———

Count Basie adopted his own late-life signature song. "Fly Me to the Moon" was a cabaret ballad crooned by Frank Sinatra that made listeners believe, at least for its two minutes, that they could make the lunar journey. It also reminded Basie watchers of two things: It had the same spirit as the Count's earlier uplifting standard, "One O'Clock Jump," although the tempo of "Jump" was faster, its form shorter, and its harmony simpler. And unlike the ever-evolving Louis Armstrong and Duke Ellington, Count Basie was reassuringly true to type.

That type preferred the shadows, in this case letting America's favorite crooner become the face of a tune that was one of Sinatra's all-time best-sellers. But there was no other bandleader Swoonatra would have wanted backing up the recording he did in 1964 of the Hall of Fame song that Bart Howard wrote a decade earlier and a hundred versions of which already had been turned into vinyl. It was originally titled "In Other Words," but was re-named to capture the spirit of soaring lyrics that evoke the moon, the stars, and "what spring is like on a-Jupiter and Mars."

It wasn't just record buyers who loved "Fly Me to the Moon," but also the men actually flying there. For that, the Count and Ol' Blue Eyes can thank Mickey Kapp, the record company executive who'd produced Louis's "Hello, Dolly!" (and encouraged Louis to personalize the lyrics by substituting his name for Dolly's). Kapp had made friends with Alan Shepard, the first American to fly in outer space, via Kapp's comedian client Bill Dana.* Kapp convinced NASA that the Walkman-like cassette recorders that astronauts from Apollo 7 onward used to log mission notes could be put to a second use to relieve the monotony of days of staring at and listening to next to nothing.

———

* Dana's feebleminded alter ego was José Jiménez, whose routine always opened with a heav-ily accented, "My name José Jiménez." Today that routine would be considered demeaning, but in the 1950s and '60s it was considered hilarious by, among others, Shepard and his NASA mates, especially when José started pretending to be a spaceman. The idea to remake the character into an astronaut (the first in outer space) came from playwright and screenwriter Neil Simon. Genzlinger, "Mickey Kapp."
  Kapp and Shepard, meanwhile, became close enough friends that the producer was in-vited to speak at the astronaut's funeral. Kamp, "Music on the Moon."

"They *could* put music on the tapes for the ride up, and then record over it with their notes later, because who cares?" Kapp said, revealing fifty years afterward a secret that nobody whispered at the time, to safeguard NASA's no-nonsense image and so no one would need to pay for the recordings. "So I would program their music."

Kapp wasn't the only music man with NASA ties. PR maven Al Bishop worked for RCA, out of Cape Canaveral, and was pals with Gene Cernan, one of two lunar-module pilots on Apollo 10, the dress rehearsal for the first moon landing. Bishop and Cernan sat on the floor taping the astronaut's favorite vinyl recordings of spaceworthy songs, a list that included Basie and Sinatra's version of "Fly Me to the Moon." And it wasn't just the Apollo crew who listened to the inspired if scratchy recording, but the millions of Americans tuning in on TV who heard ground control tell the spacemen orbiting more than 100,000 miles away, "I'm surprised you all haven't set this to music."

"You want music?" Cernan quipped. Then he played most of "Fly Me," adding at the end, with Basie-like soft sell, "Just wanted to send some thoughts back to you."*

---

* As good as the real story was, "Fly Me" producer Quincy Jones went one better, telling the *New York Times* and others that the Basie-Sinatra tune also made it onto Apollo 11 and was "the first music played on the moon." NASA, however, says that's simply not true. Email to author from Brian Odom, NASA.

But the song has become part of American space lore, played at the space agency's fiftieth anniversary gala, the fortieth anniversary of Apollo 11, and the 2012 national memorial service for Neil Armstrong. Buzz Aldrin, who was with Armstrong on that first moon walk, joked, "I have heard Frank Sinatra sing 'Fly me to the Moon' almost *too* many times. So I'm interested in composing a new song, entitled 'Get your ass to Mars!'" BuzzAldrinHere, "I am Buzz Aldrin, Engineer, American Astronaut . . . ," Reddit, July 7, 2014, https://www.reddit.com/r/IAmA/comments/2a5vg8/i_am_buzz_aldrin_engineer_american_astronaut_and/.

BREAKTHROUGH BATTLES

MARTIN LUTHER KING JR. knew better than anyone what it would take to pull off a revolution capable of reshaping the soul of America and at long last leveling the playing field for American Negroes.

First you had to have followers and allies who were prepared to challenge not just racist leaders but the cultural bedrock of a racist nation. Nobody's outcry was more heartfelt and unexpected than that of Louis Armstrong, who shortly after the 1957 Little Rock school crisis offered this knife-edge rebuke that made headlines from Boston to Budapest: "The way they are treating my people in the South, the Government can go to hell." Satchmo mocked segregationist governor Orval Faubus of Arkansas as a "mother-fucker" (to make it fit for print, he and the reporter toned it down to "un-educated plow boy"), and derided war-hero president Dwight Eisenhower as "two-faced" and having "no guts" for failing early on to protect the brave Black kids desegregating Little Rock's Central High.

A successful revolution also needed inspirational anthems and symbols. Duke more than rose to the occasion by composing transformative works like *Black, Brown and Beige* and writing *Jump for Joy,* a play that banished Uncle Tom from the stage and American life and that insisted it was time to stop turning the other cheek.

A mass movement required money, too, for everything from bringing people to rallies to bailing them out of jail. Count Basie wrote checks, while his wife Catherine Basie not only raised bagfuls more, but played pivotal roles in civil rights groups in New York and beyond.

Most of all, with Negroes constituting just 10 percent of the population, you needed support in white America. No trio did as much as Duke, Satchmo, and the Count to set the table for the insurrection by opening white America's ears and souls to the grace of their music and their personalities, demonstrating the virtues of Black artistry and Black humanity. They toppled color barriers on radio and TV; in jukeboxes, films, newspapers, and newsmagazines; and in the White House, concert halls, and living rooms from the Midwest and both coasts to the Heart of Dixie. But they did it carefully, knowing that to do otherwise in their Jim Crow era would have been suicidal. If James Brown, Chuck Berry, and Little Richard are rightfully credited with opening the door to the acceptance of Black music, it was Louis Armstrong, Count Basie, and Duke Ellington who inserted the key in the lock.

Whether or not young activists who dismissed the aging musicians as Uncle Toms understood that, the Reverend King did. That was why he went to Chicago to see Duke and *Jump for Joy,* embraced Catherine Basie and Lucille Armstrong along with their husbands, and appreciated how the dance hall's "joyful rhythms" and "language of soul" provided the countermelody for his movement. "Jazz speaks for life," King wrote to the organizers of the Berlin Jazz Festival in 1964. "Much of the power of our Freedom Movement in the United States has come from this music. It has strengthened us with its sweet rhythms when courage began to fail. It has calmed us with its rich harmonies when spirits were down."

Three years later he told the Negro National Association of Radio Announcers, "You have paved the way for social and political change by creating a powerful cultural bridge between Black and white. School integration is much easier now that they share a common music, a common language, and enjoy the same dances . . . You have taken the power which Old [Uncle] Sam had buried deep in his soul, and through our amazing technology, performed a cultural conquest that surpasses even Alexander The Great and the culture of classical Greece."

Other leaders and luminaries joined King in recognizing the revolutionary power of jazz and its practitioners. Malcolm X unabashedly adored the Count and Duke. Ralph Ellison preached the gospel of Satchmo. Jackie Robinson tapped his love of jazz and jazzmen to raise money for King's Southern Christian Leadership Conference. Even Frank Sinatra, a surprising anti-racism activist, got the message. "Maybe the political scientists will never find the cure for intolerance," said the Sultan of Swoon. "Until they do, I challenge anyone to come up with a more effective prescription than Duke Ellington's music, and Duke Ellington's performance as a human being."*

---

* While Ellington, Armstrong, and Basie were Sinatra fans, not everyone was. Producer Norman Granz said Sinatra told racist jokes, including this one: "I'm happy to be back in Las Vegas; the dressing room they gave me was Lena Horne's, who appeared here before me and, man, you couldn't get in for all the watermelon rinds." Hershorn, *Norman Granz,* 359–60.

Louis's activism was the most counterintuitive, since he was the one most disparaged as an Oreo and a sellout. That hurt because he'd worked so hard to dig out of a life of Louisiana-style racism and despair born of the Battle-field. He'd hoped fellow Blacks would acknowledge and appreciate how his becoming world-famous helped them along with him.

Satchmo and his mixed-race sidemen traveled the South long before the freedom riders did, and before it was safe to do so. No Black had ever starred on commercially sponsored network radio before he took over for Rudy Vallée on NBC's *Fleischmann's Yeast Hour* in 1937, back when Jackie Robinson was eighteen and the only Reverend King who mattered was eight-year-old Martin's daddy. Still in his thirties, Louis became the first of his race to be featured in mainstream American films or lead an all-white band in Europe. Until Armstrong, no jazz musician of any color had made the cover of *Time* magazine (1949) or of *Life* (1966), none had published a memoir until his *Swing That Music* (1936), and none had dazzled British royalty (King George V in 1932). The NAACP thought enough of his contributions to make him an honorary member for life. "As time went on and I made a reputation," he said, "I had it put in my contracts that I wouldn't *play* no place I couldn't *stay*. I was the first Negro in the business to crack them big white hotels—Oh, yeah! I pioneered, Pops!"

The public could see all of that at the time. We now know even more about his attitudes and activism, thanks to the release of hundreds of hours of his private tape recordings. They include not just racy jokes and random musings, but tortured reactions to what he labeled the "shame" of racism. He blasted famous Negroes he thought were false prophets, insisting that Marcus Garvey and Josephine Baker were exploiters, not healers. But he adored Martin Luther King Jr., making audiotapes of hour after hour of the TV coverage of his assassination in 1968. He made the tapes for the same reason he wrote a series of memoirs, so the world would someday know how torn he was. Sometimes he counseled friends to endure racial blows, other times he boasted about doing just the opposite. When a white workman disrespected him, he shouted into the recorder the insults he'd shot back at the laborer, explaining, "You try to be a gentleman, they won't let you, that's all. I'm just showing you what we have to go through."

Daily battles like that were exhausting, but he used his wit to mask his despair. Before a performance at New York's Basin Street East nightclub in the 1950s, pianist Erroll Garner stuck his head into the trumpeter's dressing room to ask, "Hey, Pops, how's everything?" Louis: "White folks still in the lead."

The problem was that for every sign of resistance, he offered critics a kowtowing image they didn't understand and couldn't stomach. The worst came in 1949 when, as New Orleans's newly crowned King of the Zulus, he donned blackface makeup, broad white lipstick, black tights underneath a cellophane grass skirt, and a crown of red-feathered cardboard, then paraded on a float with a drunk entourage through twenty miles of city streets, tossing twenty thousand coconuts to two hundred thousand fans. Was he the "greatest mockery the Negro race has ever been subjected to," as portrayed by O. C. W. Taylor, a respected Black journalist in New Orleans? Or was the Mardi Gras Zulu Parade rather "a broad, dark satire on the expensive white goings-on in another part of town," as *Time* suggested in its cover profile of Armstrong that February? Wearing the crown the way he did on the front of the magazine and in his hometown—not to mention having his ninety-one-year-old grandmother Josephine on hand and having the mayor present him with ceremonial keys to the city that had once locked him up—was "a thing I've dreamed of all my life," Louis said. "After that I'll be ready to die."

If Taylor and others couldn't see in Armstrong a quiet subversive, the FBI did. It started tracking him in the late 1940s, when Louis's name turned up in the address book of an unidentified person in whom the agency was interested. The bureau noted when dynamite was exploded near an auditorium where he was playing in Knoxville, but gave no indication it was investigating. While his file grew to twenty-seven pages, a letter from Director J. Edgar Hoover included this typed observation: "Armstrong's life is a good argument against the theory that Negroes are inferior."*

The Little Rock incident especially captivated the FBI, with good reason. In 1957, two weeks after the Arkansas National Guard kept nine Black children out of Central High, Louis took off his gloves and ditched his invisibility. He no doubt was frustrated at having repeatedly been shamed in the Black press. Even more, he joined millions of Americans who raged at TV images of white mobs cursing and spitting at what became known as the Little Rock Nine—teenagers who, by order of the Supreme Court's 1954 *Brown v. Board of Education* decision, were set to integrate Little Rock's all-white high school. It wasn't just white protesters eager to keep the school all white, but troops sent in by the governor to support the segregationists.

---

* Taylor, too, was an Armstrong fan in the end. When Louis came back to New Orleans in 1965, Taylor penned a tribute to him set to the tune of "Hello, Dolly!" and including the line "There's no one in the world whom we love more." "Letter from O. C. W. Taylor—1965," LAHM, https://collections.louisarmstronghouse.org/asset-detail/1009810.

Louis actually was seething a week before his now-famous "go to hell" tirade against President Eisenhower and Governor Faubus, which makes clear it wasn't a spur-of-moment outburst. "That Governor, I mean, I bet you right now, he's got a little colored mammy there nursing his baby," Satchmo told a radio announcer in Spokane. "There ain't a white man in the South that don't have a colored man he's crazy about. So when you see those things like that, I just sum it up, I say, well, it's one of them okey-doke's, that's all it is. That's the slang way of saying it's a shame."

Nine days later he let loose with an even angrier screed, this time talking to Larry Lubenow, a twenty-one-year-old University of North Dakota student freelancing at the *Grand Forks Herald,* who'd wormed his way into the trumpeter's hotel suite by convincing the bell captain to let him deliver a lobster dinner.* Lubenow's editor had told him that in the unlikely event he landed an interview, there was to be "no politics." But the self-described "rabble-rouser and liberal" couldn't resist, and neither could Satchmo. He told stories of touring through Jim Crow's Southland, then sang an obscenity-infused version of "The Star-Spangled Banner." Even a student reporter could recognize the scoop handed to him when the normally gun-shy performer aimed both barrels at the governor and president. "It's getting almost so bad a colored man hasn't got any country," Armstrong told Lubenow, who skipped that evening's Satchmo concert so he could rush back to the paper to write his story. Lubenow's editors were skeptical that the famous music maker really had sounded off like that and sent the cub reporter back to the hotel the next morning for confirmation. "Don't take nothing out of that story. That's just what I said, and still say," said Armstrong, then he signed the yellow copy paper, scratching at the bottom, "solid."

A handful of Negro celebrities applauded Armstrong, with Jackie Robinson congratulating him for expressing "a feeling that is becoming rampant among Negroes" and the *Chicago Defender* writing, "He may not have been grammatical, but he was eloquent." Yet actor and dancer Sammy Davis Jr. lambasted him, saying, "For years Louis Armstrong has been important in the newspapers. They have always been ready to give space if he had anything to say that really was important, and he never has. Now this happens.

---

* Armstrong's stopover also made history because he was the first Black to stay at the Dakota Hotel, Grand Fork's finest. And that city had a tie with Little Rock: it was hometown to federal judge Ronald Davies, who'd cleared the way to desegregate all-white Central High.

As for Lubenow, he got $3.50 for writing the story that shook the world, but his editor was upset at the flaunting of his "no politics" edict, and a week later Lubenow was gone from the paper. Margolick, "The Day Louis Armstrong Made Noise."

I don't think it's honest.""* And Thurgood Marshall, who'd helped convince the Supreme Court to outlaw school segregation and would become the first Black Justice, said one reason his fellow Negroes were so delighted by all that Satchmo had said about Little Rock was because "he's the No. 1 Uncle Tom! The worst in the U.S.!"

Caucasian commentators were harsher, with syndicated columnist Jim Bishop saying he was dismayed by "the enormity of the damage Armstrong has done to the United States," and asking, "What have you done for your people, except hurt them?" WBKH, the radio station in Hattiesburg, Mississippi, banned his records from its airwaves. And in Nebraska, a reader wrote to the *Lincoln Journal Star,* "I would suggest that we give him a passport and one-way ticket to Russia, where he could be happy. Old Satchmo is now exhibiting exactly the attitude that causes the southern people to refuse to integrate."

The best reply to those attacks came from white music critic Ralph J. Gleason: "Louis Armstrong invented no labor saving devices, designed no terrible weapons of destruction, yet he will be remembered as long as our culture lasts . . . Armstrong took jazz, the legacy of the Negro race, and gave it to the world. We should be grateful forever."

Louis himself responded characteristically, with colorful language and without seeming to give an inch.† Fellow Negroes, he explained in a taped conversation from 1959, wanted him to "stop talking about white folks that way." To which he said, "Kiss my ass." But the criticism wounded him more than he admitted, and left him gun-shy going forward. Understandably. When he kept silent he was branded an Uncle Tom; when he spoke up his activist accusers left him dangling.‡ "Some folks, even some of my own people, have felt that I've been 'soft' on the race issue," he confided to the Black-focused *Ebony* in 1960.§ "How can they say that? I've pioneered in breaking

---

* Davis, who himself was attacked for being too racially submissive, later changed his mind, like most of Satchmo's critics. He gave Louis an acting as well as a singing part in his 1966 semi-autobiographical film, *A Man Called Adam.*

† One place he gave ground was with President Eisenhower, who, two and a half weeks into the Little Rock crisis, federalized the Arkansas National Guard and ordered it to safeguard the Negro students. "This is the greatest country," Louis declared, adding that he'd written the president saying, "If you decide to walk into the schools with the colored kids, take me along, daddy. God bless you." "Musician Backs Move," *New York Times.*

‡ Joe Glaser was among those who left Louis dangling. While the manager stood behind his client regarding Little Rock, he was determined that Louis not alienate his mainly white audiences.

§ The great saxophonist Sonny Rollins was one of those folks. "As the civil rights movement was beginning to gain some momentum, we thought, 'Oh, gee, Louis Armstrong is, you

the color line in many Southern states (Georgia, Mississippi, Texas) with mixed bands—Negro and white. I've taken a lot of abuse, put up with a lot of jazz, even been in some pretty dangerous spots through no fault of my own for almost forty years." Three years later he told the same magazine why he wasn't on the picket lines: "If I'd be out somewhere marching with a sign and some cat hits me in my chops, I'm finished. A trumpet man gets hit in the chops and he's through. If my people don't dig me the way I am, I'm sorry. If they don't go along with me giving my dough instead of marching, well— every cat's entitled to his opinion. But that's the way I figure I can help out and still keep on working."

Would police in hot spots like Birmingham and Selma really beat up an international icon like Louis Armstrong? "They would beat Jesus," Louis said, "if he was black and marched." As for the desegregation drive roiling the South in the 1960s, Louis left no doubt where he stood: "Integration is the greatest thing that has happened since the days of the boll weevil."

The continuing rap on Louis was that Little Rock was a one-time burst of conscience, but it wasn't. Two years later he announced that he'd boycott his native Louisiana, which fifteen years before had given him a kingly welcome, until it loosened newly tightened Jim Crow statutes. "I can't even play in my own hometown, 'cause I've got white cats in the band," he agonized in an *Ebony* interview. "All I'd have to do is take all colored cats down there and I could make a million bucks. But to hell with the money. If we can't play down there like we play everywhere else we go, we don't play. So this is what burns me up everytime some damn fool says something about 'Tomming.'"

It was the trumpeter's artistry and majesty, not his stand on civil rights, that grabbed the attention of Texas attorney Charles Black. "He was the first genius I had ever seen," explained Black, who first heard Louis at Austin's Driskill Hotel back in 1931 and twenty years later worked alongside Thurgood Marshall on the *Brown v. Board of Education* case. "It is impossible to overstate the significance of a sixteen-year-old Southern boy's seeing genius, for the first time, in a black. We literally never saw a black man, then, in any but a servant's capacity . . .

"That October night, I was standing in the crowd with a 'good old boy' from Austin High. We listened together for a long time. Then he turned to me . . . and pronounced the judgment of the time and place: 'After all, he's

---

know, sort of an Uncle Tom–ish guy,'" Rollins says, but later "I felt so ashamed of myself for not realizing what he had gone through . . . ashamed that I was so ignorant." Author interview of Sonny Rollins.

nothing but a God damn nigger!' The good old boy did not await, perhaps fearing [a] reply. He walked one way and I the other. Through many years now, I have felt that it was just then that I started walking toward the *Brown* case, where I belonged . . . Louis opened my eyes wide, and put to me a choice. Blacks, the saying went, were 'all right in their place.' What was the 'place' of such a man, and of the people from which he sprung?"

That was the kind of questioning Louis hoped his virtuosity would spawn. He was a quiet insurgent—more Booker T. Washington than W. E. B. Du Bois. But "the true revolutionary," trumpeter Lester Bowie recognized, "is one that's not apparent. I mean the revolutionary that's waving a gun out in the streets is never effective; the police just arrest him. But the police don't ever know about the guy that smiles and drops a little poison in their coffee. Well, Louis, in that sense, was that sort of revolutionary, a true revolutionary."[*]

———

Duke's version of subversion, while comparably low-pitched and noncon-frontational, was more straightforward.

He held benefits for the Scottsboro Boys, nine young Negroes unjustly convicted of raping two white women in 1931, and for causes ranging from ending poll taxes to housing the poor. He desegregated venues across the country, from New York's Paramount Theater, Memphis's Orpheum, and St. Louis's Avalon, to swank Ciro's on Hollywood's Sunset Boulevard, dance halls across Texas and Louisiana, and the Academy Awards. Duke collected a closetful of honorary degrees, including from Yale, but none touched him like the one from Dunbar, the elite all-Black high school in Washington. His 1929 radio broadcasts from the Cotton Club were, in the words of historian Philip K. Eberly, "the first important national propagation of black music by a pop group" and "the first encounter most white Americans had with black music." Forty years later, he became the first African American to get the nation's highest civilian honor, the Medal of Freedom.[†]

———

[*] As for those who decried Louis's Southern drawl and jargon, Negro columnist Evelyn Cunningham had this rejoinder: "So Louis should talk like a proper Bostonian when his whole background and heritage are in the South? . . . What do you want out of Louis Armstrong? Blood?" Cunningham, "Louis' Critics Should Jump in Lake."

[†] Benny Goodman generally is credited with assembling the first integrated jazz band, in 1935, but trombonist Juan Tizol said he and Ellington achieved that milestone when they started playing together six years earlier. Tizol's skin tone was white, and he wasn't African American. But because he was from Puerto Rico, he said, he was caught in a racial catch-22: club owners considered him Caucasian and gave the band a hard time for mixing the races, but journalists and authors considered him Black and denied the band the kudos it deserved for breaking that critical racial barrier. Serrano, *Juan Tizol: His Caravan Through American Life*, 137–39.

Timuel Black, the Chicago soldier turned activist, benefited from Duke's barrier breaking. It was the early 1940s, and Ellington was playing at the Marigold Room on Chicago's northwest side, "where blacks were not supposed to go . . . At the ticket window, the clerk says, 'Sorry, we're sold out.' Now, we can plainly see that white customers are still buying tickets and going in." That's when Duke intervened for the first time, telling the nervous manager, "These are my guests, and if they can't enjoy my performance, this show is over." Timuel and his friends were ushered to a table at the back, behind a curtain, where they couldn't see the stage and white customers couldn't see them. Duke stepped in again, repeating, "These are my guests, and if they can't enjoy my performance, this show is over." Timuel picks up the story: "It turned out to be a glorious evening . . . It's one of the ways we began to bring about social justice and social change, the change that comes when people can share a common, enjoyable experience across racial, national, ethnic, and religious differences."

Beyond the patrons of posh nightclubs, anyone who turned on a radio or read newspaper reviews bore witness to Ellington's pushback against racist norms. Long before universities instituted Black Studies programs, Duke celebrated Black achievement and pride through tunes like "King Fit the Battle of Alabam," suites such as *Black, Brown and Beige,* theatrical productions like *Jump for Joy,* and even his sacred concerts. As early as the 1920s, he proposed renaming jazz "Negro music"; while that didn't happen, it was how he always described his genre. He insisted on remaining publicly apolitical and nonpartisan, but nonetheless was a masterful if clandestine influencer. "I started my own civil rights movement in the Thirties," Ellington said, looking back. "I don't think there's been any doubt how we felt concerning prejudice," he added. "But still the best way for me to be effective is through music."*

His rakish demeanor and cultured speech, in person and on-screen, along with his capacity to beguile journalists, deflected the accusations of

---

And for nearly every breakthrough that was recognized, there were reminders of ongoing indignities, as singer Tony Bennett recalled: "When Duke and I were the first performers to open Miami's Americana Hotel in 1956, Duke couldn't attend the press party. It was Florida, it was the South, and the hotel was segregated. Any white man with 50 cents in his pocket could buy a beer at the bar. But the creative genius who brought in customers by the thousands couldn't sit next to him. That was America then." Bennett and Simon, *Just Getting Started,* 185–86.

* Blackness became the theme and title for other Ellington songs, including "Black and Tan Fantasy" (1927), "Black Beauty" (1928), and "Black Butterfly" (1936).

clowning and Tomming that critics aimed at Satchmo. They forgave Duke his jungle act on the Cotton Club plantation, along with the fact that his audiences over the years were 95 percent white.* Negro publications and white ones hailed him as a "race leader" beginning in the 1930s, and NAACP chief Walter White and top lawyer Thurgood Marshall both considered him a close friend.

But with the dawn of the civil rights era in the 1950s, activists demanded more. In January 1951, when he was due to play to a segregated audience in Richmond, Virginia, the local NAACP chapter threatened to set up a picket line. Duke canceled the appearance, but said "vicious" boycotts like that threatened the livelihood of Black bands like his. He was mad and, uncharacteristically, he showed it. "What about the toilets and water fountain[s] in colored waiting rooms, why don't they do something about that? Why pick on entertainment investments?" he asked reporters. His anger spilled out again ten months later when he talked to a reporter at the *Argus,* the Black paper in St. Louis. "We [Black Americans] ain't ready yet" to battle segregation, he argued. He described legal efforts to desegregate as "a silly thing." A more logical approach would be to "get together one hundred million dollars and then we can do something."

Not surprisingly, Duke's phrasing ignited a firestorm, no matter that he insisted, "What has been published is the exact opposite of what I actually said." In truth, the *Argus* story mostly got it right, although it lacked context and was intended to trigger controversy. The bandleader did believe that raising money would let groups like the NAACP hire full-time organizers and take its campaign nationwide, which was why he helped collect that money. He was in fact skeptical of soapbox orations and short-lived marches, but he also was in awe of Martin Luther King and the young Negroes bravely defying Jim Crow. And, as he wrote in his rebuttal to the *Argus* article, "I can see nothing wrong in admitting that colored people are not doing all they can to abolish segregation, and that much more can be done. I stand by that contention."

Even as he fumed, he learned. Starting in the 1950s he pushed back against playing to the whites-only crowds he'd once accepted as a fact of life everywhere from the Cotton Club to the Southland, and in 1961 he took another

---

* Not everyone forgave. "Ellington is straight out of the 1930s—Stepnfetchit and Mr. Bojangles!" a reviewer for an alternative weekly in North Carolina wrote in 1969. "He epitomizes plastic—his mannerisms, gestures, greased down hair, and the repetitious 'we all really love you' were just too much." Cohen, *Duke Ellington's America,* 403.

giant step. From then on, he wrote this clause into his contracts: "The artist or artists have the prerogative of canceling this contract, if in any instance an audience is segregated because of race or color." It wasn't ironclad—he made exceptions in members-only clubs in places like Texas and Virginia—but he was doing more than most Black performers.

The NAACP recognized those efforts in 1959 by awarding him its cherished Spingarn Medal, for "the highest or noblest achievement by an American Negro during the previous year or years." (Previous winners included Martin Luther King Jr. and the Little Rock Nine, and the following year it was Langston Hughes.) In 1971, *Ebony* would name him to its list of the "100 Most Influential Black Americans." (Others on the list included Ralph Abernathy, who succeeded King as leader of the Southern Christian Leadership Conference; and Angela Davis, the Marxist, feminist, and activist.) The honor he likely relished most, however, was a Rochester newspaper's commentary on the unifying magic of an Ellington concert in the divisive year of 1968: "Whites and Blacks mingled in a tribute that extinguished barriers of color or race; they stood shoulder to shoulder; they smiled at each other; some brought lightweight folding chairs; red-headed white kids played tag with spic and span black children around the pillars at one end of the plaza; white and black teenyboppers argued the merits of sax and clarinet. The magic of the Duke and his music made one people of them, one admiring people."*

But as momentum for civil rights picked up in the late 1950s and '60s, accusations and insults again were hurled his way, including from his son Mercer and other band members. Duke needed to be doing more, they said, and so this most private of men dipped his toes in, starting in Baltimore. In the winter of 1960, students frustrated with the snail's pace of polite desegregation staged sit-ins demanding Negroes be served at whites-only restaurants and stores. Duke was performing at Johns Hopkins, and his hosts told him about the Blue Jay, a nearby eatery whose owner turned away Black students but said he'd serve a "proper nigger" like Ellington. Duke's first reaction was a customary no, yet after listening to the young people's persistent pleas, the sixty-year-old composer relented with a "let's go."

It was a turning point for the Blue Jay, the Hopkins students, and Duke. Newspapers across the country picked up the story, with headlines

---

* There was nothing new about that magic, which during World War II convinced a kamikaze pilot not to fly his suicide mission. "He heard Duke Ellington, and that saved him," recalls Ellington sideman Art Baron, who says the story was widely circulated among band members. "This music . . . something happened to him." Author interview of Art Baron.

screaming, "Duke Ellington Joins Sitdowners; Can't Eat," and photos show-ing the rakish maestro being ushered out of the Blue Jay by a Baltimore pa-trolman. "We are happy that Duke Ellington saw fit to go into the restaurant and be refused," wrote the *Amsterdam News*. "We are happy because when the restaurant refused Mr. Ellington, it had turned its racial bias full circle. Earlier, it had refused the little average 'nobody' Negro. But Duke Ellington is not a 'nobody.' Duke Ellington is a 'somebody' Negro. His name is almost as well known at Buckingham Palace as it is in Baltimore."

His political narrative, like most chapters in Duke Ellington's life, was rife with paradoxes. Was he the leftist his FBI file might suggest—supporting such alleged Communist or Communist-front groups as the All-Harlem Youth Conference and Veterans of the Abraham Lincoln Brigade? The House Committee on Un-American Activities also pointed fingers, while the Communist Party's *Daily Worker* newspaper embraced the bandleader's activities. But the Ellington file, as with so many others the FBI kept during the Cold War, seldom fact-checked rumors that it repeated and almost never provided historical context. In this case, the bureau failed to make clear that Russia was our ally during World War II, and a beleaguered bulwark against Nazi invaders that loyal Americans felt compelled to support. The Com-munist Party USA, meanwhile, was an ardent foe of Jim Crow. The FBI's thirty-six-page compilation did, however, include these lines from an article Ellington penned: "I've never been interested in politics in my whole life" and "the only 'Communism' I know is that of Jesus Christ."*

If anything, his politics increasingly skewed conservative and libertarian. Communism's antireligious bent was an affront to Duke's faith. So was its anticapitalism, because, said Mercer, his father "liked the idea of one day becoming rich." He was for prayer in schools and against abortion on de-mand. In 1956 he recorded an ad for the U.S. propaganda network Radio Free Europe proclaiming, "Jazz leaves lots of room for individual expression, and in the Communist-dominated countries, jazz and individual expression are two things that are not wanted." And while he joined Count Basie and other celebrities in campaigning for Democrat Franklin Roosevelt in his last presidential campaign in 1944, twenty-five years later he warmly embraced Republican president Richard Nixon.†

---

* The article, titled "No Red Songs for Me," ran in the *New Leader*, a liberal anti-Communist journal whose managing editor was Daniel James, the first husband of Ruth Ellington.

† Duke also bought into conspiracy theories, Mercer and others said—whether it was Com-munists orchestrating the civil rights movement or the Ku Klux Klan being behind the Ken-nedy and King assassinations. That came as no surprise to anyone familiar with his fear of

What seemed like contradictions were, in Ellington's mind, dualities. Was his music jazz or Negro folk? Was his faith Methodist like his father's, Baptist like his mother's, or perhaps universalist? As for his politics, his conservatism fit naturally with his middle-class upbringing and his royal demeanor. Much as Satchmo was a mutineer disguised as a bootlicker, so Duke was a traditionalist masquerading as a hipster. He knew he couldn't take up arms over every indignity, so he was strategic and at times Machiavellian. "I am a Negro and I brag about it every day," he told a newspaper reporter back in 1941.

The Reverend King understood those paradoxes, said Marian Logan, which was why Duke and Martin embraced when they first met on that Chicago street corner "as though they [had known] each other forever."

———

Nobody was better at infiltration and circumvention than Bill Basie. He believed in the cause of Negro rights as passionately as his brethren bandleaders, but he waged his campaign so discreetly that the FBI never considered him worthy of a file, the NAACP and the Black press didn't give him awards or much coverage, and young activists neither attacked nor applauded. Which was just how the Count liked it.

Everyone knew that Basie could make listeners bob their feet and rush to the dance floor, but few noticed that his was the first Black band to play at Pittsburgh's stately William Penn Hotel back in 1937. Or that just after, at Philadelphia's Nixon Grand Theater, he solicited signatures for an antilynching petition. In 1939, he toured with a revue called *Meet the People* that took swipes at segregation much like those in Ellington's *My People* twenty-four years later. In 1945, the Count told the managers of Kansas City's whites-only Tower Theatre, "If you don't want my people, then you don't want my music." Basie followed through on the ultimatum and turned down the gig. The *Amsterdam News* was so surprised and delighted that it wrote, "Associate this statement with Count Basie and automatically one would think this is the theme of a new Basie hit tune." The Count, the paper added, "is the first of the boogie-woogie band leaders to make the drastic step. If others follow his lead, both the entertainers and the laity feel the situation can be remedied." All of which led Basie trumpeter Sweets Edison to boast, "We started integration."

In Oakland in 1939, the racial situation was reversed: Basie playing to an

———

dropped buttons, repaired trousers, or gifts of socks, shoes, and slippers. Robert Udkoff interview; and Mercer Ellington, *Duke Ellington in Person,* 157–58.

audience of Blacks and whites at Sweet's Ballroom, where he smashed attendance records. Four thousand fans were having a ball when a white police sergeant "barged into the hall, heading a police detail, and promulgated a decree that whites and Negroes could not fraternize and dance together," according to a newspaper account. The officer then "took the microphone to announce that this dance was tendered by our 'colored friends' and that white people would have to leave the dance floor and go to the balcony where they were welcome as observers."

Basie confronted the same Jim Crow outrages as Armstrong and Ellington, perhaps even more egregious ones, since his audience was blacker and poorer, with plumbers, maids, and chauffeurs instead of doctors, lawyers, and teachers. "I can't remember when I had not experienced discrimination. That's how the world was ever since I started performing back in the '20s," the Count said. "But you don't let that stop you if you know what you want to be." In 1937, he appeared with Billie Holiday at Detroit's Fox Theatre. "Detroit was between race riots then, and after three performances the first day, the theater management went crazy. They claimed they had so many complaints about all those Negro men up there on the stage with those bare-legged white girls, all hell cut loose backstage. The next thing we knew, they revamped the whole show," Billie remembered. "When the chorus line opened the show, they'd fitted them out with special black masks and mammy dresses . . . When he saw what was happening, Basie flipped. But there was nothing he could do. We had signed the contracts to appear, and we had no control over what the panicky theater managers did."

Ten years later the Count was discussing business with his press agent on the corner of Broadway and Fifty-First Street in Manhattan. "Basie took his notebook out of his pocket to make notations of several appointments," a reporter wrote. "No sooner had he started writing than one of New York's finest grabbed his arm, demanded to see the notebook and informed the Count that he was under arrest. 'You bookies are getting nervier every day,' declared the bluecoat to the flabbergasted Basie . . . John Law examined the notebook and got the shock of his life when he saw that the man he was about to arrest as a bookie was none other than the famous Count Basie."*

---

* Another time Basie was mistaken for a car-park attendant. It happened just after he finished a concert at the Academy of Music in Philadelphia where he received ten standing ovations. "Bill and I were out in the parking lot after the performance when a white man tossed him his car keys," recalled Tony Bennett. "I'm not sure how I would have reacted in Bill's shoes . . . But Count Basie was a bandleader. He knew how to kid, cajole, and josh people in his way. 'Get your own car, buddy,' he told the man. 'I'm tired, I've been parking them all night.' It was

The Count could have given the policeman a long lecture on how, not far from where they were standing, he'd toppled a barrier by being the first Black swing band to perform at majestic Carnegie Hall, and he'd do the same at the storied Starlight Roof of the Waldorf-Astoria and the 5,920-seat Roxy Theatre. He launched a music-publishing business that aimed to "give a break to deserving young Negro songwriters." He cut a record—an ode to boxing champ Joe Louis—with civil rights icons Paul Robeson and Richard Wright. And in 1959, he and Ella Fitzgerald would become the first African-can Americans to collect Grammy awards (he actually won two, for Best Jazz Performance Group and Best Performance by a Dance Band, both for work the year before). His list of breakthroughs was as long as Duke's and Satchmo's but he received less credit because he bragged less. On one of the rare occasions when he did bring up race, in 1941, it was seeking a middle ground. Jazz, he said, is "a medium between white and colored music with characteristics of both."*

Blacks like Basie had to let things go more often than they'd have liked, just to survive. His endurance and theirs might have been easier had he, Armstrong, and Ellington shared stories of Jim Crow outrages and, more to the point, ways to respond. They didn't, because each was too consumed with his own affairs, too private, and because the topic was too raw. The result was a missed opportunity.

The low-pressure Count reached his boiling point one afternoon in the late 1950s, when his bandmates were refused service in a small tavern in Gettysburg, Pennsylvania. "Basie walked up to the manager, looked at him coldly, and said, 'You want us to go out in the street and drink it? You want us to get arrested for breaking the law?'" reported jazz writer Nat Hentoff. "The manager was shaken but stubborn, and the musicians decided to at least leave a memory behind. The biggest members of the band—'The Killers'— Eddie Jones, Billy Mitchell, Henry Coker—began to roam around the tavern in the manner of lions deciding just which part of their prey they'd savor

---

the response of a genius. The guy got his car, and the Count kept his nobility." Bennett and Simon, *Just Getting Started*, 41.

* While he was a sometime activist, the Count also was cautious and prudish, which was why, according to producer Teddy Reig, "he once refused to appear on a bill with Dick Gregory because the [Black] comedian was doing 'racial jokes.'" He likewise was taken aback by satirist Lenny Bruce's vulgarity, asking a friend, "What gives with that white guy?" Reig, *Reminiscing in Tempo*, 59.

But there was no wariness when, in 1981, he became the first Black man selected for the annual Kennedy Center Honors in Washington, D.C. Honorees sat in boxes next to President Ronald Reagan and his wife, Nancy. Abdul, "Count Basie Honored at White House."

first. Basie watched the scene, made no move to stop it, and in fact quite evidently enjoyed the morality play. The band wasn't served, but at least it hadn't slunk away."

Like Duke and Satchmo, the Count generally let his music speak for him. His songs didn't offer the lessons in Black history that Duke's did, and his performances didn't raise worries about Tomming that Satchmo's did. As always, Basie was steady and soft, but he had a secret weapon that let him protest without seeming to: his wife Katy. She was more eloquent than him, and more political.

The Basies ran barbecues in their backyard to benefit the NAACP. She devoted her time and leadership skills, along with her and Bill's money, to civil rights groups. She was there at the March on Washington, worked on Jack Kennedy's presidential campaign, and knew well National Urban League boss Whitney Young, NAACP leader Roy Wilkins, and Coretta and Martin King. "[The Count] was a civil rights midget and she was a Goliath," said family friend and neighbor Aaron Woodward. That activism wasn't easy. On one side, more reserved friends preferred to see her stay home and not rock boats. On the other, radicals like the Black Panthers dismissed her interracial approach as accommodationist and called her a "white pig," according to friend Bonnie Grier. "Black extremists had threatened to bomb her St. Albans home because she had invited both whites and Negroes to parties. 'If they come at me with a gun,' she said, 'I'll take some of them with me.'"

Woodward said he'd heard her make similar promises, adding that "Catherine Basie carried a pearl handled .38 revolver. Catherine Basie would fight you if it was necessary. She would. But she would go and she would try to bring people together—white people and Black people; people with money, people without money. She was a magnet . . . not that [Bill Basie] wasn't aware, he's not hiding. He stood up, he was strong when he needed to be. But he was a band leader."

The Count made an exception to his say-as-little-as-possible rule in 1960, in the thick of the sit-in movement that Ellington connected with in Baltimore. Basie didn't join the demonstrators, but he called their activism "beautiful" and said, "They're starting a real move and I am 100 per cent for it." Intimidating Negro leaders into backing down was not just wrong but wouldn't work, he argued: "They're trying to knock us down but we get right up again." As for Martin Luther King, "Like the cats would put it, he's *saying* something."

OVERSEAS AMBASSADORS

THE EXUBERANT CROWDS in New Orleans had crowned Louis Armstrong the pretend King of the Zulus during Mardi Gras in 1949. But in 1960 when he visited the Belgian Congo, not far from the fountainhead of the Zulu people, the Congolese feted him like the real thing. Tom-tommers drummed a greeting reserved for tribal chiefs and hailed him as "Ambassador Extraordinary of the United States." Grass-skirted tribesmen painted in violet and ochre carried him through the streets of Leopoldville on a homemade throne mounted on poles, a company of police and soldiers leading the way. His hosts had hoped to draw 1,500 people to his concert at King Baudouin Stadium, but so popular was Satchmo that ten thousand churning fans packed the stands. While they chanted "Satcheemo," he shouted back, in wretchedly accented French, "Merci beaucoup, beaucoup."

His proudest triumph during his twenty-four-hour trip defied even the power of diplomats and kings. As he told it, "There was fighting and they stopped the war because I played there that night." That wasn't merely Satchmo telling tales. The Congo was embroiled in a deadly civil conflict, with civilians caught between rampaging troops. But as one headline hollered, "They Called Truce to Dig Louis." The Associated Press trumpeted, "'Wizard' Satchmo Unites the Congo!" The warring sides, the AP explained, "joined forces to provide a heavily armed cordon 'round Satchmo and his party." They actually danced and cheered side by side at that night's concert, although they resumed their bloody fighting once Louis left the country.

Like many less developed countries at the time, Congo stood as a proxy in the bitter one-upmanship between the Soviets and the Americans. The U.S. government helped underwrite his trip because, as the *New York Times* reported, it saw the trumpeter as "a secret sonic weapon." An earlier piece in Africa's *Drum* magazine quipped, "Satchmo Blows Up the World." He, more than anybody, made the blue note into a universal musical language and demonstrated that hot jazz could thaw the Cold War. Africans were especially stirred by this famous African American returning to the continent from which his ancestors had been dragooned onto slave ships. "No other American attraction could [possibly] elicit same goodwill and publicise our interests in this area!" one U.S. ambassador in Africa wrote of Armstrong's two-month swing across the continent. But as Moscow Radio warned at the time, and we now know was true, the CIA exploited his Congo visits to divert attention from a U.S.-supported coup by strongman Mobutu Sese Seko and the confinement, torture, and eventual assassination of nationalist prime minister Patrice Lumumba. Satchmo's situation "was far more sinister than he could have possibly realised," colonization scholar Susan Williams wrote. "[Armstrong] would have been appalled to know that the man from the embassy with whom he dined was actually a CIA official who was cold-bloodedly plotting the death of the democratically elected prime minister."

Each of the three maestros acted as an informal ambassador in mid-century, traveling to dozens of countries from Asia to Latin America and across Europe. At first they sought only the artistic acceptance and lucrative paydays that eluded them in America. Over time, the State Department started picking up the tabs and setting itineraries that served political as well as musical objectives. They performed their foot-stomping jazz on both sides of the Iron Curtain, for overflow audiences, taking their all-American music and riveting personal stories to listeners who couldn't get enough. It made them international sensations and helped make *chahss*, as the Congolese called jazz, a world favorite and a lingua franca.

Duke, the Count, and Satchmo served the needs of the U.S. government because they were patriots. There was pushback, but less from activists worried about Black artists being used to score propaganda points for a racist nation than from an old guard opposed to promoting Negro art and sinful music. During their foreign travels the music makers largely kept to themselves their feelings about the police dogs and water cannons that were battering fellow Negroes back home even as the world celebrated them as emblems of American inclusiveness. "The reason I don't bother with politics is the words is so big that by the time they break them down to my size the joke is over," was Armstrong's sweet but disingenuous reply when overseas reporters pressed for his views, echoing Ellington's and Basie's deflections.

In more candid moments, all three let loose with what they really thought. In 1957, Duke traced the Soviet Union's one-upping America in the race for space directly to "this racial problem." Whereas Russia "doesn't permit race prejudice . . . to interfere with scientific progress," he wrote, "because so many Americans persist in the notion of the master race, millions of Negroes are deprived of proper schooling, denied the right to vote on who will spend their tax money and are the last hired and first fired in those industries necessary for the progress of the country . . . Everybody has to get in the game if we are playing to win." The Count likewise made clear that he was traveling the world, even when he was wheelchair-bound, because it freed him from the racial vituperations back home.

Satchmo, whose role as a planetary plenipotentiary for jazz and for America earned him the new moniker of Ambassador Satch, was more direct. The U.S. government could and should "put its foot down" to stop race troubles, he told reporters in Buenos Aires in 1957, "but, you know, the government is run by Southerners." Photographer Lisl Steiner heard him go a surprising step further when she was taking pictures in his hotel room. The American ambassador to Argentina called to ask that Louis perform "The Star-Spangled Banner." "Mr. Ambassador," the trumpeter said, "you can go and fuck yourself because I can't even get a hotel room in Times Square!"

———

Duke did his traveling in the quiet style that was his trademark, but he logged more taxpayer-funded miles than any jazzman of the era and raised consciousness about his country as well as his music.

The first overseas trip—in 1933, to England, France, and the Netherlands—was a landmark. He helped elevate jazz's stature from a popular novelty to an art on par with and more rollicking than the staid classical forms familiar to snobbish Europeans. Fans launched Ellington record clubs complete with lectures, recitals, and group discussions. The BBC paid its steepest fee ever for a live broadcast by a band, and music writers in America heeded the raves in the British and French press. His record sales soared. And Europe gave Duke and his sidemen a respite from Jim Crow, as drummer Sonny Greer recounted: "We stayed in the biggest hotels, baby . . . They flew the American flag for us." Duke never forgot that reception, saying, "Jazz acquired the core of its international audience in the early '30s, not as a woman of ill repute, not as a lady, but as an art form—THE American art form."

Once bitten, Duke would go back repeatedly to Europe and beyond. He found a trip to Germany in 1950 particularly unforgettable: "I had occasion to drink beer with people who claimed—and had witnesses to the fact—they had been seized by the Gestapo for playing or even possessing our records." He also heard about "a couple of kids on a farm in France, brother and sister,

[who] buried their jazz records and refused to leave when the German soldiers came. The Nazis ransacked the house, then discovered the freshly
turned earth. They dug in, took out the records, and to the surprise of the
frightened youngsters, all they did was wrap them back up, throw them over
their shoulders, and march away."*

He had vivid memories of London, too, where he'd met a Prince of Wales,
a Duke of Kent, and, best of all, Queen Elizabeth II. A year after they were
introduced in 1958, he composed for her *The Queen's Suite,* a six-movement
melody that draws on natural landscapes—a mockingbird in Florida,
Northern Lights seen from a Canadian roadside, lightning bugs and croak-
ing frogs along the Ohio River. He underwrote the exquisite recording, cut
a single golden disc, mailed it to Buckingham Palace, and ensured the piece
wasn't publicly released while he was alive. After he died, the composition
appeared on an album that won the Grammy Award for Best Jazz Performance by a Big Band.[†]

The orchestra embarked on its first government-sponsored tour in 1963,
part of a Kennedy administration charm initiative, and the timing was ideal.
The State Department targeted countries in South Asia and the Middle East
that were close enough to the Soviet Union to be jittery in the wake of the
October 1962 Cuban Missile Crisis, especially Turkey, whose U.S.-supplied
Jupiter rockets Jack and Bobby Kennedy secretly bargained away in return
for Russia removing its warheads from Cuba. The trip also came as U.S. racial violence was again making headlines worldwide. First there were bomb-
ings and riots in Birmingham, then civil rights leader Medgar Evers was
gunned down, and that June Gov. George Wallace stood in the schoolhouse
door at the University of Alabama, vowing, "segregation now, segregation
tomorrow, and segregation forever." The jazzmen's "kind of cultural diplomacy, soft propaganda, was one of the ways that the foundation was laid for
the thaw in Cold War relations that took hold in the 1970s, even as it undermined the Soviet dictatorship by demonstrating the vitality of American
culture," said Charles Sam Courtney, a young foreign service officer assigned
as Ellington's escort in Turkey. Duke "wanted to contribute to a possible less-
ening of tensions in any way that he could."

---

* Ellington had his own bad memories of Nazi Germany. During a tour of Europe in 1939,
his train was stranded for six hours in Hamburg, with Hitler's troops ominously swarming
around. Hasse, *Beyond Category: The Life and Genius of Duke Ellington,* 222.
† Biographer Don George said Ellington also "played double piano with the King of England,
who told him, 'I have five hundred of your records.' He taught the King the Charleston—
'Come on, King, you can do it.'" George, *Sweet Man,* 124.

He did contribute, in ways the Foggy Bottom planners couldn't have imagined. In Pakistan, the embassy reported that "no other American visitor except Mrs. Jacqueline Kennedy received such a popular ovation from the press in recent years." In Iraq, both shows sold out despite an ongoing coup that sent the city into curfew, saw air force jets attack the presidential palace, and interrupted phone service. As with Armstrong in the Congo, Ellington's performances provided calm amid the chaos and were, the State Department attested, the "one cultural event that had the power to suspend the curfew." When journalists asked for an eyewitness account of the violence that would claim 250 lives, Duke lit a cigarette, then reported, "Those cats were swinging, man!"

Behind the scene things were less serene, although they were swinging, as newly minted foreign service officer Tom Simons saw and recorded. The Ellingtonians were "almost without exception excellent ambassadors and representatives of an America which the world might better know, for its profit and our own." At the same time, he saw them as "the worst disciplined big band in America." The jazzmen preferred cabarets to embassy receptions, carousing to sightseeing, nighttime to daylight hours, and unmarried women to any other companions. They rightfully wondered why they played almost exclusively for "prestige audiences"—and other Americans—rather than the "man in the street whom they saw clustered around tea-shop radios," and "why they should be sent halfway around the world, at significant expense, to play for people who already liked jazz." Simons lived in perpetual fear that "were some private activities of group members to become public, this publicity would hurt the image, not only of the group, but of the nation which they necessarily represented at every moment."

Duke himself was even more of a conundrum. "He is a gentleman from head to toe, entirely concentrated on his music, his comfort and his reputation," said Simons, who'd just earned his doctorate in history from Harvard. But the bandleader couldn't dress himself without a valet, canceled offstage functions at the last minute, suffered perpetual real or imagined illnesses, and never even tried to rein in band members who were boozing, carousing, and ignoring Simons's entreaties. Then there was Fernanda de Castro Monte, "a lady whose presence was a constant source of acute embarrassment and apprehension to American officials." The worry, of course, was the same "third rail" as back home—that a Black man shouldn't be with a white woman, especially one who, as Simons wrote, "was tall, impressive and always strikingly blonde and dressed . . . Ellington also insisted, to the general hilarity of those who were so informed, that the lady was a writer helping him to translate a libretto into French . . . The escort saw no evidence at any time that this claim had any basis whatsoever in fact." The State Department thought about dispatching a higher-ranking official "to separate Duke from Fernanda," Simons recalled sixty years later, but he said he could handle it and he did, barely: "Both Ellington and his friend were conscious of the dangers of adverse publicity which her presence brought with it. They were willing to do anything to avoid them, short of separating."*

The trip was successful enough that the State Department made Ellington its poster child for overseas adventures. Simons, meanwhile, reported that, after fourteen weeks with the band, he "had no appetite, little strength and few nerves left." The silver lining, he says looking back, was that he and Duke "became friends." When the young diplomat and his wife met Ellington in Geneva years later, the bandleader invited them backstage, then to his hotel for a meal and a gift from Fernanda—"a beautiful Japanese kimono which," Simons adds, "my wife still has."

Ellington eventually made two State Department trips to Africa and ones to Eastern Europe and South America, all of which would help him win a Presidential Gold Medal in 1966 for his "unofficial ambassadorial duties around the world." His transcendent trip, however, wasn't until 1971, to the Soviet Union, the hottest of hot spots. Again, the timing was fortuitous: a decade after Nikita Khrushchev had begun opening Russia to Western ideas and music, and a year before President Nixon, an Ellington fan, would travel to Moscow for a red-letter summit. While it was Ellington's first visit to the USSR, he was already familiar to tens of millions of Russians, Ukrainians, and other Soviets, many of whom had been tuning in—for an hour a night, every night year-round, for nearly twenty years—to Willis Conover's *Jazz Hour* over Voice of America radio. While Conover routinely aired tunes by Count Basie and Louis Armstrong, his opening theme song was Ellington's signature, "Take the 'A' Train."[†]

---

* Greg Zorthian, whose father was a public affairs officer in the U.S. Embassy in New Delhi, said Duke's mysterious illness that had him bow out of the tour for two weeks was, in fact, a reaction to being told Fernanda couldn't accompany him on that leg. "We took them on a shopping trip," says Greg, who was nine at the time, "to buy jewelry for his mistress." Author interview of Greg Zorthian.

What a nine-year-old couldn't understand was that Duke simply was bone-weary, spending 174 days traveling abroad that tumultuous year of 1963. Hasse, *Beyond Category: The Life and Genius of Duke Ellington*, 352.

† One sign of how well jazz jibed with America's political goals during the Cold War was that during the 1956 Hungarian Revolution, insurrectionists whistled fragments of jazz as passwords. Cohen, *Duke Ellington's America*, 412.

Now lucky listeners got to hear and see him live. The Ellington band played in five cities from Moscow to Minsk, at venues ranging from 1,300 seats to 10,000. In Kiev, tickets were so hard to come by that the local police band decided, as one member confided, to "put our uniforms on and then there was no trouble getting in." The tour was "an immense success," wrote Joe Presel, Ellington's official escort. "A success for the Ellingtons, most of whom genuinely enjoyed their stay in the USSR, a success for the Soviet State Concert Bureau which obviously made a great deal of money out of the tour, a success for the American Government, in that the audience reaction was extraordinarily good, that a top American presentation had performed well as cultural ambassadors and that there were no major incidents, and a success to those Soviet citizens, about 115,000 of them, who were able to see Ellington perform."

The jazz tours weren't the first cultural exchanges between Cold War adversaries, but they were a very different sort. Soviets joked at the time that such interchanges meant "we'll send our violinists from Odessa and the Moscow Symphony Orchestra to New York, and you send us your New York Philharmonic violinists from Odessa who'd emigrated to America." By contrast, these hard-drinking, hard-playing trumpeters, drummers, and bass players were patently American and totally exciting.

Russian journalists, however, cared more about race than music, perhaps because they worked for official organs eager to exploit America's vulnerabilities. Duke rarely obliged. The State Department had provided a six-page, single-spaced set of "Suggestions on Methods of Answering the Critic of the United States Abroad," but this instinctive conciliator didn't need coaching on what to say.* As Presel reported, the pianist would "point out that he had received the Medal of Freedom, America's highest honor, and that he was an 'American' composer. He was uninterested, he said, in people's color and assumed that they were indifferent to his. The Soviet journalists normally found this a baffling line of thought." As always, the image that lasted was of an elegant Black man who showed rather than told a story of racial progress.†

---

* In his quixotic write-in campaign for president in 1964, Dizzy Gillespie vowed to name Duke his secretary of state, saying, "He's a natural and can con anybody." Gillespie and Fraser, *To BE, or Not*, 458.

† American journalists were obsessed with the story of Ellington's tastes in food, and especially his love for (and inability to get enough of) steaks. He solved the problem in several ways: Reuben's, one of his favorite Manhattan eateries, flew in prime cuts. His pal Bob Udkoff taught Russian cooks how to make a U.S.-style cheeseburger. And he grew to enjoy borscht and caviar. Cohen, *Duke Ellington's America*, 551–52.

Hedrick Smith saw the reaction to Ellington through a ground-level lens. He started as Moscow bureau chief for the *New York Times* just before Ellington got to Moscow, and he came to learn through his journalism and research for a bestselling book that Russians' antipathy to the West traced back nearly three hundred years to the imperialist Peter the Great. But there was a competing current of Westernizers, and when the State Department "sent these jazz guys to the Soviet bloc as American ambassadors, they were tapping into [that] wellspring of fascination, admiration, excitement, energy, of Communist-educated but Western-curious youth . . . The Soviet system had built up an ideological and psychological firewall. But the jazz broke through it. The music broke through it. Ellington broke through it."

The world was so embracing that Ellington, like Armstrong and Basie, considered not just visiting but living overseas. But all three were patriots and, despite the indignities they endured, they were too American to live anywhere else for long. Jazz, Duke told the world, was "the American Idiom," and he demonstrated his stars-and-stripes spirit during World War II and after by performing at military bases, helping Uncle Sam peddle war bonds, and taping shows for Armed Services Radio. While any musician could do that, few could compose music that, like the freedom-loving anthems of Aaron Copland and George Gershwin, was unmistakably spawned by and true to these United States. In Duke's case, it grew out of a belief that the American promise of a more perfect union—one that included Blacks like him—was both possible and inevitable.

"That's the Negro's life," he said. "Dissonance is our way of life in America. We are something apart, yet an integral part."

———

Count Basie jetted around the world for thirty years, but flew so far below the radar that his adventures got none of the fanfare of Duke's and Satchmo's.

Like all comparably aged American men during World War II, the Count

———

In India, the remedy was different. "Duke would only eat steak, U.S. steak, and in India cows are sacred," recalls Greg Zorthian. A limited supply of beef was airlifted to the embassy commissary, he adds, and "it fell to my mother to have to go to all her friends to beg for those carefully hoarded steaks." Zorthian interview.

Then there was the issue of soft drinks. He was now drinking six or seven glasses of Coke a day, spiced with spoonfuls of sugar and fresh lime or lemon juice. That was a problem in Russia because Coke wasn't doing business there yet, but with help from the U.S. Embassy and Pepsi, Duke got what he needed. Cohen, *Duke Ellington's America*, 544; and author interview of Mercedes Ellington.

had to register for the draft. But like Ellington and Armstrong, Basie wasn't called to fight. That's likely because all three were too old, although for a brief time the upper age for draftees was raised to forty-five, which made all of them eligible. Yet whereas in the aftermath of the Japanese attack on Pearl Harbor Armstrong said, "I'm ready willing and able," Basie was more reticent. "Somebody kept trying to tell me everything was going to be all right because I'd most likely be brought in as a musician and wouldn't have to do any fighting," the Count wrote later. "I said I ain't going to take all that training and stuff. I ain't going out on them maneuvers jumping in foxholes with them goddamn snakes and things out there in them swamps. I said I wouldn't, and I meant that. There was nothing they could do to me that was going to be worse than what them snakes were going to make me do to myself."

He made up for that hesitancy by performing for GI Joes and reminding them of the cultural as well as political freedoms for which they fought. Even more, he brought an upbeat view of America to our friends overseas and to our foes. Hitler and his minions banned jazz, which they dubbed "nigger music," and they especially loathed its Black performers and Jewish enablers. But forbidden fruit is always more tempting, and Basie became an underground favorite. "The most esteemed members of the Nazi hierarchy were the Luftwaffe pilots and they were the ones that Hitler promoted as the Aryan ideal. But to Hitler's consternation their favorite music was American jazz. They loved Count Basie. They didn't want to listen to Nazi German beer hall songs," said jazz historian Will Friedwald. "It's just really, really ironic that, you know, the guys that Hitler valued the most loved African Americans and Jews and all the people that the Nazis were supposed to hate.

"During World War II, especially, Basie was the home front. Basie represented American culture."

In Italy, the family of dictator Benito Mussolini loved the fact that Italian Americans like Louis Prima were among American jazz pioneers, and they loved jazzmen like Bill Basie. Small surprise, then, that the Count topped the first postwar poll of Italian music fans. "Basie's triumph in this poll is further proof of his world-wide popularity," said the *Pittsburgh Courier*.

A decade after the war, the Basie band toured Europe, from France to Denmark, Sweden, Holland, Belgium, Switzerland, and Germany. "They floored everyone, including myself," pianist-composer Mary Lou Williams recalled of his Paris performance. "I couldn't sit down during the concert, I couldn't stop dancing." The highlight of his overseas travels came in Britain in 1957. First he dazzled the audience during a two-set performance at the Royal Festival Hall, attended by Princess Margaret and a grand success even though all the sheet music for the trip had been left behind in America.* Margaret liked the early-evening, two-hour concert enough that she returned for a later performance where, as the press reported, "on more than one occasion, she led the applause."†

The princess must have raved to her sister because, seven months later, Queen Elizabeth II invited Basie back to play at a charity event for the Artists' Benevolent Fund. Nearly every member of Elizabeth's immediate family already had proven themselves jazz lovers, and now the Count treated the queen to "The Kid from Red Bank." Then he let Sonny Payne rip with his patented solo on "Old Man River." The audience at the London Palladium stood to applaud and, in the receiving line, Prince Philip whispered to Count Basie, "Oh, you had them swinging." Basie called it "one of the biggest thrills of my life . . . I was introduced to the queen. You can't beat that, not in Great Britain . . . The headlines we got for that one short set were really something. 'BASIE BAND IS ROYAL SENSATION.'"

The next morning produced a disturbing postscript when the band was kicked out of its apartment in London's West End. Basie was staying elsewhere, and he tried to put the best face on the eviction: "I guess some of the fellows and some of their happy fans must have gotten a little too carried away with all the celebration and after-partying . . . I don't think it had anything to do with color . . . You were attracting the wrong people or maybe just too many people."

A State Department tour of Southeast Asia fourteen years later proved considerably less enjoyable. The Vietnam War was raging, and two stops—Burma and Laos—were too near the action for the Count's comfort. "I was mostly just scared all of the time," he recalled. "They were shooting at planes over there . . . I was in one of those little three-seaters, and you could sit back there and look down on where all that trouble was." He was right to be afraid, but never followed through on his threat to abandon the tour. In the end, he said, "we found fans and made new friends at every stopover."

Many of those new fans and friends had actually been listening to him

---

* Basie said it was an accident that the music wasn't taken, but saxophonist Frank Wess said he'd heard the Count say, "I am not going to pay for that overweight 'cause y'all don't look at it no way; y'all looking out there in the audience." Basie, *Good Morning Blues*, 320; and Alfred Green, *Rhythm Is My Beat*, 140.

† A year before, Margaret loved hearing Satchmo. He dedicated to her the song "Mahogany Hall Stomp," named after a notorious New Orleans brothel, and she "took off her fur wrap, lit a cigarette and clutched her programme, nodding and stamping like all the other fans to the wild rhythm of the jazz men." Martlew, "'Satchmo' Plays for Margaret."

over the decades over the Voice of America or Armed Forces broadcasts. He also bonded with producer George Wein, who accompanied him nearly everywhere and saw a graciousness uncharacteristic of big-name stars. Wein had promised to accompany Basie to Laos on a paratrooper transport, but that would have meant leaving Wein's seventy-seven-year-old father alone in Burma. Basie wouldn't hear of it, saying, "Get out of here; you go back to your father and stay with him." Like Ellington, said Wein, Basie "was a road rat accustomed to the grueling pace of the road."

In Asia, the producer observed one key difference between the Count and the other two bandleaders. "I was puzzled by his attitude toward encores—he wouldn't take any," said Wein, who helped launch jazz festivals in Newport and New Orleans. "Audiences surged to their feet at the end of each performance, shouting for more . . . But no matter how great the ovation, Basie never went back onstage." The Count tried to explain, "I learned a lesson at Birdland: You've got to leave an audience hungry for more, so they come back the next time." Wein: "Bill—when's the next time you'll be in Rangoon?" That night, Wein added, the Count "played an encore. In fact, he played encores after that on all of his foreign tours."

———

Satchmo had been jazz's champion globetrotter since the summer of 1932, when he made his first trip to England. The stories about that visit are legion, and some are true. He did have trouble finding a good hotel that would take him, because of his skin color. The Prince of Wales showed up to hear him three times in a single week, but what Walter Winchell wrote—that the King and Queen came, and that Louis told him "ah'm gonna swing the nex' one fer you—Rex!"—was, as Satchmo himself concluded, "a lot of hooey." (That didn't stop him from repeating the story, with the added flair of saying he'd dedicated "You Rascal You" to that same George V.)

He traipsed back and forth to Europe over the decades, but never stayed as long or had as little fun as in 1933. He battled with his managers, cycling through three of them. His lips throbbed, forcing him to take what jazz savant Dan Morgenstern called "the longest vacation of his entire career— from spring to fall of 1934." He lived in Paris most of that time, not returning to America until January 1935, without a band, a manager, or a record label.*

———

* The *Pittsburgh Courier* said he was thinking about settling permanently in England, and the *New York Amsterdam News* said he'd applied for British citizenship. But he was too all-American to have ever seriously contemplated abandoning his homeland. "Louie to Stay in Europe," *Pittsburgh Courier*; and "Armstrong Is Being Panned," *New York Amsterdam News*.

One sign of Louis's loyalty to his homeland was that, just after Pearl Harbor, he inserted

But his time away gave him a chance to reflect not just on jazz but on race, as he told a reporter in Sweden: "Us Negroes have created Jazz. White musicians have followed us, but they haven't reached us yet and I think they never will. Because this music is namely an expression for something that lives within us and that white men never fully will understand. The liberation from slavery explains how the jazz was born. The negro has created two kinds of music. First there are these melancholic spirituals, the folk songs from the time of the slavery. And now jazz, which is a reaction, because now we dare to laugh and smile—we got human dignity."

Every foreign trip manifested a further evolution of Louis's sensibilities, his grasp of world affairs, and his sense of humor. Told in 1956 that the foreign ministers from the Big Four wartime powers were meeting in Geneva at the same time he was playing there, and that unifying Germany was high on their agenda, he quipped, "Why, man, we've already unified it. We came thru Germany playing this ol' happy music, and if them Germans wasn't unified, then this ain't ol' Satchmo talking to you." In 1957, to the delight of the U.S. government, his sixty-seven concerts in five Latin American capitals knocked the Soviet Sputnik splash off the front pages and magazine covers and made clear, as *Variety* reported, that "as a goodwill ambassador [Satchmoismo's] tour was surefire." Two years later, following his performances in Israel and Lebanon, the Egyptian press accused Ambassador Satch of spying for Israel, and Lebanon said he couldn't come back. Satchmo: "I don't read the Egyptian newspapers. I speak every language except Greek and what they're saying is all Greek to me."

The State Department never tried to measure his cumulative impact, but journalists did, repeatedly, with one writing that Armstrong "has traveled more diplomatic miles than [then secretary of state] John Foster Dulles and has done more to further the cause of American culture abroad than Walt Disney and Jayne Mansfield combined."

While he seldom looked back, one worldly matter deeply disappointed Louis: that the State Department didn't invite him to represent America behind the Iron Curtain. The idea had been in the talking stage, until his

---

into his repertoire "The Star-Spangled Banner." It wasn't a rote rendition. "I was with James Baldwin listening to Louis, and he played a great set. And then he ended with 'The Star-Spangled Banner,'" said Dan Morgenstern, who knew Baldwin thought Armstrong was too clownish. "And then James turned to me and said, 'You know, that's the first time I've liked that song.' What he heard from Louis did away with all the stuff that was accumulated around it. And just the purity that Louis brought to it made him appreciate it." Jenkins, *Louis Armstrong's Black & Blues*.

"no guts" blast against President Eisenhower. But while he'd never make it to Russia, in 1965 Satchmo organized his own tour to Prague, Bucharest, Belgrade, Sofia, and, most fun of all, East Berlin. "West Berlin was swinging, and Louis said: 'Let's go to West Berlin,'" bassist Arvell Shaw recalled. "Can't do that with papers from Russians in East Berlin and from the U.S. Louis said, 'Let's go anyway.' So we got on the bus—Checkpoint Charlie—to go through the Berlin Wall. We got to the East German side, and the Russian soldiers and East German police had their guns out. One of the guards looked at us and said 'Louis Armstrong.' He called out all the guards, got Louis' autograph and waved us all on. And when we got to the American side, a six-foot-seven sergeant from Texas—oh, he was fierce!—said, 'How'd you get through here? Where are your papers?' And he got out handcuffs. Sergeant looks and says, 'Satchmo—this is Satchmo!' He called the guards and they got autographs and waved us on.

"Every night we went back and forth. When the American ambassador heard, he said: 'How'd you do that? I can't do that!'"

None of his travels moved him as much as his trips to Africa. He went first in 1957, in a visit paid for by CBS and arranged by celebrated correspondent Edward R. Murrow, who was producing a documentary called *The Saga of Satchmo*. Ghanaian prime minister Kwame Nkrumah gave Louis a royal reception, tens of thousands of frenzied fans greeted him at Accra's Old Polo Grounds, and he was toasted by tribesmen, dancers, and drummers, after which he asked, "Did you see that little old plump woman? When she danced, man, she was like my mother Mary Ann."

The sixty-year-old trumpeter was back in 1960–61 for a twenty-seven-city tour that included his Congo visit, this time courtesy of Pepsi-Cola and U.S. taxpayers. What Pepsi wanted was clear in its ads: "You like Satchmo. Pepsi brings you Satchmo. Therefore you like Pepsi." What the State Department wanted wouldn't be entirely apparent for decades, as experts sifted through evidence of links to the Lumumba assassination and other Cold War ventures. Asked about matters of race or politics, Louis gave just the answer the State Department would have scripted: "Music's the same everywhere."*

He gave a more heartfelt answer when he teamed up a year later with

---

* Asked by the *New York Times* how he felt about being crowned Ambassador Satch—a tag bestowed by George Avakian, who produced Armstrong's album of that title—Satchmo said it "*is* nice, you know. Specially when the chicks, they say, 'Hellew there, Ambassador Satch.' And the cats, 'How you doin' there, ol' Ambassador Satchie-matchie . . . I'm not lookin' to be on no high pedestal." Millstein, "Africa Harks to Satch's Horn."

composer and pianist Dave Brubeck and his wife Iola on a satiric musical, *The Real Ambassadors*. The show captured the contradictions of America sending out Black goodwill ambassadors like Satchmo, Duke, and the Count at a moment when those men couldn't bank on basic civility back home. And it made Louis into the human-rights champion the Brubecks believed he was. The production opened with the narrator claiming that the hero, clearly meant to be Armstrong, has the "ability to keep his opinions to himself." Then a voice (Armstrong's) declared, "Lady, if you could read my mind, your head would bust wide open . . . What *we* need is a goodwill tour of Mississippi."

While the musical was performed just once, at the 1962 Monterey Jazz Festival, its songs were recorded a year earlier by Columbia. Dave Brubeck said he wrote numbers like "They Say I Look Like God" as parodies, but hearing Satchmo sing them showed "a side of Louie that I didn't know existed, and I don't think the audience really knew. They knew him for the person that was always full of joy and everything, but here he was so deep," with tears forming as he intoned:

> They Say I look like God!
> Could God be black? My God!
> If all are made in the image of Thee,
> Could Thou perchance a Zebra be?

"Goose pimple," Louis said when he was done. "I got goose pimple on this one."

PART VI

LAST ACTS

LONG-LIVED

THESE WERE SUPPOSED to be the Count's years of ease and joy, a time to reflect on his monumental achievements. And that was how he'd tell the story even though the reality was, as usual with him, more layered.

Just before Christmas in 1971, Bill, Catherine, and Diane moved full-time to the Bahamas, trading their spacious home, Olympic-sized pool, and celebrity-stocked neighborhood in Queens for the coastal beauty and physical isolation of Freeport, which Katy had fallen in love with during a vacation there. She struggled with the transition, given her reign as belle of Addisleigh Park and the supportive communities she'd built for their mentally and physically challenged daughter, Diane. It was harder still for Bill, who hadn't even been consulted. He'd lived nearly all his life in the New York area and loved being around the corner from pals like Milt Hinton, Ella Fitzgerald, and Mercer Ellington. Just getting to the Bahamas meant long and inconvenient flights.

Katy claimed the move would liberate them from city stresses. That made sense, given her run-ins with burglars and extremists. Several years earlier a trio of shotgun-toting thugs invaded their home, making off with $250 in cash before flippantly wishing her and Diane a Merry Christmas. Months before, thieves stole from her car four new pairs of curtains, dozens of freshly laundered sheets, and a spare tire and rim. Most daunting, Black radicals who thought Catherine wasn't sufficiently radical had threatened violence. She took the risk seriously enough not only to take out a gun license and buy that .38 Special, but also to become an auxiliary member of the local police force. Just to be sure they were protected once they got to the more frontier-like West Indies, she purchased a gleaming Remington rifle.

None of that worried her quite as much as the Count himself, however. She intended Freeport to test Bill's vow to give up his mistresses, gambling, and other bad behavior. "He basically said, 'I'll do anything, anything you want.' She wanted to sell the house," recalled family friend Aaron Woodward, who said their island home cost about $500,000, which was ten times what they'd paid for the house in St. Albans.*

"Kate and I were talking about something or other," Bill remembered. "[She said,] 'You know that little house you liked so much down on the island? Well, you'd better try to get two or three more gigs together, because I've put four or five dollars down on it' . . . And that was the beginning of our love palace. It really was the start of something big for me, for just me and Katy and our daughter, Diane, and Graf the puppy. That's when we really started living as a real family. It was our house of happiness."

Basie kept his promise to spend more time at home, flying to the islands on his days off and focusing on family to the point where his new house didn't even have a piano. Diane adjusted to her new surroundings, where she could walk outdoors, with assistance, and use a treadmill during the rare spells of bad weather. Katy rested easier, too, having quickly paid off the new house, set up a trust for Diane, and taken other steps to ensure that, should Bill's good behavior falter, she and her daughter would be protected. The Count, meanwhile, was taking to the lifestyle that was more his due. Now he dined regularly with A-listers, including Ronald Reagan and Frank Sinatra. No more beat-up jalopies or bare-bones buses. Everything was first-class now, from his and Katy's cabin on the *Queen Elizabeth 2* to seats in airplanes and rooms in hotels that not that long ago had refused to even book him.

This new life in the Bahamas seemed like just the thing, with their manicured lawn on a two-acre lot, pink-marbled walls and floors, and crystal chandeliers. But the initial reason for going there, as he'd acknowledge, was "to help get myself out of the doghouse one more time." His letters home suggest staying straight wasn't easy. In a three-page handwritten one to Diane in 1979 he wrote, "I know I have caused a hurt on your mother and she is very bitter." In another that same day he implied he'd been banished again from his home: "Now after so many years of life I'm alone. Nobodys [sic] fault but my own." There were love missives, too, including one where he got sexy: "Do you know that I'm getting so I must sleep behind you or I can't get too good. 'Old man huh?'"

It might indeed have been a blissful time if he'd stayed healthy. Five years

---

* The Count said that, while they sold their New York house, "we held on to the pool so it would still be available to the kids" in the neighborhood. Basie, *Good Morning Blues,* 357.

after the move he had a heart attack that required him to slow down. Several years after that he suffered shingles, then a viral infection that left him with arthritis bad enough that he needed a wheelchair and scooter to get around. He took furloughs, but wouldn't hear of retiring. With Basie-like humor, he called his arthritis "Arthur," saying, "Arthur is giving me trouble today." Now he had constant pain to mask as well as his feelings. "It was Winston Churchill who once described Soviet Russia as 'a riddle wrapped in a mystery inside an enigma.' That line comes to mind when I think of Count Basie," wrote writer and broadcaster Alex Barris. "He was a complex man who created music of great simplicity. He was a private man who spent much of his life in public. He showed the world a mask of impassivity that hid a wealth of deeply felt emotions."

Oscar Peterson, one of Basie's favorite collaborators, jazz's greatest pianists, and the BBC's favorite TV hosts, was better than most at penetrating the veils. "Many interviews remain clearly etched on my mind, for all kinds of reasons; but if I had to nominate my absolute favourite it would be the one with Bill Basie," Peterson wrote. "He was anxious about the stiffness creeping through his hands. 'I hope I don't embarrass you today,' he confided, 'but the old fingers haven't been operating too well recently. I just don't seem to be able to feel the board the way I like, and sometimes my hands feel cold, so cold.' I took his hands in mine and massaged them, saying that I was sure he'd be in his usual fine fettle. Suddenly his mood changed: he pulled his hands away, looked at me with that famous stare, and said, 'Knowing you and your gorilla self, that ain't gonna stop you from washing me away!' . . .

"I shall always remember how he sat there at the piano—this beautiful man, slightly hunched, at last beginning to show the wear and tear of nearly 50 years on the road (or perhaps I had refused to recognize the signs until now)," added Peterson. "I sympathized deeply, and wondered how many of his admirers knew what this man was putting himself through every night when he climbed onto the bandstand and fronted the orchestra."

Basie's graciousness with Peterson reflected the modesty that this icon of swing demonstrated with other virtuosos of his era, including Edward Ellington and Louis Armstrong. He called Satchmo "the king," adding, "Nobody could touch him." And he said that while musicians had showed him how to find the beat, Duke showed him "how to dress that beat in a mink coat." The two played together in 1961, making an album called *First Time! The Count Meets the Duke*. "It was the hardest, toughest two weeks of my life. Nobody should have to play alongside of that guy," Basie said. "You know what? He wanted ME to take a solo on A Train. His own tune, if you please. Duke's own tune. You know what I did? I ran for the door.'"

The Count never slowed down. The band kept getting dates, and he kept calling the tunes, even when his hands didn't cooperate. Sometimes, in private chats with his callow sidemen, he reflected on how far he and America had come. At the band's last concert before the Christmas break in 1981, "we were staying at a really famous hotel called the Muehlebach" in Kansas City, remembers drummer Gregg Field. "Basie looked at me and he smiled. He said, 'You know, the first time I came here, I had to walk in the back door. Now they give me the suite.'"

About a year later, Quincy Jones recalled, Basie was playing at the Palladium in Los Angeles and Jones had just produced Michael Jackson's bestselling album *Thriller:* "The Count was in a wheelchair: he looked tired but exuberant. After the concert they wheeled him over to me backstage. He reached up and touched my arm. With those huge nostrils typically flared open, his eyes wide, he said, 'Man—that shit you and Michael did, me and Duke would never even dream about nothin' that big. You hear me? We wouldn't even dare to *dream* about it.'"

Bill and Katy were doing better in their Bahamas phase than they had since the early years when he pursued her and she pretended to resist. She went on the road with him as often as possible, to help and so they could be together. With Diane in mind, he organized a dinner-dance concert in the Bahamas, with his friends Sarah Vaughan and Ella Fitzgerald, to raise money for a school building for "The Exceptional Children of Freeport, Grand Bahama." But illness again intervened, Katy's this time. "She was at home in Freeport, where she had been since late fall because her doctor had

---

* The Count's actions belied his words, according to saxophonist John Williams, who was there and remembers when Basie "stood, pointed at Ellington, and Ellington looked embarrassed and smiled . . . Basie was saying, 'I'm the leader, you're the sideman.'" Two other ways Basie quietly asserted himself at that recording session, according to Williams, were by showing up at "the very last moment" and by teasing Duke about his long hair. Author interview of John Williams.

Producer Teddy Reig remembered that Basie refused to say a few words alongside Duke at the end of the record, or even to pose with him for pictures: "Later, in the car I asked him what that was all about. 'I'm not gonna fuck with Duke,' he answered. 'He'll start talking some shit and I'll sound like I never went to school.' Then I asked about the photos. He said . . . 'Duke'll put on some costume that'll make me look like I never owned a suit!'" Reig, *Reminiscing in Tempo,* 56.

Ellington and Basie ran the two hottest bands of the mid-1900s, but whereas Basie would challenge to a cutting contest anyone else, including the great Chick Webb, he steered clear of Ellington.

advised her to stay home and take it easy and watch her weight," he said, trying to make sense of her sudden and fatal heart attack. "I knew she was not in the best health, but all during the time while I was at home during the Christmas break, she didn't seem to be having serious problems either. She was just her usual self, and that's the way she was when I came back to work in January, and that's how she sounded on the telephone every day. Then all of a sudden she was *gone*. My Katy, my baby."

That was in the spring of 1983, when he was seventy-eight and she was just sixty-nine. "I decided that the best thing for me to do was come right on back out on the road a couple of days after the funeral. And I have no doubt at all in my mind that this is what she wanted me to do," he wrote in his memoir. "That is exactly where I intend to be for as long as I keep on having as much satisfaction and enjoyment as I'm still getting out of it. I certainly don't have any plans for retirement in the foreseeable future, since I am still playing music, or at least *trying* to play it, as much as I ever did."

———

Louis also couldn't imagine retiring, which he saw as tantamount to dying. "Whatya gonna do? You goin' in a room and bite your nails?" he asked when a reporter asked him about abandoning his music. He was equally adamant about not leaving Corona, the melting-pot, middle-class neighborhood in Queens where Lucille had picked out their clapboard-framed house decades before. By the early 1960s she was eager to buy in a leafier and loftier community. "Lucille and I began talking about moving Louis from the poky little house in Queens to a big estate further out on Long Island, a more suitable residence for the great American virtuoso," said journalist and friend Ernie Anderson. "Lucille was thrilled at this prospect and I was about to take the idea to Joe Glaser."

Then Louis got wind of the plan. "I absolutely forbid it. I've just gotten to know my neighbours here," he informed Lucille and Ernie. He told another journalist why he loved Corona: "We're right out here with the rest of the colored folk and the Puerto Ricans and Italians and the Hebrew cats. We don't need to move out in the suburbs to some big mansion with lots of servants and yardmen and things. What for? What the hell I care about living in a 'fashionable' neighborhood? Ain't nobody cutting off the lights and gas here 'cause we didn't pay the bills. The Frigidaire is full of food. What more do we need?"

That reticence revealed Louis's truest self—a kid from the backstreets of New Orleans who had no airs and pushed back against his wife's dreams of upward mobility. His two-story house, built in 1910 and just seven blocks from Shea Stadium, was the only one he'd ever own, with the exception of an even more modest one in Chicago where he and Lil lived briefly. It had everything he needed and all the things he'd been proud to buy for Lucille. The kitchen was straight out of the *Jetsons* cartoon, with cabinets lacquered in a deep turquoise. The blender and can opener were flush mounted, the Sub-Zero was the most expensive refrigerator available, and the stove came with six burners, two broilers, two ovens, and a small placard reading, "Custom Made by Crown for Mr. and Mrs. Louis Armstrong."

Silver-foil wallpaper encased their bedroom suite, with side-by-side twin beds that allowed autonomy or intimacy, depending on Lucille's and Louis's moods. The dressing room was the size of most city people's bedrooms, with built-in drawers, racks for hundreds of suits, and a scale. His study was his private lair, off-limits to everyone else. He stocked the cabinet with Jack Daniel's and other liquors he couldn't afford in his New Orleans and Chicago years, penned thousands of letters from the curved mahogany desk, and on the recessed reel-to-reel tape recorder and record player he played nearly nonstop music from the likes of W. C. Handy, Marian Anderson, and the Armstrong All-Stars. On one dark-paneled wall hung his favorite decoration, an oil portrait of himself signed by the artist Benedetto, an old friend and admirer better known as Tony Bennett. "You out-Rembrandted Rembrandt," Armstrong told the singer-painter.

Like the Basies, the Armstrongs bought their adjoining lot. Rather than a swimming pool, Lucille and Louis filled theirs with a Japanese garden, bricked patio, wet bar with cabinets, gas grill encased in wrought iron, cedar pergola, bathroom, and fishpond stocked with colorful Japanese koi. It became a gathering spot not just for neighbors, but for nearby jazzmen like Cannonball Adderley, Dizzy Gillespie, Jimmy Rushing, and Clark Terry. A hired man helped maintain the yard while a young woman cooked, ironed, cleaned, and contemplated her good luck, telling a friend, "Can you believe it? Here I am, working in Louis Armstrong's house."*

His part of Corona reminded Louis of the camaraderie of his boyhood New Orleans. At night he'd order Chinese from the Dragon Seed. The next morning he'd pull on Bermuda shorts, socks, slippers, and a hat, and march the two blocks to Joe's Artistic Barber Shop, where he'd long ago been crowned the king of Queens. Waiting his turn in the iron chair, he'd hold

---

* With help from her staff, Lucille always had waiting for Louis a New Orleans–style casserole of red beans, vegetables including collard greens or candied sweet potatoes, along with cornbread, mineral water, and beer. Ernie Anderson, "Louis Armstrong: A Personal Memoir."

court on the sidewalk, perched on a stool with a ripped seat cover. "He didn't like me to put him ahead of anybody," remembered Joe Gibson, who cut Satchmo's hair along with Ossie Davis's and Muhammad Ali's. "He was never in a hurry." Louis called Joe's the Soul Barber Shop, and wrote that "we Soulees speak the same languages—slanguages."

When one of the neighborhood kids learned that Louis was home, there'd soon be a pack of urchins on the bandleader's stoop. Satchmo would buy everyone ice cream if the Good Humor man rolled by, or toss them candy, all the while lecturing on why they should stay in school longer than he had. One of those kids, Denise Pease, recalled that "when Uncle Louis would come home, he was magical . . . He would give the children a fifty-cent piece. And he wanted to make sure that we had money to go to college. That's what the fifty cents was supposed to be used for. But we didn't use it for that, uh, we used it to go to the nearest grocery store and buy candy. Uncle Louis and Miss Lucille didn't have children of their own, but they kind of adopted the children of the neighborhood."

Celebrity also had downsides. "Can't even go to a baseball game," he told a reporter. "Went to one Dodgers–White Sox World Series game and cats was climbing all over my box seat. Some of the players asked what in hell was all that commotion up in the stands. Sometimes them big crowds can spook you. Get to pressing you and grabbing your clothes. You get a funny feeling that they might trample on you."

Louis was crazy about dogs. He had a Boston terrier named General, replaced years later by two schnauzers: Trumpet, his gift to Lucille, and Trinket, a present from dog lover Joe Glaser. He also fell more deeply in love with his last and most enduring wife. Through the 1960s he spent more time at home, and less with his mistresses. Lucille had learned when to press and when to back off, as she explained to a journalist in 1964: "Let's say the eye sees what it wants to see . . . I have partial vision on purpose. I don't see these things. I know Louis loves me . . . I don't believe in surprises in our marriage. I call Louis when I am going to join him when he is on tour."

They had their fights, but he'd learned to argue with his mouth, not his fists. "If something bothered him, you knew it, in no uncertain terms, right then and there," said Lucille. "And then after it's over, 'Well, come on. Let's go have dinner.' He's had his say and that's the end of it."

He approached young musicians the same way at first, launching what felt like a generational war when he said, "This rock and roll stuff they play, that's not music. Anyone with a shrill harsh voice can do that. Don't mean nothing." He was even more dismissive of bebop, telling a journalist eager for a headline, "Bop is slop. Jujitsu music."* But once he'd vented he relented. Rock 'n' roll, he explained, "got beat and life." To those who complained rock was too loud, he offered this counsel: "They can turn the television set down." Later, he told *Harper's* that "there's room for all kinds of music. I dig it all: country, jazz, pop, swing, blues, ragtime."

Some called him a moldy fig, and though his genre-bending years were past, he brushed off such talk. "Music don't know no age," he said when he was fifty-four. "I feel the same as when I was twenty-eight." The next year—in between concerts and cities—he told another journalist, "I don't mind traveling and that's where the audiences are—in the towns and cities . . . I want to hear that applause." Clarinetist Joe Muranyi said that Louis simply "liked people. And he liked poor people. And he liked crippled people and fat ladies. He loved the humanity aspect."

David Halberstam showed up in Atlanta in 1957 intending to pen what he called a "twilight-of-career piece" on Louis. "It's perfectly true that he paces himself carefully, but the essence of the trumpet is all there, still able to touch a man in almost any mood; and the voice, deep and gravelly, is still expressive, light and flirtatious or deep and sentimental," wrote Halberstam, who'd go on to win a Pulitzer Prize for his *New York Times* coverage of the Vietnam War.

After decades of touring and jam-packed performances, Armstrong could now reach a bigger audience than ever through television. During that Golden Age, turning on the set meant welcoming into your home Buffalo Bob and his pal Howdy Doody, Lucy and Ricky Ricardo, Sgt. Joe Friday, and Louis Armstrong. Satchmo was omnipresent, winningly retelling his stock stories on nearly every variety show alongside such hosts as Ed Sullivan, Perry Como, Dean Martin, Jackie Gleason, David Frost, Pearl Bailey, Dick Cavett, Johnny Carson, and Flip Wilson. He was even on ABC's rock-and-roll-centered *Shindig!*

Louis and Duke got together in New York in 1961 to record their first true collaboration, seventeen songs formatted into a pair of albums entitled *Together for the First Time* and *The Great Reunion*. What came to be known as "the Great Summit" could have been a disaster. Two aging legends who'd spent

---

* Dizzy Gillespie, an avatar for bebop, shot back, calling New Orleans music "Uncle Tom music" and branding Armstrong and his ilk as "squares." The two eventually made up—"what I had considered Pops's grinning in the face of racism," Gillespie conceded, was in fact "his absolute refusal to let anything, even anger about racism, steal the joy from his life and erase his fantastic smile"—and they became fast friends. Riccardi, *Heart Full of Rhythm*, 324; and Gillespie and Fraser, *To BE, or Not*, 296.

thirty years competing in popularity polls now had to share a stage. Each possessed a sizable ego, and both were accustomed to the limelight. Over their two days in an RCA studio, Ellington played the piano and composed the tunes, but Armstrong made them his. "Midway through, Ellington unveiled a piece of music he had written long ago (words as well as music) but had never performed successfully (several studio attempts remained unissued)," Dan Morgenstern remembered. "He claimed that he'd composed this piece, 'Azalea,' with Louis in mind.

"The trumpeter and singer put on his hornrimmed glasses—something that gave him a studious appearance—and looked intently at the music sheet, then nodded his head. Ellington moved to the piano, and Louis began to play the not-at-all-simple melody as if it truly had been written for him, and then negotiated the tricky Ellingtonian lyrics, with some bizarre rhymes, as if it were a Shakespeare sonnet. Ellington beamed." That experience, Morgenstern adds, helped Duke overcome his unacknowledged but unmistakable snobbery toward the less-refined Satchmo: "'Azalea' made it clear what level of artist and man this was."

Count Basie said never recording with Louis was "one of my big regrets." But he recalled how the two shared a program card at a theater in Philadelphia late in their careers. Thad Jones, one of Basie's trumpeters, wasn't there early in the set, "so we just went on and hit, and I heard those trumpets and heard that goddamn audience going wild and looked up there, and old Pops had snuck up and was sitting in Thad's chair; and when we got to the trumpet solo spot, he took it and you never heard so much clapping. Old Pops was having a ball. As it turned out, Thad did arrive before the set was over, but he made Louis stay right on out there in the first chair. That was something nobody could ever forget . . . After that, old Pops would check by every day, just in case Thad got held up again."

Armstrong, however, finally was feeling his years. Early in 1965 he at last made it under the Iron Curtain. That fall he headed to New Orleans, which he'd avoided for ten years over its refusal to let integrated ensembles like his perform. The city had repealed that law, and Louis returned as promised, greeted like the Zulu king he'd been a generation before. That same year he talked for the first time about quitting the music scene.

His teeth hurt, and his lips. His heart pounded too hard, the veins in his legs throbbed, and, as he said, "all hotels are alike—bed, bureau, two pillows . . . That's my life." Rather than easing his way, Joe Glaser took him at his optimistic word and booked a schedule that fall and winter that would have challenged a twenty-year-old, starting with forty-two consecutive one-nighters. Louis generally stuck to his narrative that "you don't quit when you're still strong and enjoy your work." But in the summer of 1965 he told a journalist, in a conversation he thought wouldn't be published then if ever, that "all I want to do is get the hell out of this grind while I still have my health, so Lucille and I can enjoy what's left of our lives as civilians. I don't want to be Satchmo anymore . . . So mark my words: about a year and a half from now, old Satchmo is gonna disappear—me and Lucille will go underground for about six months—and when we come up again it's gonna be as Mr. and Mrs. Armstrong, civilians, period."

As for what would follow, "I'd like to give trumpet lessons to little kids . . . But once I laid down that horn I'll never pick it up in public again."

Two years later another journalist, Larry L. King, accompanied him on the road and, at the end of a ten-day stint in Atlantic City, saw close-up the trumpeter's creeping exhaustion: "After he dressed we walked along the Steel Pier . . . The noisy crowds had been dispersed and the gates locked . . . Pops lit a cigarette and leaned on a restraining fence to smoke. For long moments he looked up at the full moon, and watched the surf come and go. The glow from his cigarette faintly illuminated the dark old face in repose and I thought of some ancient tribal chieftain musing by his campfire, majestic and mystical. There was only the rush of water, gently roaring and boasting at the shore.

"'Listen to it, Pops,' he said in his low, chesty rumble. 'Whole world's turned on. Don't you dig its pretty sounds?'"

———

Duke Ellington was even less inclined than Satchmo or the Count to leave the life of music that he loved. But he might have had to if not for the miraculous rebirth he underwent in the summer of 1956 on the bandstand of an upstart jazz festival in Newport, Rhode Island.

Duke came to the seaside city looking to the outside world like a slumping fifty-seven-year-old. Big bands were an anachronism in the rocking 'n' rolling era of Elvis Presley's "Hound Dog" and Little Richard's "Slippin' and Slidin'." Many of Ellington's featured musicians were gone. Short of cash, his band traveled now in pedestrian buses, not elegant Pullman sleepers, and overseas adventures were put on hold. Duke dug deeper than ever into his pockets and royalties to cover the red ink. The summer before, he'd spent a humbling six weeks accompanying a water show called Aquacade in Flushing, New York. Newport—a community of old mansions, glistening naval destroyers, and tony tourists like those in Bing Crosby's new film *High Society*, shot nearby—didn't know or care much about Duke or jazz. Finding housing for Ellington's Black music makers had proven as challenging as in the Southland. Four sidemen couldn't be found and were likely working off a bender, which led him to limit his opening set to twelve minutes and three numbers, including "The Star-Spangled Banner." Then came a three-hour wait before he'd be back for what he saw as the show-ending "exit music," leading him to complain to organizer George Wein, "What are we—the animal act, the acrobats?"* Worst of all, Duke knew that *Time* magazine was crafting a cover story on him, that reporter Carter Harman was in the audience, and that unless his review was a rave, it could be the bandleader's professional obituary.

It all boiled down not to the new suite Duke had composed to honor the festival, which was in just its third year, but to "Diminuendo and Crescendo in Blue," a 1937 Ellington piece the band knew, but not well, and that Duke inserted at the last instant. Halfway through, Paul Gonsalves was tapped for a lengthy solo, a good idea given his skill on the tenor sax yet risky given his addictions to narcotics and booze and the fact he'd just told Duke, "I don't think I've played it but once." Ellington: "You just keep blowing until I tell you to stop." Gonsalves let loose for twenty-seven choruses that perfectly thread the line between bare simplicity and heavy fireworks. The volcanic effect was magnified when, after his seventh take and at about midnight of this last night of the festival, a platinum-blond girl in a black dress sprang out of her box seat and began dancing, prompting others in the cucumber-cool audience to gyrate like rock 'n' rollers and convincing those streaming to the exits to turn back.† Just offstage, backup drummer Jo Jones egged on the band by thwacking a rolled-up copy of the *Christian Science Monitor*, spurring first the reeds, then the trombones, and finally the entire orchestra to ricochet the bounding beat. (Duke dubbed Jones as "the man in the pit with the git-wit-it git.") Duke himself hollered "ah-HA!" then "Higher!" and, in the words of trumpeter Clark Terry, the bandleader was "almost dancing."

"Literally acres of people stood on their chairs, cheering and clapping," said record producer George Avakian, who was crouched on the edge of the stage. "Halfway through Paul's solo, it had become an enormous single living organism, reacting in waves like huge ripples to the music played before it."

---

* That, Wein explained later, was the exact way he'd programmed the show a few nights before with Count Basie, letting him whet the audience's appetite up front, then sate it at the end. Wein and Chinen, *Myself Among Others*, 153.

† That dancer, normally referred to just by her hair color and clothing, was Elaine Anderson, the daughter of a movie theater owner who'd dreamed of a career in ballet or modern dance but ended up as a community activist in Boston.

Fearful of injuries to the thousands of milling fans, "George Wein and one of the officers tried to signal to Duke to stop. Duke, sensing that to stop now might really cause a riot, chose instead to soothe the crowd down with a couple of quiet numbers." Finally, well after midnight, with his sax men still winding down, Duke assured fans, "You're very beautiful, very sweet, and we do love you madly."

The buzz afterward electrified almost as much as the concert. Few remembered that Count Basie and Satchmo Armstrong were the star attractions the nights before. All the talk was about Duke. *Ellington at Newport,* the first album ever cut at a jazz festival, sold hundreds of thousands of copies, Duke's all-time bestseller and a Library of Congress pick for the National Recording Registry. Paul Gonsalves had cemented the tenor sax as the hippest of the big band instruments, and himself as Mr. Cool. Most important, Carter Harman delivered a rhapsodic verdict in *Time,* writing that the Newport performance "marked not only the turning point in one concert; it confirmed a turning point in a career. The big news was something that the whole jazz world had long hoped to hear: the Ellington band was once again the most exciting thing in the business. Ellington himself had emerged from a long period of quiescence and was once again bursting with ideas and inspiration."[*]

Duke was elated, saying, "I was born in 1956 at the Newport festival."[†]

The truth was that he'd been reinventing himself all his life, aging in a way that remains a model for artists and everybody. As a kid in Washington he'd transformed from a sign painter to a piano-playing bandleader, and in his early days in New York he added arranger and composer to his résumé. In the Roaring Twenties Duke competed against Fletcher Henderson for headlines and fans, and forty years later he was going up against the Beatles and John Coltrane. No other band, not the Beatles or even Count Basie, lasted that long without a break.

Between 1966 and 1971, Ellington received a dozen honorary doctorates, from powerhouses like Yale, Brown, Howard, and the Berklee School of Music. One of the few prizes to elude him was the Pulitzer, although a

---

[*] Almost as sweet to the competitive Ellington was Harman's casual mention that "most bandleaders who thrived in the golden '30s are partly or completely out of the business . . . Benny Goodman plays occasional weekend dates, Tommy and Jimmy Dorsey have combined their bands. Artie Shaw is out of the music business, Cab Calloway is appearing as a solo singing act." Harman, "Jazz Man Duke Ellington."

[†] While Newport could give, it proved the following year it could take away, when the story line was how old and out of sorts Louis Armstrong was at his birthday celebration there.

three-man jury had recommended a special citation in 1965 for a lifetime of compositions. When the advisory board said no, Ellington glibly replied: "Fate is being kind to me. Fate doesn't want me to be famous too young." He added later that "my reward is hearing what I've done." His actual reward was all the free press he got when the Pulitzers turned him down.*

Duke stuck to a simple formula: give crowds old favorites like "Mood Indigo" and "Take the 'A' Train," and they'd be more receptive to his high-brow ballet or a pop arrangement from *Mary Poppins*.† Even his hair (a short ponytail tinted with henna and shined with pomade), jewelry (an earring), and clothing (velvet moccasins and psychedelic jackets) were evolving.‡ Tired of being asked about his age and evolutions, he told columnist Art Buchwald in 1961 that "Macy's been in the business 50 years, but they're not selling the same stuff they did in 1920." His sister Ruth said Duke got that attitude from his father, who'd said, "I'd rather wear out than rust out." Vocalist Herb Jeffries called him "the greatest hippie I ever knew."

Audience applause kept him young, the same way it did Satchmo and the Count, although his contracts now ensured a bed in his dressing room. One thing Duke didn't have that his fellow maestros did was a home and lair to head back to for rejuvenation. There were apartments where he could stay in New York, most obviously the one he kept for Evie. But he was an irregular visitor, preferring to lavish her with flowers, fruit, and candy than with his company; when he did stay, he'd make excuses for leaving to see his other mistresses.

---

* Duke laid bare to jazz writer Nat Hentoff his true hurt at not getting the prize, saying, "Most Americans still take it for granted that European-based music—classical music, if you will—is the only really respectable kind. What we do, what other black musicians do, has always been like the kind of man you wouldn't want your daughter to associate with." The Pulitzer Board eventually recognized its errant ways when, on the centennial of Duke's birth, it posthumously awarded him a special citation for his life's work. Hentoff, *Listen to the Stories*, 9.

† The ballet was *The River*, which put to music and dance the natural flow of water. Commissioned by the American Ballet Theater for famed choreographer Alvin Ailey, it never actually was finished, but it still premiered in 1970 at Lincoln Center, with the *New York Times* calling it "a delight." He also was writing an opera called *Queenie Pie*, a work of interracial satire loosely based on the life of cosmetics mogul Madam C. J. Walker. It, too, never was finished, and while it wasn't staged during Duke's lifetime, a new version was premiered in 2014 by the Long Beach Opera. Barnes, "Dance: Unfinished 'River.'"

‡ The red could have come from his hair straightener, or from a dye to keep him looking young. Whatever the origin, the result was yet another nickname: Piano Red. His sister Ruth's hair also got noticed, especially when it was topped, in pictures from the White House and elsewhere, by a wig of flowing blond hair.

It wasn't Evie but Ruth who accompanied him to the White House for a seventieth birthday bash hosted in 1969 by President Richard Nixon, who played "Happy Birthday" on the East Room piano. Master politician that he was, Nixon opened the White House's after-dinner entertainment to TV cameras for the first time ever, knowing that Duke and the all-star collection of musicians playing in his honor would offend nobody and that Negroes would notice, as *Time* did, that "never before had a White House dinner been so dominated by Negroes."*

For his part, Duke exchanged four kisses with the president, playfully explaining that it was "one for each cheek." He told the audience, "There is no place I would rather be tonight, except in my mother's arms." Ellington had been to the White House before, exchanging private words with Presidents Harry Truman and Dwight Eisenhower. When Lyndon Johnson was commander in chief, Duke visited seven times, twice to entertain and the rest as a guest. All of which partly made up for being rebuffed or ignored when he'd tried to meet with presidents ranging from Herbert Hoover and Franklin Roosevelt to John Kennedy. Nothing, however, topped what Nixon said in his birthday toast: "I think you would be interested to know that many years ago, the father of our guest of honor, in this very room, serving as one of the butlers in the White House, helped to serve state dinners . . .

"I, and many others here, have been guests at state dinners," the president told his dinner guests. "I have been here when an emperor has been toasted. I have been here when we have raised our glasses to a king, to a queen, to presidents, and to prime ministers. But in studying the history of all the great dinners held in this room, never before has a duke been toasted. So tonight I ask you to all rise and join me in raising our glasses to the greatest duke of them all. Duke Ellington."

---

*Around this same time the Nixon White House called Louis Armstrong to say they'd like to honor him, too. His response, according to friend Jack Bradley: "Fuck that shit. Why didn't they do it before? The only reason he would want me to play there now is to make some niggers happy." Giddins, *Satchmo*, 168.

LAST DAYS AND LASTING MEMORIES

I N THE LAST two years of his life Louis Armstrong lacked the strength to blast the horn or belt out lyrics the way he had since he was a boy, so he increasingly turned to the other forms of expression he'd fine-tuned over a lifetime: writing letters and essays, recording reminiscences, and organizing his library-sized collection of newspaper clippings, photos, taped music, and phonograph records. Ever a man of excess, he'd leave behind not just one memoir, which would have outdone any jazzman before him, but four of them, each with a different rhythm and cadence. Convinced that scattered conversations weren't sufficient to fill in his narrative, over his final twenty-four months he recorded an eye-popping 150 reels of audiotape capturing three hundred hours of his private life and musical passions.*

It was storytelling as performance art, all done with a clear purpose. After decades of reading about his life as chronicled by countless newspaper reporters, magazine writers, and biographers, Satchmo was determined to tell it his way in the end. So exhaustive was his effort that even his body tried to check out. Twice his doctors were ready to pronounce him dead but he snapped back, to continue his two-fingered typing and talking into the tape machine.

The autobiographies offer a lens into his evolving thinking and the legacy he wanted to craft. The first, the 1936 *Swing That Music,* had been edited into conventional style that stripped it of its zesty slang, rule-breaking grammar, and other Satchmo punch and bite. The second, the 1954 *My Life in New Orleans,* wound up truer to his original wording but was still pruned of the embryonic manuscript's charm and improvisation. What has been

---

* In total, Louis left behind 750 tapes varying in length from one to three hours, for a total of about 1,500 hours of talk and tunes.

retrieved of the third, *The Satchmo Story,* is a paean to his lifelong devotion to "that *good shit,*" marijuana. Louis began the last, *Louis Armstrong + the Jewish Family in New Orleans, La.,* from his hospital bed in 1969. Inspired by the Jewish doctor who'd just saved his life, he handwrote a seventy-seven-page tribute to the Karnofsky family of Lithuanian Jews who gave him a job and sense of self-worth, then dedicated it to his Jewish manager, Joe Glaser, who died at New York's Beth Israel Hospital at the same time Louis was being treated there. It also reflected wounds that simmered in Satchmo's old age—that the New Orleans of his youth was "so Digustingly Segregated and Prejudiced," and that "I have always done *great* things about *uplifting* my race (the Negroes, *of course*) but *wasn't appreciated.*"

Beyond the written words, Louis tapped into the African American tradition of oral storytelling. His taped conversations delved into nearly every crevice and moment of his life. He told lurid jokes, insisted that New Orleans trumpeter Bunk Johnson "didn't teach me shit," read the Gettysburg Address, drunkenly lured Lucille to their oversized bed, justified his painful split with his mentor King Oliver, and expounded on the "sex habits of Negro women." The recordings streamed his consciousness, laying out the narratives of his people and his times in parallel with his personal story. He'd started traveling with a typewriter in 1922 and with the best available taping equipment in 1950, recording from his hotel rooms, dressing suites, and wood-paneled study back home in Corona. He decorated his boxes of reels with clipped pictures, telegrams, postcards, and newsprint, then laminated the collages with Scotch tape. Sometimes friends and colleagues didn't find out until later that their after-hours conversations had been captured. No editors needed or permitted this time. The point was unguarded authenticity. The endless files were indexed using the first letter of the last word of the entry. ("Mood Indigo," for instance, would be under *I.*)

Why spend so much of his precious free time stooped over a typewriter or talking into a tape machine? He did it to keep in touch with friends and fans, and to give writers grist for their profiles. He did it because it was fun, made more so by a green ink pen and green typing ribbon. Most of all he took the time and effort so what he called "posterity" would know who he was and what he really thought. He believed deep down that his stories from the Battlefield and in battles beyond could inspire others. They did and still do.

They also demonstrate that, near the end, he was thinking about more than music and joy. "The Negroes always hated the Jewish people who never *harmed* anybody, but they stuck together," he wrote in *Louis Armstrong +*

the Jewish Family. "By doing that, they *had* to have *success.* Negroes *never* did stick together and they *never* will. They hold too much *malice—Jealousy* deep down in their hearts for the *few* Negroes who *tries.*" He also railed against "the poor white Trash" who guzzled mint juleps or bad whiskey, then "would Torture the poor Darkie, as innocent as he may be." That fourth memoir wouldn't be published until a quarter century after Louis's death, probably because it was buried amid twelve linear feet of other papers, or perhaps because it was so raw.

Seldom had any public figure—politician, artist, cleric, or scribe—left behind a multimedia library like Louis Armstrong's. It could and did fill a museum. None of which should have been a surprise from a genre-busting trumpeter and groundbreaking singer. He carried a dictionary and thesaurus everywhere, teaching himself the vocabulary he hadn't stuck around to learn in school. He melded conventional forms with made-up ones the way jazz improvisers did, instinctively. *Colored* became "cullud" because that's how it sounded where he came from. Same with "suh" instead of *sir.* And an Uppity Negro like Jelly Roll Morton was, in Satchmo speak, "a big Bragadossa."* He employed apostrophes, parentheses, dashes, interjections, rhetorical questions, and underlinings not in the way grammarian William Strunk taught, but to play to readers' ears. There were these lines from a 1967 letter to a U.S. soldier in Vietnam: "I'd like to 'step in here for a 'Minute or 'so' to "tell you how much—I 'feel to know that 'you are a 'Jazz *fan,* and 'Dig' that 'Jive . . . And now I'll do you 'Just like the 'Farmer did the 'Potato— I'll 'Plant you 'Now and 'Dig you 'later."

He explained at the end of one tape, "I usually say nice things about human beings, if they deserve it. I never wanted to be any more than I am, and what I don't have I don't need it anywoo . . . I don't feel ashamed at all. My life has always been an open book. So I have nothing to hide."

He confronted his own mortality for the first time in Italy in June 1954, when he had a heart attack that left him on his knees gasping for breath, and that his doctors tried to cover up for fear it could impair his career. Louis recovered, but in September 1968 he turned up at Dr. Gary Zucker's office in New York short of breath, with a swollen belly, legs, and face. He was hospitalized for acute heart failure, and responded well to oxygen therapy and diuretics. He was back for an extended stay the following February, during which his heart stopped for a full twenty seconds. Zucker: "The man was

---

* He also took regular shots at Coleman Hawkins, Benny Goodman, Bunk Johnson, Sidney Bechet, Fletcher Henderson, and other jazzmen he thought were dicty or disrespectful.

dead." Thankfully doctors in Beth Israel's intensive care unit shocked him back to life.

He still did occasional TV appearances and stage performances, including a memorable two-week booking at the Waldorf Hotel in March 1971. Zucker had warned him he could die onstage, but the doctor agreed to make twice-a-day visits to Louis in his hotel suite after the trumpeter pleaded, "Doctor, you don't understand. My whole life, my whole soul, my whole spirit is to blooooow this hoooooorn. My people are waiting for me. I cannot let them down." At the hotel he crawled into bed between shows, never left the building, had to be helped on and off the podium, and once vomited in the elevator. His last Waldorf performance, on March 13, was his last anywhere, and he cried as he left the bandstand after singing "Boy from New Orleans." His last words onstage were these fitting lyrics:

All through the years folks, I've had a ball . . .
You were very kind to old Satchmo.
Just a boy from New Orleans.

Two days later a diseased kidney triggered another heart attack and sent him back to Beth Israel. Two weeks after that his heart failed yet again, and this time it was Lucille who pronounced him clinically dead after he stopped breathing for thirty seconds. Luckily his doctors were there, restoring his heartbeat and inserting a breathing tube into his windpipe. Over the course of months, and with Lucille at his bedside sixteen hours a day, Louis's health stabilized enough for him to move from intensive care to a private room. Finally—after a phone call to Lucille at two thirty in the morning demanding, "Get me out of this damned hospital. I can't look any longer at the nurses in their uniforms"—he was freed to head home.

Once there, he took stock of all he'd survived recently: three heart attacks, four bouts of pneumonia, a lung puncture, and serious infections of the liver, kidneys, and gall bladder. His weight, once at 230 pounds, had dropped to 113. His voice was hoarser than ever, and his second day home he cut his knee during a fall. Lucille had to hoist him out of bed every four hours to change his sheets, then wash, shave, and feed him. After protesting that "I am not a cripple yet," he agreed to use a new motorized lift to take him up and down the stairs, ultimately making a game of it. He settled into a routine that included short walks around the house, with evenings spent watching the Yankees, the Mets, or, if they were playing at the same time, both on side-by-side TV sets. He made new reel-to-reels, this time of his own music, occasionally blew his trumpet, and still smoked cigarettes.

"I live for my wife and myself. Just for Lucille and Louis," he told an interviewer for a German magazine, explaining that he called her "his old lady" in public and "Beloved" when it was just the two of them. "We live simple and good. We do respect the world, and the world does respect us. I think, our Life is wonderful." Asked about the racial politics of the day, Louis and Lucille chimed in unison, "We don't make a difference between black, yellow, red and white . . . We believe in people."

Trying to convince himself and the world that he had at least one comeback left in him, on June 23, 1971, Louis invited journalists to his home. He entertained them by blowing "Sleepy Time" on the trumpet, then, pointing to himself, he announced, "See that cat? You can't kill him, man. That cat ain't ever gonna die." Eleven days later, on July 4, he invited friends to his garden terrace to celebrate what he said was his seventy-first birthday, although he likely was a month shy of turning seventy. The day after that he called his doctor to say he was ready for the next tour of the All-Stars, beginning in California.

On July 6, at five thirty in the morning, Lucille saw that he'd stopped breathing, this time for good. The cause of death, his physicians agreed, was "kidney failure, attributable to heart failure."

This man who scripted everything had imagined a year earlier what his funeral would look like, with the kind of New Orleans–style farewell he'd relished as a kid. The turnout exceeded his dreams. Twenty-five thousand fans—old women with shopping bags, young executives on lunch hour, the Cadet Corps of Central Harlem—said last goodbyes while his body was displayed in a velvet-lined open coffin at the New York National Guard Armory on Park Avenue. He wore a navy blue suit, pink shirt, and pink and silver tie, with a starched white handkerchief in his left hand and a gold plaque above his head reading, "Louis Satchmo Armstrong." Lil rode with Lucille to the funeral, where thousands were lined up outside Corona's Congregational Church. Honorary pallbearers included Count Basie and Duke Ellington, who would later say that Louis was "born poor, died rich, and never hurt anyone on the way." The music, organized by the status-conscious Lucille, wasn't the raucous sendoff Louis imagined, but that came just after in New Orleans, where a brass band and fifteen thousand mourners gathered for a City Hall sendoff.

There were page-one obituaries in newspapers around the globe, along with twenty thousand letters of condolence.* None matched the final fire-works that Satchmo himself had imagined when, almost a year to the day earlier, he told the *New York Times,* "When I go to the Gate, I'll play a duet with Gabriel. Yeah, we'll play 'Sleepy Time Down South' and 'Hello, Dolly!' Then he can blow a couple that he's been playing up there all the time. He wants to be remembered for his music, just like I do."

———

Like Satchmo, Duke remained true to type until the very end. That meant rather than telling the world more of his personal story, he turned even more inward, not even revealing to his son how sick he was until he had no choice. Duke got less warning than Louis of the health issues that would be his un-doing, and stayed on the road more despite his weakened condition and worsened cancer prognosis.

The difference between the two men shines through in how they ap-proached their memoirs. Duke didn't begin working on his until after his publisher's deadline had come and gone, and he was determined there and everywhere to present the fairy-tale version of his life. "Once upon a time a very pretty lady and very handsome gentleman met and fell in love and got married, and God blessed them with this wonderful baby boy, you know? And they held him in the palm of their hands, and nurtured him and spoiled him until he was about seven, eight years old," he told an inter-viewer. "The minute they put his feet on the ground, he ran out the front door, out across the front lawn, out across the street. The minute he got on the other side of the street, somebody said: 'Hey, Edward, up this way.' And the boy was me, incidentally. We got to the next corner, and he says: 'Hey, Edward, right. Go up there and turn left. You can't miss it.' And it's been going on that way ever since.

"That's the story. That's my biography."

He maintained that tone throughout *Music Is My Mistress.* Separate chapters told breezy stories of more than one hundred individual side-men, collaborators, and acquaintances, but there were none devoted to his wife, Edna Ellington; lifelong companion, Evie Ellis; or overseas mis-tress, Fernanda de Castro Monte. No spilling of the beans, either, about the gangsters who enabled his early career, the drugs and drinking that plagued the band, his perpetual battles with Jim Crow, or anything else

———

* A letter from New Zealand was addressed to "Mrs. Satchmo, Queens, New York, America," and one from Paris was "Lady Louis Armstrong, New York, USA." Both reached Lucille. Cogs-well, *Offstage Story of Satchmo,* 49.

unpleasant. His memoir was, as his Smithsonian biographer said, "the literary equivalent of his conceit 'We love you madly.'" One more character is noticeably absent from Duke's autobiography: Duke.

"He talks about everybody but himself, it's an old trick of his!" said Mercer. "We've written the Good Book, and now we'll write the Bad Book," Duke told his son when the first copies were printed. "He had no intention of writing another, of course," Mercer added. "He didn't forget those who had cheated or abused him but if he never precisely forgave, he didn't let memories sour his life."

Closed-mouthed and elliptical though he was, Ellington wanted the world to know that he'd spent his life trying to change more than its tastes in music. Rather than simply saying that, like Armstrong did, Duke wove it between the lines of his autobiography. "I have contributed to the cause of the advancement of colored people," he wrote three-quarters of the way through the 523-page book. "Much of my work is inspired by this objective."

Biographers pressed perpetually for him to say more, with little luck. Derek Jewell, a music critic at the *Sunday Times* of London, spent a decade trying to convince Ellington to let him "do a proper book and to travel with him and be with him all the time and write things down. And he always used to say, you know, 'What a great idea. We'll do that next year.' It was always 'next year.' And I learned, after a time, that this was his method of actually putting it off . . . He hated the very idea of biographies." Jewell did write a biography, but not until after Duke was dead, and he conceded that "there were many parts of his life about which I knew nothing first-hand."

Duke had always avoided the subject of death, so it's no surprise that he kept the news of his cancer secret. In the spring of 1973 the band was playing in Houston, and as part of a public health program, everyone agreed to be tested for emphysema. Duke's results raised enough of an alarm that he was advised to have follow-up exams when he got back to New York. Six months later his cancer diagnosis was confirmed, and an autopsy would determine that the tumors originated in his lymph ducts, then spread to his lungs and beyond.

He was visibly fatigued that fall when he debuted his *Third Sacred Concert* at Westminster Abbey in London, requiring a wheelchair at the airport on his way to Sweden. Mournful tones infused the music he composed and played then. But he never was explicit about how sick he was, not even with Mercer, who explained later, "I believe the main reason he kept denying the seriousness of his condition, and kept it from me, was that he thought the fewer people who knew about it, the better the secret would be kept. But there was no real possibility of keeping it secret. In fact, it might have been more constructive for people to have known about his condition rather than his having to take some of the abuse he did from critics and writers who were not at all kind about various affectations he developed. For example, he was often panned for being camera shy, but he knew the cancer was showing in his facial lines. He knew the picture would show not just an aging person, but a person who was sick."

Doctors removed his thyroid gland in December 1973. That didn't check the progress of his disease, and barely slowed his schedule. He soon was back performing at New York's Rainbow Grill, then on to Florida, Illinois, Michigan, Indiana, South Dakota, Missouri, Iowa, Connecticut, Ohio, New Jersey, Minnesota, and Washington, D.C., where he collapsed at a concert. Three days after his performances in March 1974 in Sturgis, Michigan, Duke was admitted for the last time to New York's Columbia Presbyterian Hospital.

During those final two months of his life he seesawed between his normal rose-tinted take and the intruding dark realities. Ruth and Mercer installed an electric piano in his hospital room, and he pushed ahead with a comic opera, ballet, and other new works. His eyesight deteriorated, and to compensate his handwriting nearly tripled in size.* The pain grew and with it, depression, as reflected in his saying no not just to the grapes he loved but to his dietary mainstay of steaks. A doctor pronounced his latest cancer findings "a catastrophe." Pneumonia set in at the end. There were distractions, but none were uplifting. He'd learned that November that his friend and doctor Arthur Logan fell to his death from a viaduct in upper Manhattan in a case that is still being debated as murder or suicide. Duke was devastated in a way he'd been just twice before, at the passings of his mother, then Billy Strayhorn. That May, while Duke was in the hospital, bandmates Paul Gonsalves and Tyree Glenn died within four days of one another, although Duke was spared that news.† In the middle of everything, Evie—who'd been at his bedside every day, bringing him food and staying into the evenings— discovered that she, too, had cancer, which spread to her lungs.

While Evie would never see Duke again after she was operated on, he called her constantly, trying to cheer her up. Taking her place at the hos-

---

* One of his last notes to himself read, "No problem. I'm easy to please. I just want to have everybody in the palm of my hand." Mercer Ellington, *Duke Ellington in Person*, 210.
† The bodies of Duke, Paul, and Tyree would lie in state together briefly in the funeral home chapel.

pital was Fernanda, who had the good sense to leave his room when Duke dialed Evie. Frank Sinatra visited and President Nixon called. Duke spoke frequently by phone to his old manager Irving Mills. Another regular visitor, especially at night when no one could chase her away, was West Coast mistress Betty McGettigan, who claimed she was alone with him when he died, with Duke saying, "Don't leave me. I love you. Come with me."

Duke's funeral was as much of a scene as Satchmo's.* Mourners—including Count Basie—filed past his open casket for fourteen hours, at the rate of five hundred an hour. "He's up there now with the Louis Armstrongs," said seventy-one-year-old Frisco Bowman, a drummer and guitarist who'd played alongside Ellington in 1923. The next day, ten thousand fans packed the Episcopal Cathedral Church of St. John the Divine, with Katy and Bill Basie in the front pew. The Count wept unselfconsciously and told those around him, "I loved him."

Duke was "loved throughout the whole world, at all levels of society, by Frenchmen and Germans, by English and Irish, by Arabs and Jews, by Indians and Pakistanis, by atheists and devout Catholics, and by communist and fascist alike," music critic and Ellington ghostwriter Stanley Dance said in his eulogy. "It is Memorial Day, when those who died for the free world are properly remembered. Duke Ellington never lost faith in this country, and he served it well." It wasn't just his country. Duke was, as the BBC's Alistair Cooke reported, "a credit to his race. The human race, that is."

———

Basie, the youngest of the maestros, was the last one left, and his final days were decidedly different from Ellington's or Armstrong's.

Unlike Satchmo, the Count had no interest in baring his soul or testing his writing chops. And he was nowhere near as artful a dodger as Duke. Asked by a journalist in 1975 how his memoir was coming, Basie kidded, "Pretty good. I've been working on it for about fifteen years now. I'm up to page eight." It was no joke to Albert Murray, one of the most talented authors in the music world and the Count's chosen ghostwriter. He traveled with the Basie band for six years, miniature Sony tape recorder in hand, trying every way he knew to get the bandleader talking about the Pendergast political machine in Kansas City, the politics of the Bennie Moten band, or the wild

———

* Funeral director John Joyce said the Ellington family alone had about thirty-five limousines, with 110 in total in the cortege. Fifty city policemen were there, along with a dozen church guards and federal security people. "It was like a service for a head of state," Joyce concluded. Interview of John Joyce, September 21, 1983, Yale.

days of the Reno Club. Basie's unwavering and maddening answer: "Why the hell should I get into that?"

"If the story he has chosen to tell is thereby made short on scandalous self-exposé, it is also short on outrageous self-inflation. If it is short on explanation, it is also short on false claims and pretentiousness," said the ever-gracious Murray. In private, Murray told friends how exasperated he was, feeling that working with Basie had disrupted his writing career and his equilibrium.

It's also true that the Basie-Murray collaboration, *Good Morning Blues*, perfectly exhibits the real-life Count. He told friends that he wanted to be remembered not as the Holy Man or King of Swing, but as a "nice guy." And he ended his book with these Basie-like lines, "I'm not saying this is the end. I'm just saying that's all for now. I'm saying: *to be continued, until we meet again*. Meanwhile, keep on listening and tapping your feet."

As with his fellow icons, however, there was more to his story than listening and tapping. Jim Crow had restricted where the Count could sleep, eat, or simply be, even when he was, as he wrote, "the hottest attraction in the biggest theaters and auditoriums or the top night spot in town . . . I already knew about all of that beforehand just as you would just have to know about what you have to go through to become a prizefighter or a football player . . . I'll just say that I was not surprised when things got strange in one way or another. I'll just say that I didn't intend to let anything stop me if I could help it, and that should tell you something."

It did.

Basie spent the year after Katy's death mainly on the road, mourning her and maintaining a rigorous schedule that included a two-week tour of Japan. "I can still remember the morning I received a tearful phone call from Bill Basie asking me to write something for his recently deceased wife," said composer Sammy Nestico. "I recall her dignified presence, and how she made us all feel like family. I think it is the only melancholy song that I have ever written. In 1984, on our final session together, we recorded 'Katy.'"

In between gigs, the Count headed back to Freeport and daughter Diane. It was a lonely existence there, with the two of them sitting together for non-verbal meals at the big glass table in the formal dining room. Both had aides on hand to help with their disabilities. "I still feel her," Bill said of Katy. "I talk to her every day; most assuredly three times a day in prayer." He spent his days working out on a treadmill or in the solar-heated swimming pool, trying to strengthen his legs, and watching on TV *The Price Is Right*, Westerns, or baseball, Diane by his side, each in their special rocking chair.

It wasn't just arthritis that was eating away at his body and causing him pain now, but cancer of the pancreas that he knew was unstoppable. He performed for the final time in April 1984, with Ella Fitzgerald at the University of Vermont. He died two weeks later at a hospital in Florida, at age seventy-nine—a year to the month after Katy's death, having completed *Good Morning Blues* but before its publication. His funeral took place at the Abyssinian Baptist Church in Harlem, blocks from the honky-tonks where he had launched his career sixty years earlier. Flowers in the shape of a grand piano stood beside the altar, with a note from Frank Sinatra reading, "You'll always be with me. I love you." Friends who were there included John Hammond, who kick-started Basie's career, along with Quincy Jones, Billy Eckstine, Sarah Vaughan, and George Wein. Vocalist Joe Williams sang "Come Sunday," the spiritual written by Duke Ellington, who had died a decade before.

Two tributes best captured the understated Count. "Basie wound up being considered a musical genius of sorts, ironically, not despite the modesty of his talents but rather because of it," wrote culture critic Gerald Early. "So much like the music he played," Basie was "the mighty burning of the unassuming." Quincy Jones said, "Basie reminded me of everything I'd come from. My dad. Jazz. My past. My dignity. He wasn't a complicated man. He was pure hip, old-time, down-home goodness. He harked back to the days when we played music not to get over: we just wanted to be good."

EPILOGUE: LEGACIES

THEY'RE IN SEPARATE burial grounds now, but jazz's Holy Trinity remain bound by the spiritual rhythms that linked them in life.

Duke Ellington has accomplished in his settled hereafter what eluded him in his restless earthly existence, surrounding himself with those he cherished most. Thanks largely to him, New York's Civil War–era Woodlawn Cemetery became jazz's preferred final resting place. Across a tree-lined street from the Ellington plot lies Miles Davis, who once gushed that "musicians should get together one certain day and get down on their knees and thank Duke." Near him in Jazz Corner or up the rolling hills are Duke's master percussionist Sonny Greer, two of his favorite brass men, Cootie Williams and Clark Terry, King of the Vibes Lionel Hampton along with King Oliver, and George Wein, the Newport Jazz impresario who brought Duke's career back from the ghost in the 1950s.*

Duke always insisted that his family was the center of his universe, and now they enfold him in perpetuity. Evie Ellis died two years after him and is buried to his right, with a headstone and *New York Times* obituary finally assigning her the last name she coveted: Ellington. On Duke's other side rest Daisy, the mother he worshipped, and J.E., his courtly father. Ruth, who outlived her brother by a full generation, lies on the far side of their parents, with her second husband. Nearby are the bandleader's aunt, his cousins and nephew, and Evelyn Ellington, Mercer's first wife. Duke "wanted everybody to be together for a change," says Mercedes, Mercer's daughter.

The only one missing is Mercer, who orchestrated the plot arrangements and other details that were too painful for the death-averse Duke. But Mercer made clear his abiding ambivalence to his dad when he decided to be buried

---

* Other jazz artists have asked to be "as close to Duke as possible," according to Woodlawn staff.

not in the Bronx with his extended family, but at Arlington National Cemetery, which was his right as an Army veteran and was nearer Edna Ellington, his mother and Duke's only wife. "I think it was [Mercer's] last slap in the face to [Duke]," explains Mercedes. "I guess he finally got away from his father."

Count Basie's burial choices likewise speak to his essential character. This reserved man arranged to be cremated in a private ceremony after his funeral, and he shared his headstone—reading "William Count Basie"—with his beloved Katy. Their graveyard on Long Island isn't far from their old home in Addisleigh Park, but an intended world away from where his birth family was interred outside Red Bank. Buried next to Bill and Katy and cremated like him is their daughter, Diane, who defied her doctors' dour expectations and her parents' wildest hopes, outliving them by nearly forty years.

As for Satchmo, he is buried near his Corona home, at Flushing Cemetery. His preferred nickname, Satchmo, bracketed by quotation marks, is etched above "Louis Armstrong" on his simple black gravestone. Buried beside him is his most abiding wife, Lucille, who died in 1983 from a heart attack while in Boston for a concert in Louis's honor.* Clarence, the cousin whom Satchmo called his son and who survived him by a quarter of a century, spent his last years at a nursing home in the Bronx and is entombed in New Jersey, an hour's drive from Louis.†

The three maestros also were united in death by their abundant fortunes. Basie likely left the largest estate, which was thanks to Katy's adroit planning and was fortunate given Diane's need for decades of round-the-clock care at the home she was moved to in Florida. Ellington had the least cash on hand and the greatest debts, but was guaranteed the biggest royalties given his thousands of compositions. With no will, it was left to Mercer to clean up his tax liabilities and to all of his descendants to argue over what each would collect. Louis, by contrast, was explicit: he gave $5,000 to Clarence, whose expenses he'd covered all along; $5,000 to his sister Mama Lucy, who died in 1987 in New Orleans; and everything else—first thought to be $500,000, but which may have been five times that—to Lucille.

---

* In her widowhood, Lucille had a boyfriend who, according to Ricky Riccardi, "she basically hid" and might have been living on the third floor of the Corona house. That house was declared a historic landmark first by the U.S. government and then the City of New York, and today is a museum. Riccardi interview.

† Clarence died too poor for a funeral and was slated to be buried in an unmarked grave in a potter's field, but Louis's friends raised the money for a proper sendoff and burial. Cogswell, *Offstage Story of Satchmo,* 159; Riccardi, "'My Adopted Son,'" LAHM; and email to author from David Ostwald.

Their rhythm, however, always mattered more than the money, and music remained, in Ellington's lexicon, each one's true mistress. Louis had no band to bequeath, but Duke did. Mercer led it from just after his father's death in 1974 until his own in 1996, at which point it went to Mercer's youngest son, Paul, who never knew his illustrious grandfather. Basie's current band has a closer connection to the Count, with a vocalist and trombonist he hired. But it's less through reboots that the Ellington, Basie, and Armstrong music still resonates than through eternal re-airing of their timeless originals.

America has its own peculiar ways of marking legacies of icons like these, starting with their combined twenty-one Grammy awards. The Post Office honored Armstrong with a stamp, after Chad, Niger, Tanzania, and eight other countries had done so. His native New Orleans failed to save from the wrecking balls the houses where he grew up, but named after him its airport, a thirty-one-acre park, and a summertime music festival. Duke, too, got commemorative stamps, and he devoted ten full pages in his memoir to the rest of his tributes, from being named honorary deputy sheriff in Lackawanna County, Pennsylvania, to receiving a ceremonial key to Bull Connor's Birmingham. The Count collected his own laurels, with streets, a theater, a dormitory, a school, and a stamp named after him.

All that delighted the jazzmen, but they would have been most proud of their influence on those who came after. They helped spawn Cool Jazz and Motown, along with Bebop and Hip Hop. Bob Dylan and B. B. King acknowledged their debts. So did the Beatles and Bing Crosby, Ella Fitzgerald and Bob Marley, Wynton Marsalis and Jon Batiste, who explained his reverence in religious terms: Basie set the doctrine, Duke defined the spirit, and Satchmo was the deity. And it wasn't just jazzmen who were touched by this hallowed trio. They inspired, in transformational ways, Martin Luther King Jr., Malcolm X, James Baldwin, and Bill Clinton, whose walls are adorned with pictures of Duke, the Count, and Satchmo.

Libraries are filled with the stories of Ellington, Basie, and Armstrong, but what's stunning is how what was said about each of them individually applies to them collectively. All captured America with their melodies and their passion. Each said he was a music maker first and last, when in reality they also were cultural and racial revolutionaries. All thrived professionally for an unheard-of half century and defined their eras as few others did. Dizzy Gillespie, the Ambassador of Jazz, was talking about Satchmo but it could as easily have been Duke or the Count when he declared, "No him, no me."

ACKNOWLEDGMENTS

The Pullman porters were my gift that is still giving. First they shared their inspired stories about rising from the rails to reshape their world. Then they said I had to write about their favorite athlete, Satchel Paige, and I had a grand time doing that. The book they wanted most was on their three best-loved passengers and friends—Duke, the Count, and Satchmo—and here we are.

Jill Kneerim was a different sort of treasure. She helped me hatch the ideas for all nine of my books, oversaw the writing and rewriting of proposals, found just the right publishers and editors, edited the nearly finished manuscripts, worked alongside the publisher and me on marketing plans, and held my hand throughout. Mentor, indeed, even from her hospice bed.

The only one who gave more, from start to the last word, was Lisa Frusztajer, my wife and partner, editor and sounding board.

Making the arduous book process seem easier was Deborah Brody, first when she was the publisher at Houghton Mifflin Harcourt, then as an editorial director at HarperCollins, which bought HMH. It's rare that an author can use the words *inspired editor* and *steadfast friend* to describe the same person, rarer when that editor joins you at jazz clubs to hear and see your story play out. Her editing my book at her new imprint wouldn't have worked without the enthusiastic buy-in of two HarperCollins colleagues, Morrow Group President Liate Stehlik, who lived up to her reputation as a friend of poets and writers, and Peter Hubbard, the intellectually curious good guy who runs Mariner Books.

Copy editor Mark Steven Long demonstrated a dead-on grasp of usage and logic, while David Palmer deftly and patiently managed in-house production. Weighing in with more blue-chip assistance were art director Brian Moore, cover designer Pete Garceau, proofreaders Bob Castillo and Justine Gardner, editing boss Laura Brady, attorney Andrew Jacobs, and the perfect pair of promoters, Sarah Falter and Deanna Bailey. Then there was the marvelous Emma Effinger, who held my hand and answered my questions on everything from assembling photos to obtaining permissions.

Before I handed in my manuscript to Deb, Peter, Liate, and the rest of the team at HarperCollins, a group that I call Team Jazzmen read all or parts of it. Trumpeter and vocalist Wendell Brunious knows jazz and New Orleans better than just about anyone. Nobody has chronicled Louis Armstrong more thoroughly and thoughtfully than Ricky Riccardi, research chief at the Armstrong House Museum, or offered a more nuanced take on Duke Ellington than cultural historian Harvey Cohen. Gwen Thompkins is an NPR veteran, a New Orleans native, and a radio-show host. Loren Schoenberg plays the sax, conducts, teaches, and ran the National Jazz Museum in Harlem. All saved me from more mistakes than I'll admit, and helped me see more clearly my subjects and their contributions.

Friends also dug into what I had written, offering context and texture. Biographer Sally Jacobs showed, again, how gifted she is at writing, editing, and thinking. Journalist and author Eileen McNamara had something invaluable to say about each chapter. Environmentalist and author Philip Warburg reminded me that his creative antenna is pitch-perfect. Jazz aficionado Dan Hamilton offered valuable feedback in the warp-speed time you'd expect of a reporter and editor.

In addition to all of that, and before it, veteran editor David Sobel took out his red pencil and, through word fixes and big-picture critiques, gave me the confidence to hand out the manuscript to my other readers and to hand it in to HarperCollins. It's the third of my books that David has helped with, and I now count him as a loyal friend as well as literary craftsman.

Earlier biographers of my trio—from Gary Giddins to Geoffrey Ward and Laurence Bergreen—graciously assisted with this one, as did a long list of generous scholars of music, race, and history, all named in the Bibliography. Jazz writer, producer, and archivist Dan Morgenstern was the first person I interviewed, and he never complained when I kept coming back. Equally instructive and indulgent were scores of musicians, from Wynton Marsalis, Jon Batiste, and Sonny Rollins to a pair of Carringtons, Terri Lyne and her dad, Sonny. Joy Rosenthal helped me understand the Basie estate that she's nobly overseen. Attorney Charles Walton aided in my quest for government records, as did Michael McGoings, a retired judge, friend, and son of an amazing Pullman porter. And I was lucky to have enthusiastic assistance from these archivists at the collections that mattered most to me: Ricky at the Louis Armstrong House Museum, Kay Peterson at the Smithsonian, Elizabeth Surles at Rutgers' Institute of Jazz Studies, and Melissa Weber at

Tulane's Hogan Jazz Archive, where Tad Jones's papers make clear he'd have written an essential book if he'd lived long enough.

It's impossible for me to imagine assembling a book without help from student and professional researchers, and a stream of them helped with chores ranging from library and internet searches to transcribing interviews and proofing quotes. The ones who stayed longest were Debbie Bloom, Jack Maniaci, Zoe Rosenberger, Ann Simpson, Matthew Winkler, and Karen Yetra.

As essential as editors and interns are enablers. Mine, close to home, were Alec and Amanda, Marina and Bear, and Nellie, who were patient and supportive beyond expectation or reason. Also there with perspective and encouragement, as always, were John Allen, Teri Bergman, Natalie Brody, Jim Cahill, Jerry and Susan Cohen, Andrew Dreyfus, Kitty and Mike Dukakis, the Frusztajers—Olga, Nina, Mischa, and Edina—Jessie Gottsegen, Suzanne and Norman Goldberg, Dick Hamilton, Jim and Gin Hoeck, Henry Hyde, Lynne and Bill Kovach, Joanne and Arthur Massaro, Bill and Debbie Mills, Phil Odence, Ash Rao and Janis Gogan, Don and Judy Skwar, Don and Ariela Tye, Eileen Tye, Mark Tye, Richard Wolman, and all my Health Coverage fellows and fellow Niemans. My then hundred-year-old mother, Dottie Tye, was there cheering from the start, as always, but sadly not at the finish. Nor was my friend and father-in-law, Bill Frusztajer, whom I loved talking to about books and everything. Sadly gone as well are Cotuit pal Sue Hamilton, *Globe* buddy Don MacGillis, and college mentor George Morgan, father of Brown's now-old New Curriculum.

A special thanks to publisher Bruce Nichols, who helped me realize that the way to tell this story was through a trio of voices. I thought that writing about three people, I'd spend a third of the time on each that I had with bios of single subjects. That, of course, was naive. I needed to devote the attention to each as if he was the sole focus. That's evident in my stack of 8,200 pages of typed notes and interview transcripts.[*]

But don't feel sorry for me. Can you imagine better company to keep during a Covid lockdown than Satchmo, Duke, or the Count? And can you imagine a sweeter treat from your publisher—after spending three years with a bullying Senator Joe McCarthy—than spending the next three with the most rollicking and uplifting artists of their era? While I'm glad to be done, I'm sorry to see it end. As my Pullman porter friends predicted, this gorgeous universe of rhythm will be part of me forever.

---

[*] I am donating my tapes, transcripts, and files to the Louis Armstrong House Museum in Queens, which will make them available for public viewing and listening.

NOTES

ABBREVIATIONS

HJA: Hogan Jazz Archive, Tulane University
IJS: Institute of Jazz Studies, Rutgers University
LAHM: Louis Armstrong House Museum
SI: Smithsonian National Museum of American History
Yale: Duke Ellington Oral History Collection, Yale University Archives

Key phrases and page numbers indicate where numbered notes would have appeared, and sources refer to the text just before that.

PREFACE: A ROAD MAP

ix *a piano stool*: Giddins, *Visions of Jazz*, 171.

x "Any *Nigger*": Email to author from Loren Schoenberg; interview of George Avakian, September 28, 1993, SI; and Armstrong, *In His Own Words*, 17.

xiii *our musical everyman*: Wilson, *Satchmo: The Wonderful World of Louis Armstrong, Jazz Profiles*, NPR; and author interviews with Christian McBride and Wynton Marsalis.

CHAPTER 1: SATCHMO'S BATTLEFIELD

3 *and shoeless children*: His mother could have been as young as sixteen or as old as nineteen, based on her conflicting answers on census forms, the only public records available for her, and on her obituary.

3 *Waif's Home preferred 1901*: Louis's birthday may be the most argued happening in jazz. The manifest when he boarded the S.S. *Majestic* in 1932 showed 1900, adding to the confusion produced by the public records. A *New Orleans Democrat* account of his arrest in 1912 agreed, saying he was twelve. Among the questions raised by the swirl of dates are these: Had he altered his age to make himself either eligible or ineligible for service during World War I—or perhaps to nail a job in a juke joint or with old man Karnofsky?

Louis Armstrong's Application for Social Security Account Number, February 9, 1943; Social Security Death Index, July 1971; and Registration Cards for World War I and World War II. Passenger list S.S. *Majestic*, 1932.

4 *a fresh century*: Baptismal Register, 1901, New Orleans Sacred Heart of Jesus, Office of Archives and Records, Archdiocese of New Orleans.

Ricky Riccardi, research director at LAHM and Armstrong's trusted biographer, says Louis and his mother believed his birth date was July 4, which is good enough for Ricky, and he thinks the right year was 1901. But he adds, "I don't say that with any 100 percent accuracy." Author interview of Riccardi.

4   *"glad to be here"*: Riccardi, "Happy Birthday, Pops!"

4   *"when we were poor"*: Armstrong, *Swing that Music,* 124.

5   *called Jane Alley:* Again, just who was living at 723 Jane Alley then, and who owned it, depends on which version of the stories one believes. Census records say it was owned in 1900 by Louis's uncle, Isaac Myles, a relative on the Albert side of the family, not Josephine and William's.

5   *"they called their rooms"*: Armstrong, *Satchmo: My Life,* 7–8.

5   *"Marandy said, 'Yassum'"*: Giddins, *Satchmo,* 52. Riccardi adds this explainer to the "moonlit night" tale: "We have a tape of Louis and friends backstage at the Chicago Theater in 1954 and one white friend, Dwight 'Dite' Myers, tells it as a joke, right down to the name 'Marandy.' Louis was listening to those tapes again beginning in 1969 and it's possible he heard it, laughed, and slipped it into his own story" in the last of his memoirs, *Louis Armstrong + the Jewish Family.* Riccardi email.

6   *"the rear seats"*: Armstrong, *Satchmo: My Life,* 14.

7   *"out of my sight"*: Armstrong, *Satchmo: My Life,* 8 and 28–29.

7   *"Old Lady" Magg:* Armstrong, *Satchmo: My Life,* 9–10; Sanders, "Reluctant Millionaire"; and Brothers, *Louis Armstrong's New Orleans,* 52.

7   *"for days and days"*: Armstrong, *Satchmo: My Life,* 19.

8   *"gave me a present"*: Armstrong, *Satchmo: My Life,* 20 and 117–18.

8   *game called coon can:* Armstrong, *Satchmo: My Life,* 26, 85, and 93; Brothers, *Louis Armstrong's New Orleans,* 90; and Bergreen, *An Extravagant Life,* 41.

8   *"back of my shirt"*: Armstrong, *Satchmo: My Life,* 86–87 and 199. At Storyville's height, there were about two thousand prostitutes working out of 250 brothels.

9   *a Star of David:* Tad Jones files, HJA; and Armstrong, *In His Own Words,* 15.

9   *"to our mothers"*: Armstrong, *Satchmo: My Life,* 34; and Armstrong, *Swing That Music,* 4.

10 *apprehended in 1910:* Karst, "New Details Emerge"; emails to author from James Karst; and Jones and Chilton, *Louis Armstrong Story,* 56. The clerk for Orleans Parish Juvenile Court said Armstrong was in and out of the Waif's Home during his early teens, mainly for stealing newspapers that he in turn sold on the streets. Giddins, *Satchmo,* 66.

10 *came to tragic ends:* Karst, "Willie Telfry Was Arrested"; Karst, "Tragic Life of Red Sun"; and Goffin, *Horn of Plenty,* 282.

10 *"from behind me"*: Armstrong, *Satchmo: My Life,* 33–35; and Armstrong, *Swing That Music,* 1.

10 *drunks, thieves, and harlots:* In one of his evolving narratives on that night, Louis said the arresting detective was "high up on a horse." In most others the arresting officer was behind him, on foot. "Louis Armstrong in Paris," HJA.

11 *"the negro Waif's Home"*: Tad Jones files; Armstrong, *Satchmo: My Life,* 35; and "Few Juveniles Arrested," *Times-Democrat.*

11 *hopes for a future:* Armstrong, *Swing that Music,* 5.

11 *"learn how to pitch"*: Paige, *Maybe I'll Pitch Forever,* 24–26.

11 *at grammar schools:* Tad Jones files.

12 *the whole school watching:* Brothers, *Louis Armstrong's New Orleans,* 100.

12 *"as I wanted"*: Armstrong, *Satchmo: My Life,* 37; and Armstrong, *Swing That Music,* 6.

12 *only lasted a day:* Armstrong, *Satchmo: My Life,* 37 and 53; and Tad Jones files.

12 *while other boys clapped:* Tad Jones files.

13 *"'Home Sweet Home' on that"*: Meryman, "An Authentic American Genius."

13 *to the Waif's Home:* Brothers, *Louis Armstrong's New Orleans,* 108.

13 *Gatemouth and Satchelmouth:* Armstrong, *Satchmo: My Life,* 45; and Armstrong, *Swing That Music,* 6.

13 *after he'd arrived:* Some researchers believe that he might have been in and out of the Home between January 1, 1913, and his final release in the summer of 1914, rather than being there for eighteen months straight. Jones's wife said he was in for five years. Cogs-

well, *Offstage Story of Satchmo,* 31; and Buckingham, "Louis Armstrong and the Waifs' Home."

13 *becoming a man:* Armstrong, *Swing That Music,* 23; Armstrong, *Satchmo: My Life,* 51; and Collier, *An American Genius,* 105.

14 *"married at the home":* Armstrong, *Swing That Music,* 6; Armstrong, *Satchmo: My Life,* 51; and Krebs, "Louis Armstrong, Jazz Trumpeter and Singer, Dies."

14 *and Nasty Slim:* Brothers, *Louis Armstrong's New Orleans,* 79–80.

14 *"the bigwigs of music":* Armstrong, *Satchmo: My Life,* 24.

15 *"Can't Nobody Harm' Ya":* Louis sometimes attributed that hard-learned advice to a bouncer named Slippers.

15 *"Sweetheart on the outside":* Armstrong, *In His Own Words,* 160.

15 *of course he did:* Armstrong, *Satchmo: My Life,* 101–2 and 121–22; and Armstrong, *In His Own Words,* 85.

15 *another four years:* Armstrong, *Satchmo: My Life,* 157–58.

15 *the elder Hatfield:* Armstrong, *Satchmo: My Life,* 80–81. Public records in New Orleans show several men by that name whose age and other particulars could be a match for the old white fellow Louis identified as having impregnated Flora.

16 *called "feeble-minded":* Armstrong, *Satchmo: My Life,* 160–62; and Bergreen, *An Extravagant Life,* 139.

16 *with unfamiliar scores:* Armstrong, *Satchmo: My Life,* 191–93.

16 *"they* loved *us":* Armstrong, *Satchmo: My Life,* 189.

16 *"KING OLIVER":* Goffin, *Horn of Plenty,* 149.

CHAPTER 2: THE COUNT'S SHROUDED ROOTS IN RED BANK

18 *"ask those questions":* Linda Kuehl interview of Basie, March 3, 1977, SI.

18 *hopes raised, then dashed:* Every public record about Lillian has a different year of birth, ranging from 1871 to 1886. I picked 1877 because that was on the Count's birth certificate. Public records also offer different clues of her siblings, but no definitive proof: she might have had just one, Victoria, or there could also have been three brothers—Jessie, Alexander, and Henry. Bill remembered two uncles, Alex and Henry.

18 *as opposed to Lillian:* Basie, *Good Morning Blues,* 24.

18 *opportunities denied their parents:* Again, Count Basie's information was off, putting his father's birth in 1870, not 1874, and saying he had three siblings instead of six.

19 *"[He] didn't discourage me":* Basie, *Good Morning Blues,* 130; and Kuehl interview.

20 *"for the elephants":* Basie, *Good Morning Blues,* xi–xii and 28–29.

21 *to pull it off:* Basie, *Good Morning Blues,* xi–xii and 28–33.

21 *"what he did up there":* Kuehl interview; and Basie, *Good Morning Blues,* 33.

21 *"musician or a criminal":* Basie, *Good Morning Blues,* 39 and 42; author interview of Judy Carmichael.

22 *"world of show business":* Basie, *Good Morning Blues,* 45.

22 *"music was my ticket":* Basie, *Good Morning Blues,* 46.

22 *New York Giants stayed:* Basie, *Good Morning Blues,* 50.

23 *"something like that":* Basie, *Good Morning Blues,* 56–57 and 93.

23 *"little tasting going on":* Basie, *Good Morning Blues,* 57–59.

23 *"lessons I ever had":* Basie, *Good Morning Blues,* 69–70.

23 *"from New York":* Basie, *Good Morning Blues,* 84.

CHAPTER 3: DUKE'S CAPITAL EXPERIENCE

24 *to go to school:* Ulanov, *Duke Ellington,* 1; Cohen, *Duke Ellington's America,* 16; and Collier, *Duke Ellington,* 12.

24 *"He made it"*: Interviews of Bernice Wiggins and Juanita Middleton, September 6, 1983, Yale.

25 *"here and there"*: Interview of Ruth Ellington, November 11, 1977, Yale.

25 *called "beyond category"*: Edward Kennedy Ellington, *Music Is My Mistress*, 378.

26 *white police ranks*: Ellington biographer A. H. Lawrence says there were no Black senior officers at that time and no evidence that James Kennedy held that post.

26 *and school principals*: Ruth Ellington interview; Cohen, *Duke Ellington's America*, 13; Wiggins interview; and Tucker, *Ellington: The Early Years*, 19.

26 *"as beautiful as mine"*: Edward Kennedy Ellington, *Music Is My Mistress*, 6; and Ruth Ellington interview.

26 *"an aura of conviviality"*: Ulanov, *Duke Ellington*, 2; Cohen, *Duke Ellington's America*, 13; Nicholson, *Reminiscing in Tempo*, 5; Edward Kennedy Ellington, *Music Is My Mistress*, 12; and Carter Harman interviews of Duke Ellington, SI, 1956 and 1964.

27 *her life's devotion*: Washington, D.C., death certificate; and Lawrence, *Duke Ellington and His World*, 2.

27 *"the school door"*: Edward Kennedy Ellington, *Music Is My Mistress*, 6–9.

27 *"hurt and self-pity"*: Duke Ellington, "My Path of Prayer."

28 *in a department store*: Teachout, *Duke: A Life of Duke Ellington*, 24.

29 *"who's what color"*: Ruth Ellington interview.

29 *mantra of Black militants*: *Beyond Category* radio series; and interviews of Duke Ellington, 1964, Yale.

29 *publicity man did so*: Tucker, *Ellington: The Early Years*, 201; and Harman interviews.

30 *"'I was in Cleveland'"*: Edward Kennedy Ellington, *Music Is My Mistress*, 23.

30 *"discussed with authority"*: Edward Kennedy Ellington, *Music Is My Mistress*, 30.

30 *"Get em ice cold"*: Edward Kennedy Ellington, *Music Is My Mistress*, 9 and 22.

31 *named Marietta Clinkscales*: The teacher's name is sometimes given as Klingscale, Klinkscales, Klinkscale, and Chinkscales.

31 *knotted and neck tight*: Ulanov, *Duke Ellington*, 12.

31 *"here comes Duke"*: Mercer Ellington, *Duke Ellington in Person*, 33.

31 *"in any school"*: Edward Kennedy Ellington, *Music Is My Mistress*, 32–33.

32 *"bled to death"*: Stewart, *Boy Meets Horn*, 7 and 33.

32 *"pussy, not money"*: Edward Kennedy Ellington, *Music Is My Mistress*, 12 and 22; Harman interviews; Teachout, *Duke: A Life of Duke Ellington*, 40.

32 *baby boy, Mercer Kennedy Ellington*: Crawford, "A Visit with Mrs. Duke Ellington"; Teachout, *Duke: A Life of Duke Ellington*, 40; Harman interviews; and Ulanov, *Duke Ellington*, 9.

32 *dying at birth*: Crawford, "A Visit with Mrs. Duke Ellington."

33 *child's birth mother*: Lawrence, *Duke Ellington and His World*, 410; Hill, "Secret Grief of Jazz Charmer"; author interviews of Judy Udkoff, Dan Morgenstern, and Mercedes Ellington; Ruth Ellington Certificate of Live Birth, Health Department of the District of Columbia, July 2, 1915; and Ruth Ellington interview.

There is one more mystery surrounding Edward Kennedy Ellington's earliest years: whether the District of Columbia, the city of his birth, has his birth certificate. Officials say they do, but add that records like those aren't publicly available until 125 years after an individual's birth. But when we asked last year, with support from Mercedes Ellington and knowledge that the 125-year limit was just a year away, the District gave us his younger sister Ruth Ellington's birth certificate but inexplicably wouldn't release Duke's.

33 *"to someone else"*: Mercer Ellington, *Duke Ellington in Person*, 128.

CHAPTER 4: NIGHTSPOTS

37 *"a community pillar"*: Douglas, *Terrible Honesty*, 74.

38 *"tall, tan and terrific"*: Haskins, *Cotton Club*, 33 and 75; and Bailey, "Cotton Club Girls."

38 *conquering America:* Jewell, *Duke: A Portrait of Duke Ellington,* 41.
39 *"A great place":* Interview of Duke Ellington, February 1, 1973, Yale.
39 *"never lost his smile":* Pierpont, "Black, Brown, and Beige."
39 *"gag than anything else":* Edward Kennedy Ellington, *Music Is My Mistress,* 36–37.
40 *"booze than anybody ever":* Edward Kennedy Ellington, *Music Is My Mistress,* 73 and 75.
40 *let Ellington go:* Lawrence, *Duke Ellington and His World,* 105; and Jewell, *Duke: A Portrait of Duke Ellington,* 42.
40 *"characters of our time":* Edward Kennedy Ellington, *Music Is My Mistress,* 76; and Tucker, *Duke Ellington Reader,* 71–72.
41 *"chance to work at it":* Tucker, *Duke Ellington Reader,* 41–43.
41 *eventually the globe:* Teachout, *Duke: A Life of Duke Ellington,* 89.
42 *"at the Cotton Club":* Interview of Derek Jewell, March 24, 1981, Yale.
42 *all-American art:* Bergreen, *An Extravagant Life,* 238.
43 *another nearby speakeasy:* Ulanov, *Duke Ellington,* 117; and Haskins, *Cotton Club,* 59.
43 *an insatiable libido:* Applegate, *Madam: The Biography of Polly Adler,* 224.
44 *"hidden in their mattresses":* Edward Kennedy Ellington, *Music Is My Mistress,* 67.
45 *"but a happy town":* Basie, *Good Morning Blues,* 157; and Shapiro and Hentoff, *Jazz Makers,* 235.
47 *a routine tonsillectomy:* Basie, *Good Morning Blues,* 146; and Marre, *Count Basie: Through His Own Eyes.*
48 *"the Count is Here":* Basie, *Good Morning Blues,* 17 and 147.
48 *"a dignified beggar":* Driggs and Haddix, *Kansas City Jazz,* 127; Pearson, *Goin' to Kansas City,* 137; and Stanley Dance, *World of Count Basie,* 268.
49 *license and everywhere else:* Basie, *Good Morning Blues,* 17 and 131.
49 *New York City's East Side:* Driggs and Haddix, *Kansas City Jazz,* 143; and Stanley Dance, *World of Count Basie,* 13.
50 *"things for us":* Hammond and Townsend, *John Hammond on Record,* 167 and 170; and Basie, *Good Morning Blues,* 166.
50 *"out of Kansas City":* Basie, *Good Morning Blues,* 178 and 196.
51 *the not-so-old Confederacy:* Gene Anderson, *Original Hot Five Recordings;* Kenney, *Recorded Music in American Life;* and author interview of and emails to author from Tim Samuelson.
52 *"the Windy City for good":* Mezzrow and Wolfe, *Really the Blues,* 129; and Hampton and Haskins, *Hamp: An Autobiography,* 37.
53 *played in public just twice:* The first was on February 27, 1926, when, after cutting six sides the previous day, the band performed in front of ten thousand fans at the Chicago Coliseum in a concert organized by OKeh. A long-forgotten second show was July 10, 1928, at a picnic for the Waiters' Union local at Seventy-Ninth Street and Archer Avenue.
53 *"but it was fun":* Riccardi, "90 Years of Louis Armstrong and His Hot Five"; Lyttelton, *The Best of Jazz,* 130–5; Riccardi email.
53 *"go wrong with Louis":* Ory and Koenig, "The Hot Five Sessions."
54 *"on the South Side":* Edward Kennedy Ellington, *Music Is My Mistress,* 131.
55 *"the air would play it":* Condon, *We Called It Music,* 133.
56 *after-hours spot or two:* Brothers, *Master of Modernism,* 176.
57 *"crazy, screaming it":* Brothers, *Master of Modernism,* 191–92; and Larry L. King, "Everybody's Louie."
57 *"a private bath":* Brothers, *Master of Modernism,* 283; and Armstrong, *Satchmo: My Life,* 234.
57 *"married to me, too":* Lil Armstrong, "Satchmo and Me"; and email from Brynna Farris, Franklin Library, Fisk University.
57 *"the right way, huh":* Lil Armstrong, "Satchmo and Me."
58 *"it means pound plenty":* Magee, *Uncrowned King of Swing,* 72.
58 *Lil and Chicago:* Magee, *Uncrowned King of Swing,* 72; and Brothers, *Master of Modernism,* 122.

59   *near-perfect last chorus:* Denton, "On 'West End Blues.'"

59   *"imagined or conceived of":* Holiday and Dufty, *Lady Sings the Blues,* 9–10; and Nolan, *Three Chords for Beauty's Sake,* 25.

60   *for his fellow pianist:* Edward Kennedy Ellington, *Music Is My Mistress,* 100–102.

60   *"up there hearing him":* Basie, *Good Morning Blues,* 176–77, 302–3, 340, and 371.

60   *a record together:* Brothers, *Master of Modernism,* 300.

60   *"king for nothing":* Edward Kennedy Ellington, *Music Is My Mistress,* 236 and 418.

61   *from the get-go:* Email to author from Dan Morgenstern.

CHAPTER 5: LIFE ON THE ROCKY ROAD

63   *"burn them afterwards":* Interview of Robert Udkoff, March 11, 1991, SI.

63   *"Disorder is the order":* Teachout, *Pops: A Life of Louis Armstrong,* 226–27.

64   *"mothered some mean sons":* Larry L. King, "Everybody's Louie."

64   *"to forget," he said:* Marre, *Count Basie: Through His Own Eyes.*

64   *"what I was doing":* Basie, *Good Morning Blues,* 382.

65   *"the excitement was intense":* "Webb 'Cuts' Basie in Swing Battle," *DownBeat.* The magazine's name went from *down beat* to *Down Beat* to *DownBeat.* To avoid confusion, all entries here are spelled *DownBeat,* which is how it has been known since 2002. Jazz-research@groups.io.

65   *that wasn't Basieland:* Vail, *Count Basie: Swingin' the Blues,* 16–24.

65   *a vaudeville show:* "The Duke—Where and When," Ellington on the Web, http://tdwaw.ellington web.ca/TDWAW1.html.

65   *"almost a whole year":* Jo Jones, *Rifftide,* 84–85; and Ward and Burns, *Jazz: A History of America's Music,* 250.

66   *"and I never have":* Basie, *Good Morning Blues,* 382.

66   *and whispered, "Touchdown":* Soll, "The Night Basie Played Against the Packers—and Won."

66   *"to sign contracts":* Hasse, *Beyond Category: The Life and Genius of Duke Ellington,* 378; and "An Interview with Busy Duke Ellington," *Chicago Defender.*

67   *with a beer:* Horricks, *Count Basie and His Orchestra,* 21; George, *Sweet Man,* 104; Parks, *To Smile in Autumn,* 120; Taubman, "Satchmo Wears His Crown Gaily"; and Hinton and Berger, *Bass Line,* 207–8.

67   Guide to Gambling: Cogswell, *Offstage Story of Satchmo,* 89; Berrett, *Louis Armstrong Companion,* 102–3; "Louis the First," *Time;* Balliett, "King Louis"; and M. H. Miller, "Louis Armstrong, the King of Queens."

      Riccardi points out that the organic chemistry text was a gift to Louis on his seventieth birthday, inscribed to him by the author.

68   *"tree would dry up":* Hentoff, *Jazz Life,* 26–27.

68   *came in blackface:* Autobiography of Quincy Jones, 181; and Douglas, *Terrible Honesty,* 79.

69   *"reach over your shoulder":* Boyer, "Hot Bach—II."

69   *"coaching third base":* Autobiography of Clark Terry, 166; and Alfred Green, *Rhythm Is My Beat,* 82.

69   *singer Tony Watkins:* Interview of Eddie Barefield, November 21, 1978, SI; and interview of Tony Watkins, November 19, 1982, Yale.

70   *"out of there":* Gillespie and Fraser, *To BE, or Not,* 446.

70   *"That would be Utopia":* Love, "Chords & Discords"; Armstrong, "Daddy, How the Country Has Changed!"; and Boyer, "Hot Bach—II."

70   *"ask questions later":* "Takes More'n Tenn. Bomb to Stop Satchmo," *New York Post;* Riccardi, "'I'm Still Louis Armstrong—Colored,'" LAHM; and Armstrong, *Satchmo: My Life,* 146.

71   *christened Jerry:* Hinton and Berger, *Bass Line,* 116.

71   *"so smart after all":* Alfred Green, *Rhythm Is My Beat,* 78; and Alexander, "'For Posterity.'"

71   *"covered with condoms":* Ward and Burns, *Jazz: A History of America's Music,* 250; and Gitler, *Swing to Bop,* 13.

72 "without *federal troops*": Cohen, *Duke Ellington's America*, 254; and Jewell, *Duke: A Portrait of Duke Ellington*, 77.

CHAPTER 6: GETTING THERE

74 "*and room service*": Edward Kennedy Ellington, *Music Is My Mistress*, 85–86.

74 "*Joe [Oliver]'s eyes*": Armstrong, *Satchmo: My Life*, 228.

75 "*music to me*": Basie, *Good Morning Blues*, 57.

75 "*in his own bed*": Stewart, *Boy Meets Horn*, 133.

75 *during World War II*: Tucker, *Duke Ellington Reader*, 330.

76 "*all of you niggers*": Riccardi, *Heart Full of Rhythm*, 90–91.

76 "*ourselves and our wives*": "Darktown Stage Troupe to Face Judge," *Commercial Appeal*; Raeburn, "'I'll Be Glad When You're Dead,'" 346–47; and Max Jones, *Jazz Talking*, 136–37.

76 "*because he was black*": Snitzer, *Glorious Days and Nights*, 26; and author interview of Herb Snitzer.

77 "*spread out and relax*": *Autobiography of Clark Terry*, 114.

77 *the Iron Lung*: Gourse, *Every Day: The Story of Joe Williams*, 48.

78 "*Blue Goose bus*": Crow, *Jazz Anecdotes*, 77–78.

78 "'*No Suh Boss*'": Armstrong, *In His Own Words*, 104–5.

78 "*rough out there*": Marre, *Count Basie: Through His Own Eyes*.

79 "*I mean, 18 maniacs*": Collier, *Duke Ellington*, 325; and Harman interviews of Duke Ellington.

79 "*deal with business problems*": Hentoff, "Incompleat Duke Ellington."

79 "*people there you know*": Stanley Dance, *World of Duke Ellington*, 79–80.

79 "*fell back to sleep*": Teachout, *Duke: A Life of Duke Ellington*, 304.

81 "*a train freak*": Claire Gordon, *My Unforgettable Jazz Friends*, 258; Boyer, "Hot Bach—I"; and Ulanov, *Duke Ellington*, 270.

81 "*would of taught him*": Boyer, "Hot Bach—I."

82 "*the old pressure on*": Stewart, *Boy Meets Horn*, 147.

82 "*lying there smiling*": Max Jones, *Jazz Talking*, 112–13.

83 *just for his shoes*: Serrano, *Juan Tizol: His Caravan Through American Life*, 130–31; and Stewart, *Boy Meets Horn*, 149.

CHAPTER 7: SETTING THE THEMES

84 *civil rights icon Paul Robeson*: Actor-sportsman-activist Paul Robeson recorded a number of what were derisively called coon songs, including "Ma Curly-Headed Baby" and "That's Why Darkies Were Born."

85 "*Harvard cat visibly wilted*": Brothers, *Master of Modernism*, 441; Bigard, *With Louis and the Duke*, 123–24; Teachout, *Pops: A Life of Louis Armstrong*, 326; and Ernie Anderson, "Joe Glaser & Louis Armstrong." "Sleepy Time" actually had a trio of songwriters—Clarence Muse, Leon René, and his brother Otis René.

85 "*it lives with me*": Riccardi, *What a Wonderful World*, 61; and Wein and Stiber, *Louis Armstrong at Newport*.

86 *such an offensive word*: Hicks, "Louis Armstrong Makes New D . . . . y Recording."

86 *Enough said*: Brothers, *Master of Modernism*, 443.

87 "*That's what they do*": Riccardi, *What a Wonderful World*, 60.

87 "*slavery time down south*": Riccardi, *Heart Full of Rhythm*, 131.

88 "*the riffs just stuck*": Basie, *Good Morning Blues*, 162.

88 "*writing of the tune*": Russell, *Jazz Style in Kansas City*, 136.

88 "*He did, too*": McDaniels, "Buster Smith"; Russell, *Jazz Style in Kansas City*, 136–37; Daniels, *One O'Clock Jump*, 178–79; and Pearson, *Goin' to Kansas City*, 139–40.

89 *Carnegie Hall in 1938:* Hammond and Townsend, *John Hammond on Record,* 178–80; and Stearns, *Story of Jazz,* 213.

89 *an early blues number:* Gleason, *Celebrating the Duke, and Louis,* 164.

90 *kissed and made up:* Jewell, *Duke: A Portrait of Duke Ellington,* 100; and Duke Ellington interviews, Yale.

90 *"got every contrast":* Jewell, *Duke: A Portrait of Duke Ellington,* 76.

90 *"'East St. Louis Toodle-oo'":* Stanley Dance, *World of Duke Ellington,* 7; and Edward Kennedy Ellington, *Music Is My Mistress,* 106.

90 *"letter to a friend":* Hajdu, *Lush Life,* 55–56.

91 *"rest of the stuff":* Hajdu, *Lush Life,* 84.

91 *"way up in Harlem":* Hajdu, *Lush Life,* 97.

92 *at Duke Ellington's:* Edward Kennedy Ellington, *Music Is My Mistress,* 156. "'A' Train" actually is more sophisticated than critics acknowledge, as Harvey Cohen points out, adding, "Try playing it sometime." Cohen email.

CHAPTER 8: THE LANGUAGE OF JAZZ

94 *didn't require quotes:* Jones and Chilton, *Louis Armstrong Story,* 45–48; and Riccardi, "The Eternal Debate: Louis vs. Louie."

94 *"too late to eat":* Gleason, *Celebrating the Duke, and Louis,* 53.

95 *worked briefly for Louis:* Shapiro and Hentoff, *Hear Me Talkin' to Ya,* 11; and Bergreen, *An Extravagant Life,* 52.

95 *"Cootie, cootie, cootie":* Tucker, *Duke Ellington Reader,* 491.

97 *a marriage breakfast:* Basie, *Good Morning Blues,* 257.

97 *Ellington hated categories:* Stanley Dance, *World of Duke Ellington,* 2.

97 *trying a second time:* Love, "Chords & Discords," 27.

98 *nor too sluggish:* Charles Hersch, "Poisoning Their Coffee."

98 *"have not understood":* Armstrong, *Swing That Music,* 78 and 135–36.

98 *"my hip boots on":* Edward Kennedy Ellington, *Music Is My Mistress,* 179; Jewell, *Duke: A Portrait of Duke Ellington,* 21; and Harman interviews of Duke Ellington.

98 *"the we was royal":* Jewell, *Duke: A Portrait of Duke Ellington,* 51.

CHAPTER 9: ON CENTER STAGE

99 *hidden in his shoes:* Nestico, *Gift of Music,* 74.

99 *"if you look at it":* Basie, *Good Morning Blues,* 69.

99 *"and mind would follow":* *Beyond Category* radio series; and Giddins, *Visions of Jazz,* 184.

100 *the dance-band era:* Cooper, "Basie Insists Swing."

100 *"And very signature":* *Autobiography of Clark Terry,* 112–13.

100 *early Duke or Satchmo:* Pearson, *Goin' to Kansas City,* 136; author interviews of Nelson Harrison and Duff Jackson; and Hentoff, *Jazz Life,* 143–46.

101 *"most of all, swing":* Tucker, "Count Basie and the Piano That Swings."

101 *"it's only one note":* *Autobiography of Quincy Jones,* 245; Tucker, "Count Basie and the Piano That Swings"; and Marre, *Count Basie: Through His Own Eyes.*

101 *"cutting butter":* Tucker, "Count Basie and the Piano That Swings"; Basie, *Good Morning Blues,* 370.

102 *"brass I used to use":* Alkyer and Enright, *DownBeat: The Great Jazz Interviews,* 15.

102 *Count played, they danced:* John S. Wilson, "Count Basie, 79, Band Leader and Master of Swing, Dead"; Hinton and Berger, *Bass Line,* 187; and Alfred Green, *Rhythm Is My Beat,* 124.

102 *"rammed home the climax":* "Big-Band Jazz," *Time.*

102 *"It was unbelievable":* Author interview of Gary Giddins.

103 *"like that Basie band":* Jo Jones, *Rifftide,* 47.

103 "changes made," Basie warned: Alkyer and Enright, DownBeat: The Great Jazz Interviews, 15.
103 electrifying Count Basie Orchestra: Hentoff, Jazz Life, 144; and interview of Clark Terry, February 23, 1989, East Stroudsburg University.
103 "play him Count Basie": Author interview of Tom Reney.
104 "on an instrument": Author interview of Will Friedwald; and interview of Mercer Ellington, March 1, 1980, Yale.
104 "they'd take their time": Harman interviews of Duke Ellington.
105 "happening in the air": Wilson, Teddy Wilson Talks Jazz, 105.
105 "give me the best": Harman interviews of Duke Ellington; and Autobiography of Clark Terry, 133.
105 "if he had retired": Hasse, Beyond Category: The Life and Genius of Duke Ellington, 317.
106 "reels and breakdowns": Tucker, Duke Ellington Reader, 60.
107 "written by Ellington": Mercer Ellington interview, March 1, 1980.
107 "his own persona": Author interview of Mercedes Ellington.
107 "at least temporary happiness": Basie, Good Morning Blues, 303; and Tucker, Duke Ellington Reader, 53.
107 "and her bones": Harman interviews of Duke Ellington.
108 "mass singing of slaves": Tucker, Duke Ellington Reader, 53; and "Duke Ellington's Rehearsals a Bedlam of Discord," Baltimore Afro-American.
108 "it doesn't happen": Edward Kennedy Ellington, Music Is My Mistress, 458.
108 "known as 'symphonic jazz'": Tucker, Duke Ellington Reader, 73 and 110–11.
109 interest in, conducting: ASCAP has a softer system for issuing writing credits—letting the song's author credit anyone she or he wants, even if it is just to honor them—and by that count, Armstrong "wrote" as many as 120 songs.
109 bell of his trumpet: Ward and Burns, Jazz: A History of America's Music, 118; and author interview of Enrico Rava.
109 "supports the heavens": Crouch, Notes of a Hanging Judge, 255–56.
109 "would come out magnificent": Wilson, Satchmo: The Wonderful World of Louis Armstrong.
110 "this one superstar": Wilson, Satchmo: The Wonderful World of Louis Armstrong.
110 "and started to sing": Cogswell, Offstage Story of Satchmo, 28.
110 "his peculiar art": Larry L. King, "Everybody's Louie"; Krebs, "Louis Armstrong, Jazz Trumpeter and Singer, Dies"; and Armstrong, Swing That Music, xvi.
111 "long may he reign": Author interview of Ed Eckstein; Cohen email; and Ken Murray, "Louis, Bix Had Most Influence on Der Bingle."
111 "mention Charlie Chaplin": Bankhead, "An Appreciation of Louis Armstrong."

CHAPTER 10: THE SIDEMEN

115 "my favorite human being": Edward Kennedy Ellington, Music Is My Mistress, 159.
116 "'permission to fire me'": Harman interviews of Duke Ellington; Edward Kennedy Ellington, Music Is My Mistress, 111; Carney, "All I Want Is to Stay with Duke"; and interview of Juan Tizol, November 15, 1978, SI.
116 "and so was I": Simmen, "Harry Carney: An Encounter."
117 "keeping them there": Clayton, Buck Clayton's Jazz World, 62; Mercer Ellington interview, July 22, 1979, Yale; Watkins interview; Jewell, Duke: A Portrait of Duke Ellington, 105; and Stewart, Boy Meets Horn, 193.
117 "a genius like that": Interview of Sonny Greer, January 1979, SI.
117 low-strung, and strung-out: Autobiography of Clark Terry, 133 and 143.
118 "You do from Ellington": Max Jones, Jazz Talking, 11; and Teachout, Duke: A Life of Duke Ellington, 115.
118 and Lawrence Brown: Hasse, Beyond Category: The Life and Genius of Duke Ellington, 351.

119   *one of Duke's suits:* Interview of Lawrence Brown, July 1976, SI; Mercer Ellington, *Duke Ellington in Person,* 138 and 161; Jenkins, "Reminiscing in Tempo"; Hasse, *Beyond Category: The Life and Genius of Duke Ellington,* 81; and Jewell, *Duke: A Portrait of Duke Ellington,* 165.

119   *eventually came back:* Hasse, *Beyond Category: The Life and Genius of Duke Ellington,* 279.

119   *Terry sheepishly recalled:* Interview of Milt Hinton, October 14, 1977, Yale; and *Autobiography of Clark Terry,* 126.

120   *"'Take me with you'":* Hentoff, *At the Jazz Band Ball,* 22.

121   *"finished at dawn":* Teachout, *Duke: A Life of Duke Ellington,* 194.

121   *"Billy went with truth":* Brothers, *Help! The Beatles,* 136.

121   *"old-fashioned chauvinism":* Mercer Ellington, *Duke Ellington in Person,* 157–58; and Hasse, *Beyond Category: The Life and Genius of Duke Ellington,* 233.

121   *"the world would understand":* Teachout, *Duke: A Life of Duke Ellington,* 333; and Brothers, *Help! The Beatles,* 139.

122   *"'not gonna pay for that'":* Wein and Chinen, *Myself Among Others,* 164; and author interview of Tom Simons.

122   *"the guitar player":* Jordan and Scanlan, *Rhythm Man,* 1–2.

123   *"leave with him":* Alfred Green, *Rhythm Is My Beat,* 110 and 152; and Giddins interview.

123   *became a septet:* Alfred Green, *Rhythm Is My Beat,* 92.

123   *"gone out with anyone else":* Interview of Buddy Tate, October 28, 1984, University of California, Santa Barbara; and Max Jones, *Jazz Talking,* 105.

124   *"'Okay, let's go'":* *Autobiography of Clark Terry,* 119.

124   *"everything he had to say":* Rowe and Britell, *Jazz Tales from Jazz Legends,* 41–2.

124   *in dough. But still:* Interviews of Frank Foster, 1998, SI.

124   *the police pension fund:* Hentoff, *Jazz Life,* 49.

124   *"'cost a hundred dollars'":* Clayton, *Buck Clayton's Jazz World,* 95 and 99.

125   *he'd been sacked:* Harold Jones, *Singer's Drummer,* 82; and Voce, "Still Clinging to the Wreckage."

125   *home from school:* "Has Ex-Convict Brewer Let Count Basie Down?" and "Count Basie's Composer Confesses Killing Woman," *Chicago Defender.*

125   *"'a gun on the boss'":* Giddins interview.

125   *"I'd go to sleep":* Feather, *From Satchmo to Miles,* 120; and Büchmann-Møller, *You Just Fight for Your Life,* 94.

126   *"get him out":* Author interview of Alyn Shipton.

126   *"what am I going to do":* Alfred Green, *Rhythm Is My Beat,* 152.

127   *"Zutty from then on":* Riccardi, *Heart Full of Rhythm,* 32–33.

127   *"and his big ideas":* Stanley Dance, *The World of Earl Hines,* 54; and Freeman, "We'll Get Along Without Hines' Ego."

127   *the injured party:* Russell, "Armstrong Interview Notes"; Freeman, "We'll Get Along Without Hines' Ego"; and Teachout, *Pops: A Life of Louis Armstrong,* 148.

128   *"I'll be the leader":* Morgenstern, *Living with Jazz,* 78; Riccardi, *Heart Full of Rhythm,* 332; and Russell, "Armstrong Interview Notes."

128   *"you won't be there":* James, "A Year with Satchmo, 1931–32"; Riccardi, *What a Wonderful World,* 255; and *Autobiography of Pops Foster,* 189.

128   *"That was it":* Riccardi, *What a Wonderful World,* 212; and author interview of Jewel Brown.

129   *"love, love, love":* Maxine Gordon, *Sophisticated Giant,* 45.

129   *forced him to leave:* Delatiner, "Bassist Follows Armstrong Trail."

129   *"in his music":* Riccardi, *Heart Full of Rhythm,* 334–35.

CHAPTER 11: SIDE WOMEN

132   *"the masculine orchestras":* Roy, "Lil Armstrong Rivals Her Famous Hubby."

132   *"greatest of jazz musicians":* John S. Wilson, "Mary Lou Williams, a Jazz Great, Dies"; and

Gathright, "Mary Lou Williams, Missionary of Jazz." Just how many full or half siblings Williams had is unclear, given conflicting census and genealogical data.

133 *"I couldn't stop dancing"*: Kernodle, *Soul on Soul,* 162; and Dahl, *Morning Glory,* 72 and 237.

133 *"like soul on soul"*: *Soul on Soul* became the title of Tammy Kernodle's biography of Williams. Dahl, *Morning Glory,* 132–33; and Edward Kennedy Ellington, *Music Is My Mistress,* 169.

133 *a male bastion*: Whitehead, *Why Jazz?,* 48–49; and Von Eschen, *Satchmo Blows Up the World,* 21.

134 *"That was her bank"*: Meryman, "An Authentic American Genius."

134 *she prayerfully chanted*: Hamlin, "Billie Holiday's Bio."

135 *wrote in Lady Sings the Blues*: Holiday's memoir gets wrong this fact along with others, as she was with the band a year, not two, and was making more money than any other member. Clarke, *Billie Holiday: Wishing on the Moon,* 128–34.

135 *"them in our heads"*: Holiday and Dufty, *Lady Sings the Blues,* 62 and 69–70.

135 *"as fast as we could"*: Holiday and Dufty, *Lady Sings the Blues,* 68; Clarke, *Billie Holiday: Wishing on the Moon,* 130 and 134; and Basie, *Good Morning Blues,* 211.

136 *a hospital in Freetown*: Divergent records place her year of birth sometime between 1914 and 1917.

136 *"to be looked at"*: Interview of Maria Cole, July 5, 1980, Yale; and Edward Kennedy Ellington, *Music Is My Mistress,* 220.

136 *"It was very exciting"*: Interview of Kay Davis, July 21, 1980, Yale; and Edward Kennedy Ellington, *Music Is My Mistress,* 219.

137 *"to hear music"*: Interview of Lu Elliott, May 17, 1981, Yale; and Judy Carmichael, *Swinger!,* 252.

137 *"'her, not him'"*: Jewel Brown interview.

137 *"shot at the gate"*: Dahl, *Morning Glory,* 60–61.

138 *"let me do this again"*: Lu Elliott interview; and Marre, *Count Basie: Through His Own Eyes.*

CHAPTER 12: MANAGERS AND MOBSTERS

139 *"But from you"*: Larry L. King, "Everybody's Louie"; and Riccardi, *Heart Full of Rhythm,* 143.

140 *first sight of blood*: Another version of the story says that Joe refused to go to medical school, which disappointed not just his dad but the other docs in the family.

140 *"south side physician"*: "Diploma Mill for Physicians Laid to Doctors," *Chicago Tribune.*

140 *the brink of bankruptcy*: *People of the State of Illinois v. Joseph G. Glaser,* Supreme Court of Illinois.

141 *their white handlers*: Larry L. King, "Everybody's Louie"; and Riccardi, *Heart Full of Rhythm,* 161–67.

141 *"'bout its daddy"*: Meryman, "An Authentic American Genius"; Breslin, "A Normal Day with Joe Glaser."

142 *following him everywhere*: Riccardi, *Heart Full of Rhythm,* 63–74.

142 *his ravaged lips*: Riccardi, *Heart Full of Rhythm,* 166.

143 *in perfect cursive*: Breslin, "A Normal Day with Joe Glaser."

143 *shines, niggers, and schvartzes*: Ernie Anderson, "Joe Glaser & Louis Armstrong."

144 *the Hot Five*: Ernie Anderson, "Joe Glaser & Louis Armstrong."

144 *they shortchanged Black artists*: Armstrong, "Daddy, How the Country Has Changed!"

144 *and abhorred Joe*: Bigard, *With Louis and the Duke,* 116.

144 *"'Give the people a show'"*: Meryman, "An Authentic American Genius"; and Larry L. King, "Everybody's Louie."

145 *"a dozen shirts"*: Meryman, "An Authentic American Genius"; and Giddins, *Satchmo,* 129.

145 *Louis told a friend*: Teachout, *Pops: A Life of Louis Armstrong,* 317; and Breslin, "A Normal Day with Joe Glaser."

145 *"an old trick"*: Teachout, *Pops: A Life of Louis Armstrong,* 270; Hampton and Haskins, *Hamp:*

An Autobiography, 124; Larry L. King, "Everybody's Louie"; and Collier, *An American Genius,* 270.

146 *"your goddam throat'":* Wein and Chinen, *Myself Among Others,* 300; Collier, *An American Genius,* 160; and Crouch, "Laughin' Louis Armstrong."

146 *"I love you, Pops'":* Larry L. King, "Everybody's Louie."

146 *"the treasure he was":* Edward Kennedy Ellington, *Music Is My Mistress,* 234–35.

146 *"teach or something":* Meryman, *Louis Armstrong—A Self-Portrait,* 36.

147 *"washed and ironed":* Ernie Anderson, "Louis Armstrong: A Personal Memoir."

147 *"I left the office":* Ernie Anderson, "Louis Armstrong: A Personal Memoir"; Collier, *An American Genius,* 314–15; and Riccardi, *What a Wonderful World,* 26–27.

147 *Frenchy was gone:* Bigard, *With Louis and the Duke,* 116; Darensbourg, *Jazz Odyssey,* 166; and Riccardi, *What a Wonderful World,* 237.

148 *"who's painting their signs":* Cohen, *Duke Ellington's America,* 21; Hasse, *Beyond Category: The Life and Genius of Duke Ellington,* 47; and Edward Kennedy Ellington, *Music Is My Mistress,* 32.

148 *"about doing records, Duke":* The time of year and even the year of that momentous Mills-Ellington encounter changed depending on who was recounting, but Mark Tucker, the most complete chronicler of Ellington's early years, says it likely was 1926. As for the manager's name change, his marriage license suggested that he changed his first name first, becoming Irving Minsky, with Mills a later add-on. Tucker, *Ellington: The Early Years,* 197.

149 *fast talker like Irving Mills:* Ulanov, *Duke Ellington,* 57–58.
     While his son Bob and most Ellington biographers believed Mills was born after his parents came to New York, census records and his marriage license make clear it was in Russia. Emails to author from Bill Edwards.

149 *"always ahead of ourselves":* Interview of Irving Mills, April 23, 1981, Yale.

150 *"response from your editors":* "Advertising Manual: Duke Ellington and His Famous Orchestra," Mills Dance Orchestras (undated).

150 *284 separate stories:* Teachout, *Duke: A Life of Duke Ellington,* 125.

150 *"Gillette razor blade":* Sonny Greer interview.

150 *marketing master plan:* Cohen, *Duke Ellington's America,* 59 and 81–82.

151 *"in those days":* Cohen, *Duke Ellington's America,* 49 and 141; "Mills's Music," *Time;* Mills interview; and Mercer Ellington interview, July 22, 1979.

151 *white man running interference:* Ulanov, *Duke Ellington,* 126.

152 *"Massa Irving Mills":* Powell, "My Grandfather's Branded."

152 *a $3,500 version:* Ulanov, *Duke Ellington,* 206–7; and Nicholson, *Reminiscing in Tempo,* 207–8.

152 *"the best of friends":* Mills interview.

153 *"bring him back too":* Tucker, *Duke Ellington Reader,* 231; and Bigard, *With Louis and the Duke,* 50.

153 *Duke's first biographer:* Ulanov, *Duke Ellington,* 263; and Robert Udkoff interview.

154 *on the payroll:* Stewart, *Boy Meets Horn,* 149–50.

154 *pay Celley $6,000:* Ulanov, *Duke Ellington,* 263–64; and Cohen, *Duke Ellington's America,* 366–67. Ellington also accused his longtime accountant, William Mittler, of stealing, but in the end he paid $9,000 to settle a lawsuit Mittler brought against him.

154 *"neither fish nor fowl":* Mercer Ellington, *Duke Ellington in Person,* 136–37.

155 *"tell him that I did":* Francis Davis, *Outcats,* 9.

155 *"a very costly affair":* Interview of Cress Courtney, April 8, 1978, Yale.

155 *control their fates:* Cohen, *Duke Ellington's America,* 182–83.

156 *rest of Ellington's life:* Teachout, *Duke: A Life of Duke Ellington,* 276; Wein and Chinen, *Myself Among Others,* 168; and Cohen, *Duke Ellington's America,* 364.

156 *"can do for anybody":* Interview of Stanley Dance, April 8, 1978; and Edward Kennedy Ellington, *Music Is My Mistress,* 89.

156 *"wanted to be Jewish"*: Hersch, *Jews and Jazz*, 2.
156 *"eager to grab credit"*: Randy Sandke interview of Avakian, 2003; and Avakian interview, September 28, 1993.
156 *"he's responsible for me"*: Basie, *Good Morning Blues*, 295; and Pearson, *Goin' to Kansas City*, 142.
157 *"sounds better in person"*: Simon, *Big Bands*, 81.
158 *"one goddamn payroll"*: Basie, *Good Morning Blues*, 358–59.
158 *"defer to a Count"*: Wein and Chinen, *Myself Among Others*, 151.

CHAPTER 13: CRITICAL AUDIENCES AND PROFESSIONAL CRITICS

159 *"the back was enthusiastic"*: Swaffer, "I Heard Yesterday."
159 *"as James Joyce"*: Teachout, *Pops: A Life of Louis Armstrong*, 187.
160 *"'blow your goddamn nose'"*: Larry L. King, "Everybody's Louie."
160 *"race would ever produce"*: Tucker, *Duke Ellington Reader*, 51 and 111.
160 *"artists of his race"*: Tucker, *Duke Ellington Reader*, 120.
160 *"yoke of foreign dictatorship"*: Tucker, *Duke Ellington Reader*, 80–81.
161 *"BG got $2,500"*: Avakian, "'Barrelhouse Benny' Drops Decision."
161 *"but a human being"*: Author interview of Mort Sahl.
161 *"a kind of king"*: Interview of Alvin Ailey, September 7, 1983, Yale.
161 *vinyls and the wireless*: Brothers, *Master of Modernism*, 38.
162 *photographer Jack Bradley*: Teachout, *Pops: A Life of Louis Armstrong*, 326.
162 *"law to get to it"*: Ellison, *Conversations with Ralph Ellison*, 314.
162 *"jeans and T-shirts"*: Author interview of Nelson Harrison; and Giddins interview.
162 *"that title for weeks"*: Parks, *To Smile in Autumn*, 118.
163 *"the most powerful thing"*: Enstice and Rubin, *Jazz Spoken Here*, 66.
163 *"to show their support"*: Timuel Black, *Sacred Ground*, 44 and 61.
163 *the gunslinger's favorite numbers*: Larry L. King, "Everybody's Louie"; and Boyer, "Hot Bach—I."
163 *"one wishes to be"*: Drew, *On the Road with Duke Ellington*.
164 *"did not escape"*: Berrett, *Louis Armstrong Companion*, 72.
164 *"comparison with any other"*: Wells, *Night People*, 71; "Philadelphia Theater-Goers Go for Count Basie's 'Swing,'" *Pittsburgh Courier*; Dawbarn, "Basie Voted World's Top Jazzman"; and Avakian, "'Barrelhouse Benny' Drops Decision."
164 *"against Duke Ellington"*: Tucker, *Duke Ellington Reader*, 72–74; Voce, "It Don't Mean a Thing"; and Payne, "Story Behind Ellington's White House Fete."
165 *"no end of sludge"*: "Black Rascal," *Time*; "Louis the First," *Time*; and Kempton, "Louis Armstrong's Legacy Plays On."
165 *"and stay on"*: Riccardi, *Heart Full of Rhythm*, 243–44; Tucker, *Duke Ellington Reader*, 120; and Feather, "Rise and Fall of the Basie Band."
165 *"a beautiful flower anymore"*: Tucker, *Duke Ellington Reader*, 369.

CHAPTER 14: FAMILY UNFRIENDLY

169 *almost to his lip*: Mercer Ellington, *Duke Ellington in Person*, 13; Lawrence, *Duke Ellington and His World*, 134–35; and Jewell, *Duke: A Portrait of Duke Ellington*, 31.
170 *"used in our family"*: Kakutani, "Life as Ellington's Son"; Francis Davis, *Outcats*, 5; and Mercer Ellington, *Duke Ellington in Person*, 7 and 18.
170 *talk his heart out*: Lawrence, *Duke Ellington and His World*, 152; and Ulanov, *Duke Ellington*, 113–14.
170 *"Everything was for Edward"*: Ruth Ellington interview; Mercedes Ellington interview, June 30, 1980, Yale; and Cohen, *Duke Ellington's America*, 183.

171 *"I'm still jealous"*: Crawford, "A Visit with Mrs. Duke Ellington."

171 *"might have been both"*: Mercedes Ellington interview, Yale.

171 *"and I was hers"*: Interview of Lawrence Brown and Barney Bigard, June 1976, SI; Collier, *Duke Ellington*, 102; "Duke Ellington's Duchess," *Jet;* and author interview of Mercedes Ellington.

172 *"I'm home to dine"*: Lawrence, *Duke Ellington and His World*, 152; and Ruth Ellington interview.

172 *"come off it"*: Ulanov, *Duke Ellington*, 163–64; and Mercer Ellington, *Duke Ellington in Person*, 68–69.

172 *"really did straighten up"*: Harman interviews of Duke Ellington; and Edward Kennedy Ellington, *Music Is My Mistress*, 86.

173 *that family bond*: Jewell, *Duke: A Portrait of Duke Ellington*, 92–93; and Ruth Ellington interview.

173 *"I didn't say anything"*: Ruth Ellington interview; and Edward Kennedy Ellington, *Music Is My Mistress*, 44.

173 *"on the road"*: Ruth Ellington interview.

174 *"service and a Cadillac"*: Mercer Ellington, *Duke Ellington in Person*, 79.

174 *"position to help others"*: Mercer Ellington, *Duke Ellington in Person*, 21 and 90.

174 *"my appreciation of him"*: Interview of Joya Sherrill, November 21, 1979, Yale; and Mercer Ellington, *Duke Ellington in Person*, 55.

174 *"he'd call him 'Pop'"*: Mercedes Ellington and Brower, *Duke Ellington: An American Composer and Icon*, 17–20.

175 *"never a direct way"*: Author interview of Edward Kennedy Ellington II.

176 *"out of there fast"*: Basie, *Good Morning Blues*, 135 and 153.

176 *"coming back again"*: Basie, *Good Morning Blues*, 229–30.

176 *"those one-nighters"*: Basie, *Good Morning Blues*, 259. Columnist Danton Walker wrote in January 1943 that Bill and Catherine had just eloped. Walker, "New York Letter."

177 *out of childhood*: "151 Out-of-Town Pairs Get Baltimore Wedding Permits," *Baltimore Afro-American;* Calvin, "Thru Harlem"; and King County Washington Marriage Certificate, July 13, 1950.

177 *"out on the road"*: Basie, *Good Morning Blues*, 333–34.

178 *back in Red Bank*: Hinton and Berger, *Bass Line*, 177 and 186.

178 *and kidney stones*: Basie, *Good Morning Blues*, 265; Marre, *Count Basie: Through His Own Eyes;* and "Report of Guardian Ad Litem, Diane Basie," Surrogate's Court of the State of New York, March 11, 2011.

179 *too critical of him*: Bartley, "'The One Who Counts with Count'"; author interviews of Aaron Woodward and Pamela Jackson; Marre, *Count Basie: Through His Own Eyes;* and letter from Count to Catherine, July 31, 1965, IJS.

179 *"exactly what he did"*: Author interview of Carmen Bradford.

180 *"never have been married"*: Armstrong, *Satchmo: My Life*, 151–58; and Armstrong, *Swing That Music*, 37.

180 *"get some sleep"*: Divorce filings, *Louis Armstrong v. Daisy Armstrong*, Clerk of the Circuit Court of Cook County, August 30, 1923, and February 11, 1925; and Jones and Chilton, *Louis: The Louis Armstrong Story*, 56.

181 *"few real hard ones"*: Armstrong, *Satchmo: My Life*, 178–79.

181 *a lawyer Lil arranged*: Brothers, *Master of Modernism*, 113.

181 *"her wants and necessities"*: Lillian-Louis Armstrong divorce proceedings, Cook County, Illinois, 1931; Lil-Louis divorce papers, Tad Jones files; and interview of Lillian Harden Armstrong, July 1, 1959, HA.

182 *"support of said child"*: Brothers, *Master of Modernism*, 120–21 and 321; Riccardi, *Heart Full of Rhythm*, 333; Armstrong, *In His Own Words*, 97; and Lil-Louis divorce papers, Tad Jones files.

182 *her writings and interviews:* Armstrong, *In His Own Words,* 26 and 86; Riccardi, *Heart Full of Rhythm,* 334; Albertson, "Lil Hardin Armstrong—A Fond Remembrance"; and author interview of Riccardi.

182 *her ever-present mother:* Cogswell, *Offstage Story of Satchmo,* 142.

182 *"all you know":* Letter from Armstrong to Walter Winchell, January 19, 1942, LAHM.

183 *"nobody had been around":* Another time, when a rightfully jealous Alpha was trying to choke him backstage, Louis hit her on the chin hard enough to knock her out. Or so said biographer Robert Goffin, a Belgian whom Louis fed original material and paid for his services, but who sometimes embellished facts and invented pseudo–New Orleans patois. Goffin, *Horn of Plenty,* 296–97.

183 *the United States:* Russell, "Armstrong Interview Notes."

183 *she lived until 1960:* Ernie Anderson, "Joe Glaser & Louis Armstrong"; and Riccardi, *Heart Full of Rhythm,* 262. Alpha died at a swank address in Beverly Hills that as of August 2023 is valued at more than $8 million. Zillow, https://www.zillow.com/homedetails/709-N -Roxbury-Dr-Beverly-Hills-CA-90210/20521552_zpid/.

184 *"anything nice [about me]":* Mama Lucy's first marriage was at just nineteen, her second at forty-four, according to the marriage licenses from New Orleans. Interview of Phoebe Jacobs, August 31, 2010, LAHM.

184 *"woman is rare today":* As Lucille put it, "He couldn't cook in my pots and I'll not blow his horn, we each had our own position." Wilson, *Satchmo: The Wonderful World of Louis Armstrong;* Teachout, *Pops: A Life of Louis Armstrong,* 230; and Armstrong, "Why I Like Dark Women."

185 *on the planet:* McLendon, "Mrs. Satchmo Goes Where Louie Toots"; Bowers, "The Great Woman Who's Behind Great 'Satchmo'"; and Armstrong, *In His Own Words,* 10.

185 *after it was issued:* In the space marked date of marriage, someone wrote, "Don't know."

185 *"one of them Russell":* Riccardi, *Heart Full of Rhythm,* 262.

CHAPTER 15: MISTRESSES AND MISOGYNY

186 *if not his carousing:* Ward and Burns, *Jazz: A History of America's Music,* 290.

186 *"But that's another story":* Basie, *Good Morning Blues,* 357.

186 *"'You're a lying motherfucker'":* Author interview of Ed Eckstine. Billy was born with his name spelled Eckstein, not Eckstine, but changed it after a promoter told him his legal name sounded like he was Jewish, "and that folks didn't show up, you know, in the Black community because it was a Jewish guy," explains Ed. "So the following week when he performed, the guy put on the marquee, 'Tonight, colored singing sensation Billy Eckstine.'" Ed uses the Eckstine spelling to pay tribute to his father, he says, although his email uses his grandparents' Eckstein.

187 *"take me home":* Hinton and Berger, *Bass Line,* 186–87.

187 *"four times a year":* "Blonde Sues Billy Daniels," *Chicago Defender;* and "Count Basie Is Coming Home," *New York Amsterdam News.*

187 *"jump thru you":* letters from Count to Catherine: May 8, 1957, January 20, 1960, April 24, 1962, and August 8, 1963 (the dates on the postmarks are difficult to make out), IJS.

188 *tug at Katy's heartstrings:* letter from Count to Catherine, July 31, 1965, IJS.

188 *"By Mrs. Count Basie":* Basie files, IJS.

188 *"almost 10 carats":* Marre, *Count Basie: Through His Own Eyes.*

189 *"a king's palace":* Jo Jones, *Rifftide,* 101.

189 *"trouble around here":* Author interview of Linda Gerber; and "The Count," *60 Minutes,* January 28, 1979.

190 *keys to the dukedom:* Lawrence, *Duke Ellington and His World,* 401; George, *Sweet Man,* 109; Teachout, *Duke: A Life of Duke Ellington,* 140; and Claire Gordon, *My Unforgettable Jazz Friends,* 274.

190 *the family music company*: Mercer Ellington, *Duke Ellington in Person*, 78.
191 *"'wait for the money'"*: Mercer Ellington, *Duke Ellington in Person*, 78.
191 *she never was enough*: Recognizing her role as Duke's fierce protector, band members gave Evie the nickname Thunderbird.
192 *"became his slave"*: George, *Sweet Man*, 141.
192 *"could hardly believe it"*: Mercer Ellington, *Duke Ellington in Person*, 126.
192 *but wasn't concerned*: Mercer Ellington, *Duke Ellington in Person*, 205–6.
193 *"'I reminded him of him'"*: Interview of Betty McGettigan, July 15, 1980, Yale; and McGettigan, "Waltzing to a Tango."
193 *"she didn't believe me"*: Author interview of Mary McGettigan.
194 *"before you were born"*: Avakian interview, March 17, 1978, Yale; McLeese, "100 Reasons to Remember Duke"; Teachout, *Duke: A Life of Duke Ellington*, 3; and Jewell, *Duke: A Portrait of Duke Ellington*, 132–33.
194 *"I douche with Lavoris"*: *Autobiography of Clark Terry*, 142; and George, *Sweet Man*, 147.
194 *"the Soviet Army"*: Duke Ellington, "Sex Is No Sin"; and Teachout, *Duke: A Life of Duke Ellington*, 177.
195 *"second fiddle to no one"*: George, *Sweet Man*, 155; and Edward Kennedy Ellington, *Music Is My Mistress*, 447.
195 *they are "uncountable"*: Author interviews of Riccardi and Thomas Brothers.
195 *a Fleetwood Cadillac*: Armstrong, *In His Own Words*, 84; and Riccardi, *Heart Full of Rhythm*, 233.
196 *"but [will] marry nary"*: Lamar, "Louis Armstrong Faces Trouble with 4th Wife."
196 *"ballin' all the time"*: Letter from Louis Armstrong to Joe Glaser, August 2, 1955, LAHM; and "Lost Tapes": *Voice of America Jazz Hour*, BBC Radio 4, 1956.
197 *"cute little Baby"*: Bigard interview, SI; Armstrong letter to Glaser; and Preston-Folta and Millner, *Little Satchmo*, 101. Sharon wasn't the only one claiming to be an Armstrong heir. Hollywood Herb Armstrong, a jazz singer in Australia, said he is "the product of the lovechild generation" and that his grandmother, seamstress Iola Bates, was Louis's unofficial wife. Noonan, "Blowing the Trumpet."
And Louis wasn't the only jazzman who had young people saying they were his offspring. "They call themselves April and Edward Ellington," says Mercedes Ellington. "They introduced themselves to me in Canada and said, 'We are Duke Ellington's children' . . . I was like so excited. I said to my father, 'Guess who I met?' and my father started laughing. He says, 'Oh, I know who they are. Their father was the bass player in the band, when the band was in Canada. Their mother was a nurse, and she hung out with the band.'" Author interview of Mercedes Ellington.
197 *"ifs' and ans' about it"*: Armstrong, *In His Own Words*, 158; and Armstrong letter to Glaser.

CHAPTER 16: KEEPING THE FAITH

198 *"the Sin in Syncopation"*: Carmody, "Baptist Ministers Refuse to Endorse"; and Riccardi, *Heart Full of Rhythm*, 226.
199 *"hit the floor"*: Ernie Anderson, "Joe Glaser & Louis Armstrong"; and Berrett, *Louis Armstrong Companion*, 166–67.
199 *"spiritual and mental plane"*: Daniels, *Lester Leaps In*, 185–86.
199 *"bringing light into darkness"*: Cohen, *Duke Ellington's America*, 446 and 467.
200 *"I have ever done"*: Edward Kennedy Ellington, *Music Is My Mistress*, 266–69.
200 *"she'd 'Come 'to"*: Armstrong, *In His Own Words*, 170; and Brothers, *New Orleans*, 30–40.
200 *the Big Easy*: Armstrong, *Satchmo: My Life*, 11; and Millstein, "Africa Harks to Satch's Horn."
201 *"Jewish star for luck"*: Berrett, *Louis Armstrong Companion*, xv.
201 *"I Love Her So"*: Author interview of Eric Schneider.
201 *LOVE GOD*: Ruth Ellington interview; and Boyer, "Hot Bach—I."

202 *"in my life I prayed"*: George, *Sweet Man*, 104–6.
202 *"God does not understand"*: Interview of John Gensel, December 14, 1979, Yale; and Elam, "Endless Ellington Era."
202 *"the* Sacred Concerts*"*: Edward Kennedy Ellington, *Music Is My Mistress*, 261; and Lawrence, *Duke Ellington and His World*, 404.
202 *into their services*: Cohen, *Duke Ellington's America*, 458 and 470–71.
203 *"consecration of the world"*: Cohen, *Duke Ellington's America*, 469–70.
203 *"cross back on"*: Edward Kennedy Ellington, *Music Is My Mistress*, 282.

CHAPTER 17: CRAVINGS AND DEPENDENCIES

204 *"'Can he run'"*: Frank Foster interviews; Marre, *Count Basie: Through His Own Eyes*; Feather, "Rise and Fall of the Basie Band"; and Alfred Green, *Rhythm Is My Beat*, 45.
205 *"aboard the plane"*: Autobiography of Quincy Jones, 181–82.
205 *"owned Basie's band"*: Autobiography of Quincy Jones, 36.
205 *their daughter Diane's*: Basie, *Good Morning Blues*, 285 and 364; and author interview of Morgenstern.
205 *"excuse to keep working"*: Giddins, *Visions of Jazz*, 171.
206 *whiff of marijuana*: Jo Jones, *Rifftide*, 58; and Marre, *Count Basie: Through His Own Eyes*.
206 *"Not much. Not enough"*: Basie, *Good Morning Blues*, 198 and 306.
206 *"a champion partier"*: Author interviews of Dave Stahl and Duff Jackson.
207 *chauffeur him around*: Parks, *To Smile in Autumn*, 121.
207 *sever a bond*: Rowe and Britell, *Jazz Tales from Jazz Legends*, 27; and Mercer Ellington, *Duke Ellington in Person*, 154.
207 *"twist a button loose"*: Stewart, *Jazz Masters of the 30s*, 93.
208 *her granddad saying*: Author interview of Mercedes Ellington.
208 *"over his left shoulder"*: Mercer Ellington, *Duke Ellington in Person*, 35 and 154.
208 *four teaspoons of sugar*: Edward Kennedy Ellington, *Music Is My Mistress*, 75.
209 *"He was too sober"*: Author interview of Harriet Choice.
209 *from the boss's car*: "Nab Duke Band Group for Dope," *Chicago Defender*; and "Jailed in Narcotics Case," *New York Times*.
210 *"children you ever saw"*: Hentoff, "Incompleat Duke Ellington."
210 *"among jazz musicians"*: Winick and Nyswander, "Psychotherapy of Successful Musicians"; and Winick, "Use of Drugs by Jazz Musicians."
210 *"Lady, King, Bird"*: Winick, "Use of Drugs by Jazz Musicians."
211 *"people with asthma smoke"*: Stanley Dance, *World of Earl Hines*, 146.
211 *"like it or you don't"*: Armstrong, *In His Own Words*, 112–13.
211 *"sit on the toilet"*: Armstrong, *In His Own Words*, 113; Hinton and Berger, *Bass Line*, 207; and Riccardi, *What a Wonderful World*, 93.
212 *"I wired you, eh"*: Letter from Armstrong to Mezz Mezzrow, September 18, 1932, Oberlin College Library.
212 *"'please forive me'"*: Gillespie and Fraser, *To BE, or Not*, 285; and Clayton, *Buck Clayton's Jazz World*, 46.
213 *"a few of the nurses"*: Brothers, *Master of Modernism*, 390; Riccardi, *Heart Full of Rhythm*, 58–62; and Berton, *Remembering Bix*, 389.
213 *to Louis, not her*: Hinton and Berger, *Bass Line*, 209; and Riccardi, *Heart Full of Rhythm*, 87.
214 *"Nothing impossible, man"*: Riccardi, *What a Wonderful World*, 85–93.
214 *"say, 'Fuck you'"*: Riccardi, *Heart Full of Rhythm*, 92–93; and Giddins, *Satchmo*, 130.
214 *"a dope fiend"*: Armstrong, *In His Own Words*, 113–14.
215 *"don't tell anyone"*: Larry L. King, "Everybody's Louie"; and Teachout, *Pops: A Life of Louis Armstrong*, 357.

CHAPTER 18: TOILET TRUTHS, FOOD FETISHES, AND OTHER MEDICAL MATTERS

216   *"Yes, mother"*: Armstrong, *Satchmo: My Life*, 16 and 20.

217   *"No shit"*: Riccardi, *What a Wonderful World*, 144.

217   *"in your stomach"*: Berrett, *Louis Armstrong Companion*, 99–101.

217   *five-foot-six-inch frame*: Riccardi, *What a Wonderful World*, 143–44.

218   *here and overseas*: Schiff also treated the rest of the band when he went overseas, and even handled its payroll. Zucker interview, LAHM.

218   *"do the same thing"*: Armstrong, *In His Own Words*, 188.

218   *"nothing had happened"*: Meryman, "An Authentic American Genius"; and Armstrong, *Satchmo: My Life*, 20–21.

218   *"like a skin flap"*: Collier, *An American Genius*, 41; and Zucker interview, LAHM.

219   *away from his art*: Larry L. King, "Everybody's Louie"; and Ernie Anderson, "Joe Glaser & Louis Armstrong."

219   *on long trips, methedrine*: Larry L. King, "Everybody's Louie"; and Krupnick, "Have Satchelmouth—Will Travel."

219   *"some good, ya dig"*: Larry L. King, "Everybody's Louie."

219   *a doctor's (unrefillable) prescription*: Colegrave, "It Ain't the Money"; and Krupnick, "Have Satchelmouth—Will Travel."

220   *"no chance of pyorrhea"*: Colegrave, "It Ain't the Money"; and Armstrong, "Care of the Lip."

220   *"Louis would wake up"*: Hinton and Berger, *Bass Line*, 208.

220   *"should I say, disgustingly"*: Armstrong, "Ulceratedly Yours."

221   *"when I came out"*: Edward Kennedy Ellington, *Music Is My Mistress*, 205–10.

221   *"in front of the public"*: George, *Sweet Man*, 149; and Enstice and Rubin, *Jazz Spoken Here*, 129.

221   *"on the table at the same time"*: Edward Kennedy Ellington, *Music Is My Mistress*, 400–401.

221   *Old Orchard Beach*: Tucker, *Duke Ellington Reader*, 215.

222   *"lost thirty pounds"*: Edward Kennedy Ellington, *Music Is My Mistress*, 390.

222   *with tired feet*: Hentoff, "Incompleat Duke Ellington"; Jewell, *Duke: A Portrait of Duke Ellington*, 200; and Balliett, *American Musicians II*, 400.

222   *"communists, financiers, or both"*: Mercer Ellington, *Duke Ellington in Person*, 157.

223   *"let anything bug you"*: Jewell, *Duke: A Portrait of Duke Ellington*, 131–32 and 201; and Edward Kennedy Ellington, *Music Is My Mistress*, 209.

223   *"he hates planes"*: Hajdu, *Lush Life*, 230; and Hentoff, "Incompleat Duke Ellington."

223   *"playing dress-up"*: George, *Sweet Man*, 241; and Hajdu, *Lush Life*, 193.

224   *at age twelve*: "William Basie, Musician, in Hospital Here," *Kansas City Call*; and Voce, "Still Clinging to the Wreckage."

224   *"for his bag"*: Horricks, *Count Basie and His Orchestra*, 21.

224   *"which is the body"*: Gourse, *Every Day: The Story of Joe Williams*, 210.

225   *"every five or six weeks"*: Basie, *Good Morning Blues*, 373–77.

226   *"great receptions as before"*: Basie, *Good Morning Blues*, 378–81.

226   *"smoothly from that point"*: Basie, *Good Morning Blues*, 378 and 381; and Nestico, *Gift of Music*, 76.

CHAPTER 19: FOLLOW THE MONEY

227   *released from his contract*: Cohen, *Duke Ellington's America*, 106–8 and 262–64.

227   *"nothing from record sales"*: Hammond and Townsend, *John Hammond on Record*, 171.

228   *"Louis Armstrong—colored"*: Sanders, "Reluctant Millionaire."

229   *"sandwich in his pocket"*: Cohen, *Duke Ellington's America*, 349–51 and 373; and Teachout, *Duke: A Life of Duke Ellington*, 344–45.

230 *"or make money"*: Hasse, *Beyond Category: The Life and Genius of Duke Ellington*, 274–75; Cohen, *Duke Ellington's America*, 88–89 and 351; and Wilson, "Duke Ellington, a Master of Music, Dies."

230 *Glenn Miller five times*: Jewell, *Duke: A Portrait of Duke Ellington*, 22 and 103.

230 *the Count was played out*: Clayton, *Buck Clayton's Jazz World*, 99; and Daniels, *One O'Clock Jump*, 168.

230 *"on reduced salaries"*: Daniels, *One O'Clock Jump*, 168–73; and Alfred Green, *Rhythm Is My Beat*, 90.

230 *"music you like"*: Basie, *Good Morning Blues*, 381–82.

231 *"sustain but to break"*: Armstrong, "Why I Like Dark Women," 68.

231 *he was hardly reluctant*: Sanders, "Reluctant Millionaire."

231 *"dead as he is"*: Cogswell, *Offstage Story of Satchmo*, 103; Fox, "Ambassador Armstrong," 294; and Sanders, "Reluctant Millionaire."

232 *"when it was so popular"*: Basie, *Good Morning Blues*, 325–26.

232 *"It was a mess"*: Author interview of Mercedes Ellington.

233 *"we sure look pretty"*: Stewart, *Jazz Masters of the 30s*, 84; and Harman, "Jazz Man Duke Ellington."

233 *"Ellington never did"*: Cohen, *Duke Ellington's America*, 288.

233 *"we don't even know about"*: Ruth Ellington interview.

233 *"Duke paid for all of it"*: *Autobiography of Clark Terry*, 147.

233 *"other saints and sinners"*: Stewart, *Jazz Masters of the 30s*, 89–90; and Stewart, *Boy Meets Horn*, 156.

234 *"'And always be fair'"*: Stahl interview; and *Autobiography of Quincy Jones*, 101.

234 *"any discussion about it"*: Basie, *Good Morning Blues*, 381.

234 *"no strings attached"*: Sanders, "Reluctant Millionaire."

CHAPTER 20: ARTISTS *AND* ENTERTAINERS

237 *"make it seven percent"*: Teachout, *Pops: A Life of Louis Armstrong*, 221.

237 *"nice things about me"*: *Miles: The Autobiography*, 313 and 83.

238 *"for the white man"*: Ossie Davis, *Life Lit by Some Large Vision*, 161.

238 *"call him Uncle Tom"*: Riccardi, *Heart Full of Rhythm*, 8–9.

238 *"I ain't the only one"*: Ossie Davis, *Life Lit by Some Large Vision*, 161–62.

239 *"you can't play nothing"*: Meryman, "An Authentic American Genius"; and Riccardi, "'I'm Still Louis Armstrong—Colored.'"

239 *on Billboard's Hot 100*: Meryman, "An Authentic American Genius."

240 *his mother's Pentecostal church*: Riccardi, "Louis Armstrong and Comedy, Parts 1 and 2," LAHM; and Teachout, *Pops: A Life of Louis Armstrong*, 326.

240 *"exhibition of pseudo-jazz"*: Riccardi, *Heart Full of Rhythm*, 243–44; and Keepnews, "Lemme Take This Chorus."

240 *"don't worry about that few"*: Riccardi, "'I'm Still Louis Armstrong—Colored.'"

241 *"white girl—in their acts"*: Teachout, *Pops: A Life of Louis Armstrong*, 223.

241 *the best-song Oscar*: Green, "Artists and Models"; and Riccardi, *What a Wonderful World*, 245.

241 *"Cause I'm colored"*: Riccardi, "'I'm Still Louis Armstrong—Colored.'"

242 *"you wanted it cut"*: Author interview of Harold Reddick.

242 *stoop to prevail*: Ellison, *Invisible Man*, 8.

243 *"a throat of gravel"*: Reddick interview; Bilovsky, "Satchel Paige—Bittersweet Tale of a Sad 'Clown'"; and Ellison, *Collected Essays*, 106.

243 *"you're not serious"*: Reich, "Jazz Giant's Private Views Show Anger Behind Smile."

243 *"black—like us"*: Parks, "Jazz."

244 *"expensive organisation going"*: Hentoff, *Listen to the Stories*, 17; and Hasse, *Beyond Category: The Life and Genius of Duke Ellington*, 238.

245 *"the surface than above"*: Tucker, *Duke Ellington Reader*, 173; Jewell, *Duke: A Portrait of Duke Ellington*, 15; and Stewart, *Jazz Masters of the 30s*, 80.

245 *mistress Fredi Washington*: Whitehead, *Play the Way You Feel*, 288.

245 *Negro* New York Age: Cohen, *Duke Ellington's America*, 104; Whitehead, *Play the Way You Feel*, 168; Hasse, *Beyond Category: The Life and Genius of Duke Ellington*, 184; and Teachout, *Duke: A Life of Duke Ellington*, 97 and 104.

246 *"so little as Count Basie"*: Hentoff, "One More Time: Travels of Count Basie."

CHAPTER 21: RESETTING THE THEMES

247 *snarling German shepherds*: Cohen, *Duke Ellington's America*, 394–95.

248 *"everything you want to say"*: Cohen, *Duke Ellington's America*, 393–95; and Nicholson, *Reminiscing in Tempo*, 347–48.

248 *"quite a moment"*: Interview of Marian Logan, February 27, 1978, Yale.

249 *in all of Hollywood*: Cohen, *Duke Ellington's America*, 189–91; Mercer Ellington, *Duke Ellington in Person*, 182; Caponi-Tabery, *Jump for Joy*, 179.

249 *Jump was shuttered*: Caponi-Tabery, *Jump for Joy*, 182–86; Teachout, *Duke: A Life of Duke Ellington*, 229; and Duke Ellington, typescript outline for *Jump for Joy*, 1941, Georgetown University Special Collections.

249 *"the world was not ready"*: Edward Kennedy Ellington, *Music Is My Mistress*, 176.

250 *spent decades nurturing*: Edward Kennedy Ellington, *Music Is My Mistress*, 182.

250 *"never got quite white"*: Harmon interviews; Teachout, *Duke: A Life of Duke Ellington*, 238; and Cohen, *Duke Ellington's America*, 213–14. Cohen called it "quite right" but the original recording sounds like "quite white."

250 *"they restricted each other"*: Enstice and Rubin, *Jazz Spoken Here*, 121.

251 *talking about himself here*: Edward Kennedy Ellington, *Music Is My Mistress*, 182; and Cohen, *Duke Ellington's America*, 229.

251 *"in them to languish"*: Cohen, *Duke Ellington's America*, 226.

251 *"the blues is real jazz"*: Tucker, *Duke Ellington Reader*, 166–67 and 177.

251 *"all people and all lands"*: Cohen, *Duke Ellington's America*, 234.

251 *road of racial critique*: Lawrence, *Duke Ellington and His World*, 319–20.

252 *"into these two weeks"*: Breslin, "Satchmo."

253 *"pandemonium broke out"*: Ward and Burns, *Jazz: A History of America's Music*, 436.

254 *"my teenage audience"*: Riccardi, "It's Awful Nice to Be Up There Among All Them Beatles," LAHM; Riccardi, "50 Years of 'Hello, Dolly!'"; Riccardi, *What a Wonderful World*, 223; and Breslin, "Satchmo."

254 *co-composer Bob Thiele*: The other writer was George David Weiss. Weiss's son points out that the theme and concept were Thiele's doing, while the music and lyrics came from Weiss. Riccardi email.

254 *with lines like these*: Riccardi, *What a Wonderful World*, 258–59.

255 *"that's the secret. Yeaah"*: Wilson, *Satchmo: The Wonderful World of Louis Armstrong*.

256 *"program their music"*: Kamp, "Music on the Moon."

256 *"thoughts back to you"*: "Apollo 10: Day 2, Part 8," Apollo Flight Journal, NASA, https://history.nasa.gov/afj/ap10fj/as10-day2-pt8.html.

CHAPTER 22: BREAKTHROUGH BATTLES

257 *Little Rock's Central High*: "Louis Armstrong, Barring Soviet Tour, Denounces Eisenhower and Gov. Faubus," *New York Times*.

258 *"when spirits were down"*: Zambito, "That Lives Large in Jazz."

258 *"culture of classical Greece"*: Martin Luther King Jr., "Transforming a Neighborhood into a Brotherhood."

258 *"performance as a human being"*: Cohen, *Duke Ellington's America*, 575.

259 *"I pioneered, Pops"*: Larry L. King, "Everybody's Louie."

259 *"we have to go through"*: Reich, "Jazz Giant's Private Views Show Anger Behind Smile."

259 *"still in the lead"*: Riccardi, *What a Wonderful World*, 278.

260 *"ready to die"*: "Louis and New Orleans," *DownBeat*; and "Louis the First," *Time*.

260 *"Negroes are inferior"*: Armstrong FBI files; and Bergreen, *An Extravagant Life*, 472.

261 *"saying it's a shame"*: Riccardi, "Louis Armstrong and Little Rock."

261 at the bottom, *"solid"*: Margolick, "The Day Louis Armstrong Made Noise."

262 *"worst in the U.S."*: "Eartha, Lena Agree with 'Satchmo,'" *Pittsburgh Courier*; Margolick, "The Day Louis Armstrong Made Noise"; "Satchmo no Spokesman," *Pittsburgh Courier*; and Wallace, "Mike Wallace Asks Thurgood Marshall."

262 *"refuse to integrate"*: Bishop, "Enormity of Satchmo's Damage to US"; and Riccardi, "Louis Armstrong and Little Rock."

262 *"should be grateful forever"*: Gleason, "Perspectives."

263 *"still keep on working"*: Armstrong, "Daddy, How the Country Has Changed!"; and Sanders, "Reluctant Millionaire."

263 *"the boll weevil"*: "Louis Armstrong Scores Beating of Selma Negroes"; and Armstrong, "Daddy, How the Country Has Changed!"

263 *"something about 'Tomming'"*: Sanders, "Reluctant Millionaire."

264 *"from which he sprung"*: Charles Black, "My World with Louis Armstrong."

264 *"a true revolutionary"*: Berrett, *Louis Armstrong Companion*, 187.

264 the Medal of Freedom: Cohen, *Duke Ellington's America*, 57 and 66.

265 *"and religious differences"*: Timuel Black, *Sacred Ground*, 49.

265 *"effective is through music"*: Cohen, *Duke Ellington's America*, 401–2.

266 *"we can do something"*: Cohen, *Duke Ellington's America*, 299 and 301.

267 most Black performers: Cohen, *Duke Ellington's America*, 390.

267 *"one admiring people"*: "Race Relations—Good and Bad," *Democrat and Chronicle*.

268 *"it is in Baltimore"*: "Duke Ellington Joins Sitdowners," *Baltimore Afro-American*; and Cohen, *Duke Ellington's America*, 386–89.

268 *"that of Jesus Christ"*: Duke Ellington FBI files.

268 president Richard Nixon: Mercer Ellington interview, July 22, 1979; Cohen, *Duke Ellington's America*, 261 and 510; Erenberg, *Swingin' the Dream*, 202; and Stowe, *Swing Changes*, 70.

269 back in 1941: "Duke Ellington Says *DownBeat* Article Gave Wrong Impression," *Pittsburgh Courier*.

269 *"each other forever"*: Marian Logan interview.

269 *"We started integration"*: "James Rushing Coming Home with Count Basie's Band," *Black Dispatch* (Oklahoma City, OK); "Philadelphia Theatre-Goers Go for Count Basie's 'Swing,'" *Pittsburgh Courier*; Erenberg, *Swingin' the Dream*, 147; "Basie Skips Theatre for Barring Negro Customers," *New York Amsterdam News*; and Daniels, *Lester Leaps In*, 200.

270 *"welcome as observers"*: "Basie Breaks Record, but Not Jim Crow," *Chicago Defender*.

270 *"panicky theater managers did"*: Marre, *Count Basie: Through His Own Eyes*; and Holiday and Dufty, *Lady Sings the Blues*, 68.

270 *"the famous Count Basie"*: "How Basie Received Big Scare," *Chicago Defender*.

271 *"characteristics of both"*: "Count Basie Opens at Lincoln Hotel," *Pittsburgh Courier*; "Basie Forms Own Music Firm with Milt Ebbins," *Pittsburgh Courier*; and "The Count Classifies the Duke, the Earl, and the Hawk Tops," *Metronome*.

272 *"it hadn't slunk away"*: Hentoff, *Jazz Life*, 147.

272 *"he was a band leader"*: Marre, *Count Basie: Through His Own Eyes*.

272 *"he's saying something"*: Dunnigan, "Count Basie Speaks Out"; and Hentoff, *Jazz Life*, 147.

CHAPTER 23: OVERSEAS AMBASSADORS

274 *"elected prime minister"*: Belair, "United States Has Secret Sonic Weapon"; Susan Williams, *White Malice*, 330; Riccardi, "'Satchmo Charms Congo Cats,'" LAHM; Hofmann, "Satchmo Plays for Congo's Cats"; Millstein, "Africa Harks to Satch's Horn"; and Von Eschen, *Satchmo Blows Up the World*, 61–71.

274 *Ellington's and Basie's deflections*: Ingalls, "Armstrong Horn Wins Nairobi, Too."

275 *vituperations back home*: Tucker, *Duke Ellington Reader*, 294–96.

275 *"in Times Square"*: Riccardi, "'Satchmo Charms Congo Cats.'"

275 *"THE American art form"*: Sonny Greer interview; and Duke Ellington, "A Royal View of Jazz."

276 *"and march away"*: Duke Ellington, "A Royal View of Jazz."

276 *"any way that he could"*: Courtney, *Ignorant Armies*, 99.

277 *"cats were swinging, man"*: Cohen, *Duke Ellington's America*, 438–39; Von Eschen, *Satchmo Blows Up the World*, 132–33; and Edward Kennedy Ellington, *Music Is My Mistress*, 329.

277 *"represented at every moment"*: Simons, "Ellington Orchestra Tour of the Near East and South Asia."

278 *"short of separating"*: Simons, "Ellington Orchestra Tour"; and author interview of Tom Simons.

278 *"my wife still has"*: Simons, "Ellington Orchestra Tour"; Simons interview; and email to author from Simons.

278 *"Take the 'A' Train"*: Cohen, *Duke Ellington's America*, 500.

279 *"to see Ellington perform"*: Presel, "Duke Ellington in the USSR."

279 *story of racial progress*: Cohen, *Duke Ellington's America*, 428; and Presel, "Duke Ellington in the USSR."

280 *"Ellington broke through it"*: Author interview of Hedrick Smith.

280 *both possible and inevitable*: Edward Kennedy Ellington, *Music Is My Mistress*, 309; and Hasse, *Beyond Category: The Life and Genius of Duke Ellington*, 277–78.

280 *"yet an integral part"*: Tucker, *Duke Ellington Reader*, 150.

281 *"do to myself"*: Riccardi, *Heart Full of Rhythm*, 254; and Basie, *Good Morning Blues*, 252–53.

281 *"Basie represented American culture"*: Author interview of Will Friedwald; and Marre, *Count Basie: Through His Own Eyes*.

281 the *Pittsburgh Courier*: "Count Basie Cops Overseas Ork Poll," *Pittsburgh Courier*.

282 *"she led the applause"*: Dahl, *Morning Glory*, 237.

282 *"'ROYAL SENSATION'"*: Basie, *Good Morning Blues*, 320–24; and Alfred Green, *Rhythm Is My Beat*, 140–41.

282 *"just too many people"*: Basie, *Good Morning Blues*, 324.

282 *"friends at every stopover"*: Basie, *Good Morning Blues*, 359–60.

283 *"pace of the road"*: Wein and Chinen, *Myself Among Others*, 302–3.

283 *"his foreign tours"*: Wein and Chinen, *Myself Among Others*, 301–2.

283 *that same George V*: Riccardi, *Heart Full of Rhythm*, 117–40.

284 *"we got human dignity"*: Morgenstern and Brask, *Jazz People*, 94; and Riccardi, *Heart Full of Rhythm*, 148.

284 *"all Greek to me"*: "Satchmo Will Make Reds 'Dig' the Blues," *Chicago Tribune*; "Satchmo Swamps Sputnik in South Am," *Variety*; and "Cairo Calls Satchmo a Spy for Israel," *Washington Post*.

284 *"Jayne Mansfield combined"*: Krupnick, "Have Satchelmouth—Will Travel."

285 *against President Eisenhower*: The State Department missed a huge opportunity by not sending Armstrong behind the Iron Curtain during the Little Rock crisis. That would have made "a powerful statement about freedom in a democratic society," historian Harvey Cohen points out, even as it "undercut images of African American subservience." Cohen, *Duke Ellington's America*, 417.

285 *"I can't do that"*: Von Eschen, *Satchmo Blows Up the World*, 11–12.

285 *"my mother Mary Ann"*: "Just Very," *Time*.

285 *"Music's the same everywhere"*: Von Eschen, *Satchmo Blows Up the World*, 67.

286 *"goodwill tour of Mississippi"*: Von Eschen, *Satchmo Blows Up the World*, 82–83.

286 *"goose pimple on this one"*: Giddins, *Satchmo*; and Riccardi, *What a Wonderful World*, 206.

CHAPTER 24: LONG-LIVED

289 *a gleaming Remington rifle*: Barner, "'Yule-Spirit' Yeggs Rob Basie's Wife."

290 *"house of happiness"*: Basie, *Good Morning Blues*, 357–58.

290 *"Old man huh'"*: Basie, *Good Morning Blues*, 357; and letters from Count to Catherine: June 20, 1979, and December 14, 1979, IJS.

291 *"deeply felt emotions"*: Barris, "Minimalistic Beauty."

291 *"fronted the orchestra"*: Peterson, *Jazz Odyssey*, 282–83.

292 *"ran for the door"*: Basie, *Good Morning Blues*, 96; and Cooper, "Basie Insists Swing Has Never 'Been Away,'" *Chicago Defender*.

292 *"give me the suite'"*: Author interview of Gregg Field.

292 *"to dream about it'"*: *Autobiography of Quincy Jones*, 244–45.

293 *"as much as I ever did"*: Basie, *Good Morning Blues*, 380–81; and Basie files, IJS.

293 *"to Joe Glaser"*: Kennedy, "Music Don't Know No Age"; and Ernie Anderson, "Joe Glaser & Louis Armstrong."

293 *"What more do we need"*: Ernie Anderson, "Joe Glaser & Louis Armstrong"; and Sanders, "Reluctant Millionaire."

294 *told the singer-painter*: Duke, "Louis Armstrong, The Jazzman Next Door."

294 *"in Louis Armstrong's house"*: Cogswell, *Offstage Story of Satchmo*, 45–46.

295 *"the same languages—slanguages"*: O'Grady, "What a Wonderful Shave."

295 *"children of the neighborhood"*: Filstrup, "Neighbor Spotlight: Denise Pease Remembers 'Uncle Louis,'" LAHM.

295 *"might trample on you"*: Larry L. King, "Everybody's Louie."

295 *"he is on tour"*: Riccardi, *Heart Full of Rhythm*, 296.

295 *"that's the end of it"*: Interview of Lucille Armstrong on the show *Positively Black*, NBC New York, May 21, 1972.

296 *"swing, blues, ragtime'"*: Halberstam, "A Day with Satchmo"; Krupnick, "Have Satchelmouth—Will Travel"; "Ambassador Satch Sounds Off"; and Larry L. King, "Everybody's Louie."

296 *"loved the humanity aspect"*: Kennedy, "Music Don't Know No Age"; Halberstam, "A Day with Satchmo"; and Riccardi, *Heart Full of Rhythm*, 256.

297 *"artist and man this was"*: Morgenstern, "The Armstrong I Knew"; and email to author from Morgenstern.

297 *"got held up again"*: Basie, *Good Morning Blues*, 362–63.

298 *"in public again"*: Meryman, *Louis Armstrong—A Self-Portrait*, 55; and Riccardi, *What a Wonderful World*, 242–43.

298 *"dig its pretty sounds'"*: Larry L. King, "Everybody's Louie."

299 *bandleader's professional obituary*: Harman, "Jazz Man Duke Ellington"; Hasse, *Beyond Category: The Life and Genius of Duke Ellington*, 316–17; and Cohen, *Duke Ellington's America*, 322.

299 *was "almost dancing"*: Avakian interview, March 17, 1978; Edward Kennedy Ellington, *Music Is My Mistress*, 241; and Cohen, *Duke Ellington's America*, 323.

300 *"love you madly"*: Tucker, *Duke Ellington Reader*, 290–92; and Wein and Chinen, *Myself Among Others*, 155.

300 *"ideas and inspiration"*: Harman, "Jazz Man Duke Ellington."

300 *"at the Newport festival"*: Jewell, *Duke: A Portrait of Duke Ellington*, 110.

301 *"greatest hippie I ever knew"*: Cohen, *Duke Ellington's America*, 493, 514, and 516.

302 *"of them all. Duke Ellington"*: Faine, *Ellington at the White House*, 81–82.

CHAPTER 25: LAST DAYS AND LASTING MEMORIES

304 *but* wasn't appreciated: Armstrong, *In His Own Words*, 9, 15, and 33.

304 *would be under* I: Armstrong tape 1987.3.218, LAHM.

305 *it was so raw*: Armstrong, *In His Own Words*, 9 and 17.

305 "'Dig you 'later'": Armstrong, *In His Own Words*, 25, 169, and 172.

305 "*nothing to hide*": Alexander, "'For Posterity.'"

306 *these fitting lyrics*: Riccardi, *What a Wonderful World*, 292.

307 "*We believe in people*": Sandford, "Louis Armstrong: I Live!"; and Riccardi, "Louis' Sick Days," LAHM.

307 *beginning in California*: Riccardi, "That Cat Ain't Never Gonna Die," LAHM.

308 "*just like I do*": Carmody, "Mourners Pay Tribute to Armstrong"; Edward Kennedy Ellington, *Music Is My Mistress*, 236; and Shenker, "'Just Plain Old Satchmo' Turns 70 Sweetly."

308 "*That's my biography*": Duke Ellington interview, February 1, 1973.

309 *from Duke's autobiography: Duke*: Hasse, *Beyond Category: The Life and Genius of Duke Ellington*, 383.

309 "*sour his life*": Mercer Ellington, *Duke Ellington in Person*, 172.

309 "*inspired by this objective*": Edward Kennedy Ellington, *Music Is My Mistress*, 379.

309 "*I knew nothing first-hand*": Jewell interview, March 24, 1981.

310 "*person who was sick*": Mercer Ellington, *Duke Ellington in Person*, 193–94.

311 "*Come with me*": Jewell, *Duke: A Portrait of Duke Ellington*, 226–29; Mercer Ellington, *Duke Ellington in Person*, 197–211; and Betty McGettigan interview, July 15, 1980.

311 "*The human race, that is*": Buckley, "Fellow Musicians Among 12,500 at Services for Duke Ellington"; "Duke Ellington's Friends, Great and Small, Pay Their Respects," *New York Times*; George, *Sweet Man*, 256; Tucker, *Duke Ellington Reader*, 382 and 384; and Cooke, "Letter from America."

312 "*should I get into that*": Barris, "Minimalistic Beauty"; and Murray, *Blue Devils of Nada*, 40.

312 *and his equilibrium*: Murray, *Blue Devils of Nada*, 41; and author interviews of Loren Schoenberg and Dan Morgenstern.

312 "*tapping your feet*": Basie, *Good Morning Blues*, 385.

312 "*tell you something*": Basie, *Good Morning Blues*, 382–83.

312 "*we recorded 'Katy'*": Nestico, *Gift of Music*, 77.

312 *their special rocking chair*: Noel, "Count Basie's Quiet Retreat."

313 "*wanted to be good*": Early, *Tuxedo Junction*, 278; and *Autobiography of Quincy Jones*, 245.

EPILOGUE: LEGACIES

315 *ghost in the 1950s*: Feather, "1st Blindfold Test Miles Davis."

Miles Davis "did not want to die and had no role in his resting place," leaving that to his heirs, who "selected Woodlawn because of the jazz musicians there," says Susan Olsen, the cemetery's historian. Davis is in a sarcophagus. Email to author from Olsen.

Duke bought his family plot in 1959, for $8,584, Olsen says, and "after Duke's death, Mercer automatically became the owner and he would have authorized interments and gravestones." Daisy and J.E. were moved to Woodlawn the same year Duke bought the parcel and more than twenty years after they were entombed at Washington's Columbian Harmony Cemetery. Harmony had announced that it was closing, with developers taking over the property that had long been one of D.C.'s most popular Black burial grounds and the thirty-seven thousand graves being transplanted to a site in Maryland. Duke was distraught. With help from a colleague, he had his father's and mother's remains dug up from Harmony, moved by train to his new plot at Woodlawn, and buried again under the direction of the Rev. John Gensel, the jazz minister.

316 *"away from his father"*: Author interview of Mercedes Ellington.

316 *five times that—to Lucille:* Last will and testament of Louis Armstrong, LAHM; and Riccardi interview.

317 *twenty-one Grammy awards:* Duke won eleven, the Count nine, and Satchmo one.

317 *"No him, no me":* Okrent, "Pops Is Still Tops."

7

BIBLIOGRAPHY

INTERVIEWS AND CORRESPONDENCE

Jeffrey Adler, Emmanuel Akyeampong, Adele Alexander, Michael Allemana, Honore Allen, Dee Askew, Rob Bamberger, Clarence Banks, Michael Baptiste, Scotty Barnhart, Art Baron, Dave Basse, Jon Batiste, Carol Beckwith-Cohen, Dina Bennett, David Berger, David G. Berger, Laurence Bergreen, Joshua Berrett, Jason Berry, Fred Bieber, Scott Billington, Eric Boeren, Vilray Blair Bolles, Vaughn Booker, Bobby Bradford, Carmen Bradford, Jack Bradley, Taylor Branch, Jerry Brock, Thomas Brothers, Jewel Brown, Wendell Brunious, Clyde Bullard, Gary Burton, Artie Butler, Richard Campanella, Mark Cantor, Dale Carley, Judy Carmichael, Susanne Caro, Sonny Carrington, Terri Carrington, James Carter, Waldo Carter, Anna Celenza, Harriet Choice, Evan Christopher, John Clayton, Bill Clinton, Michael Cogswell, Harvey Cohen, Anthony Coleman, Tom Cosentino, Stephanie Crease, Stanley Crouch, Michael Cuscuna, Yair Dagan, Linda Dahl, Francis Davis, Matthew Delmont, Ken Demme, Scott DeVeaux, Joel Dinerstein, Anita Dixon, Dave Douglas, Eve Duke, Gerald Early, Cleve Eaton, Jennifer Eckhoff, Ed Eckstein, Jonathan Eig, Edward Kennedy Ellington II, Mercedes Ellington, Freddi Evans, Brynna Farris, Randy Fertel, Maristella Feustle, Gregg Field, Carmen Fields, Sharon Folta-Armstrong, George Freeman, Will Friedwald, Krin Gabbard, Jim Gallert, Dave Garrow, John Gennari, Linda Gerber, Sonny Gibson, Gary Giddins, Matt Glaser, Kristin Booth Glen, Russell Gloyd, Marv Goldberg, Dick Golden, April Goltz, Alfred Green, Denny Griffin, Chuck Haddix, David Hadju, Jason Hammond, Jay Harris, Nelson Harrison, Rusty Hassan, Keith Hatschek, Carolyn Heard, John Heard, Charlotte Hinton, Morris Hodara, Jonathan Holloway, Bill Holman, Andrew Homzy, Duff Jackson, Maurice Jackson, Pamela Jackson, Reuben Jackson, Ahmad Jamal, Stephen James, Leroy Jones, Sheila Jordan, Melba Joyce, Jacob Karno, James Karst, Robert Kenny, Tammy Kernodle, David Kertzer, Wolfram Knauer, Larry Kopitnik, David Kunian, Jim Kweskin, John Laband, Robert Lacey, Steven Lasker, James Leary, Wilma Lehr, Dave Liebman, Steve Little, John Litweiler, Chris Lornell, Joe Lovano, Allen Lowe, Myra Luftman, Stephen Maitland-Lewis, Howard Mandel, Wynton Marsalis, Terry Martin, Allaudin Mathieu, Christian McBride,

John McCusker, John McDonough, Lonnie McFadden, Mary McGettigan, Donald McGlynn, Pat Metheny, Phillippe Milanta, Butch Miles, Doug Miller, Jason Miller, Keith Miller, Dan Morgenstern, Joe Muccioli, David Murray, Michael Mwenso, Marc Myers, Suzanne Jones Myers, Walter Naegle, Sammy Nestico, James Newton, Jeffrey Nussbaum, Susan Olsen, Hank O'Neal, David Ostwald, Jimmy Owens, David Palmquist, Patrick Parr, Robin Parson, Kathy Peiss, Lewis Porter, Adam Powell, Larry Powell, Joseph Presel, Sharon Preston-Folta, Vince Prudente, Bruce Raeburn, Ben Ratliff, Enrico Rava, Tom Reney, Ricky Riccardi, Marc Rice, Larry Ridley, Gilda Rogers, Sonny Rollins, Joy Rosenthal, Lincoln Ross, Dennis Rowland, Willie Ruff, Mort Sahl, Matt Sakakeeny, Kalamu Ya Salaam, Tim Samuelson, Geri Sanders, Randy Sandke, Phil Schaap, Bobby Schiffman, Eric Schneider, Loren Schoenberg, Thomas Sciacca, Doc Severinsen, Alyn Shipton, Ben Sidran, Thomas Simons, Bria Skonberg, Hedrick Smith, Herb Snitzer, Dick Spotswood, Dave Stahl, Marvin Stamm, Walter Stern, Carol Sudhalter, Jeff Sultanof, John Szwed, Louis Tavecchio, Dave Taylor, Gwen Thompkins, Lori Tucker, Steve Turre, Judy Udkoff, Jayne Uyenoyama, Gianni Valenti, John Valenti, Don Vappie, Meg Ventrudo, Elijah Wald, Maurice Wallace, Geoff Ward, Peter Watrous, Melissa Weber, George Wein, Fred Wesley, Hollie West, Michael White, Kevin Whitehead, John Williams, Dennis Wilson, Aaron Woodward, Bill Worley, Davey Yarborough, and Greg Zorthian.

BOOKS, THESES, AND UNPUBLISHED WORKS

Ackermann, Karl. *A Map of Jazz: Crossroads of Music and Human Rights*. Thornwood, NY: WriteSpace, 2020.

Albertson, Chris. *Bessie*. New Haven, CT: Yale University Press, 2003.

———. *Louis Armstrong*. Alexandria, VA: Time-Life Records, 1978.

Alkyer, Frank, and Ed Enright, eds. *DownBeat: The Great Jazz Interviews: A 75th Anniversary Anthology*. New York: Hal Leonard, 2009.

Allen, Walter C., and Brian A. L. Rust. *King Joe Oliver*. London: Sidgwick and Jackson, 1958.

Anderson, Gene H. *The Original Hot Five Recordings of Louis Armstrong*. Hillsdale, NY: Pendragon, 2007.

Appel, Alfred, Jr. *Jazz Modernism: From Ellington and Armstrong to Matisse and Joyce*. New York: Alfred A. Knopf, 2002.

Applegate, Debby. *Madam: The Biography of Polly Adler, Icon of the Jazz Age*. New York: Doubleday, 2021.

Armstrong, Louis. Last will and testament of Louis Armstrong. February 10, 1970. LAHM.

———. *Louis Armstrong + the Jewish Family in New Orleans, La., the Year of 1907*. 1969. LAHM.

———. *Louis Armstrong: In His Own Words, Selected Writings*. Edited by Thomas Brothers. New York: Oxford University Press, 1999.

———. *Satchmo: My Life in New Orleans*. New York: Da Capo, 1986.

———. *The Satchmo Story*. 1959. LAHM.

———. *Swing That Music*. New York: Da Capo, 1936.

Baldwin, James. *Sonny's Blues and Other Stories*. New York: Penguin, 1995.

Balliett, Whitney. *American Musicians II: Seventy-One Portraits in Jazz*. New York: Oxford, 1996.

———. *Ecstasy at the Onion: Thirty-One Pieces on Jazz*. Indianapolis: Bobbs-Merrill, 1971.

Bankhead, Tallulah. *Tallulah: My Autobiography*. Jackson: University Press of Mississippi, 2004.

Barker, Danny. *A Life in Jazz*. New Orleans: The Historic New Orleans Collection, 2016.

Basie, Count. *Good Morning Blues: The Autobiography of Count Basie*. As told to Albert Murray. New York: Random House, 1985.

Basile, John A. *Cape Cod Jazz: From Colombo to the Columns*. Charleston, SC: History Press, 2017.

Bechet, Sidney. *Treat It Gentle: An Autobiography*. Cambridge, MA: Da Capo, 2002.

Behrens, John. *America's Music Makers: Big Bands & Ballrooms, 1912–2011*. Bloomington, IN: AuthorHouse, 2011.

Bennett, Tony, and Scott Simon. *Just Getting Started*. New York: Harper, 2016.

Bergreen, Laurence. *Louis Armstrong: An Extravagant Life*. New York: Broadway, 1997.

Bernhardt, Clyde E. B. *I Remember: Eighty Years of Black Entertainment, Big Bands, and the Blues*. As told to Sheldon Harris. Philadelphia: University of Pennsylvania Press, 1986.

Berrett, Joshua. *The Louis Armstrong Companion: Eight Decades of Commentary*. New York: Schirmer, 1999.

———, ed. *Louis Armstrong & Paul Whiteman: Two Kings of Jazz*. New Haven, CT: Yale University Press, 2004.

Berry, Jason, Jonathan Foose, and Tad Jones. *Up from the Cradle of Jazz: New Orleans Music Since World War II*. Lafayette: University of Louisiana at Lafayette Press, 2009.

Berton, Ralph. *Remembering Bix: A Memoir of the Jazz Age*. Cambridge, MA: Da Capo, 2000.

Bigard, Barney. *With Louis and the Duke: The Autobiography of a Jazz Clarinetist*. Edited by Barry Martyn. New York: Oxford, 1986.

Black, Timuel D., Jr. *Sacred Ground: The Chicago Streets of Timuel Black*. As told to Susan Klonsky. Edited by Bart Schultz. Evanston: Northwestern University Press, 2019.

Blesh, Rudi. *Shining Trumpets: A History of Jazz*. New York: Knopf, 1958.

Boujut, Michel. *Louis Armstrong*. New York: Rizzoli, 1998.

Bradbury, David. *Armstrong*. London: Haus, 2003.

Brothers, Thomas. *Help! The Beatles, Duke Ellington, and the Magic of Collaboration*. New York: W. W. Norton, 2018.

———. *Louis Armstrong, Master of Modernism*. New York: Norton, 2014.

———. *Louis Armstrong's New Orleans*. New York: Norton, 2006.

Brower, Steven. *Satchmo: The Wonderful World and Art of Louis Armstrong*. New York: Abrams, 2009.

Brown, Sandford. *Louis Armstrong: Swinging, Singing, Satchmo*. New York: Franklin Watts, 1993.

Büchmann-Møller, Frank. *You Just Fight for Your Life: The Story of Lester Young*. New York: Praeger, 1990.

Buckner, Reginald T., and Steven Weiland, eds. *Jazz in Mind: Essays on the History and Meanings of Jazz*. Detroit: Wayne State University Press, 1991.

Buerkle, Jack V., and Danny Barker. *Bourbon Street Black: The New Orleans Black Jazzman*. New York: Oxford, 1973.

Burke, Diane Mutti, Jason Roe, and John Herron, eds. *Wide-Open Town: Kansas City in the Pendergast Era*. Lawrence: University Press of Kansas, 2018.

Bushell, Garvin. *Jazz from the Beginning*. As told to Mark Tucker. New York: Da Capo, 1998.

Calloway, Cab, and Bryant Rollins. *Of Minnie the Moocher & Me*. New York: Crowell, 1976.

Caponi-Tabery, Gena. *Jump for Joy: Jazz, Basketball, and Black Culture in 1930s America*. Amherst: University of Massachusetts Press, 2008.

Carlon, Mick. *Girl Singer*. Fredonia, NY: Leapfrog Press, 2015.

———. *Riding on Duke's Train*. Teaticket, MA: Leapfrog Press, 2011.

Carmichael, Hoagy. *The Stardust Road*. Bloomington: Indiana University Press, 1983.

Carmichael, Judy. *Swinger! A Jazz Girl's Adventures from Hollywood to Harlem*. Scotts Valley, CA: CreateSpace, 2017.

Carter-Kennedy, Carolyn. *The Lucille Armstrong Story: A Lady with a Vision*. Bloomington, IN: iUniverse, 2010.

Cerulli, Dom, Burt Korall, and Mort Nasatir, eds. *The Jazz Word*. New York: Da Capo, 1987.

Chambers, J. K. *Sweet Thunder: Duke Ellington's Music in Nine Themes*. Toronto: Milestones, Music & Art, 2019.

Chapman, Con. *Rabbit's Blues: The Life and Music of Johnny Hodges*. New York: Oxford, 2019.

Charles, Ray, and David Ritz. *Brother Ray: Ray Charles' Own Story*. New York: Da Capo, 1992.

Charters, Samuel. *A Trumpet Around the Corner: The Story of New Orleans Jazz*. Jackson: University Press of Mississippi, 2008.

Cheatham, Doc. *I Guess I'll Get the Papers and Go Home: The Life of Doc Cheatham*. Edited by Alyn Shipton. New York: Cassell, 1996.

Chilton, John. *Ride, Red, Ride: The Life of Henry "Red" Allen*. New York: Cassell, 1999.

———. *Sidney Bechet: The Wizard of Jazz*. New York: Da Capo, 1996.

———. *The Song of the Hawk: The Life and Recordings of Coleman Hawkins*. Ann Arbor: University of Michigan Press, 1990.

Chilton, Karen. *Hazel Scott: The Pioneering Journey of a Jazz Pianist from Café Society to Hollywood to HUAC*. Ann Arbor: University of Michigan Press, 2008.

Clarke, Donald. *Billie Holiday: Wishing on the Moon*. Cambridge, MA: Da Capo, 2002.

Clayton, Buck. *Buck Clayton's Jazz World*. Assisted by Nancy Miller Elliott. New York: Oxford, 1987.

Cogswell, Michael. *Louis Armstrong: The Offstage Story of Satchmo*. Portland, OR: Collectors, 2003.

Cohen, Harvey G. *Duke Ellington's America*. Chicago: University of Chicago Press, 2010.

Collier, James Lincoln. *Duke Ellington*. New York: Oxford, 1987.

———. *Louis Armstrong: An American Genius*. New York: Oxford, 1983.

Condon, Eddie. *We Called It Music: A Generation of Jazz*. Narration by Thomas Sugrue. New York: Da Capo, 1992.

Courtney, Charles Sam. *Ignorant Armies: Tales and Morals of an Alien Empire*. Victoria, BC: Trafford, 2007.

Cox, Karen L. *Dreaming of Dixie: How the South Was Created in American Popular Culture*. Chapel Hill: University of North Carolina Press, 2011.

Crosby, Bing. *Call Me Lucky*. As told to Pete Martin. New York: Da Capo, 1993.

Crouch, Stanley. *Notes of a Hanging Judge: Essays and Reviews, 1979–1989*. New York: Oxford, 1990.

Crow, Bill. *Jazz Anecdotes: Second Time Around*. New York: Oxford, 2005.

Crowder, Steve. "Black Folk Medicine in Southern Appalachia." Master's thesis, East Tennessee State University, 2001.

Dahl, Linda. *Morning Glory: A Biography of Mary Lou Williams*. Berkeley: University of California Press, 2001.

Dance, Helen Oakley. *Stormy Monday: The T-Bone Walker Story*. Baton Rouge: Louisiana State University Press, 1987.

Dance, Stanley. *The World of Count Basie*. New York: Charles Scribner's Sons, 1980.

———. *The World of Duke Ellington*. New York: Scribner's, 1970.

———. *The World of Earl Hines*. New York: Scribner's, 1977.

Daniels, Douglas Henry. *Lester Leaps In: The Life and Times of Lester "Pres" Young*. Boston: Beacon, 2002.

———. *One O'Clock Jump: The Unforgettable History of the Oklahoma City Blue Devils*. Boston: Beacon, 2006.

Darensbourg, Joe. *Jazz Odyssey: The Autobiography of Joe Darensbourg*. As told to Pete Vacher. Baton Rouge: Louisiana State University, 1988.

Davenport, Lisa E. *Jazz Diplomacy: Promoting America in the Cold War Era*. Jackson: University Press of Mississippi, 2009.

Davis, Angela Y. *Blues Legacies and Black Feminism: Gertrude "Ma" Rainey, Bessie Smith, and Billie Holiday*. New York: Vintage, 1999.

Davis, Francis. *Jazz and Its Discontents: A Francis Davis Reader*. Cambridge, MA: Da Capo, 2004.

———. *Outcasts: Jazz Composers, Instrumentalists, and Singers*. New York: Oxford, 1990.

Davis, Miles. *Miles: The Autobiography*. With Quincy Troupe. New York: Simon & Schuster, 1989.

Davis, Ossie. *Life Lit by Some Large Vision: Selected Speeches and Writings*. New York: Atria, 2006.

Dickerson, James L. *Just for a Thrill: Lil Hardin Armstrong, First Lady of Jazz*. Jackson, MS: Sartoris Literary Group, 2018.

Dietrich, Kurt. *Duke's 'Bones: Ellington's Great Trombonists*. Rottenburg, Germany: Advance Music, 1995.

Dinerstein, Joel. *Jazz: A Quick Immersion*. New York: Tibidabo Publishing, 2020.

———. *Swinging the Machine: Modernity, Technology, and African American Culture Between the World Wars*. Amherst: University of Massachusetts Press, 2003.

Dodds, Baby. *The Baby Dodds Story*. As told to Larry Gara. Baton Rouge: Louisiana State University, 1992.

Dodge, Roger Pryor. *Hot Jazz and Jazz Dance: Collected Writings, 1929–1964*. New York: Oxford, 1995.

Douglas, Ann. *Terrible Honesty: Mongrel Manhattan in the 1920s*. New York: Farrar, Straus and Giroux, 1995.

Driggs, Frank, and Chuck Haddix. *Kansas City Jazz: From Ragtime to Bebop—A History*. New York: Oxford, 2005.

Dupuis, Robert. *Bunny Berigan: Elusive Legend of Jazz*. Baton Rouge: Louisiana State University, 1993.

Dylan, Bob. *Chronicles*. New York: Simon & Schuster, 2004.

Early, Gerald Lyn, ed. *The Sammy Davis Jr. Reader*. New York: Farrar, Straus and Giroux, 2001.

———. *Tuxedo Junction: Essays on American Culture*. New York: Ecco Press, 1989.

Ellington, Edward Kennedy. *Duke Ellington Anthology: Piano, Vocal, Guitar*. Milwaukee: Hal Leonard, 2008.

———. *Music Is My Mistress*. Garden City, NY: Doubleday, 1973.

Ellington, Mercedes, and Steven Brower. *Duke Ellington: An American Composer and Icon*. New York: Rizzoli, 2016.

Ellington, Mercer. *Duke Ellington in Person: An Intimate Memoir*. With Stanley Dance. Boston: Houghton Mifflin, 1978.

Ellison, Ralph. *The Collected Essays of Ralph Ellison*. Edited by John F. Callahan. New York: Modern Library, 1995.

———. *Conversations with Ralph Ellison*. Edited by Maryemma Graham and Amritjit Singh. Jackson: University Press of Mississippi, 1995.

———. *Invisible Man*. New York: Vintage, 1995.

———. *Living with Music: Ralph Ellison's Jazz Writings*. Edited by Robert G. O'Meally. New York: Modern Library, 2001.

———. *Shadow and Act*. New York: Vintage, 1972.

Ellison, Ralph, and Albert Murray. *Trading Twelves: The Selected Letters of Ralph Ellison and Albert Murray*. Edited by Albert Murray and John F. Callahan. New York: Modern Library, 2000.

Enstice, Wayne, and Paul Rubin. *Jazz Spoken Here: Conversations with Twenty-Two Musicians*. Baton Rouge: Louisiana State University, 1992.

Erenberg, Lewis A. *Swingin' the Dream: Big Band Jazz and the Rebirth of American Culture*. Chicago: University of Chicago, 1998.

Evans, Freddi Williams. *Congo Square: African Roots in New Orleans*. Lafayette: University of Louisiana at Lafayette Press, 2011.

Faine, Edward Allan. *Ellington at the White House, 1969*. Takoma Park, MD: IM Press, 2013.

FBI file. Louis Armstrong. https://archive.org/details/LouisArmstrongFBI/page/n25/mode/2up.

———. Edward Kennedy Ellington. https://vault.fbi.gov/Edward%20Kennedy%20%28Duke%29%20Ellington.

——. Joe Glaser. https://www.maryferrell.org/php/showlist.php?docset=1248&sort=agency.

Feather, Leonard. *The Encyclopedia of Jazz*. New York: Da Capo, 1984.

——. *The Encyclopedia of Jazz in the Sixties*. New York: Bonanza, 1966.

——. *From Satchmo to Miles*. New York: Stein and Day, 1972.

Fernett, Gene. *Swing Out: Great Negro Dance Bands*. New York: Da Capo, 1993.

Fertel, Randy. *The Gorilla Man and the Empress of Steak: A New Orleans Family Memoir*. Jackson: University Press of Mississippi, 2011.

——. *A Taste for Chaos: The Art of Literary Improvisation*. New Orleans: Spring Journal, 2015.

Firestone, Ross. *Swing, Swing, Swing: The Life & Times of Benny Goodman*. New York: Norton, 1993.

Foster, Pops. *The Autobiography of Pops Foster: New Orleans Jazzman*. As told to Tom Stoddard. San Francisco: Backbeat, 2005.

Fox, Ted, and James Otis Smith. *Showtime at the Apollo: The Epic Tale of Harlem's Legendary Theater*. New York: Abrams ComicArts, 2018.

Franceschina, John. *Duke Ellington's Music for the Theater*. Jefferson, NC: McFarland, 2001.

Frankl, Ron. *Duke Ellington: Bandleader and Composer*. Danbury, CT: Grolier, 1988.

Frazier, E. Franklin. *Black Bourgeoisie*. New York: Free Press, 1997.

Freeman, Bud. *Crazeology: The Autobiography of a Chicago Jazzman*. As told to Robert Wolf. Urbana: University of Illinois Press, 1989.

Friedwald, Will. *The Great Jazz and Pop Vocal Albums*. New York: Pantheon, 2017.

Gabbard, Krin. *Better Git It in Your Soul: An Interpretive Biography of Charles Mingus*. Oakland: University of California Press, 2016.

——, ed. *Representing Jazz*. Durham, NC: Duke University Press, 1995.

Gammond, Peter, ed. *Duke Ellington: His Life and Music*. London: Phoenix House, 1958.

Garrett, Charles Hiroshi. *Struggling to Define a Nation: American Music and the Twentieth Century*. Berkeley: University of California Press, 2008.

Gates, Henry Louis, Jr., and Cornel West. *The Future of the Race*. New York: Knopf, 1996.

Gennari, John. *Blowin' Hot and Cool: Jazz and Its Critics*. Chicago: University of Chicago, 2006.

George, Don R. *Sweet Man: The Real Duke Ellington*. New York: G. P. Putnam's Sons, 1981.

Giddins, Gary. *Faces in the Crowd: Musicians, Writers, Actors, and Filmmakers*. New York: Da Capo, 1996.

——. *Riding on a Blue Note: Jazz and American Pop*. New York: Da Capo, 2000.

——. *Satchmo*. New York: Doubleday, 1988.

——. *Visions of Jazz: The First Century*. New York: Oxford, 1998.

——. *Weather Bird: Jazz at the Dawn of Its Second Century*. New York: Oxford, 2004.

Giddins, Gary, and Scott Knowles DeVeaux. *Jazz*. New York: Norton, 2009.

Gilbert, David W. *The Product of Our Souls: Ragtime, Race, and the Birth of the Manhattan Musical Marketplace*. Chapel Hill: University of North Carolina Press, 2015.

Gillespie, Dizzy, and Al Fraser. *To BE, or Not . . . to BOP: Memoirs*. Garden City, NY: Doubleday, 1979.

Gioia, Ted. *The History of Jazz*. New York: Oxford, 1997.

Gitler, Ira. *Swing to Bop: An Oral History of the Transition in Jazz in the 1940s*. New York: Oxford, 1985.

Gleason, Ralph J. *Celebrating the Duke, and Louis, Bessie, Billie, Bird, Carmen, Miles, Dizzy, and Other Heroes*. Boston: Little, Brown, 1975.

——. *Conversations in Jazz: The Ralph J. Gleason Interviews*. Edited by Toby Gleason. New Haven, CT: Yale University Press, 2016.

Goddard, Chris. *Jazz Away from Home*. New York: Paddington Press, 1979.

Goffin, Robert. *Horn of Plenty: The Story of Louis Armstrong*. Translated by James F. Bezou. New York: Allen, Towne & Heath, 1947.

Gordon, Claire P. *My Unforgettable Jazz Friends: Duke, Benny, Nat, Rex . . .* Arroyo Grande, CA: Phase V Press, 2004.

Gordon, Maxine. *Sophisticated Giant: The Life and Legacy of Dexter Gordon.* Oakland: University of California Press, 2018.

Gourse, Leslie. *Every Day: The Story of Joe Williams.* New York: Da Capo, 1985.

———. *Louis' Children: American Jazz Singers.* New York: Quill, 1984.

Graham, Charles. *The Great Jazz Day.* Cambridge, MA: Da Capo, 2000.

Green, Alfred. *Rhythm Is My Beat: Jazz Guitar Great Freddie Green and the Count Basie Sound.* Lanham, MD: Rowman & Littlefield, 2015.

Green, Edward, and Evan Spring, eds. *The Cambridge Companion to Duke Ellington.* Cambridge, UK: Cambridge University Press, 2014.

Griffin, Dennis N., and Jazzin' Jeanne Brei. *House Party Tonight: The Career of Legendary Saxophonist Don Hill.* Las Vegas: Houdini, 2012.

Hair, William Ivy. *Carnival of Fury: Robert Charles and the New Orleans Race Riot of 1900.* Baton Rouge: Louisiana State University, 2008.

Hajdu, David. *Lush Life: A Biography of Billy Strayhorn.* New York: Farrar, Straus and Giroux, 1996.

Hall, Gwendolyn Midlo. *Africans in Colonial Louisiana: The Development of Afro-Creole Culture in the Eighteenth Century.* Baton Rouge: Louisiana State University, 1992.

Hammond, John, and Irving Townsend. *John Hammond on Record: An Autobiography.* New York: Ridge, 1977.

Hampton, Lionel, and James Haskins. *Hamp: An Autobiography.* New York: Warner, 1989.

Handy, W. C. *Father of the Blues: An Autobiography.* Edited by Arna Bontemps. New York: Da Capo, 1991.

Harker, Brian Cameron. "The Early Musical Development of Louis Armstrong, 1901–1928." PhD diss., Columbia University, 1997.

Haskins, James. *The Cotton Club.* New York: Hippocrene, 1994.

Hasse, John Edward. *Beyond Category: The Life and Genius of Duke Ellington.* New York: Simon & Schuster, 1993.

Heat-Moon, William Least. *Blue Highways: A Journey into America.* Boston: Little, Brown, 1999.

Hennessey, Thomas J. *From Jazz to Swing: African-American Jazz Musicians and Their Music, 1890–1935.* Detroit: Wayne State University Press, 1994.

Hentoff, Nat. *At the Jazz Band Ball: Sixty Years on the Jazz Scene.* Berkeley: University of California Press, 2010.

———. *The Jazz Life.* New York: Da Capo, 1978.

———. *Listen to the Stories: Nat Hentoff on Jazz and Country Music.* Cambridge, MA: Da Capo, 2000.

———. *The Nat Hentoff Reader.* Cambridge, MA: Da Capo, 2001.

Hersch, Charles. *Jews and Jazz: Improvising Ethnicity.* New York: Routledge, 2017.

———. *Subversive Sounds: Race and the Birth of Jazz in New Orleans.* Chicago: University of Chicago, 2007.

Hershorn, Tad. *Norman Granz: The Man Who Used Jazz for Justice.* Berkeley: University of California Press, 2011.

Hinton, Milt, and David G. Berger. *Bass Line: The Stories and Photographs of Milt Hinton.* Philadelphia: Temple University Press, 1988.

Hodeir, André. *Jazz: Its Evolution and Essence.* Translated by David Noakes. New York: Grove, 1956.

Hodes, Art, and Chadwick Hansen, eds. *Selections from the Gutter: Portraits from "The Jazz Record."* Berkeley: University of California Press, 1977.

Holiday, Billie, and William Dufty. *Lady Sings the Blues: The 50th Anniversary Edition.* New York: Harlem Moon, 2006.

Holland, Michelle Linsey. "Where East Texas Dances: The Cooper Club of Henderson, Rusk County, and Popular Dance Bands, 1932–1942." PhD diss., Baylor University, 2007.

Horne, Gerald. *Jazz and Justice: Racism and the Political Economy of the Music.* New York: Monthly Review Press, 2019.

Horricks, Raymond. *Count Basie and His Orchestra: Its Music and Its Musicians*. New York: Citadel Press, 1957.

Hoskins, Robert H. B. *Louis Armstrong: Biography of a Musician*. Los Angeles: Holloway House, 1979.

Howland, John. *Ellington Uptown: Duke Ellington, James P. Johnson, & the Birth of Concert Jazz*. Ann Arbor: University of Michigan Press, 2009.

Jackson, Jeffrey H. *Making Jazz French: Music and Modern Life in Interwar Paris*. Durham, NC: Duke University Press, 2003.

Jackson, Mahalia, and Evan McLeod Wylie. *Movin' On Up*. New York: Avon, 1969.

Jewell, Derek. *Duke: A Portrait of Duke Ellington*. New York: Norton, 1977.

Johnson, Bruce. *Jazz Diaspora: Music and Globalisation*. New York: Routledge, 2020.

Jones, Harold. *Harold Jones: The Singer's Drummer*. As told to Gil Jacobs and Joe Agro. Bloomington, IN: AuthorHouse, 2011.

Jones, Jo. *Rifftide: The Life and Opinions of Papa Jo Jones*. As told to Albert Murray. Minneapolis: University of Minnesota Press, 2011.

Jones, LeRoi [Amiri Baraka]. *Blues People: The Negro Experience in White America and the Music That Developed from It*. New York: Morrow Quill, 1963.

Jones, Max. *Jazz Talking: Profiles, Interviews, and Other Riffs on Jazz Musicians*. New York: Da Capo, 2000.

Jones, Max, and John Chilton. *Louis: The Louis Armstrong Story, 1900–1971*. Boston: Little, Brown, 1971.

Jones, Max, John Chilton, and Leonard Feather. *Salute to Satchmo*. London: IPC Specialist and Professional Press, 1970.

Jones, Quincy. *Q: The Autobiography of Quincy Jones*. New York: Doubleday, 2001.

Jordan, Steve, and Tom Scanlan. *Rhythm Man: Fifty Years in Jazz*. Ann Arbor: University of Michigan Press, 1993.

Josephson, Barney, and Terry Trilling-Josephson. *Café Society: The Wrong Place for the Right People*. Urbana: University of Illinois Press, 2009.

Kaminsky, Max, and V. E. Hughes. *Jazz Band: My Life in Jazz*. New York: Da Capo, 1981.

Kempton, Murray. *America Comes of Middle Age: Columns, 1950–1962*. New York: Viking, 1972.

Kenney, William Howland. *Chicago Jazz: A Cultural History, 1904–1930*. New York: Oxford, 1994.

———. *Jazz on the River*. Chicago: University of Chicago, 2005.

———. *Recorded Music in American Life: The Phonograph and Popular Memory, 1890–1945*. New York: Oxford, 1999.

Kernodle, Tammy L. *Soul on Soul: The Life and Music of Mary Lou Williams*. Urbana: University of Illinois Press, 2020.

Kiple, Kenneth F., and Virginia Himmelsteib King. *Another Dimension to the Black Diaspora: Diet, Disease, and Racism*. New York: Cambridge University Press, 1981.

Kirk, Andy. *Twenty Years on Wheels*. As told to Amy Lee. Ann Arbor: University of Michigan Press, 1989.

Kliment, Bud. *Count Basie: Bandleader and Musician*. New York: Chelsea House, 1992.

Lambert, Constant. *Music Ho! A Study of Music in Decline*. London: Penguin, 1948.

Lambert, G. E. *Kings of Jazz Duke Ellington*. New York: A. S. Barnes, 1961.

Lavezzoli, Peter. *The King of All, Sir Duke: Ellington and the Artistic Revolution*. New York: Continuum, 2001.

Lawrence, A. H. *Duke Ellington and His World: A Biography*. New York: Routledge, 2001.

Lees, Gene. *Cats of Any Color: Jazz, Black and White*. Cambridge, MA: Da Capo, 2001.

Lefkovitz, Aaron E. *Louis Armstrong, Duke Ellington, and Miles Davis: A Twentieth-Century Transnational Biography*. Lanham, MD: Lexington, 2018.

Leonard, Neil. *Jazz: Myth and Religion*. New York: Oxford, 1987.

Leur, Walter van de. *Something to Live For: The Music of Billy Strayhorn*. New York: Oxford, 2002.

Lewis, David Levering. *When Harlem Was in Vogue*. New York: Penguin, 1997.

Long, Alecia P. *The Great Southern Babylon: Sex, Race, and Respectability in New Orleans, 1865–1920*. Baton Rouge: Louisiana State University, 2004.

Love, Preston. *A Thousand Honey Creeks Later: My Life in Music from Basie to Motown*. Hanover: University Press of New England, 1997.

Lyons, Jimmy, and Ira Kamin. *Dizzy, Duke, the Count and Me: The Story of the Monterey Jazz Festival*. San Francisco: San Francisco Examiner, 1978.

Lyons, Len. *The Great Jazz Pianists*. New York: Da Capo, 1989.

Lyttelton, Humphrey. *The Best of Jazz: Basin Street to Harlem*. New York: Penguin, 1980.

Magee, Jeffrey. *The Uncrowned King of Swing: Fletcher Henderson and Big Band Jazz*. New York: Oxford, 2005.

Marsalis, Wynton. *Jazz ABZ: An A to Z Collection of Jazz Portraits*. Cambridge, MA: Candlewick, 2005.

McCarthy, Albert J. *Louis Armstrong*. (Kings of Jazz). New York: A. S. Barnes, 1961.

McCusker, John. *Creole Trombone: Kid Ory and the Early Years of Jazz*. Jackson: University Press of Mississippi, 2012.

McDougal, Dennis. *The Last Mogul: Lew Wasserman, MCA, and the Hidden History of Hollywood*. New York: Da Capo, 2001.

McPartland, Marian. *Marian McPartland's Jazz World: All in Good Time*. Urbana: University of Illinois Press, 2003.

Meckna, Michael. *Satchmo: The Louis Armstrong Encyclopedia*. Westport, CT: Greenwood, 2004.

Meryman, Richard. *Louis Armstrong—A Self-Portrait*. New York: Eakins, 1966.

Mezzrow, Mezz, and Bernard Wolfe. *Really the Blues*. New York: New York Review Books, 2016.

Miller, Marc H., and Donald Bogle, eds. *Louis Armstrong: A Cultural Legacy*. Seattle: University of Washington Press, 1994. Published in association with the Queens Museum of Art, New York.

Miller, Paul Eduard, ed. *Esquire's 1946 Jazz Book*. New York: Smith & Durrell, 1946.

Mingus, Charles. *Beneath the Underdog: His World as Composed by Mingus*. Edited by Nel King. New York: Vintage, 1991.

———. *Mingus Speaks*. Interviews by John F. Goodman. Berkeley: University of California Press, 2013.

Mitchell, Sarah. "Bodies of Knowledge: The Influence of Slaves on the Antebellum Medical Community." Master's thesis, Virginia Tech University, 1997.

Monson, Ingrid T. *Freedom Sounds: Civil Rights Call Out to Jazz and Africa*. New York: Oxford, 2007.

Morgan, Alun. *Count Basie*. New York: Hippocrene, 1984.

Morgenstern, Dan. *Living with Jazz*. New York: Pantheon, 2004.

Morgenstern, Dan, and Ole Brask. *Jazz People*. New York: Harry N. Abrams, 1976.

Morris, Ronald L. *Wait Until Dark: Jazz and the Underworld, 1880–1940*. Bowling Green, OH: Bowling Green University Popular Press, 1980.

Morrison, Toni. *Jazz*. New York: Vintage International, 2004.

Murray, Albert. *The Blue Devils of Nada: A Contemporary American Approach to Aesthetic Statement*. New York: Vintage, 1997.

———. *From the Briarpatch File: On Context, Procedure, and the American Identity*. New York: Pantheon, 2001.

———. *Murray Talks Music: Albert Murray on Jazz and Blues*. Edited by Paul Devlin. Minneapolis: University of Minnesota Press, 2016.

———. *Stomping the Blues*. Minneapolis: University of Minnesota Press, 2017.

Myers, Marc. *Why Jazz Happened*. Berkeley: University of California Press, 2013.

Nestico, Sammy. *The Gift of Music: The Autobiography of Sammy Nestico*. Carlsbad, CA: Sammy Nestico Publishing, 2009.

Newton, Francis. *The Jazz Scene*. London: Penguin, 1961.

Nicholson, Stuart. *Reminiscing in Tempo: A Portrait of Duke Ellington*. Boston: Northern University Press, 1999.

Nolan, Tom. *Three Chords for Beauty's Sake: The Life of Artie Shaw*. New York: Norton, 2010.

O'Neal, Hank. *The Ghosts of Harlem: Sessions with Jazz Legends*. Nashville: Vanderbilt University Press, 2009.

Paige, Satchel, and David Lipman. *Maybe I'll Pitch Forever: A Great Baseball Player Tells the Hilarious Story Behind the Legend*. Lincoln: University of Nebraska Press, 1993.

Panassié, Hugues. *Louis Armstrong*. New York: Scribner's, 1971.

Parks, Gordon. *To Smile in Autumn: A Memoir*. Minneapolis: University of Minnesota Press, 2009.

Payne, Les, and Tamara Payne. *The Dead Are Arising: The Life of Malcolm X*. New York: Liveright, 2020.

Pearson, Nathan W., Jr. *Goin' to Kansas City*. Urbana: University of Illinois Press, 1987.

Peiss, Kathy. *Zoot Suit: The Enigmatic Career of an Extreme Style*. Philadelphia: University of Pennsylvania Press, 2011.

Peress, Maurice. *Dvořák to Duke Ellington: A Conductor Explores America's Music and Its African American Roots*. New York: Oxford, 2004.

Peretti, Burton W. *The Creation of Jazz: Music, Race, and Culture in Urban America*. Urbana: University of Illinois Press, 1992.

Peterson, Oscar. *A Jazz Odyssey: My Life in Jazz*. Edited by Richard Palmer. New York: Continuum, 2003.

Placksin, Sally. *American Women in Jazz: 1900 to the Present, Their Words, Lives, and Music*. New York: Wideview, 1982.

Porter, Horace A. *Jazz Country: Ralph Ellison in America*. Iowa City: University of Iowa Press, 2001.

Preston-Folta, Sharon, and Denene Millner. *Little Satchmo: Living in the Shadow of My Father Louis Daniel Armstrong*. Scotts Valley, CA: CreateSpace, 2012.

Prial, Dunstan. *The Producer: John Hammond and the Soul of American Music*. New York: Picador, 2007.

Rampersad, Arnold. *The Life of Langston Hughes*. 2 vols. New York: Oxford, 1986 and 1988.

Ramsey, Frederic, Jr., and Charles Edward Smith, eds. *Jazzmen: The Story of Hot Jazz Told in the Lives of the Men Who Created It*. New York: Limelight Editions, 1985.

Ratliff, Ben. *Coltrane: The Story of a Sound*. New York: Picador, 2008.

Rattenbury, Ken. *Duke Ellington: Jazz Composer*. New Haven, CT: Yale University Press, 1990.

Reich, Howard. *Let Freedom Swing: Collected Writings on Jazz, Blues, and Gospel*. Evanston, IL: Northwestern University Press, 2010.

Reiff, Melanie. "Unexpected Activism: A Study of Louis Armstrong and Charles Mingus as Activists Using James Scott's Theory of Public Versus Hidden Transcripts." Summer Research, University of Puget Sound, 2010.

Reig, Teddy. *Reminiscing in Tempo: The Life and Times of a Jazz Hustler*. With Edward Berger. Lanham, MD: Scarecrow, 1990.

Riccardi, Ricky. *Heart Full of Rhythm: The Big Band Years of Louis Armstrong*. New York: Oxford, 2020.

———. *What a Wonderful World: The Magic of Louis Armstrong's Later Years*. New York: Vintage, 2012.

Rose, Al. *Storyville, New Orleans: Being an Authentic, Illustrated Account of the Notorious Red-Light District*. Tuscaloosa: University of Alabama Press, 1974.

Rose, Frank. *The Agency: William Morris and the Hidden History of Show Business*. New York: HarperBusiness, 1995.

Rowe, Monk, and Romy Britell. *Jazz Tales from Jazz Legends: Oral Histories from the Fillius Jazz Archive at Hamilton College*. Clinton, NY: Richard W. Couper Press, 2015.

Ruff, Willie. *A Call to Assembly: An American Success Story*. New York: Penguin, 1993.

Russell, Ross. *Jazz Style in Kansas City and the Southwest*. Berkeley: University of California Press, 1971.

Sandke, Randall. *Where the Dark and the Light Folks Meet: Race and the Mythology, Politics, and Business of Jazz*. Lanham, MD: Scarecrow, 2010.

Santoro, Gene. *Myself When I Am Real: The Life and Music of Charles Mingus*. New York: Oxford, 2000.

Schiffman, Jack. *Harlem Heyday: A Pictorial History of Modern Black Show Business and the Apollo Theatre*. Buffalo, NY: Prometheus, 1984.

Schuller, Gunther. *Early Jazz: Its Roots and Musical Development*. New York: Oxford, 1968.

———. *The Swing Era: The Development of Jazz, 1930–1945*. New York: Oxford, 1989.

Serrano, Basilio. *Juan Tizol: His Caravan Through American Life and Culture*. Bloomington, IN: Xlibris, 2012.

Shaik, Fatima. *Economy Hall: The Hidden History of a Free Black Brotherhood*. New Orleans: Historic New Orleans Collection, 2021.

Shapiro, Nat, and Nat Hentoff, eds. *Hear Me Talkin' to Ya: The Story of Jazz as Told by the Men Who Made It*. New York: Dover, 1966.

———. *The Jazz Makers: Essays on the Greats of Jazz*. New York: Da Capo, 1979.

Shaw, Arnold. *52nd Street: The Street of Jazz*. New York: Da Capo, 1977.

Sidran, Ben. *Black Talk*. New York: Da Capo, 1981.

———. *Talking Jazz: An Oral History*. New York: Da Capo, 1995.

———. *There Was a Fire: Jews, Music and the American Dream*. Madison, WI: Nardis Books, 2021.

Simon, George T. *The Big Bands*. New York: Macmillan, 1967.

———. *Simon Says: The Sights and Sounds of the Swing Era, 1935–1955*. New Rochelle, NY: Arlington House, 1971.

Smith, Charles Edward. *The Jazz Record Book*. With Frederick Ramsey Jr., Charles Payne Rogers, and William Russell. New York: Smith & Durrell, 1942.

Snitzer, Herb. *Glorious Days and Nights: A Jazz Memoir*. Jackson: University Press of Mississippi, 2011.

Starr, S. Frederick. *Red and Hot: The Fate of Jazz in the Soviet Union*. New York: Oxford, 1983.

Stearns, Marshall Winslow. *The Story of Jazz*. New York: Oxford, 1956.

Stein, Daniel. *Music Is My Life: Louis Armstrong, Autobiography, and American Jazz*. Ann Arbor: University of Michigan Press, 2012.

Stern, Walter C. *Race and Education in New Orleans: Creating the Segregated City, 1764–1960*. Baton Rouge: Louisiana State University, 2018.

Stewart, Rex. *Boy Meets Horn*. Ann Arbor: University of Michigan Press, 1991.

———. *Jazz Masters of the 30s*. New York: Da Capo, 1980.

Stowe, David W. *Swing Changes: Big-Band Jazz in New Deal America*. Cambridge, MA: Harvard University Press, 1994.

Stratemann, Klaus. *Louis Armstrong on the Screen*. Copenhagen: JazzMedia, 1996.

Stricklin, David. *Louis Armstrong: The Soundtrack of the American Experience*. Lanham, MD: Rowman & Littlefield, 2015.

Sudhalter, Richard M. *Stardust Melody: The Life and Music of Hoagy Carmichael*. New York: Oxford, 2002.

Sultanof, Jeff. *Experiencing Big Band Jazz: A Listener's Companion*. Lanham, MD: Rowman & Littlefield, 2017.

Szwed, John F. *Billie Holiday: The Musician and the Myth*. New York: Penguin, 2016.

———. *So What: The Life of Miles Davis*. New York: Simon & Schuster, 2002.

Teachout, Terry. *Duke: A Life of Duke Ellington*. New York: Gotham, 2013.

———. *Pops: A Life of Louis Armstrong*. Boston: Houghton Mifflin, 2009.

Terkel, Studs. *And They All Sang: Adventures of an Eclectic Disc Jockey*. New York: New Press, 2005.

Terry, Clark. *Clark: The Autobiography of Clark Terry*. With Gwen Terry. Berkeley: University of California Press, 2011.

Toledano, Ralph de, ed. *Frontiers of Jazz*. Gretna, LA: Pelican, 1994.

Tormé, Mel. *My Singing Teachers*. New York: Oxford, 1994.

Traill, Sinclair, and Gerald Lascelles. *Just Jazz 3*. London: Landsborough, 1959.

Travis, Dempsey J. *An Autobiography of Black Jazz*. Chicago: Urban Research Institute, 1983.

——. *The Louis Armstrong Odyssey: From Jane Alley to America's Jazz Ambassador*. Chicago: Urban Research Press, 1997.

Tucker, Mark. *Ellington: The Early Years*. Urbana: University of Illinois Press, 1991.

Tucker, Mark, ed. *The Duke Ellington Reader*. New York: Oxford, 1993.

Tye, Larry. *Rising from the Rails: Pullman Porters and the Making of the Black Middle Class*. New York: Holt, 2004.

——. *Satchel: The Life and Times of an American Legend*. New York: Random House, 2009.

Ulanov, Barry. *Duke Ellington*. New York: Da Capo, 1975.

Vacca, Richard. *The Boston Jazz Chronicles: Faces, Places, and Nightlife 1937–1962*. Belmont, MA: Troy Street, 2012.

Vacher, Peter. *Soloists and Sidemen: American Jazz Stories*. London: Northway, 2004.

——. *Swingin' on Central Avenue: African American Jazz in Los Angeles*. Lanham, MD: Rowman & Littlefield, 2015.

Vail, Ken. *Count Basie: Swingin' the Blues 1936–1950*. Lanham, MD: Scarecrow, 2003.

Valk, Jeroen de. *Ben Webster: His Life and Music*. Berkeley: Berkeley Hills Books, 2001.

Von Eschen, Penny M. *Satchmo Blows Up the World: Jazz Ambassadors Play the Cold War*. Cambridge, MA: Harvard University Press, 2004.

Walser, Robert, ed. *Keeping Time: Reading in Jazz History*. New York: Oxford, 1999.

Ward, Geoffrey C. *Unforgivable Blackness: The Rise and Fall of Jack Johnson*. New York: Vintage, 2006.

Ward, Geoffrey C., and Ken Burns. *Jazz: A History of America's Music*. New York: Knopf, 2000.

Wein, George, and Nate Chinen. *Myself Among Others: A Life in Music*. Cambridge, MA: Da Capo, 2003.

Wells, Dicky. *The Night People: The Jazz Life of Dicky Wells*. As told to Stanley Dance. Washington, D.C.: Smithsonian Institution Press, 1991.

Westerberg, Hans. *Boy from New Orleans: Louis "Satchmo" Armstrong: On Records, Films, Radio and Television*. Copenhagen: JazzMedia, 1981.

Whitehead, Kevin. *New Dutch Swing*. New York: Billboard, 1998.

——. *Play the Way You Feel: The Essential Guide to Jazz Stories on Film*. New York: Oxford, 2020.

——. *Why Jazz? A Concise Guide*. New York: Oxford, 2011.

Wilkerson, Isabel. *The Warmth of Other Suns: The Epic Story of America's Great Migration*. New York: Vintage, 2011.

Willems, Jos. *All of Me: The Complete Discography of Louis Armstrong*. Lanham, MD: Scarecrow, 2006.

Williams, Martin. *Jazz Masters of New Orleans*. New York: Macmillan, 1967.

——. *The Jazz Tradition*. New York: Oxford, 1983.

Williams, Martin, ed. *Jazz Panorama*. New York: Collier, 1964.

Williams, Susan. *White Malice: The CIA and the Covert Recolonization of Africa*. New York: PublicAffairs, 2021.

Wilmer, Valerie. *Jazz People*. New York: Da Capo, 1977.

Wilson, Edmund. *The Twenties: From Notebooks and Diaries of the Period*. New York: Farrar, Straus and Giroux, 1975.

Wilson, Teddy. *Teddy Wilson Talks Jazz*. With Ari Ligthart and Van Humphrey Loo. New York: Continuum, 2001.

Winick, Charles. *The Narcotic Addiction Problem*. New York: American Social Health Association, 1968.

X, Malcolm. *The Autobiography of Malcolm X*. As told to Alex Haley. New York: Grove, 1965.

Zolotow, Maurice. *Never Whistle in a Dressing Room; or, Breakfast in Bedlam*. New York: E. P. Dutton, 1944.

ARTICLES AND BROADCASTS

Abdul, Raoul. "Count Basie Honored at White House, Kennedy Center." *New York Amsterdam News,* December 12, 1981.

Ackermann, Karl. "Blue Highways and Suite Music: The Territory Bands, Part I." June 25, 2018. https://www.allaboutjazz.com/blue-highways-and-sweet-music-the-territory-bands-part-i-count-basie-by-karl-ackermann.

Adams, Eddie. "'Satchmo' Appeared to Sense Hotel Date Was Last." *Blade* (Toledo, OH), July 11, 1971.

Agee, James. "Films." *Nation,* August 2, 1947.

Albertson, Chris. "Lil Hardin Armstrong." Memphis Music Hall of Fame, 2016. https://memphis musichalloffame.com/inductee/lilhardinarmstrong/.

———. "Lil Hardin Armstrong—A Fond Remembrance." *Saturday Review,* September 25, 1971.

Aldrin, Buzz [BuzzAldrinHere]. "I Am Buzz Aldrin, Engineer, American Astronaut, and the Second Person to Walk on the Moon During the Apollo 11 Moon Landing. AMA!" Reddit, July 8, 2014. https://www.reddit.com/r/IAmA/comments/2a5vg8/i_am_buzz_aldrin_engineer _american_astronaut_and/.

Alexander, Ben. "'For Posterity': The Personal Audio Recordings of Louis Armstrong." *American Archivist* (Spring–Summer 2008).

Allen, Zita D. "Dance and the Duke: Through the Eyes of Mercer Ellington." *New York Amsterdam News,* August 21, 1976.

Allison, Brian. "Grainger Meets Duke Ellington." Hoard House: News from the Grainger Museum, July 2009.

Amory, Cleveland. "Straight from the Trumpet's Mouth." *New York Times Book Review,* October 10, 1954.

Anderson, Ernie. "Joe Glaser & Louis Armstrong: A Memoir by Ernie Anderson." Pts. 1 and 2. *Storyville,* December 1, 1994, and March 1, 1995.

———. "Louis Armstrong: A Personal Memoir." *Storyville,* December 1, 1991.

Anderson, Gene. "The Origin of Armstrong's Hot Fives and Hot Sevens." *College Music Symposium* (2003).

Anderson, Omer. "Soundtracks Should Be Sold Separately—Hefti." *Billboard,* July 18, 1964.

Anslinger, Harry J. "Marijuana: Assassin of Youth." *American Magazine,* July 1937.

Appelbaum, Larry. "Louis Armstrong/Duke Ellington: The Great Summit Complete Sessions." *JazzTimes,* October 1, 2000.

Arkansas Gazette. "Four Negro Notables Join Satchmo in Knocking Ike." September 20, 1957.

Arlt, Helen. "Welcome Home Satchmo." *Second Line,* September–October 1965.

Armstrong, Lil Hardin. "Satchmo and Me." *American Music* (Spring 2007).

Armstrong, Louis. "Bunk Didn't Teach Me." *Record Changer,* July–August 1950.

———. "Care of the Lip." *Record Changer,* July–August 1950.

———. "Daddy, How the Country Has Changed!" *Ebony,* May 1961.

———. "Europe—with Kicks." *Holiday Magazine,* June 1950.

———. "Jazz on a High Note." *Esquire,* December 1951.

———. "Joe Oliver Is Still King." *Record Changer,* July–August 1950.

———. "Louis and Letters." To Leonard Feather. *Metronome,* April 1945.

———. "Louis Armstrong at Home." Edited by Thomas Brothers. *JazzTimes,* October 2000.

———. "Louis on the Spot." Interview. *Record Changer,* July–August 1950.

———. "Says Joe Louis Took It Like a Man, So Should We." *Pittsburgh Courier,* July 4, 1936.

———. "60-Year-Old 'Bunk' Johnson, Louis' Tutor, Sits in the Band." *DownBeat,* August 15, 1941.

———. "Stomping Piano Man." *New York Times Book Review,* June 18, 1950.

———. "Ulceratedly Yours." *DownBeat,* July 14, 1950.

———. "Why I Like Dark Women." *Ebony,* August 1954.

———. "Yesterday, Today, and Tomorrow." *DownBeat,* July 15, 1965.

Armstrong, Lucille, and Pat Cunnington. "Life with Louis." January 1, 1952, LAHM.

———. "Louis' Favorite Dish." *Record Changer,* July–August 1950.

Atkinson, Brooks. "Swinging Shakespeare's 'Dream' with Benny Goodman, Louis Armstrong and Maxine Sullivan." *New York Times,* November 30, 1939.

Atlanta Daily World. "Time Features Duke Ellington." August 19, 1956.

Avakian, George. "'Barrelhouse Benny' Drops Decision to 'Kansas City Killer' at Garden." *Tempo,* July 1938.

Bailey, A. Peter. "The Cotton Club Girls." *Ebony,* December 1985.

Bakker, Dick M. "Louis and the Females." *Micrography,* February 1972.

Balliett, Whitney. "Jazz." *New Yorker,* July 19, 1958.

———. "King Louis." *New Yorker,* August 8, 1994.

———. "New York Drummers." *New Yorker,* November 5, 1979.

Baltimore Afro-American. "Armstrong, in Suit, Says He's Not Unique." January 16, 1932.

———. "'Black Rascal' Sold 100,000 Records." June 18, 1932.

———. "Critic Calls Louis Armstrong Modern Angel Gabriel." April 15, 1933.

———. "Duke Ellington Joins Sitdowners; Can't Eat." March 5, 1960.

———. "Duke Ellington's Rehearsals a Bedlam of Discord." May 19, 1934.

———. "Duke Ellington to Tour South." August 4, 1934.

———. "Is He Through?" April 20, 1935.

———. "'Jazz Is Too Good for Americans,' Says Bandleader Dizzy Gillespie." May 25, 1957.

———. "Louis Armstrong Gets Six Months for Dope." March 21, 1931.

———. "151 Out-of-Town Pairs Get Baltimore Wedding Permits." May 3, 1947.

———. "Plasters $2000 Fine on Duke Ellington." September 5, 1931.

Bankhead, Tallulah. "An Appreciation of Louis Armstrong." *Flair,* November 1950.

———. "Louis the End—and Beginning." *DownBeat,* July 14, 1950.

———. "The World's Greatest Musician." *Ebony,* December 19, 1952.

Barner, George. "'Yule-Spirit' Yeggs Rob Basie's Wife." *New York Amsterdam News,* December 18, 1965.

Barnes, Clive. "Dance: Unfinished 'River.'" *New York Times,* June 26, 1970.

Barris, Alex. "Minimalistic Beauty: A Profile of Count Basie." *Jazz Report,* Spring 1998.

Bartley, Sylvia. "'The One Who Counts with Count.'" *New York Amsterdam News,* July 17, 1948.

Beaty, Roger E. "The Neuroscience of Musical Improvisation." *Neuroscience & Biobehavioral Reviews,* April 2015.

Belair, Felix, Jr. "United States Has Secret Sonic Weapon—Jazz." *New York Times,* November 6, 1955.

Bernstein, Adam. "Donald 'Tee' Carson, 70; Protege of Count Basie." *Washington Post,* February 15, 2000.

Berrett, Joshua. "Louis Armstrong and Opera." *Musical Quarterly* (Summer 1992).

Bertrand, Maglyn. "Armstrong as an OKeh Artist." *West End Blog,* October 9, 2020. https://louis armstrongfellowsblog.wordpress.com/2020/10/09/armstrong-as-an-okeh-artist/.

Beyer, Gregory. "The Matriarch of New York Jazz Looks Back at Life with Louis Armstrong." *Wall Street Journal,* August 31, 2010.

Beyond Category (radio series). Produced and hosted by Dick Golden, George Washington University. Aired 2004–2007 on XM Satellite Radio.

Billboard. "Satchmo Socko." August 30, 1947.

Bilovsky, Frank. "Satchel Paige—Bittersweet Tale of a Sad 'Clown.'" *Philadelphia Sunday Bulletin,* August 14, 1966.

Bishop, Jim. "Enormity of Satchmo's Damage to US." *Daily World* (Opelousas, LA), January 3, 1958.

Black, Charles L., Jr. "My World with Louis Armstrong." *Yale Review,* October 1979.

Black Dispatch (Oklahoma City). "Count Basie, Nation's Number One Swing Band, to Play Here Next Week." September 7, 1940.

——. "James Rushing Coming Home with Count Basie's Band for Easter Dance." April 16, 1938.

Blue Light. "Irving Mills Publicity Materials from 1930s" (Spring 2018).

Blumenfeld, Larry. "Second Line: Ten Trumpeters Talkin' About Louis." *Jazziz*, July 1995.

Blumenthal, Ralph. "Digging for Satchmo's Roots in the City That Spawned Him." *New York Times*, August 15, 2000.

——. "Satchmo with His Tape Recorder Running." *New York Times*, August 3, 1999.

Bolton, Clint. "When Satchmo was Zulu." *Second Line*, Summer 1973.

Bonnie, Richard J., and Charles H. Whitebread II. "The Forbidden Fruit and the Tree of Knowledge: An Inquiry into the Legal History of American Marijuana Prohibition." *Virginia Law Review* (October 1970).

Borneman, Ernest. "Diary—68 Hours Without Sleep." *Blue Light* (Autumn 2016).

Bowers, Carolyn A. "The Great Woman Who's Behind Great 'Satchmo.'" *Chicago Defender*, January 16, 1971.

Boyer, Richard O. "The Hot Bach—I." *New Yorker*, June 24, 1944.

——. "The Hot Bach—II." *New Yorker*, July 1, 1944.

Bradley, Jack. "The Man Who Revolutionized Jazz. IV." *Saturday Review*, July 4, 1970.

Breck, Park. "This Isn't Bunk; Bunk Taught Louis." *DownBeat*, June 1939.

Breslin, Jimmy. "A Normal Day with Joe Glaser." *New York Herald Tribune*, November 15, 1964.

——. "Satchmo." *New York Herald Tribune*, March 19, 1964.

——. "Switching Channels on JFK Memories." *Newsday*, December 24, 1991.

Brown, Roxanne. "Who Left What Behind: Wills of Famous Blacks." *Ebony*, February 1989.

Brownsville Herald. "Jazzman's Kin Killed." May 21, 1968.

Buckingham, Will. "Louis Armstrong and the Waifs' Home." *The Jazz Archivist* 24 (2011).

Buckley, Tom. "Fellow Musicians Among 12,500 at Services for Duke Ellington." *New York Times*, May 28, 1974.

Burley, Dan. "How About Our Maestros as Disk Jocks? Has Radio Unwritten Law?" *New York Amsterdam News*, September 13, 1947.

——. "Music Union Cracks Down." *New York Amsterdam News*, October 21, 1939.

——. "Says Duke's Concert Advanced Race 20 Years." *New York Amsterdam News*, January 30, 1943.

California Eagle. "Racketeers After Louis Armstrong." May 1, 1931.

Calloway, Earl. "Duke Ellington: A Perspective on His Music." *Pittsburgh Courier*, November 11, 1978.

——. "Duke Ellington Honored by Musicians." *Chicago Defender*, September 9, 1972.

Calvin, Dolores. "Mrs. 'Satchmo' Is Career Girl for Husband's Wants." *Chicago Defender*, June 2, 1945.

——. "Thru Harlem." *Chicago Defender*, January 23, 1943.

Campbell, Mary. "They Still Dig Old (70) Satchmo." *Washington Post*, June 28, 1970.

Carmody, Deirdre. "Mourners Pay Tribute to Armstrong." *New York Times*, July 9, 1971.

Carmody, John. "Baptist Ministers Refuse to Endorse the 'Worldly' Music of Duke Ellington." *Washington Post*, December 1, 1966.

Carney, Harry. "All I Want Is to Stay with Duke." *Melody Maker*, October 11, 1958.

Cawthra, Benjamin. "Duke Ellington's 'Jump for Joy' and the Fight for Equality in Wartime Los Angeles." *Southern California Quarterly* (Spring 2016).

Cerra, Steven A. "An Interview at Mid-Career with Bob Brookmeyer." *JazzProfiles*. https://jazzprofiles.blogspot.com/2015/05/an-interview-at-mid-career-with-bob.html.

Chicago Defender. "All Musical Roads Lead Home for Duke Ellington Sidemen." October 4, 1962.

——. "Anderson, Hughes, Ellington, Delegates at First World Festival of Negro Arts." March 5, 1966.

——. "Armstrong Accosted by Gangsters; Trumpet Ace Has Trio Arrested." April 25, 1931.

——. "Ask Basie to Snub Mo. Dance Date." September 16, 1968.

———. "Basie Breaks Record, but Not Jim Crow." October 21, 1939.

———. "Blonde Sues Billy Daniels." August 28, 1954.

———. "Count Basie May Drop Band for Benny Tour." November 16, 1940.

———. "Count Basie's Composer Confesses Killing Woman." December 13, 1941.

———. "Count Basie Wins Managerial Fight; to Keep Band." December 7, 1940.

———. "Duke Ellington Back in Harlem." October 5, 1935.

———. "Duke Ellington's Band Plays Cincy." July 21, 1934.

———. "Duke Ellington Tours the South." January 6, 1934.

———. "Former Ellington Star and Nurse Write on Solidarity." May 26, 1945.

———. "Has Ex-Convict Brewer Let Count Basie Down?" October 11, 1941.

———. "How Basie Received Big Scare." June 22, 1946.

———. "An Interview with Busy Duke Ellington." September 28, 1967.

———. "London Raves over Duke Ellington's Sizzling Music." July 1, 1933.

———. "London's Complaint of Our Louis Armstrong Explained." June 23, 1934.

———. "Louis Armstrong Given Thirty Days: Had Broken California's Poison Law." March 21, 1931.

———. "Louis Armstrong Nabbed on Drug Felony Charge." November 29, 1930.

———. "Miss Lillian Hardin Is Bride of Louis Armstrong." February 16, 1924.

———. "Mrs. Louis Armstrong Off on Tour of the South." September 7, 1935.

———. "Musician Billy Strayhorn Is Dead at 51." June 3, 1967.

———. "Nab Duke Band Group for Dope." February 18, 1961.

———. "Wolcott Langford's Manager Gets 10 Yrs." February 11, 1928.

Chicago Tribune. "'Black and Tan' Resorts Raided by Schoemaker." December 26, 1926.

———. "Bomb Concert of 'Satchmo' in Dixie City." February 20, 1957.

———. "Child Attacker Finally Tried; Gets 10 Years." February 8, 1928.

———. "A Conversation with Duke Ellington." October 7, 1967.

———. "Court Refuses Glaser's Move for New Trial." February 26, 1928.

———. "Diploma Mill for Physicians Laid to Doctors." April 19, 1916.

———. "Glaser, Married to Girl Accuser, Refused Mercy." March 2, 1928.

———. "Glaser Saved from Prison by Supreme Court." June 21, 1929.

———. "Joe Glaser Is Ordered to Pay Alimony to Wife." January 27, 1931.

———. "Joe Glaser Sued by Wife." January 15, 1931.

———. "Judge Attacks Sunset Cabaret, Fining Owners." January 12, 1927.

———. "Marshal Royal, 82; Music Director of Count Basie's Band for 20 Years." May 24, 1995.

———. "Mercer Ellington, 76, Kept Duke's Band Alive." February 10, 1996.

———. "Miss Elaine Harless Introduced to Society." December 19, 1913.

———. "Rev. Williamson Assails Police and 'Vice Graft.'" September 18, 1922.

———. "Richard Boone, Trombonist Who Played with Basie." February 12, 1999.

———. "Satchmo Will Make Reds 'Dig' the Blues." November 7, 1955.

———. "Tells of $5,000 Offer by Glaser to Drop Charges." February 24, 1928.

———. "To Decide Action Today on Return of Glaser's Wife." June 18, 1928.

———. "Vote to Indict Joe Glaser in Liquor Robbery." April 9, 1935.

———. "Weil, Laureate of Former City Regime, Jailed." April 19, 1931.

Chideya, Farai. "Revisiting Louis Armstrong in the Context of Civil Rights." *News & Notes,* NPR, aired November 22, 2006.

Chinen, Nate. "Satchmo's Story, Music Substituting for Words." *New York Times,* September 1, 2010.

Choice, Harriet. "Duke Ellington Is Dead; An Era of Great Jazz Ends." *Chicago Tribune,* May 25, 1974.

———. "Duke Ellington—from Russia with Love." *Chicago Tribune,* December 5, 1971.

———. "Duke Ellington: The Monarch of American Music." *Chicago Tribune,* April 28, 1974.

Cleveland Call and Post. "Dizzy Gillespie Cites Example of How Musician Shouldn't Act." May 25, 1957.

———. "Duke's Secretary Given Long Term." July 26, 1952.

Cogley, John. "Duke Ellington, at 67, Is Starting a New Chapter." *New York Times,* August 13, 1966.

Cohen, Harvey G. "Visions of Freedom: Duke Ellington in the Soviet Union." *Popular Music,* October 2011.

Colegrave, Albert M. "It Ain't the Money." Scripps Howard News Service, September 26, 1958.

Collier, James Lincoln. "The Faking of Jazz." *New Republic,* November 18, 1985.

Commercial Appeal (Memphis, TN). "Darktown Stage Troupe to Face Judge Instead of Arkansas Audience." October 7, 1931.

Cook, Christopher Joseph. "'An Utter Disregard for the Law': Law, Order, and the Criminal Element in the Robert Charles Riot of 1900." *Louisiana History* (Winter 2019).

Cooke, Alistair. "Letter from America." May 31, 1974. https://www.bbc.co.uk/programmes/articles /21Fqwq7wvLCF8vlbQy75WwC/duke-ellington-31-may-1974.

Cooke, Marvel. "Negro Musicians Win Many First Places in Poll." *New York Amsterdam News,* April 26, 1941.

Cooper, Morton. "Basie Insists Swing Has Never 'Been Away.'" *Chicago Defender,* February 9, 1963.

Cosentino, Tom. "What I Learned From Clarence Armstrong." *Jazz Lives* (blog), February 27, 2010. https://jazzlives.wordpress.com/tag/tom-cosentino/.

Cowans, Russel J. "Composer's Mother Dies: Remains of Mrs. Ellington Are Shipped to D.C." *Baltimore Afro-American,* June 1, 1935.

Crawford, Marc. "Count Basie Takes Crack at Jazz Myths." *Pittsburgh Courier,* February 4, 1956.

———. "A Visit with Mrs. Duke Ellington." *Ebony,* March 1959.

Crouch, Stanley. "Duke Ellington: Artist of the Century." *JazzTimes,* December 1, 1999.

———. "Laughin' Louis Armstrong." *Village Voice,* August 14, 1978.

———. "Louis Armstrong: The Jazz Musician." *Time,* June 8, 1998.

———. "Wherever He Went, Joy Was Sure to Follow." *New York Times,* March 12, 2000.

Crowther, Bosley. "'New Orleans,' Study in Jazz, at Winter Garden." *New York Times,* June 20, 1947.

———. "No 'Philadelphia Story,' This." *New York Times,* August 10, 1956.

Cunningham, Evelyn. "Give 'Satchmo' the Spingarn Medal." *Pittsburgh Courier,* September 28, 1957.

———. "Louis' Critics Should Jump in Lake." *Pittsburgh Courier,* June 8, 1957.

Daily Express (UK). "Satchmo's Column." May 14, 1956.

Daily Record (Long Branch, NJ). "Red Bank Boy Deead." August 29, 1911.

Daily Register (Red Bank, NJ). "A Bicycle Parade." September 13, 1899.

———. "A Church Incorporated." January 28, 1903.

———. "A Colored Association." March 4, 1914.

———. "Colored Republican Meeting." February 3, 1915.

———. "Feast and a Speech." May 2, 1934.

———. "Indicted Officials Come from Varied Backgrounds." December 18, 1969.

———. "Middletown Village News." May 10, 1899.

———. "Money for Boy Scouts." May 20, 1914.

———. "Mrs. Mary Basie Turner." November 26, 1958.

———. "Mrs. Susan Barber." October 10, 1900.

———. "Personal." March 28, 1917.

———. "Racing for a Championship." August 1, 1900.

———. "Red Bank and Vicinity." September 26, 1878.

———. "To Attend Convention." August 13, 1919.

———. "Won $2.50 in Piano Playing." January 12, 1921.

Daily Standard (Red Bank, NJ). "Woman Fined for Swearing and Two Tramps Sent Up." June 21, 1902.

Dance, Stanley. "A Drum Is a Woman." *Melody Maker,* September 7, 1957.

——. "The Great Ellington Soloists." *Jazz Journal,* May 1954.

——. "Louis Armstrong: American Original." *Saturday Review,* July 4, 1970.

——. "Three Ellington Firsts." *Jazz* (1962).

Davis, Ellsworth. "Harry Carney, Noted Ellington Saxophonist." *Washington Post,* October 12, 1974.

Davis, Francis. "The Loss of Count Basie." *Atlantic Monthly,* August 1984.

Davis, Frank Marshall. "Duke Ellington, Who Goes to the Movies Between Shows, Wrote Song Hit 'Solitude,' Three Years Ago." *Pittsburgh Courier,* January 26, 1935.

Davis, Stephen. "Count Basie: 'Super Chief.'" *Rolling Stone,* July 6, 1972.

Dawbarn, Bob. "Basie Voted World's Top Jazzman." *Melody Maker,* October 12, 1957.

Decatur Evening Herald. "Fight Manager in Toils Again." March 6, 1928.

Delatiner, Barbara. "Bassist Follows Armstrong Trail." *New York Times,* March 22, 1987.

Democrat and Chronicle (Rochester, NY). "Race Relations—Good and Bad." August 3, 1968.

——. "South Africa Denies Visa to Satchmo." December 3, 1964.

Denton, Brian. "On 'West End Blues.'" November 23, 2016. https://brianedenton.medium.com/on-west-end-blues-73151f301ba7.

Des Moines Register. "Glaser Sued for $10,000." January 29, 1930.

Dexter, Dave, Jr. "Billie Holiday for the First Time Tells Why She Left Shaw & Basie: 'Too Many Bad Kicks.'" *DownBeat,* November 1, 1939.

Dhakal, Kiran, Martin Norgaard, and Mukesh Dhamala. "Enhanced White Matter Fiber Tracts in Advanced Jazz Improvisers." *Brain Sciences,* April 2021.

Dinerstein, Joel. "Swinging into the Future." *American Scholar,* December 7, 2020.

Dishneau, David. "Ellington's 'Jump for Joy' Back After 50 Years." *Los Angeles Times,* January 4, 1992.

Doughty, Bob, and Barbara Klein. "Willis Conover, 1920–1996: He Brought Jazz, 'the Music of Freedom,' to the World." *People in America.* https://learningenglish.voanews.com/a/a-23-2009-01-31-voa1-83140482/129453.html.

DownBeat. "Band Review." March 7, 1956.

——. "Louis and New Orleans." January 7, 1960.

——. "Louis Denies He Was Undisturbed by Racial Barrier." September 5, 1956.

——. "Music World Salutes the Duke." November 5, 1952.

——. "Newport Jazz Festival." August 8, 1957.

——. "Passing of a Legend: Agent Joe Glaser, 72." July 24, 1969.

——. "Satchmo Speaks Twice." October 31, 1957.

——. "Webb 'Cuts' Basie in Swing Battle." February 1938.

Drew, Robert, dir. *On the Road with Duke Ellington.* New York: Docurama, 1974.

Duckett, Alfred. "Duke Ellington Employs a 'Stray Horn' Not as Instrument—as an Arranger." *Chicago Defender,* August 21, 1954.

Duke, Lynne. "Louis Armstrong, The Jazzman Next Door." *Washington Post,* October 29, 2003.

Dunnigan, Alice A. "Count Basie Speaks Out, Supports Student 'Sit-Ins.'" *Pittsburgh Courier,* April 2, 1960.

Early, Gerald. "'And I Will Sing of Joy and Pain for You': Louis Armstrong and the Great Jazz Traditions." *Callaloo* (Spring–Summer 1984).

Ebony. "Diets of the Stars." May 1960.

——. "What Men Notice About Women." January 1950.

Edgers, Geoff. "Louis Armstrong's Museum Has Gone Silent, but 'Pops' Is Still Talking." *Washington Post,* April 13, 2020.

Edwards, Brent Hayes. "Louis Armstrong and the Syntax of Scat." *Critical Inquiry* (Spring 2002).

Eggler, Bruce. "Lost Louis." *Times-Picayune* (New Orleans), August 5, 2001.

Elam, Joe. "Endless Ellington Era." *New York Amsterdam News,* July 27, 1974.

Ellington, Duke. "The Charles Melville Interview." Network Three, BBC. Transcribed by Steve Voce. *DEMS Bulletin,* April–July 2001.

———. "The Dankworth-Lyttelton Interview." *Monitor,* BBC. Transcribed by Steve Voce. *DEMS Bulletin,* April–July 2001.

———. "Duke Ellington Explains His Views on Communications and the Artist." *Washington Post,* December 3, 1966.

———. "Duke Ellington Rates the Masters of Swing and Jazz Music." *New York Amsterdam News,* August 5, 1939.

———. "The Most Essential Instrument." *Jazz Journal,* December 1965.

———. "My Path of Prayer." *Guideposts,* February 1971.

———. "Reminiscing: With the Duke." *Baltimore Afro-American,* August 1, 1942.

———. "A Royal View of Jazz." *Jazz: A Quarterly of American Music* (Spring 1959).

———. "Sex Is No Sin." *Ebony,* May 1954.

Epps, Brittany. "Seeking Satch Competition: The Sons of Satchmo." *OffBeat,* August 1, 2010.

Evening Journal (Lubbock, TX). "Bandleader Duke Ellington, Manager of Globetrotters Jailed in San Antonio." February 14, 1952.

Feather, Leonard. "Basie's from the Old School." *Metronome,* July 1947.

———. "Billy Strayhorn—The Young Duke." *Jazz,* January 1943.

———. "Duke Ellington Says He Never Makes Uncomplimentary Remarks." *Metronome,* August 1947.

———. "1st Blindfold Test Miles Davis." *DownBeat,* September 21, 1955.

———. "Life with Feather: Part V of a Critic's Autobiography, Remembering 'Pops.'" *DownBeat,* July 15, 1965.

———. "Man of Many Faces." *DownBeat,* July 24, 1969.

———. "Pops Pops Top on Sloppy Bop." *Metronome,* October 1949.

———. "Recollections of a Regal Count." *Los Angeles Times,* May 6, 1984.

———. "The Rhythm Section." *Esquire,* February 1946.

———. "The Rise and Fall of the Basie Band." *Melody Maker,* January 20, 1968.

———. "Satchmo Remembers the Big Magaffa." *Los Angeles Times,* June 22, 1969.

———. "Trumpeter's Jubilee." *New York Times,* October 26, 1941.

Fellers, Li. "Bill Yancey, 70; Bassist Toured with Fitzgerald, Ellington." *Chicago Tribune,* January 27, 2004.

Ferguson, Otis. "Speaking of Jazz: I." *New Republic,* August 2, 1939.

Fertel, Randy. "The Birth of Jazz and the Jews of South Rampart Street." *Tikkun,* October 4, 2011.

Filstrup, Adriana. "Neighbor Spotlight: Denise Pease Remembers 'Uncle Louis.'" https://virtualexhibits.louisarmstronghouse.org/2020/08/12/neighbor-spotlight-denise-pease/.

Finnigan, Joe. "Count Basie, Back from Europe with Story for Bands Crossing Ocean." *Chicago Defender,* April 4, 1959.

Firestone, David. "Louisiana: An Airport Named Armstrong." *New York Times,* July 7, 2001.

Fisher, Larry. "Clark Terry Discusses His Experiences with the Bands of Duke Ellington and Count Basie." *Note* (Fall–Winter 2021).

Fitzgerald, Colin. "African American Slave Medicine of the 19th Century." *Undergraduate Review* (2016).

Fort Lauderdale News. "Africans Deny Visa to 'Satchmo.'" December 2, 1964.

———. "'Bama Won't Let Satchmo Perform." December 7, 1964.

Fortune. "Introducing Duke Ellington." August 1933.

Franklyn, Frank. "Believes Musicians Are Derelict by Not Protecting Their Own Interests." *Philadelphia Tribune,* December 3, 1936.

Fraser, C. Gerald. "Cootie Williams, Ellington Trumpeter, Dead." *New York Times,* September 16, 1985.

Freedman, Samuel G. "Jazz World Bids Farewell to Basie in Harlem." *New York Times,* May 1, 1984.

Freeman, Don. "We'll Get Along Without Hines' Ego, Says Armstrong." *DownBeat,* February 22, 1952.

Fox, Jack. "Ambassador Armstrong." *Saga: The Magazine for Men,* October 1960.

Gabbard, Krin. "The Eloquent Firing of Charles Mingus." *Blue Light* (Spring 2018).

Gaines-Carter, Patrice. "Ellington: The Duke of Musical Royalty." *Washington Post,* April 29, 1989.

Gardner, Chappy. "Louis Armstrong Arrested in Big Dope Scandal." *Pittsburgh Courier,* December 6, 1930.

Gathright, Jenny. "Mary Lou Williams, Missionary of Jazz." *All Things Considered,* NPR, aired September 11, 2019.

Gazette and Daily (York, PA). "Armstrong Is Right." September 21, 1957.

Genzlinger, Neil. "Mickey Kapp, Who Made Mixtapes for Astronauts, Dies at 88." *New York Times,* July 8, 2019.

Gershen, Marty. "Satchmo to Toot for Troops in Berlin." *Stars and Stripes,* October 4, 1961.

Giddins, Gary. "Satchuated." *Village Voice,* April 15, 2003.

Giles Wantuck, Susan. "Louis Armstrong's Daughter to Appear at Tampa Jazz Club Show." https://wusf news.wusf.usf.edu/culture/2015-04-17/louis-armstrongs-daughter-to-appear-at-tampa-jazz -club-show.

Gill, James. "Trumpeting Armstrong's Darker Side." *Times-Picayune* (New Orleans), August 22, 2004.

Gillespie, John Birks. "Jazz Is Too Good for Americans." *Esquire,* June 1957.

———. "Louis Armstrong 1900–1971." *New York Times,* July 18, 1971.

Gilmore, Eddy. "Trumpet Blowing Ambassador." *Kilgore (TX) News Herald,* May 27, 1956.

Gioia, Ted. "When Duke Ellington Made a Record for Just One Person—Queen Elizabeth." *Honest Broker,* September 9, 2022. https://tedgioia.substack.com/p/when-duke-ellington-made-a -record.

Gish, Lillian, Rube Goldberg, Maurice Chevalier, Ted Shawn, Edward Steichen, Louis Armstrong, et al. "Good-bye to All of You." *Esquire,* December 1969.

Gitler, Ira. "Mingus Speaks—and Bluntly." *DownBeat,* July 21, 1960.

Glaser, Matt. "Satchmo, The Philosopher." *Village Voice,* June 5, 2001.

Gleason, Ralph J. "Perspectives." *DownBeat,* February 6, 1958.

Glenn, Tyree. "Unforgettable 'Satchmo.'" *Reader's Digest,* December 1971.

Goddard, Jacqui. "Louis Armstrong's Secret Daughter Revealed, 42 Years After His Death." *Telegraph* (London), December 15, 2012.

Goffin, Robert. "Jazzmen's Greatest Kicks." *Esquire,* August 1944.

Goines, Leonard. "The Basie and Ellington Bands: A Blues Comparison." Black Musicians Conference and Festival, Amherst, MA, February 28, 1995.

Goldberg, Marv. "Apollo Theater Shows," 2019. https://www.uncamarvy.com/ApolloTheater Shows/apollo.html

Gottlieb, Bill. "Armstrong Devoted to Dieting But Loses No Weight in Jazz." *Washington Post,* June 30, 1946.

Gourse, Leslie. "Count Basie Plus Joe Williams Equals Harmony." *New York Amsterdam News,* November 21, 1981.

Green, Abel. "Artists and Models." *Variety,* August 4, 1937.

Greenbaum, Lucy. "Saga of 'Satchmo.'" *New York Times Book Review,* May 4, 1947.

Halberstam, David. "A Day with Satchmo." *Reporter,* May 2, 1957.

Hamlin, Jesse. "Billie Holiday's Bio, 'Lady Sings the Blues,' May Be Full of Lies, But It Gets at Jazz Great's Core." *San Francisco Chronicle,* September 18, 2006.

Hammond, John. "Count Basie Marks 20th Anniversary." *DownBeat,* November 2, 1955.

Harker, Brian. "Louis Armstrong and the Clarinet." *American Music* (Summer 2003).

Harman, Carter. "Jazz Man Duke Ellington." *Time,* August 20, 1956.

Harrington, Richard. "Brunch with Count Basie." *Washington Post,* December 7, 1981.

———. "Count Basie, the Jazz Monarch." *Washington Post,* April 27, 1984.

———. "Ellington Birthday Bash." *Washington Post,* April 28, 1993.

Harris, Meunier H. "An Ellington Investigation." *Jazz Notes,* May 1949.

Harris, Stan, dir. *Duke Ellington . . . We Love You Madly!* Munich, DE: Tandem Productions, 1973.

Hasse, John Edward. "The Concert That Changed Music History." *Wall Street Journal,* December 24, 2018.

———. "Fresh Talents, Unprecedented Heights." *Wall Street Journal,* February 11, 2020.

———. "Jazz Jams for Justice and Profit." *Wall Street Journal,* July 1, 2019.

———. "'Strange Fruit': Still Haunting at 80." *Wall Street Journal,* April 30, 2019.

Henderson, Fletcher. "He Made the Band Swing." *Record Changer,* July–August 1950.

Henshaw, Laurie. "Relaxing at the Dorchester." *Melody Maker,* January 19, 1963.

Hentoff, Nat. "Dr. Jazz and His Son, the Professor." *New York Times Magazine,* April 14, 1974.

———. "The Duke." *DownBeat,* January 9, 1957.

———. "The Everlasting Louis Armstrong." *JazzTimes,* August 6, 2010.

———. "The Incompleat Duke Ellington." *Show,* July–August 1964.

———. "One More Time: Travels of Count Basie." *Jazz Review,* January 1961.

Hepburn, Dave. "Basie-Levy Rift Widens; Count to Quit Roulette." *New York Amsterdam News,* May 19, 1962.

———. "Duke Ellington Busier, More Energetic Than Ever." *New York Amsterdam News,* March 9, 1963.

Herdener, Marcus, Thierry Humbel, Fabrizio Esposito, Benedikt Habermeyer, Katja Cattapan-Ludewig, and Erich Seifritz. "Jazz Drummers Recruit Language-Specific Areas for the Processing of Rhythmic Structure." *Cerebral Cortex* (March 2014).

Hersch, Charles. "'Let Freedom Ring!': Free Jazz and African-American Politics." *Cultural Critique* (Winter 1995).

———. "Poisoning Their Coffee: Louis Armstrong and Civil Rights." *Polity* (2002).

Hersch, Fred. "Fred Hirsch's Life In & Out of Jazz." *Out,* October 2, 2017. https://www.out.com/music/2017/10/02/fred-hirschs-life-out-jazz.

Hess, Harry. "The Diligent Duke of Ellington." *Esquire,* August 1946.

Heughan, G. W. K. "An Historical Calendar of Duke Ellington's Career." *Jazz Journal,* January 1963.

Hicks, James L. "Louis Armstrong Makes New D . . . y Recording." *Baltimore Afro-American,* January 8, 1952.

Hill, Amelia. "Secret Grief of Jazz Charmer." *Guardian,* April 28, 2001.

Hodges, Johnny. "Johnny Hodges—An Interview with Henry Whiston." *Jazz Journal,* January 1966.

Hodgson, Simon. "A Hell of a Businessman: A Biography of Joe Glaser." *Inside A.C.T.* http://blog.act-sf.org/2016/01/a-hell-of-businessman-biography-of-joe.html.

Hofmann, Paul. "Satchmo Plays for Congo's Cats." *New York Times,* October 29, 1960.

Holden, Stephen. "Product of 20 Minutes: A Million-Dollar Song." *New York Times,* December 19, 1988.

Horricks, Raymond. "Duke Ellington Plays." *Jazz Journal,* January 1954.

Hutchinson, Louise. "Lil Armstrong Recalls Chicago's 'Swing Time' of the 1920s." *Chicago Tribune,* March 28, 1965.

Ingalls, Leonard. "Armstrong Horn Wins Nairobi, Too." *New York Times,* November 7, 1960.

James, George. "A Year with Satchmo, 1931–32." *Jazz Journal International,* January 1992.

Jarrett, Vernon. "Armstrong Was No Uncle Tom." *Chicago Tribune,* July 15, 1971.

———. "Louis Armstrong: Jazz Prime Minister." *Chicago Tribune,* July 11, 1971.

Jazz Notes. "Things Ain't What They Use to Be: Random Recollections of Ellingtonia." September 1949.

Jenkins, Freddie. "Reminiscing in Tempo." Interview. *Storyville,* April–May 1973.

Jenkins, Sacha, dir. and prod. *Louis Armstrong's Black & Blues.* Documentary, Apple TV+, 2022.

Jet. "Bury Ellington's First Lady Beside Him in N.Y." April 29, 1976.

———. "Duke Ellington's Duchess." February 2, 1967.

———. "Louis Armstrong's Wife Seized in Hawaii for Dope." January 14, 1954.

———. "Nab 4 Duke Ellington Bandsmen on Dope Counts." February 23, 1961.

——. "White, Negro Celebrities Back Satchmo's Blast at Ike." October 3, 1957.

——. "Why Louis Armstrong Can't Go Home Again." November 26, 1959.

——. "Words of the Week." April 17, 1958.

Johnson, David. "'Jump for Joy': Duke Ellington's Celebratory Musical." Indiana Public Media, February 5, 2008. https://indianapublicmedia.org/nightlights/jump-for-joy-duke-ellingtons -celebratory-musical.php.

Jolley, Levi. "Louis Armstrong's Ex-Manager Takes Receipts at Dance." *Baltimore Afro-American*, July 13, 1935.

Jones, Angela. "Project Named After Satchmo." *New York Amsterdam News*, December 25, 1982.

Jones, Chris. "Behind a Great Trumpeter, the Notorious Joe Glaser." *Chicago Tribune*, January 31, 2016.

Jones, Dalton Anthony. "Louis Armstrong's 'Karnofsky Document': The Reaffirmation of Social Death and the Afterlife of Emotional Labor." *Music & Politics* (Winter 2015).

Jones, Max. "Duke and Basie Combine." *Melody Maker*, March 17, 1962.

——. "Duke—Whose Hand on the Tiller?" *Melody Maker*, January 23, 1965.

——. "Louis Blasts Jim Crow." *Melody Maker*, December 12, 1959.

——. "Tchaikovsky Would Have Approved." *Melody Maker*, December 10, 1960.

——. "With Duke and Louis in Paris." *Melody Maker*, January 7, 1961.

Kael, Pauline. "Keep Going." *New Yorker*, January 3, 1970.

Kakutani, Michiko. "Life as Ellington's Son Was Mostly 'Mood Indigo.'" *New York Times*, March 29, 1981.

Kamp, David. "Music on the Moon: Meet Mickey Kapp, Master of Apollo 11's Astro-Mixtapes." *Vanity Fair*, December 14, 2018.

Kansas City Call. "Gossip." July 25, 1930.

——. "Midnight Show for Flood Sufferers Fills Lincoln Theatre." Undated.

——. "Mrs. Vivian Winn Basie Asks Divorce." January 26, 1934.

——. "New York to Claim Bennie Moten." February 20, 1931.

——. "Vivian Basie Is New Clerk at General Hospital No. 2." February 24, 1933.

——. "William Basie, Musician, in Hospital Here." Undated.

Karst, James. "Buddy Bolden's Blues." *64 Parishes* (Summer 2020).

——. "Fragments of Louis Armstrong When He Was on the Cusp of Greatness." *Times-Picayune* (New Orleans), March 19, 2017.

——. "New Details Emerge About Satchmo's Arrest at 9." *Times-Picayune* (New Orleans), April 30, 2017.

——. "The Tragic Life of Red Sun, Comic Figure in Louis Armstrong Book." *Times-Picayune* (New Orleans), March 18, 2018.

——. "What Became of the Colored Waifs Home Band After Louis Armstrong Left?" *Times-Picayune* (New Orleans), January 21, 2018.

——. "Willie Telfry Was Arrested with Louis Armstrong, but He Followed a Different Path." *Times-Picayune* (New Orleans), February 19, 2018.

——. "Young Satchmo." *64 Parishes*, Summer 2019.

Keepnews, Orrin. "Lemme Take This Chorus." *Record Changer*, April 1948.

Keepnews, Peter. "Benny Powell, 80, Played Trombone with Count Basie." *New York Times*, July 4, 2010.

——. "Jimmy Woode, Ex-Ellington Bassist, Dies at 78." *New York Times*, April 30, 2005.

Kempton, Murray. "Birthday Party." *New York Post*, July 1957.

——. "Louis Armstrong's Legacy Plays On." *Newsday*, December 15, 1994.

——. "'Prisoners to the Luck of the Day.'" *Washington Post*, December 24, 1987.

Kennedy, William. "Music Don't Know No Age." *GQ*, August 1992.

Kilgallen, Dorothy. "The Count's Looking for Base." *Washington Post*, April 22, 1962.

——. "Ellington Integrates Texas Cheers." *Washington Post*, September 25, 1961.

———. "Swing Set." *Hearst's International Combined with Cosmopolitan,* March 1940.

———. "Voice of Broadway." *Shreveport Times,* July 6, 1958.

———. "Watch Out, Europe; Here Comes Music!" *Washington Post,* March 31, 1956.

King, Larry L. "Everybody's Louie." *Harper's,* November 1967.

King, Martin Luther, Jr. "Transforming a Neighborhood into a Brotherhood." National Association of TV and Radio Announcers, August 1967. https://www.rimaregas.com/2015/09/12/transcript-martin-luther-kings-speech-to-natra1967-first-half-msm-on-blog42/ and https://www.rimaregas.com/2015/09/12/transcript-martin-luther-kings-speech-to-natra1967-second-half-racism-on-blog42/.

Koppel, Niko. "Collector Shares Mementos and Memories of Jazz Legend." *New York Times,* September 28, 2008.

Koster, Rick. "'Black Benny' Williams, Louis' Hero." *OffBeat,* September 1, 2000.

Krebs, Albin. "Louis Armstrong, Jazz Trumpeter and Singer, Dies." *New York Times,* July 7, 1971.

Krupnick, Jerry. "Have Satchelmouth—Will Travel: The Louis Armstrong Story." *Newark Star-Ledger,* November 3, 1957.

Lacy, Sam. "Theatrical Whirl." *Baltimore Afro-American,* May 21, 1955.

Lamar, Lawrence F. "Louis Armstrong Faces Trouble with 4th Wife." *New York Amsterdam News,* September 15, 1945.

Lancashire, David. "Louis Armstrong's Marijuana Use Told." *Chicago Tribune,* September 29, 1971.

Larkin, R. L. "Are Colored Bands Doomed as Big Money Makers?" *DownBeat,* December 1, 1940.

Lasker, Steven. "Backstory in Black and White." January 2018. https://alhirschfeldfoundation.org/spotlight/backstory-black-and-white.

———. "Dating Duke and Edna's Breakup—and the Infamous Slashing Incident." *Blue Light* (Autumn 2013).

———. "Liner Notes for Ellington, Duke." *The Complete 1936–1940 Variety, Vocalion and Okeh Small Group Sessions.* Mosaic Records, 2006.

———. "Selling Ellington." *Blue Light* (Autumn 2017).

Lees, Gene. "The Anchorite." Pts. 1, 2, and 3. *Jazzletter,* June, July, and August 2004.

Lehren, Andrew W. "Jazz and the FBI: Guilty Until Proven Innocent." *JazzTimes,* April 25, 2019.

Leland, John. "Live From Satchmo's Den." *New York Times,* October 9, 2003.

Lelyveld, Joseph. "Friends Bid Louis Armstrong a Nostalgic Farewell at Simple Service." *New York Times,* July 10, 1971.

Levin, Floyd. "The Night Louis Armstrong Kissed Me!" *American Rag,* July 2001.

Library of Congress. "Today in History—April 29." https://www.loc.gov/item/today-in-history/april-29/#duke-ellington.

Lord, Tom. "The Jazz Discography." https://www.lordisco.com.

Los Angeles Sentinel. "Count Basie Believes There Is Room for Bop." March 17, 1949.

Los Angeles Times. "Armstrong Home—'I Never Felt Better.'" July 3, 1959.

———. "Armstrong Seriously Ill; Spirits High." June 26, 1959.

———. "Cheering Fans Mob Armstrong in Buenos Aires." October 29, 1957.

———. "Cry For More: Satchmo Gets Royal Ovation." December 19, 1956.

———. "Irate Trumpeter: Russia Trip Out, Satchmo Assails U.S." September 19, 1957.

———. "Louis Armstrong Meets Pope Paul." February 8, 1968.

Love, Preston. "Chords & Discords." *Sounds & Fury,* July–August 1965.

Lowe, Bill. "The Basie Lineage." Presentation at Black Musicians Conference, University of Massachusetts, February 28, 1995.

Lyons, Leonard. "Gabors Psychoanalyze Selves." *San Mateo Times,* September 27, 1957.

Lyttelton, Humphrey. "If They Criticize Duke I May Get Violent." *Melody Maker,* October 11, 1958.

Manchester Guardian. "Louis Armstrong Taken Ill: Influenza Condition." June 24, 1959.

Margolick, David. "The Day Louis Armstrong Made Noise." *New York Times,* September 23, 2007.

Marre, Jeremy, dir. *Count Basie: Through His Own Eyes.* London, UK: Eagle Rock Productions, 2018.

Marsh, Julia. "Friend 'Stole' $70K from Jazz Legend's Disabled Daughter." *New York Post,* October 17, 2015.

Martin, Douglas. "Arvell Shaw, 79, Jazz Bassist; Played with Louis Armstrong." *New York Times,* December 10, 2002.

Martin, Louis. "For Satchmo All Hands Clapped." *Chicago Defender,* July 10, 1971.

Martlew, Norman. "'Satchmo' Plays for Margaret." *Daily Mirror,* May 10, 1956.

Mathiasen, Jørgen. "Duke Ellington's Production as a Composer." *DEMS Bulletin,* December 2004–March 2005.

McCarthy, James. "Count Basie in Come Back." *Black Dispatch,* December 19, 1942.

McClure, Susan A. "Parallel Usage of Medicinal Plants by Africans and Their Caribbean Descendants." *Economic Botany* (July–September 1982).

McDaniels, Jack. "Buster Smith." *DownBeat,* July 11, 1956.

McDonough, Buddy. "Basie Tribute A Success." *Pittsburgh Courier,* May 19, 1984.

McElfresh, Pat. "Basie: Back on Road with New Lifestyle." *Jazz,* Spring 1977.

McGettigan, Betty. "Waltzing to a Tango." Differnet, 2005. www.differnet.com/Tango/.

McGregor, Craig. "Armstrong: 'His Tragedy Is One We All Share.'" *New York Times,* August 8, 1971.

McKinley, James C., Jr. "Woman Declares Louis Armstrong Was Her Father." *New York Times,* December 13, 2012.

McLeese, Don. "100 Reasons to Remember Duke." *National Post,* April 30, 1999.

McLellan, Joseph. "Duke's Last Work: Intrigue in the Ellington Estate." *Washington Post,* July 7, 1981.

McLendon, Winzola. "Mrs. Satchmo Goes Where Louie Toots." *Washington Post,* August 11, 1960.

Melody Maker. "Alabama Students Demand Louis." January 2, 1965.

———. "Case." November 14, 1953.

———. "Count Basie Is Tops Among the U. S. Big Bands." August 24, 1957.

———. "Count Versus Duke." October 11, 1958.

———. "French Mustard Is No Hotter than Basie, Say French." April 3, 1954.

———. "Jazz Records." May 20, 1972.

———. "Pre-Dawn Drugs Raid on Ellington Men." February 18, 1961.

———. "The Press and Louis." January 5, 1957.

———. "Royalty Salutes the Basie Band." April 20, 1957.

Meryman, Richard. "An Authentic American Genius." *Life,* April 15, 1966.

Metronome. "The Count Classifies the Duke, the Earl, and the Hawk Tops." May 1941.

———. "The Daniel Louis Satchmo Armstrong: A Man of Substance." September 1959.

———. "Lombardo Grooves Louis!" September 1949.

———. "Paul Robeson to Sing with Count Basie." September 1941.

———. "Three Chicks for Duke." November 1944.

Michelson, Art. "'Satchmo' Changes Mind on Ike." *Quad City Times,* September 25, 1957.

Micucci, Matt. "Louis Armstrong and the Colored Waif's Home for Boys." *Jazziz,* July 4, 2016.

Miele, Dave. "The Promise of Louis Armstrong." *Jazz Improv* (Winter 2007).

Mikell, Robert S. "The Legacy of Louis Armstrong's Music Teacher Peter Davis." *Syncopated Times,* July 27, 2019.

———. "Peter Davis (ca. 1887–1971)." *BlackPast,* September 18, 2017.

Milkowski, Bill. "Money Jungle." *DownBeat,* June 2013.

Miller, M. H. "Louis Armstrong, the King of Queens." *T: The New York Times Style Magazine,* February 23, 2020.

Miller, Paul Eduard. "Is the Duke Declining?" *Hollywood Note,* June 1946.

Mills, Bob. "Irving Mills." Red Hot Jazz Archive, 2000. https://syncopatedtimes.com/irving-mills-1894-1985/.

Millstein, Gilbert. "Africa Harks to Satch's Horn." *New York Times Magazine,* November 20, 1960.

———. "Louis Armstrong, King of Jazz." *Reader's Digest New Treasury for Young Readers,* 1963.

Monmouth Inquirer (Freehold, NJ). "Childs—Basie." July 5, 1900.

Monroe, Al. "How Count Basie Paid $25,000 for His Own Contract Is Told." *Chicago Defender,* March 24, 1945.

Monthly Film Bulletin. "The Five Pennies." January 1, 1959.

Moon, Fletcher F. "So 'Fisk' ticated Ladies and Gentlemen: Highlights from 150 Years of Fisk University's Musical Tradition, Impact, and Influence." 2016. https://digitalscholarship.tnstate.edu /lib/15.

Morgenstern, Dan. "The Armstrong I Knew." *Annual Review of Jazz Studies* (1999).

———. "Pops in Perspective." *Jazz Journal,* May 1962.

———. "Three Giants." *Jazz Journal,* February 1960.

Morgenstern, Dan, ed. "Roses for Satchmo." *DownBeat,* July 9, 1970.

Murray, James P. "A New Song Every Day." *New York Amsterdam News,* June 1, 1974.

Murray, Ken. "Louis, Bix Had Most Influence on Der Bingle." *DownBeat,* July 14, 1950.

Nag, Ashoke. "Christie's Celebrates 100 Years of Popular Culture with Pop Culture Online-Only Sale." *Economic Times,* November 28, 2013.

Nashville Banner. "Fisk Student Group to Urge Desegregation." March 13, 1957.

Negro South. "New Orleans' Own Louis Armstrong: 30 Years A Jazz Great." April 1946.

Nerges, Chester. "Blue Notes." *Chicago Defender,* May 16, 1931.

New Journal and Guide (Norfolk, VA). "The Duchess of Ellington." October 21, 1933.

———. "Duke Ellington Invading South for First Time." July 14, 1934.

———. "Duke Ellington Sidemen Charged with Having Dope." February 18, 1961.

New Orleans Beat Street Magazine, August 2003.

New York Afro-American. "Lou Armstrong Says Gangsters Pester Him." October 17, 1931.

New York Amsterdam News. "Armstrong-Connie Court Fight Ends." January 20, 1932.

———. "Armstrong Is Being Panned." April 28, 1934.

———. "Basie Skips Theatre for Barring Negro Customers." June 30, 1945.

———. "Basie Top Negro Band in Disc Poll." July 25, 1942.

———. "Basie Will Train Hank." February 8, 1941.

———. "Count Basie Is Coming Home; Cathy Is Waiting." April 10, 1965.

———. "Count Basie Resident in Exclusive Addisleigh Park." April 19, 1947.

———. "Dance Bands in Japan Playing Basie's Music." March 15, 1947.

———. "Duke Ellington Sued." October 3, 1964.

———. "Eddie South and Arcadians Will Head Apollo Program." November 3, 1934.

———. "Ex-Convict, Given Job by Count Basie as Music Arranger Sought in 9 States." October 4, 1941.

———. "Louis Armstrong, The Man Still Going Strong." October 31, 1970.

———. "No Improvement in Lip of Star Trumpeteer." April 13, 1935.

———. "Popular Musician Faced by British Color Bar." June 28, 1933.

———. "Ten Best Dressed Women Are Named." March 19, 1960.

———. "Tribute to Strayhorn." June 17, 1967.

———. "Trumpeter Fights Ban." January 13, 1932.

New York Daily News. "Satch Sorry, Not Sore." December 3, 1964.

New York Herald Tribune. "Satchmo: 'They Would Beat Jesus If He Was Black.'" March 11, 1965.

New Yorker. "Goings On About Town." October 20, 1928.

———. "Goings On About Town." June 29, 1929.

———. "Goings On About Town." December 7, 1929.

New York Post. "Takes More'n Tenn. Bomb to Stop Satchmo." February 20, 1957.

New York Times. "American Ragtime Sweeping Europe." June 28, 1913.

———. "Armstrong Cites Gains." November 30, 1957.

———. "Armstrong—Clarence Hatfield." September 9, 1998.

———. "Armstrong Hurts Lip." November 23, 1957.

———. "Armstrong in Hospital." June 24, 1959.

———. "Armstrong Is Better." June 27, 1959.

———. "Armstrong Leaves Hospital." June 30, 1959.

———. "Armstrong's Agent Awaits Word on Ban." December 8, 1964.

———. "Armstrong's Jazz 'Sends' a Princess." May 10, 1956.

———. "Armstrong Very Ill." June 26, 1959.

———. "Bonus at Jazz Concert." July 9, 1956.

———. "Duke Ellington's Friends, Great and Small, Pay Their Respects." May 26, 1974.

———. "Duke Ellington Will Tour Soviet." May 8, 1971.

———. "Edward Jones, 68, Bassist with Count Basie." June 8, 1997.

———. "Ellington's Widow Dies." April 10, 1976.

———. "'Hot Chocolates' Is High Spirited." June 21, 1929.

———. "Irving Mills Dies at 91; Jazz Music Publisher." April 23, 1985.

———. "Jailed in Narcotics Case." July 17, 1952.

———. "Joseph G. Glaser Is Dead at 72; Booking Agent for Many Stars." June 8, 1969.

———. "Lester Young, 49, a Jazz Musician." March 16, 1959.

———. "Louis Armstrong Back." July 3, 1959.

———. "Louis Armstrong Barred by Alabama University." December 7, 1964.

———. "Louis Armstrong, Barring Soviet Tour, Denounces Eisenhower and Gov. Faubus." September 19, 1957.

———. "Louis Armstrong Here." December 6, 1957.

———. "Louis Armstrong Improved." June 25, 1959.

———. "Louis Armstrong 'Just Fine.'" June 28, 1959.

———. "Louis Armstrong Offers Friendly Horn to Big 4." May 14, 1959.

———. "Louis Armstrong Scores Beating of Selma Negroes." March 11, 1965.

———. "Louis Armstrong, 65, Hailed by Teen-Agers." July 5, 1965.

———. "Louis Armstrong's Life, as He Saw It." *Indian Express*, November 18, 2018. https://indianexpress.com/article/entertainment/music/louis-armstrong-the-louis-armstrong-house-museum-archives-5452046/.

———. "Louis Armstrong Storms Stadium." July 15, 1956.

———. "Musician Backs Move." September 26, 1957.

———. "Night Club Notes." October 19, 1935.

———. "Rio Greets Armstrong." November 26, 1957.

Nichols, E. J., and W. L. Werner. "Hot Jazz Jargon." *Vanity Fair,* November 1935.

Nocera, Joe. "Louis Armstrong, the Real Ambassador." *New York Times,* May 1, 2015.

Noel, Pamela. "Count Basie's Quiet Retreat in the Bahamas." *Ebony,* January 1984.

Noonan, Kathleen. "Blowing the Trumpet on the Legacy of Louis." *Courier-Mail* (Brisbane, Australia), September 1, 2007.

Norgaard, Martin. "How Jazz Musicians Improvise: The Central Role of Auditory and Motor Patterns." *Music Perception* (February 2014).

Norgaard, Martin, Jonathan Spencer, and Mariana Montiel. "Testing Cognitive Theories by Creating a Pattern-Based Probabilistic Algorithm for Melody and Rhythm in Jazz Improvisation." *Psychomusicology: Music, Mind, and Brain* (December 2013).

Oakland Tribune. "Ellington Widow Dies." April 9, 1976.

Oakley, Helen M. "Critics Tear Hair over 'Dukes' New Tunes." *DownBeat,* March 1936.

Observer (London). "Profile—'Satchmo.'" May 13, 1956.

O'Grady, Jim. "What a Wonderful Shave." *New York Times,* October 5, 2003.

OKeh Records. "Get 'Heebie Jeebies' with Louis Armstrong and his Hot Five." Advertisement. *Chicago Defender,* May 1, 1926.

———. "Louis Armstrong Ain't Misbehavin.'" Advertisement. *Chicago Defender,* September 28, 1929.

——. "Louis Armstrong King of the Trumpet—Starring in 'Connie's Hot Chocolates.'" Advertisement. *Chicago Defender*, September 14, 1929.

Okrent, Daniel. "Pops Is Still Tops. Oh Yeah!" *Time*, August 28, 2000.

O'Meally, Robert G. "Checking Our Balances: Ellison on Armstrong's Humor." *boundary 2* (Summer 2003).

Ory, Kid. "The Hot Five Sessions." As told to Lester Koenig. *Record Changer*, July–August 1950.

Ostwald, David H. "Louis Armstrong, Civil Rights Pioneer." *New York Times*, August 3, 1991.

Ottley, Roi. "'Jazz' Acquires Flashy Clothes as 'Swing' in Fascinating and Colorful Saga of Satch." *New York Amsterdam News*, December 12, 1936.

Pace, Eric. "Edmund Anderson, 89, a Muse to Ellington." *New York Times*, July 19, 2002.

Page, Walter. "All About My Life in Music." *Jazz Review*, November 1958.

Palmer, Robert. "Louis Armstrong's Archives." *New York Times*, October 12, 1987.

Panassié, Hughes, and Madeleine Gautier. "Louis Armstrong Off Stage." *Jazz Journal*, May 1956.

Parks, Gordon. "Jazz." *Esquire*, December 1975.

Payne, Ethel L. "Story Behind Ellington's White House Fete." *Chicago Defender*, May 5, 1969.

Pearson, Drew. "'Satchmo' Armstrong." *New York Mirror*, December 14, 1957.

Petters, John. "Louis Armstrong—The World's Greatest Jazz Vocalist." *Just Jazz*, August 2001.

Peyton, Dave. "The Musical Bunch." *Chicago Defender*, July 20, 1929.

——. "The Worries of an Orchestra Leader." *Chicago Defender*, November 7, 1925.

Philadelphia Tribune. "Ellington's Aide Jailed for Dope." July 19, 1952.

——. "Name Cigar for Lou." October 8, 1931.

Piazza, Tom. "The Little Record Labels That Could (and They Did)." *New York Times*, November 6, 1994.

Pick, Margaret Moos. "My Heart: The Story of Lil Hardin Armstrong." Riverwalk Jazz Collection. Stanford Archive of Recorded Sound, Stanford, CA.

Pierpont, Claudia Roth. "Black, Brown, and Beige: Duke Ellington's Music and Race in America." *New Yorker*, May 10, 2010.

Pittsburgh Courier. "Armstrong Indignant Over Race Ban Story." July 28, 1956.

——. "Armstrong's 'Axe' Gasses Ghanese Fans." June 2, 1956.

——. "Armstrong's Rift, Rumor Is Afloat." December 26, 1931.

——. "Basie Forms Own Music Firm with Milt Ebbins." November 17, 1945.

——. "Basie Launches Sepia Band Policy at Avodon." December 7, 1946.

——. "Count Basie Cops Overseas Ork Poll." August 17, 1946.

——. "Count Basie Opens at Lincoln Hotel; Race Attractions on Upbeat in N. Y." November 6, 1943.

——. "Duke Ellington Says *DownBeat* Article Gave Wrong Impression." February 8, 1941.

——. "Eartha, Lena Agree with 'Satchmo.'" September 28, 1957.

——. "Ellington Is Presented with Courier Loving Cup; Record Crowd Out." January 9, 1932.

——. "Ellington's Negro Opera Not Being Peddled." December 10, 1938.

——. "Ex-Louis Armstrong Clarinetist Among Those Living in Ghana." December 12, 1959.

——. "Handy Man to Duke Gets Four Years." July 26, 1952.

——. "'Life' Lists 'King' Oliver, 'Duke' Ellington, 'Count' Basie, 'Prince Louie' in Swing Parade." August 13, 1938.

——. "Louie Armstrong Had No Place to Toot Horn; Crowds Followed Him." September 19, 1931.

——. "Louie to Stay in Europe." October 28, 1933.

——. "Louis Armstrong Admits He's Worth Over $100,000." November 25, 1939.

——. "Louis Armstrong Gets Six Months for Dope." March 21, 1931.

——. "Louis Armstrong Goes to Boston for New 'High;' Gets $8,000 Per." March 14, 1936.

——. "Louis Armstrong Offers to Donate His Services to Aid in Relief of Flood Victims." April 4, 1936.

——. "Louis Armstrong Out; Sentence Cut Short." March 28, 1931.

——. "Louie Armstrong to Undergo Operation." March 28, 1936.

——. "Louis Armstrong, Who Once Made 260 Consecutive 'High C's' and Finished on 'Top F', Is Daddy of Swing Music." March 28, 1936.

——. "Philadelphia Theatre-Goers Go for Count Basie's 'Swing.'" April 24, 1937.

——. "Satchmo Flips His Wig." September 28, 1957.

——. "Satchmo No Spokesman." October 12, 1957.

——. "'Satchmo' Tells Off Ike, U.S.!: Turns Down Paid Trip to Russia!" September 28, 1957.

Porter, Lewis. "Hear the Earliest Surviving Radio Broadcast by Duke Ellington, A Historic Find." October 4, 2018. https://www.wbgo.org/music/2018-10-04/hear-the-earliest-surviving-radio-broadcast-by-duke-ellington-a-historic-find-in-deep-dive.

——. "Odds 'n' Ends About Duke Ellington, Thelonious Monk, Lester Young and 'Jazz' Itself." March 7, 2019. https://www.wbgo.org/music/2019-03-07/deep-dive-odds-n-ends-about-duke-ellington-thelonious-monk-lester-young-and-jazz-itself.

——. "Putting Louis Armstrong in Context." May 3, 2019. https://www.wbgo.org/music/2019-05-03/deep-dive-putting-louis-armstrong-in-context.

Powe. "The Five Pennies." *Variety*, May 6, 1959.

Powell, A. Clayton, Jr. "My Grandfather's Branded, Our Musicians Are Slaves, Owned Body and Soul, Work for Massa [*sic*] Mills." *New York Amsterdam News*, November 21, 1936.

Presel, Joseph A. "Duke Ellington in the USSR." U.S. State Department, September–October 1971.

Prideaux, Ed. "Not a Wonderful World: Why Louis Armstrong Was Hated by So Many." *Guardian* (UK), December 17, 2020.

Provizer, Steve. "Jazz Commentary: Louis Armstrong as Negotiator." October 2, 2020. https://artsfuse.org/213078/jazz-commentary-louis-armstrong-as-negotiator/.

Purslow, Alan. "Louis & Me—A Love Story." *Jassman*, 2011.

Raeburn, Bruce Boyd. "'I'll Be Glad When You're Dead': Louis Armstrong's Smack Down with White Authority and His First Films, 1930–1932." *Southern Quarterly* (Fall 2013–Winter 2014).

——. "Louis and Women." Delivered at North Carolina Jazz Festival, University of North Carolina, March 2, 2001.

Ratcliffe, Robert M. "Telling Off Louis Armstrong's Critics!" *Pittsburgh Courier*, October 19, 1957.

Ratliff, Ben. "Al Grey, 74, a Sly Trombonist Who Played with Count Basie." *New York Times*, March 27, 2000.

——. "Buddy Tate, 87, Saxophonist for Basie's Band." *New York Times*, February 13, 2001.

——. "Harry (Sweets) Edison, 83, Trumpeter for Basie Band, Dies." *New York Times*, July 29, 1999.

——. "Trumpets, Diaries and Cocktail Jiggers." *New York Times*, October 15, 2003.

Rawlins, Bill. "Satchmo and Cash Paired for TV Show." *Sun-Democrat* (Paducah, KY), December 3, 1970.

Reckdahl, Kathy. "In Central City, New Marker Notes 1900 New Orleans 'Mass Lynching.'" Updated December 19, 2020. https://www.nola.com/news/crime_police/article_ca7abefc-4171-11eb-a3aa-c35babfbe7de.html.

Reich, Howard. "Duke Is Still Tops." *Chicago Tribune*, December 13, 1995.

——. "50 Years Later, Pegasus Puts Ellington's Fiery Musical Back Together." *Chicago Tribune*, October 6, 1991.

——. "Hotter Near the Lake." *Chicago Tribune*, September 5, 1993.

——. "Jazz Giant's Private Views Show Anger Behind Smile." *Chicago Tribune*, July 29, 2001.

——. "Satchmo in Chicago." *Chicago Tribune*, April 9, 1995.

——. "Satchmo Through the Looking Glass." *Chicago Tribune*, July 2, 2000.

——. "Silent for 35 Years, Ellington's Restored Musical Celebrates Black Culture, Composer's Genius." *Chicago Tribune*, May 11, 1998.

Riccardi, Ricky. "Ambassador Satchmo Meets Tricky Dick? Not So Fast . . ." October 18, 2014. https://dippermouth.blogspot.com/2014/10/ambassador-satch-meets-tricky-dick-not.html.

———. "The Eternal Debate: Louis vs. Louie." January 18, 2020. https://dippermouth.blogspot .com/2020/01/the-eternal-debate-louis-vs-louie.html.

———. "50 Years of 'Hello, Dolly!'" December 03, 2013. https://dippermouth.blogspot.com/2013 /12/50-years-of-hello-dolly.html.

———. "50 Years of the Slivovice Interview." May 22, 2015. https://dippermouth.blogspot.com /2015/05/50-years-of-sliviovice-interview.html.

———. "Happy Birthday, Pops! (The Case for July 4, 1901 . . .)." July 4, 2015. https://dippermouth. blogspot.com/2015/07/happy-birthday-pops-case-for-july-4-1901.html.

———. "'I'm Still Louis Armstrong—Colored': Louis Armstrong and the Civil Rights Era." May 2020. https://virtualexhibits.louisarmstronghouse.org/2020/05/11/im-still-louis-armstrong-colored -louis-armstrong-and-the-civil-rights-era/.

———. "'It's Awful Nice to Be Up There Among All Them Beatles': The Story of 'Hello, Dolly!'" December 3, 2021. https://virtualexhibits.louisarmstronghouse.org/2021/12/03/its-awful-nice -to-be-up-there-among-all-them-beatles-the-story-of-hello-dolly/.

———. "Louis Armstrong and Comedy Part 1: Early Influences Bert Williams and Bill 'Bojangles' Robinson." October 14, 2020. https://virtualexhibits.louisarmstronghouse.org/2020/10/14/louis -armstrong-and-comedy-part-1-early-influences-bert-williams-and-bill-bojangles-robinson/.

———. "Louis Armstrong and Comedy Part 2: 'Always a Showman!' 1922–1933." October 20, 2020. https://virtualexhibits.louisarmstronghouse.org/2020/10/20/louis-armstrong-and-comedy -part-2-always-a-showman-1922-1933/.

———. "Louis Armstrong and Little Rock: 60 Years Later." September 29, 2017. https://dippermouth .blogspot.com/2017/09/louis-armstrong-and-little-rock-60.html.

———. "Louis Armstrong, Joe Glaser and 'Satchmo at the Waldorf.'" June 6, 2015. https://dippe rmouth.blogspot.com/2015/06/louis-armstrong-joe-glaser-and-satchmo.html.

———. "Louis' Sick Days: Louis Armstrong's 1971 'Jasmin' Interview." June 11, 2021. https://virt ualexhibits.louisarmstronghouse.org/2021/06/11/louis-sick-days-louis-armstrongs-1971 -jasmin-interview/.

———. "More on Louis Armstrong and the Colored Waifs Home: 1910–1913." December 22, 2014. https://dippermouth.blogspot.com/2014/12/louis-armstrong-and-colored-waifs-home.html.

———. "'My Adopted Son': The Story of Clarence Hatfield Armstrong." January 26, 2023. https ://virtualexhibits.louisarmstronghouse.org/2023/01/26/my-adopted-son-the-story-of -clarence-hatfield-armstrong/.

———. "90 Years of Louis Armstrong and His Hot Five!" November 12, 2015. https://dipper mouth.blogspot.com/2015/11/90-years-of-louis-armstrong-and-his-hot.html.

———. "'Satchmo Charms Congo Cats': Louis Armstrong and Leopoldville, 60 Years Later." October 28, 2020. https://virtualexhibits.louisarmstronghouse.org/2020/10/28/satchmo -charms-congo-cats-louis-armstrong-and-leopoldville-60-years-later/.

———. "'That Cat Ain't Never Gonna Die': Louis Armstrong's Final Collages and Last Birthday Party." July 1, 2021. https://virtualexhibits.louisarmstronghouse.org/2021/07/01/as-long-as -youre-breathing-youve-got-a-chance-the-final-collages-and-the-last-birthday-party/.

Richards, David. "Stumbling 'Satchmo.'" *Washington Post,* August 7, 1987.

Richman, John. "Louis Armstrong—100 Years, Thanks a Million." *Just Jazz,* August 2001.

Rickard, John. "'The Unknown Satchmo,' A BBC Radio Documentary." *Just Jazz,* August 2001.

Rink, Janet. "Satchmo Comes Home." *Dixie,* October 31, 1965.

Roberts, Porter. "Debunking Mr. Joe Glaser (Louis Armstrong's Manager)." *Pittsburgh Courier,* May 2, 1936.

Robertson, Nan. "Duke Ellington, 70, Honored at White House." *New York Times,* April 30, 1969.

Robinson, Major. "Hear Count Basie May Join Benny Goodman's Band." *Chicago Defender,* November 9, 1940.

Rough, Lisa. "Louis Armstrong and Cannabis: The Jazz Legend's Lifelong Love of 'the Gage.'" Updated July 28, 2020. https://www.leafly.com/news/lifestyle/louis-armstrong-and-cannabis.

Rowe, Billy. "Count Basie's Blessing to the World." *New York Amsterdam News,* May 12, 1984.

Rowe, Isadora. "Ike Wins Satchmo's Applause!" *Pittsburgh Courier,* October 5, 1957.

——. "NY Promoter Charges Bias in Ban of Basie Gillespie." *Pittsburgh Courier,* January 26, 1957.

Roy, Rob. "Lil Armstrong Rivals Her Famous Hubby." *Chicago Defender,* September 29, 1934.

Russell, William. "Armstrong Interview Notes." *Blue Note,* November 29, 1953.

Salzman, Eric. "Armstrong, Back After Illness, Plays and Sings at the Stadium." *New York Times,* July 5, 1959.

Sanders, Charles L. "Louis Armstrong—The Reluctant Millionaire." *Ebony,* November 1964.

Sandford, Miriam. "Louis Armstrong: I Live! Only I Can't Play the Trumpet Yet." *Jasmin,* July 16, 1971. English translation, LAHM.

Saxonis, Bill. "Ellington and Civil Rights: A Delicate Balance," 26th International Duke Ellington Study Group Conference, Georgetown University, March 2020.

Schwartz, Ben. "What Louis Armstrong Really Thinks." *New Yorker,* February 25, 2014.

Scott, Patrick. "No Jazz at Funeral at Satchmo's Request." *Globe and Mail* (Toronto), 1971.

——. "A Tired Old Pal Remembers Satchmo." *Globe and Mail* (Toronto), July 9, 1971, LAHM.

Scott, Walter. "Walter Scott's Personality Parade." *Parade,* July 17, 1977.

——. "Walter Scott's Personality Parade." *Parade,* November 15, 1981.

See, Hilda. "Critic Finds L. Armstrong Here 'To Rest.'" *Chicago Defender,* January 21, 1933.

——. "Switch to Combos Has 'Spotlighted' Surviving Orks." *Chicago Defender,* July 2, 1955.

Shah, Diane K. "On Q." *New York Times Magazine,* November 18, 1990.

Sheffield, Maceo B. "It Happened to the Duke in Illinois." *Pittsburgh Courier,* April 18, 1942.

Sheidlower, Noah. "Explore Queens' Addisleigh Park, the 'African-American Gold Coast of NY.'" June 23, 2020. https://untappedcities.com/2020/06/23/explore-queens-addisleigh-park-the-african-american-gold-coast-of-ny/.

Shenker, Israel. "'Just Plain Old Satchmo' Turns 70 Sweetly." *New York Times,* July 4, 1970.

Simmen, Johnny. "Harry Carney: An Encounter." *Cadence,* July 1987.

Simon, George T. "Bebop's the Easy Out, Claims Louis." *Metronome,* March 1948.

Simons, Thomas W., Jr. "Ellington Orchestra Tour of the Near East and South Asia." U.S. State Department, Fall 1963.

Slotnik, Daniel E. "Marty Napoleon, 93, Pianist Who Played with Armstrong." *New York Times,* May 4, 2015.

Smith, Charles Edward. "Collecting Hot." *Esquire,* February 1934.

Smith, Isadora. "Duke Ellington Rated 'Joe Louis' of Music." *Pittsburgh Courier,* July 16, 1938.

Snelson, Floyd G. "Story of Duke Ellington's Rise to Kingship of Jazz Reads Like Fiction." *Pittsburgh Courier,* December 19, 1931.

Snitzer, Herb. "On the Road with Pops." *Jazz Improv* (Winter 2007).

Soll, Rick. "The Night Basie Played Against the Packers—and Won." *Chicago Tribune,* June 2, 1975.

Spencer, Joe. "Big Question: Who'll Be the New Leader of Basie Band?" *New York Amsterdam News,* May 26, 1984.

Springfield Leader and Press (Springfield, MO). "'Satch' Fractures Protocol, Plays Stomp for Princess." May 10, 1956.

Stein, Daniel. "The Performance of Jazz Autobiography." *Genre* (June 2004).

Steiner, Ken. "Duke Ellington and the Rise of Radio: The Cotton Club Era," 26th International Duke Ellington Study Group Conference, Georgetown University, March 2020.

Sterling, Dana. "Roots of Jazz Run Deep in Tulsa Area." *Tulsa World,* February 9, 1997.

Stone, Roger. "Nixon Unknowingly 'Muled' for Pot Smuggling Louis Armstrong?" *Niagara Falls Reporter,* September 2, 2014.

Strayhorn, Billy. "The Ellington Effect." *DownBeat,* November 5, 1952.

Strongin, Theodore. "Acting Mayor Presents Medal to the Duke (Ellington, That Is)." *New York Times,* August 3, 1965.

Sullivan, Ed. "Talk of the Town." *Washington Post,* September 13, 1935.

Swaffer, Hannen. "I Heard Yesterday." *Daily Herald* (UK), July 25, 1932.

Sylvester, Robert. "Dream Street." *New York Daily News,* July 12, 1966.

Szulo, Tad. "Hot Jazz Trails Hot Jets to Rio." *New York Times,* November 21, 1957.

Tamarkin, Jeff. "Satchmo at the National Press Club: Red Beans and Rice-ly Yours." *JazzTimes,* August 2012.

Tapley, Mel. "Hundreds Mourn Basie." *New York Amsterdam News,* May 5, 1984.

———. "Schomburg Celebrates Ellington." *New York Amsterdam News,* November 11, 1989.

Tarby, Russ. "When Jack Ruby Robbed Jewel Brown." *Syncopated Times,* March 1, 2016.

Taubman, Howard. "The 'Duke' Invades Carnegie Hall." *New York Times,* January 17, 1943.

———. "Satchmo Wears His Crown Gaily." *New York Times,* January 29, 1950.

Teachout, Terry. "A Face of Armstrong, but Not the Image." *New York Times,* July 29, 2001.

———. "Satchmo and the Jews." *Commentary,* November 2009.

ten Hove, B. "The Iron Duke." *Rhythm,* May 1936.

Thayer, James Stewart. "Armstrong Heads Dizzy's List." *Seattle Daily Times,* February 14, 1982.

Thompkins, Gwen. "An Eight-Second Film of 1915 New Orleans and the Mystery of Louis Armstrong's Happiness." *New Yorker,* July 8, 2019.

Thomson, David. "Whatever Happened to Satchmo?" *Independent,* July 4, 2000.

Time. "The Beautiful Persons." June 28, 1963.

———. "Big-Band Jazz." January 11, 1954.

———. "Black Rascal." June 13, 1932.

———. "December Records." December 15, 1930.

———. "Jazz? Swing? It's Ragtime." November 5, 1945.

———. "Just Very." June 4, 1956.

———. "Last Trumpet for the First Trumpeter." July 19, 1971.

———. "Louis the First." February 21, 1949.

———. "The Man on Cloud No. 7." November 8, 1954.

———. "Mills's Music." March 22, 1937.

———. "Muggles." September 7, 1931.

———. "Music Is Music." May 22, 1950.

———. "New Musical in Manhattan." December 11, 1939.

———. "The New Pictures." November 23, 1936.

———. "The New Pictures." August 6, 1956.

———. "New Plays in Manhattan." July 1, 1929.

———. "People." May 21, 1956.

———. "Reverend Satchelmouth." April 29, 1946.

———. "Satchmo: The Musical Autobiography of Louis Armstrong." October 7, 1957.

———. "Song Suppressed." June 24, 1940.

———. "Whoa-ho-ho-ho-ho-ho!" January 20, 1936.

Times-Democrat (New Orleans). "Few Juveniles Arrested." January 2, 1913.

Todd, George. "Ellington's Doctorate: At Roseland." *New York Amsterdam News,* June 23, 1973.

Tucker, George. "Manhattan." *Daily News Journal* (Murfreesboro, TN), February 25, 1942.

Tucker, Mark. "Count Basie and the Piano That Swings the Band." *Popular Music,* 1985.

US News & World Report. "They Crossed the Iron Curtain to Hear American Jazz." December 1955.

Van Blaine, Lloyd. "His PR Man Writes on Louis Armstrong." *New York Amsterdam News,* July 17, 1971.

Variety. "Ambassador Satch Sounds Off." January 29, 1958.

———. "Armstrong's Collapse at Spoleto Festival." June 24, 1959.

———. "Drug Charge Against Jazz Band Musicians." November 19, 1930.

———. "Glaser-Stein, Inc." December 15, 1943.

———. "Joe Glaser, Stein Set for Coast Huddle on ABC Buy of MCA's 50%." August 28, 1946.

———. "Louis Packin' His Satchmo for S. American Bow." June 19, 1957.

——. "Satchmo Swamps Sputnik in South Am." December 4, 1957.

Voce, Steve. "It Don't Mean a Thing." *Jazz Journal,* September 1968.

——. "Still Clinging to the Wreckage." *Jazz Journal,* March 2016.

Vuijsje, Bert. "Jazz in the Netherlands." In *The History of European Jazz: The Music, Musicians and Audience in Context,* edited by Francesco Martinelli. Sheffield, UK: Equinox Publishing, 2018.

Waddell, Robert. "Satchmo's on a Stamp, So the Music's Starting." *New York Times,* September 3, 1995.

Waggoner, Walter. "U. S. Voting Ways Are a Hit of Fair." *New York Times,* April 22, 1958.

Walker, Danton. "New York Letter." *Philadelphia Inquirer,* January 12, 1943.

Wallace, Mike. "Mike Wallace Asks Thurgood Marshall: Is a Civil War Brewing in the South?" *New York Post,* September 30, 1957.

Washington Post. "Armstrong Blasts U.S., Cancels Soviet Trip." September 19, 1957.

——. "Armstrong Not Welcome in Lebanon." November 18, 1959.

——. "Cairo Calls Satchmo a Spy for Israel." November 13, 1959.

——. "Dope Charges Hold 4 Members in Ellington Band." February 10, 1961.

——. "Louis Armstrong Fuss Blows Out in Alabama." December 8, 1964.

——. "Louis Armstrong, Great Jazzman, Dies at 71." July 7, 1971.

——. "Satchmo Armstrong Ill of Pneumonia in Italy." June 24, 1959.

——. "Satchmo Fights Heart Disturbances and Pneumonia, Makes Late Rally." June 26, 1959.

——. "Satchmo, Well, Motors to Rome." June 30, 1959.

Watrous, Peter. "Polishing the Image of Louis Armstrong." *New York Times,* December 14, 1994.

Weaver, Jim. "Jazz and Ellingtonia." *Jazz,* December 1943.

Weiler, A. H. "The Five Pennies." *New York Times,* June 19, 1959.

Wein, George, and Sidney J. Stiber. *Louis Armstrong at Newport,* 1970. Courtesy of Ambassador Entertainment Inc.

West, Hollie I. "Duke Ellington: A Big Band Leader for More Than 40 Years." *Washington Post,* April 27, 1969.

——. "Mercer Ellington: Conducting a Legacy." *Washington Post,* July 23, 1974.

——. "A Portrait of the Duke." *Washington Post,* April 30, 1977.

Whorton, James. "Civilization and the Colon: Constipation as 'the Disease of Diseases.'" *Western Journal of Medicine* (December 2000).

Wiggins, Edgar A. "Duke Ellington's Band a Hit in France and Belgium." *Chicago Defender,* April 22, 1939.

Williams, Bob. "The Hawkins-Armstrong Feud." *Afro-American,* May 19, 1934.

Williams, Cootie. "Reminiscing with Cootie." *Storyville,* June–July 1977.

Wilson, Earl. "It Happened Last Night." *Sarasota Herald-Tribune,* March 8, 1971.

Wilson, John S. "Adderley, Mulligan, Armstrong Give Jazz Concert for C.O.R.E." *New York Times,* June 29, 1961.

——. "Barney Josephson, Owner of Cafe Society Jazz Club, Is Dead at 86." *New York Times,* September 30, 1988.

——. "Billy Strayhorn: Alter Ego for the Duke." *New York Times,* June 6, 1965.

——. "Count Basie, 79, Band Leader and Master of Swing, Dead." *New York Times,* April 27, 1984.

——. "Duke Ellington, a Master of Music, Dies at 75." *New York Times,* May 25, 1974.

——. "Duke Ellington Still the Pioneer." *New York Times,* April 2, 1961.

——. "'Hard Times, Good Times' of Marty Napoleon." *New York Times,* March 23, 1984.

——. "Jazz Is Tested at Stadium." *New York Times,* July 16, 1956.

——. "Jazzmen Doubling as Narrators." *New York Times,* September 29, 1957.

——. "Jimmy Rushing, Blues Singer with Intense Voice, Dies at 68." *New York Times,* June 9, 1972.

——. "Kool Festival, a Tribute to Basie, Opens Today." *New York Times,* June 22, 1984.

——. "Louis Armstrong and Quintet Play." *New York Times,* December 28, 1959.

——. "Mary Lou Williams, a Jazz Great, Dies." *New York Times,* May 30, 1981.

———. "Russell Procope, 72, Clarinetist with Ellington 29 Years, Dead." *New York Times*, January 23, 1981.

———. "A Touch of the Duke from Russell Procope." *New York Times*, July 20, 1979.

Wilson, Nancy. "Billie Holiday: 'Lady Sings the Blues.'" *Jazz Profiles*, NPR, aired October 3, 2007.

———. "Louis Armstrong: 'The Man and His Music.'" Pts. 1 and 2. *Satchmo: The Wonderful World of Louis Armstrong, Jazz Profiles*, NPR, aired August 1 and 8, 2007.

———. "Louis Armstrong: 'The Singer.'" *Satchmo: The Wonderful World of Louis Armstrong, Jazz Profiles*, NPR, aired August 22, 2007.

———. "Louis Armstrong: 'The Trumpeter.'" *Satchmo: The Wonderful World of Louis Armstrong, Jazz Profiles*, NPR, aired August 15, 2007.

Winick, Charles. "The Use of Drugs by Jazz Musicians." *Social Problems* (January 1959).

Winick, Charles, and Nyswander, Marie. "Psychotherapy of Successful Musicians Who Are Drug Addicts." *American Journal of Orthopsychiatry* (July 1961).

Winnipeg Free Press. "US People Keeping Calm, Satchmo Says." December 10, 1941.

Woodlawn Cemetery & Conservancy. "The Jazz Legacy of the Woodlawn Cemetery."

Wooley, John. "Clarence Love: King of Sweet Inducted into Jazz Hall of Fame." *Tulsa World*, June 10, 1990.

Wyckoff, Geraldine. "Louis Armstrong: Born on the Fourth of July?" *OffBeat*, August 1, 2013.

Yardley, William. "Frank Wess, 91, Saxophonist and Flutist with the Basie Band, Dies." *New York Times*, November 3, 2013.

Zambito, Tony. "The Essay by Martin Luther King Jr. That Lives Large In Jazz." January 21, 2019. https://jazzbuffalo.org/2019/01/21/the-essay-by-martin-luther-king-jr-that-lives-large-in -jazz/.

Zanesville Signal. "Duke Ellington Cancels Appearance." August 7, 1945.

Zirpolo, Michael P. "In Duke's Head." *Duke Ellington Society of Sweden Bulletin*, December 2006.

INDEX

ABOUT THE AUTHOR

LARRY TYE is the bestselling author of *Bobby Kennedy* and *Satchel,* as well as *Demagogue, Superman, The Father of Spin, Home Lands,* and *Rising from the Rails,* and coauthor, with Kitty Dukakis, of *Shock.* Previously an award-winning reporter at the *Boston Globe* and a Nieman fellow at Harvard University, he now runs the Boston-based Health Coverage Fellowship. He lives on Cape Cod.

ABOUT

MARINER BOOKS

MARINER BOOKS traces its beginnings to 1832 when William Ticknor cofounded the Old Corner Bookstore in Boston, from which he would run the legendary firm Ticknor and Fields, publisher of Ralph Waldo Emerson, Harriet Beecher Stowe, Nathaniel Hawthorne, and Henry David Thoreau. Following Ticknor's death, Henry Oscar Houghton acquired Ticknor and Fields and, in 1880, formed Houghton Mifflin, which later merged with venerable Harcourt Publishing to form Houghton Mifflin Harcourt. HarperCollins purchased HMH's trade publishing business in 2021 and reestablished their storied lists and editorial team under the name Mariner Books.

Uniting the legacies of Houghton Mifflin, Harcourt Brace, and Ticknor and Fields, Mariner Books continues one of the great traditions in American bookselling. Our imprints have introduced an incomparable roster of enduring classics, including Hawthorne's *The Scarlet Letter*, Thoreau's *Walden*, Willa Cather's *O Pioneers!*, Virginia Woolf's *To the Lighthouse*, W.E.B. Du Bois's *Black Reconstruction*, J.R.R. Tolkien's *The Lord of the Rings*, Carson McCullers's *The Heart Is a Lonely Hunter*, Ann Petry's *The Narrows*, George Orwell's *Animal Farm* and *Nineteen Eighty-Four*, Rachel Carson's *Silent Spring*, Margaret Walker's *Jubilee*, Italo Calvino's *Invisible Cities*, Alice Walker's *The Color Purple*, Margaret Atwood's *The Handmaid's Tale*, Tim O'Brien's *The Things They Carried*, Philip Roth's *The Plot Against America*, Jhumpa Lahiri's *Interpreter of Maladies*, and many others. Today Mariner Books remains proudly committed to the craft of fine publishing established nearly two centuries ago at the Old Corner Bookstore.